BUTTERWOR

CONTRACT,

BUTTERWORTHS STUDENT STATUTES

Contract, Tort and Restitution

Third edition

STEVE HEDLEY, MA, LLB

University Lecturer and Fellow in Law,

Christ's College, Cambridge

Butterworths
LexisNexis™

Members of the LexisNexis Group worldwide

United Kingdom	LexisNexis Butterworths Tolley, a Division of Reed Elsevier (UK) Ltd, Halsbury House, 35 Chancery Lane, LONDON WC2A 1EL and 4 Hill Street, EDINBURGH EH2 3JZ
Argentina	LexisNexis Argentina, BUENOS AIRES
Australia	LexisNexis Butterworths, CHATSWOOD, New South Wales.
Austria	LexisNexis Verlag ARD Orac GmbH & Co KG, VIENNA
Canada	LexisNexis Butterworths MARKHAM, Ontario
Chile	LexisNexis Chile Ltda, SANTIAGO DE CHILE
Czech Republic	Nakladatelství Orac sro, PRAGUE
France	Editions du Juris-Classeur SA, PARIS
Hong Kong	LexisNexis Butterworths, HONG KONG
Hungary	HVG-Orac, BUDAPEST
India	LexisNexis Butterworths, NEW DELHI
Ireland	Butterworths (Ireland) Ltd, DUBLIN
Italy	Giuffrè Editore, MILAN
Malaysia	Malayan Law Journal Sdn Bhd, KUALA LUMPUR
New Zealand	LexisNexis Butterworths, WELLINGTON
Poland	Wydawnictwo Prawnicze LexisNexis, WARSAW
Singapore	LexisNexis Butterworths, SINGAPORE
South Africa	Butterworths SA, DURBAN
Switzerland	Stämpfli Verlag AG, BERNE
USA	LexisNexis, DAYTON, OHIO

A CIP Catalogue record for this book is available from the British Library.

ISBN 0 406 96031 3

Typeset by Kerrypress Ltd, Luton, Bedfordshire

Printed in England by Clays Ltd, St Ives plc

Preface

Relatively few changes have been needed for this new edition.

The Electronic Communications Act 2000 is an attempt to grapple with novel means of making contracts, with what results it is much too early to tell. Law reform proceeds in rather glacial fashion, though it has now at last been possible to include the text of the new privity legislation (the Contracts (Rights of Third Parties) Act 1999).

My thanks go to all at Butterworths who have helped to produce this new edition.

I would be happy to receive any comments or suggestions for improvement!

Steve Hedley

steve.hedley@law.cam.ac.uk

24 August 2002

Contents

PART I

STATUTES

Statute of Frauds (1677)

1677 CHAPTER 3

An Act for prevention of Frauds and Perjuryes

4 No action against executors, etc, upon a special promise, or upon any agreement, or contract for sale of lands, etc, unless agreement, etc, be in writing, and signed

. . . noe action shall be brought . . . whereby to charge the defendant upon any speciall promise to answere for the debt default or miscarriages of another person . . . unlesse the agreement upon which such action shall be brought or some memorandum or note thereof shall be in writeing and signed by the partie to be charged therewith or some other person thereunto by him lawfully authorized.

NOTES

First words omitted repealed by the Statute Law Revision Act 1883 and the Statute Law Revision Act 1948; second words omitted repealed by the Law Reform (Enforcement of Contracts) Act 1954, s 1; third words omitted repealed by the Law of Property Act 1925, s 207, Sch 7, and the Law Reform (Enforcement of Contracts) Act 1954, s 1.

Fires Prevention (Metropolis) Act 1774

1774 CHAPTER 78

An Act . . . for the more effectually preventing Mischiefs by Fire within the Cities of London and Westminster and the Liberties thereof, and other the Parishes, Precincts, and Places within the Weekly Bills of Mortality, the Parishes of Saint Mary-le-bon, Paddington, Saint Pancras and Saint Luke at Chelsea, in the County of Middlesex . . .

NOTES

Words omitted repealed by the Statute Law Revision Act 1887.

86 No action to lie against a person where the fire accidentally begins

And . . . no action, suit or process whatever shall be had, maintained or prosecuted against any person in whose house, chamber, stable, barn or other building, or on whose estate any fire shall . . . accidentally begin, nor shall any recompence be made by such person for any damage suffered thereby, any law, usage or custom to the contrary notwithstanding: . . . provided that no contract or agreement made between landlord and tenant shall be hereby defeated or made void.

NOTES

First words omitted repealed by the Statute Law Revision Act 1888; second words omitted repealed by the Statute Law Revision Act 1948; final words omitted repealed by the Statute Law Revision Act 1958.

Statute of Frauds Amendment Act 1828

1828 CHAPTER 14

An Act for rendering a written Memorandum necessary to the Validity of certain Promises and Engagements

[9th May 1828]

6 Action not maintainable on representations of character, etc, unless they be in writing signed by the party chargeable

No action shall be brought whereby to charge any person upon or by reason of any representation or assurance made or given concerning or relating to the character, conduct, credit, ability, trade, or dealings of any other person, to the intent or purpose that such other person may obtain credit, money, or goods upon, unless such representation or assurance be made in writing, signed by the party to be charged therewith.

Parliamentary Papers Act 1840

1840 CHAPTER 9

An Act to give summary Protection to Persons employed in the Publication of Parliamentary Papers

[14th April 1840]

1 Proceedings, criminal or civil, against persons for publication of papers printed by order of Parliament to be stayed upon delivery of a certificate and affidavit to the effect that such publication is by order of either House of Parliament

. . . It shall and may be lawful for any person or persons who now is or are, or hereafter shall be, a defendant or defendants in any civil or criminal proceeding commenced or prosecuted in any manner soever, for or on account or in respect of the publication of any such report, paper, votes, or proceedings by such person or persons, or by his, her, or their servant or servants, by or under the authority of either House of Parliament, to bring before the court in which such proceeding shall have been or shall be so commenced or prosecuted, or before any judge of the same (if one of the superior courts at Westminster), first giving twenty-four hours notice of his intention so to do to the prosecutor or plaintiff in such proceeding, a certificate under the hand of the lord high chancellor of Great Britain, or the lord keeper of the great seal, or of the speaker of the House of Lords, for the time being, or of the clerk of the Parliaments, or of the speaker of the House of Commons, or of the clerk of the same house, stating that the report, paper, votes, or proceedings, as the case may be, in respect whereof such civil or criminal proceeding shall have been commenced or prosecuted, was published by such person or persons, or by his, her, or their servant or servants, by order or under the authority of the House of Lords or of the House of Commons, as the case may be, together with an affidavit verifying such certificate; and such court or judge shall thereupon immediately stay such civil or criminal proceeding; and the same, and every writ or process issued therein, shall be and shall be deemed and taken to be finally put an end to, determined, and superseded by virtue of this Act.

NOTES

Words omitted repealed by the Statute Law Revision (No 2) Act 1890.

2 Proceedings to be stayed when commenced in respect of a copy of an authenticated report, etc

. . . In case of any civil or criminal proceeding hereafter to be commenced or prosecuted for or on account or in respect of the publication of any copy of such report, paper, votes, or proceedings, it shall be lawful for the defendant or defendants at any stage of the proceedings to lay before the court or judge such report, paper, votes, or proceedings, and such copy, with an affidavit verifying such report, paper, votes, or proceedings, and the correctness of such copy, and the court or judge shall immediately stay such civil or criminal proceeding; and the same, and every writ or process issued therein, shall be and shall be deemed and taken to be finally put an end to, determined, and superseded by virtue of this Act.

NOTES

Words omitted repealed by the Statute Law Revision (No 2) Act 1888, and the Statute Law Revision Act 1958.

3 In proceedings for printing any extract or abstract of a paper, it may be shown that such extract was bona fide made

. . . It shall be lawful in any civil or criminal proceeding to be commenced or prosecuted for printing any extract from or abstract of such report, paper, votes, or proceedings, to give in evidence . . . such report, paper, votes, or proceedings, and to show that such extract or abstract was published bona fide and without malice; and if such shall be the opinion of the jury, a verdict of not guilty shall be entered for the defendant or defendants.

NOTES

Words omitted repealed by the Statute Law Revision (No 2) Act 1888, and the Statute Law Revision Act 1958.

4 Act not to affect the privileges of Parliament

Provided always . . . that nothing herein contained shall be deemed or taken, or held or construed, directly or indirectly, by implication or otherwise, to affect the privileges of Parliament in any manner whatsoever.

NOTES

Words omitted repealed by the Statute Law Revision (No 2) Act 1888.

Libel Act 1843

1843 CHAPTER 96

An Act to amend the Law respecting defamatory Words and Libel

[24th August 1843]

1 Offer of an apology admissible in evidence in mitigation of damages in action for defamation

. . . In any action for defamation it shall be lawful for the defendant (after notice in writing of his intention so to do, duly given to the plaintiff at the time of filing or delivering the plea in such action,) to give in evidence, in mitigation of damages, that he made or offered an apology to the plaintiff for such defamation before the commencement of the action, or as soon afterwards as he had an opportunity of doing so, in case the action shall have been commenced before there was an opportunity of making or offering such apology.

NOTES

Words omitted repealed by the Statute Law Revision Act 1891.

2 In an action against a newspaper for libel, the defendant may plead that it was inserted without malice and without negligence, and that he has published or offered to publish an apology

. . . In an action for libel contained in any public newspaper or other periodical publication it shall be competent to the defendant to plead that such libel was inserted in such newspaper or other periodical publication without actual malice, and without gross negligence, and that before the commencement of the action, or at the earliest opportunity afterwards, he inserted in such newspaper or other periodical publication a full apology for the said libel, or, if the newspaper or periodical publication in which the said libel appeared should be ordinarily published at intervals exceeding one week, had offered to publish the said apology in any newspaper or periodical publication to be selected by the plaintiff in such action; . . . and . . . to such plea to such action it shall be competent to the plaintiff to reply generally, denying the whole of such plea.

NOTES

Words omitted repealed by the Statute Law Revision Act 1891, and the Statute Law Revision Act 1892.

10 Commencement and extent of Act

. . . Nothing in this Act contained shall extend to Scotland.

NOTES

Words omitted repealed by the Statute Law Revision Act 1874 (No 2).

Libel Act 1845

1845 CHAPTER 75

An Act to amend an Act passed in the Session of Parliament held in the Sixth and Seventh Years of the Reign of Her present Majesty, intituled "An Act to amend the Law respecting defamatory Words and Libel"

[31st July 1845]

2 Defendant not to file such plea without paying money into court by way of amends

. . . It shall not be competent to any defendant in such action, whether in England or in Ireland, to file any such plea, without at the same time making a payment of money into court by way of amends . . . , but every such plea so filed without payment of money into court shall be deemed a nullity, and may be treated as such by the plaintiff in the action.

NOTES

Words omitted repealed by the Statute Law Revision Act 1891.

Gaming Act 1845

1845 CHAPTER 109

An Act to amend the Law concerning Games and Wagers

[8th August 1845]

18 Contracts by way of gaming to be void, and wagers or sums deposited with stakeholders not to be recoverable at law—Saving for subscriptions for prizes

< . . . > *All contracts or agreements, whether by parole or in writing, by way of gaming or wagering, shall be null and void; and* < . . . > *no suit shall be brought or maintained in any court of law and equity for recovering any sum of money or valuable thing alleged to be won upon any wager, or which shall have been deposited in the hands of any person to abide the event on which any wager shall have been made: Provided always, that this enactment shall not be deemed to apply to any subscription or contribution, or agreement to subscribe or contribute, for or towards any plate, prize, or sum of money to be awarded to the winner or winners of any lawful game, sport, pastime, or exercise.*

NOTES

Repealed in relation to Northern Ireland by the Betting, Gaming, Lotteries and Amusements (Northern Ireland) Order 1985, SI 1985/1204, art 187(4), Sch 21.

Words omitted repealed by the Statute Law Revision Act 1891.

Apportionment Act 1870

1870 CHAPTER 35

An Act for the better Apportionment of Rents and other periodical Payments

[1st August 1870]

1 Short title

This Act may be cited for all purposes as "The Apportionment Act 1870."

2 Rents, etc to be apportionable in respect of time

. . . All rents, annuities, dividends, and other periodical payments in the nature of income (whether reserved or made payable under an instrument in writing or otherwise) shall, like interest on money lent, be considered as accruing from day to day, and shall be apportionable in respect of time accordingly.

NOTES

Words omitted repealed by the Statute Law Revision (No 2) Act 1893.

3 Apportioned part of rent, etc to be payable when the next entire portion shall have become due

The apportioned part of any such rent, annuity, dividend, or other payment shall be payable or recoverable in the case of a continuing rent, annuity, or other such payment when the entire portion of which such apportioned part shall form part shall become due and payable, and not before, and in the case of a rent, annuity, or other such payment determined by re-entry, death, or otherwise when the next entire portion of the same would have been payable if the same had not so determined, and not before.

5 Interpretation

In the construction of this Act—

The word "rents" includes rent service, rentcharge, and rent seck, and also tithes and all periodical payments or renderings in lieu of or in the nature of rent or tithe.

The word "annuities" includes salaries and pensions.

The word "dividends" includes (besides dividends strictly so called) all payments made by the name of dividend, bonus, or otherwise out of the revenue of trading or other public companies, divisible between all or any of the members of such respective companies, whether such payments shall be usually made or declared, at any fixed times or otherwise; and all such divisible revenue shall, for the purposes of this Act, be deemed to have accrued by equal daily increment during and within the period for or in respect of which the payment of the same revenue shall be declared or expressed to be made, but the said word "dividend" does not include payments in the nature of a return or reimbursement of capital.

6 Act not to apply to policies of assurance

Nothing in this Act contained shall render apportionable any annual sums made payable in policies of assurance of any description.

7 Nor where stipulation made to the contrary

The provisions of this Act shall not extend to any case in which it is or shall be expressly stipulated that no apportionment shall take place.

Slander of Women Act 1891

1891 CHAPTER 51

An Act to amend the Law relating to the Slander of Women

[5th August 1891]

1 Amendment of law

Words spoken and published . . . which impute unchastity or adultery to any woman or girl shall not require special damage to render them actionable.

Provided always, that in any action for words spoken and made actionable by this Act, a plaintiff shall not recover more costs than damages, unless the judge shall certify that there was reasonable ground for bringing the action.

NOTES

Words omitted repealed by the Statute Law Revision Act 1908.

2 Short title and extent

This Act may be cited as the Slander of Women Act 1891 and shall not apply to Scotland.

Gaming Act 1892

1892 CHAPTER 9

An Act to amend the Act of the eighth and ninth Victoria, chapter one hundred and nine, intituled "An Act to amend the Law concerning Games and Wagers"

[20th May 1892]

1 Promises to repay sums paid under contracts void by 8 & 9 Vict c 109 to be null and void

Any promise, express or implied, to pay any person any sum of money paid by him under or in respect of any contract or agreement rendered null and void by the Gaming Act 1845 or to pay any sum of money by way of commission, fee, reward, or otherwise in respect of any such contract, or of any services in relation thereto or in connection therewith, shall be null and void, and no action shall be brought or maintained to recover any such sum of money.

2 Short title

This Act may be cited as the Gaming Act 1892.

Law of Property Act 1925

1925 CHAPTER 20

An Act to consolidate the enactments relating to Conveyancing and the Law of Property in England and Wales

[9th April 1925]

PART II

CONTRACTS, CONVEYANCES AND OTHER INSTRUMENTS

Contracts

41 Stipulations not of the essence of a contract

Stipulations in a contract, as to time or otherwise, which according to rules of equity are not deemed to be or to have become of the essence of the contract, are also construed and have effect at law in accordance with the same rules.

49 Applications to the court by vendor and purchaser

(1) A vendor or purchaser of any interest in land, or their representatives respectively, may apply in a summary way to the court, in respect of any requisitions or objections, or any claim for compensation, or any other question arising out of or connected with the contract (not being a question affecting the existence or validity of the contract), and the court may make such order upon the application as to the court may appear just, and may order how and by whom all or any of the costs of and incident to the application are to be borne and paid.

(2) Where the court refuses to grant specific performance of a contract, or in any action for the return of a deposit, the court may, if it thinks fit, order the repayment of any deposit.

(3) This section applies to a contract for the sale or exchange of any interest in land.

[(4) The county court has jurisdiction under this section where the land which is to be dealt with in the court does not exceed [£30,000] in capital value . . .]

NOTES

Sub-s (4): inserted by the County Courts Act 1984, s 148(1), Sch 2, para 2; sum in square brackets substituted and words omitted repealed by SI 1991/724, art 2(3)(a), (8), Schedule, Part I.

Conveyances and other Instruments

56 Persons taking who are not parties and as to indentures

(1) A person may take an immediate or other interest in land or other property, or the benefit of any condition, right of entry, covenant or agreement over or respecting land or other property, although he may not be named as a party to the conveyance or other instrument.

(2) A deed between parties, to effect its objects, has the effect of an indenture though not indented or expressed to be an indenture.

PART IV

EQUITABLE INTERESTS AND THINGS IN ACTION

136 Legal assignments of things in action

(1) Any absolute assignment by writing under the hand of the assignor (not purporting to be by way of charge only) of any debt or other legal thing in action, of which express notice in writing has been given to the debtor, trustee or other person from whom the assignor would have been entitled to claim such debt or thing in action, is effectual in law (subject to equities having priority over the right of the assignee) to pass and transfer from the date of such notice—

(a) the legal right to such debt or thing in action;
(b) all legal and other remedies for the same; and
(c) the power to give a good discharge for the same without the concurrence of the assignor:

Provided that, if the debtor, trustee or other person liable in respect of such debt or thing in action has notice—

(a) that the assignment is disputed by the assignor or any person claiming under him; or
(b) of any other opposing or conflicting claims to such debt or thing in action;

he may, if he thinks fit, either call upon the persons making claim thereto to interplead concerning the same, or pay the debt or other thing in action into court under the provisions of the Trustee Act 1925.

(2) This section does not affect the provisions of the Policies of Assurance Act 1867.

[(3) The county court has jurisdiction (including power to receive payment of money or securities into court) under the proviso to subsection (1) of this section where the amount or value of the debt or thing in action does not exceed [£30,000].]

NOTES

Sub-s (3): inserted by the County Courts Act 1984, s 148(1), Sch 2, para 4; sum in square brackets substituted by SI 1991/724, art 2(5), (8), Schedule, Part I.

PART XII

CONSTRUCTION, JURISDICTION, AND GENERAL PROVISIONS

209 Short title, commencement, extent

(1) This Act may be cited as the Law of Property Act 1925.

(2) . . .

(3) This Act extends to England and Wales only.

NOTES

Sub-s (2): repealed by the Statute Law Revision Act 1950.

Third Parties (Rights Against Insurers) Act 1930

1930 CHAPTER 25

An Act to confer on third parties rights against insurers of third-party risks in the event of the insured becoming insolvent, and in certain other events

[10th July 1930]

1 Rights of third parties against insurers on bankruptcy, etc, of the insured

(1) Where under any contract of insurance a person (hereinafter referred to as the insured) is insured against liabilities to third parties which he may incur, then—

(a) in the event of the insured becoming bankrupt or making a composition or arrangement with his creditors; or

(b) in the case of the insured being a company, in the event of a winding-up order [or an administration order] being made, or a resolution for a voluntary winding-up being passed, with respect to the company, or of a receiver or manager of the company's business or undertaking being duly appointed, or of possession being taken, by or on behalf of the holders of any debentures secured by a floating charge, of any property comprised in or subject to the charge [or of [a voluntary arrangement proposed for the purposes of Part I of the Insolvency Act 1986 being approved under that Part]];

if, either before or after that event, any such liability as aforesaid is incurred by the insured, his rights against the insurer under the contract in respect of the liability shall, notwithstanding anything in any Act or rule of law to the contrary, be transferred to and vest in the third party to whom the liability was so incurred.

(2) Where [the estate of any person falls to be administered in accordance with an order under section [421 of the Insolvency Act 1986]], then, if any debt provable in bankruptcy [(in Scotland, any claim accepted in the sequestration)] is owing by the deceased in respect of a liability against which he was insured under a contract of

insurance as being a liability to a third party, the deceased debtor's rights against the insurer under the contract in respect of that liability shall, notwithstanding anything in [any such order], be transferred to and vest in the person to whom the debt is owing.

(3) In so far as any contract of insurance made after the commencement of this Act in respect of any liability of the insured to third parties purports, whether directly or indirectly, to avoid the contract or to alter the rights of the parties thereunder upon the happening to the insured of any of the events specified in paragraph (a) or paragraph (b) of subsection (1) of this section or upon the [estate of any person falling to be administered in accordance with an order under section [421 of the Insolvency Act 1986]], the contract shall be of no effect.

(4) Upon a transfer under subsection (1) or subsection (2) of this section, the insurer shall, subject to the provisions of section three of this Act, be under the same liability to the third party as he would have been under to the insured, but—

- (a) if the liability of the insurer to the insured exceeds the liability of the insured to the third party, nothing in this Act shall affect the rights of the insured against the insurer in respect of the excess; and
- (b) if the liability of the insurer to the insured is less than the liability of the insured to the third party, nothing in this Act shall affect the rights of the third party against the insured in respect of the balance.

(5) For the purposes of this Act, the expression "liabilities to third parties", in relation to a person insured under any contract of insurance, shall not include any liability of that person in the capacity of insurer under some other contract of insurance.

(6) This Act shall not apply—

- (a) where a company is wound up voluntarily merely for the purposes of reconstruction or of amalgamation with another company; or
- (b) to any case to which subsections (1) and (2) of section seven of the Workmen's Compensation Act 1925 applies.

NOTES

Sub-s (1): words in first and second (outer) pairs of square brackets inserted by the Insolvency Act 1985, s 235, Sch 8, para 7; words in third (inner) pair of square brackets substituted by the Insolvency Act 1986, s 439(2), Sch 14.

Sub-s (2): words in first (outer) and final pairs of square brackets substituted by the Insolvency Act 1985, s 235, Sch 8, para 7; words in second (inner) pair of square brackets substituted by the Insolvency Act 1986, s 439(2), Sch 14; words in third pair of square brackets inserted by the Bankruptcy (Scotland) Act 1985, s 75(1), Sch 7, Part I, para 6(1).

Sub-s (3): words in first (outer) pair of square brackets substituted by the Insolvency Act 1985, s 235, Sch 8, para 7; words in second (inner) pair of square brackets substituted by the Insolvency Act 1986, s 439(2), Sch 14.

2 Duty to give necessary information to third parties

(1) In the event of any person becoming bankrupt or making a composition or arrangement with his creditors, or in the event of [the estate of any person falling to be administered in accordance with an order under section [421 of the Insolvency

Act 1986]], or in the event of a winding-up order [or an administration order] being made, or a resolution for a voluntary winding-up being passed, with respect to any company or of a receiver or manager of the company's business or undertaking being duly appointed or of possession being taken by or on behalf of the holders of any debentures secured by a floating charge of any property comprised in or subject to the charge it shall be the duty of the bankrupt, debtor, personal representative of the deceased debtor or company, and, as the case may be, of the trustee in bankruptcy, trustee, liquidator, [administrator,] receiver, or manager, or person in possession of the property to give at the request of any person claiming that the bankrupt, debtor, deceased debtor, or company is under a liability to him such information as may reasonably be required by him for the purpose of ascertaining whether any rights have been transferred to and vested in him by this Act and for the purpose of enforcing such rights, if any, and any contract of insurance, in so far as it purports, whether directly or indirectly, to avoid the contract or to alter the rights of the parties thereunder upon the giving of any such information in the events aforesaid or otherwise to prohibit or prevent the giving thereof in the said events shall be of no effect.

[(1A) The reference in subsection (1) of this section to a trustee includes a reference to the supervisor of a [voluntary arrangement proposed for the purposes of, and approved under, Part I or Part VIII of the Insolvency Act 1986].]

(2) If the information given to any person in pursuance of subsection (1) of this section discloses reasonable ground for supposing that there have or may have been transferred to him under this Act rights against any particular insurer, that insurer shall be subject to the same duty as is imposed by the said subsection on the persons therein mentioned.

(3) The duty to give information imposed by this section shall include a duty to allow all contracts of insurance, receipts for premiums, and other relevant documents in the possession or power of the person on whom the duty is so imposed to be inspected and copies thereof to be taken.

NOTES

Sub-s (1): words in first (outer), third and fourth pairs of square brackets substituted or inserted by the Insolvency Act 1985, s 235, Sch 8, para 7; words in second (inner) pair of square brackets substituted by the Insolvency Act 1986, s 439(2), Sch 14.

Sub-s (1A): inserted by the Insolvency Act 1985, s 235, Sch 8, para 7; words in square brackets therein substituted by the Insolvency Act 1986, s 439(2), Sch 14.

3 Settlement between insurers and insured persons

Where the insured has become bankrupt or where in the case of the insured being a company, a winding-up order [or an administration order] has been made or a resolution for a voluntary winding-up has been passed, with respect to the company, no agreement made between the insurer and the insured after liability has been incurred to a third party and after the commencement of the bankruptcy or winding-up [or the day of the making of the administration order], as the case may be, nor any waiver, assignment, or other disposition made by, or payment made to the insured after the commencement [or day] aforesaid shall be effective to defeat or affect the rights transferred to the third party under this Act, but those rights shall be the same as if no such agreement, waiver, assignment, disposition or payment had been made.

NOTES

Words in square brackets inserted by the Insolvency Act 1985, s 235, Sch 8, para 7.

5 Short title

This Act may be cited as the Third Parties (Rights Against Insurers) Act 1930.

Law Reform (Miscellaneous Provisions) Act 1934

1934 CHAPTER 41

An Act to amend the law as to the effect of death in relation to causes of action and as to the awarding of interest in civil proceedings

[25th July 1934]

1 Effect of death on certain causes of action

(1) Subject to the provisions of this section, on the death of any person after the commencement of this Act all causes of action subsisting against or vested in him shall survive against, or, as the case may be, for the benefit of, his estate. Provided that this subsection shall not apply to causes of action for defamation . . .

[(1A) The right of a person to claim under section 1A of the Fatal Accidents Act 1976 (bereavement) shall not survive for the benefit of his estate on his death.]

(2) Where a cause of action survives as aforesaid for the benefit of the estate of a deceased person, the damages recoverable for the benefit of the estate of that person:—

[(a) shall not include—
  (i) any exemplary damages;
  (ii) any damages for loss of income in respect of any period after that person's death;]

(b) . . .

(c) where the death of that person has been caused by the act or omission which give rise to the cause of action, shall be calculated without reference to any loss or gain to his estate consequent on his death, except that a sum in respect of funeral expenses may be included.

(3) . . .

(4) Where damage has been suffered by reason of any act or omission in respect of which a cause of action would have subsisted against any person if that person had not died before or at the same time as the damage was suffered, there shall be

deemed, for the purposes of this Act, to have been subsisting against him before his death such cause of action in respect of that act or omission as would have subsisted if he had died after the damage was suffered.

(5) The rights conferred by this Act for the benefit of the estates of deceased persons shall be in addition to and not in derogation of any rights conferred on the dependants of deceased persons by the Fatal Accidents Acts 1846 to 1908 . . . and so much of this Act as relates to causes of action against the estates of deceased persons shall apply in relation to causes of action under the said Acts as it applies in relation to other causes of action not expressly excepted from the operation of subsection (1) of this section.

(6) In the event of the insolvency of an estate against which proceedings are maintainable by virtue of this section, any liability in respect of the cause of action in respect of which the proceedings are maintainable shall be deemed to be a debt provable in the administration of the estate, notwithstanding that it is a demand in the nature of unliquidated damages arising otherwise than by a contract, promise or breach of trust.

(7) . . .

NOTES

Sub-s (1): words omitted repealed by the Law Reform (Miscellaneous Provisions) Act 1970, s 7, Schedule, and the Administration of Justice Act 1982, ss 4(2), 75, Sch 9, Part I.

Sub-s (1A): inserted by the Administration of Justice Act 1982, ss 4(1), 73(1).

Sub-s (2): para (a) substituted by the Administration of Justice Act 1982, ss 4(2), 73(3), (4); para (b) repealed by the Law Reform (Miscellaneous Provisions) Act 1970, s 7, Schedule.

Sub-s (3): repealed by the Proceedings Against Estates Act 1970, s 1.

Sub-s (5): words omitted repealed by the Carriage by Air Act 1961, s 14(3), Sch 2.

Sub-s (7): repealed by the Statute Law Revision Act 1950.

4 Short title and extent

(1) This Act may be cited as the Law Reform (Miscellaneous Provisions) Act 1934.

(2) This Act shall not extend to Scotland or Northern Ireland.

Law Reform (Married Women and Tortfeasors) Act 1935

1935 CHAPTER 30

An Act to amend the law relating to the capacity, property, and liabilities of married women, and the liabilities of husbands; and to amend the law relating to proceedings against, and contribution between, tortfeasors

[22nd August 1935]

PART I
CAPACITY, PROPERTY, AND LIABILITIES OF MARRIED WOMEN; AND LIABILITIES OF HUSBANDS

3 Abolition of husband's liability for wife's torts and ante-nuptial contracts, debts, and obligations

Subject to the provisions of this Part of this Act, the husband of a married woman shall not, by reason only of his being her husband, be liable—

(a) in respect of any tort committed by her whether before or after the marriage, or in respect of any contract entered into, or debt or obligation incurred, by her before the marriage; or

(b) to be sued, or made a party to any legal proceeding brought, in respect of any such tort, contract, debt, or obligation.

4 Savings

(1) Nothing in this Part of this Act shall—

(a) during coverture which began before the first day of January eighteen hundred and eighty-three, affect any property to which the title (whether vested or contingent, and whether in possession, reversion, or remainder) of a married woman accrued before that date, except property held for her separate use in equity;

(b) affect any legal proceeding in respect of any tort if proceedings had been instituted in respect thereof before the passing of this Act;

(c) enable any judgment or order against a married woman in respect of a contract entered into, or debt or obligation incurred, before the passing of this Act, to be enforced in bankruptcy or to be enforced otherwise than against her property.

(2) For the avoidance of doubt it is hereby declared that nothing in this Part of this Act—

(a) renders the husband of a married woman liable in respect of any contract entered into, or debt or obligation incurred, by her after the marriage in respect of which he would not have been liable if this Act had not been passed;

(b) exempts the husband of a married woman from liability in respect of any contract entered into, or debt or obligation (not being a debt or obligation arising out of the commission of a tort) incurred, by her after the marriage in respect of which he would have been liable if this Act had not been passed;

(c) prevents a husband and wife from acquiring, holding, and disposing of, any property jointly or as tenants in common, or from rendering themselves, or being rendered, jointly liable in respect of any tort, contract, debt or obligation, and of suing and being sued either in tort or in contract or otherwise, in like manner as if they were not married;

(d) prevents the exercise of any joint power given to a husband and wife.

PART III
SUPPLEMENTARY

8 Short title, extent and construction of references

(1) This Act may be cited as the Law Reform (Married Women and Tortfeasors) Act 1935.

(2) This Act shall not extend to Scotland or to Northern Ireland.

(3) Any reference in this Act to any other enactment or to any provision of any other enactment shall, unless the context otherwise requires, be construed as a reference to that enactment, or that provision, as the case may be, as amended by any subsequent enactment including this Act.

Law Reform (Frustrated Contracts) Act 1943

1943 CHAPTER 40

An Act to amend the law relating to the frustration of contracts

[5th August 1943]

1 Adjustment of rights and liabilities of parties to frustrated contracts

(1) Where a contract governed by English law has become impossible of performance or been otherwise frustrated, and the parties thereto have for that reason been discharged from the further performance of the contract, the following provisions of this section shall, subject to the provisions of section two of this Act, have effect in relation thereto.

(2) All sums paid or payable to any party in pursuance of the contract before the time when the parties were so discharged (in this Act referred to as "the time of discharge") shall, in the case of sums so paid, be recoverable from him as money

received by him for the use of the party by whom the sums were paid, and, in the case of sums so payable, cease to be so payable:

Provided that, if the party to whom the sums were so paid or payable incurred expenses before the time of discharge in, or for the purpose of, the performance of the contract, the court may, if it considers it just to do so having regard to all the circumstances of the case, allow him to retain or, as the case may be, recover the whole or any part of the sums so paid or payable, not being an amount in excess of the expenses so incurred.

(3) Where any party to the contract has, by reason of anything done by any other party thereto in, or for the purpose of, the performance of the contract, obtained a valuable benefit (other than a payment of money to which the last foregoing subsection applies) before the time of discharge, there shall be recoverable from him by the said other party such sum (if any), not exceeding the value of the said benefit to the party obtaining it, as the court considers just, having regard to all the circumstances of the case and, in particular,—

(a) the amount of any expenses incurred before the time of discharge by the benefited party in, or for the purpose of, the performance of the contract, including any sums paid or payable by him to any other party in pursuance of the contract and retained or recoverable by that party under the last foregoing subsection, and

(b) the effect, in relation to the said benefit, of the circumstances giving rise to the frustration of the contract.

(4) In estimating, for the purposes of the foregoing provisions of this section, the amount of any expenses incurred by any party to the contract, the court may, without prejudice to the generality of the said provisions, include such sum as appears to be reasonable in respect of overhead expenses and in respect of any work or services performed personally by the said party.

(5) In considering whether any sum ought to be recovered or retained under the foregoing provisions of this section by any party to the contract, the court shall not take into account any sums which have, by reason of the circumstances giving rise to the frustration of the contract, become payable to that party under any contract of insurance unless there was an obligation to insure imposed by an express term of the frustrated contract or by or under any enactment.

(6) Where any person has assumed obligations under the contract in consideration of the conferring of a benefit by any other party to the contract upon any other person, whether a party to the contract or not, the court may, if in all the circumstances of the case it considers it just to do so, treat for the purposes of subsection (3) of this section any benefit so conferred as a benefit obtained by the person who has assumed the obligations as aforesaid.

2 Provision as to application of this Act

(1) This Act shall apply to contracts, whether made before or after the commencement of this Act, as respects which the time of discharge is on or after the first day of July, nineteen hundred and forty-three, but not to contracts as respects which the time of discharge is before the said date.

(2) This Act shall apply to contracts to which the Crown is a party in like manner as to contracts between subjects.

(3) Where any contract to which this Act applies contains any provision which, upon the true construction of the contract, is intended to have effect in the event of circumstances arising which operate, or would but for the said provision operate, to frustrate the contract, or is intended to have effect whether such circumstances arise or not, the court shall give effect to the said provision and shall only give effect to the foregoing section of this Act to such extent, if any, as appears to the court to be consistent with the said provision.

(4) Whether it appears to the court that a part of any contract to which this Act applies can properly be severed from the remainder of the contract, being a part wholly performed before the time of discharge, or so performed except for the payment in respect of that part of the contract of sums which are or can be ascertained under the contract, the court shall treat that part of the contract as if it were a separate contract and had not been frustrated and shall treat the foregoing section of this Act as only applicable to the remainder of that contract.

(5) This Act shall not apply—

- (a) to any charterparty, except a time charterparty or a charterparty by way of demise, or to any contract (other than a charterparty) for the carriage of goods by sea; or
- (b) to any contract of insurance, save as is provided by subsection (5) of the foregoing section; or
- (c) to any contract to which [section 7 of the Sale of Goods Act 1979] (which avoids contracts for the sale of specific goods which perish before the risk has passed to the buyer) applies, or to any other contract for the sale, or for the sale and delivery, of specific goods, where the contract is frustrated by reason of the fact that the goods have perished.

NOTES

Sub-s (5): words in square brackets substituted by the Sale of Goods Act 1979, s 63, Sch 2, para 2.

3 Short title and interpretation

(1) This Act may be cited as the Law Reform (Frustrated Contracts) Act 1943.

(2) In this Act the expression "court" means, in relation to any matter, the court or arbitrator by or before whom the matter falls to be determined.

Law Reform (Contributory Negligence) Act 1945

1945 CHAPTER 28

An Act to amend the law relating to contributory negligence and for purposes connected therewith

[15th June 1945]

1 Apportionment of liability in case of contributory negligence

(1) Where any person suffers damage as the result partly of his own fault and partly of the fault of any other person or persons, a claim in respect of that damage shall not be defeated by reason of the fault of the person suffering the damage, but the damages recoverable in respect thereof shall be reduced to such extent as the court thinks just and equitable having regard to the claimant's share in the responsibility for the damage:

Provided that—

(a) this subsection shall not operate to defeat any defence arising under a contract;

(b) where any contract or enactment providing for the limitation of liability is applicable to the claim, the amount of damages recoverable by the claimant by virtue of this subsection shall not exceed the maximum limit so applicable.

(2) Where damages are recoverable by any person by virtue of the foregoing subsection subject to such reduction as is therein mentioned, the court shall find and record the total damages which would have been recoverable if the claimant had not been at fault.

(3), (4) . . .

(5) Where, in any case to which subsection (1) of this section applies, one of the persons at fault avoids liability to any other such person or his personal representative by pleading the Limitation Act 1939, or any other enactment limiting the time within which proceedings may be taken, he shall not be entitled to recover any damages . . . from that other person or representative by virtue of the said subsection.

(6) Where any case to which subsection (1) of this section applies is tried with a jury, the jury shall determine the total damages which would have been recoverable if the claimant had not been at fault and the extent to which those damages are to be reduced.

(7) . . .

NOTES

Sub-ss (3), (5): words omitted repealed by the Civil Liability (Contribution) Act 1978, s 9(2), Sch 2.

Sub-s (4): repealed by the Fatal Accidents Act 1976, s 6(2), Sch 2.

Sub-s (7): repealed by the Carriage by Air Act 1961, s 14(3), Sch 2.

3 Saving for Maritime Conventions Act 1911, and past cases

(1) This Act shall not apply to any claim to which section one of the Maritime Conventions Act 1911, applies and that Act shall have effect as if this Act had not been passed.

(2) This Act shall not apply to any case where the Acts or omissions giving rise to the claim occurred before the passing of this Act.

4 Interpretation

The following expressions have the meanings hereby respectively assigned to them, that is to say—

"court" means, in relation to any claim, the court or arbitrator by or before whom the claim falls to be determined;

"damage" includes loss of life and personal injury;

. . .

"fault" means negligence, breach of statutory duty or other act or omission which gives rise to a liability in tort or would, apart from this Act, give rise to the defence of contributory negligence.

NOTES

Words omitted repealed by the Fatal Accidents Act 1976, s 6(2), Sch 2, and the National Insurance (Industrial Injuries) Act 1946, s 89 (1), Sch 9.

7 Short title and extent

This Act may be cited as the Law Reform (Contributory Negligence) Act 1945.

Crown Proceedings Act 1947

1947 CHAPTER 44

An Act to amend the law relating to the civil liabilities and rights of the Crown and to civil proceedings by and against the Crown, to amend the law relating to the civil liabilities of persons other than the Crown in certain cases involving the affairs or property of the Crown, and for purposes connected with the matters aforesaid

[31st July 1947]

PART I
SUBSTANTIVE LAW

2 Liability of the Crown in tort

(1) Subject to the provisions of this Act, the Crown shall be subject to all those liabilities in tort to which, if it were a private person of full age and capacity, it would be subject:—

(a) in respect of torts committed by its servants or agents;
(b) in respect of any breach of those duties which a person owes to his servants or agents at common law by reason of being their employer; and
(c) in respect of any breach of the duties attaching at common law to the ownership, occupation, possession or control of property:

Provided that no proceedings shall lie against the Crown by virtue of paragraph (*a*) of this subsection in respect of any act or omission of a servant or agent of the Crown unless the act or omission would apart from the provisions of this Act have given rise to a cause of action in tort against that servant or agent or his estate.

(2) Where the Crown is bound by a statutory duty which is binding also upon persons other than the Crown and its officers, then, subject to the provisions of this Act, the Crown shall, in respect of a failure to comply with that duty, be subject to all those liabilities in tort (if any) to which it would be so subject if it were a private person of full age and capacity.

(3) Where any functions are conferred or imposed upon an officer of the Crown as such either by any rule of the common law or by statute, and that officer commits a tort while performing or purporting to perform those functions, the liabilities of the Crown in respect of the tort shall be such as they would have been if those functions had been conferred or imposed solely by virtue of instructions lawfully given by the Crown.

(4) Any enactment which negatives or limits the amount of the liability of any Government department[, part of the Scottish Administration] or officer of the Crown in respect of any tort committed by that department[, part] or officer shall, in the case of proceedings against the Crown under this section in respect of a tort committed by that department[, part] or officer, apply in relation to the Crown as it

would have applied in relation to that department[, part] or officer if the proceedings against the Crown had been proceedings against that department[, part] or officer.

(5) No proceedings shall lie against the Crown by virtue of this section in respect of anything done or omitted to be done by any person while discharging or purporting to discharge any responsibilities of a judicial nature vested in him, or any responsibilities which he has in connection with the execution of judicial process.

(6) No proceedings shall lie against the Crown by virtue of this section in respect of any act, neglect or default of any officer of the Crown, unless that officer has been directly or indirectly appointed by the Crown and was at the material time paid in respect of his duties as an officer of the Crown wholly out of the Consolidated Fund of the United Kingdom, moneys provided by Parliament, [the Scottish Consolidated Fund] . . ., or any other Fund certified by the Treasury for the purposes of this subsection or was at the material time holding an office in respect of which the Treasury certify that the holder thereof would normally be so paid.

NOTES

Sub-s (4): words ", part of the Scottish Administration" in square brackets inserted by SI 1999/1042, art 4, Sch 2, para 4(1), (2).

Date in force: 20 May 1999: see SI 1999/1042, art 1(2)(b).

Sub-s (4): word ", part" in square brackets in each place it occurs inserted by SI 1999/1042, art 4, Sch 2, para 4(1), (2).

Date in force: 20 May 1999: see SI 1999/1042, art 1(2)(b).

Sub-s (6): words "the Scottish Consolidated Fund" in square brackets inserted by SI 1999/1820, art 4, Sch 2, Pt I, para 21.

Date in force: 1 July 1999: see SI 1999/1820, art 1(2).

Sub-s (6): words omitted repealed by the Statute Law (Repeals) Act 1981.

PART VI
EXTENT, COMMENCEMENT, SHORT TITLE, ETC

52 Extent of Act

Subject to the provisions hereinafter contained with respect to Northern Ireland, this Act shall not affect the law enforced in courts elsewhere than in England and Scotland, or the procedure in any such courts.

54 Short title and commencement

(1) This Act may be cited as the Crown Proceedings Act 1947.

(2) . . .

NOTES

Sub-s (2): repealed by the Statute Law Revision Act 1950.

Law Reform (Personal Injuries) Act 1948

1948 CHAPTER 41

An Act to abolish the defence of common employment, to amend the law relating to the measure of damages for personal injury or death, and for purposes connected therewith.

[30th June 1948]

1 Common employment

(1) It shall not be a defence to an employer who is sued in respect of personal injuries caused by the negligence of a person employed by him, that that person was at the time the injuries were caused in common employment with the person injured.

(2) Accordingly the Employers' Liability Act 1880 shall cease to have effect, and is hereby repealed.

(3) Any provision contained in a contract of service or apprenticeship, or in an agreement collateral thereto, (including a contract or agreement entered into before the commencement of this Act) shall be void in so far as it would have the effect of excluding or limiting any liability of the employer in respect of personal injuries caused to the person employed or apprenticed by the negligence of persons in common employment with him.

6 Short title and commencement

(1) This Act may be cited as the Law Reform (Personal Injuries) Act 1948.

(2) Section one and subsection (1) of section two of this Act shall apply only where the cause of action accrues on or after the day appointed for the National Insurance (Industrial Injuries) Act 1946 to take effect, but subsections (4) and (5) of the said section two shall apply whether the cause of action accrued or the action was commenced before or after the commencement of this Act.

National Parks and Access to the Countryside Act 1949

1949 CHAPTER 97

An Act to make provision for National Parks and the establishment of a National Parks Commission; to confer on the Nature Conservancy and local authorities powers for the establishment and maintenance of nature reserves; to make further provision for the recording, creation, maintenance and improvement of public paths and for securing access to open country, and to amend the law relating to rights of way; to confer further powers for preserving and enhancing natural beauty; and for matters connected with the purposes aforesaid

[16th December 1949]

PART V
ACCESS TO OPEN COUNTRY

60 Rights of public where access agreement or order in force

(1) Subject to the following provisions of this Part of this Act, where an access agreement or order is in force as respects any land a person who enters upon land comprised in the agreement or order for the purpose of open-air recreation without breaking or damaging any wall, fence, hedge or gate, or who is on such land for that purpose after having so entered thereon, shall not be treated as a trespasser on that land or incur any other liability by reason only of so entering or being on the land:

Provided that this subsection shall not apply to land which for the time being is excepted land as hereinafter defined.

(2) Nothing in the provisions of the last foregoing subsection shall entitle a person to enter or be on any land, or to do anything thereon, in contravention of any prohibition contained in or having effect under any enactment.

(3) An access agreement or order may specify or provide for imposing restrictions subject to which persons may enter or be upon land by virtue of subsection (1) of this section, including in particular, but without prejudice to the generality of this subsection, restrictions excluding the land or any part thereof at particular times from the operation of the said subsection (1); and that subsection shall not apply to any person entering or being on the land in contravention of any such restriction or failing to comply therewith while he is on the land.

(4) Without prejudice to the provisions of the last foregoing subsection, subsection (1) of this section shall have effect subject to the provisions of the Second Schedule to this Act as to the general restrictions to be observed by persons having access to land by virtue of the said subsection (1).

(5) For the purposes of this Part of this Act, the expression "excepted land" means land which for the time being is of any of the following descriptions, that is to say—

(a) agricultural land, other than such land which is agricultural land by reason only that it affords rough grazing for livestock;
(b) land comprised in a declaration for the time being in force under subsection (2) of section nineteen of this Act or that subsection as applied by section twenty-one of this Act;
(c) land covered by buildings or the curtilage of such land;
(d) land used for the purpose of a park, garden or pleasure ground, being land which was so used at the date when the relevant access agreement or order was made;
(e) land used for the getting of minerals by surface working (including quarrying), land used for the purposes of a railway (including a light railway) or tramway, or land used for the purposes of a golf course, racecourse or aerodrome;
(f) land (not falling within the foregoing paragraphs of this subsection) covered by works used for the purposes of a statutory undertaking [or a telecommunications code system] or the curtilage of such land;
(g) land as respects which development is in course of being carried out which will result in the land becoming such land as is specified in paragraph (c), (e) or (f) of this subsection;
(h) land to which section one hundred and ninety-three of the Law of Property Act 1925 for the time being applies:

Provided that land which is for the time being comprised in an access agreement or order shall not become excepted land, by reason of any development carried out thereon, or any change of use made thereof, if the development or change of use is one for which under the Act of 1947 planning permission is required and either that permission has not been granted or any condition subject to which it was granted has been contravened or has not been complied with.

NOTES

Sub-s (5): words in square brackets in para (f) inserted by the Telecommunications Act 1984, s 109, Sch 4, para 28.

66 Effect of access agreement or order on rights and liabilities of owners

(1) A person interested in any land comprised in an access agreement or order, not being excepted land, shall not carry out any work thereon whereby the area to which the public are able to have access by virtue of the agreement or order is substantially reduced:

Provided that nothing in this subsection shall affect the doing of anything whereby any land becomes excepted land.

(2) The operation of subsection (1) of section sixty of this Act in relation to any land shall not increase the liability, under any enactment not contained in this Act or

under any rule of law, of a person interested in that land or adjoining land in respect of the state thereof or of things done or omitted thereon.

(3) Any restriction arising under a covenant or otherwise as to the use of any land comprised in an access agreement or order, shall have effect subject to the provisions of this Part of this Act, and any liability of a person interested in such land in respect of such a restriction shall be limited accordingly.

(4) For the purposes of any enactment or rule of law as to the circumstances in which the dedication of a highway or the grant of an easement may be presumed, or may be established by prescription, the use by the public or by any person of a way across land at any time while it is comprised in an access agreement or order shall be disregarded.

PART VI
GENERAL, FINANCIAL AND SUPPLEMENTARY

Supplementary Provisions

115 Short title and extent

(1) This Act may be cited as the National Parks and Access to the Countryside Act 1949.

(2) This Act, except Part III thereof and so much of this Part thereof as relates to the said Part III, shall not extend to Scotland; and this Act shall not extend to Northern Ireland.

Defamation Act 1952

1952 CHAPTER 66

An Act to amend the law relating to libel and slander and other malicious falsehoods

[30th October 1952]

2 Slander affecting official, professional or business reputation

In an action for slander in respect of words calculated to disparage the plaintiff in any office, profession, calling, trade or business held or carried on by him at the time of the publication, it shall not be necessary to allege or prove special damage, whether or not the words are spoken of the plaintiff in the way of his office, profession, calling, trade or business.

3 Slander of title, etc

(1) In an action for slander of title, slander of goods or other malicious falsehood, it shall not be necessary to allege or prove special damage—

(a) if the words upon which the action is founded are calculated to cause pecuniary damage to the plaintiff and are published in writing or other permanent form; or

(b) if the said words are calculated to cause pecuniary damage to the plaintiff in respect of any office, profession, calling, trade or business held or carried on by him at the time of the publication.

(2) Section one of this Act shall apply for the purposes of this section as it applies for the purposes of the law of libel and slander.

5 Justification

In an action for libel or slander in respect of words containing two or more distinct charges against the plaintiff, a defence of justification shall not fail by reason only that the truth of every charge is not proved if the words not proved to be true do not materially injure the plaintiff's reputation having regard to the truth of the remaining charges.

6 Fair comment

In an action for libel or slander in respect of words consisting partly of allegations of fact and partly of expression of opinion, a defence of fair comment shall not fail by reason only that the truth of every allegation of fact is not proved if the expression of opinion is fair comment having regard to such of the facts alleged or referred to in the words complained of as are proved.

9 Extension of certain defences to broadcasting

(1) Section three of the Parliamentary Papers Act 1840 (which confers protection in respect of proceedings for printing extracts from or abstracts of parliamentary papers) shall have effect as if the reference to printing included a reference to broadcasting by means of wireless telegraphy.

(2), (3) . . .

NOTES

Sub-ss (2), (3): repealed by the Defamation Act 1996, s 16, Sch 2.

10 Limitation on privilege at elections

A defamatory statement published by or on behalf of a candidate in any election to a local government authority [to the Scottish Parliament] or to Parliament shall not be deemed to be published on a privileged occasion on the ground that it is material to a question in issue in the election, whether or not the person by whom it is published is qualified to vote at the election.

NOTES

Words "to the Scottish Parliament" in square brackets inserted by the Scotland Act 1998, s 125, Sch 8, para 10.

Date in force: 19 November 1998: (no specific commencement provision).

11 Agreements for indemnity

An agreement for indemnifying any person against civil liability for libel in respect of the publication of any matter shall not be unlawful unless at the time of the publication that person knows that the matter is defamatory, and does not reasonably believe there is a good defence to any action brought upon it.

12 Evidence of other damages recovered by plaintiff

In any action for libel or slander the defendant may give evidence in mitigation of damages that the plaintiff has recovered damages, or has brought actions for damages, for libel or slander in respect of the publication of words to the same effect as the words on which the action is founded, or has received or agreed to receive compensation in respect of any such publication.

13 Consolidation of actions for slander, etc

Section five of the Law of Libel Amendment Act 1888 (which provides for the consolidation, on the application of the defendants, of two or more actions for libel by the same plaintiff) shall apply to actions for slander and to actions for slander of title, slander of goods or other malicious falsehood as it applies to actions for libel; and references in that section to the same, or substantially the same, libel shall be construed accordingly.

16 Interpretation

(1) Any reference in this Act to words shall be construed as including a reference to pictures, visual images, gestures and other methods of signifying meaning.

(2) . . .

(3) . . .

(4) . . .

NOTES

Sub-s (2): repealed by the Defamation Act 1996, s 16, Sch 2.

Sub-s (3): repealed by the Defamation Act 1996, s 16, Sch 2.

Date in force (in relation to England and Wales): 28 February 2000: see SI 2000/222, art 3(b)(i)–(vi).

Date in force (in relation to Scotland): 31 March 2001: see SSI 2001/98, art 3(b)(i).

Sub-s (4): repealed by the Cable and Broadcasting Act 1984, s 57(2), Sch 6.

18 Short title, commencement, extent and repeals

(1) This Act may be cited as the Defamation Act 1952 and shall come into operation one month after the passing of this Act.

(2) This Act . . . shall not extend to Northern Ireland.

(3) . . .

NOTES

Sub-s (2): words omitted repealed by the Northern Ireland Constitution Act 1973, s 41(1), Sch 6, Part I.

Sub-s (3): repealed by the Statute Law (Repeals) Act 1974.

Occupiers' Liability Act 1957

1957 CHAPTER 31

An Act to amend the law of England and Wales as to the liability of occupiers and others for injury or damage resulting to persons or goods lawfully on any land or other property from dangers due to the state of the property or to things done or omitted to be done there, to make provision as to the operation in relation to the Crown of laws made by the Parliament of Northern Ireland for similar purposes or otherwise amending the law of tort, and for purposes connected therewith

[6 June 1957]

Liability in tort

1 Preliminary

(1) The rules enacted by the two next following sections shall have effect, in place of the rules of the common law, to regulate the duty which an occupier of premises owes to his visitors in respect of dangers due to the state of the premises or to things done or omitted to be done on them.

(2) The rules so enacted shall regulate the nature of the duty imposed by law in consequence of a person's occupation or control of premises and of any invitation or permission he gives (or is to be treated as giving) to another to enter or use the premises, but they shall not alter the rules of the common law as to the persons on whom a duty is so imposed or to whom it is owed; and accordingly for the purpose of the rules so enacted the persons who are to be treated as an occupier and as his visitors are the same (subject to subsection (4) of this section) as the persons who would at common law be treated as an occupier and as his invitees or licensees.

(3) The rules so enacted in relation to an occupier of premises and his visitors shall also apply, in like manner and to the like extent as the principles applicable at common law to an occupier of premises and his invitees or licensees would apply, to regulate—

(a) the obligations of a person occupying or having control over any fixed or moveable structure, including any vessel, vehicle or aircraft; and

(b) the obligations of a person occupying or having control over any premises or structure in respect of damage to property, including the property of persons who are not themselves his visitors.

(4) A person entering any premises in exercise of rights conferred by virtue of an access agreement or order under the National Parks and Access to the Countryside Act 1949, is not, for the purposes of this Act, a visitor of the occupier of those premises.

[(4) A person entering any premises in exercise of rights conferred by virtue of—

(a) section 2(1) of the Countryside and Rights of Way Act 2000, or

(b) an access agreement or order under the National Parks and Access to the Countryside Act 1949,

is not, for the purposes of this Act, a visitor of the occupier of the premises.]

NOTES

Sub-s (4): substituted by the Countryside and Rights of Way Act 2000, s 13(1).

Date in force: to be appointed: see the Countryside and Rights of Way Act 2000, s 103(3).

2 Extent of occupier's ordinary duty

(1) An occupier of premises owes the same duty, the "common duty of care", to all his visitors, except in so far as he is free to and does extend, restrict, modify or exclude his duty to any visitor or visitors by agreement or otherwise.

(2) The common duty of care is a duty to take such care as in all the circumstances of the case is reasonable to see that the visitor will be reasonably safe in using the premises for the purposes for which he is invited or permitted by the occupier to be there.

(3) The circumstances relevant for the present purpose include the degree of care, and of want of care, which would ordinarily be looked for in such a visitor, so that (for example) in proper cases—

(a) an occupier must be prepared for children to be less careful than adults; and

(b) an occupier may expect that a person, in the exercise of his calling, will appreciate and guard against any special risks ordinarily incident to it, so far as the occupier leaves him free to do so.

(4) In determining whether the occupier of premises has discharged the common duty of care to a visitor, regard is to be had to all the circumstances, so that (for example)—

(a) where damage is caused to a visitor by a danger of which he had been warned by the occupier, the warning is not to be treated without more as absolving the occupier from liability, unless in all the circumstances it was enough to enable the visitor to be reasonably safe; and

(b) where damage is caused to a visitor by a danger due to the faulty execution of any work of construction, maintenance or repair by an independent contractor employed by the occupier, the occupier is not to be treated without more as answerable for the danger if in all the circumstances he had acted reasonably in entrusting the work to an independent contractor and had taken such steps (if any) as he reasonably ought in order to satisfy himself that the contractor was competent and that the work had been properly done.

(5) The common duty of care does not impose on an occupier any obligation to a visitor in respect of risks willingly accepted as his by the visitor (the question

whether a risk was so accepted to be decided on the same principles as in other cases in which one person owes a duty of care to another).

(6) For the purposes of this section, persons who enter premises for any purpose in the exercise of a right conferred by law are to be treated as permitted by the occupier to be there for that purpose, whether they in fact have his permission or not.

3 Effect of contract on occupier's liability to third party

(1) Where an occupier of premises is bound by contract to permit persons who are strangers to the contract to enter or use the premises, the duty of care which he owes to them as his visitors cannot be restricted or excluded by that contract, but (subject to any provision of the contract to the contrary) shall include the duty to perform his obligations under the contract, whether undertaken for their protection or not, in so far as those obligations go beyond the obligations otherwise involved in that duty.

(2) A contract shall not by virtue of this section have the effect, unless it expressly so provides, of making an occupier who has taken all reasonable care answerable to strangers to the contract for dangers due to the faulty execution of any work of construction, maintenance or repair or other like operation by persons other than himself, his servants and persons acting under his direction and control.

(3) In this section "stranger to the contract" means a person not for the time being entitled to the benefit of the contract as a party to it or as the successor by assignment or otherwise of a party to it or as the successor by assignment or otherwise of a party to it, and accordingly includes a party to the contract who has ceased to be so entitled.

(4) Where by the terms or conditions governing any tenancy (including a statutory tenancy which does not in law amount to a tenancy) either the landlord or the tenant is bound, though not by contract, to permit persons to enter or use premises of which he is the occupier, this section shall apply as if the tenancy were a contract between the landlord and the tenant.

(5) This section, in so far as it prevents the common duty of care from being restricted or excluded, applies to contracts entered into and tenancies created before the commencement of this Act, as well as to those entered into or created after its commencement; but, in so far as it enlarges the duty owed by an occupier beyond the common duty of care, it shall have effect only in relation to obligations which are undertaken after that commencement or which are renewed by agreement (whether express or implied) after that commencement.

Liability in contract

5 Implied term in contracts

(1) Where persons enter or use, or bring or send goods to, any premises in exercise of a right conferred by contract with a person occupying or having control of the premises, the duty he owes them in respect of dangers due to the state of the premises or to things done or omitted to be done on them, in so far as the duty

depends on a term to be implied in the contract by reason of its conferring that right, shall be the common duty of care.

(2) The foregoing subsection shall apply to fixed and moveable structures as it applies to premises.

(3) This section does not affect the obligations imposed on a person by or by virtue of any contract for the hire of, or for the carriage for reward of persons or goods in, any vehicle, vessel, aircraft or other means of transport, or by or by virtue of any contract of bailment.

(4) This section does not apply to contracts entered into before the commencement of this Act.

8 Short title etc

(1) This Act may be cited as the Occupiers' Liability Act 1957.

(2) This Act shall not extend to Scotland, nor to Northern Ireland except in so far as it extends the powers of the Parliament of Northern Ireland.

(3) This Act shall come into force on the first day of January, nineteen hundred and fifty-eight.

Law Reform (Husband and Wife) Act 1962

1962 CHAPTER 48

An Act to amend the law with respect to civil proceedings between husband and wife

[1st August 1962]

1 Actions in tort between husband and wife

(1) Subject to the provisions of this section, each of the parties to a marriage shall have the like right of action in tort against the other as if they were not married.

(2) Where an action in tort is brought by one of the parties to a marriage against the other during the subsistence of the marriage, the court may stay the action if it appears—

- (a) that no substantial benefit would accrue to either party from the continuation of the proceedings; or
- (b) that the question or questions in issue could more conveniently be disposed of on an application made under section seventeen of the Married Women's Property Act 1882 (determination of questions between husband and wife as to the title to or possession of property);

and without prejudice to paragraph (*b*) of this subsection the court may, in such an action, either exercise any power which could be exercised on an application under the said section seventeen, or give such directions as it thinks fit for the disposal under that section of any question arising in the proceedings.

(3) . . .

(4) This section does not extend to Scotland.

NOTES

Sub-s (3): repealed by SI 1998/2940, art 4.
Date in force: 26 April 1999: see SI 1998/2940, art 1, and SI 1998/3132.

3 Short title, repeal, interpretation, saving and extent

(1) This Act may be cited as the Law Reform (Husband and Wife) Act 1962.

(2) . . .

(3) The references in subsection (1) of section one and subsection (1) of section two of this Act to the parties to a marriage include references to the persons who were parties to a marriage which has been dissolved.

(4) This Act does not apply to any cause of action which arose, or would but for the subsistence of a marriage have arisen, before the commencement of this Act.

(5) This Act does not extend to Northern Ireland.

NOTES

Sub-s (2): repealed by the Statute Law (Repeals) Act 1974.

Nuclear Installations Act 1965

1965 CHAPTER 57

An Act to consolidate the Nuclear Installations Act 1959 and 1965

[5th August 1965]

Duty of licensee, etc, in respect of nuclear occurrences

7 Duty of licensee of licensed site

(1) [Subject to subsection (4) below,] where a nuclear site licence has been granted in respect of any site, it shall be the duty of the licensee to secure that—

(a) no such occurrence involving nuclear matter as is mentioned in subsection (2) of this section causes injury to any person or damage to any property of any person other than the licensee, being injury or damage arising out of or resulting from the radioactive properties, or a combination of those and any toxic, explosive or other hazardous properties, of that nuclear matter; and

(b) no ionising radiations emitted during the period of the licensee's responsibility—

(i) from anything caused or suffered by the licensee to be on the site which is not nuclear matter; or

(ii) from any waste discharged (in whatever form) on or from the site,

cause injury to any person or damage to any property of any person other than the licensee.

(2) The occurrences referred to in subsection (1)(a) of this section are—

(a) any occurrence on the licensed site during the period of the licensee's responsibility, being an occurrence involving nuclear matter;

(b) any occurrence elsewhere than on the licensed site involving nuclear matter which is not excepted matter and which at the time of the occurrence—

(i) is in the course of carriage on behalf of the licensee as licensee of that site; or

(ii) is in the course of carriage to that site with the agreement of the licensee from a place outside the relevant territories; and

(iii) in either case, is not on any other relevant site in the United Kingdom;

(c) any occurrence elsewhere than on the licensed site involving nuclear matter which is not excepted matter and which—

(i) having been on the licensed site at any time during the period of the licensee's responsibility; or

(ii) having been in the course of carriage on behalf of the licensee as licensee of that site,

has not subsequently been on any relevant site, or in the course of any relevant carriage, or (except in the course of relevant carriage) within the territorial limits of a country which is not a relevant territory.

(3) In determining the liability by virtue of subsection (1) of this section in respect of any occurrence of the licensee of a licensed site, any property which at the time of the occurrence is on that site, being—

(a) a nuclear installation; or

(b) other property which is on that site—

(i) for the purpose of use in connection with the operation, or the cessation of the operation, by the licensee of a nuclear installation which is or has been on that site; or

(ii) for the purpose of the construction of a nuclear installation on that site,

shall, notwithstanding that it is the property of some other person, be deemed to be the property of the licensee.

[(4) Section 8 of this Act shall apply in relation to sites occupied by the Authority.]

NOTES

Sub-s (1): words in square brackets inserted by SI 1990/1918, reg 2, Schedule, para 2(a).
Sub-s (4): inserted by SI 1990/1918, reg 2, Schedule, para 2(b).

9 Duty of Crown in respect of certain sites

If a government department uses any site for any purpose which, if section 1 of this Act applied to the Crown, would require the authority of a nuclear site licence in respect of that site, section 7 of this Act shall apply in like manner as if—

(a) the Crown were the licensee under a nuclear site licence in respect of that site; and
(b) any reference to the period of the licensee's responsibility were a reference to any period during which the department occupies the site.

Right to compensation in respect of breach of duty

12 Right to compensation by virtue of ss 7 to 10

(1) Where any injury or damage has been caused in breach of a duty imposed by section 7, 8, 9 or 10 of this Act—
(a) subject to sections 13(1), (3) and (4), 15 and 17(1) of this Act, compensation in respect of that injury or damage shall be payable in accordance with section 16 of this Act wherever the injury or damage was incurred;
(b) subject to subsections (3) and (4) of this section and to section 21(2) of this Act, no other liability shall be incurred by any person in respect of that injury or damage.

(2) Subject to subsection (3) of this section, any injury or damage which, though not caused in breach of such a duty as aforesaid, is not reasonably separable from injury or damage so caused shall be deemed for the purposes of subsection (1) of this section to have been so caused.

(3) Where any injury or damage is caused partly in breach of such a duty as aforesaid and partly by an emission of ionising radiations which does not constitute such a breach, subsection (2) of this section shall not affect any liability of any person in respect of that emission apart from this Act, but a claimant shall not be entitled to recover compensation in respect of the same injury or damage both under this Act and otherwise than under this Act.

[(3A) Subject to subsection (4) of this section, where damage to any property has been caused which was not caused in breach of a duty imposed by section 7, 8, 9 or 10 of this Act but which would have been caused in breach of such a duty if in subsection (1)(a) or (b) of the said section 7 the words "other than the licensee" or in subsection (1) of the said section 10 the words "other than that operator" had not been enacted, no liability which, apart from this subsection, would have been incurred by any person in respect of that damage shall be so incurred except—
(a) in pursuance of an agreement to incur liability in respect of such damage entered into in writing before the occurrence of the damage; or
(b) where the damage was caused by an act or omission of that person done with intent to cause injury or damage.]

(4) Subject to section 13(5) of this Act, nothing in subsection (1)(b) [or in subsection (3A)] of this section shall affect—
(a) . . .
(b) the operation of the Carriage by Air Act 1932, the Carriage by Air Act 1961 or the Carriage by Air (Supplementary Provisions) Act 1962 in relation to any international carriage to which a convention referred to in the Act in question applies; or

(c) the operation of any Act which may be passed to give effect to the Convention on the Contract for the International Carriage of Goods by Road signed at Geneva on 19th May 1956.

NOTES

Sub-s (3A): inserted by the Nuclear Installations Act 1969, s 1.

Sub-s (4): words in square brackets inserted by the Nuclear Installations Act 1969, s 1; words omitted repealed by the Carriage of Goods by Sea Act 1971, s 6(3).

13 Exclusion, extension or reduction of compensation in certain cases

(1) Subject to subsections (2) and (5) of this section, compensation shall not be payable under this Act in respect of injury or damage caused by a breach of duty imposed by section 7, 8, 9 or 10 thereof if the injury or damage—

(a) was caused by such an occurrence as is mentioned in section 7(2)(b) or (c) or 10(2)(b) of this Act which is shown to have taken place wholly within the territorial limits of one, and one only, of the relevant territories other than the United Kingdom; or

(b) was incurred within the territorial limits of a country which is not a relevant territory.

(2) In the case of a breach of duty imposed by section 7, 8 or 9 of this Act, subsection (1)(b) of this section shall not apply to injury or damage incurred by, or by persons or property on, a ship or aircraft registered in the United Kingdom.

(3) Compensation shall not be payable under this Act in respect of injury or damage caused by a breach of a duty imposed by section 10 of this Act in respect of such carriage as is referred to in subsection (1)(a)(ii) of that section unless the agreement so referred to was expressed in writing.

(4) The duty imposed by section 7, 8, 9, 10 or 11 of this Act—

(a) shall not impose any liability on the person subject to that duty with respect to injury or damage caused by an occurrence which constitutes a breach of that duty if the occurrence, or the causing thereby of the injury or damage, is attributable to hostile action in the course of any armed conflict, including any armed conflict within the United Kingdom; but

(b) shall impose such a liability where the occurrence, or the causing thereby of the injury or damage, is attributable to a natural disaster, notwithstanding that the disaster is of such an exceptional character that it could not reasonably have been foreseen.

(5) Where, in the case of an occurrence which constitutes a breach of a duty imposed by section 7, 8, 9 or 10 of this Act, a person other than the person subject to that duty makes any payment in respect of injury or damage caused by that occurrence and—

(a) the payment is made in pursuance of any of the international conventions referred to in the Acts mentioned in section 12(4) of this Act; or

(b) the occurrence took place [or the injury or damage was incurred] within the territorial limits of a country which is not a relevant territory, and the payment is made by virtue of a law of that country and by a person who has his principal place of business in a relevant territory or is acting on behalf of such a person,

the person making the payment may make the like claim under this Act for compensation of the like amount, if any, [(subject to subsection (5A) of this section)], as would have been available to him if—

(i) the injury in question had been suffered by him or, as the case may be, the property suffering the damage in question had been his; and

(ii) subsection (1) of this section had not been passed.

[(5A) The amount that a person may claim by virtue of subsection (5) of this section shall not exceed the amount of the payment made by him and, in the case of a claim made by virtue of paragraph (b) of that subsection, shall not exceed the amount applicable under section 16(1) or (2) of this Act to the person subject to the duty in question.]

(6) The amount of compensation payable to or in respect of any person under this Act in respect of any injury or damage caused in breach of a duty imposed by section 7, 8, 9 or 10 of this Act may be reduced by reason of the fault of that person if, but only if, and to the extent that, the causing of that injury or damage is attributable to any act of that person committed with the intention of causing harm to any person or property or with reckless disregard for the consequences of his act.

NOTES

Sub-s (5): first words in square brackets inserted by the Nuclear Installations Act 1969, s 3; final words in square brackets substituted by the Energy Act 1983, s 27.

Sub-s (5A): inserted by the Energy Act 1983, s 27.

Bringing and satisfaction of claims

15 Time for bringing claims under ss 7 to 11

(1) Subject to subsection (2) of this section and to section 16(3) of this Act, but notwithstanding anything in any other enactment, a claim by virtue of any of sections 7 to 11 of this Act may be made at any time before, but shall not be entertained if made at any time after, the expiration of thirty years from the relevant date, that is to say, the date of the occurrence which gave rise to the claim or, where that occurrence was a continuing one, or was one of a succession of occurrences all attributable to a particular happening on a particular relevant site or to the carrying out from time to time on a particular relevant site of a particular operation, the date of the last event in the course of that occurrence or succession of occurrences to which the claim relates.

(2) Notwithstanding anything in subsection (1) of this section, a claim in respect of injury or damage caused by an occurrence involving nuclear matter stolen from, or lost, jettisoned or abandoned by, the person whose breach of a duty imposed by section 7, 8, 9 or 10 of this Act gave rise to the claim shall not be entertained if the occurrence takes place after the expiration of the period of twenty years beginning with the day when the nuclear matter in question was so stolen, lost, jettisoned or abandoned.

16 Satisfaction of claims by virtue of ss 7 to 10

(1) The liability of any person to pay compensation under this Act by virtue of a duty imposed on that person by section 7, 8 or 9 thereof shall not require him to make in respect of any one occurrence constituting a breach of that duty payments by way of such compensation exceeding in the aggregate, apart from payments in respect of interest or costs, [[£140 million] or, in the case of the licencees of such sites as may be prescribed, [£10 million]].

[(1A) The Secretary of State may with the approval of the Treasury by order increase or further increase either or both of the amounts specified in subsection (1) of this section; but an order under this subsection shall not affect liability in respect of any occurrence before (or beginning before) the order comes into force.]

(2) A relevant foreign operator shall not be required by virtue of section 10 of this Act to make any payment by way of compensation in respect of an occurrence—

- (a) if he would not have been required to make that payment if the occurrence had taken place in his home territory and the claim had been made by virtue of the relevant foreign law made for purposes corresponding to those of section 7, 8 or 9 of this Act; or
- (b) to the extent that the amount required for the satisfaction of the claim is not required to be available by the relevant foreign law made for purposes corresponding to those of section 19(1) of this Act and has not been made available under section 18 of this Act or by means of a relevant foreign contribution.

(3) Any claim by virtue of a duty imposed on any person by section 7, 8, 9 or 10 of this Act—

- (a) to the extent to which, by virtue of subsection (1) or (2) of this section, though duly established, it is not or would not be payable by that person; or
- (b) which is made after the expiration of the relevant period; or
- (c) which, being such a claim as is mentioned in section 15(2) of this Act, is made after the expiration of the period of twenty years so mentioned; or
- (d) which is a claim the full satisfaction of which out of funds otherwise required to be, or to be made, available for the purpose is prevented by section 21(1) of this Act,

shall be made to the appropriate authority, that is to say—

- (i) in the case of a claim by virtue of the said section 8 the Minister of Technology;
- (ii) in the case of a claim by virtue of the said section 9 (other than a claim in connection with a site used by a department of the Government of Northern Ireland), the Minister in charge of the government department concerned [or where the government department concerned is a part of the Scottish Administration the Scottish Ministers];
- (iii) in any other case, the Minister,

and, if established to the satisfaction of the appropriate authority, and to the extent to which it cannot be satisfied out of sums made available for the purpose under section 18 of this Act or by means of a relevant foreign contribution, shall be satisfied by the appropriate authority to such extent and out of funds provided by such means as Parliament may determine.

(4) Where in pursuance of subsection (3) of this section a claim has been made to the appropriate authority, any question affecting the establishment of the claim or as to the amount of any compensation in satisfaction of the claim may, if the authority thinks fit, be referred for decision to the appropriate court, that is to say, to whichever of the High Court, the Court of Session and the high Court of Justice in Northern Ireland would, but for the provisions of this section, have had jurisdiction in accordance with section 17(1) and (2) of this Act to determine the claim; and the claimant may appeal to that court from any decision of the authority on any such question which is not so referred; and on any such reference or appeal—

(a) the authority shall be entitled to appear and be heard; and
(b) notwithstanding anything in any Act, the decision of the court shall be final.

(5) In this section, the expression "the relevant period" means the period of ten years beginning with the relevant date within the meaning of section 15(1) of this Act.

NOTES

Sub-s (1): first words in square brackets substituted by the Energy Act 1983, s 27, sums in square brackets therein substituted by SI 1994/909, art 2.

Sub-s (1A): inserted by the Energy Act 1983, s 27.

Sub-s (3): in para (ii) words from "or where the" to "the Scottish Ministers" in square brackets inserted by SI 1999/1820, art 4, Sch 2, Pt I, para 38(1), (2).

Date in force: 1 July 1999: see SI 1999/1820, art 1(2).

Cover for compensation

18 General cover for compensation by virtue of ss 7 to 10

(1) In the case of any occurrence in respect of which one or more persons incur liability by virtue of section 7, 8, 9 or 10 of this Act or by virtue of any relevant foreign law made for purposes corresponding to those of any of those sections, but subject to subsections (2) [to (4B)] of this section and to sections 17(3)(b) and 21(1) of this Act, there shall be made available out of moneys provided by Parliament such sums as, when aggregated—

(a) with any funds required by, or by any relevant foreign law made for purposes corresponding to those of, section 19(1) of this Act to be available for the purpose of satisfying claims in respect of that occurrence against any licensee or relevant foreign operator; and
(b) in the case of a claim by virtue of any such foreign law, with any relevant foreign contributions towards the satisfaction of claims in respect of that occurrence[; and
(c) in the case of an occurrence in respect of which the Authority incurs liability, with any amounts payable under a contract of insurance or other arrangements for satisfying claims in respect of that occurrence against the Authority,]

may be necessary to ensure that all claims in respect of that occurrence made within the relevant period and duly established, excluding, but without prejudice to, any claim in respect of interest or costs, are satisfied up to [the aggregate amount specified in subsection (1A) of this section].

[(1A) The aggregate amount referred to in subsection (1) of this section is the equivalent in sterling of 300 million special drawing rights on—

(a) the day (or first day) of the occurrence in question, or

(b) if the Secretary of State certifies that another day has been fixed in relation to the occurrence in accordance with an international agreement, that other day.

(1B) The Secretary of State may with the approval of the Treasury by order increase or further increase the sum expressed in special drawing rights in subsection (1A) of this section; but an order under this subsection shall not have effect in respect of an occurrence before (or beginning before) the order comes into force.]

(2) Subsection (1) of this section shall not apply to any claim by virtue of such a relevant foreign law as is mentioned in that subsection in respect of injury or damage incurred within the territorial limits of a country which is not a relevant territory or to any claim such as is mentioned in section 15(2) of this Act which is not made within the period of twenty years so mentioned.

(3) Where any claim such as is mentioned in subsection (1) of this section is satisfied wholly or partly out of moneys provided by Parliament under that subsection, there shall also be made available out of moneys so provided such sums as are necessary to ensure the satisfaction of any claim in respect of interest or costs in connection with the first-mentioned claim.

[(4) In relation to liability by virtue of any relevant foreign law, there shall be left out of account for the purposes of subsection (1) of this section any claim which, though made within the relevant period, was made after the expiration of any period of limitation imposed by that law and permitted by a relevant international agreement.

(4A) Where—

(a) a relevant foreign law provides in pursuance of a relevant international agreement for sums additional to those referred to in subsection (1)(a) of this section to be made available out of public funds, but

(b) the maximum aggregate amount of compensation for which it provides in respect of an occurrence in pursuance of that agreement is less than that specified in subsection (1A) of this section,

then, in relation to liability by virtue of that law in respect of the occurrence, subsection (1) of this section shall have effect as if for the reference to the amount so specified there were substituted a reference to the maximum aggregate amount so provided.

(4B) Where a relevant foreign law does not make the provision mentioned in subsection (4A)(a) of this section, then in relation to liability by virtue of that law in respect of any occurrence—

(a) subsection (1) of this section shall not have effect unless the person (or one of the persons) liable is a licensee, the Authority or the Crown; and
(b) if a licensee, the Authority or the Crown is liable, subsection (1) shall have effect as if for the reference to the amount specified in subsection (1A) there were substituted a reference to the amount which would be applicable to that person under section 16(1) of this Act in respect of the occurrence (or, if more than one such person is liable, to the aggregate of the amounts which would be so applicable) if it had constituted a breach of duty under section 7, 8 or 9 of this Act.]

(5) Any sums received by the Minister by way of a relevant foreign contribution towards the satisfaction of any claim by virtue of section 7, 8, 9 or 10 of this Act shall be paid into the Exchequer.

(6) In this section, the expression "the relevant period" has the same meaning as in section 16 of this Act.

NOTES

Sub-s (1): first and final words in square brackets substituted by the Energy Act 1983, s 28; para (c) inserted by the Atomic Energy Act 1989, s 3.
Sub-ss (1A), (4A), (4B): inserted by the Energy Act 1983, s 28.
Sub-s (4): substituted by the Energy Act 1983, s 28.

19 Special cover for licensee's liability

(1) Subject to section 3(5) of this Act and to subsection (3) of this section, where a nuclear site licence has been granted in respect of any site, the licensee shall make such provision (either by insurance or by some other means) as the Minister may with the consent of the Treasury approve for sufficient funds to be available at all times to ensure that any claims which have been or may be duly established against the licensee as licensee of that site by virtue of section 7 of this Act or any relevant foreign law made for purposes corresponding to those of section 10 of this Act (excluding, but without prejudice to, any claim in respect of interest or costs) are satisfied up to [the required amount] in respect of each severally of the following periods, that is to say—
(a) the current cover period, if any;
(b) any cover period which ended less than ten years before the time in question;
(c) any earlier cover period in respect of which a claim remains to be disposed of, being a claim made—
  (i) within the relevant period within the meaning of section 16 of this Act; and
  (ii) in the case of a claim such as is mentioned in section 15(2) of this Act, also within the period of twenty years so mentioned;

and for the purposes of this section the cover period in respect of which any claim is to be treated as being made shall be that in which the beginning of the relevant period aforesaid fell.

[(1A) In this section "the required amount", in relation to the provision to be made by a licensee in respect of a cover period, means an aggregate amount equal to the amount applicable under section 16(1) of this Act to the licensee, as licensee of the site in question, in respect of an occurrence within that period.]

(2) In this Act, the expression "cover period" means [, subject to the following provisions of this section, the period of the licensee's responsibility;] and for the purposes of this definition the period of the licensee's responsibility shall be deemed to include any time after the expiration of that period during which it remains possible for the licensee to incur any liability by virtue of section 7(2)(b) or (*c*) of this Act, or by virtue of any relevant foreign law made for purposes corresponding to those of section 10 of this Act.

[(2A) When the amount applicable under section 16(1) of this Act to a licensee of a site changes as a result of—

(a) the coming into force of an order under section 16(1A) or of regulations made for the purposes of section 16(1), or

(b) an alteration relating to the site which brings it within, or takes it outside, the description prescribed by such regulations,

the current cover period relating to him as licensee of that site shall end and a new cover period shall begin.]

[(2B) The current cover period continues to run (and no new cover period begins) on the grant of a new nuclear site licence to the same licensee in respect of a site consisting of or including the site in respect of which his existing nuclear site licence is in force.]

(3) Where in the case of any licensed site the provision required by subsection (1) of this section is to be made otherwise than by insurance and, apart from this subsection, provision would also fall to be so made by the same person in respect of two or more other sites, the requirements of that subsection shall be deemed to be satisfied in respect of each of those sites if funds are available to meet such claims as are mentioned in that subsection in respect of all the sites collectively, and those funds would for the time being be sufficient to satisfy the requirements of that subsection in respect of those two of the sites in respect of which those requirements are highest:

Provided that the Minister may in any particular case at any time direct either that this subsection shall not apply or that the funds available as aforesaid shall be of such amount higher than that provided for by the foregoing provisions of this subsection, but lower than that necessary to satisfy the requirements of the said subsection (1) in respect of all the sites severally, as may be required by the direction.

(4) Where, by reason of the gravity of any occurrence which has resulted or may result in claims such as are mentioned in subsection (1) of this section against a licensee as licensee of a particular licensed site, or having regard to any previous occurrences which have resulted or may result in such claims against the licensee, the Minister thinks it proper so to do, he shall by notice in writing to the licensee direct that a new cover period for the purposes of the said subsection (1) shall begin in respect of that site on such date not earlier than two months after the date of the service of the notice as may be specified therein.

(5) If at any time while subsection (1) of this section applies in relation to any licensed site the provisions of that subsection are not complied with in respect of that site, the licensee shall be guilty of an offence and be liable—

(a) [the prescribed sum] or to imprisonment for a term not exceeding three months, or to both;

(b) on conviction on indictment, to a fine . . . , or to imprisonment for a term not exceeding two years, or to both.

NOTES

Sub-s (1): words in square brackets substituted by the Energy Act 1983, s 27.

Sub-ss (1A), (2A): inserted by the Energy Act 1983, s 27.

Sub-s (2): words in square brackets substituted with retrospective effect by the Atomic Energy Act 1989, s 4(1)(a).

Sub-s (2B): inserted with retrospective effect by the Atomic Energy Act 1989, s 4(1)(b).

Sub-s (5): first words in square brackets substituted by virtue of the Magistrates' Courts Act 1980, s 32(2); words omitted repealed by virtue of the Criminal Law Act 1977, s 32(1).

Miscellaneous and general

30 Short title and commencement

(1) This Act may be cited as the Nuclear Installations Act 1965.

(2) This Act shall come into force on such day as Her Majesty may by Order in Council appoint; and a later day may be appointed for the purposes of section 17(5) than that appointed for the purposes of the other provisions of this Act.

Misrepresentation Act 1967

1967 CHAPTER 7

An Act to amend the law relating to innocent misrepresentations and to amend sections 11 and 35 of the Sale of Goods Act 1893

[22nd March 1967]

1 Removal of certain bars to rescission for innocent misrepresentation

Where a person has entered into a contract after a misrepresentation has been made to him, and—

(a) the misrepresentation has become a term of the contract; or

(b) the contract has been performed;

or both, then, if otherwise he would be entitled to rescind the contract without alleging fraud, he shall be so entitled, subject to the provisions of this Act, notwithstanding the matters mentioned in paragraphs (*a*) and (*b*) of this section.

2 Damages for misrepresentation

(1) Where a person has entered into a contract after a misrepresentation has been made to him by another party thereto and as a result thereof he has suffered loss, then, if the person making the misrepresentation would be liable to damages in respect thereof had the misrepresentation been made fraudulently, that person shall be so liable notwithstanding that the misrepresentation was not made fraudulently, unless he proves that he had reasonable ground to believe and did believe up to the time the contract was made that the facts represented were true.

(2) Where a person has entered into a contract after a misrepresentation has been made to him otherwise than fraudulently, and he would be entitled, by reason of the misrepresentation, to rescind the contract, then, if it is claimed, in any proceedings arising out of the contract, that the contract ought to be or has been rescinded the court or arbitrator may declare the contract subsisting and award damages in lieu of rescission, if of opinion that it would be equitable to do so, having regard to the nature of the misrepresentation and the loss that would be caused by it if the contract were upheld, as well as to the loss that rescission would cause to the other party.

(3) Damages may be awarded against a person under subsection (2) of this section whether or not he is liable to damages under subsection (1) thereof, but where he is so liable any award under the said subsection (2) shall be taken into account in assessing his liability under the said subsection (1).

[3 Avoidance of provision excluding liability for misrepresentation]

[If a contract contains a term which would exclude or restrict—

(a) any liability to which a party to a contract may be subject by reason of any misrepresentation made by him before the contract was made; or

(b) any remedy available to another party to the contract by reason of such a misrepresentation,

that term shall be of no effect except in so far as it satisfies the requirement of reasonableness as stated in section 11(1) of the Unfair Contract Terms Act 1977; and it is for those claiming that the term satisfies that requirement to show that it does.]

NOTES

Substituted by the Unfair Contract Terms Act 1977, s 8(1).

5 Saving for past transactions

Nothing in this Act shall apply in relation to any misrepresentation or contract of sale which is made before the commencement of this Act.

6 Short title, commencement and extent

(1) This Act may be cited as the Misrepresentation Act 1967.

(2) This Act shall come into operation at the expiration of the period of one month beginning with the date on which it is passed.

(3) This Act . . . does not extend to Scotland.

(4) This Act does not extend to Northern Ireland.

NOTES

Sub-s (3): words omitted repealed by the Sale of Goods Act 1979, ss 62, 63, Sch 3.

Criminal Law Act 1967

1967 CHAPTER 58

An Act to amend the law of England and Wales by abolishing the division of crimes into felonies and misdemeanours and to amend and simplify the law in respect of matters arising from or related to that division or the abolition of it; to do away (within or without England and Wales) with certain obsolete crimes together with the torts of maintenance and champerty; and for purposes connected therewith

[21st July 1967]

PART I
FELONY AND MISDEMEANOUR

3 Use of force in making arrest, etc

(1) A person may use such force as is reasonable in the circumstances in the prevention of crime, or in effecting or assisting in the lawful arrest of offenders or suspected offenders or of persons unlawfully at large.

(2) Subsection (1) above shall replace the rules of the common law on the question when force used for a purpose mentioned in the subsection is justified by that purpose.

11 Extent of Part I, and provision for Northern Ireland

(1) Subject to subsections (2) to (4) below, this Part of this Act shall not extend to Scotland or to Northern Ireland.

(2) Subsection (1) above shall not restrict the operation of this Part of this Act—

- (a) in so far as it affects—
  - (i) . . .; or
  - (ii) the Army Act 1955, the Air Force Act 1955 or the Naval Discipline Act 1957; or
  - (iii) section 2 of the Forfeiture Act 1870 or any other enactment or rule of law relating to any parliamentary disqualification or other disability or penal consequence arising from an offence being felony; or
- (b) in so far as (by paragraph 10 of Schedule 2) it amends the Regimental Debts Act 1893.

(3), (4) . . .

NOTES

Sub-s (2): words omitted repealed by the Extradition Act 1989, s 37(1), Sch 2.
Sub-s (3): repealed by the Public Order Act 1986, s 40(3), Sch 3.
Sub-s (4): repealed by the Northern Ireland Constitution Act 1973, s 41(1), Sch 6, Part I.

PART III
SUPPLEMENTARY

14 Civil rights in respect of maintenance and champerty

(1) No person shall, under the law of England and Wales, be liable in tort for any conduct on account of its being maintenance or champerty as known to the common law, except in the case of a cause of action accruing before this section has effect.

(2) The abolition of criminal and civil liability under the law of England and Wales for maintenance and champerty shall not affect any rule of that law as to the cases in which a contract is to be treated as contrary to public policy or otherwise illegal.

15 Short title

This Act may be cited as the Criminal Law Act 1967.

Theatres Act 1968

1968 CHAPTER 54

An Act to abolish censorship of the theatre and to amend the law in respect of theatres and theatrical performances

[26th July 1968]

Provisions with respect to performances of plays

4 Amendment of law of defamation

(1) For the purposes of the law of libel and slander (including the law of criminal libel so far as it relates to the publication of defamatory matter) the publication of words in the course of a performance of a play shall, subject to section 7 of this Act, be treated as publication in permanent form.

(2) The foregoing subsection shall apply for the purposes of section 3 (slander of title, etc) of the Defamation Act 1952 as it applies for the purposes of the law of libel and slander.

(3) In this section "words" includes pictures, visual images, gestures and other methods of signifying meaning.

(4) This section shall not apply to Scotland.

7 Exceptions for performances given in certain circumstances

(1) Nothing in sections 2 to 4 of this Act shall apply in relation to a performance of a play given on a domestic occasion in a private dwelling.

(2) Nothing in sections 2 to 6 of this Act shall apply in relation to a performance of a play given solely or primarily for one or more of the following purposes, that is to say—

- (a) rehearsal; or
- (b) to enable—
  - (i) a record or cinematograph film to be made from or by means of the performance; or
  - (ii) the performance to be broadcast; or
  - [(iii) the performance to be included in a programme service (within the meaning of the Broadcasting Act 1990) other than a sound or television broadcasting service;]

but in any proceedings for an offence under section 2, . . . or 6 of this Act alleged to have been committed in respect of a performance of a play or an offence at common law alleged to have been committed in England and Wales by the publication of defamatory matter in the course of a performance of a play, if it is proved that the performance was attended by persons other than persons directly connected with the giving of the performance or the doing in relation thereto of any of the things mentioned in paragraph (b) above, the performance shall be taken not to have been given solely or primarily for one or more of the said purposes unless the contrary is shown.

(3) In this section—

"broadcast" means broadcast by wireless telegraphy (within the meaning of the Wireless Telegraphy Act 1949), whether by way of sound broadcasting or television;

"cinematograph film" means any print, negative, tape or other article on which a performance of a play or any part of such a performance is recorded for the purposes of visual reproduction;

"record" means any record or similar contrivance for reproducing sound, including the sound-track of a cinematograph film;

. . .

NOTES

Sub-s (2): sub-para (b)(iii) substituted by the Broadcasting Act 1990, s 203(1), Sch 20, para 13; figure omitted repealed by the Public Order Act 1986, s 40(3), Sch 3.

Sub-s (3): words omitted repealed by the Cable and Broadcasting Act 1984, s 57, Sch 5, para 21(2), Sch 6.

Miscellaneous and general

20 Short title, commencement, extent and application to Isles of Scilly

(1) This Act may be cited as the Theatres Act 1968.

(2) The provisions of this Act mentioned in subsection (3) below shall come into force on the passing of this Act, and the other provisions of this Act shall come into force on the expiration of a period of two months beginning with the date on which this Act is passed; but a licence granted under this Act during that period, and any requirements imposed under section 17(2) during that period, shall not come into force before the expiration of that period.

(3) The provisions of this Act referred to in subsection (2) above are the following—

(a) sections 1(2), 12(4), 14, 17(2), 18(1) and this section;

(b) section 17(3) so far as it relates to section 14 or to paragraph 7 of Schedule 1;

(c) Schedule 1.

(4) This Act does not extend to Northern Ireland.

(5) In relation to the Isles of Scilly this Act shall have effect as if they were a county and as if for any reference to the council of a county there were substituted a reference to the Council of the Isles of Scilly.

Civil Evidence Act 1968

1968 CHAPTER 64

An Act to amend the law of evidence in relation to civil proceedings, and in respect of the privilege against self-incrimination to make corresponding amendments in relation to statutory powers of inspection or investigation

[25th October 1968]

PART II
MISCELLANEOUS AND GENERAL

Convictions, etc as evidence in civil proceedings

11 Convictions as evidence in civil proceedings

(1) In any civil proceedings the fact that a person has been convicted of an offence by or before any court in the United Kingdom or by a court-martial there or elsewhere shall (subject to subsection (3) below) be admissible in evidence for the purpose of proving, where to do so is relevant to any issue in those proceedings, that he committed that offence, whether he was so convicted upon a plea of guilty or otherwise and whether or not he is a party to the civil proceedings; but no conviction other than a subsisting one shall be admissible in evidence by virtue of this section.

(2) In any civil proceedings in which by virtue of this section a person is proved to have been convicted of an offence by or before any court in the United Kingdom or by a court-martial there or elsewhere—

(a) he shall be taken to have committed that offence unless the contrary is proved; and
(b) without prejudice to the reception of any other admissible evidence for the purpose of identifying the facts on which the conviction was based, the contents of any document which is admissible as evidence of the conviction, and the contents of the information, complaint, indictment or charge-sheet on which the person in question was convicted, shall be admissible in evidence for that purpose.

(3) Nothing in this section shall prejudice the operation of section 13 of this Act or any other enactment whereby a conviction or a finding of fact in any criminal proceedings is for the purposes of any other proceedings made conclusive evidence of any fact.

(4) Where in any civil proceedings the contents of any document are admissible in evidence by virtue of subsection (2) above, a copy of that document, or of the material part thereof, purporting to be certified or otherwise authenticated by or on behalf of the court or authority having custody of that document shall be admissible in evidence and shall be taken to be a true copy of that document or part unless the contrary is shown.

(5) Nothing in any of the following enactments, that is to say—
(a) [[section 1C] of the Powers of Criminal Courts Act 1973] (under which a conviction leading to . . . discharge is to be disregarded except as therein mentioned);
(b) section 9 of the Criminal Justice (Scotland) Act 1949 (which makes similar provision in respect of convictions on indictment in Scotland); and
(c) section 8 of the Probation Act (Northern Ireland) 1950 (which corresponds to the said section 12) or any corresponding enactment of the Parliament of Northern Ireland for the time being in force,

shall affect the operation of this section; and for the purposes of this section any order made by a court of summary jurisdiction in Scotland under section 1 or section 2 of the said Act of 1949 shall be treated as a conviction.

(6) In this section "court-martial" means a court-martial constituted under the Army Act 1955, the Air Force Act 1955 or the Naval Discipline Act 1957 or a disciplinary court constituted under *section 50* [section 52G] of the said Act of 1957, and in relation to a court-martial "conviction", . . . , means a finding of guilty which is, or falls to be treated as, the finding of the court, and "convicted" shall be construed accordingly.

NOTES

Sub-s (5): words in first (outer) pair of square brackets substituted by the Powers of Criminal Courts Act 1973, ss 56(1), 60(2), Sch 5, para 31, words in second (inner) pair of square brackets substituted and words omitted repealed, by the Criminal Justice Act 1991, ss 100, 101(2), Sch 11, para 5, Sch 13.

Sub-s (6): words in square brackets substituted and words omitted repealed by the Armed Forces Act 1996, ss 5, 35(2), Sch 1, para 100, Sch 7, Pt II.

13 Conclusiveness of convictions for purposes of defamation actions

(1) In an action for libel or slander in which the question whether [the plaintiff] did or did not commit a criminal offence is relevant to an issue arising in the action, proof that at the time when that issue falls to be determined, [he] stands convicted of that offence shall be conclusive evidence that he committed that offence; and his conviction thereof shall be admissible in evidence accordingly.

(2) In any such action as aforesaid in which by virtue of this section [the plaintiff] is proved to have been convicted of an offence, the contents of any document which is admissible as evidence of the conviction, and the contents of the information, complaint, indictment or charge-sheet on which [he] was convicted, shall, without prejudice to the reception of any other admissible evidence for the purpose of identifying the facts on which the conviction was based, be admissible in evidence for the purpose of identifying those facts.

[(2A) In the case of an action for libel or slander in which there is more than one plaintiff—

(a) the references in subsections (1) and (2) above to the plaintiff shall be construed as references to any of the plaintiffs, and

(b) proof that any of the plaintiffs stands convicted of an offence shall be conclusive evidence that he committed that offence so far as that fact is relevant to any issue arising in relation to his cause of action or that of any other plaintiff.]

(3) For the purposes of this section a person shall be taken to stand convicted of an offence if but only if there subsists against him a conviction of that offence by or before a court in the United Kingdom or by a court-martial there or elsewhere.

(4) Subsections (4) to (6) of section 11 of this Act shall apply for the purposes of this section as they apply for the purposes of that section, but as if in the said subsection (4) the reference to subsection (2) were a reference to subsection (2) of this section.

(5) The foregoing provisions of this section shall apply for the purposes of any action begun after the passing of this Act, whenever the cause of action arose, but shall not apply for the purposes of any action begun before the passing of this Act or any appeal or other proceedings arising out of any such action.

NOTES

Sub-ss (1), (2): words in square brackets substituted by the Defamation Act 1996, s 12(1).
Sub-s (2A): inserted by the Defamation Act 1996, s 12(1).

General

20 Short title, repeals, extent and commencement

(1) This Act may be cited as the Civil Evidence Act 1968.

(2) . . .

(3) This Act shall not extend to Scotland or, . . . to Northern Ireland.

(4) The following provisions of this Act, namely sections 13 to 19, this section (except subsection (2)) and the Schedule, shall come into force on the day this Act is passed, and the other provisions of this Act shall come into force on such day as the Lord Chancellor may by order made by statutory instrument appoint; and different days may be so appointed for different purposes of this Act or for the same purposes in relation to different courts or proceedings or otherwise in relation to different circumstances.

NOTES

Sub-s (2): repeals the Evidence Act 1938, ss 1, 2, 6(1)(in part).

Sub-s (3): words omitted repealed by the Northern Ireland Constitution Act 1973, s 41(1), Sch 6, Part I.

Employer's Liability (Defective Equipment) Act 1969

1969 CHAPTER 37

An Act to make further provision with respect to the liability of an employer for injury to his employee which is attributable to any defect in equipment provided by the employer for the purposes of the employer's business; and for purposes connected with the matter aforesaid.

[25th July 1969]

1 Extension of employer's liability for defective equipment

(1) Where after the commencement of this Act—

(a) an employee suffers personal injury in the course of his employment in consequence of a defect in equipment provided by his employer for the purposes of the employer's business; and

(b) the defect is attributable wholly or partly to the fault of a third party (whether identified or not),

the injury shall be deemed to be also attributable to negligence on the part of the employer (whether or not he is liable in respect of the injury apart from this subsection), but without prejudice to the law relating to contributory negligence and to any remedy by way of contribution or in contract or otherwise which is available to the employer in respect of the injury.

(2) In so far as any agreement purports to exclude or limit any liability of an employer arising under subsection (1) of this section, the agreement shall be void.

(3) In this section—

"business" includes the activities carried on by any public body;

"employee" means a person who is employed by another person under a contract of service or apprenticeship and is so employed for the purposes of a business carried on by that other person, and "employer" shall be construed accordingly;

"equipment" includes any plant and machinery, vehicle, aircraft and clothing;

"fault" means negligence, breach of statutory duty or other act or omission which gives rise to liability in tort in England and Wales or which is wrongful and gives rise to liability in damages in Scotland; and

"personal injury" includes loss of life, any impairment of a person's physical or mental condition and any disease.

(4) This section binds the Crown, and persons in the service of the Crown shall accordingly be treated for the purposes of this section as employees of the Crown if they would not be so treated apart from this subsection.

2 Short title, commencement and extent

(1) This Act may be cited as the Employer's Liability (Defective Equipment) Act 1969.

(2) This Act shall come into force on the expiration of the period of three months beginning with the date on which it is passed.

(3) . . .

(4) This Act . . . does not extend to Northern Ireland.

NOTES

Sub-ss (3), (4): words omitted repealed by the Northern Ireland Constitution Act 1973, s 41, Sch 6, Part I.

Employers' Liability (Compulsory Insurance) Act 1969

1969 CHAPTER 57

An Act to require employers to insure against their liability for personal injury to their employees; and for purposes connected with the matter aforesaid.

[22nd October 1969]

1 Insurance against liability for employees

(1) Except as otherwise provided by this Act, every employer carrying on any business in Great Britain shall insure, and maintain insurance, under one or more approved policies with an authorised insurer or insurers against liability for bodily injury or disease sustained by his employees, and arising out of and in the course of their employment in Great Britain in that business, but except in so far as regulations otherwise provide not including injury or disease suffered or contracted outside Great Britain.

(2) Regulations may provide that the amount for which an employer is required by this Act to insure and maintain insurance shall, either generally or in such cases or

classes of case as may be prescribed by the regulations, be limited in such manner as may be so prescribed.

(3) For the purposes of this Act—

(a) "approved policy" means a policy of insurance not subject to any conditions or exceptions prohibited for those purposes by regulations;

[(b) "authorised insurer" means—

(i) a person who has permission under Part 4 of the Financial Services and Markets Act 2000 to effect and carry out contracts of insurance of a kind required by this Act and regulations made under this Act, or

(ii) an EEA firm of the kind mentioned in paragraph 5(d) of Schedule 3 to the Financial Services and Markets Act 2000, which has permission under paragraph 15 of that Schedule to effect and carry out contracts of insurance of a kind required by this Act and regulations made under this Act;]

(c) "business" includes a trade or profession, and includes any activity carried on by a body of persons, whether corporate or unincorporate;

(d) except as otherwise provided by regulations, an employer not having a place of business in Great Britain shall be deemed not to carry on business there.

[(3A) Subsection (3)(b) must be read with—

(a) section 22 of the Financial Services and Markets Act 2000;

(b) any relevant order under that section; and

(c) Schedule 2 to that Act.]

NOTES

Sub-s (3): para (b) substituted by SI 2001/3649, art 280(1), (2).
Date in force: 1 December 2001: see SI 2001/3649, art 1.
Sub-s (3A): inserted by SI 2001/3649, art 280(1), (3).
Date in force: 1 December 2001: see SI 2001/3649, art 1.

2 Employees to be covered

(1) For the purposes of this Act the term "employee" means an individual who has entered into or works under a contract of service or apprenticeship with an employer whether by way of manual labour, clerical work or otherwise, whether such contract is expressed or implied, oral or in writing.

(2) This Act shall not require an employer to insure—

(a) in respect of an employee of whom the employer is the husband, wife, father, mother, grandfather, grandmother, step-father, step-mother, son, daughter, grandson, granddaughter, stepson, stepdaughter, brother, sister, half-brother or half-sister; or

(b) except as otherwise provided by regulations, in respect of employees not ordinarily resident in Great Britain.

7 Short title, extent and commencement

(1) This Act may be cited as the Employers' Liability (Compulsory Insurance) Act 1969.

(2) This Act shall not extend to Northern Ireland.

(3) This Act shall come into force for any purpose on such date as the Secretary of State may by order contained in a statutory instrument appoint, and the purposes for which this Act is to come into force at any time may be defined by reference to the nature of an employer's business, or to that of an employee's work, or in any other way.

Taxes Management Act 1970

1970 CHAPTER 9

An Act to consolidate certain of the enactments relating to income tax, capital gains tax and corporation tax, including certain enactments relating also to other taxes
[12th March 1970]

PART IV
ASSESSMENT AND CLAIMS

[30 Recovery of overpayment of tax, etc]

[(1) Where an amount of [income tax or capital gains tax] has been repaid to any person which ought not to have been repaid to him, that amount of tax may be assessed and recovered as if it were unpaid tax.

[(1A) Subsection (1) above shall not apply where the amount of tax which has been repaid is assessable under section 29 of this Act.]

[(1B) Subsections (2) to (8) of section 29 of this Act shall apply in relation to an assessment under subsection (1) above as they apply in relation to an assessment under subsection (1) of that section; and subsection (4) of that section as so applied shall have effect as if the reference to the loss of tax were a reference to the repayment of the amount of tax which ought not to have been repaid.]

(2) In any case where—

(a) a repayment of tax has been increased in accordance with section [824 . . . of the principal Act or section] [283 of the 1992 Act] (supplements added to repayments of tax, etc.); and

(b) the whole or any part of that repayment has been paid to any person but ought not to have been paid to him; and

(c) that repayment ought not to have been increased either at all or to any extent;

then the amount of the repayment assessed under subsection (1) above may include an amount equal to the amount by which the repayment ought not to have been increased.

[(2A) . . .]

(3) In any case where—

(a) a payment, other than a repayment of tax to which subsection (2) above applies, is increased in accordance with section [824 or 825 of the principal Act or section] [283 of the 1992 Act]; and
(b) that payment ought not to have been increased either at all or to any extent;

then an amount equal to the amount by which the payment ought not to have been increased may be assessed and recovered as if it were unpaid income tax . . ..

[(3A) . . .]

[(4) An assessment to income tax under this section shall be made under Case VI of Schedule D.]

[(4A) . . .]

[(5) An assessment under this section shall not be out of time under section 34 of this Act if it is made before the end of whichever of the following ends the later, namely—
(a) the [year of assessment] following that in which the amount assessed was repaid or paid as the case may be, or
(b) where a return delivered by the person concerned. . . is enquired into by an officer of the Board, the period ending with the day on which, by virtue of section [28A(1)] of this Act, [the enquiry is] completed.]

(6) Subsection (5) above is without prejudice to [section 36] of this Act.

(7) In this section any reference to an amount repaid or paid includes a reference to an amount allowed by way of set-off.]

NOTES

Substituted by the Finance Act 1982, s 149(1).

Sub-s (1): words "income tax or capital gains tax" in square brackets substituted by the Finance Act 1998, s 117(3), Sch 19, para 13(2).

Date in force: this amendment has effect in relation to accounting periods ending on or after 1 July 1999 (being the date appointed under s 199 of the Finance Act 1994 for the purposes of Chapter III of Part IV of that Act): see the Finance Act 1998, s 117(4) and SI 1998/3173, art 2.

Sub-s (1A): inserted, in relation to amounts of tax repaid on or after 26 July 1990, by the Finance Act 1990, s 105.

Sub-s (1B): inserted, in relation to income tax and capital gains tax as respects the year 1996–97 and subsequent years of assessment, and in relation to corporation tax as respects accounting periods ending on or after 1 July 1999, by the Finance Act 1994, s 196, Sch 19, para 4(1), in accordance with s 199(2), (3) thereof.

Sub-s (2): in para (a) words in square brackets beginning with the word "824" substituted by the Income and Corporation Taxes Act 1988, s 844, Sch 29, para 32.

Sub-s (2): in para (a) words omitted repealed by the Finance Act 1998, ss 117(3), 165, Sch 19, para 13(3), Sch 27, Pt III(28).

Date in force: this repeal has effect in relation to accounting periods ending on or after 1 July 1999 (being the date appointed under s 199 of the Finance Act 1994 for the purposes of Chapter III of Part IV of that Act): see the Finance Act 1998, s 117(4) and SI 1998/3173, art 2.

Sub-s (2): in para (a) words "283 of the 1992 Act" in square brackets substituted by the Taxation of Chargeable Gains Act 1992, s 290(1), Sch 10, para 2(6).

Sub-s (2A): inserted by the Finance (No 2) Act 1987, s 88(1), (7), in relation to accounting periods ending after 30 September 1993.

Sub-s (2A): repealed by the Finance Act 1998, ss 117(3), 165, Sch 19, para 13(4), Sch 27, Pt III(28).

Date in force: this repeal has effect in relation to accounting periods ending on or after 1 July 1999 (being the date appointed under s 199 of the Finance Act 1994 for the purposes of Chapter III of Part IV of that Act): see the Finance Act 1998, s 117(4) and SI 1998/3173, art 2.

Sub-s (3): in para (a) words "824 or 825 of the principal Act or section" in square brackets substituted by the Income and Corporation Taxes Act 1988, s 844, Sch 29, para 32.

Sub-s (3): in para (a) words "283 of the 1992 Act" in square brackets substituted by the Income and Corporation Taxes Act 1988, s 844, Sch 29, para 32.

Sub-s (3): words omitted repealed by the Finance Act 1998, ss 117(3), 165, Sch 19, para 13(5), Sch 27, Pt III(28).

Date in force: this repeal has effect in relation to accounting periods ending on or after 1 July 1999 (being the date appointed under s 199 of the Finance Act 1994 for the purposes of Chapter III of Part IV of that Act): see the Finance Act 1998, s 117(4) and SI 1998/3173, art 2.

Sub-s (3A): inserted by the Finance (No 2) Act 1987, s 88(2), (7), in relation to accounting periods ending after 30 September 1993.

Sub-s (3A): repealed by the Finance Act 1998, ss 117(3), 165, Sch 19, para 13(6), Sch 27, Pt III(28).

Date in force: this repeal has effect in relation to accounting periods ending on or after 1 July 1999 (being the date appointed under s 199 of the Finance Act 1994 for the purposes of Chapter III of Part IV of that Act): see the Finance Act 1998, s 117(4) and SI 1998/3173, art 2.

Sub-s (4): substituted by the Finance Act 1998, s 117(3), Sch 19, para 13(7).

Date in force: this amendment has effect in relation to accounting periods ending on or after 1 July 1999 (being the date appointed under s 199 of the Finance Act 1994 for the purposes of Chapter III of Part IV of that Act): see the Finance Act 1998, s 117(4) and SI 1998/3173, art 2.

Sub-s (4A): inserted by the Finance (No 2) Act 1987, s 88(4), (7), in relation to accounting periods ending after 30 September 1993.

Sub-s (4A): repealed by the Finance Act 1998, ss 117(3), 165, Sch 19, para 13(8), Sch 27, Pt III(28).

Date in force: this repeal has effect in relation to accounting periods ending on or after 1 July 1999 (being the date appointed under s 199 of the Finance Act 1994 for the purposes of Chapter III of Part IV of that Act): see the Finance Act 1998, s 117(4) and SI 1998/3173, art 2.

Sub-s (5): substituted, in relation to income tax and capital gains tax as respects the year 1996–97 and subsequent years of assessment, and in relation to corporation tax as respects accounting periods ending on or after 1 July 1999, by the Finance Act 1994, s 196, Sch 19, para 4(2), in accordance with s 199(2), (3) thereof.

Sub-s (5): in para (a) words "year of assessment" in square brackets substituted by the Finance Act 1998, s 117(3), Sch 19, para 13(9).

Date in force: this amendment has effect in relation to accounting periods ending on or after 1 July 1999 (being the date appointed under s 199 of the Finance Act 1994 for the purposes of Chapter III of Part IV of that Act): see the Finance Act 1998, s 117(4) and SI 1998/3173, art 2.

Sub-s (5): in para (b) words omitted repealed by the Finance Act 2001, ss 88(1), 110, Sch 29, Pt 5, para 23(1), (2)(a), Sch 33, Pt 2(13).

Date in force: this repeal has effect as from 11 May 2001 in relation to returns whether made before or after that date, and whether relating to periods before or after that date: see the Finance Act 2001, s 88(3).

Sub-s (5): in para (b) reference to "28A(1)" in square brackets substituted by the Finance Act 2001, s 88(1), Sch 29, Pt 5, para 23(1), (2)(b).

Date in force: this amendment has effect as from 11 May 2001 in relation to returns whether made before or after that date, and whether relating to periods before or after that date: see the Finance Act 2001, s 88(3).

Sub-s (5): words "the enquiry is" in square brackets substituted by the Finance Act 2001, s 88(1), Sch 29, Pt 5, para 23(1), (2)(c).

Date in force: this amendment has effect as from 11 May 2001 in relation to returns whether made before or after that date, and whether relating to periods before or after that date: see the Finance Act 2001, s 88(3).

Sub-s (6): words "section 36" in square brackets substituted by the Finance Act 1989, s 149(3).

Relief for excessive assessments

33 Error or mistake

[(1) If a person who has paid income tax or capital gains tax under an assessment (whether a self-assessment or otherwise) alleges that the assessment was excessive by reason of some error or mistake in a return, he may by notice in writing at any time not later than five years after the 31st January next following the year of assessment to which the return relates, make a claim to the Board for relief.]

(2) On receiving the claim the Board shall inquire into the matter and shall, subject to the provisions of this section, give by way of repayment such relief < . . . > in respect of the error or mistake as is reasonable and just:

. . .

[(2A) No relief shall be given under this section in respect of—

(a) an error or mistake as to the basis on which the liability of the claimant ought to have been computed where the return was in fact made on the basis or in accordance with the practice generally prevailing at the time when it was made; or

(b) an error or mistake in a claim which is included in the return.]

(3) In determining the claim the Board shall have regard to all the relevant circumstances of the case, and in particular shall consider whether the granting of relief would result in the exclusion from charge to tax of any part of the profits of the claimant, and for this purpose the Board may take into consideration the liability of the claimant and assessments made on him in respect of chargeable periods other than that to which the claim relates.

(4) If any appeal is brought from the decision of the Board on the claim the Special Commissioners shall hear and determine the appeal in accordance with the principles to be followed by the Board in determining claims under this section; and neither the appellant nor the Board shall be entitled to [appeal under section 56A of this Act against the determination of the Special Commissioners except] on a point of law arising in connection with the computation of profits.

[(4A) . . .]

(5) In this section "profits"—

(a) in relation to income tax, means income, [and]
(b) in relation to capital gains tax, means chargeable gains,
(c) . . .

NOTES

Sub-s (1): substituted by the Finance Act 1998, s 117(3), Sch 19, para 15(2).

Date in force: this amendment has effect in relation to accounting periods ending on or after 1 July 1999 (being the date appointed under s 199 of the Finance Act 1994 for the purposes of Chapter III of Part IV of that Act): see the Finance Act 1998, s 117(4) and SI 1998/3173, art 2.

Sub-s (2): first words omitted repealed by the Finance Act 1971, ss 37(2), 38, 69(7), Sch 14, Part II, with effect for the year 1973–74 and subsequent years of assessment.

Sub-s (2): second words omitted repealed by the Finance Act 1994, ss 196, 258, Sch 19, para 8(2), Sch 26, Pt V.

Date in force: this repeal has effect, in relation to income tax and capital gains tax, as respects the year 1996–97 and subsequent years of assessment: see the Finance Act 1994, s 199(2)(a).

Date in force: this repeal has effect, in relation to corporation tax, as respects accounting periods ending on or after 1 July 1999: see the Finance Act 1994, s 199(2)(b) and SI 1998/3173, art 2.

Sub-s (2A): inserted by the Finance Act 1994, s 196, Sch 19, para 8(2).

Date in force: this amendment has effect, in relation to income tax and capital gains tax, as respects the year 1996–97 and subsequent years of assessment: see the Finance Act 1994, s 199(2)(a).

Date in force: this amendment has effect, in relation to corporation tax, as respects accounting periods ending on or after 1 July 1999: see the Finance Act 1994, s 199(2)(b) and SI 1998/3173, art 2.

Sub-s (4): words from "appeal under" to "Special Commissioners except" in square brackets substituted by SI 1994/1813, reg 2(1), Sch 1, para 2.

Sub-s (4A): inserted by the Development Land Tax Act 1976, s 41, Sch 8, para 5; repealed, in respect of any disposal taking place on or after 19 March 1985, by virtue of the Finance Act 1985, s 98(6), Sch 27, Part X.

Sub-s (5): word "and" in square brackets at the end of para (a) inserted by the Finance Act 1998, s 117(3), Sch 19, para 15(3).

Date in force: this amendment has effect in relation to accounting periods ending on or after 1 July 1999 (being the date appointed under s 199 of the Finance Act 1994 for the purposes of Chapter III of Part IV of that Act): see the Finance Act 1998, s 117(4) and SI 1998/3173, art 2.

Sub-s (5): para (c) repealed by the Finance Act 1998, ss 117(3), 165, Sch 19, para 15(3), Sch 27, Pt III(28).

Date in force: this repeal has effect in relation to accounting periods ending on or after 1 July 1999 (being the date appointed under s 199 of the Finance Act 1994 for the purposes of Chapter III of Part IV of that Act): see the Finance Act 1998, s 117(4) and SI 1998/3173, art 2.

PART XII
GENERAL

119 Commencement and construction

(1) This Act shall come into force for all purposes on 6th April 1970 to the exclusion of the corresponding enactments repealed by the principal Act.

(2) This Act, and the repeals made by the principal Act, have effect subject to Schedule 4 to this Act.

(3) This Act, so far as it relates to income tax or corporation tax, shall be construed as one with the principal Act.

(4) This Act, so far as it relates to chargeable gains, shall be construed as one with [the [1992 Act]].

[(5) . . .]

NOTES

Sub-s (4): words in square brackets beginning with the word "the" substituted by the Capital Gains Tax Act 1979, s 157(2), Sch 7, para 8(a).

Sub-s (4): words "1992 Act" in square brackets substituted by the Taxation of Chargeable Gains Act 1992, s 290(1), Sch 10, para 2(2).

Sub-s (5): inserted by the Development Land Tax Act 1976, s 41, Sch 8, para 33; repealed, in respect of any disposal taking place on or after 19 March 1985, by virtue of by the Finance Act 1985, s 98(6), Sch 27, Part X.

Animals Act 1971

1971 CHAPTER 22

An Act to make provision with respect to civil liability for damage done by animals and with respect to the protection of livestock from dogs; and for purposes connected with those matters

[12th May 1971]

Strict liability for damage done by animals

1 New provisions as to strict liability for damage done by animals

(1) The provisions of sections 2 to 5 of this Act replace—

(a) the rules of the common law imposing a strict liability in tort for damage done by an animal on the ground that the animal is regarded as ferae naturea or that its vicious or mischievous propensities are known or presumed to be known;

(b) subsections (1) and (2) of section 1 of the Dogs Act 1906 as amended by the Dogs (Amendment) Act 1928 (injury to cattle or poultry); and

(c) the rules of the common law imposing a liability for cattle trespass.

(2) Expressions used in those sections shall be interpreted in accordance with the provisions of section 6 (as well as those of section 11) of this Act.

2 Liability for damage done by dangerous animals

(1) Where any damage is caused by an animal which belongs to a dangerous species, any person who is a keeper of the animal is liable for the damage, except as otherwise provided by this Act.

(2) Where damage is caused by an animal which does not belong to a dangerous species, a keeper of the animal is liable for the damage, except as otherwise provided by this Act, if—

(a) the damage is of a kind which the animal, unless restrained, was likely to cause or which, if caused by the animal, was likely to be severe; and

(b) the likelihood of the damage or of its being severe was due to characteristics of the animal which are not normally found in animals of the same species or are not normally so found except at particular times or in particular circumstances: and

(c) those characteristics were known to that keeper or were at any time known to a person who at that time had charge of the animal as that keeper's servant or, where that keeper is the head of a household, were known to another keeper of the animal who is a member of that household and under the age of sixteen.

3 Liability for injury done by dogs to livestock

Where a dog causes damage by killing or injuring livestock, any person who is a keeper of the dog is liable for the damage, except as otherwise provided by this Act.

4 Liability for damage and expenses due to trespassing livestock

(1) Where livestock belonging to any person strays on to land in the ownership or occupation of another and—

(a) damage is done by the livestock to the land or to any property on it which is in the ownership or possession of the other person; or

(b) any expenses are reasonably incurred by that other person in keeping the livestock while it cannot be restored to the person to whom it belongs or while it is detained in pursuance of section 7 of this Act, or in ascertaining to whom it belongs;

the person to whom the livestock belongs is liable for the damage or expenses, except as otherwise provided by this Act.

(2) For the purposes of this section any livestock belongs to the person in whose possession it is.

5 Exceptions from liability under sections 2 to 4

(1) A person is not liable under sections 2 to 4 of this Act for any damage which is due wholly to the fault of the person suffering it.

(2) A person is not liable under section 2 of this Act for any damage suffered by a person who has voluntarily accepted the risk thereof.

(3) A person is not liable under section 2 of this Act for any damage caused by an animal kept on any premises or structure to a person trespassing there, if it is proved either—

(a) that the animal was not kept there for the protection of persons or property; or

(b) (if the animal was kept there for the protection of persons or property) that keeping it there for that purpose was not unreasonable.

(4) A person is not liable under section 3 of this Act if the livestock was killed or injured on land on to which it had strayed and either the dog belonged to the occupier or its presence on the land was authorised by the occupier.

(5) A person is not liable under section 4 of this Act where the livestock strayed from a highway and its presence there was a lawful use of the highway.

(6) In determining whether any liability for damage under section 4 of this Act is excluded by subsection (1) of this section the damage shall not be treated as due to the fault of the person suffering it by reason only that he could have prevented it by fencing; but a person is not liable under that section where it is proved that the straying of the livestock on to the land would not have occurred but for a breach by any other person, being a person having an interest in the land, of a duty to fence.

6 Interpretation of certain expressions used in sections 2 to 5

(1) The following provisions apply to the interpretation of sections 2 to 5 of this Act.

(2) A dangerous species is a species—

(a) which is not commonly domesticated in the British Islands; and

(b) whose fully grown animals normally have such characteristics that they are likely, unless restrained, to cause severe damage or that any damage they may cause is likely to be severe.

(3) Subject to subsection (4) of this section, a person is a keeper of an animal if—

(a) he owns the animal or has it in his possession; or

(b) he is the head of a household of which a member under the age of sixteen owns the animal or has it in his possession;

and if at any time an animal ceases to be owned by or to be in the possession of a person, any person who immediately before that time was a keeper thereof by virtue of the preceding provisions of this subsection continues to be a keeper of the animal until another person becomes a keeper thereof by virtue of those provisions.

(4) Where an animal is taken into and kept in possession for the purpose of preventing it from causing damage or of restoring it to its owner, a person is not a keeper of it by virtue only of that possession.

(5) Where a person employed as a servant by a keeper of an animal incurs a risk incidental to his employment he shall not be treated as accepting it voluntarily.

Detention and sale of trespassing livestock

7 Detention and sale of trespassing livestock

(1) The right to seize and detain any animal by way of distress damage feasant is hereby abolished.

(2) Where any livestock strays on to any land and is not then under the control of any person the occupier of the land may detain it, subject to subsection (3) of this section, unless ordered to return it by a court.

(3) Where any livestock is detained in pursuance of this section the right to detain it ceases—

- (a) at the end of a period of forty-eight hours, unless within that period notice of the detention has been given to the officer in charge of a police station and also, if the person detaining the livestock knows to whom it belongs, to that person; or
- (b) when such amount is tendered to the person detaining the livestock as is sufficient to satisfy any claim he may have under section 4 of this Act in respect of the livestock; or
- (c) if he has no such claim, when the livestock is claimed by a person entitled to its possession.

(4) Where livestock has been detained in pursuance of this section for a period of not less than fourteen days the person detaining it may sell it at a market or by public auction, unless proceedings are then pending for the return of the livestock or for any claim under section 4 of this Act in respect of it.

(5) Where any livestock is sold in the exercise of the right conferred by this section and the proceeds of the sale, less the costs thereof and any costs incurred in connection with it, exceed the amount of any claim under section 4 of this Act which the vendor had in respect of the livestock, the excess shall be recoverable from him by the person who would be entitled to the possession of the livestock but for the sale.

(6) A person detaining any livestock in pursuance of this section is liable for any damage caused to it by a failure to treat it with reasonable care and supply it with adequate food and water while it is so detained.

(7) References in this section to a claim under section 4 of this Act in respect of any livestock do not include any claim under that section for damage done by or expenses incurred in respect of the livestock before the straying in connection with which it is detained under this section.

Animals straying on to highway

8 Duty to take care to prevent damage from animals straying on to the highway

(1) So much of the rules of the common law relating to liability for negligence as excludes or restricts the duty which a person might owe to others to take such care

as is reasonable to see that damage is not caused by animals straying on to a highway is hereby abolished.

(2) Where damage is caused by animals straying from unfenced land to a highway a person who placed them on the land shall not be regarded as having committed a breach of the duty to take care by reason only of placing them there if—

(a) the land is common land, or is land situated in an area where fencing is not customary, or is a town or village green; and

(b) he had a right to place the animals on that land.

Protection of livestock against dogs

9 Killing of or injury to dogs worrying livestock

(1) In any civil proceedings against a person (in this section referred to as the defendant) for killing or causing injury to a dog it shall be a defence to prove—

(a) that the defendant acted for the protection of any livestock and was a person entitled to act for the protection of that livestock; and

(b) that within forty-eight hours of the killing or injury notice thereof was given by the defendant to the officer in charge of a police station.

(2) For the purposes of this section a person is entitled to act for the protection of any livestock if, and only if—

(a) the livestock or the land on which it is belongs to him or to any person under whose express or implied authority he is acting; and

(b) the circumstances are not such that liability for killing or causing injury to the livestock would be excluded by section 5(4) of this Act.

(3) Subject to subsection (4) of this section, a person killing or causing injury to a dog shall be deemed for the purposes of this section to act for the protection of any livestock if, and only if, either—

(a) the dog is worrying or is about to worry the livestock and there are no other reasonable means of ending or preventing the worrying; or

(b) the dog has been worrying livestock, has not left the vicinity and is not under the control of any person and there are no practicable means of ascertaining to whom it belongs.

(4) For the purposes of this section the condition stated in either of the paragraphs of the preceding subsection shall be deemed to have been satisfied if the defendant believed that it was satisfied and had reasonable ground for that belief.

(5) For the purposes of this section—

(a) an animal belongs to any person if he owns it or has it in his possession; and

(b) land belongs to any person if he is the occupier thereof.

Supplemental

10 Application of certain enactments to liability under sections 2 to 4

For the purposes of the Fatal Accidents Acts 1846 to 1959, the Law Reform (Contributory Negligence) Act 1945 and [the Limitation Act 1980] any damage for which a person is liable under sections 2 to 4 of this Act shall be treated as due to his fault.

NOTES

Words in square brackets substituted by the Limitation Act 1980, s 40(2), Sch 3, para 10.

11 General interpretation

In this Act—

"common land", and "town or village green" have the same meanings as in the Commons Registration Act 1965;

"damage" includes the death of, or injury to, any person (including any disease and any impairment of physical or mental condition);

"fault" has the same meaning as in the Law Reform (Contributory Negligence) Act 1945;

"fencing" includes the construction of any obstacle designed to prevent animals from straying;

"livestock" means cattle, horses, asses, mules, hinnies, sheep, pigs, goats and poultry, and also deer not in the wild state and, in sections 3 and 9, also, while in captivity, pheasants, partridges and grouse;

"poultry" means the domestic varieties of the following, that is to say, fowls, turkeys, geese, ducks, guinea-fowls, pigeons, peacocks and quails; and

"species" includes sub-species and variety.

12 Application to Crown

(1) This Act binds the Crown, but nothing in this section shall authorise proceedings to be brought against Her Majesty in her private capacity.

(2) Section 38(3) of the Crown Proceedings Act 1947 (interpretation of references to Her Majesty in her private capacity) shall apply as if this section were contained in that Act.

13 Short title, repeal, commencement and extent

(1) This Act may be cited as the Animals Act 1971.

(2) . . .

(3) This Act shall come into operation on 1st October 1971.

(4) This Act does not extend to Scotland or to Northern Ireland.

NOTES

Sub-s (2): amends the Dogs Act 1906, s 1, and the Dogs (Amendment) Act 1928, s 1(1).

Unsolicited Goods and Services Act 1971

1971 CHAPTER 30

An Act to make provision for the greater protection of persons receiving unsolicited goods, and to amend the law with respect to charges for entries in directories

[12th May 1971]

1 Rights of recipient of unsolicited goods

(1) In the circumstances specified in the following subsection, a person who after the commencement of this Act receives unsolicited goods, may as between himself and the sender, use, deal with or dispose of them as if they were an unconditional gift to him, and any right of the sender to the goods shall be extinguished.

(2) The circumstances referred to in the preceding subsection are that the goods were sent to the recipient with a view to his acquiring them, that the recipient has no reasonable cause to believe that they were sent with a view to their being acquired for the purposes of a trade or business and has neither agreed to acquire nor agreed to return them, and either—

(a) that during the period of six months beginning with the day on which the recipient received the goods the sender did not take possession of them and the recipient did not unreasonably refuse to permit the sender to do so; or

(b) that not less than thirty days before the expiration of the period aforesaid the recipient gave notice to the sender in accordance with the following subsection, and that during the period of thirty days beginning with the day on which the notice was given the sender did not take possession of the goods and the recipient did not unreasonably refuse to permit the sender to do so.

(3) A notice in pursuance of the preceding subsection shall be in writing and shall—

(a) state the recipient's name and address and, if possession of the goods in question may not be taken by the sender at that address, the address at which it may be so taken;

(b) contain a statement, however expressed, that the goods are unsolicited,

and may be sent by post.

(4) In this section "sender", in relation to any goods, includes any person on whose behalf or with whose consent the goods are sent, and any other person claiming through or under the sender or any such person.

NOTES

Repealed by SI 2000/2334, reg 22(1), (2).

Date in force: 31 October 2000 (in relation to goods sent after that date): see SI 2000/2334, regs 1(1), 22(4).

2 Demands and threats regarding payment

(1) A person who, not having reasonable cause to believe there is a right to payment, in the course of any trade or business makes a demand for payment, or asserts a present or prospective right to payment, for what he knows are unsolicited goods sent (after the commencement of this Act) to another person with a view to his acquiring them [for the purposes of his trade or business], shall be guilty of an offence and on summary conviction shall be liable to a fine not exceeding [level 4 on the standard scale].

(2) A person who, not having reasonable cause to believe there is a right to payment, in the course of any trade or business and with a view to obtaining any payment for what he knows are unsolicited goods sent as aforesaid—

(a) threatens to bring any legal proceedings; or

(b) places or causes to be placed the name of any person on a list of defaulters or debtors or threatens to do so; or

(c) invokes or causes to be invoked any other collection procedure or threatens to do so,

shall be guilty of an offence and shall be liable on summary conviction to a fine not exceeding [level 5 on the standard scale].

NOTES

Sub-s (1): words "for the purposes of his trade or business" in square brackets inserted by SI 2000/2334, reg 22(1), (3).

Date in force: 31 October 2000 (in relation to goods sent after that date): see SI 2000/2334, regs 1(1), 22(4).

Maximum fines increased and converted to levels on the standard scale by virtue of the Criminal Justice Act 1982, ss 37, 38, 46.

3 Directory entries

[(1) A person ("the purchaser") shall not be liable to make any payment, and shall be entitled to recover any payment made by him, by way of charge for including or arranging for the inclusion in a directory of an entry relating to that person or his trade or business, unless—

(a) there has been signed by the purchaser or on his behalf an order complying with this section,

(b) there has been signed by the purchaser or on his behalf a note complying with this section of his agreement to the charge and before the note was signed, a copy of it was supplied, for retention by him, to him or a person acting on his behalf, or

(c) there has been transmitted by the purchaser or a person acting on his behalf an electronic communication which includes a statement that the purchaser agrees to the charge and the relevant condition is satisfied in relation to that communication.]

(2) A person shall be guilty of an offence punishable on summary conviction with a fine not exceeding [the prescribed sum] if, in a case where a payment in respect of a charge would, in the absence of an order or note of agreement to the charge complying with this section [and in the absence of an electronic communication in

relation to which the relevant condition is satisfied], be recoverable from him in accordance with the terms of subsection (1) above, he demands payment, or asserts a present or prospective right to payment, of the charge or any part of it, without knowing or having reasonable cause to believe [that—

(a) the entry to which the charge relates was ordered in accordance with this section,

(b) a proper note of the agreement has been duly signed, or

(c) the requirements set out in subsection (1)(c) above have been met].

(3) For the purposes of subsection (1) above, an order for an entry in a directory must be made by means of an order form or other stationery belonging to the [purchaser and bearing, in print, his name and address (or one or more of his addresses);] and the note required by this section of a person's agreement to a charge *must state the amount of the charge immediately above the place for signature, and—*

(a) must identify the directory or proposed directory, and give the following particulars of it—

(i) the proposed date of publication of the directory or of the issue in which the entry is to be included and the name and address of the person producing it;

(ii) if the directory or that issue is to be put on sale, the price at which it is to be offered for sale and the minimum number of copies which are to be available for sale;

(iii) if the directory or that issue is to be distributed free of charge (whether or not it is also to be put on sale), the minimum number of copies which are to be so distributed; and

(b) must set out or give reasonable particulars of the entry in respect of which the charge would be payable [shall comply with the requirements of regulations under section 3A of this Act applicable thereto].

[(3A) In relation to an electronic communication which includes a statement that the purchaser agrees to a charge for including or arranging the inclusion in a directory of any entry, the relevant condition is that—

(a) before the electronic communication was transmitted the information referred to in subsection (3B) below was communicated to the purchaser, and

(b) the electronic communication can readily be produced and retained in a visible and legible form.

(3B) that information is—

(a) the following particulars—

(i) the amount of the charge;
(ii) the name of the directory or proposed directory;
(iii) the name of the person producing the directory;
(iv) the geographic address at which that person is established;
(v) if the directory is or is to be available in printed form, the proposed date of publication of the directory or of the issue in which the entry is to be included;
(vi) if the directory or the issue in which the entry is to be included is to be put on sale, the price at which it is to be offered for sale and the minimum number of copies which are to be available for sale;
(vii) if the directory or the issue in which the entry is to be included is to be distributed free of charge (whether or not it is also to be put on sale), the minimum number of copies which are to be so distributed;
(viii) if the directory is or is to be available in a form other than in printed form, adequate details of how it may be accessed; and

(b) reasonable particulars of the entry in respect of which the charge would be payable.

(3C) In this section "electronic communication" has the same meaning as in the Electronic Communications Act 2000.]

(4) Nothing in this section shall apply to a payment due under a contract entered into before the commencement of this Act, or entered into by the acceptance of an offer made before that commencement.

NOTES

Sub-s (1): substituted by SI 2001/2778, arts 2, 3.

Date in force: 31 August 2001: see SI 2001/2778, art 1.

Sub-s (2): words "the prescribed sum" in square brackets substituted by virtue of the Magistrates' Courts Act 1980, s 32(2).

Sub-s (2): words from "and in the" to "condition is satisfied" in square brackets inserted by SI 2001/2778, art 4(a).

Date in force: 31 August 2001: see SI 2001/2778, art 1.

Sub-s (2): paras (a)–(c) and word "that" immediately preceding them substituted by SI 2001/2778, art 4(b).

Date in force: 31 August 2001: see SI 2001/2778, art 1.

Sub-s (3): words from "purchaser and bearing" to "of his addresses);" in square brackets substituted by SI 2001/2778, art 5.

Date in force: 31 August 2001: see SI 2001/2778, art 1.

Sub-s (3): words from "must state" to "would be payable" in italics repealed and subsequent words in square brackets substituted with savings by the Unsolicited Goods and Services (Amendment) Act 1975, ss 2(1), 4(4).

Date in force: to be appointed: see the Unsolicited Goods and Services (Amendment) Act 1975, s 4(3).

Sub-ss (3A)–(3C): inserted by SI 2001/2778, art 6.

Date in force: 31 August 2001: see SI 2001/2778, art 1.

[3A Contents and form of notes of agreement, invoices and similar documents]

[(1) For the purposes of this Act, the Secretary of State may make regulations as to the contents and form of notes of agreement, invoices and similar documents; and, without prejudice to the generality of the foregoing, any such regulations may—

- (a) require specified information to be included,
- (b) prescribe the manner in which specified information is to be included,
- (c) prescribe such other requirements (whether as to presentation, type, size, colour or disposition of lettering, quality or colour of paper or otherwise) as the Secretary of State may consider appropriate for securing that specified information is clearly brought to the attention of the recipient of any note of agreement, invoice or similar document,
- (d) make different provision for different classes or descriptions of notes of agreement, invoices and similar documents or for the same class or description in different circumstances,
- (e) contain such supplementary and incidental provisions as the Secretary of State may consider appropriate.

(2) Any reference in this section to a note of agreement includes any such copy as is mentioned in section 3(1) of this Act.

(3) Regulations under this section shall be made by statutory instrument and shall be subject to annulment in pursuance of a resolution of either House of Parliament.]

NOTES

Inserted by the Unsolicited Goods and Services (Amendment) Act 1975, s 1.

4 Unsolicited publications

(1) A person shall be guilty of an offence if he sends or causes to be sent to another person any book, magazine or leaflet (or advertising material for any such publication) which he knows or ought reasonably to know is unsolicited and which describes or illustrates human sexual techniques.

(2) A person found guilty of an offence under this section shall be liable on summary conviction to a fine not exceeding [level 5 on the standard scale].

(3) A prosecution for an offence under this section shall not in England and Wales be instituted except by, or with the consent of, the Director of Public Prosecutions.

NOTES

Sub-s (2): enhanced penalty on a subsequent conviction abolished, maximum fine on any conviction increased and converted to a level on the standard scale, by virtue of the Criminal Justice Act 1982, ss 35, 37, 38, 46.

5 Offences by corporations

(1) Where an offence under this Act which has been committed by a body corporate is proved to have been committed with the consent or connivance of, or to be attributable to any neglect on the part of, any director, manager, secretary, or other similar officer of the body corporate, or of any person who was purporting to

act in any such capacity, he as well as the body corporate shall be guilty of that offence and shall be liable to be proceeded against and punished accordingly.

(2) Where the affairs of a body corporate are managed by its members, this section shall apply in relation to the acts or defaults of a member in connection with his functions of management as if he were a director of the body corporate.

6 Interpretation

(1) In this Act, unless the context or subject matter otherwise requires,—

"acquire" includes hire;

"send" includes deliver, and "sender" shall be construed accordingly;

"unsolicited" means, in relation to goods sent to any person, that they are sent without any prior request made by him or on his behalf.

[(2) For the purposes of this Act any invoice or similar document stating the amount of any payment and not complying with the requirements of regulations under section 3A of this Act applicable thereto shall be regarded as asserting a right to the payment.]

NOTES

Sub-s (2): substituted by the Unsolicited Goods and Services (Amendment) Act 1975, s 2(2).

7 Citation, commencement and extent

(1) This Act may be cited as the Unsolicited Goods and Services Act 1971.

(2) This Act shall come into force at the expiration of three months beginning with the day on which it is passed.

(3) This Act does not extend to Northern Ireland.

Defective Premises Act 1972

1972 CHAPTER 35

An Act to impose duties in connection with the provision of dwellings and otherwise to amend the law of England and Wales as to liability for injury or damage caused to persons through defects in the state of premises

[29th June 1972]

1 Duty to build dwellings properly

(1) A person taking on work for or in connection with the provision of a dwelling (whether the dwelling is provided by the erection or by the conversion or enlargement of a building) owes a duty—

(a) if the dwelling is provided to the order of any person, to that person; and

(b) without prejudice to paragraph (*a*) above, to every person who acquires an interest (whether legal or equitable) in the dwelling;

to see that the work which he takes on is done in a workmanlike or, as the case may be, professional manner, with proper materials and so that as regards that work the dwelling will be fit for habitation when completed.

(2) A person who takes on any such work for another on terms that he is to do it in accordance with instructions given by or on behalf of that other shall, to the extent to which he does it properly in accordance with those instructions, be treated for the purposes of this section as discharging the duty imposed on him by subsection (1) above except where he owes a duty to that other to warn him of any defects in the instructions and fails to discharge that duty.

(3) A person shall not be treated for the purposes of subsection (2) above as having given instructions for the doing of work merely because he has agreed so the work being done in a specified manner, with specified materials or to a specified design.

(4) A person who—

(a) in the course of a business which consists of or includes providing or arranging for the provision of dwellings or installations in dwellings; or

(b) in the exercise of a power of making such provision or arrangements conferred by or by virtue of any enactment;

arranges for another to take on work for or in connection with the provision of a dwelling shall be treated for the purposes of this section as included among the persons who have taken on the work.

(5) Any cause of action in respect of a breach of the duty imposed by this section shall be deemed, for the purposes of the Limitation Act 1939, the Law Reform (Limitation of Actions, &c) Act 1954 and the Limitation Act 1963, to have accrued at the time when the dwelling was completed, but if after that time a person who has done work for or in connection with the provision of the dwelling does further work to rectify the work he has already done, any such cause of action in respect of that further work shall be deemed for those purposes to have accrued at the time when the further work was finished.

2 Cases excluded from the remedy under section 1

(1) Where—

(a) in connection with the provision of a dwelling or its first sale or letting for habitation any rights in respect of defects in the state of the dwelling are conferred by an approved scheme to which this section applies on a person having or acquiring an interest in the dwelling; and

(b) it is stated in a document of a type approved for the purposes of this section that the requirements as to design or construction imposed by or under the scheme have, or appear to have, been substantially complied with in relation to the dwelling;

no action shall be brought by any person having or acquiring an interest in the dwelling for breach of the duty imposed by section 1 above in relation to the dwelling.

(2) A scheme to which this section applies—

(a) may consist of any number of documents and any number of agreements or other transactions between any number of persons; but

(b) must confer, by virtue of agreements entered into with persons having or acquiring an interest in the dwellings to which the scheme applies, rights on such persons in respect of defects in the state of the dwellings.

(3) In this section "approved" means approved by the Secretary of State, and the power of the Secretary of State to approve a scheme or document for the purposes of this section shall be exercisable by order, except that any requirements as to construction or design imposed under a scheme to which this section applies may be approved by him without making any order or, if he thinks fit, by order.

(4) The Secretary of State—

(a) may approve a scheme or document for the purposes of this section with or without limiting the duration of his approval; and

(b) may by order revoke or vary a previous order under this section or, without such an order, revoke or vary a previous approval under this section given otherwise than by order.

(5) The production of a document purporting to be a copy of an approval given by the Secretary of State otherwise than by order and certified by an officer of the Secretary of State to be a true copy of the approval shall be conclusive evidence of the approval, and without proof of the handwriting or official position of the person purporting to sign the certificate.

(6) The power to make an order under this section shall be exercisable by statutory instrument which shall be subject to annulment in pursuance of a resolution by either House of Parliament.

(7) Where an interest in a dwelling is compulsorily acquired—

(a) no action shall be brought by the acquiring authority for breach of the duty imposed by section 1 above in respect of the dwelling; and

(b) if any work for or in connection with the provision of the dwelling was done otherwise than in the course of a business by the person in occupation of the dwelling at the time of the compulsory acquisition, the acquiring authority and not that person shall be treated as the person who took on the work and accordingly as owing that duty.

3 Duty of care with respect to work done on premises not abated by disposal of premises

(1) Where work of construction, repair, maintenance or demolition or any other work is done on or in relation to premises, any duty of care owed, because of the doing of the work, to persons who might reasonably be expected to be affected by defects in the state of the premises created by the doing of the work shall not be abated by the subsequent disposal of the premises by the person who owed the duty.

(2) This section does not apply—

(a) in the case of premises which are let, where the relevant tenancy of the premises commenced, or the relevant tenancy agreement of the premises was entered into, before the commencement of this Act;

(b) in the case of premises disposed of in any other way, when the disposal of the premises was completed, or a contract for their disposal was entered into, before the commencement of this Act; or

(c) in either case, where the relevant transaction disposing of the premises is entered into in pursuance of an enforceable option by which the consideration for the disposal was fixed before the commencement of this Act.

4 Landlord's duty of care in virtue of obligation or right to repair premises demised

(1) Where premises are let under a tenancy which puts on the landlord an obligation to the tenant for the maintenance or repair of the premises, the landlord owes to all persons who might reasonably be expected to be affected by defects in the state of the premises a duty to take such care as is reasonable in all the circumstances to see that they are reasonably safe from personal injury or from damage to their property caused by a relevant defect.

(2) The said duty is owed if the landlord knows (whether as the result of being notified by the tenant or otherwise) or if he ought in all the circumstances to have known of the relevant defect.

(3) In this section "relevant defect" means a defect in the state of the premises existing at or after the material time and arising from, or continuing because of, an act or omission by the landlord which constitutes or would if he had had notice of the defect, have constituted a failure by him to carry out his obligation to the tenant for the maintenance or repair of the premises; and for the purposes of the foregoing provision "the material time" means—

(a) where the tenancy commenced before this Act, the commencement of this Act; and

(b) in all other cases, the earliest of the following times, that is to say—

(i) the time when the tenancy commences;

(ii) the time when the tenancy agreement is entered into;

(iii) the time when possession is taken of the premises in contemplation of the letting.

(4) Where premises are let under a tenancy which expressly or impliedly gives the landlord the right to enter the premises to carry out any description of maintenance or repair of the premises, then, as from the time when he first is, or by notice or otherwise can put himself, in a position to exercise the right and so long as he is or can put himself in that position, he shall be treated for the purposes of subsections (1) to (3) above (but for no other purpose) as if he were under an obligation to the tenant for that description of maintenance or repair of the premises; but the landlord shall not owe the tenant any duty by virtue of this subsection in respect of any defect in the state of the premises arising from, or continuing because of, a failure to carry out an obligation expressly imposed on the tenant by the tenancy.

(5) For the purposes of this section obligations imposed or rights given by any enactment in virtue of a tenancy shall be treated as imposed or given by the tenancy.

(6) This section applies to a right of occupation given by contract or any enactment and not amounting to a tenancy as if the right were a tenancy, and "tenancy" and cognate expressions shall be construed accordingly.

5 Application to Crown

This Act shall bind the Crown, but as regards the Crown's liability in tort shall not bind the Crown further than the Crown is made liable in tort by the Crown Proceedings Act 1947.

6 Supplemental

(1) In this Act—

"disposal", in relation to premises, includes a letting, and an assignment or surrender of a tenancy, of the premises and the creation by contract of any other right to occupy the premises, and "dispose" shall be construed accordingly;

"personal injury" includes any disease and any impairment of a person's physical or mental condition;

"tenancy" means—

- (a) a tenancy created either immediately or derivatively out of the freehold, whether by a lease or underlease, by an agreement for a lease or underlease or by a tenancy agreement, but not including a mortgage term or any interest arising in favour of a mortgagor by his attorning tenant to his mortgagee; or
- (b) a tenancy at will or a tenancy on sufferance; or
- (c) a tenancy, whether or not constituting a tenancy at common law, created by or in pursuance of any enactment;

and cognate expressions shall be construed accordingly.

(2) Any duty imposed by or enforceable by virtue of any provision of this Act is in addition to any duty a person may owe apart from that provision.

(3) Any term of an agreement which purports to exclude or restrict, or has the effect of excluding or restricting, the operation of any of the provisions of this Act, or any liability arising by virtue of any such provision, shall be void.

(4) . . .

NOTES

Words omitted repeal the Occupiers' Liability Act 1957, s 4

7 Short title, commencement and extent

(1) This Act may be cited as the Defective Premises Act 1972.

(2) This Act shall come into force on 1st January 1974.

(3) This Act does not extend to Scotland or Northern Ireland.

Supply of Goods (Implied Terms) Act 1973

1973 CHAPTER 13

An Act to amend the law with respect to the terms to be implied in contracts of sale of goods and hire-purchase agreements and on the exchange of goods for trading stamps, and with respect to the terms of conditional sale agreements: and for connected purposes

[18th April 1973]

Hire-purchase agreements

[8 Implied terms as to title]

[(1) In every hire-purchase agreement, other than one to which subsection (2) below applies, there is—

- (a) an implied [term] on the part of the creditor that he will have a right to sell the goods at the time when the property is to pass; and
- (b) an implied [term] that—
  - (i) the goods are free, and will remain free until the time when the property is to pass, from any charge or encumbrance not disclosed or known to the person to whom the goods are bailed or (in Scotland) hired before the agreement is made, and
  - (ii) that person will enjoy quiet possession of the goods except so far as it may be disturbed by any person entitled to the benefit of any charge or encumbrance so disclosed or known.

(2) In a hire-purchase agreement, in the case of which there appears from the agreement or is to be inferred from the circumstances of the agreement an intention that the creditor should transfer only such title as he or a third person may have, there is—

- (a) an implied [term] that all charges or encumbrances known to the creditor and not known to the person to whom the goods are bailed or hired have been disclosed to that person before the agreement is made; and
- (b) an implied [term] that neither—
  - (i) the creditor; nor
  - (ii) in a case where the parties to the agreement intend that any title which may be transferred shall be only such title as a third person may have, that person; nor
  - (iii) anyone claiming through or under the creditor or that third person otherwise than under a charge or encumbrance disclosed or known to the person to whom the goods are bailed or hired, before the agreement is made;

will disturb the quiet possession of the person to whom the goods are bailed or hired.

[(3) As regards England and Wales and Northern Ireland, the term implied by subsection (1)(a) above is a condition and the terms implied by subsections (1)(b), (2)(a) and (2)(b) above are warranties.]]

NOTES

Substituted by the Consumer Credit Act 1974, s 192(3)(a), Sch 4, para 35.

Sub-ss (1), (2): words in square brackets substituted by the Sale and Supply of Goods Act 1994, s 7, Sch 2 para 4(2)(a).

Sub-s (3): inserted by the Sale and Supply of Goods Act 1994, s 7, Sch 2 para 4(2)(b).

[9 Bailing or hiring by description]

[(1) Where under a hire-purchase agreement goods are bailed or (in Scotland) hired by description, there is an implied [term] that the goods will correspond with the description, and if under the agreement the goods are bailed or hired by reference to a sample as well as a description, it is not sufficient that the bulk of the goods corresponds with the sample if the goods do not also correspond with the description.

[(1A) As regards England and Wales and Northern Ireland, the term implied by subsection (1) above is a condition.]

(2) Goods shall not be prevented from being bailed or hired by description by reason only that, being exposed for sale, bailment or hire, they are selected by the person to whom they are bailed or hired.]

NOTES

Substituted by the Consumer Credit Act 1974, s 192(3)(a), Sch 4, para 35.

Sub-s (1): word in square brackets substituted by the Sale and Supply of Goods Act 1994, s 7, Sch 2, para 4(3)(a).

Sub-s (1A): inserted by the Sale and Supply of Goods Act 1994, s 7, Sch 2, para 4(3)(b).

[10 Implied undertakings as to quality or fitness]

[(1) Except as provided by this section and section 11 below and subject to the provisions of any other enactment, including any enactment of the Parliament of Northern Ireland, or the Northern Ireland Assembly, there is no implied [term] as to the quality or fitness for any particular purpose of goods bailed or (in Scotland) hired under a hire-purchase agreement.

[(2) Where the creditor bails or hires goods under a hire purchase agreement in the course of a business, there is an implied term that the goods supplied under the agreement are of satisfactory quality.

(2A) For the purposes of this Act, goods are of satisfactory quality if they meet the standard that a reasonable person would regard as satisfactory, taking account of any description of the goods, the price (if relevant) and all the other relevant circumstances.

(2B) For the purposes of this Act, the quality of goods includes their state and condition and the following (among others) are in appropriate cases aspects of the quality of goods—

(a) fitness for all the purposes for which goods of the kind in question are commonly supplied,
(b) appearance and finish,
(c) freedom from minor defects,
(d) safety, and
(e) durability.

(2C) The term implied by subsection (2) above does not extend to any matter making the quality of goods unsatisfactory—

(a) which is specifically drawn to the attention of the person to whom the goods are bailed or hired before the agreement is made,
(b) where that person examines the goods before the agreement is made, which that examination ought to reveal, or
(c) where the goods are bailed or hired by reference to a sample, which would have been apparent on a reasonable examination of the sample.]

(3) Where the creditor bails or hires goods under a hire-purchase agreement in the course of a business and the person to whom the goods are bailed or hired, expressly or by implication, makes known—

(a) to the creditor in the course of negotiations conducted by the creditor in relation to the making of the hire-purchase agreement, or
(b) to a credit-broker in the course of negotiations conducted by that broker in relation to goods sold by him to the creditor before forming the subject matter of the hire-purchase agreement,

any particular purpose for which the goods are being bailed or hired, there is an implied [term] that the goods supplied under the agreement are reasonably fit for that purpose, whether or not that is a purpose for which such goods are commonly supplied, except where the circumstances show that the person to whom the goods are bailed or hired does not rely, or that it is unreasonable for him to rely, on the skill or judgment of the creditor or credit-broker.

(4) An implied [term] as to quality or fitness for a particular purpose may be annexed to a hire-purchase agreement by usage.

(5) The preceding provisions of this section apply to a hire-purchase agreement made by a person who in the course of a business is acting as agent for the creditor as they apply to an agreement made by the creditor in the course of a business, except where the creditor is not bailing or hiring in the course of a business and either the person to whom the goods are bailed or hired knows that fact or reasonable steps are taken to bring it to the notice of that person before the agreement is made.

(6) In subsection (3) above and this subsection—

(a) "credit-broker" means a person acting in the course of a business of credit brokerage.
(b) "credit brokerage" means the effecting of introductions of individuals desiring to obtain credit—

(i) to persons carrying on any business so far as it relates to the provision of credit, or
(ii) to other persons engaged in credit brokerage.]

[(7) As regards England and Wales and Northern Ireland, the terms implied by subsections (2) and (3) above are conditions.]

NOTES

Substituted by the Consumer Credit Act 1974, s 192(3)(a), Sch 4, para 35.

Sub-ss (1), (3), (4): words in square brackets substituted by the Sale and Supply of Goods Act 1994, s 7, Sch 2, para 4(4)(b).

Sub-ss (2)–(2C): substituted, for sub-s (2) as originally enacted, by the Sale and Supply of Goods Act 1994, s 7, Sch 2, para 4(4)(a).

Sub-s (7): inserted by the Sale and Supply of Goods Act 1994, s 7, Sch 2, para 4(4)(c).

[11 Samples]

[[(1)] Where under a hire-purchase agreement goods are bailed or (in Scotland) hired by reference to a sample, there is an implied [term]—

(a) that the bulk will correspond with the sample in quality; and
(b) that the person to whom the goods are bailed or hired will have a reasonable opportunity of comparing the bulk with the sample; and
(c) that the goods will be free from any defect, [making their quality unsatisfactory], which would not be apparent on reasonable examination of the sample.]

[(2) As regards England and Wales and Northern Ireland, the term implied by subsection (1) above is a condition.]

NOTES

Substituted by the Consumer Credit Act 1974, s 192(3)(a), Sch 4, para 35.

Sub-s (1): numbered as such, and words in square brackets substituted, by the Sale and Supply of Goods Act 1994, s 7, Sch 2, para 4(5)(a)–(c).

Sub-s (2): inserted by the Sale and Supply of Goods Act 1994, s 7, Sch 2, para 4(5)(d).

[11A Modification of remedies for breach of statutory condition in non-consumer cases]

[(1) Where in the case of a hire purchase agreement—

(a) the person to whom goods are bailed would, apart from this subsection, have the right to reject them by reason of a breach on the part of the creditor of a term implied by section 9, 10 or 11(1)(a) or (c) above, but
(b) the breach is so slight that it would be unreasonable for him to reject them,

then, if the person to whom the goods are bailed does not deal as consumer, the breach is not to be treated as a breach of condition but may be treated as a breach of warranty.

(2) This section applies unless a contrary intention appears in, or is to be implied from, the agreement.

(3) It is for the creditor to show—

(a) that a breach fell within subsection (1)(b) above, and

(b) that the person to whom the goods were bailed did not deal as consumer.

(4) The references in this section to dealing as consumer are to be construed in accordance with Part I of the Unfair Contract Terms Act 1977.

(5) This section does not apply to Scotland.]

NOTES

Inserted by the Sale and Supply of Goods Act 1994, s 7, Sch 2, para 4(6).

[12 Exclusion of implied terms]

[An express term does not negative a term implied by this Act unless inconsistent with it.]

NOTES

Substituted by the Sale and Supply of Goods Act 1994, s 7, Sch 2 para 4(7).

[14 Special provisions as to conditional sale agreements]

[(1) [Section 11(4) of the Sale of Goods Act 1979] (whereby in certain circumstances a breach of a condition in a contract of sale is treated only as a breach of warranty) shall not apply to [a conditional sale agreement where the buyer deals as consumer within Part I of the Unfair Contract Terms Act 1977 . . .].

(2) In England and Wales and Northern Ireland a breach of a condition (whether express or implied) to be fulfilled by the seller under any such agreement shall be treated as a breach of warranty, and not as grounds for rejecting the goods and treating the agreement as repudiated, if (but only if) it would have fallen to be so treated had the condition been contained or implied in a corresponding hire-purchase agreement as a condition to be fulfilled by the creditor.]

NOTES

Substituted by the Consumer Credit Act 1974, s 192(3)(a), Sch 4, para 36.

Sub-s (1): first words in square brackets substituted by the Sale of Goods Act 1979, s 63, Sch 2, para 16; second words in square brackets substituted by the Unfair Contract Terms Act 1977, s 31(3), Sch 3; words omitted repealed by the Statute Law (Repeals) Act 1981.

[15 Supplementary]

[(1) In sections 8 to 14 above and this section—

"business" includes a profession and the activities of any government department (including a Northern Ireland department), [or local or public authority];

"buyer" and "seller" includes a person to whom rights and duties under a conditional sale agreement have passed by assignment or operation of law;

. . .

"conditional sale agreement" means an agreement for the sale of goods under which the purchase price or part of it is payable by instalments, and the property in the goods is to remain in the seller (notwithstanding that the buyer is to be in possession of the goods) until such conditions as to the payment of instalments or otherwise as may be specified in the agreement are fulfilled;

. . .

"creditor" means the person by whom the goods are bailed or (in Scotland) hired under a hire-purchase agreement or the person to whom his rights and duties under the agreement have passed by assignment or operation of law; and

"hire-purchase agreement" means an agreement, other than a conditional sale agreement, under which—

(a) goods are bailed or (in Scotland) hired in return for periodical payments by the person to whom they are bailed or hired, and

(b) the property in the goods will pass to that person if the terms of the agreements are complied with and one or more of the following occurs—

(i) the exercise of an option to purchase by that person,

(ii) the doing of any other specified act by any party to the agreement,

(iii) the happening of any other specified event.

(2) . . .

(3) In section 14(2) above "corresponding hire-purchase agreement" means, in relation to a conditional sale agreement, a hire-purchase agreement relating to the same goods as the conditional sale agreement and made between the same parties and at the same time and in the same circumstances and, as nearly as may be, in the same terms as the conditional sale agreement.

(4) Nothing in sections 8 to 13 above shall prejudice the operation of any other enactment including any enactment of the Parliament of Northern Ireland or the Northern Ireland Assembly or any rule of law whereby any [term], other than one relating to quality or fitness, is to be implied in any hire-purchase agreement.]

NOTES

Substituted by the Consumer Credit Act 1974, s 192(3)(a), Sch 4, para 36.

Sub-s (1): in definition "business" words in square brackets substituted, and definition "consumer sale" repealed, by the Unfair Contract Terms Act 1977, s 31(3), (4), Schs 3, 4; definition omitted repealed by the Sale and Supply of Goods Act 1994, s 7, Sch 2, para 4(9)(a).

Sub-s (2): repealed by the Sale and Supply of Goods Act 1994, s 7, Sch 2 para 4(9)(b), Sch 3.

Sub-s (4): word in square brackets substituted by the Sale and Supply of Goods Act 1994, s 7, Sch 2, para 4(9)(c).

Miscellaneous

18 Short title, citation, interpretation, commencement, repeal and saving

(1) This Act may be cited as the Supply of Goods (Implied Terms) Act 1973.

(2) . . .

(3) This Act shall come into operation at the expiration of a period of one month beginning with the date on which it is passed.

(4) . . .

(5) This Act does not apply to contracts of sale or hire-purchase agreements made before its commencement.

NOTES

Sub-s (2): repealed by the Sale of Goods Act 1979, s 63(2), Sch 3.

Sub-s (4): repeals the Hire-Purchase Act 1965, ss 17–20, 29(3)(c), the Hire-Purchase (Scotland) Act 1965, ss 17–20, 29(3)(c) and the Hire- Purchase Act (Northern Ireland) 1966, ss 17–20, 29(3)(c).

Health and Safety at Work etc Act 1974

1974 CHAPTER 37

An Act to make further provision for securing the health, safety and welfare of persons at work, for protecting others against risks to health or safety in connection with the activities of persons at work, for controlling the keeping and use and preventing the unlawful acquisition, possession and use of dangerous substances, and for controlling certain emissions into the atmosphere; to make further provision with respect to the employment medical advisory service; to amend the law relating to building regulations, and the Building (Scotland) Act 1959; and for connected purposes

[31st July 1974]

PART I
HEALTH, SAFETY AND WELFARE IN CONNECTION WITH WORK, AND CONTROL OF DANGEROUS SUBSTANCES AND CERTAIN EMISSIONS INTO THE ATMOSPHERE

General duties

2 General duties of employers to their employees

(1) It shall be the duty of every employer to ensure, so far as is reasonably practicable, the health, safety and welfare at work of all his employees.

(2) Without prejudice to the generality of an employer's duty under the preceding subsection, the matters to which that duty extends include in particular—

(a) the provision and maintenance of plant and systems of work that are, so far as is reasonably practicable, safe and without risks to health;

(b) arrangements for ensuring, so far as is reasonably practicable, safety and absence of risks to health in connection with the use, handling, storage and transport of articles and substances;

(c) the provision of such information, instruction, training and supervision as is necessary to ensure, so far as is reasonably practicable, the health and safety at work of his employees;

(d) so far as is reasonably practicable as regards any place of work under the employer's control, the maintenance of it in a condition that is safe and without risks to health and the provision and maintenance of means of access to and egress from it that are safe and without such risks;

(e) the provision and maintenance of a working environment for his employees that is, so far as is reasonably practicable, safe, without risks to health, and adequate as regards facilities and arrangements for their welfare at work.

(3) Except in such cases as may be prescribed, it shall be the duty of every employer to prepare and as often as may be appropriate revise a written statement of his general policy with respect to the health and safety at work of his employees and the organisation and arrangements for the time being in force for carrying out that policy, and to bring the statement and any revision of it to the notice of all his employees.

(4) Regulations made by the Secretary of State may provide for the appointment in prescribed cases by recognised trade unions (within the meaning of the regulations) of safety representatives from amongst the employees, and those representatives shall represent the employees in consultations with the employers under subsection (6) below and shall have such other functions as may be prescribed.

(5) . . .

(6) It shall be the duty of every employer to consult any such representatives with a view to the making and maintenance of arrangements which will enable him and his employees to co-operate effectively in promoting and developing measures to ensure the health and safety at work of the employees, and in checking the effectiveness of such measures.

(7) In such cases as may be prescribed it shall be the duty of every employer, if requested to do so by the safety representatives mentioned in [subsection (4)] above, to establish, in accordance with regulations made by the Secretary of State, a safety committee having the function of keeping under review the measures taken to ensure the health and safety at work of his employees and such other functions as may be prescribed.

NOTES

Sub-s (5): repealed by the Employment Protection Act 1975, ss 116, 125(3), Sch 15, para 1, Sch 18.

Sub-s (7): words in square brackets substituted by the Employment Protection Act 1975, ss 116, 125(3), Sch 15, para 1, Sch 18.

3 General duties of employers and self-employed to persons other than their employees

(1) It shall be the duty of every employer to conduct his undertaking in such a way as to ensure, so far as is reasonably practicable, that persons not in his employment who may be affected thereby are not thereby exposed to risks to their health or safety.

(2) It shall be the duty of every self-employed person to conduct his undertaking in such a way as to ensure, so far as is reasonably practicable, that he and other

persons (not being his employees) who may be affected thereby are not thereby exposed to risks to their health or safety.

(3) In such cases as may be prescribed, it shall be the duty of every employer and every self-employed person, in the prescribed circumstances and in the prescribed manner, to give to persons (not being his employees) who may be affected by the way in which he conducts his undertaking the prescribed information about such aspects of the way in which he conducts his undertaking as might affect their health or safety.

4 General duties of persons concerned with premises to persons other than their employees

(1) This section has effect for imposing on persons duties in relation to those who—

(a) are not their employees; but

(b) use non-domestic premises made available to them as a place of work or as a place where they may use plant or substances provided for their use there,

and applies to premises so made available and other non-domestic premises used in connection with them.

(2) It shall be the duty of each person who has, to any extent, control of premises to which this section applies or of the means of access thereto or egress therefrom or of any plant or substance in such premises to take such measures as it is reasonable for a person in his position to take to ensure, so far as is reasonably practicable, that the premises, all means of access thereto or egress therefrom available for use by persons using the premises, and any plant or substance in the premises or, as the case may be, provided for use there, is or are safe and without risks to health.

(3) Where a person has, by virtue of any contract or tenancy, an obligation of any extent in relation to—

(a) the maintenance or repair of any premises to which this section applies or any means of access thereto or egress therefrom; or

(b) the safety of or the absence of risks to health arising from plant or substances in any such premises;

that person shall be treated, for the purposes of subsection (2) above, as being a person who has control of the matters to which his obligation extends.

(4) Any reference in this section to a person having control of any premises or matter is a reference to a person having control of the premises or matter in connection with the carrying on by him of a trade, business or other undertaking (whether for profit or not).

The Health and Safety Commission and the Health and Safety Executive

10 Establishment of the Commission and the Executive

(1) There shall be two bodies corporate to be called the Health and Safety Commission and the Health and Safety Executive which shall be constituted in accordance with the following provisions of this section.

(2) The Health and Safety Commission (hereafter in this Act referred to as "the Commission") shall consist of a chairman appointed by the Secretary of State and not less than six nor more than nine other members appointed by the Secretary of State in accordance with subsection (3) below.

(3) Before appointing the members of the Commission (other than the chairman) the Secretary of State shall—

- (a) as to three of them, consult such organisations representing employers as he considers appropriate;
- (b) as to three others, consult such organisations representing employees as he considers appropriate; and
- (c) as to any other members he may appoint, consult such organisations representing local authorities and such other organisations, including professional bodies, the activities of whose members are concerned with matters relating to any of the general purposes of this Part, as he considers appropriate.

(4) The Secretary of State may appoint one of the members to be deputy chairman of the Commission.

(5) The Health and Safety Executive (hereafter in this Act referred to as "the Executive") shall consist of three persons of whom one shall be appointed by the Commission with the approval of the Secretary of State to be the director of the Executive and the others shall be appointed by the Commission with the like approval after consultation with the said director.

(6) The provisions of Schedule 2 shall have effect with respect to the Commission and the Executive.

(7) The functions of the Commission and of the Executive, and of their officers and servants, shall be performed on behalf of the Crown.

[(8) For the purposes of any civil proceedings arising out of those functions, the Crown Proceedings Act 1947 and the Crown Suits (Scotland) Act 1857 shall apply to the Commission and the Executive as if they were government departments within the meaning of the said Act of 1947 or, as the case may be, public departments within the meaning of the said Act of 1857.]

NOTES

Sub-s (8): inserted by the Employment Protection Act 1975, s 116, Sch 15, para 3.

Health and safety regulations and approved codes of practice

15 Health and safety regulations

[(1) Subject to the provisions of section 50, the Secretary of State. . . shall have power to make regulations under this section for any of the general purposes of this Part (and regulations so made are in this Part referred to as "health and safety regulations").]

(2) Without prejudice to the generality of the preceding subsection, health and safety regulations may for any of the general purposes of this Part make provision for any of the purposes mentioned in Schedule 3.

(3) Health and safety regulations—
- (a) may repeal or modify any of the existing statutory provisions;
- (b) may exclude or modify in relation to any specified class of case any of the provisions of sections 2 to 9 or any of the existing statutory provisions;
- (c) may make a specified authority or class of authorities responsible, to such extent as may be specified, for the enforcement of any of the relevant statutory provisions.

(4) Health and safety regulations—
- (a) may impose requirements by reference to the approval of the Commission or any other specified body or person;
- (b) may provide for references in the regulations to any specified document to operate as references to that document as revised or re-issued from time to time.

(5) Health and safety regulations—
- (a) may provide (either unconditionally or subject to conditions, and with or without limit of time) for exemptions from any requirement or prohibition imposed by or under any of the relevant statutory provisions;
- (b) may enable exemptions from any requirement or prohibition imposed by or under any of the relevant statutory provisions to be granted (either unconditionally or subject to conditions, and with or without limit of time) by any specified person or by any person authorised in that behalf by a specified authority.

(6) Health and safety regulations—
- (a) may specify the persons or classes of persons who, in the event of a contravention of a requirement or prohibition imposed by or under the regulations, are to be guilty of an offence, whether in addition to or to the exclusion of other persons or classes of persons;
- (b) may provide for any specified defence to be available in proceedings for any offence under the relevant statutory provisions either generally or in specified circumstances;
- (c) may exclude proceedings on indictment in relation to offences consisting of a contravention of a requirement or prohibition imposed by or under any of the existing statutory provisions, sections 2 to 9 or health and safety regulations;
- (d) may restrict the punishments [(other than the maximum fine on conviction on indictment)] which can be imposed in respect of any such offence as is mentioned in paragraph (c) above;
- [(e) in the case of regulations made for any purpose mentioned in section 1(1) of the Offshore Safety Act 1992, may provide that any offence consisting of a contravention of the regulations, or of any requirement or prohibition imposed by or under them, shall be punishable on conviction on indictment by imprisonment for a term not exceeding two years, or a fine, or both.]

(7) Without prejudice to section 35, health and safety regulations may make provision for enabling offences under any of the relevant statutory provisions to be treated as having been committed at any specified place for the purpose of bringing any such offence within the field of responsibility of any enforcing authority or conferring jurisdiction on any court to entertain proceedings for any such offence.

(8) Health and safety regulations may take the form of regulations applying to particular circumstances only or to a particular case only (for example, regulations applying to particular premises only).

(9) If an Order in Council is made under section 84 (3) providing that this section shall apply to or in relation to persons, premises or work outside Great Britain then, notwithstanding the Order, health and safety regulations shall not apply to or in relation to aircraft in flight, vessels, hovercraft or offshore installations outside Great Britain or persons at work outside Great Britain in connection with submarine cables or submarine pipelines except in so far as the regulations expressly so provide.

(10) In this section "specified" means specified in health and safety regulations.

NOTES

Sub-s (1): substituted by the Employment Protection Act 1975, s 116, Sch 15, para 6.

Sub-s (1): words omitted repealed by SI 2002/794, art 5(2), Sch 2.

Date in force: 27 March 2002: see SI 2002/794, art 1(2).

Sub-s (6): in para (d) words "(other than the maximum fine on conviction on indictment)" in square brackets inserted by the Criminal Law Act 1977, s 65, Sch 12.

Sub-s (6): para (e) insertd by the Offshore Safety Act 1992, s 4(1), (6).

17 Use of approved codes of practice in criminal proceedings

(1) A failure on the part of any person to observe any provision of an approved code of practice shall not of itself render him liable to any civil or criminal proceedings; but where in any criminal proceedings a party is alleged to have committed an offence by reason of a contravention of any requirement or prohibition imposed by or under any such provision as is mentioned in section 16(1) being a provision for which there was an approved code of practice at the time of the alleged contravention, the following subsection shall have effect with respect to that code in relation to those proceedings.

(2) Any provision of the code of practice which appears to the court to be relevant to the requirement or prohibition alleged to have been contravened shall be admissible in evidence in the proceedings; and if it is proved that there was at any material time a failure to observe any provision of the code which appears to the court to be relevant to any matter which it is necessary for the prosecution to prove in order to establish a contravention of that requirement or prohibition, that matter shall be taken as proved unless the court is satisfied that the requirement or prohibition was in respect of that matter complied with otherwise than by way of observance of that provision of the code.

(3) In any criminal proceedings—

(a) a document purporting to be a notice issued by the Commission under section 16 shall be taken to be such a notice unless the contrary is proved; and

(b) a code of practice which appears to the court to be the subject of such a notice shall be taken to be the subject of that notice unless the contrary is proved.

Miscellaneous and supplementary

47 Civil liability

(1) Nothing in this Part shall be construed—

(a) as conferring a right of action in any civil proceedings in respect of any failure to comply with any duty imposed by sections 2 to 7 or any contravention of section 8; or

(b) as affecting the extent (if any) to which breach of a duty imposed by any of the existing statutory provisions is actionable; or

(c) as affecting the operation of section 12 of the Nuclear Installations Act 1965 (right to compensation by virtue of certain provisions of that Act).

(2) Breach of a duty imposed by health and safety regulations . . . shall, so far as it causes damage, be actionable except in so far as the regulations provide otherwise.

(3) No provision made by virtue of section 15(6)(b) shall afford a defence in any civil proceedings, whether brought by virtue of subsection (2) above or not; but as regards any duty imposed as mentioned in subsection (2) above health and safety regulations . . . may provide for any defence specified in the regulations to be available in any action for breach of that duty.

(4) Subsections (1)(a) and (2) above are without prejudice to any right of action which exists apart from the provisions of this Act, and subsection (3) above is without prejudice to any defence which may be available apart from the provisions of the regulations there mentioned.

(5) Any term of an agreement which purports to exclude or restrict the operation of subsection (2) above, or any liability arising by virtue of that subsection, shall be void, except in so far as health and safety regulations . . . provide otherwise.

(6) In this section "damage" includes the death of, or injury to, any person (including any disease and any impairment of a person's physical or mental condition).

NOTES

Sub-ss (2), (3), (5): words omitted repealed by the Employment Protection Act 1975, ss 116, 125(3), Sch 15, para 14, Sch 18.

PART IV
MISCELLANEOUS AND GENERAL

84 Extent, and application of Act

(1) This Act, except—
(a) Part I and this Part so far as may be necessary to enable regulations under section 15 . . . to be made and operate for the purpose mentioned in paragraph 2 of Schedule 3; and
(b) paragraph . . . 3 of Schedule 9,

does not extend to Northern Ireland.

(2) Part III, except section 75 and Schedule 7, does not extend to Scotland.

(3) Her Majesty may by Order in Council provide that the provisions of Parts I and II and this Part shall, to such extent and for such purposes as may be specified in the Order, apply (with or without modification) to or in relation to persons, premises, work, articles, substances and other matters (of whatever kind) outside Great Britain as those provisions apply within Great Britain or within a part of Great Britain so specified.

For the purposes of this subsection "premises", "work" and "substance" have the same meaning as they have for the purposes of Part I.

(4) An Order in Council under subsection (3) above—
(a) may make different provision for different circumstances or cases;
(b) may (notwithstanding that this may affect individuals or bodies corporate outside the United Kingdom) provide for any of the provisions mentioned in that subsection, as applied by such an Order, to apply to individuals whether or not they are British subjects and to bodies corporate whether or not they are incorporated under the law of any part of the United Kingdom;
(c) may make provision for conferring jurisdiction on any court or class of courts specified in the Order with respect to offences under Part I committed outside Great Britain or with respect to causes of action arising by virtue of section 47 (2) in respect of acts or omissions taking place outside Great Britain, and for the determination, in accordance with the law in force in such part of Great Britain as may be specified in the Order, of questions arising out of such acts or omissions;
(d) may exclude from the operation of section 3 of the Territorial Waters Jurisdiction Act 1878 (consents required for prosecutions) proceedings for offences under any provision of Part I committed outside Great Britain;
(e) may be varied or revoked by a subsequent Order in Council under this section;

and any such Order shall be subject to annulment in pursuance of a resolution of either House of Parliament.

(5) . . .

(6) Any jurisdiction conferred on any court under this section shall be without prejudice to any jurisdiction exercisable apart from this section by that or any other court.

NOTES

Sub-s (1): in para (a) words omitted repealed by the Employment Protection Act 1975, ss 116, 125(3), Sch 15, para 20, Sch 18; in para (b) words omitted repealed by the House of Commons Disqualification Act 1975, s 10(2), Sch 3.

Sub-s (5): repealed by the Offshore Safety Act 1992, ss 3(1), 7(2), Sch 2.

85 Short title and commencement

(1) This Act may be cited as the Health and Safety at Work etc Act 1974.

(2) This Act shall come into operation on such day as the Secretary of State may by order made by statutory instrument appoint, and different days may be appointed under this subsection for different purposes.

(3) An order under this section may contain such transitional provisions and savings as appear to the Secretary of State to be necessary or expedient in connection with the provisions thereby brought into force, including such adaptations of those provisions or any provision of this Act then in force as appear to him to be necessary or expedient in consequence of the partial operation of this Act (whether before or after the day appointed by the order).

Consumer Credit Act 1974

1974 CHAPTER 39

An Act to establish for the protection of consumers a new system, administered by the Director General of Fair Trading, of licensing and other control of traders concerned with the provision of credit, or the supply of goods on hire or hire-purchase, and their transactions, in place of the present enactments regulating moneylenders, pawnbrokers and hire-purchase traders and their transactions, and for related matters

[31st July 1974]

PART IX
JUDICIAL CONTROL

Extortionate credit bargains

137 Extortionate credit bargains

(1) If the court finds a credit bargain extortionate it may reopen the credit agreement so as to do justice between the parties.

(2) In this section and sections 138 to 140—

(a) "credit agreement" means any agreement [(other than an agreement which is an exempt agreement as a result of section 16(6C))] between an individual (the "debtor") and any other person (the "creditor") by which the creditor provides the debtor with credit of any amount, and
(b) "credit bargain"—
  (i) where no transaction other than the credit agreement is to be taken into account in computing the total charge for credit, means the credit agreement, or
  (ii) where one or more other transactions are to be so taken into account, means the credit agreement and those other transactions, taken together.

NOTES

Sub-s (2): in para (a) words from "(other than an agreement" to "section 16(6C))" in square brackets inserted by SI 2001/544, art 90(1), (6).

Date in force: 1 September 2002 (being 9 months after the Financial Services and Markets Act 2000, s 19 came into force): see SI 2001/3538, art 2(1) and SI 2001/544, art 2(1).

138 When bargains are extortionate

(1) A credit bargain is extortionate if it—
(a) requires the debtor or a relative of his to make payments (whether unconditionally, or on certain contingencies) which are grossly exorbitant, or
(b) otherwise grossly contravenes ordinary principles of fair dealing.

(2) In determining whether a credit bargain is extortionate, regard shall be had to such evidence as is adduced concerning—
(a) interest rates prevailing at the time it was made,
(b) the factors mentioned in subsections (3) to (5), and
(c) any other relevant considerations.

(3) Factors applicable under subsection (2) in relation to the debtor include—
(a) his age, experience, business capacity and state of health; and
(b) the degree to which, at the time of making the credit bargain, he was under financial pressure, and the nature of that pressure.

(4) Factors applicable under subsection (2) in relation to the creditor include—
(a) the degree of risk accepted by him, having regard to the value of any security provided;
(b) his relationship to the debtor; and
(c) whether or not a colourable cash price was quoted for any goods or services included in the credit bargain.

(5) Factors applicable under subsection (2) in relation to a linked transaction include the question how far the transaction was reasonably required for the protection of debtor or creditor, or was in the interest of the debtor.

139 Reopening of extortionate agreements

(1) A credit agreement may, if the court thinks just, be reopened on the ground that the credit bargain is extortionate—

(a) on an application for the purpose made by the debtor or any surety to the High Court, county court or sheriff court; or

(b) at the instance of the debtor or a surety in any proceedings to which the debtor and creditor are parties, being proceedings to enforce the agreement, any security relating to it, or any linked transaction; or

(c) at the instance of the debtor or a surety in other proceedings in any court where the amount paid or payable under the credit agreement is relevant.

(2) In reopening the agreement, the court may, for the purpose of relieving the debtor or a surety from payment of any sum in excess of that fairly due and reasonable, by order—

(a) direct accounts to be taken, or (in Scotland) an accounting to be made, between any persons,

(b) set aside the whole or part of any obligation imposed on the debtor or surety by the credit bargain or any related agreement,

(c) require the creditor to repay the whole or part of any sum paid under the credit bargain or any related agreement by the debtor or a surety, whether paid to the creditor or any other person,

(d) direct the return to the surety of any property provided for the purposes of the security, or

(e) alter the terms of the credit agreement or any security instrument.

(3) An order may be made under subsection (2) notwithstanding that its effect is to place a burden on the creditor in respect of an advantage unfairly enjoyed by another person who is a party to a linked transaction.

(4) An order under subsection (2) shall not alter the effect of any judgment.

(5) In England and Wales, an application under subsection (1)(a) shall be brought only in the county court in the case of—

(a) a regulated agreement, or

(b) an agreement (not being a regulated agreement) under which the creditor provides the debtor with fixed-sum credit . . . or running-account credit . . ..

[(5A) . . .]

(6) In Scotland an application under subsection (1)(a) may be brought in the sheriff court for the district in which the debtor or surety resides or carries on business.

(7) In Northern Ireland an application under subsection (1)(a) may be brought in the county court in the case of—

(a) a regulated agreement, or

(b) an agreement (not being a regulated agreement) under which the creditor provides the debtor with fixed-sum credit not exceeding [£15,000] or running-account credit on which the credit limit does not exceed [£15,000].

NOTES

Sub-s (5): in para (b) words omitted repealed by SI 1991/724, art 2(1), (8), Schedule, Part I.

Sub-s (5A): inserted by the Administration of Justice Act 1982, s 37, Sch 3, Part II, para 4; repealed by SI 1991/724, art 2(8), Schedule, Part I.

Sub-s (7): sums in square brackets substituted by virtue of the County Courts (Financial Limits) Order (Northern Ireland) 1993, SR 1993/282, art 2, Schedule.

PART XII
SUPPLEMENTAL

Miscellaneous

193 Short title and extent

(1) This Act may be cited as the Consumer Credit Act 1974.

(2) This Act extends to Northern Ireland.

Rehabilitation of Offenders Act 1974

1974 CHAPTER 53

An Act to rehabilitate offenders who have not been reconvicted of any serious offence for periods of years, to penalise the unauthorised disclosure of their previous convictions, to amend the law of defamation, and for purposes connected therewith

[31st July 1974]

4 Effect of rehabilitation

(1) Subject to sections 7 and 8 below, a person who has become a rehabilitated person for the purposes of this Act in respect of a conviction shall be treated for all purposes in law as a person who has not committed or been charged with or prosecuted for or convicted of or sentenced for the offence or offences which were the subject of that conviction; and, notwithstanding the provisions of any other enactment or rule of law to the contrary, but subject as aforesaid—

- (a) no evidence shall be admissible in any proceedings before a judicial authority exercising its jurisdiction or functions in Great Britain to prove that any such person has committed or been charged with or prosecuted for or convicted of or sentenced for any offence which was the subject of a spent conviction; and
- (b) a person shall not, in any such proceedings, be asked, and, if asked, shall not be required to answer, any question relating to his past which cannot be answered without acknowledging or referring to a spent conviction or spent convictions or any circumstances ancillary thereto.

(2) Subject to the provisions of any order made under subsection (4) below, where a question seeking information with respect to a person's previous convictions, offences, conduct or circumstances is put to him or to any other person otherwise than in proceedings before a judicial authority—

(a) the question shall be treated as not relating to spent convictions or to any circumstances ancillary to spent convictions, and the answer thereto may be framed accordingly; and

(b) the person questioned shall not be subjected to any liability or otherwise prejudiced in law by reason of any failure to acknowledge or disclose a spent conviction or any circumstances ancillary to a spent conviction in his answer to the question.

(3) Subject to the provisions of any order made under subsection (4) below,—

(a) any obligation imposed on any person by any rule of law or by the provisions of any agreement or arrangement to disclose any matters to any other person shall not extend to requiring him to disclose a spent conviction or any circumstances ancillary to a spent conviction (whether the conviction is his own or another's); and

(b) a conviction which has become spent or any circumstances ancillary thereto, or any failure to disclose a spent conviction or any such circumstances, shall not be a proper ground for dismissing or excluding a person from any office, profession, occupation or employment, or for prejudicing him in any way in any occupation or employment.

(4) The Secretary of State may by order—

(a) make such provisions as seems to him appropriate for excluding or modifying the application of either or both of paragraphs *(a)* and *(b)* of subsection (2) above in relation to questions put in such circumstances as may be specified in the order;

(b) provide for such exceptions from the provisions of subsection (3) above as seem to him appropriate, in such cases or classes of case, and in relation to convictions of such a description, as may be specified in the order.

(5) For the purposes of this section and section 7 below any of the following are circumstances ancillary to a conviction, that is to say—

(a) the offence or offences which were the subject of that conviction;

(b) the conduct constituting that offence or those offences; and

(c) any process or proceedings preliminary to that conviction, any sentence imposed in respect of that conviction, any proceedings (whether by way of appeal or otherwise) for reviewing that conviction or any such sentence, and anything done in pursuance of or undergone in compliance with any such sentence.

(6) For the purposes of this section and section 7 below "proceedings before a judicial authority" includes, in addition to proceedings before any of the ordinary courts of law, proceedings before any tribunal, body or person having power—

(a) by virtue of any enactment, law, custom or practice;

(b) under the rules governing any association, institution, profession, occupation or employment; or

(c) under any provision of an agreement providing for arbitration with respect to questions arising thereunder;

to determine any question affecting the rights, privileges, obligations or liabilities of any person, or to receive evidence affecting the determination of any such question.

8 Defamation actions

(1) This section applies to any action for libel or slander begun after the commencement of this Act by a rehabilitated person and founded upon the publication of any matter imputing that the plaintiff has committed or been charged with or prosecuted for or convicted of or sentenced for an offence which was the subject of a spent conviction.

(2) Nothing in section 4(1) above shall affect an action to which this section applies where the publication complained of took place before the conviction in question became spent, and the following provisions of this section shall not apply in any such case.

(3) Subject to subsections (5) and (6) below, nothing in section 4(1) above shall prevent the defendant in an action to which this section applies from relying on any defence of justification or fair comment or of absolute or qualified privilege which is available to him, or restrict the matters he may establish in support of any such defence.

(4) Without prejudice to the generality of subsection (3) above, where in any such action malice is alleged against a defendant who is relying on a defence of qualified privilege, nothing in section 4(1) above shall restrict the matters he may establish in rebuttal of the allegation.

(5) A defendant in any such action shall not by virtue of subsection (3) above be entitled to rely upon the defence of justification if the publication is proved to have been made with malice.

(6) Subject to subsection (7) below a defendant in any such action shall not, by virtue of subsection (3) above, be entitled to rely on any matter or adduce or require any evidence for the purpose of establishing (whether under [section 14 of the Defamation Act 1996] or otherwise) the defence that the matter published constituted a fair and accurate report of judicial proceedings if it is proved that the publication contained a reference to evidence which was ruled to be inadmissible in the proceedings by virtue of section 4(1) above.

(7) Subsection (3) above shall apply without the qualifications imposed by subsection (6) above in relation to—

(a) any report of judicial proceedings contained in any bona fide series of law reports which does not form part of any other publication and consists solely of reports of proceedings in courts of law; and

(b) any report or account of judicial proceedings published for bona fide educational, scientific or professional purposes, or given in the course of any lecture, class or discussion given or held for any of those purposes.

(8) In the application of this section to Scotland—

(a) for the reference in subsection (1) to libel and slander there shall be substituted a reference to defamation;

(b) for references to the plaintiff and the defendant there shall be substituted respectively references to the pursuer and the defender; and

(c) for references to the defence of justification there shall be substituted references to the defence of veritas.

NOTES

Sub-s (6): words "section 14 of the Defamation Act 1996" in square brackets substituted by the Defamation Act 1996, s 14(4).

Date in force: 1 April 1999: see SI 1999/817, art 2(a).

11 Citation commencement and extent

(1) This Act may be cited as the Rehabilitation of Offenders Act 1974.

(2) This Act shall come into force on 1st July 1975 or such earlier day as the Secretary of State may by order appoint.

(3) This Act shall not apply to Northern Ireland.

Congenital Disabilities (Civil Liability) Act 1976

1976 CHAPTER 28

An Act to make provision as to civil liability in the case of children born disabled in consequence of some person's fault; and to extend the Nuclear Installations Act 1965, so that children so born in consequence of a breach of duty under that Act may claim compensation

[22nd July 1976]

1 Civil liability to child born disabled

(1) If a child is born disabled as the result of such an occurrence before its birth as is mentioned in subsection (2) below, and a person (other than the child's own mother) is under this section answerable to the child in respect of the occurrence, the child's disabilities are to be regarded as damage resulting from the wrongful act of that person and actionable accordingly at the suit of the child.

(2) An occurrence to which this section applies is one which—

- (a) affected either parent of the child in his or her ability to have a normal, healthy child; or
- (b) affected the mother during her pregnancy, or affected her or the child in the course of its birth, so that the child is born with disabilities which would not otherwise have been present.

(3) Subject to the following subsections, a person (here referred to as "the defendant") is answerable to the child if he was liable in tort to the parent or would, if sued in due time, have been so; and it is no answer that there could not have been such liability because the parent suffered no actionable injury, if there was a breach of legal duty which, accompanied by injury, would have given rise to the liability.

(4) In the case of an occurrence preceding the time of conception, the defendant is not answerable to the child if at that time either or both of the parents knew the risk

of their child being born disabled (that is to say, the particular risk created by the occurrence); but should it be the child's father who is the defendant, this subsection does not apply if he knew of the risk and the mother did not.

(5) The defendant is not answerable to the child, for anything he did or omitted to do when responsible in a professional capacity for treating or advising the parent, if he took reasonable care having due regard to then received professional opinion applicable to the particular class of case; but this does not mean that he is answerable only because he departed from received opinion.

(6) Liability to the child under this section may be treated as having been excluded or limited by contract made with the parent affected, to the same extent and subject to the same restrictions as liability in the parent's own case; and a contract term which could have been set up by the defendant in an action by the parent, so as to exclude or limit his liability to him or her, operates in the defendant's favour to the same, but no greater, extent in an action under this section by the child.

(7) If in the child's action under this section it is shown that the parent affected shared the responsibility for the child being born disabled, the damages are to be reduced to such extent as the court thinks just and equitable having regard to the extent of the parent's responsibility.

[1A Extension of section 1 to cover infertility treatments]

[(1) In any case where—

(a) a child carried by a woman as the result of the placing in her of an embryo or of sperm and eggs or her artificial insemination is born disabled,

(b) the disability results from an act or omission in the course of the selection, or the keeping or use outside the body, of the embryo carried by her or of the gametes used to bring about the creation of the embryo, and

(c) a person is under this section answerable to the child in respect of the act or omission,

the child's disabilities are to be regarded as damage resulting from the wrongful act of that person and actionable accordingly at the suit of the child.

(2) Subject to subsection (3) below and the applied provisions of section 1 of this Act, a person (here referred to as "the defendant") is answerable to the child if he was liable in tort to one or both of the parents (here referred to as "the parent or parents concerned") or would, if sued in due time, have been so; and it is no answer that there could not have been such liability because the parent or parents concerned suffered no actionable injury, if there was a breach of legal duty which, accompanied by injury, would have given rise to the liability.

(3) The defendant is not under this section answerable to the child if at the time the embryo, or the sperm and eggs, are placed in the woman or the time of her insemination (as the case may be) either or both of the parents knew the risk of their child being born disabled (that is to say, the particular risk created by the act or omission).

(4) Subsections (5) to (7) of section 1 of this Act apply for the purposes of this section as they apply for the purposes of that but as if references to the parent or the parent affected were references to the parent or parents concerned.]

NOTES

Inserted by the Human Fertilisation and Embryology Act 1990, s 44.

2 Liability of woman driving when pregnant

A woman driving a motor vehicle when she knows (or ought reasonably to know) herself to be pregnant is to be regarded as being under the same duty to take care for the safety of her unborn child as the law imposes on her with respect to the safety of other people; and if in consequence of her breach of that duty her child is born with disabilities which would not otherwise have been present, those disabilities are to be regarded as damage resulting from her wrongful act and actionable accordingly at the suit of the child.

3 Disabled birth due to radiation

(1) Section 1 of this Act does not affect the operation of the Nuclear Installations Act 1965 as to liability for, and compensation in respect of, injury or damage caused by occurrences involving nuclear matter or the emission of ionising radiations.

(2) For the avoidance of doubt anything which—

(a) affects a man in his ability to have a normal, healthy child; or
(b) affects a woman in that ability, or so affects her when she is pregnant that her child is born with disabilities which would not otherwise have been present,

is an injury for the purposes of that Act.

(3) If a child is born disabled as the result of an injury to either of its parents caused in breach of a duty imposed by any of sections 7 to 11 of that Act (nuclear site licensees and others to secure that nuclear incidents do not cause injury to persons, etc), the child's disabilities are to be regarded under the subsequent provisions of that Act (compensation and other matters) as injuries caused on the same occasion, and by the same breach of duty, as was the injury to the parent.

(4) As respects compensation to the child, section 13 (6) of that Act (contributory fault of person injured by radiation) is to be applied as if the reference there to fault were to the fault of the parent.

(5) Compensation is not payable in the child's case if the injury to the parent preceded the time of the child's conception and at that time either or both of the parents knew the risk of their child being born disabled (that is to say, the particular risk created by the injury).

4 Interpretation and other supplementary provisions

(1) References in this Act to a child being born disabled or with disabilities are to its being born with any deformity, disease or abnormality, including predisposition (whether or not susceptible of immediate prognosis) to physical or mental defect in the future.

(2) In this Act—

(a) "born" means born alive (the moment of a child's birth being when it first has a life separate from its mother), and "birth" has a corresponding meaning; and

(b) "motor vehicle" means a mechanically propelled vehicle intended or adapted for use on roads

[and references to embryos shall be construed in accordance with section 1 of the Human Fertilisation and Embryology Act 1990].

(3) Liability to a child under section 1 [1A] or 2 of this Act is to be regarded—

(a) as respects all its incidents and any matters arising or to arise out of it; and

(b) subject to any contrary context or intention, for the purpose of construing references in enactments and documents to personal or bodily injuries and cognate matters,

as liability for personal injuries sustained by the child immediately after its birth.

(4) No damages shall be recoverable under [any] of those sections in respect of any loss of expectation of life, nor shall any such loss be taken into account in the compensation payable in respect of a child under the Nuclear Installations Act 1965 as extended by section 3, unless (in either case) the child lives for at least 48 hours.

[(4A) In any case where a child carried by a woman as the result of the placing in her of an embryo or of sperm and eggs or her artificial insemination is born disabled, any reference in section 1 of this Act to a parent includes a reference to a person who would be a parent but for sections 27 to 29 of the Human Fertilisation and Embryology Act 1990.]

(5) This Act applies in respect of births after (but not before) its passing, and in respect of any such birth it replaces any law in force before its passing, whereby a person could be liable to a child in respect of disabilities with which it might be born; but in section 1(3) of this Act the expression "liable in tort" does not include any reference to liability by virtue of this Act, or to liability by virtue of any such law.

(6) References to the Nuclear Installations Act 1965 are to that Act as amended; and for the purposes of section 28 of that Act (power by Order in Council to extend the Act to territories outside the United Kingdom) section 3 of this Act is to be treated as if it were a provision of that Act.

NOTES

Sub-ss (2), (3): words in square brackets inserted by the Human Fertilisation and Embryology Act 1990, s 44(2).

Sub-s (4): word in square brackets substituted by the Human Fertilisation and Embryology Act 1990, s 44(2).

Sub-s (4A): inserted by the Human Fertilisation and Embryology Act 1990, s 35(4).

6 Citation and extent

(1) This Act may be cited as the Congenital Disabilities (Civil Liability) Act 1976.

(2) This Act extends to Northern Ireland but not to Scotland.

Fatal Accidents Act 1976

1976 CHAPTER 30

An Act to consolidate the Fatal Accidents Acts.

[22nd July 1976]

[1 Right of action for wrongful act causing death]

[(1) If death is caused by any wrongful act, neglect or default which is such as would (if death had not ensued) have entitled the person injured to maintain an action and recover damages in respect thereof, the person who would have been liable if death had not ensued shall be liable to an action for damages, notwithstanding the death of the person injured.

(2) Subject to section 1A(2) below, every such action shall be for the benefit of the dependants of the person ("the deceased") whose death has been so caused.

(3) In this Act "dependant" means—

- (a) the wife or husband or former wife or husband of the deceased;
- (b) any person who—
  - (i) was living with the deceased in the same household immediately before the date of the death; and
  - (ii) had been living with the deceased in the same household for at least two years before that date; and
  - (iii) was living during the whole of that period as the husband or wife of the deceased;
- (c) any parent or other ascendant of the deceased;
- (d) any person who was treated by the deceased as his parent;
- (e) any child or other descendant of the deceased;
- (f) any person (not being a child of the deceased) who, in the case of any marriage to which the deceased was at any time a party, was treated by the deceased as a child of the family in relation to that marriage;
- (g) any person who is, or is the issue of, a brother, sister, uncle or aunt of the deceased.

(4) The reference to the former wife or husband of the deceased in subsection (3)(*a*) above includes a reference to a person whose marriage to the deceased has been annulled or declared void as well as a person whose marriage to the deceased has been dissolved.

(5) In deducing any relationship for the purposes of subsection (3) above—
- (a) any relationship of affinity shall be treated as a relationship by consanguinity, any relationship of the half blood as a relationship of the whole blood, and the stepchild of any person as his child, and
- (b) an illegitimate person shall be treated as the legitimate child of his mother and reputed father.

(6) Any reference in this Act to injury includes any disease and any impairment of a person's physical or mental condition.]

NOTES

Substituted by the Administration of Justice Act 1982, s 3.

[1A Bereavement]

[(1) An action under this Act may consist of or include a claim for damages for bereavement.

(2) A claim for damages for bereavement shall only be for the benefit—
- (a) of the wife or husband of the deceased; and
- (b) where the deceased was a minor who was never married—
  - (i) of his parents, if he was legitimate; and
  - (ii) of his mother, if he was illegitimate.

(3) Subject to subject (5) below, the sum to be awarded as damages under this section shall be [£10,000].

(4) Where there is a claim for damages under this section for the benefit of both the parents of the deceased, the sum awarded shall be divided equally between them (subject to any deduction falling to be made in respect of costs not recovered from the defendant).

(5) The Lord Chancellor may by order made by statutory instrument, subject to annulment in pursuance of a resolution of either House of Parliament, amend this section by varying the sum for the time being specified in subsection (3) above.]

NOTES

Inserted by the Administration of Justice Act 1982, s 3.

Sub-s (3): sum "£10,000" in square brackets substituted by SI 2002/644, art 2.

Date in force: 1 April 2002 (in relation to causes of action which accrue on or after that date): see SI 2002/644, art 1.

[2 Persons entitled to bring the action]

[(1) The action shall be brought by and in the name of the executor or administrator of the deceased.

(2) If—
- (a) there is no executor or administrator of the deceased, or
- (b) no action is brought within six months after the death by and in the name of an executor or administrator of the deceased.

the action may be brought by and in the name of all or any of the persons for whose benefit an executor or administrator could have brought it.

(3) Not more than one action shall lie for and in respect of the same subject matter of complaint.

(4) The plaintiff in the action shall be required to deliver to the defendant or his solicitor full particulars of the persons for whom and on whose behalf the action is brought and of the nature of the claim in respect of which damages are sought to be recovered.]

NOTES

Substituted by the Administration of Justice Act 1982, s 3.

[3 Assessment of damages]

[(1) In the action such damages, other than damages for bereavement, may be awarded as are proportioned to the injury resulting from the death to the dependants respectively.

(2) After deducting the costs not recovered from the defendant any amount recovered otherwise than as damages for bereavement shall be divided among the dependants in such shares as may be directed.

(3) In an action under this Act where there fall to be assessed damages payable to a widow in respect of the death of her husband there shall not be taken account the re-marriage of the widow or her prospects of re-marriage.

(4) In an action under this Act where there fall to be assessed damages payable to a person who is a dependant by virtue of section 1(3)(*b*) above in respect of the death of the person with whom the dependant was living as husband or wife there shall be taken into account (together with any other matter that appears to the court to be relevant to the action) the fact that the dependant had no enforceable right to financial support by the deceased as a result of their living together.

(5) If the dependants have incurred funeral expenses in respect of the deceased, damages may be awarded in respect of those expenses.

(6) Money paid into court in satisfaction of a cause of action under this Act may be in one sum without specifying any person's share.]

NOTES

Substituted by the Administration of Justice Act 1982, s 3.

[4 Assessment of damages: disregard of benefits]

[In assessing damages in respect of a person's death in an action under this Act, benefits which have accrued or will or may accrue to any person from his estate or otherwise as a result of his death shall be disregarded.]

NOTES

Substituted by the Administration of Justice Act 1982, s 3.

5 Contributory negligence

Where any person dies as the result partly of his own fault and partly of the fault of any other person or persons, and accordingly if an action were brought for the benefit of the estate under the Law Reform (Miscellaneous Provisions) Act 1934 the damages recoverable would be reduced under section 1(1) of the Law Reform (Contributory Negligence) Act 1945, any damages recoverable in an action . . . under this Act shall be reduced to a proportionate extent.

NOTES

Words omitted repealed by the Administration of Justice Act 1982, s 3, s 75, Sch 9, Part I.

7 Short title, etc

(1) This Act may be cited as the Fatal Accidents Act 1976.

(2) This Act shall come into force on 1st September 1976, but shall not apply to any cause of action arising on a death before it comes into force.

(3) This Act shall not extend to Scotland or Northern Ireland.

Resale Prices Act 1976

1976 CHAPTER 53

An Act to consolidate those provisions of the Resale Prices Act 1964 still having effect, Part II of the Restrictive Trade Practices Act 1956, and related enactments; and to repeal the provisions of the Resale Prices Act 1964 and the Restrictive Trade Practices Act 1968 which have ceased to have any effect

[26 October 1976]

PART I
PROHIBITION OF COLLECTIVE RESALE PRICE MAINTENANCE

1 Collective agreement by suppliers

(1) It is unlawful for any two or more persons carrying on business in the United Kingdom as suppliers of any goods to make or carry out any agreement or arrangement by which they undertake—

(a) to withhold supplies of goods for delivery in the United Kingdom from dealers (whether party to the agreement or arrangement or not) who resell or have resold goods in breach of any condition as to the price at which those goods may be resold;

(b) to refuse to supply goods for delivery in the United Kingdom to such dealers except on terms and conditions which are less favourable than those applicable in the case of other dealers carrying on business in similar circumstances; or

(c) to supply goods only to persons who undertake or have undertaken—

(i) *to withhold supplies of goods as described in paragraph (a) above; or*
(ii) *to refuse to supply goods as described in paragraph (b) above.*

(2) It is unlawful for any two or more such persons to make or carry out any agreement or arrangement authorising—

(a) *the recovery of penalties (however described) by or on behalf of the parties to the agreement or arrangement from dealers who resell or have resold goods in breach of any such condition as is described in paragraph (a) of subsection (1) above; or*
(b) *the conduct of any domestic proceedings in connection therewith.*

NOTES

Whole Act repealed by the Competition Act 1998, ss 1, 74(3), Sch 14, Pt I as from a day to be appointed; for transitional provisions and savings see Sch 13, Pts II–IV thereto.

PART III
GENERAL AND SUPPLEMENTAL

30 Short title, extent and commencement

(1) This Act may be cited as the Resale Prices Act 1976.

(2) This Act extends to Northern Ireland.

(3) This Act shall come into operation on such day as the Secretary of State may appoint by order made by statutory instrument.

NOTES

Repealed as noted to s 1.

Torts (Interference with Goods) Act 1977

1977 CHAPTER 32

An Act to amend the law concerning conversion and other torts affecting goods
[22nd July 1977]

Preliminary

1 Definition of "wrongful interference with goods"

In this Act "wrongful interference", or "wrongful interference with goods", means—

(a) conversion of goods (also called trover),
(b) trespass to goods,
(c) negligence so far as it results in damage to goods or to an interest in goods,

(d) subject to section 2, any other tort so far as it results in damage to goods or to an interest in goods

[and references in this Act (however worded) to proceedings for wrongful interference or to a claim or right to claim for wrongful interference shall include references to proceedings by virtue of Part I of the Consumer Protection Act 1987 [or Part II of the Consumer Protection (Northern Ireland) Order 1987] (product liability) in respect of any damage to goods or to an interest in goods or, as the case may be, to a claim or right to claim by virtue of that Part in respect of any such damage].

NOTES

Words in square brackets inserted by the Consumer Protection Act 1987, s 48, Sch 4; words in square brackets therein inserted by SI 1987/2049, art 35(1), Sch 3, para 3.

Detention of goods

2 Abolition of detinue

(1) Detinue is abolished.

(2) An action lies in conversion for loss or destruction of goods which a bailee has allowed to happen in breach of his duty to his bailor (that is to say it lies in a case which is not otherwise conversion, but would have been detinue before detinue was abolished).

3 Form of judgment where goods are detained

(1) In proceedings for wrongful interference against a person who is in possession or in control of the goods relief may be given in accordance with this section, so far as appropriate.

(2) The relief is—

(a) an order for delivery of the goods, and for payment of any consequential damages, or

(b) an order for delivery of the goods, but giving the defendant the alternative of paying damages by reference to the value of the goods, together in either alternative with payment of any consequential damages, or

(c) damages.

(3) Subject to rules of court—

(a) relief shall be given under only one of paragraphs (a), (b) and (c) of subsection (2),

(b) relief under paragraph (a) of subjection (2) is at the discretion of the court, and the claimant may choose between the others.

(4) If it is shown to the satisfaction of the court that an order under subsection (2)(a) has not been complied with, the court may—

(a) revoke the order, or the relevant part of it, and

(b) make an order for payment of damages by reference to the value of the goods.

(5) Where an order is made under subsection (2)(b) the defendant may satisfy the order by returning the goods at any time before execution of judgment, but without prejudice to liability to pay any consequential damages.

(6) An order for delivery of the goods under subsection (2)(a) or (b) may impose such conditions as may be determined by the court, or pursuant to rules of court, and in particular, where damages by reference to the value of the goods would not be the whole of the value of the goods, may require an allowance to be made by the claimant to reflect the difference.

For example, a bailor's action against the bailee may be one in which the measure of damages is not the full value of the goods, and then the court may order delivery of the goods, but require the bailor to pay the bailee a sum reflecting the difference.

(7) Where under subjection (1) or subsection (2) of section 6 an allowance is to be made in respect of an improvement of the goods, and an order is made under subsection (2)(a) or (b), the court may assess the allowance to be made in respect of the improvement, and by the order require, as a condition for delivery of the goods, that allowance to be made by the claimant.

(8) This section is without prejudice—
- (a) to the remedies afforded by section 133 of the Consumer Credit Act 1974, or
- (b) to the remedies afforded by sections 35, 42 and 44 of the Hire-Purchase Act 1965, or to those sections of the Hire-Purchase Act (Northern Ireland) 1966 (so long as those sections respectively remain in force), or
- (c) to any jurisdiction to afford ancillary or incidental relief.

4 Interlocutory relief where goods are detained

(1) In this section "proceedings" means proceedings for wrongful interference.

(2) On the application of any person in accordance with rules of court, the High Court shall, in such circumstances as may be specified in the rules, have power to make an order providing for the delivery up of any goods which are or may become the subject matter of subsequent proceedings in the court, or as to which any question may arise in proceedings.

(3) Delivery shall be, as the order may provide, to the claimant or to a person appointed by the court for the purpose, and shall be on such terms and conditions as may be specified in the order.

(4) The power to make rules of court under section [84 of the Supreme Court Act 1981] or under section 7 of the Northern Ireland Act 1962 shall include power to make rules of court as to the manner in which an application for such an order can be made, and as to the circumstances in which such an order can be made; and any such rules may include such incidental, supplementary and consequential provisions as the authority making the rules may consider necessary or expedient.

(5) The preceding provisions of this section shall have effect in relation to county courts as they have effect in relation to the High Court, and as if in those provisions references to rules of court and to section [84] of the said Act of [1981] or section 7 of the Northern Ireland Act 1962 included references to county court rules and to

[section 75 of the County Courts Act 1984] or [Article 47 of the County Courts (Northern Ireland) Order 1980].

NOTES

Sub-s (4): words in square brackets substituted by the Supreme Court Act 1981, s 152 (1), Sch 5.

Sub-s (5): first and second amendments made by the Supreme Court Act 1981, s 152 (1), Sch 5; third words in square brackets substituted by the County Courts Act 1984, s 148(1), Sch 2, Pt V, para 64; final amendment made by the County Courts (Northern Ireland) Order 1980, SI 1980/397, art 68 (2), Sch 1, Part II.

Damages

5 Extinction of title on satisfaction of claim for damages

(1) Where damages for wrongful interference are, or would fall to be, assessed on the footing that the claimant is being compensated—

(a) for the whole of his interest in the goods, or

(b) for the whole of his interest in the goods subject to a reduction for contributory negligence,

payment of the assessed damages (under all heads), or as the case may be settlement of a claim for damages for the wrong (under all heads), extinguishes the claimant's title to that interest.

(2) In subsection (1) the reference to the settlement of the claim includes—

(a) where the claim is made in court proceedings, and the defendant has paid a sum into court to meet the whole claim, the taking of that sum by the claimant, and

(b) where the claim is made in court proceedings, and the proceedings are settled or compromised, the payment of what is due in accordance with the settlement or compromise, and

(c) where the claim is made out of court and is settled or compromised, the payment of what is due in accordance with the settlement or compromise.

(3) It is hereby declared that subsection (1) does not apply where damages are assessed on the footing that the claimant is being compensated for the whole of his interest in the goods, but the damages paid are limited to some lesser amount by virtue of any enactment or rule of law.

(4) Where under section 7(3) the claimant accounts over to another person (the "third party") so as to compensate (under all heads) the third party for the whole of his interest in the goods, the third party's title to that interest is extinguished.

(5) This section has effect subject to any agreement varying the respective rights of the parties to the agreement, and where the claim is made in court proceedings has effect subject to any order of the court.

6 Allowance for improvement of the goods

(1) If in proceedings for wrongful interference against a person (the "improver") who has improved the goods, it is shown that the improver acted in the mistaken but

honest belief that he had a good title to them, an allowance shall be made for the extent to which, at the time as at which the goods fall to be valued in assessing damages, the value of the goods is attributable to the improvement.

(2) If, in proceedings for wrongful interference against a person ("the purchaser") who has purported to purchase the goods—

(a) from the improver, or

(b) where after such a purported sale the goods passed by a further purported sale on one or more occasions, on any such occasion,

it is shown that the purchaser acted in good faith, an allowance shall be made on the principle set out in subsection (1).

For example, where a person in good faith buys a stolen car from the improver and is sued in conversion by the true owner the damages may be reduced to reflect the improvement, but if the person who bought the stolen car from the improver sues the improver for failure of consideration, and the improver acted in good faith, subsection (3) below will ordinarily make a comparable reduction in the damages he recovers from the improver.

(3) If in a case within subsection (2) the person purporting to sell the goods acted in good faith, then in proceedings by the purchaser for recovery of the purchase price because of failure of consideration, or in any other proceedings founded on that failure of consideration, an allowance shall, where appropriate, be made on the principle set out in subsection (1).

(4) This section applies, with the necessary modifications, to a purported bailment or other disposition of goods as it applies to a purported sale of goods.

Liability to two or more claimants

7 Double liability

(1) In this section "double liability" means the double liability of the wrongdoer which can arise—

(a) where one of two or more rights of action for wrongful interference is founded on a possessory title, or

(b) where the measure of damages in an action for wrongful interference founded on a proprietary title is or includes the entire value of the goods, although the interest is one of two or more interests in the goods.

(2) In proceedings to which any two or more claimants are parties, the relief shall be such as to avoid double liability of the wrongdoer as between those claimants.

(3) On satisfaction, in whole or in part, of any claim for an amount exceeding that recoverable if subsection (2) applied, the claimant is liable to account over to the other person having a right to claim to such extent as will avoid double liability.

(4) Where, as the result of enforcement of a double liability, any claimant is unjustly enriched to any extent, he shall be liable to reimburse the wrongdoer to that extent.

For example, if a converter of goods pays damages first to a finder of the goods, and then to the true owner, the finder is unjustly enriched unless he accounts over to the true owner under subsection (3); and then the true owner is unjustly enriched and becomes liable to reimburse the converter of the goods.

8 Competing rights to the goods

(1) The defendant in an action for wrongful interference shall be entitled to show, in accordance with rules of court, that a third party has a better right than the plaintiff as respects all or any part of the interest claimed by the plaintiff, or in right of which he sues, and any rule of law (sometimes called *jus tertii*) to the contrary is abolished.

(2) Rules of court relating to proceedings for wrongful interference may—
- (a) require the plaintiff to give particulars of his title,
- (b) require the plaintiff to identify any person who, to his knowledge, has or claims any interest in the goods,
- (c) authorise the defendant to apply for directions as to whether any person should be joined with a view to establishing whether he has a better right than the plaintiff, or has a claim as a result of which the defendant might be doubly liable,
- (d) where a party fails to appear on an application within paragraph (c), or to comply with any direction given by the court on such an application, authorise the court to deprive him of any right of action against the defendant for the wrong either unconditionally, or subject to such terms or conditions as may be specified.

(3) Subsection (2) is without prejudice to any other power of making rules of court.

9 Concurrent actions

(1) This section applies where goods are the subject of two or more claims for wrongful interference (whether or not the claims are founded on the same wrongful act, and whether or not any of the claims relates also to other goods).

(2) Where goods are the subject of two or more claims under section 6 this section shall apply as if any claim under section 6(3) were a claim for wrongful interference.

(3) If proceedings have been brought in a county court on one of those claims, county court rules may waive, or allow a court to waive, any limit (financial or territorial) on the jurisdiction of county courts in [the County Courts Act 1984] or the County Courts [(Northern Ireland) Order 1980] so as to allow another of those claims to be brought in the same county court.

(4) If proceedings are brought on one of the claims in the High Court, and proceedings on any other are brought in a county court, whether prior to the High Court proceedings or not, the High Court may, on the application of the defendant, after notice has been given to the claimant in the county court proceedings—
- (a) order that the county court proceedings be transferred to the High Court, and

(b) order security for costs or impose such other terms as the court thinks fit.

NOTES

Sub-s (3): first words in square brackets substituted by the County Courts Act 1984, s 148(1), Sch 2, Pt V, para 65; second words in square brackets substituted by the County Courts (Northern Ireland) Order 1980, SI 1980/397, art 68(2), Sch 1, Pt II.

Conversion and trespass to goods

10 Co-owners

(1) Co-ownership is no defence to an action founded on conversion or trespass to goods where the defendant without the authority of the other co-owner—

- (a) destroys the goods, or disposes of the goods in a way giving a good title to the entire property in the goods, or otherwise does anything equivalent to the destruction of the other's interest in the goods, or
- (b) purports to dispose of the goods in a way which would give a good title to the entire property in the goods if he was acting with the authority of all co-owners of the goods.

(2) Subsection (1) shall not effect the law concerning execution or enforcement of judgments, or concerning any form of distress.

(3) Subsection (1)(a) is by way of restatement of existing law so far as it relates to conversion.

11 Minor amendments

(1) Contributory negligence is no good defence in proceedings founded on conversion, or on intentional trespass to goods.

(2) Receipt of goods by way of pledge is conversion if the delivery of the goods is conversion.

(3) Denial of title is not of itself conversion.

Uncollected goods

12 Bailee's power of sale

(1) This section applies to goods in the possession or under the control of a bailee where—

- (a) the bailor is in breach of an obligation to take delivery of the goods or, if the terms of the bailment so provide, to give directions as to their delivery, or
- (b) the bailee could impose such an obligation by giving notice to the bailor, but is unable to trace or communicate with the bailor, or
- (c) the bailee can reasonably expect to be relieved of any duty to safeguard the goods on giving notice to the bailor, but is unable to trace or communicate with the bailor.

(2) In the cases in Part I of Schedule 1 to this Act a bailee may, for the purposes of subsection (1), impose an obligation on the bailor to take delivery of the goods,

or as the case may be to give directions as to their delivery, and in those cases the said Part I sets out the methods of notification.

(3) If the bailee—
- (a) has in accordance with Part II of Schedule 1 to this Act given notice to the bailor of his intention to sell the goods under this subsection, or
- (b) has failed to trace or communicate with the bailor with a view to giving him such a notice, after having taken reasonable steps for the purpose,

and is reasonably satisfied that the bailor owns the goods, he shall be entitled, as against the bailor, to sell the goods.

(4) Where subsection (3) applies but the bailor did not in fact own the goods, a sale under this section, or under section 13, shall not give a good title as against the owner, or as against a person claiming under the owner.

(5) A bailee exercising his powers under subsection (3) shall be liable to account to the bailor for the proceeds of sale, less any costs of sale, and—
- (a) the account shall be taken on the footing that the bailee should have adopted the best method of sale reasonably available in the circumstances, and
- (b) where subsection (3)(a) applies, any sum payable in respect of the goods by the bailor to the bailee which accrued due before the bailee gave notice of intention to sell the goods shall be deductible from the proceeds of sale.

(6) A sale duly made under this section gives a good title to the purchaser as against the bailor.

(7) In this section, section 13, and Schedule 1 to this Act,
- (a) "bailor" and "bailee" include their respective successors in title, and
- (b) references to what is payable, paid or due to the bailee in respect of the goods include references to what would be payable by the bailor to the bailee as a condition of delivery of the goods at the relevant time.

(8) This section, and Schedule 1 to this Act, have effect subject to the terms of the bailment.

(9) This section shall not apply where the goods were bailed before the commencement of this Act.

13 Sale authorised by the court

(1) If a bailee of the goods to which section 12 applies satisfies the court that he is entitled to sell the goods under section 12, or that he would be so entitled if he had given any notice required in accordance with Schedule 1 to this Act, the court—
- (a) may authorise the sale of the goods subject to such terms and conditions, if any, as may be specified in the order, and
- (b) may authorise the bailee to deduct from the proceeds of sale any costs of sale and any amount due from the bailor to the bailee in respect of the goods, and
- (c) may direct the payment into court of the net proceeds of sale, less any amount deducted under paragraph (b), to be held to the credit of the bailor.

(2) A decision of the court authorising a sale under this section shall, subject to any right of appeal, be conclusive, as against the bailor, of the bailee's entitlement to sell the goods, and gives a good title to the purchaser as against the bailor.

(3) In this section "the court" means the High Court or a county court, [and a county court shall have jurisdiction in the proceedings save that, in Northern Ireland, a county court shall only have jurisdiction in proceedings if the value of the goods does not exceed the county court limit mentioned in Article 10(1) of the County Courts (Northern Ireland) Order 1980].

NOTES

Sub-s (3): words in square brackets substituted by the High Court and County Courts Jurisdiction Order 1991, SI 1991/724, art 2(1), (8), Schedule.

Supplemental

14 Interpretation

(1) In this Act, unless the context otherwise requires—

. . .

"enactment" includes an enactment contained in an Act of the Parliament of Northern Ireland or an Order in Council made under the Northern Ireland (Temporary Provisions) Act 1972, or in a Measure of the Northern Ireland Assembly,

"goods" includes all chattels personal other than things in action and money,

"High Court" includes the High Court of Justice in Northern Ireland.

(2) References in this Act to any enactment include references to that enactment as amended, extended or applied by or under that or any other enactment.

NOTES

Sub-s (1): words omitted repealed by SI 1991/724, art 2(8), Schedule, Part I; for transitional provisions in relation to Crown proceedings, and savings, see arts 11, 12 thereof.

16 Extent and application to the Crown

(1) Section 15 shall extend to Scotland, but otherwise this Act shall not extend to Scotland.

(2) This Act, except section 15, extends to Northern Ireland.

(3) This Act shall bind the Crown, but as regards the Crown's liability in tort shall not bind the Crown further than the Crown is made liable in tort by the Crown Proceedings Act 1947.

17 Short title, etc

(1) This Act may be cited as the Torts (Interference with Goods) Act 1977.

(2) This Act shall come into force on such day as the Lord Chancellor may by order contained in a statutory instrument appoint, and such an order may appoint different dates for different provisions or for different purposes.

(3) Schedule 2 to this Act contains transitional provisions.

SCHEDULE 1
UNCOLLECTED GOODS

Section 12

PART I
POWER TO IMPOSE OBLIGATION TO COLLECT GOODS

1 (1) For the purposes of section 12(1) a bailee may, in the circumstances specified in this Part of this Schedule, by notice given to the bailor impose on him an obligation to take delivery of the goods.

(2) The notice shall be in writing, and may be given either—
- (a) by delivering it to the bailor, or
- (b) by leaving it at his proper address, or
- (c) by post.

(3) The notice shall—
- (a) specify the name and address of the bailee, and give sufficient particulars of the goods and the address or place where they are held, and
- (b) state that the goods are ready for delivery to the bailor, or where combined with a notice terminating the contract of bailment, will be ready for delivery when the contract is terminated, and
- (c) specify the amount, if any, which is payable by the bailor to the bailee in respect of the goods and which became due before the giving of the notice.

(4) Where the notice is sent by post it may be combined with a notice under Part II of this Schedule if the notice is sent by post in a way complying with paragraph 6(4).

(5) References in this Part of this Schedule to taking delivery of the goods include, where the terms of the bailment admit, references to giving directions as to their delivery.

(6) This Part of this Schedule is without prejudice to the provisions of any contract requiring the bailor to take delivery of the goods.

Goods accepted for repair or other treatment

2 If a bailee has accepted goods for repair or other treatment on the terms (expressed or implied) that they will be re-delivered to the bailor when the repair or other treatment has been carried out, the notice may be given at any time after the repair or other treatment has been carried out.

Goods accepted for valuation or appraisal

3 If a bailee has accepted goods in order to value or appraise them, the notice may be given at any time after the bailee has carried out the valuation or appraisal.

Storage, warehousing, etc

4 (1) If a bailee is in possession of goods which he has held as custodian, and his obligation as custodian has come to an end, the notice may be given at any time after the ending of the obligation, or may be combined with any notice terminating his obligation as custodian.

(2) This paragraph shall not apply to goods held by a person as mercantile agent, that is to say by a person having in the customary course of his business as a mercantile agent authority either to sell goods or to consign goods for the purpose of sale, or to buy goods, or to raise money on the security of goods.

Supplemental

5 Paragraphs 2, 3 and 4 apply whether or not the bailor has paid any amount due to the bailee in respect of the goods, and whether or not the bailment is for reward, or in the course of business, or gratuitous.

PART II
NOTICE OF INTENTION TO SELL GOODS

6 (1) A notice under section 12 (3) shall

(a) specify the name and address of the bailee, and give sufficient particulars of the goods and the address or place where they are held, and

(b) specify the date on or after which the bailee proposes to sell the goods, and

(c) specify the amount, if any, which is payable by the bailor to the bailee in respect of the goods, and which became due before the giving of the notice.

(2) The period between giving of the notice and the date specified in the notice as that on or after which the bailee proposes to exercise the power of sale shall be such as will afford the bailor a reasonable opportunity of taking delivery of the goods.

(3) If any amount is payable in respect of the goods by the bailor to the bailee, and became due before giving of the notice, the said period shall be not less than three months.

(4) The notice shall be in writing and shall be sent by post in a registered letter, or by the recorded delivery service.

7 (1) The bailee shall not give a notice under section 12 (3), or exercise his right to sell the goods pursuant to such a notice, at a time when he has notice that, because of a dispute concerning the goods, the bailor is questioning or refusing to pay all or any part of what the bailee claims to be due to him in respect of the goods.

(2) This paragraph shall be left out of account in determining under section 13 (1) whether a bailee of goods is entitled to sell the goods under section 12, or would be so entitled if he had given any notice required in accordance with this Schedule.

Supplemental

8 For the purposes of this Schedule, and of section 26 of the Interpretation Act 1889 in its application to this Schedule, the proper address of the person to whom a notice is to be given shall be—

(a) in the case of a body corporate, a registered or principal office of the body corporate, and

(b) in any other case, the last known address of the person.

SCHEDULE 2
TRANSITIONAL

Section 17

1. This Act shall not affect any action or arbitration brought before the commencement of this Act or any proceedings brought to enforce a decision in the action or arbitration.

2. Subject to paragraph 1, this Act applies to acts or omissions before it comes into force as well as to later ones, and for the purposes of the Limitation Act 1939, the Statute of Limitations (Northern Ireland) 1958, or any other limitation enactment, the cause of action shall be treated as having accrued at the time of the act or omission even if proceedings could not have been brought before the commencement of this Act.

For the purposes of this Schedule, any claim by way of set-off or counterclaim shall be deemed to be a separate action, and to have been brought on the same date as the action in which the set-off or counterclaim is pleaded.

Unfair Contract Terms Act 1977

1977 CHAPTER 50

An Act to impose further limits on the extent to which under the law of England and Wales and Northern Ireland civil liability for breach of contract, or for negligence or other breach of duty, can be avoided by means of contract terms and otherwise, and under the law of Scotland civil liability can be avoided by means of contract terms

[26th October 1977]

PART I
AMENDMENT OF LAW FOR ENGLAND AND WALES AND NORTHERN IRELAND

Introductory

1 Scope of Part I

(1) For the purposes of this Part of this Act, "negligence" means the breach—

(a) of any obligation, arising from the express or implied terms of a contract, to take reasonable care or exercise reasonable skill in the performance of the contract;

(b) of any common law duty to take reasonable care or exercise reasonable skill (but not any stricter duty);

(c) of the common duty of care imposed by the Occupiers' Liability Act 1957 or the Occupiers' Liability Act (Northern Ireland) 1957.

(2) This Part of this Act is subject to Part III; and in relation to contracts, the operation of sections 2 to 4 and 7 is subject to the exceptions made by Schedule 1.

(3) In the case of both contract and tort, sections 2 to 7 apply (except where the contrary is stated in section 6(4)) only to business liability, that is liability for breach of obligations or duties arising—

(a) from things done or to be done by a person in the course of a business (whether his own business or another's); or

(b) from the occupation of premises used for business purposes of the occupier;

and references to liability are to be read accordingly [but liability of an occupier of premises for breach of an obligation or duty towards a person obtaining access to the premises for recreational or educational purposes, being liability for loss or damage suffered by reason of the dangerous state of the premises, is not a business liability of the occupier unless granting that person such access for the purposes concerned falls within the business purposes of the occupier].

(4) In relation to any breach of duty or obligation, it is immaterial for any purpose of this Part of this Act whether the breach was inadvertent or intentional, or whether liability for it arises directly or vicariously.

NOTES

Sub-s (3): words in square brackets inserted, in relation to England and Wales, by the Occupiers' Liability Act 1984, s 2.

Avoidance of liability for negligence, breach of contract, etc

2 Negligence liability

(1) A person cannot by reference to any contract term or to a notice given to persons generally or to particular persons exclude or restrict his liability for death or personal injury resulting from negligence.

(2) In the case of other loss or damage, a person cannot so exclude or restrict his liability for negligence except in so far as the term or notice satisfies the requirement of reasonableness.

(3) Where a contract term or notice purports to exclude or restrict liability for negligence a person's agreement to or awareness of it is not of itself to be taken as indicating his voluntary acceptance of any risk.

3 Liability arising in contract

(1) This section applies as between contracting parties where one of them deals as consumer or on the other's written standard terms of business.

(2) As against that party, the other cannot by reference to any contract term—
- (a) when himself in breach of contract, exclude or restrict any liability of his in respect of the breach; or
- (b) claim to be entitled—
  - (i) to render a contractual performance substantially different from that which was reasonably expected of him, or
  - (ii) in respect of the whole or any part of his contractual obligation, to render no performance at all,

except in so far as (in any of the cases mentioned above in this subsection) the contract term satisfies the requirement of reasonableness.

4 Unreasonable indemnity clauses

(1) A person dealing as consumer cannot by reference to any contract term be made to indemnify another person (whether a party to the contract or not) in respect

of liability that may be incurred by the other for negligence or breach of contract, except in so far as the contract term satisfies the requirement of reasonableness.

(2) This section applies whether the liability in question—
- (a) is directly that of the person to be indemnified or is incurred by him vicariously;
- (b) is to the person dealing as consumer or to someone else.

Liability arising from sale or supply of goods

5 "Guarantee" of consumer goods

(1) In the case of goods of a type ordinarily supplied for private use or consumption, where loss or damage—
- (a) arises from the goods proving defective while in consumer use; and
- (b) results from the negligence of a person concerned in the manufacture or distribution of the goods,

liability for the loss or damage cannot be excluded or restricted by reference to any contract term or notice contained in or operating by reference to a guarantee of the goods.

(2) For these purposes—
- (a) goods are to be regarded as "in consumer use" when a person is using them, or has them in his possession for use, otherwise than exclusively for the purposes of a business; and
- (b) anything in writing is a guarantee if it contains or purports to contain some promise or assurance (however worded or presented) that defects will be made good by complete or partial replacement, or by repair, monetary compensation or otherwise.

(3) This section does not apply as between the parties to a contract under or in pursuance of which possession or ownership of the goods passed.

6 Sale and hire-purchase

(1) Liability for breach of the obligations arising from—
- (a) [section 12 of the Sale of Goods Act 1979] (seller's implied undertakings as to title, etc);
- (b) section 8 of the Supply of Goods (Implied Terms) Act 1973 (the corresponding thing in relation to hire-purchase),

cannot be excluded or restricted by reference to any contract term.

(2) As against a person dealing as consumer, liability for breach of the obligations arising from—
- (a) [section 13, 14 or 15 of the 1979 Act] (seller's implied undertakings as to conformity of goods with description or sample, or as to their quality or fitness for a particular purpose);
- (b) section 9, 10 or 11 of the 1973 Act (the corresponding things in relation to hire-purchase),

cannot be excluded or restricted by reference to any contract term.

(3) As against a person dealing otherwise than as consumer, the liability specified in subsection (2) above can be excluded or restricted by reference to a contract term, but only in so far as the term satisfies the requirement of reasonableness.

(4) The liabilities referred to in this section are not only the business liabilities defined by section 1(3), but include those arising under any contract of sale of goods or hire-purchase agreement.

NOTES

Sub-ss (1), (2): words in square brackets substituted by the Sale of Goods Act 1979, s 63, Sch 2, para 19.

7 Miscellaneous contracts under which goods pass

(1) Where the possession or ownership of goods passes under or in pursuance of a contract not governed by the law of sale of goods or hire-purchase, subsections (2) to (4) below apply as regards the effect (if any) to be given to contract terms excluding or restricting liability for breach of obligation arising by implication of law from the nature of the contract.

(2) As against a person dealing as consumer, liability in respect of the goods' correspondence with description or sample, or their quality or fitness for any particular purpose, cannot be excluded or restricted by reference to any such term.

(3) As against a person dealing otherwise than as consumer, that liability can be excluded or restricted by reference to such a term, but only in so far as the term satisfies the requirement of reasonableness.

[(3A) Liability for breach of the obligations arising under section 2 of the Supply of Goods and Services Act 1982 (implied terms about title etc in certain contracts for the transfer of the property in goods) cannot be excluded or restricted by references to any such term.]

(4) Liability in respect of—

(a) the right to transfer ownership of the goods, or give possession; or

(b) the assurance of quiet possession to a person taking goods in pursuance of the contract,

cannot [(in a case to which subsection (3A) above does not apply)] be excluded or restricted by reference to any such term except in so far as the term satisfies the requirement of reasonableness.

(5) This section does not apply in the case of goods passing on a redemption of trading stamps within the Trading Stamps Act 1964 or the Trading Stamps Act (Northern Ireland) 1965.

NOTES

Sub-s (3A): inserted by the Supply of Goods and Services Act 1982, s 17(2), (3).

Sub-s (4): words in square brackets inserted by the Supply of Goods and Services Act 1982, s 17(2), (3).

Other provisions about contracts

9 Effect of breach

(1) Where for reliance upon it a contract term has to satisfy the requirement of reasonableness, it may be found to do so and be given effect accordingly notwithstanding that the contract has been terminated either by breach or by a party electing to treat it as repudiated.

(2) Where on a breach the contract is nevertheless affirmed by a party entitled to treat it as repudiated, this does not of itself exclude the requirement of reasonableness in relation to any contract term.

10 Evasion by means of secondary contract

A person is not bound by any contract term prejudicing or taking away rights of his which arise under, or in connection with the performance of, another contract, so far as those rights extend to the enforcement of another's liability which this Part of this Act prevents that other from excluding or restricting.

Explanatory provisions

11 The "reasonableness" test

(1) In relation to a contract term, the requirement of reasonableness for the purposes of this Part of this Act, section 3 of the Misrepresentation Act 1967 and section 3 of the Misrepresentation Act (Northern Ireland) 1967 is that the term shall have been a fair and reasonable one to be included having regard to the circumstances which were, or ought reasonably to have been, known to or in the contemplation of the parties when the contract was made.

(2) In determining for the purposes of section 6 or 7 above whether a contract term satisfies the requirement of reasonableness, regard shall be had in particular to the matters specified in Schedule 2 to this Act; but this subsection does not prevent the court or arbitrator from holding, in accordance with any rule of law, that a term which purports to exclude or restrict any relevant liability is not a term of the contract.

(3) In relation to a notice (not being a notice having contractual effect), the requirement of reasonableness under this Act is that it should be fair and reasonable to allow reliance on it, having regard to all the circumstances obtaining when the liability arose or (but for the notice) would have arisen.

(4) Where by reference to a contract term or notice a person seeks to restrict liability to a specified sum of money, and the question arises (under this or any other Act) whether the term or notice satisfies the requirement of reasonableness, regard shall be had in particular (but without prejudice to subsection (2) above in the case of contract terms) to—

(a) the resources which he could expect to be available to him for the purpose of meeting the liability should it arise; and

(b) how far it was open to him to cover himself by insurance.

(5) It is for those claiming that a contract term or notice satisfies the requirement of reasonableness to show that it does.

12 "Dealing as consumer"

(1) A party to a contract "deals as consumer" in relation to another party if—
- (a) he neither makes the contract in the course of a business nor holds himself out as doing so; and
- (b) the other party does make the contract in the course of a business; and
- (c) in the case of a contract governed by the law of sale of goods or hire-purchase, or by section 7 of this Act, the goods passing under or in pursuance of the contract are of a type ordinarily supplied for private use or consumption.

(2) But on a sale by auction or by competitive tender the buyer is not in any circumstances to be regarded as dealing as consumer.

(3) Subject to this, it is for those claiming that a party does not deal as consumer to show that he does not.

13 Varieties of exemption clause

(1) To the extent that this Part of this Act prevents the exclusion or restriction of any liability it also prevents—
- (a) making the liability or its enforcement subject to restrictive or onerous conditions;
- (b) excluding or restricting any right or remedy in respect of the liability, or subjecting a person to any prejudice in consequence of his pursuing any such right or remedy;
- (c) excluding or restricting rules of evidence or procedure;

and (to that extent) sections 2 and 5 to 7 also prevent excluding or restricting liability by reference to terms and notices which exclude or restrict the relevant obligation or duty.

(2) But an agreement in writing to submit present or future differences to arbitration is not to be treated under this Part of this Act as excluding or restricting any liability.

14 Interpretation of Part I

In this Part of this Act—

"business" includes a profession and the activities of any government department or local or public authority;

"goods" has the same meaning as in [the Sale of Goods Act 1979]:

"hire-purchase agreement" has the same meaning as in the Consumer Credit Act 1974;

"negligence" has the meaning given by section 1(1);

"notice" includes an announcement, whether or not in writing, and any other communication or pretended communication; and "personal injury" includes any disease and any impairment of physical or mental condition.

NOTES

Words in square brackets in definition "goods" substituted by the Sale of Goods Act 1979, s 63, Sch 2, para 20.

PART III
PROVISIONS APPLYING TO WHOLE OF UNITED KINGDOM

Miscellaneous

26 International supply contracts

(1) The limits imposed by this Act on the extent to which a person may exclude or restrict liability by reference to a contract term do not apply to liability arising under such a contract as is described in subsection (3) below.

(2) The terms of such a contract are not subject to any requirement of reasonableness under section 3 or 4: and nothing in Part II of this Act shall require the incorporation of the terms of such a contract to be fair and reasonable for them to have effect.

(3) Subject to subsection (4), that description of contract is one whose characteristics are the following—

- (a) either it is a contract of sale of goods or it is one under or in pursuance of which the possession or ownership of goods passes; and
- (b) it is made by parties whose places of business (or, if they have none, habitual residences) are in the territories of different States (the Channel Islands and the Isle of Man being treated for this purpose as different States from the United Kingdom).

(4) A contract falls within subsection (3) above only if either—

- (a) the goods in question are, at the time of the conclusion of the contract, in the course of carriage, or will be carried, from the territory of one State to the territory of another; or
- (b) the acts constituting the offer and acceptance have been done in the territories of different States; or
- (c) the contract provides for the goods to be delivered to the territory of a State other than that within whose territory those acts were done.

27 Choice of law clauses

(1) Where the [law applicable to] a contract is the law of any part of the United Kingdom only by choice of the parties (and apart from that choice would be the law of some country outside the United Kingdom) sections 2 to 7 and 16 to 21 of this Act do not operate as part [of the law applicable to the contract].

(2) This Act has effect notwithstanding any contract term which applies or purports to apply the law of some country outside the United Kingdom, where (either or both)—

(a) the term appears to the court, or arbitrator or arbiter to have been imposed wholly or mainly for the purpose of enabling the party imposing it to evade the operation of this Act; or

(b) in the making of the contract one of the parties dealt as consumer, and he was then habitually resident in the United Kingdom, and the essential steps necessary for the making of the contract were taken there, whether by him or by others on his behalf.

(3) In the application of subsection (2) above to Scotland, for paragraph (b) there shall be substituted—

"(b) the contract is a consumer contract as defined in Part II of this Act, and the consumer at the date when the contract was made was habitually resident in the United Kingdom, and the essential steps necessary for the making of the contract were taken there, whether by him or by others on his behalf.".

NOTES

Sub-s (1): words in square brackets substituted by the Contracts (Applicable Law) Act 1990, s 5, Sch 4, para 4.

29 Saving for other relevant legislation

(1) Nothing in this Act removes or restricts the effect of, or prevents reliance upon, any contractual provision which—

(a) is authorised or required by the express terms or necessary implication of an enactment; or

(b) being made with a view to compliance with an international agreement to which the United Kingdom is a party, does not operate more restrictively than is contemplated by the agreement.

(2) A contract term is to be taken—

(a) for the purposes of Part I of this Act, as satisfying the requirement of reasonableness; and

(b) for those of Part II, to have been fair and reasonable to incorporate,

if it is incorporated or approved by, or incorporated pursuant to a decision or ruling of, a competent authority acting in the exercise of any statutory jurisdiction or function and is not a term in a contract to which the competent authority is itself a party.

(3) In this section—

"competent authority" means any court, arbitrator or arbiter, government department or public authority;

"enactment" means any legislation (including subordinate legislation) of the United Kingdom or Northern Ireland and any instrument having effect by virtue of such legislation; and

"statutory" means conferred by an enactment.

General

31 Commencement; amendments; repeals

(1) This Act comes into force on 1st February 1978.

(2) Nothing in this Act applies to contracts made before the date on which it comes into force; but subject to this, it applies to liability for any loss or damage which is suffered on or after that date.

(3) The enactments specified in Schedule 3 to this Act are amended as there shown.

(4) The enactments specified in Schedule 4 to this Act are repealed to the extent specified in column 3 of that Schedule.

32 Citation and extent

(1) This Act may be cited as the Unfair Contract Terms Act 1977.

(2) Part I of this Act extends to England and Wales and to Northern Ireland; but it does not extend to Scotland.

(3) Part II of this Act extends to Scotland only.

(4) This Part of this Act extends to the whole of the United Kingdom.

SCHEDULE 1
Scope of sections 2 to 4 and 7

Section 1(2)

1 Sections 2 to 4 of this Act do not extend to—
- (a) any contract of insurance (including a contract to pay an annuity on human life);
- (b) any contract so far as it relates to the creation or transfer of an interest in land, or to the termination of such an interest, whether by extinction, merger, surrender, forfeiture or otherwise;
- (c) any contract so far as it relates to the creation or transfer of a right or interest in any patent, trade mark, copyright [or design right], registered design, technical or commercial information or other intellectual property, or relates to the termination of any such right or interest;
- (d) any contract so far as it relates—
  - (i) to the formation or dissolution of a company (which means any body corporate or unincorporated association and includes a partnership), or
  - (ii) to its constitution or the rights or obligations of its corporators or members;
- (e) any contract so far as it relates to the creation or transfer of securities or of any right or interest in securities.

2 Section 2(1) extends to—
- (a) any contract of marine salvage or towage;
- (b) any charterparty of a ship or hovercraft; and
- (c) any contract for the carriage of goods by ship or hovercraft;

but subject to this sections 2 to 4 and 7 do not extend to any such contract except in favour of a person dealing as consumer.

3 Where goods are carried by ship or hovercraft in pursuance of a contract which either—

(a) specifies that as the means of carriage over part of the journey to be covered, or
(b) makes no provision as to the means of carriage and does not exclude that means,

then sections 2(2), 3 and 4 do not, except in favour of a person dealing as consumer, extend to the contract as it operates for and in relation to the carriage of the goods by that means.

4 Section 2(1) and (2) do not extend to a contract of employment, except in favour of the employee.

5 Section 2(1) does not affect the validity of any discharge and indemnity given by a person, on or in connection with an award to him of compensation for pneumoconiosis attributable to employment in the coal industry, in respect of any further claim arising from his contracting that disease.

NOTES

Para 1: the reference to a trade mark in sub-para (c) includes a reference to a service mark, by virtue of the Patents, Designs and Marks Act 1986, s 2(3), Sch 2, Part I; words in square brackets inserted by the Copyright, Designs and Patents Act 1988, s 303(1), Sch 7, para 24.

SCHEDULE 2

"GUIDELINES" FOR APPLICATION OF REASONABLENESS TEST

Sections 11(2), 24(2)

The matters to which regard is to be had in particular for the purposes of sections 6(3), 7(3) and (4), 20 and 21 are any of the following which appear to be relevant—

(a) the strength of the bargaining positions of the parties relative to each other, taking into account (among other things) alternative means by which the customer's requirements could have been met;
(b) whether the customer received an inducement to agree to the term, or in accepting it had an opportunity of entering into a similar contract with other persons, but without having to accept a similar term;
(c) whether the customer knew or ought reasonably to have known of the existence and extent of the term (having regard, among other things, to any custom of the trade and any previous course of dealing between the parties);
(d) where the term excludes or restricts any relevant liability if some condition is not complied with, whether it was reasonable at the time of the contract to expect that compliance with that condition would be practicable;
(e) whether the goods were manufactured, processed or adapted to the special order of the customer.

State Immunity Act 1978

1978 CHAPTER 33

An Act to make new provision with respect to proceedings in the United Kingdom by or against other States; to provide for the effect of judgments given against the United Kingdom in the courts of States parties to the European Convention on State Immunity; to make new provision with respect to the immunities and privileges of heads of State; and for connected purposes

[20th July 1978]

PART I
PROCEEDINGS IN UNITED KINGDOM BY OR AGAINST OTHER STATES

Immunity from jurisdiction

1 General immunity from jurisdiction

(1) A State is immune from the jurisdiction of the courts of the United Kingdom except as provided in the following provisions of this Part of this Act.

(2) A court shall give effect to the immunity conferred by this section even though the State does not appear in the proceedings in question.

Exceptions from immunity

3 Commercial transactions and contracts to be performed in United Kingdom

(1) A State is not immune as respects proceedings relating to—
- (a) a commercial transaction, entered into by the State; or
- (b) an obligation of the State which by virtue of a contract (whether a commercial transaction or not) falls to be performed wholly or partly in the United Kingdom.

(2) This section does not apply if the parties to the dispute are States or have otherwise agreed in writing; and subsection (1)(b) above does not apply if the contract (not being a commercial transaction) was made in the territory of the State concerned and the obligation in question is governed by its administrative law.

(3) In this section "commercial transaction" means—
- (a) any contract for the supply of goods or services;
- (b) any loan or other transaction for the provision of finance and any guarantee or indemnity in respect of any such transaction or of any other financial obligation; and
- (c) any other transaction or activity (whether of a commercial, industrial, financial, professional or other similar character) into which a State enters or in which it engages otherwise than in the exercise of sovereign authority;

but neither paragraph of subsection (1) above applies to a contract of employment between a State and an individual.

5 Personal injuries and damage to property

A State is not immune as respects proceedings in respect of—

(a) death or personal injury; or

(b) damage or loss of tangible property,

caused by an act or omission in the United Kingdom.

PART III

MISCELLANEOUS AND SUPPLEMENTARY

23 Short title, repeals commencement and extent

(1) This Act may be cited as the State Immunity Act 1978.

(2) . . .

(3) Subject to subsection (4) below, Parts I and II of this Act do not apply to proceedings in respect of matters that occurred before the date of the coming into force of this Act and, in particular—

(a) sections 2(2) and 13(3) do not apply to any prior agreement, and

(b) sections 3, 4 and 9 do not apply to any transaction, contract or arbitration agreement,

entered into before that date.

(4) Section 12 above applies to any proceedings instituted after the coming into force of this Act.

(5) This Act shall come into force on such date as may be specified by an order made by the Lord Chancellor by statutory instrument.

(6) This Act extends to Northern Ireland.

(7) Her Majesty may by Order in Council extend any of the provisions of this Act, with or without modification, to any dependent territory.

NOTES

Sub-s (2): repeals the Administration of Justice (Miscellaneous Provisions) Act 1938, s 13, and the Law Reform (Miscellaneous Provisions) (Scotland) Act 1940, s 7.

Civil Liability (Contribution) Act 1978

1978 CHAPTER 47

An Act to make new provision for contribution between persons who are jointly or severally, or both jointly and severally, liable for the same damage and in certain other similar cases where two or more persons have paid or may be required to pay compensation for the same damage; and to amend the law relating to proceedings against persons jointly liable for the same debt or jointly or severally, or both jointly and severally, liable for the same damage

[31st July 1978]

Proceedings for contribution

1 Entitlement to contribution

(1) Subject to the following provisions of this section, any person liable in respect of any damage suffered by another person may recover contribution from any other person liable in respect of the same damage (whether jointly with him or otherwise).

(2) A person shall be entitled to recover contribution by virtue of subsection (1) above notwithstanding that he has ceased to be liable in respect of the damage in question since the time when the damage occurred, provided that he was so liable immediately before he made or was ordered or agreed to make the payment in respect of which the contribution is sought.

(3) A person shall be liable to make contribution by virtue of subsection (1) above notwithstanding that he has ceased to be liable in respect of the damage in question since the time when the damage occurred, unless he ceased to be liable by virtue of the expiry of a period of limitation or prescription which extinguished the right on which the claim against him in respect of the damage was based.

(4) A person who has made or agreed to make any payment in bona fide settlement or compromise of any claim made against him in respect of any damage (including a payment into court which has been accepted) shall be entitled to recover contribution in accordance with this section without regard to whether or not he himself is or ever was liable in respect of the damage, provided, however, that he would have been liable assuming that the factual basis of the claim against him could be established.

(5) A judgment given in any action brought in any part of the United Kingdom by or on behalf of the person who suffered the damage in question against any person from whom contribution is sought under this section shall be conclusive in the proceedings for contribution as to any issue determined by that judgment in favour of the person from whom the contribution is sought.

(6) References in this section to a person's liability in respect of any damage are references to any such liability which has been or could be established in an action brought against him in England and Wales by or on behalf of the person who

suffered the damage; but it is immaterial whether any issue arising in any such action was or would be determined (in accordance with the rules of private international law) by reference to the law of a country outside England and Wales.

2 Assessment of contribution

(1) Subject to subsection (3) below, in any proceedings for contribution under section 1 above the amount of the contribution recoverable from any person shall be such as may be found by the court to be just and equitable having regard to the extent of that person's responsibility for the damage in question.

(2) Subject to subsection (3) below, the court shall have power in any such proceedings to exempt any person from liability to make contribution, or to direct that the contribution to be recovered from any person shall amount to a complete indemnity.

(3) Where the amount of the damages which have or might have been awarded in respect of the damage in question in any action brought in England and Wales by or on behalf of the person who suffered it against the person from whom the contribution is sought was or would have been subject to—

(a) any limit imposed by or under any enactment or by any agreement made before the damage occurred;

(b) any reduction by virtue of section 1 of the Law Reform (Contributory Negligence) Act 1945 or section 5 of the Fatal Accidents Act 1976; or

(c) any corresponding limit or reduction under the law of a country outside England and Wales;

the person from whom the contribution is sought shall not by virtue of any contribution awarded under section 1 above be required to pay in respect of the damage a greater amount than the amount of those damages as so limited or reduced.

Proceedings for the same debt or damage

3 Proceedings against persons jointly liable for the same debt or damage

Judgment recovered against any person liable in respect of any debt or damage shall not be a bar to an action, or to the continuance of an action, against any other person who is (apart from any such bar) jointly liable with him in respect of the same debt or damage.

4 Successive actions against persons liable (jointly or otherwise) for the same damage

If more than one action is brought in respect of any damage by or on behalf of the person by whom it was suffered against persons liable in respect of the damage (whether jointly or otherwise) the plaintiff shall not be entitled to costs in any of those actions, other than that in which judgment is first given, unless the court is of the opinion that there was reasonable ground for bringing the action.

Supplemental

5 Application to the Crown

Without prejudice to section 4(1) of the Crown Proceedings Act 1947 (indemnity and contribution), this Act shall bind the Crown, but nothing in this Act shall be construed as in any way affecting Her Majesty in Her private capacity (including in right of Her Duchy of Lancaster) or the Duchy of Cornwall.

6 Interpretation

(1) A person is liable in respect of any damage for the purposes of this Act if the person who suffered it (or anyone representing his estate or dependants) is entitled to recover compensation from him in respect of that damage (whatever the legal basis of his liability, whether tort, breach of contract, breach of trust or otherwise).

(2) References in this Act to an action brought by or on behalf of the person who suffered any damage include references to an action brought for the benefit of his estate or dependants.

(3) In this Act "dependants" has the same meaning as in the Fatal Accidents Act 1976.

(4) In this Act, except in section 1(5) above, "action" means an action brought in England and Wales.

7 Savings

(1) Nothing in this Act shall affect any case where the debt in question became due or (as the case may be) the damage in question occurred before the date on which it comes into force.

(2) A person shall not be entitled to recover contribution or liable to make contribution in accordance with section 1 above by reference to any liability based on breach of any obligation assumed by him before the date on which this Act comes into force.

(3) The right to recover contribution in accordance with section 1 above supersedes any right, other than an express contractual right, to recover contribution (as distinct from indemnity) otherwise than under this Act in corresponding circumstances; but nothing in this Act shall affect—

(a) any express or implied contractual or other right to indemnity; or
(b) any express contractual provision regulating or excluding contribution;

which would be enforceable apart from this Act (or render enforceable any agreement for indemnity or contribution which would not be enforceable apart from this Act).

8 Application to Northern Ireland

In the application of this Act to Northern Ireland—

(a) the reference in section 2(3)(b) to section 1 of the Law Reform (Contributory Negligence) Act 1945 or section 5 of the Fatal Accidents Act 1976 shall be construed as a reference to section 2 of the Law Reform (Miscellaneous Provisions) Act (Northern Ireland) 1948 or Article 7 of the Fatal Accidents (Northern Ireland) Order 1977;

(b) the reference in section 5 to section 4(1) of the Crown Proceedings Act 1947 shall be construed as a reference to section 4(1) of that Act as it applies in Northern Ireland;

(c) the reference in section 6(3) to the Fatal Accidents Act 1976 shall be construed as a reference to the Fatal Accidents (Northern Ireland) Order 1977;

(d) references to England and Wales shall be construed as references to Northern Ireland; and

(e) any reference to an enactment shall be construed as including a reference to an enactment of the Parliament of Northern Ireland and a Measure of the Northern Ireland Assembly.

10 Short title, commencement and extent

(1) This Act may be cited as the Civil Liability (Contribution) Act 1978.

(2) This Act shall come into force on 1st January next following the date on which it is passed.

(3) This Act, with the exception of paragraph 1 of Schedule 1 thereto, does not extend to Scotland.

Vaccine Damage Payments Act 1979

1979 CHAPTER 17

An Act to provide for payments to be made out of public funds in cases where severe disablement occurs as a result of vaccination against certain diseases or of contact with a person who has been vaccinated against any of those diseases; to make provision in connection with similar payments made before the passsing of this Act; and for purposes connected therewith

[22nd March 1979]

1 Payments to persons severely disabled by vaccination

(1) If, on consideration of a claim, the Secretary of State is satisfied

(a) that a person is, or was immediately before his death, severely disabled as a result of vaccination against any of the diseases to which this Act applies; and

(b) that the conditions of entitlement which are applicable in accordance with section 2 below are fulfilled,

he shall in accordance with this Act make a payment of [the relevant statutory sum] to or for the benefit of that person or to his personal representatives.

[(1A) In subsection (1) above "statutory sum" means [£100,000] or such other sum as is specified by the Secretary of State for the purposes of this Act by order made by statutory instrument with the consent of the Treasury; and the relevant statutory sum for the purposes of that subsection is the statutory sum at the time when a claim for payment is first made].

(2) The diseases to which this Act applies are–
- (a) diphtheria,
- (b) tetanus,
- (c) whooping cough,
- (d) poliomyelitis,
- (e) measles,
- (f) rubella,
- (g) tuberculosis,
- (h) smallpox, and
- (i) any other disease which is specified by the Secretary of State for the purposes of this Act by order made by statutory instrument.

(3) Subject to section 2(3) below, this Act has effect with respect to a person who is severely disabled as a result of a vaccination given to his mother before he was born as if the vaccination had been given directly to him and, in such circumstances as may be prescribed by regulations under this Act, this Act has effect with respect to a person who is severely disabled as a result of contracting a disease through contact with a third person who was vaccinated against it as if the vaccination had been given to him and the disablement resulted from it.

(4) For the purposes of this Act, a person is severely disabled if he suffers disablement to the extent of [60 per cent] or more, assessed as for the purposes of [section 103 of the Social Security Contributions and Benefits Act 1992 or] [section 103 of the Social Security Contributions and Benefits (Northern Ireland) Act 1992] (disablement gratuity and pension).

[(4A) No order shall be made by virtue of subsection (1A) above unless a draft of the order has been laid before Parliament and been approved by a resolution of each House.]

(5) A statutory instrument under subsection (2)(i) above shall be subject to annulment in pursuance of a resolution of either House of Parliament.

NOTES

Sub-s (1): words "the relevant statutory sum" in square brackets substituted by the Social Security Act 1985, s 23.

Sub-s (1A): inserted by the Social Security Act 1985, s 23.

Sub-s (1A): sum "£100,000" in square brackets substituted by virtue of SI 2000/1983, art 2.

Date in force: 22 July 2000: see SI 2000/1983, art 1.

Sub-s (4): words "60 per cent" in square brackets substituted by SI 2002/1592, art 2.

Date in force: 16 June 2002 (in relation to claims for payments under s 1(1) hereof which are made on or after that date): see SI 2002/1592, art 1(1), (2).

Sub-s (4): words "section 103 of the Social Security Contributions and Benefits Act 1992 or" in square brackets substituted by the Social Security (Consequential Provisions) Act 1992, s 4, Sch 2, para 53.

Sub-s (4): words "section 103 of the Social Security Contributions and Benefits (Northern Ireland) Act 1992" in square brackets substituted by the Social Security (Consequential Provisions) (Northern Ireland) Act 1992, s 4, Sch 2, para 21.

Sub-s (4A): inserted by the Social Security Act 1985, s 23.

2 Conditions of entitlement

(1) Subject to the provisions of this section, the conditions of entitlement referred to in section 1(1)(b) above are–

(a) that the vaccination in question was carried out–
  (i) in the United Kingdom or the Isle of Man, and
  (ii) on or after 5th July 1948, and
  (iii) in the case of vaccination against smallpox, before 1st August 1971;

(b) except in the case of vaccination against poliomyelitis or rubella, that the vaccination was carried out either at a time when the person to whom it was given was under the age of eighteen or at the time of an outbreak within the United Kingdom or the Isle of Man of the disease against which the vaccination was given; and

(c) that the disabled person was over the age of two on the date when the claim was made or, if he died before that date, that he died after 9th May 1978 and was over the age of two when he died.

(2) An order under section 1(2)(i) above specifying a disease for the purposes of this Act may provide that, in relation to vaccination against that disease, the conditions of entitlement specified in subsection (1) above shall have effect subject to such modifications as may be specified in the order.

(3) In a case where this Act has effect by virtue of section 1(3) above, the reference in subsection (1)(b) above to the person to whom a vaccination was given is a reference to the person to whom it was actually given and not to the disabled person.

(4) With respect to claims made after such date as may be specified in the order and relating to vaccination against such disease as may be so specified, the Secretary of State may by order made by statutory instrument—

(a) provide that, in such circumstances as may be specified in the order, one or more of the conditions of entitlement appropriate to vaccination against that disease need not be fulfilled; or

(b) add to the conditions of entitlement which are appropriate to vaccination against that disease, either generally or in such circumstances as may be specified in the order.

(5) Regulations under this Act shall specify the cases in which vaccinations given outside the United Kingdom and the Isle of Man to persons defined in the regulations as serving members of Her Majesty's forces or members of their families are to be treated for the purposes of this Act as carried out in England.

(6) The Secretary of State shall not make an order containing any provision made by virtue of paragraph (b) of subsection (4) above unless a draft of the order has been laid before Parliament and approved by a resolution of each House; and a

statutory instrument by which any other order is made under that subsection shall be subject to annulment in pursuance of a resolution of either House of Parliament.

3 Determination of claims

(1) Any reference in this Act, other than section 7, to a claim is a reference to a claim for a payment under section 1(1) above which is made—

(a) by or on behalf of the disabled person concerned or, as the case may be, by his personal representatives; and

(b) in the manner prescribed by regulations under this Act; and

[(c) on or before whichever is the later of—

(i) the date on which the disabled person attains the age of 21, or where he has died, the date on which he would have attained the age of 21; and

(ii) the end of the period of six years beginning with the date of the vaccination to which the claim relates;]

and, in relation to a claim, any reference to the claimant is a reference to the person by whom the claim was made and any reference to the disabled person is a reference to the person in respect of whose disablement a payment under subsection (1) above is claimed to be payable.

(2) As soon as practicable after he has received a claim, the Secretary of State shall give notice in writing to the claimant of his determination whether he is satisfied that a payment is due under section 1(1) above to or for the benefit of the disabled person or to his personal representatives.

(3) If the Secretary of State is not satisfied that a payment is due as mentioned in subsection (2) above, the notice in writing under that subsection shall state the grounds on which he is not so satisfied.

(4) If, in the case of any claim, the Secretary of State—

(a) is satisfied that the conditions of entitlement which are applicable in accordance with section 2 above are fulfilled, but

(b) is not satisfied that the disabled person is or, where he has died, was immediately before his death severely disabled as a result of vaccination against any of the diseases to which this Act applies,

the notice in writing under subsection (2) above shall inform the claimant [of the right of appeal conferred by section 4 below].

(5) If in any case a person is severely disabled, the question whether his severe disablement results from vaccination against any of the diseases to which this Act applies shall be determined for the purposes of this Act on the balance of probability.

NOTES

Sub-s (1): para (c) substituted by SI 2002/1592, art 3.

Date in force: 16 June 2002 (in relation to claims for payments under s 1(1) hereof which are made on or after that date): see SI 2002/1592, art 1(1), (2).

Sub-s (4): words "of the right of appeal conferred by section 4 below" in square brackets substituted by the Social Security Act 1998, s 86(1), Sch 7, para 5.

Date in force: 18 October 1999: see SI 1999/2860, art 2(c), Sch 1.

[3A Decisions reversing earlier decisions]

[(1) Subject to subsection (2) below, any decision of the Secretary of State under section 3 above or this section, and any decision of an appeal tribunal under section 4 below, may be reversed by a decision made by the Secretary of State—

(a) either within the prescribed period or in prescribed cases or circumstances; and

(b) either on an application made for the purpose or on his own initiative.

(2) In making a decision under subsection (1) above, the Secretary of State need not consider any issue that is not raised by the application or, as the case may be, did not cause him to act on his own initiative.

(3) Regulations may prescribe the procedure by which a decision may be made under this section.

(4) Such notice as may be prescribed by regulations shall be given of a decision under this section.

(5) Except as provided by section 5(4) below, no payment under section 1(1) above shall be recoverable by virtue of a decision under this section.

(6) In this section and sections 4 and 8 below "appeal tribunal" means an appeal tribunal constituted under Chapter I of Part I of the Social Security Act 1998.]

NOTES

Inserted by the Social Security Act 1998, s 45.

Date in force (sub-ss (1), (4), to the extent the making of regulations is authorised): 4 March 1999: see SI 1999/528, art 2(a), Schedule.

Date in force (sub-s (3)): 4 March 1999: see SI 1999/528, art 2(a), Schedule.

Date in force (sub-ss (1), (4) for remaining purposes, sub-ss (2), (5), (6)): 18 October 1999: see SI 1999/2860, art 2(c), Sch 1.

6 Payments to or for the benefit of disabled persons

(1) Where a payment under section 1(1) above falls to be made in respect of a disabled person who is over eighteen and capable of managing his own affairs, the payment shall be made to him.

(2) Where such a payment falls to be made in respect of a disabled person who has died, the payment shall be made to his personal representatives.

(3) Where such a payment falls to be made in respect of any other disabled person, the payment shall be made for his benefit by paying it to such trustees as the Secretary of State may appoint to be held by them upon such trusts or, in Scotland, for such purposes and upon such conditions as may be declared by the Secretary of State.

(4) The making of a claim for, or the receipt of, a payment under section 1(1) above does not prejudice the right of any person to institute or carry on proceedings in respect of disablement suffered as a result of vaccination against any disease to which this Act applies; but in any civil proceedings brought in respect of disablement resulting from vaccination against such a disease, the court shall treat a

payment made to or in respect of the disabled person concerned under section 1(1) above as paid on account of any damages which the court awards in respect of such disablement.

12 Financial provisions

(1) . . .

(2) The Secretary of State shall pay such fees as he considers appropriate to medical practitioners, as defined in [section 191 of the Social Security Administration Act 1992], who provide information or other evidence in connection with claims.

(3) The Secretary of State shall pay such travelling and other allowances as he may determine—
  (a) to persons required under this Act to undergo medical examinations;
  (b) to persons required to attend before tribunals under section 4 above; and
  (c) in circumstances where he considers it appropriate, to any person who accompanies a disabled person to such a medical examination or tribunal.

(4) There shall be paid out of moneys provided by Parliament—
  (a) any expenditure incurred by the Secretary of State in making payments under section 1(1) above;
  (b) any expenditure incurred by the Secretary of State by virtue of subsections (1) to (3) above; and
  (c) any increase in the administrative expenses of the Secretary of State attributable to this Act.

(5) Any sums repaid to the Secretary of State by virtue of section 5(4) above shall be paid into the Consolidated Fund.

NOTES

Sub-s (1): repealed by the Social Security Act 1998, s 86(1), (2), Sch 7, para 10, Sch 8.

Date in force: 18 October 1999: see SI 1999/2860, art 2(c), Sch 1.

Sub-s (2): words in square brackets substituted by the Social Security (Consequential Provisions) Act 1992, s 4, Sch 2, para 54.

13 Short title and extent

(1) This Act may be cited as the Vaccine Damage Payments Act 1979.

(2) This Act extends to Northern Ireland and the Isle of Man.

Sale of Goods Act 1979

1979 CHAPTER 54

An Act to consolidate the law relating to the sale of goods

[6th December 1979]

PART II
FORMATION OF THE CONTRACT

Contract of sale

2 Contract of sale

(1) A contract of sale of goods is a contract by which the seller transfers or agrees to transfer the property in goods to the buyer for a money consideration, called the price.

(2) There may be a contract of sale between one part owner and another.

(3) A contract of sale may be absolute or conditional.

(4) Where under a contract of sale the property in the goods is transferred from the seller to the buyer the contract is called a sale.

(5) Where under a contract of sale the transfer of the property in the goods is to take place at a future time or subject to some condition later to be fulfilled the contract is called an agreement to sell.

(6) An agreement to sell becomes a sale when the time elapses or the conditions are fulfilled subject to which the property in the goods is to be transferred.

Subject matter of contract

7 Goods perishing before sale but after agreement to sell

Where there is an agreement to sell specific goods and subsequently the goods, without any fault on the part of the seller or buyer, perish before the risk passes to the buyer, the agreement is avoided.

The price

8 Ascertainment of price

(1) The price in a contract of sale may be fixed by the contract, or may be left to be fixed in a manner agreed by the contract, or may be determined by the course of dealing between the parties.

(2) Where the price is not determined as mentioned in subsection (1) above the buyer must pay a reasonable price.

(3) What is a reasonable price is a question of fact dependent on the circumstances of each particular case.

9 Agreement to sell at valuation

(1) Where there is an agreement to sell goods on the terms that the price is to be fixed by the valuation of a third party, and he cannot or does not make the valuation, the agreement is avoided; but if the goods or any part of them have been delivered to and appropriated by the buyer he must pay a reasonable price for them.

(2) Where the third party is prevented from making the valuation by the fault of the seller or buyer, the party not at fault may maintain an action for damages against the party at fault.

[Implied terms etc]

NOTES

Substituted by the Sale and Supply of Goods Act 1994, s 7, Sch 2, para 5(10).

10 Stipulations about time

(1) Unless a different intention appears from the terms of the contract, stipulations as to time of payment are not of the essence of a contract of sale.

(2) Whether any other stipulation as to time is or is not of the essence of the contract depends on the terms of the contract.

(3) In a contract of sale "month" prima facie means calendar month.

11 When condition to be treated as warranty

[(1) This section does not apply to Scotland.]

(2) Where a contract of sale is subject to a condition to be fulfilled by the seller, the buyer may waive the condition, or may elect to treat the breach of the condition as a breach of warranty and not as a ground for treating the contract as repudiated.

(3) Whether a stipulation in a contract of sale is a condition, the breach of which may give rise to a right to treat the contract as repudiated, or a warranty, the breach of which may give rise to a claim for damages but not to a right to reject the goods and treat the contract as repudiated, depends in each case on the construction of the contract; and a stipulation may be a condition, though called a warranty in the contract.

(4) [Subject to section 35A below] where a contract of sale is not severable and the buyer has accepted the goods or part of them, the breach of a condition to be fulfilled by the seller can only be treated as a breach of warranty, and not as a ground for rejecting the goods and treating the contract as repudiated, unless there is an express or implied term of the contract to that effect.

(5) . . .

(6) Nothing in this section affects a condition or warranty whose fulfilment is excused by law by reason of impossibility or otherwise.

(7) Paragraph 2 of Schedule 1 below applies in relation to a contract made before 22 April 1967 or (in the application of this Act to Northern Ireland) 28 July 1967.

NOTES

Sub-s (1): substituted by the Sale and Supply of Goods Act 1994, s 3(2).

Sub-s (4): words in square brackets inserted by the Sale and Supply of Goods Act 1994, s 3(2).

Sub-s (5): repealed by the Sale and Supply of Goods Act 1994, s 7, Sch 2, para 5(2), Sch 3.

12 Implied terms about title, etc

(1) In a contract of sale, other than one to which subsection (3) below applies, there is an implied [term] on the part of the seller that in the case of a sale he has a right to sell the goods, and in the case of an agreement to sell he will have such a right at the time when the property is to pass.

(2) In a contract of sale, other than one to which subsection (3) below applies, there is also an implied [term] that—

- (a) the goods are free, and will remain free until the time when the property is to pass, from any charge or encumbrance not disclosed or known to the buyer before the contract is made, and
- (b) the buyer will enjoy quiet possession of the goods except so far as it may be disturbed by the owner or other person entitled to the benefit of any charge or encumbrance so disclosed or known.

(3) This subsection applies to a contract of sale in the case of which there appears from the contract or is to be inferred from its circumstances an intention that the seller should transfer only such title as he or a third person may have.

(4) In a contract to which subsection (3) above applies there is an implied [term] that all charges or encumbrances known to the seller and not known to the buyer have been disclosed to the buyer before the contract is made.

(5) In a contract to which subsection (3) above applies there is also an implied [term] that none of the following will disturb the buyer's quiet possession of the goods, namely—

- (a) the seller;
- (b) in a case where the parties to the contract intend that the seller should transfer only such title as a third person may have, that person;
- (c) anyone claiming through or under the seller or that third person otherwise than under a charge or encumbrance disclosed or known to the buyer before the contract is made.

[(5A) As regards England and Wales and Northern Ireland, the term implied by subsection (1) above is a condition and the terms implied by subsections (2), (4) and (5) above are warranties.]

(6) Paragraph 3 of Schedule 1 below applies in relation to a contract made before 18 May 1973.

NOTES

Sub-ss (1), (2), (4), (5): words in square brackets substituted by the Sale and Supply of Goods Act 1994, s 7, Sch 2, para 5(3)(a).

Sub-s (5A): inserted by the Sale and Supply of Goods Act 1994, s 7, Sch 2, para 5(3)(b).

13 Sale by description

(1) Where there is a contract for the sale of goods by description, there is an implied [term] that the goods will correspond with the description.

[(1A) As regards England and Wales and Northern Ireland, the term implied by subsection (1) above is a condition.]

(2) If the sale is by sample as well as by description it is not sufficient that the bulk of the goods corresponds with the sample if the goods do not also correspond with the description.

(3) A sale of goods is not prevented from being a sale by description by reason only that, being exposed for sale or hire, they are selected by the buyer.

(4) Paragraph 4 of Schedule 1 below applies in relation to a contract made before 18th May 1973.

NOTES

Sub-s (1): word in square brackets substituted by the Sale and Supply of Goods Act 1994, s 7, Sch 2, para 5(4)(a).

Sub-s (1A): inserted by the Sale and Supply of Goods Act 1994, s 7, Sch 2, para 5(4)(b).

14 Implied terms about quality or fitness

(1) Except as provided by this section and section 15 below and subject to any other enactment, there is no implied [term] about the quality or fitness for any particular purpose of goods supplied under a contract of sale.

[(2) Where the seller sells goods in the course of a business, there is an implied term that the goods supplied under the contract are of satisfactory quality.

(2A) For the purposes of this Act, goods are of satisfactory quality if they meet the standard that a reasonable person would regard as satisfactory, taking account of any description of the goods, the price (if relevant) and all the other relevant circumstances.

(2B) For the purposes of this Act, the quality of goods includes their state and condition and the following (among others) are in appropriate cases aspects of the quality of goods—

- (a) fitness for all the purposes for which goods of the kind in question are commonly supplied,
- (b) appearance and finish,
- (c) freedom from minor defects,
- (d) safety, and
- (e) durability.

(2C) The term implied by subsection (2) above does not extend to any matter making the quality of goods unsatisfactory—

(a) which is specifically drawn to the buyer's attention before the contract is made,

(b) where the buyer examines the goods before the contract is made, which that examination ought to reveal, or

(c) in the case of a contract for sale by sample, which would have been apparent on a reasonable examination of the sample.]

(3) Where the seller sells goods in the course of a business and the buyer, expressly or by implication, makes known—

(a) to the seller, or

(b) where the purchase price or part of it is payable by instalments and the goods were previously sold by a credit-broker to the seller, to that credit-broker,

any particular purpose for which the goods are being bought, there is an implied [term] that the goods supplied under the contract are reasonably fit for that purpose, whether or not that is a purpose for which such goods are commonly supplied, except where the circumstances show that the buyer does not rely, or that it is unreasonable for him to rely, on the skill or judgment of the seller or credit-broker.

(4) An implied [term] about quality or fitness for a particular purpose may be annexed to a contract of sale by usage.

(5) The preceding provisions of this section apply to a sale by a person who in the course of a business is acting as agent for another as they apply to a sale by a principal in the course of a business, except where that other is not selling in the course of a business and either the buyer knows that fact or reasonable steps are taken to bring it to the notice of the buyer before the contract is made.

[(6) As regards England and Wales and Northern Ireland, the terms implied by subsections (2) and (3) above are conditions.]

(7) Paragraph 5 of Schedule 1 below applies in relation to a contract made on or after 18 May 1973 and before the appointed day, and paragraph 6 in relation to one made before 18th May 1973.

(8) In subsection (7) above and paragraph 5 of Schedule 1 below references to the appointed day are to the day appointed for the purposes of those provisions by an order of the Secretary of State made by statutory instrument.

NOTES

Sub-ss (1), (3), (4): words in square brackets substituted by the Sale and Supply of Goods Act 1994, s 7, Sch 2, para 5(5)(a).

Sub-ss (2)–(2C): substituted, for sub-s (2) as originally enacted, by the Sale and Supply of Goods Act 1994, s 1(1).

Sub-s (6): substituted by the Sale and Supply of Goods Act 1994, s 7, Sch 2, para 5(5)(b).

Sale by sample

15 Sale by sample

(1) A contract of sale is a contract for sale by sample where there is an express or implied term to that effect in the contract.

(2) In the case of a contract for sale by sample there is an implied [term]—
- (a) that the bulk will correspond with the sample in quality;
- (b) . . .
- (c) that the goods will be free from any defect, [making their quality unsatisfactory], which would not be apparent on reasonable examination of the sample.

[(3) As regards England and Wales and Northern Ireland, the term implied by subsection (2) above is a condition.]

(4) Paragraph 7 of Schedule 1 below applies in relation to a contract made before 18 May 1973.

NOTES

Sub-s (2): words in square brackets substituted, and para (b) repealed, by the Sale and Supply of Goods Act 1994, ss 1(2), 7, Sch 2, para 5(6)(a), Sch 3.

Sub-s (3): substituted by the Sale and Supply of Goods Act 1994, s 7, Sch 2, para 5(6)(b).

PART IV
PERFORMANCE OF THE CONTRACT

34 Buyer's right of examining the goods

. . . Unless otherwise agreed, when the seller tenders delivery of goods to the buyer, he is bound on request to afford the buyer a reasonable opportunity of examining the goods for the purpose of ascertaining whether they are in conformity with the contract [and, in the case of a contract for sale by sample, of comparing the bulk with the sample].

NOTES

Words omitted repealed, and words in square brackets inserted by the Sale and Supply of Goods Act 1994, ss 2(2), 7, Sch 3.

35 Acceptance

(1) The buyer is deemed to have accepted the goods [subject to subsection (2) below—
- (a) when he intimates to the seller that he has accepted them, or
- (b) when the goods have been delivered to him and he does any act in relation to them which is inconsistent with the ownership of the seller.

(2) Where goods are delivered to the buyer, and he has not previously examined them, he is not deemed to have accepted them under subsection (1) above until he has had a reasonable opportunity of examining them for the purpose—
- (a) of ascertaining whether they are in conformity with the contract, and

(b) in the case of a contract for sale by sample, of comparing the bulk with the sample.

(3) Where the buyer deals as consumer or (in Scotland) the contract of sale is a consumer contract, the buyer cannot lose his right to rely on subsection (2) above by agreement, waiver or otherwise.

(4) The buyer is also deemed to have accepted the goods when after the lapse of a reasonable time he retains the goods without intimating to the seller that he has rejected them.

(5) The questions that are material in determining for the purposes of subsection (4) above whether a reasonable time has elapsed include whether the buyer has had a reasonable opportunity of examining the goods for the purpose mentioned in subsection (2) above.

(6) The buyer is not by virtue of this section deemed to have accepted the goods merely because—

(a) he asks for, or agrees to, their repair by or under an arrangement with the seller, or

(b) the goods are delivered to another under a sub-sale or other disposition.

(7) Where the contract is for the sale of goods making one or more commercial units, a buyer accepting any goods included in a unit is deemed to have accepted all the goods making the unit; and in this subsection "commercial unit" means a unit division of which would materially impair the value of the goods or the character of the unit.

(8)] Paragraph 10 of Schedule 1 below applies in relation to a contract made before 22nd April 1967 or (in the application of this Act to Northern Ireland) 28th July 1967.

NOTES

Sub-s (1): words in square brackets substituted, together with new sub-ss (2)–(7), by the Sale and Supply of Goods Act 1994, s 2(1).

Sub-ss (2)–(7): substituted, together with words in sub-s (1), by the Sale and Supply of Goods Act 1994, s 2(1).

PART VI
ACTIONS FOR BREACH OF THE CONTRACT

Seller's remedies

49 Action for price

(1) Where, under a contract of sale, the property in the goods has passed to the buyer and he wrongfully neglects or refuses to pay for the goods according to the terms of the contract, the seller may maintain an action against him for the price of the goods.

(2) Where, under a contract of sale, the price is payable on a day certain irrespective of delivery and the buyer wrongfully neglects or refuses to pay such

price, the seller may maintain an action for the price, although the property in the goods has not passed and the goods have not been appropriated to the contract.

(3) Nothing in this section prejudices the right of the seller in Scotland to recover interest on the price from the date of tender of the goods, or from the date on which the price was payable, as the case may be.

50 Damages for non-acceptance

(1) Where the buyer wrongfully neglects or refuses to accept and pay for the goods, the seller may maintain an action against him for damages for non-acceptance.

(2) The measure of damages is the estimated loss directly and naturally resulting, in the ordinary course of events, from the buyer's breach of contract.

(3) Where there is an available market for the goods in question the measure of damages is prima facie to be ascertained by the difference between the contract price and the market or current price at the time or times when the goods ought to have been accepted or (if no time was fixed for acceptance) at the time of the refusal to accept.

Buyer's remedies

51 Damages for non-delivery

(1) Where the seller wrongfully neglects or refuses to deliver the goods to the buyer, the buyer may maintain an action against the seller for damages for non-delivery.

(2) The measure of damages is the estimated loss directly and naturally resulting, in the ordinary course of events, from the seller's breach of contract.

(3) Where there is an available market for the goods in question the measure of damages is prima facie to be ascertained by the difference between the contract price and the market or current price of the goods at the time or times when they ought to have been delivered or (if no time was fixed) at the time of the refusal to deliver.

52 Specific performance

(1) In any action for breach of contract to deliver specific or ascertained goods the court may, if it thinks fit, on the plaintiff's application, by its judgment or decree direct that the contract shall be performed specifically, without giving the defendant the option of retaining the goods on payment of damages.

(2) The plaintiff's application may be made at any time before judgment or decree.

(3) The judgment or decree may be unconditional, or on such terms and conditions as to damages, payment of the price and otherwise as seem just to the court.

(4) The provisions of this section shall be deemed to be supplementary to, and not in derogation of, the right of specific implement in Scotland.

53 Remedy for breach of warranty

(1) Where there is a breach of warranty by the seller, or where the buyer elects (or is compelled) to treat any breach of a condition on the part of the seller as a breach of warranty, the buyer is not by reason only of such breach of warranty entitled to reject the goods; but he may—

(a) set up against the seller the breach of warranty in diminution or extinction of the price, or

(b) maintain an action against the seller for damages for the breach of warranty.

(2) The measure of damages for breach of warranty is the estimated loss directly and naturally resulting, in the ordinary course of events, from the breach of warranty.

(3) In the case of breach of warranty of quality such loss is prima facie the difference between the value of the goods at the time of delivery to the buyer and the value they would have had if they had fulfilled the warranty.

(4) The fact that the buyer has set up the breach of warranty in diminution or extinction of the price does not prevent him from maintaining an action for the same breach of warranty if he has suffered further damage.

[(5) This section does not apply to Scotland.]

NOTES

Sub-s (5): substituted by the Sale and Supply of Goods Act 1994, s 7, Sch 2, para 5(7).

PART VII
SUPPLEMENTARY

61 Interpretation

(1) In this Act, unless the context or subject matter otherwise requires—

"action" includes counterclaim and set-off, and in Scotland condescendence and claim and compensation;

["bulk" means a mass or collection of goods of the same kind which—

(a) is contained in a defined space or area; and

(b) is such that any goods in the bulk are interchangeable with any other goods therein of the same number or quantity;]

"business" includes a profession and the activities of any government department (including a Northern Ireland department) or local or public authority;

"buyer" means a person who buys or agrees to buy goods;

["consumer contract" has the same meaning as in section 25(1) of the Unfair Contract Terms Act 1977; and for the purposes of this Act the onus of proving that a contract is not to be regarded as a consumer contract shall lie on the seller]

"contract of sale" includes an agreement to sell as well as a sale;

"credit-broker" means a person acting in the course of a business of credit brokerage carried on by him, that is a business of effecting introductions of individuals desiring to obtain credit—

(a) to persons carrying on any business so far as it relates to the provision of credit, or

(b) to other persons engaged in credit brokerage;

"defendant" includes in Scotland defender, respondent, and claimant in a multiple poinding;

"delivery" means voluntary transfer of possession from one person to another [except that in relation to sections 20A and 20B above it includes such appropriation of goods to the contract as results in property in the goods being transferred to the buyer;]

"document of title to goods" has the same meaning as it has in the Factors Acts;

"Factors Acts" means the Factors Act 1889, the Factors (Scotland) Act 1890, and any enactment amending or substituted for the same;

"fault" means wrongful act or default;

"future goods" means goods to be manufactured or acquired by the seller after the making of the contract of sale;

"goods" includes all personal chattels other than things in action and money, and in Scotland all corporeal moveables except money; and in particular "goods" includes emblements, industrial growing crops, and things attached to or forming part of the land which are agreed to be severed before sale or under the contract of sale [and includes an undivided share in goods;]

"plaintiff" includes pursuer, complainer, claimant in a multiplepoinding and defendant or defender counter-claiming;

"property" means the general property in goods, and not merely a special property;

. . .

"sale" includes a bargain and sale as well as a sale and delivery;

"seller" means a person who sells or agrees to sell goods;

"specific goods" means goods identified and agreed on at the time a contract of sale is made [and includes an undivided share, specified as a fraction or percentage, of goods identified and agreed on as aforesaid];

"warranty" (as regards England and Wales and Northern Ireland) means an agreement with reference to goods which are the subject of a contract of sale, but collateral to the main purpose of such contract, the breach of which gives rise to a claim for damages, but not to a right to reject the goods and treat the contract as repudiated.

(2) . . .

(3) A thing is deemed to be done in good faith within the meaning of this Act when it is in fact done honestly, whether it is done negligently or not.

(4) A person is deemed to be insolvent within the meaning of this Act if he has either ceased to pay his debts in the ordinary course of business or he cannot pay his debts as they become due, . . .

(5) Goods are in a deliverable state within the meaning of this Act when they are in such a state that the buyer would under the contract be bound to take delivery of them.

[(5A) References in this Act to dealing as consumer are to be construed in accordance with Part I of the Unfair Contract Terms Act 1977; and, for the purposes of this Act, it is for a seller claiming that the buyer does not deal as consumer to show that he does not.]

(6) As regards the definition of "business" in subsection (1) above, paragraph 14 of Schedule 1 below applies in relation to a contract made on or after 18th May 1973 and before 1st February 1978, and paragraph 15 in relation to one made before 18th May 1973.

NOTES

Sub-s (1): definition "bulk", and words in square brackets in definitions "delivery", "goods" and "specific goods", inserted by the Sale of Goods (Amendment) Act 1995, s 2; definition "consumer contract" inserted, and second definition omitted repealed, by the Sale and Supply of Goods Act 1994, s 7, Sch 2, para 5(9)(a), Sch 3.

Sub-s (2): repealed by the Sale and Supply of Goods Act 1994, s 7, Sch 2, para 5(9)(b), Sch 3.

Sub-s (4): words omitted repealed by the Insolvency Act 1985, s 235, Sch 10, Part III, and the Bankruptcy (Scotland) Act 1985, s 75(2), Sch 8.

Sub-s (5A): inserted by the Sale and Supply of Goods Act 1994, s 7, Sch 2, para 5(9)(c).

64 Short title and commencement

(1) This Act may be cited as the Sale of Goods Act 1979.

(2) This Act comes into force on 1st January 1980.

Limitation Act 1980

1980 CHAPTER 58

An Act to consolidate the Limitation Acts 1939 to 1980

[13th November 1980]

PART I
ORDINARY TIME LIMITS FOR DIFFERENT CLASSES OF ACTION

Time limits under Part I subject to extension or exclusion under Part II

1 Time limits under Part I subject to extension or exclusion under Part II

(1) This Part of this Act gives the ordinary time limits for bringing actions of the various classes mentioned in the following provisions of this Part.

(2) The ordinary time limits given in this Part of this Act are subject to extension or exclusion in accordance with the provisions of Part II of this Act.

Actions founded on tort

2 Time limit for actions founded on tort

An action founded on tort shall not be brought after the expiration of six years from the date on which the cause of action accrued.

3 Time limit in case of successive conversions and extinction of title of owner of converted goods

(1) Where any cause of action in respect of the conversion of a chattel has accrued to any person and, before he recovers possession of the chattel, a further conversion takes place, no action shall be brought in respect of the further conversion after the expiration of six years from the accrual of the cause of action in respect of the original conversion.

(2) Where any such cause of action has accrued to any person and the period prescribed for bringing that action has expired and he has not during that period recovered possession of the chattel, the title of that person to the chattel shall be extinguished.

4 Special time limit in case of theft

(1) The right of any person from whom a chattel is stolen to bring an action in respect of the theft shall not be subject to the time limits under sections 2 and 3(1) of this Act, but if his title to the chattel is extinguished under section 3(2) of this Act he may not bring an action in respect of a theft preceding the loss of his title, unless the theft in question preceded the conversion from which time began to run for the purposes of section 3(2).

(2) Subsection (1) above shall apply to any conversion related to the theft of a chattel as it applies to the theft of a chattel; and, except as provided below, every conversion following the theft of a chattel before the person from whom it is stolen recovers possession of it shall be regarded for the purposes of this section as related to the theft.

If anyone purchases the stolen chattel in good faith neither the purchase nor any conversion following it shall be regarded as related to the theft.

(3) Any cause of action accruing in respect of the theft or any conversion related to the theft of a chattel to any person from whom the chattel is stolen shall be disregarded for the purpose of applying section 3(1) or (2) of this Act to his case.

(4) Where in any action brought in respect of the conversion of a chattel it is proved that the chattel was stolen from the plaintiff or anyone through whom he claims it shall be presumed that any conversion following the theft is related to the theft unless the contrary is shown.

(5) In this section "theft" includes—

- (a) any conduct outside England and Wales which would be theft if committed in England and Wales; and

(b) obtaining any chattel (in England and Wales or elsewhere) in the circumstances described in section 15(1) of the Theft Act 1968 (obtaining by deception) or by blackmail within the meaning of section 21 of that Act;

and references in this section to a chattel being "stolen" shall be construed accordingly.

[4A Time limit for actions for defamation or malicious falsehood]

[The time limit under section 2 of this Act shall not apply to an action for—

(a) libel or slander, or malicious falsehood.

(b) slander of title, slander of goods or other malicious falsehood,

but no such action shall be brought after the expiration of one year from the date on which the cause of action accrued.]

NOTES

Inserted by the Administration of Justice Act 1985, s 57(2).
Substituted by the Defamation Act 1996, s 5(2), (6).

Actions founded on simple contract

5 Time limit for actions founded on simple contract

An action founded on simple contract shall not be brought after the expiration of six years from the date on which the cause of action accrued.

6 Special time limit for actions in respect of certain loans

(1) Subject to subsection (3) below, section 5 of this Act shall not bar the right of action on a contract of loan to which this section applies.

(2) This section applies to any contract of loan which—

(a) does not provide for repayment of the debt on or before a fixed or determinable date; and

(b) does not effectively (whether or not it purports to do so) make the obligation to repay the debt conditional on a demand for repayment made by or on behalf of the creditor or on any other matter;

except where in connection with taking the loan the debtor enters into any collateral obligation to pay the amount of the debt or any part of it (as, for example, by delivering a promissory note as security for the debt) on terms which would exclude the application of this section to the contract of loan if they applied directly to repayment of the debt.

(3) Where a demand in writing for repayment of the debt under a contract of loan to which this section applies is made by or on behalf of the creditor (or, where there are joint creditors, by or on behalf of any one of them) section 5 of this Act shall thereupon apply as if the cause of action to recover the debt had accrued on the date on which the demand was made.

(4) In this section "promissory note" has the same meaning as in the Bills of Exchange Act 1882.

7 Time limit for actions to enforce certain awards

An action to enforce an award, where the submission is not by an instrument under seal, shall not be brought after the expiration of six years from the date on which the cause of action accrued.

General rule for actions on a specialty

8 Time limit for actions on a specialty

(1) An action upon a specialty shall not be brought after the expiration of twelve years from the date on which the cause of action accrued.

(2) Subsection (1) above shall not affect any action for which a shorter period of limitation is prescribed by any other provision of this Act.

Actions for sums recoverable by statute

9 Time limit for actions for sums recoverable by statute

(1) An action to recover any sum recoverable by virtue of any enactment shall not be brought after the expiration of six years from the date on which the cause of action accrued.

(2) Subsection (1) above shall not affect any action to which section 10 of this Act applies.

10 Special time limit for claiming contribution

(1) Where under section 1 of the Civil Liability (Contribution) Act 1978 any person becomes entitled to a right to recover contribution in respect of any damage from any other person, no action to recover contribution by virtue of that right shall be brought after the expiration of two years from the date on which that right accrued.

(2) For the purposes of this section the date on which a right to recover contribution in respect of any damage accrues to any person (referred to below in this section as "the relevant date") shall be ascertained as provided in subsections (3) and (4) below.

(3) If the person in question is held liable in respect of that damage—
- (a) by a judgment given in any civil proceedings; or
- (b) by an award made on any arbitration;

the relevant date shall be the date on which the judgment is given, or the date of the award (as the case may be).

For the purposes of this subsection no account shall be taken of any judgment or award given or made on appeal in so far as it varies the amount of damages awarded against the person in question.

(4) If, in any case not within subsection (3) above, the person in question makes or agrees to make any payment to one or more persons in compensation for that damage (whether he admits any liability in respect of the damage or not), the relevant date shall be the earliest date on which the amount to be paid by him is agreed between him (or his representative) and the person (or each of the persons, as the case may be) to whom the payment is to be made.

(5) An action to recover contribution shall be one to which sections 28, 32 and 35 of this Act apply, but otherwise Parts II and III of this Act (except sections 34, 37 and 38) shall not apply for the purposes of this section.

Actions in respect of wrongs causing personal injuries or death

11 Special time limit for actions in respect of personal injuries

(1) This section applies to any action for damages for negligence, nuisance or breach of duty (whether the duty exists by virtue of a contract or of provision made by or under a statute or independently of any contract or any such provision) where the damages claimed by the plaintiff for the negligence, nuisance or breach of duty consist of or include damages in respect of personal injuries to the plaintiff or any other person.

[(1A) This section does not apply to any action brought for damages under section 3 of the Protection from Harassment Act 1997.]

(2) None of the time limits given in the preceding provisions of this Act shall apply to an action to which this section applies.

(3) An action to which this section applies shall not be brought after the expiration of the period applicable in accordance with subsection (4) or (5) below.

(4) Except where subsection (5) below applies, the period applicable is three years from—

- (a) the date on which the cause of action accrued; or
- (b) the date of knowledge (if later) of the person injured.

(5) If the person injured dies before the expiration of the period mentioned in subsection (4) above, the period applicable as respects the cause of action surviving for the benefit of his estate by virtue of section 1 of the Law Reform (Miscellaneous Provisions) Act 1934 shall be three years from—

- (a) the date of death; or
- (b) the date of the personal representative's knowledge;

whichever is the later.

(6) For the purposes of this section "personal representative" includes any person who is or has been a personal representative of the deceased, including an executor who has not proved the will (whether or not he has renounced probate) but not anyone appointed only as a special personal representative in relation to settled land;

and regard shall be had to any knowledge acquired by any such person while a personal representative or previously.

(7) If there is more than one personal representative, and their dates of knowledge are different, subsection (5)(b) above shall be read as referring to the earliest of those dates.

NOTES

Sub-s (1A): inserted by the Protection from Harassment Act 1997, s 6.

[11A Actions in respect of defective products]

[(1) This section shall apply to an action for damages by virtue of any provision of Part I of the Consumer Protection Act 1987.

(2) None of the time limits given in the preceding provisions of this Act shall apply to an action to which this section applies.

(3) An action to which this section applies shall not be brought after the expiration of the period of ten years from the relevant time, within the meaning of section 4 of the said act of 1987; and this subsection shall operate to extinguish a right of action and shall do so whether or not that right of action had accrued, or time under the following provisions of this Act had begun to run, at the end of the said period of ten years.

(4) Subject to subsection (4) below, an action to which this section applies in which the damages claimed by the plaintiff consist of or include damages in respect of personal injuries to the plaintiff or any other person or loss of or damage to any property, shall not be brought after the expiration of the period of three years from whichever is the later of—

(a) the date on which the cause of action accrued; and
(b) the date of knowledge of the injured person or, in the case of loss of damage to property, the date of knowledge of the plaintiff or (if earlier) of any person in whom his cause of action was previously vested.

(5) If in a case where the damages claimed by the plaintiff consist of or include damages in respect of personal injuries to the plaintiff or any other person the injured person died before the expiration of the period mentioned in subsection (4) above, that subsection shall have effect as respects the cause of action surviving for the benefit of his estate by virtue of section 1 of the Law Reform (Miscellaneous Provisions) Act 1934 as if for the reference to that period there were substituted a reference to the period of three years from whichever is the later of—

(a) the date of death; and
(b) the date of the personal representative's knowledge.

(6) For the purposes of this section "personal representative" includes any person who is or has been a personal representative of the deceased, including an executor who has not proved the will (whether or not he has renounced probate) but not anyone appointed only as a special personal representative in relation to settled land; and regard shall be had to any knowledge acquired by any such person while a personal representative or previously.

(7) If there is more than one personal representative and their dates of knowledge are different, subsection (5)(b) above shall be read as referring to the earliest of those dates.

(8) Expressions used in this section or section 14 of this Act and in Part I of the Consumer Protection Act 1987 have the same meanings in this section or that section as in that Part; and section 1(1) of that Act (Part I to be construed as enacted for the purpose of complying with the product liability Directive) shall apply for the purpose of construing this section and the following provisions of this Act so far as they relate to an action by virtue of any provision of that Part as it applies for the purpose of construing that Part.]

NOTES

Inserted by the Consumer Protection Act 1987, s 6, Sch 1, Part I, para 1.

12 Special time limit for actions under Fatal Accidents legislation

(1) An action under the Fatal Accidents Act 1976 shall not be brought if the death occurred when the person injured could no longer maintain an action and recover damages in respect of the injury (whether because of a time limit in this Act or in any other Act, or for any other reason).

Where any such action by the injured person would have been barred by the time limit in section 11 [or 11A] of this Act, no account shall be taken of the possibility of that time limit being overridden under section 33 of this Act.

(2) None of the time limits given in the preceding provisions of this Act shall apply to an action under the Fatal Accidents Act 1976, but no such action shall be brought after the expiration of three years from—

(a) the date of death; or

(b) the date of knowledge of the person for whose benefit the action is brought;

whichever is the later.

(3) An action under the Fatal Accidents Act 1976 shall be one to which sections 28, 33 and 35 of this Act apply, and the application to any such action of the time limit under subsection (2) above shall be subject to section 39; but otherwise Parts II and III of this Act shall not apply to any such action.

NOTES

Sub-s (1): words in square brackets inserted by the Consumer Protection Act 1987, s 6, Sch 1, Part I, para 2.

13 Operation of time limit under section 12 in relation to different dependants

(1) Where there is more than one person for whose benefit an action under the Fatal Accidents Act 1976 is brought, section 12(2)(b) of this Act shall be applied separately to each of them.

(2) Subject to subsection (3) below, if by virtue of subsection (1) above the action would be outside the time limit given by section 12(2) as regards one or more, but

not all, of the persons for whose benefit it is brought, the court shall direct that any person as regards whom the action would be outside that limit shall be excluded from those for whom the action is brought.

(3) The court shall not give such a direction if it is shown that if the action were brought exclusively for the benefit of the person in question it would not be defeated by a defence of limitation (whether in consequence of section 28 of this Act or an agreement between the parties not to raise the defence, or otherwise).

14 Definition of date of knowledge for purposes of sections 11 and 12

(1) [Subject to subsection (1A) below,] In sections 11 and 12 of this Act references to a person's date of knowledge are references to the date on which he first had knowledge of the following facts—

(a) that the injury in question was significant; and
(b) that the injury was attributable in whole or in part to the act or omission which is alleged to constitute negligence, nuisance or breach of duty; and
(c) the identity of the defendant; and
(d) if it is alleged that the act or omission was that of a person other than the defendant, the identity of that person and the additional facts supporting the bringing of an action against the defendant;

and knowledge that any acts or omissions did or did not, as a matter of law, involve negligence, nuisance or breach of duty is irrelevant.

[(1A) In section 11A of this Act and in section 12 of this Act so far as that section applies to an action by virtue of section 6(1)(a) of the Consumer Protection Act 1987 (death caused by defective product) references to a person's date of knowledge are references to the date on which he first had knowledge of the following facts—

(a) such facts about the damage caused by the defect as would lead a reasonable person who had suffered such damage to consider it sufficiently serious to justify his instituting proceedings for damages against a defendant who did not dispute liability and was able to satisfy a judgment; and
(b) that the damage was wholly or partly attributable to the facts and circumstances alleged to constitute the defect; and
(c) the identity of the defendant;

but, in determining the date on which a person first had such knowledge there shall be disregarded both the extent (if any) of that person's knowledge on any date of whether particular facts or circumstances would or would not, as a matter of law, constitute a defect and, in a case relating to loss of or damage to property, any knowledge which that person had on a date on which he had no right of action by virtue of Part I of that Act in respect of the loss or damage.]

(2) For the purposes of this section an injury is significant if the person whose date of knowledge is in question would reasonably have considered it sufficiently serious to justify his instituting proceedings for damages against a defendant who did not dispute liability and was able to satisfy a judgment.

(3) For the purposes of this section a person's knowledge includes knowledge which he might reasonably have been expected to acquire—

(a) from facts observable or ascertainable by him; or

(b) from facts ascertainable by him with the help of medical or other appropriate expert advice which it is reasonable for him to seek;

but a person shall not be fixed under this subsection with knowledge of a fact ascertainable only with the help of expert advice so long as he has taken all reasonable steps to obtain (and, where appropriate, to act on) that advice.

NOTES

Sub-s (1): words in square brackets inserted by the Consumer Protection Act 1987, s 6, Sch 1, Part I, para 3.

Sub-s (1A): inserted by the Consumer Protection Act 1987, s 6, Sch 1, Part I, para 3.

Actions in respect of latent damage not involving personal injuries

[14A Special time limit for negligence actions where facts relevant to cause of action are not known at date of accrual]

[(1) This section applies to any action for damages for negligence, other than one to which section 11 of this Act applies, where the starting date for reckoning the period of limitation under subsection (4)(b) below falls after the date on which the cause of action accrued.

(2) Section 2 of this Act shall not apply to an action to which this section applies.

(3) An action to which this section applies shall not be brought after the expiration of the period applicable in accordance with subsection (4) below.

(4) That period is either—

(a) six years from the date on which the cause of action accrued; or

(b) three years from the starting date as defined by subsection (5) below, if that period expires later than the period mentioned in paragraph (a) above.

(5) For the purposes of this section, the starting date for reckoning the period of limitation under subsection (4)(b) above is the earliest date on which the plaintiff or any person in whom the cause of action was vested before him first had both the knowledge required for bringing an action for damages in respect of the relevant damage and a right to bring such an action.

(6) In subsection (5) above "the knowledge required for bringing an action for damages in respect of the relevant damage" means knowledge both—

(a) of the material facts about the damage in respect of which damages are claimed; and

(b) of the other facts relevant to the current action mentioned in subsection (8) below.

(7) For the purposes of subsection (6)(a) above, the material facts about the damage are such facts about the damage as would lead a reasonable person who had suffered such damage to consider it sufficiently serious to justify his instituting proceedings for damages against a defendant who did not dispute liability and was able to satisfy a judgment.

(8) The other facts referred to in subsection (6)(b) above are—

(a) that the damage was attributable in whole or in part to the act or omission which is alleged to constitute negligence; and
(b) the identity of the defendant; and
(c) if it is alleged that the act or omission was that of a person other than the defendant, the identity of that person and the additional facts supporting the bringing of an action against the defendant.

(9) Knowledge that any acts or omissions did or did not, as a matter of law, involve negligence is irrelevant for the purposes of subsection (5) above.

(10) For the purposes of this section a person's knowledge includes knowledge which he might reasonably have been expected to acquire—
(a) from facts observable or ascertainable by him; or
(b) from facts ascertainable by him with the help of appropriate expert advice which it is reasonable for him to seek;

but a person shall not be taken by virtue of this subsection to have knowledge of a fact ascertainable only with the help of expert advice so long as he has taken all reasonable steps to obtain (and, where appropriate, to act on) that advice.]

NOTES

Inserted by the Latent Damage Act 1986, s 1.

[14B Overriding time limit for negligence actions not involving personal injuries]

[(1) An action for damages for negligence, other than one to which section 11 of this Act applies, shall not be brought after the expiration of fifteen years from the date (or, if more than one, from the last of the dates) on which there occurred any act or omission—
(a) which is alleged to constitute negligence; and
(b) to which the damage in respect of which damages are claimed is alleged to be attributable (in whole or in part).

(2) This section bars the right of action in a case to which subsection (1) above applies notwithstanding that—
(a) the cause of action has not yet accrued; or
(b) where section 14A of this Act applies to the action, the date which is for the purposes of that section the starting date for reckoning the period mentioned in subsection (4)(b) of that section has not yet occurred;

before the end of the period of limitation prescribed by this section.]

NOTES

Inserted by the Latent Damage Act 1986, s 1.

PART II
EXTENSION OR EXCLUSION OF ORDINARY TIME LIMITS

Disability

28 Extension of limitation period in case of disability

(1) Subject to the following provisions of this section, if on the date when any right of action accrued for which a period of limitation is prescribed by this Act, the person to whom it accrued was under a disability, the action may be brought at any time before the expiration of six years from the date when he ceased to be under a disability or died (whichever first occurred) notwithstanding that the period of limitation has expired.

(2) This section shall not affect any case where the right of action first accrued to some person (not under a disability) through whom the person under a disability claims.

(3) When a right of action which has accrued to a person under a disability accrues, on the death of that person while still under a disability, to another person under a disability, no further extension of time shall be allowed by reason of the disability of the second person.

(4) No action to recover land or money charged on land shall be brought by virtue of this section by any person after the expiration of thirty years from the date on which the right of action accrued to that person or some person through whom he claims.

[(4A) If the action is one to which section 4A of this Act applies, subsection (1) above shall have effect—

- (a) in the case of an action for libel or slander, as if for the words from "at any time" to "occurred)" there were substituted the words "by him at any time before the expiration of one year from the date on which he ceased to be under a disability"; and
- (b) in the case of an action for slander of title, slander of goods or other malicious falsehood, as if for the words "six years" there were substituted the words "one year".]

(5) If the action is one to which section 10 of this Act applies, subsection (1) above shall have effect as if for the words "six years" there were substituted the words "two years".

(6) If the action is one to which section 11 or 12(2) of this Act applies, subsection (1) above shall have effect as if for the words "six years" there were substituted the words "three years".

[(7) If the action is one to which section 11A of this Act applies or one by virtue of section 6(1)(a) of the Consumer Protection Act 1987 (death caused by defective product), subsection (1) above—

- (a) shall not apply to the time limit prescribed by subsection (3) of the said section 11A or to that time limit as applied by virtue of section 12(1) of this Act; and

(b) in relation to any other time limit prescribed by this Act shall have effect as if for the word "six years" there were substituted the words "three years".]

NOTES

Sub-s (4A): inserted by the Administration of Justice Act 1985, ss 57(3), 69(5), Sch 9, para 14; substituted by the Defamation Act 1996, s 5(3), (6).

Sub-s (7): inserted by the Consumer Protection Act 1987, s 6, Sch 1, Part I, para 4.

[28A Extension for cases where the limitation period is the period under section 14A(4)(b)]

[(1) Subject to subsection (2) below, if in the case of any action for which a period of limitation is prescribed by section 14A of this Act—

(a) the period applicable in accordance with subsection (4) of that section is the period mentioned in paragraph (b) of that subsection;

(b) on the date which is for the purposes of that section the starting date for reckoning that period the person by reference to whose knowledge that date fell to be determined under subsection (5) of that section was under a disability; and

(c) section 28 of this Act does not apply to the action;

the action may be brought at any time before the expiration of three years from the date when he ceased to be under a disability or died (whichever first occurred) notwithstanding that the period mentioned above has expired.

(2) An action may not be brought by virtue of subsection (1) above after the end of the period of limitation prescribed by section 14B of this Act.]

NOTES

Inserted by the Latent Damage Act 1986, s 2(1).

Acknowledgment and part payment

29 Fresh accrual of action on acknowledgment or part payment

(1) Subsections (2) and (3) below apply where any right of action (including a foreclosure action) to recover land or an advowson or any right of a mortgagee of personal property to bring a foreclosure action in respect of the property has accrued.

(2) If the person in possession of the land, benefice or personal property in question acknowledges the title of the person to whom the right of action has accrued—

(a) the right shall be treated as having accrued on and not before the date of the acknowledgment; and

(b) in the case of a right of action to recover land which has accrued to a person entitled to an estate or interest taking effect on the determination of an entailed interest against whom time is running under section 27 of this Act, section 27 shall thereupon cease to apply to the land.

(3) In the case of a foreclosure or other action by a mortgagee, if the person in possession of the land, benefice or personal property in question or the person liable for the mortgage debt makes any payment in respect of the debt (whether of principal or interest) the right shall be treated as having accrued on and not before the date of the payment.

(4) Where a mortgagee is by virtue of the mortgage in possession of any mortgaged land and either—

(a) receives any sum in respect of the principal or interest of the mortgage debt; or

(b) acknowledges the title of the mortgagor, or his equity of redemption;

an action to redeem the land in his possession may be brought at any time before the expiration of twelve years from the date of the payment or acknowledgment.

(5) Subject to subsection (6) below, where any right of action has accrued to recover—

(a) any debt or other liquidated pecuniary claim; or

(b) any claim to the personal estate of a deceased person or to any share or interest in any such estate;

and the person liable or accountable for the claim acknowledges the claim or makes any payment in respect of it the right shall be treated as having accrued on and not before the date of the acknowledgment or payment.

(6) A payment of a part of the rent or interest due at any time shall not extend the period for claiming the remainder then due, but any payment of interest shall be treated as a payment in respect of the principal debt.

(7) Subject to subsection (6) above, a current period of limitation may be repeatedly extended under this section by further acknowledgments or payments, but a right of action, once barred by this Act, shall not be revived by any subsequent acknowledgment or payment.

30 Formal provisions as to acknowledgments and part payments

(1) To be effective for the purposes of section 29 of this Act, an acknowledgment must be in writing and signed by the person making it.

(2) For the purposes of section 29, any acknowledgment or payment—

(a) may be made by the agent of the person by whom it is required to be made under that section; and

(b) shall be made to the person, or to an agent of the person, whose title or claim is being acknowledged or, as the case may be, in respect of whose claim the payment is being made.

31 Effect of acknowledgment or part payment on persons other than the maker or recipient

(1) An acknowledgment of the title to any land, benefice, or mortgaged personalty by any person in possession of it shall bind all other persons in possession during the ensuing period of limitation.

(2) A payment in respect of a mortgage debt by the mortgagor or any other person liable for the debt, or by any person in possession of the mortgaged property, shall, so far as any right of the mortgagee to foreclose or otherwise to recover the property is concerned, bind all other persons in possession of the mortgaged property during the ensuing period of limitation.

(3) Where two or more mortgagees are by virtue of the mortgage in possession of the mortgaged land, an acknowledgment of the mortgagor's title or of his equity of redemption by one of the mortgagees shall only bind him and his successors and shall not bind any other mortgagee or his successors.

(4) Where in a case within subsection (3) above the mortgagee by whom the acknowledgment is given is entitled to a part of the mortgaged land and not to any ascertained part of the mortgage debt the mortgagor shall be entitled to redeem that part of the land on payment, with interest, of the part of the mortgage debt which bears the same proportion to the whole of the debt as the value of the part of the land bears to the whole of the mortgaged land.

(5) Where there are two or more mortgagors, and the title or equity of redemption of one of the mortgagors is acknowledged as mentioned above in this section, the acknowledgment shall be treated as having been made to all the mortgagors.

(6) An acknowledgment of any debt or other liquidated pecuniary claim shall bind the acknowledgor and his successors but not any other person.

(7) A payment made in respect of any debt or other liquidated pecuniary claim shall bind all persons liable in respect of the debt or claim.

(8) An acknowledgment by one of several personal representatives of any claim to the personal estate of a deceased person or to any share or interest in any such estate, or a payment by one of several personal representatives in respect of any such claim, shall bind the estate of the deceased person.

(9) In this section "successor", in relation to any mortgagee or person liable in respect of any debt or claim, means his personal representatives and any other person on whom the rights under the mortgage or, as the case may be, the liability in respect of the debt or claim devolve (whether on death or bankruptcy or the disposition of property or the determination of a limited estate or interest in settled property or otherwise).

Fraud, concealment and mistake

32 Postponement of limitation period in case of fraud, concealment or mistake

(1) Subject to [subsections (3) and (4A)] below, where in the case of any action for which a period of limitation is prescribed by this Act, either—

- (a) the action is based upon the fraud of the defendant; or
- (b) any fact relevant to the plaintiff's right of action has been deliberately concealed from him by the defendant; or
- (c) the action is for relief from the consequences of a mistake;

the period of limitation shall not begin to run until the plaintiff has discovered the fraud, concealment or mistake (as the case may be) or could with reasonable diligence have discovered it.

References in this subsection to the defendant include references to the defendant's agent and to any person through whom the defendant claims and his agent.

(2) For the purposes of subsection (1) above, deliberate commission of a breach of duty in circumstances in which it is unlikely to be discovered for some time amounts to deliberate concealment of the facts involved in that breach of duty.

(3) Nothing in this section shall enable any action—
  (a) to recover, or recover the value of, any property; or
  (b) to enforce any charge against, or set aside any transaction affecting, any property;

to be brought against the purchaser of the property or any person claiming through him in any case where the property has been purchased for valuable consideration by an innocent third party since the fraud or concealment or (as the case may be) the transaction in which the mistake was made took place.

(4) A purchaser is an innocent third party for the purposes of this section—
  (a) in the case of fraud or concealment of any fact relevant to the plaintiff's right of action, if he was not a party to the fraud or (as the case may be) to the concealment of that fact and did not at the time of the purchase know or have reason to believe that the fraud or concealment had taken place; and
  (b) in the case of mistake, if he did not at the time of the purchase know or have reason to believe that the mistake had been made.

[(4A) Subsection (1) above shall not apply in relation to the time limit prescribed by section 11A(3) of this Act or in relation to that time limit as applied by virtue of section 12(1) of this Act].

[(5) Sections 14A and 14B of this Act shall not apply to any action to which subsection (1)(b) above applies (and accordingly the period of limitation referred to in that subsection, in any case to which either of those sections would otherwise apply, is the period applicable under section 2 of this Act).]

NOTES

Sub-s (1): words in square brackets substituted by the Consumer Protection Act 1987, s 6, Sch 1, Part I, para 5.

Sub-s (4A): inserted by the Consumer Protection Act 1987, s 6, Sch 1, Part I, para 5.

Sub-s (5): inserted by the Latent Damage Act 1986, s 2(2).

[Discretionary exclusion of time limit for actions for defamation or malicious falsehood]

[32A Discretionary exclusion of time limit for actions for defamation or malicious falsehood]

[(1) If it appears to the court that it would be exclusion of time equitable to allow an action to proceed having regard to limit for actions the degree to which—

(a) the operation of section 4A of this Act prejudices the plaintiff or any person whom he represents, and
(b) any decision of the court under this subsection would prejudice the defendant or any person whom he represents,

the court may direct that that section shall not apply to the action or shall not apply to any specified cause of action to which the action relates.

(2) In acting under this section the court shall have regard to all the circumstances of the case and in particular to—
(a) the length of, and the reasons for, the delay on the part of the plaintiff;
(b) where the reason or one of the reasons for the delay was that all or any of the facts relevant to the cause of action did not become known to the plaintiff until after the end of the period mentioned in section 4A—
(i) the date on which any such facts did become known to him, and
(ii) the extent to which he acted promptly and reasonably once he knew whether or not the facts in question might be capable of giving rise to an action; and
(c) the extent to which, having regard to the delay, relevant evidence is likely—
(i) to be unavailable, or
(ii) to be less cogent than if the action had been brought within the period mentioned in section 4A.

(3) In the case of an action for slander of title, slander of goods or other malicious falsehood brought by a personal representative—
(a) the references in subsection (2) above to the plaintiff shall be construed as including the deceased person to whom the cause of action accrued and any previous personal representative of that person; and
(b) nothing in section 28(3) of this Act shall be construed as affecting the court's discretion under this section.

(4) In this section "the court" means the court in which the action has been brought.]

NOTES

Inserted by the Administration of Justice Act 1985, s 57(4).
Substituted by the Defamation Act 1996, s 5(4), (6).

Discretionary exclusion of time limit for actions in respect of personal injuries or death

33 Discretionary exclusion of time limit for actions in respect of personal injuries or death

(1) If it appears to the court that it would be equitable to allow an action to proceed having regard to the degree to which—
(a) the provisions of section 11 [or 11A] or 12 of this Act prejudice the plaintiff or any person whom he represents; and
(b) any decision of the court under this subsection would prejudice the defendant or any person whom he represents;

the court may direct that those provisions shall not apply to the action, or shall not apply to any specified cause of action to which the action relates.

[(1A) The court shall not under this section disapply—

(a) subsection (3) of section 11A; or

(b) where the damages claimed by the plaintiff are confined to damages for loss of or damage to any property, any other provision in its application to an action by virtue of Part I of the Consumer Protection Act 1987.]

(2) The court shall not under this section disapply section 12(1) except where the reason why the person injured could no longer maintain an action was because of the time limit in section 11 [or subsection (4) of section 11A].

If, for example, the person injured could at his death no longer maintain an action under the Fatal Accidents Act 1976 because of the time limit in Article 29 in Schedule 1 to the Carriage by Air Act 1961, the court has no power to direct that section 12(1) shall not apply.

(3) In acting under this section the court shall have regard to all the circumstances of the case and in particular to—

(a) the length of, and the reasons for, the delay on the part of the plaintiff;

(b) the extent to which, having regard to the delay, the evidence adduced or likely to be adduced by the plaintiff or the defendant is or is likely to be less cogent than if the action had been brought within the time allowed by section 11 [, by section 11A] or (as the case may be) by section 12;

(c) the conduct of the defendant after the cause of action arose, including the extent (if any) to which he responded to requests reasonably made by the plaintiff for information or inspection for the purpose of ascertaining facts which were or might be relevant to the plaintiff's cause of action against the defendant;

(d) the duration of any disability of the plaintiff arising after the date of the accrual of the cause of action;

(e) the extent to which the plaintiff acted promptly and reasonably once he knew whether or not the act or omission of the defendant, to which the injury was attributable, might be capable at that time of giving rise to an action for damages;

(f) the steps, if any, taken by the plaintiff to obtain medical, legal or other expert advice and the nature of any such advice he may have received.

(4) In a case where the person injured died when, because of section 11 [or subsection (4) of section 11A], he could no longer maintain an action and recover damages in respect of the injury, the court shall have regard in particular to the length of, and the reasons for, the delay on the part of the deceased.

(5) In a case under subsection (4) above, or any other case where the time limit, or one of the time limits, depends on the date of knowledge of a person other than the plaintiff, subsection (3) above shall have effect with appropriate modifications, and shall have effect in particular as if references to the plaintiff included references to any person whose date of knowledge is or was relevant in determining a time limit.

(6) A direction by the court disapplying the provisions of section 12(1) shall operate to disapply the provisions to the same effect in section 1(1) of the Fatal Accidents Act 1976.

(7) In this section "the court" means the court in which the action has been brought.

(8) References in this section to section 11 [or 11A] include references to that section as extended by any of the preceding provisions of this Part of this Act or by any provision of Part III of this Act.

NOTES

Sub-ss (1), (3), (4), (8): words in square brackets inserted by the Consumer Protection Act 1987, s 6, Sch 1, Part I, para 6.

Sub-s (1A): inserted by the Consumer Protection Act 1987, s 6, Sch 1, Part I, para 6.

PART III
MISCELLANEOUS AND GENERAL

36 Equitable jurisdiction and remedies

(1) The following time limits under this Act, that is to say—
- (a) the time limit under section 2 for actions founded on tort;
- [(aa) the time limit under section 4A for actions for libel or slander, or for slander of title, slander of goods or other malicious falsehood;]
- (b) the time limit under section 5 for actions founded on simple contract;
- (c) the time limit under section 7 for actions to enforce awards where the submission is not by an instrument under seal;
- (d) the time limit under section 8 for actions on a specialty;
- (e) the time limit under section 9 for actions to recover a sum recoverable by virtue of any enactment; and
- (f) the time limit under section 24 for actions to enforce a judgment;

shall not apply to any claim for specific performance of a contract or for an injunction or for other equitable relief, except in so far as any such time limit may be applied by the court by analogy in like manner as the corresponding time limit under any enactment repealed by the Limitation Act 1939 was applied before 1st July 1940.

(2) Nothing in this Act shall affect any equitable jurisdiction to refuse relief on the ground of acquiescence or otherwise.

NOTES

Sub-s (1): para (aa) inserted by the Administration of Justice Act 1985, ss 57(5), 69(5), Sch 9, para 14, substituted by the Defamation Act 1996, s 5(5), (6).

38 Interpretation

(1) In this Act, unless the context otherwise requires—

"action" includes any proceeding in a court of law, including an ecclesiastical court;

"land" includes corporeal hereditaments, tithes and rentcharges and any legal or equitable estate or interest therein . . . but except as provided above in this definition does not include any incorporeal hereditament;

"personal estate" and "personal property" do not include chattels real;

"personal injuries" includes any disease and any impairment of a person's physical or mental condition, and "injury" and cognate expressions shall be construed accordingly;

"rent" includes a rentcharge and a rentservice; "rentcharge" means any annuity or periodical sum of money charged upon or payable out of land, except a rent service or interest on a mortgage on land;

"settled land", "statutory owner" and "tenant for life" have the same meanings respectively as in the Settled Land Act 1925;

"trust" and "trustee" have the same meanings respectively as in the Trustee Act 1925; and

. . .

(2) For the purposes of this Act a person shall be treated as under a disability while he is an infant, or of unsound mind.

(3) For the purposes of subsection (2) above a person is of unsound mind if he is a person who, by reason of mental disorder [is incapable of managing and administering his property and affairs; and in this section "mental disorder" has the same meaning as in the Mental Health Act 1983].

(4) Without prejudice to the generality of subsection (3) above, a person shall be conclusively presumed for the purposes of subsection (2) above to be of unsound mind—

(a) while he is liable to be detained or subject to guardianship under [the Mental Health Act 1983 (otherwise than by virtue of section 35 or 89)]; and

[(b) while he is receiving treatment [for mental disorder] as an in-patient in any hospital within the meaning of the Mental Health Act 1983 [or independent hospital or care home within the meaning of the Care Standards Act 2000] without being liable to be detained under the said Act of 1983 (otherwise than by virtue of section 35 or 89), being treatment which follows without any interval a period during which he was liable to be detained or subject to guardianship under the Mental Health Act 1959, or the said Act of 1983 (otherwise than by virtue of section 35 or 89) or by virtue of any enactment repealed or excluded by the Mental Health Act 1959].

(5) Subject to subsection (6) below, a person shall be treated as claiming through another person if he became entitled by, through, under, or by the act of that other person to the right claimed, and any person whose estate or interest might have been barred by a person entitled to an entailed interest in possession shall be treated as claiming through the person so entitled.

(6) A person becoming entitled to any estate or interest by virtue of a special power of appointment shall not be treated as claiming through the appointor.

(7) References in this Act to a right of action to recover land shall include references to a right to enter into possession of the land or, in the case of rentcharges

and tithes, to distrain for arrears of rent or tithe, and references to the bringing of such an action shall include references to the making of such an entry or distress.

(8) References in this Act to the possession of land shall, in the case of tithes and rentcharges, be construed as references to the receipt of the tithe or rent, and references to the date of dispossession or discontinuance of possession of land shall, in the case of rent charges, be construed as references to the date of the last receipt of rent.

(9) References in Part II of this Act to a right of action shall include references to—

- (a) a cause of action;
- (b) a right to receive money secured by a mortgage or charge on any property;
- (c) a right to recover proceeds of the sale of land; and
- (d) a right to receive a share or interest in the personal estate of a deceased person.

(10) References in Part II to the date of the accrual of a right of action shall be construed—

- (a) in the case of an action upon a judgment, as references to the date on which the judgment became enforceable; and
- (b) in the case of an action to recover arrears of rent or interest, or damages in respect of arrears of rent or interest, as references to the date on which the rent or interest became due.

NOTES

Sub-s (1): words omitted from definition "land" repealed, and definition omitted repealed, by the Trusts of Land and Appointment of Trustees Act 1996, s 25(2), Sch 4; for savings in relation to entailed interests created before the commencement of that Act, and savings consequential upon the abolition of the doctrine of conversion, see s 25(4), (5) thereof.

Sub-s (3): words from "is incapable of" to "Mental Health Act 1983" in square brackets substituted by the Care Standards Act 2000, s 116, Sch 4, para 8(a).

Date in force (in relation to England): 1 April 2002: see SI 2001/4150, art 3(3)(a); for transitional provisions see SI 2001/4150, arts 3(2), 4(1), (3), (4) and SI 2002/1493, art 4 (as amended by SI 2002/1493, art 6).

Date in force (in relation to Wales): 1 April 2002: see SI 2002/920, art 3(3)(d); for transitional provisions see arts 2, 3(2), (4), (6)–(10), Sch 1 thereto.

Sub-s (4): in para (a) words from "the Mental Health Act 1983" to "35 or 89)" in square brackets substituted by the Mental Health Act 1983, s 148, Sch 4, para 55(b)(i).

Sub-s (4): para (b) substituted by the Mental Health Act 1983, s 148, Sch 4, para 55(b)(ii).

Sub-s (4) in para (b) words "for mental disorder" in square brackets inserted by the Care Standards Act 2000, s 116, Sch 4, para 8(b).

Date in force (in relation to England): 1 April 2002: see SI 2001/4150, art 3(3)(a); for transitional provisions see SI 2001/4150, arts 3(2), 4(1), (3), (4) and SI 2002/1493, art 4 (as amended by SI 2002/1493, art 6).

Date in force (in relation to Wales): 1 April 2002: see SI 2002/920, art 3(3)(d); for transitional provisions see arts 2, 3(2), (4), (6)–(10), Sch 1 thereto.

Sub-s (4): in para (b) words "or independent hospital or care home within the meaning of the Care Standards Act 2000" in square brackets substituted by the Care Standards Act 2000, s 116, Sch 4, para 8(b).

Date in force (in relation to England): 1 April 2002: see SI 2001/4150, art 3(3)(a); for transitional provisions see SI 2001/4150, arts 3(2), 4(1), (3), (4) and SI 2002/1493, art 4 (as amended by SI 2002/1493, art 6).

Date in force (in relation to Wales): 1 April 2002: see SI 2002/920, art 3(3)(d); for transitional provisions see arts 2, 3(2), (4), (6)–(10), Sch 1 thereto.

41 Short title, commencement and extent

(1) This Act may be cited as the Limitation Act 1980.

(2) This Act, except section 35, shall come into force on 1st May 1981.

(3) Section 35 of this Act shall come into force on 1st May 1981 to the extent (if any) that the section substituted for section 28 of the Limitation Act 1939 by section 8 of the Limitation Amendment Act 1980 is in force immediately before that date; but otherwise section 35 shall come into force on such day as the Lord Chancellor may by order made by statutory instrument appoint, and different days may be appointed for different purposes of that section (including its application in relation to different courts or proceedings).

(4) The repeal by this Act of section 14(1) of the Limitation Act 1963 and the corresponding saving in paragraph 2 of Schedule 2 to this Act shall extend to Northern Ireland, but otherwise this Act does not extend to Scotland or to Northern Ireland.

Highways Act 1980

1980 CHAPTER 66

An Act to consolidate the Highways Acts 1959 to 1971 and related enactments, with amendments to give effect to recommendations of the Law Commission

[13th November 1980]

PART IV
MAINTENANCE OF HIGHWAYS

Enforcement of liability for maintenance

58 Special defence in action against a highway authority for damages for non-repair of highway

(1) In an action against a highway authority in respect of damage resulting from their failure to maintain a highway maintainable at the public expense it is a defence (without prejudice to any other defence or the application of the law relating to contributory negligence) to prove that the authority had taken such care as in all the circumstances was reasonably required to secure that the part of the highway to which the action relates was not dangerous for traffic.

(2) For the purposes of a defence under subsection (1) above, the court shall in particular have regard to the following matters:—

(a) the character of the highway, and the traffic which was reasonably to be expected to use it;

(b) the standard of maintenance appropriate for a highway of that character and used by such traffic;

(c) the state of repair in which a reasonable person would have expected to find the highway;

(d) whether the highway authority knew, or could reasonably have been expected to know, that the condition of the part of the highway to which the action relates was likely to cause danger to users of the highway;

(e) where the highway authority could not reasonably have been expected to repair that part of the highway before the cause of action arose, what warning notices of its condition had been displayed;

but for the purposes of such a defence it is not relevant to prove that the highway authority had arranged for a competent person to carry out or supervise the maintenance of the part of the highway to which the action relates unless it is also proved that the authority had given him proper instructions with regard to the maintenance of the highway and that he had carried out the instructions.

(3) This section binds the Crown.

(4) . . .

NOTES

Sub-s (4): repealed by the New Roads and Street Works Act 1991, s 168(2), Sch 9.

PART XIV

MISCELLANEOUS AND SUPPLEMENTARY PROVISIONS

Savings etc

345 Short title, commencement and extent

(1) This Act may be cited as the Highways Act 1980.

(2) This Act shall come into force on 1st January 1981.

(3) This Act (except paragraph 18(c) of Schedule 24) extends to England and Wales only.

Contempt of Court Act 1981

1981 CHAPTER 49

An Act to amend the law relating to contempt of court and related matters

[27th July 1981]

Strict liability

3 Defence of innocent publication or distribution

(1) A person is not guilty of contempt of court under the strict liability rule as the publisher of any matter to which that rule applies if at the time of publication (having taken all reasonable care) he does not know and has no reason to suspect that relevant proceedings are active.

(2) A person is not guilty of contempt of court under the strict liability rule as the distributor of a publication containing any such matter if at the time of distribution (having taken all reasonable care) he does not know that it contains such matter and has no reason to suspect that it is likely to do so.

(3) The burden of proof of any fact tending to establish a defence afforded by this section to any person lies upon that person.

(4) . . .

NOTES

Sub-s (4): repeals the Administration of Justice Act 1960, s 11.

4 Contemporary reports of proceedings

(1) Subject to this section a person is not guilty of contempt of court under the strict liability rule in respect of a fair and accurate report of legal proceedings held in public, published contemporaneously and in good faith.

(2) In any such proceedings the court may, where it appears to be necessary for avoiding a substantial risk of prejudice to the administration of justice in those proceedings, or in any other proceedings pending or imminent, order that the publication of any report of the proceedings, or any part of the proceedings, be postponed for such period as the court thinks necessary for that purpose.

[(2A) Where in proceedings for any offence which is an administration of justice offence for the purposes of section 54 of the Criminal Procedure and Investigations Act 1996 (acquittal tainted by an administration of justice offence) it appears to the court that there is a possibility that (by virtue of that section) proceedings may be taken against a person for an offence of which he has been acquitted, subsection (2) of this section shall apply as if those proceedings were pending or imminent.]

(3) For the purposes of subsection (1) of this section . . . a report of proceedings shall be treated as published contemporaneously—

(a) in the case of a report of which publication is postponed pursuant to an order under subsection (2) of this section, if published as soon as practicable after that order expires;
(b) in the case of a report of committal proceedings of which publication is permitted by virtue only of subsection (3) of section 8 of the Magistrates' Courts Act 1980, if published as soon as practicable after publication is so permitted.

(4) . . .

NOTES

Sub-s (2A): inserted by the Criminal Procedure and Investigations Act 1996, s 57(3).
Sub-s (3): words omitted repealed by the Defamation Act 1996, s 16, Sch 2.
Date in force: 1 April 1999: see SI 1999/817, art 2(b).
Sub-s (4): repeals the Magistrates' Courts Act 1980, s 8(9).

Supplemental

21 Short title, commencement and extent

(1) This Act may be cited as the Contempt of Court Act 1981.

(2) The provisions of this Act relating to legal aid in England and Wales shall come into force on such day as the Lord Chancellor may appoint by order made by statutory instrument; and the provisions of this Act relating to legal aid in Scotland and Northern Ireland shall come into force on such day or days as the Secretary of State may so appoint.

Different days may be appointed under this subsection in relation to different courts.

(3) Subject to subsection (2), this Act shall come into force at the expiration of the period of one month beginning with the day on which it is passed.

(4) Sections 7, 8(3), 12, 13(1) to (3), 14, 16, 17 and 18, Parts I and III of Schedule 2 and Schedules 3 and 4 of this Act do not extend to Scotland.

(5) This Act, except sections 15 and 17 and Schedules 2 and 3, extends to Northern Ireland.

Civil Aviation Act 1982

1982 CHAPTER 16

An Act to consolidate certain enactments relating to civil aviation

[27th May 1982]

PART III
REGULATION OF CIVIL AVIATION

Trespass by aircraft and aircraft nuisance, noise, etc

76 Liability of aircraft in respect of trespass, nuisance and surface damage

(1) No action shall lie in respect of trespass or in respect of nuisance, by reason only of the flight of an aircraft over any property at a height above the ground which, having regard to wind, weather and all the circumstances of the case is reasonable, or the ordinary incidents of such flight, so long as the provisions of any Air Navigation Order and of any orders under section 62 above have been duly complied with and there has been no breach of section 81 below.

(2) Subject to subsection (3) below, where material loss or damage is caused to any person or property on land or water by, or by a person in, or an article, animal or person falling from, an aircraft while in flight, taking off or landing, then unless the loss or damage was caused or contributed to by the negligence of the person by whom it was suffered, damages in respect of the loss or damage shall be recoverable without proof of negligence or intention or other cause of action, as if the loss or damage had been caused by the wilful act, neglect, or default of the owner of the aircraft.

(3) Where material loss or damage is caused as aforesaid in circumstances in which—

(a) damages are recoverable in respect of the said loss or damage by virtue only of subsection (2) above, and

(b) a legal liability is created in some person other than the owner to pay damages in respect of the said loss or damage,

the owner shall be entitled to be indemnified by that other person against any claim in respect of the said loss or damage.

(4) Where the aircraft concerned has been bona fide demised, let or hired out for any period exceeding fourteen days to any other person by the owner thereof, and no pilot, commander, navigator or operative member of the crew of the aircraft is in the employment of the owner, this section shall have effect as if for references to the owner there were substituted references to the person to whom the aircraft has been so demised, let or hired out.

PART V
MISCELLANEOUS AND GENERAL

110 Citation and commencement

(1) This Act may be cited as the Civil Aviation Act 1982.

(2) This Act shall come into force at the expiration of the period of three months beginning with its passing.

Supply of Goods and Services Act 1982

1982 CHAPTER 29

An Act to amend the law with respect to the terms to be implied in certain contracts for the transfer of the property in goods, in certain contracts for the hire of goods and in certain contracts for the supply of a service; and for connected purposes.
[13th July 1982]

PART I
SUPPLY OF GOODS

Contracts for the transfer of property in goods

1 The contracts concerned

(1) In this Act [in its application to England and Wales and Northern Ireland] a "contract for the transfer of goods" means a contract under which one person transfers or agrees to transfer to another the property in goods, other than an excepted contract.

(2) For the purposes of this section an excepted contract means any of the following:—
- (a) a contract of sale of goods;
- (b) a hire-purchase agreement;
- (c) a contract under which the property in goods is (or is to be) transferred in exchange for trading stamps on their redemption;
- (d) a transfer or agreement to transfer which is made by deed and for which there is no consideration other than the presumed consideration imported by the deed;
- (e) a contract intended to operate by way of mortgage, pledge, charge or other security.

(3) For the purposes of this Act [in its application to England and Wales and Northern Ireland] a contract is a contract for the transfer of goods whether or not services are also provided or to be provided under the contract, and (subject to subsection (2) above) whatever is the nature of the consideration for the transfer or agreement to transfer.

NOTES

Sub-ss (1), (3): words in square brackets inserted by the Sale and Supply of Goods Act 1994, s 7, Sch 2, para 6(2).

2 Implied terms about title, etc

(1) In a contract for the transfer of goods, other than one to which subsection (3) below applies, there is an implied condition on the part of the transferor that in the case of a transfer of the property in the goods he has a right to transfer the property and in the case of an agreement to transfer the property in the goods he will have such a right at the time when the property is to be transferred.

(2) In a contract for the transfer of goods, other than one to which subsection (3) below applies, there is also an implied warranty that—

- (a) the goods are free, and will remain free until the time when the property is to be transferred, from any charge or encumbrance not disclosed or known to the transferee before the contract is made, and
- (b) the transferee will enjoy quiet possession of the goods except so far as it may be disturbed by the owner or other person entitled to the benefit of any charge or encumbrance so disclosed or known.

(3) This subsection applies to a contract for the transfer of goods in the case of which there appears from the contract or is to be inferred from its circumstances an intention that the transferor should transfer only such title as he or a third person may have.

(4) In a contract to which subsection (3) above applies there is an implied warranty that all charges or encumbrances known to the transferor and not known to the transferee have been disclosed to the transferee before the contract is made.

(5) In a contract to which subsection (3) above applies there is also an implied warranty that none of the following will disturb the transferee's quiet possession of the goods, namely—

- (a) the transferor;
- (b) in a case where the parties to the contract intend that the transferor should transfer only such title as a third person may have, that person;
- (c) anyone claiming through or under the transferor or that third person otherwise than under a charge or encumbrance disclosed or known to the transferee before the contract is made.

3 Implied terms where transfer is by description

(1) This section applies where, under a contract for the transfer of goods, the transferor transfers or agrees to transfer the property in the goods by description.

(2) In such a case there is an implied condition that the goods will correspond with the description.

(3) If the transferor transfers or agrees to transfer the property in the goods by sample as well as by description it is not sufficient that the bulk of the goods corresponds with the sample if the goods do not also correspond with the description.

(4) A contract is not prevented from falling within subsection (1) above by reason only that, being exposed for supply, the goods are selected by the transferee.

4 Implied terms about quality or fitness

(1) Except as provided by this section and section 5 below and subject to the provisions of any other enactment, there is no implied condition or warranty about the quality or fitness for any particular purpose of goods supplied under a contract for the transfer of goods.

[(2) Where, under such a contract, the transferor transfers the property in goods in the course of a business, there is an implied condition that the goods supplied under the contract are of satisfactory quality.

(2A) For the purposes of this section and section 5 below, goods are of satisfactory quality if they meet the standard that a reasonable person would regard as satisfactory, taking account of any description of the goods, the price (if relevant) and all the other relevant circumstances.

(3) The condition implied by subsection (2) above does not extend to any matter making the quality of goods unsatisfactory—

- (a) which is specifically drawn to the transferee's attention before the contract is made,
- (b) where the transferee examines the goods before the contract is made, which that examination ought to reveal, or
- (c) where the property in the goods is transferred by reference to a sample, which would have been apparent on a reasonable examination of the sample.]

(4) Subsection (5) below applies where, under a contract for the transfer of goods, the transferor transfers the property in goods in the course of a business and the transferee, expressly or by implication, makes known—

- (a) to the transferor, or
- (b) where the consideration or part of the consideration for the transfer is a sum payable by instalments and the goods were previously sold by a credit-broker to the transferor, to that credit-broker,

any particular purpose for which the goods are being acquired.

(5) In that case there is (subject to subsection (6) below) an implied condition that the goods supplied under the contract are reasonably fit for that purpose, whether or not that is a purpose for which such goods are commonly supplied.

(6) Subsection (5) above does not apply where the circumstances show that the transferee does not rely, or that it is unreasonable for him to rely, on the skill or judgment of the transferor or credit-broker.

(7) An implied condition or warranty about quality or fitness for a particular purpose may be annexed by usage to a contract for the transfer of goods.

(8) The preceding provisions of this section apply to a transfer by a person who in the course of a business is acting as agent for another as they apply to a transfer by a principal in the course of a business, except where that other is not transferring in the course of a business and either the transferee knows that fact or reasonable steps are taken to bring it to the transferee's notice before the contract concerned is made.

(9) . . .

NOTES

Sub-ss (2), (2A), (3): substituted, for sub-ss (2), (3) as originally enacted, by the Sale and Supply of Goods Act 1994, s 7, Sch 2, para 6(3).

Sub-s (9): repealed by the Sale and Supply of Goods Act 1994, s 7, Sch 2, para 6(3), Sch 3.

5 Implied terms where transfer is by sample

(1) This section applies where, under a contract for the transfer of goods, the transferor transfers or agrees to transfer the property in the goods by reference to a sample.

(2) In such a case there is an implied condition—
- (a) that the bulk will correspond with the sample in quality; and
- (b) that the transferee will have a reasonable opportunity of comparing the bulk with the sample; and
- (c) that the goods will be free from any defect, [making their quality unsatisfactory], which would not be apparent on reasonable examination of the sample.

(3) . . .

(4) For the purposes of this section a transferor transfers or agrees to transfer the property in goods by reference to a sample where there is an express or implied term to that effect in the contract concerned.

NOTES

Sub-s (2): words in square brackets substituted by the Sale and Supply of Goods Act 1994, s 7, Sch 2, para 6(4)(a).

Sub-s (3): repealed by the Sale and Supply of Goods Act 1994, s 7, Sch 2, para 6(4)(b), Sch 3.

[5A Modification of remedies for breach of statutory condition in non-consumer cases]

[(1) Where in the case of a contract for the transfer of goods—
- (a) the transferee would, apart from this subsection, have the right to treat the contract as repudiated by reason of a breach on the part of the transferor of a term implied by section 3, 4 or 5(2)(a) or (c) above, but
- (b) the breach is so slight that it would be unreasonable for him to do so,

then, if the transferee does not deal as consumer, the breach is not to be treated as a breach of condition but may be treated as a breach of warranty.

(2) This section applies unless a contrary intention appears in, or is to be implied from, the contract.

(3) It is for the transferor to show that a breach fell within subsection (1)(b) above.]

NOTES

Inserted by the Sale and Supply of Goods Act 1994, s 7, Sch 2, para 6(5).

Contracts for the hire of goods

6 The contracts concerned

(1) In this Act [in its application to England and Wales and Northern Ireland] a "contract for the hire of goods" means a contract under which one person bails or agrees to bail goods to another by way of hire, other than an excepted contract.

(2) For the purposes of this section an excepted contract means any of the following:—

- (a) a hire-purchase agreement;
- (b) a contract under which goods are (or are to be) bailed in exchange for trading stamps on their redemption.

(3) For the purposes of this Act [in its application to England and Wales and Northern Ireland] a contract is a contract for the hire of goods whether or not services are also provided or to be provided under the contract, and (subject to subsection (2) above) whatever is the nature of the consideration for the bailment or agreement to bail by way of hire.

NOTES

Sub-ss (1), (3): words in square brackets inserted by the Sale and Supply of Goods Act 1994, s 7, Sch 2, para 6(6).

7 Implied terms about right to transfer possession, etc

(1) In a contract for the hire of goods there is an implied condition on the part of the bailor that in the case of a bailment he has a right to transfer possession of the goods by way of hire for the period of the bailment and in the case of an agreement to bail he will have such a right at the time of the bailment.

(2) In a contract for the hire of goods there is also an implied warranty that the bailee will enjoy quiet possession of the goods for the period of the bailment except so far as the possession may be disturbed by the owner or other person entitled to the benefit of any charge or encumbrance disclosed or known to the bailee before the contract is made.

(3) The preceding provisions of this section do not affect the right of the bailor to repossess the goods under an express or implied term of the contract.

8 Implied terms where hire is by description

(1) This section applies where, under a contract for the hire of goods, the bailor bails or agrees to bail the goods by description.

(2) In such a case there is an implied condition that the goods will correspond with the description.

(3) If under the contract the bailor bails or agrees to bail the goods by reference to a sample as well as a description it is not sufficient that the bulk of the goods corresponds with the sample if the goods do not also correspond with the description.

(4) A contract is not prevented from falling within subsection (1) above by reason only that, being exposed for supply, the goods are selected by the bailee.

9 Implied terms about quality or fitness

(1) Except as provided by this section and section 10 below and subject to the provisions of any other enactment, there is no implied condition or warranty about the quality or fitness for any particular purpose of goods bailed under a contract for the hire of goods.

[(2) Where, under such a contract, the bailor bails goods in the course of a business, there is an implied condition that the goods supplied under the contract are of satisfactory quality.

(2A) For the purposes of this section and section 10 below, goods are of satisfactory quality if they meet the standard that a reasonable person would regard as satisfactory, taking account of any description of the goods, the consideration for the bailment (if relevant) and all the other relevant circumstances.

(3) The condition implied by subsection (2) above does not extend to any matter making the quality of goods unsatisfactory—

(a) which is specifically drawn to the bailee's attention before the contract is made,

(b) where the bailee examines the goods before the contract is made, which that examination ought to reveal, or

(c) where the goods are bailed by reference to a sample, which would have been apparent on a reasonable examination of the sample.]

(4) Subsection (5) below applies where, under a contract for the hire of goods, the bailor bails goods in the course of a business and the bailee, expressly or by implication, makes known—

(a) to the bailor in the course of negotiations conducted by him in relation to the making of the contract, or

(b) to a credit-broker in the course of negotiations conducted by that broker in relation to goods sold by him to the bailor before forming the subject matter of the contract,

any particular purpose for which the goods are being bailed.

(5) In that case there is (subject to subsection (6) below) an implied condition that the goods supplied under the contract are reasonably fit for that purpose, whether or not that is a purpose for which such goods are commonly supplied.

(6) Subsection (5) above does not apply where the circumstances show that the bailee does not rely, or that it is unreasonable for him to rely, on the skill or judgment of the bailor or credit-broker.

(7) An implied condition or warranty about quality or fitness for a particular purpose may be annexed by usage to a contract for the hire of goods.

(8) The preceding provisions of this section apply to a bailment by a person who in the course of a business is acting as agent for another as they apply to a bailment by a principal in the course of a business, except where that other is not bailing in the course of a business and either the bailee knows that fact or reasonable steps are taken to bring it to the bailee's notice before the contract concerned is made.

(9) . . .

NOTES

Sub-ss (2), (2A), (3): substituted, for sub-ss (2), (3) as originally enacted, by the Sale and Supply of Goods Act 1994, s 7, Sch 2, para 6(7).

Sub-s (9): repealed by the Sale and Supply of Goods Act 1994, s 7, Sch 2, para 6(7), Sch 3.

10 Implied terms where hire is by sample

(1) This section applies where, under a contract for the hire of goods, the bailor bails or agrees to bail the goods by reference to a sample.

(2) In such a case there is an implied condition—

- (a) that the bulk will correspond with the sample in quality; and
- (b) that the bailee will have a reasonable opportunity of comparing the bulk with the sample; and
- (c) that the goods will be free from any defect, [making their quality unsatisfactory], which would not be apparent on reasonable examination of the sample.

(3) . . .

(4) For the purposes of this section a bailor bails or agrees to bail goods by reference to a sample where there is an express or implied term to that effect in the contract concerned.

NOTES

Sub-s (2): words in square brackets substituted by the Sale and Supply of Goods Act 1994, s 7, Sch 2, para 6(8)(a).

Sub-s (3): repealed by the Sale and Supply of Goods Act 1994, s 7, Sch 2, para 6(8)(b), Sch 3.

[10A Modification of remedies for breach of statutory condition in non-consumer cases]

[(1) Where in the case of a contract for the hire of goods—

(a) the bailee would, apart from this subsection, have the right to treat the contract as repudiated by reason of a breach on the part of the bailor of a term implied by section 8, 9 or 10(2)(a) or (c) above, but

(b) the breach is so slight that it would be unreasonable for him to do so,

then, if the bailee does not deal as consumer, the breach is not to be treated as a breach of condition but may be treated as a breach of warranty.

(2) This section applies unless a contrary intention appears in, or is to be implied from, the contract.

(3) It is for the bailor to show that a breach fell within subsection (1)(b) above.]

NOTES

Inserted by the Sale and Supply of Goods Act 1994, s 7, Sch 2, para 6(9).

Exclusion of implied terms, etc

11 Exclusion of implied terms, etc

(1) Where a right, duty or liability would arise under a contract for the transfer of goods or a contract for the hire of goods by implication of law, it may (subject to subsection (2) below and the 1977 Act) be negatived or varied by express agreement, or by the course of dealing between the parties, or by such usage as binds both parties to the contract.

(2) An express condition or warranty does not negative a condition or warranty implied by the preceding provisions of this Act unless inconsistent with it.

(3) Nothing in the preceding provisions of this Act prejudices the operation of any other enactment or any rule of law whereby any condition or warranty (other than one relating to quality or fitness) is to be implied in a contract for the transfer of goods or a contract for the hire of goods.

[PART IA
SUPPLY OF GOODS AS RESPECTS SCOTLAND]

[Contracts for the transfer of property in goods]

[11A The contracts concerned]

[(1) In this Act in its application to Scotland a "contract for the transfer of goods" means a contract under which one person transfers or agrees to transfer to another the property in goods, other than an excepted contract.

(2) For the purposes of this section an excepted contract means any of the following—

(a) a contract of sale of goods;

(b) a hire-purchase agreement;
(c) a contract under which the property in goods is (or is to be) transferred in exchange for trading stamps on their redemption;
(d) a transfer or agreement to transfer for which there is no consideration;
(e) a contract intended to operate by way of mortgage, pledge, charge or other security.

(3) For the purposes of this Act in its application to Scotland a contract is a contract for the transfer of goods whether or not services are also provided or to be provided under the contract, and (subject to subsection (2) above) whatever is the nature of the consideration for the transfer or agreement to transfer.]

NOTES

This Part (ss 11A–11L) was inserted by the Sale and Supply of Goods Act 1994, s 6, Sch 1, para 1.

[11B Implied terms about title, etc]

[(1) In a contract for the transfer of goods, other than one to which subsection (3) below applies, there is an implied term on the part of the transferor that in the case of a transfer of the property in the goods he has a right to transfer the property and in the case of an agreement to transfer the property in the goods he will have such a right at the time when the property is to be transferred.

(2) In a contract for the transfer of goods, other than one to which subsection (3) below applies, there is also an implied term that—
(a) the goods are free, and will remain free until the time when the property is to be transferred, from any charge or encumbrance not disclosed or known to the transferee before the contract is made, and
(b) the transferee will enjoy quiet possession of the goods except so far as it may be disturbed by the owner or other person entitled to the benefit of any charge or encumbrance so disclosed or known.

(3) This subsection applies to a contract for the transfer of goods in the case of which there appears from the contract or is to be inferred from its circumstances an intention that the transferor should transfer only such title as he or a third person may have.

(4) In a contract to which subsection (3) above applies there is an implied term that all charges or encumbrances known to the transferor and not known to the transferee have been disclosed to the transferee before the contract is made.

(5) In a contract to which subsection (3) above applies there is also an implied term that none of the following will disturb the transferee's quiet possession of the goods, namely—
(a) the transferor;
(b) in a case where the parties to the contract intend that the transferor should transfer only such title as a third person may have, that person;
(c) anyone claiming through or under the transferor or that third person otherwise than under a charge or encumbrance disclosed or known to the transferee before the contract is made.

(6) . . .]

NOTES

This Part (ss 11A–11L) was inserted by the Sale and Supply of Goods Act 1994, s 6, Sch, 1, para 1.

Sub-s (6): inserts the Unfair Contract Terms Act 1977, s 21(3A).

[11C Implied terms where transfer is by description]

[(1) This section applies where, under a contract for the transfer of goods, the transferor transfers or agrees to transfer the property in the goods by description.

(2) In such a case there is an implied term that the goods will correspond with the description.

(3) If the transferor transfers or agrees to transfer the property in the goods by reference to a sample as well as by description it is not sufficient that the bulk of the goods corresponds with the sample if the goods do not also correspond with the description.

(4) A contract is not prevented from falling within subsection (1) above by reason only that, being exposed for supply, the goods are selected by the transferee.]

NOTES

This Part (ss 11A–11L) was inserted by the Sale and Supply of Goods Act 1994, s 6, Sch 1, para 1.

[11D Implied terms about quality or fitness]

[(1) Except as provided by this section and section 11E below and subject to the provisions of any other enactment, there is no implied term about the quality or fitness for any particular purpose of goods supplied under a contract for the transfer of goods.

(2) Where, under such a contract, the transferor transfers the property in goods in the course of a business, there is an implied term that the goods supplied under the contract are of satisfactory quality.

(3) For the purposes of this section and section 11E below, goods are of satisfactory quality if they meet the standard that a reasonable person would regard as satisfactory, taking account of any description of the goods, the price (if relevant) and all the other relevant circumstances.

(4) The term implied by subsection (2) above does not extend to any matter making the quality of goods unsatisfactory—

(a) which is specifically drawn to the transferee's attention before the contract is made,

(b) where the transferee examines the goods before the contract is made, which that examination ought to reveal, or

(c) where the property in the goods is, or is to be, transferred by reference to a sample, which would have been apparent on a reasonable examination of the sample.

(5) Subsection (6) below applies where, under a contract for the transfer of goods, the transferor transfers the property in goods in the course of a business and the transferee, expressly or by implication, makes known—

(a) to the transferor, or

(b) where the consideration or part of the consideration for the transfer is a sum payable by instalments and the goods were previously sold by a credit-broker to the transferor, to that credit-broker,

any particular purpose for which the goods are being acquired.

(6) In that case there is (subject to subsection (7) below) an implied term that the goods supplied under the contract are reasonably fit for the purpose, whether or not that is a purpose for which such goods are commonly supplied.

(7) Subsection (6) above does not apply where the circumstances show that the transferee does not rely, or that it is unreasonable for him to rely, on the skill or judgment of the transferor or credit-broker.

(8) An implied term about quality or fitness for a particular purpose may be annexed by usage to a contract for the transfer of goods.

(9) The preceding provisions of this section apply to a transfer by a person who in the course of a business is acting as agent for another as they apply to a transfer by a principal in the course of a business, except where that other is not transferring in the course of a business and either the transferee knows that fact or reasonable steps are taken to bring it to the transferee's notice before the contract concerned is made.]

NOTES

This Part (ss 11A–11L) was inserted by the Sale and Supply of Goods Act 1994, s 6, Sch 1, para 1.

[11E Implied terms where transfer is by sample]

[(1) This section applies where, under a contract for the transfer of goods, the transferor transfers or agrees to transfer the property in the goods by reference to a sample.

(2) In such a case there is an implied term—

(a) that the bulk will correspond with the sample in quality;

(b) that the transferee will have a reasonable opportunity of comparing the bulk with the sample; and

(c) that the goods will be free from any defect, making their quality unsatisfactory, which would not be apparent on reasonable examination of the sample.

(3) For the purposes of this section a transferor transfers or agrees to transfer the property in goods by reference to a sample where there is an express or implied term to that effect in the contract concerned.]

NOTES

This Part (ss 11A–11L) was inserted by the Sale and Supply of Goods Act 1994, s 6, Sch 1, para 1.

[11F Remedies for breach of contract]

[(1) Where in a contract for the transfer of goods a transferor is in breach of any term of the contract (express or implied), the other party to the contract (in this section referred to as "the transferee") shall be entitled—

(a) to claim damages; and
(b) if the breach is material, to reject any goods delivered under the contract and treat it as repudiated.

(2) Where a contract for the transfer of goods is a consumer contract and the transferee is the consumer, then, for the purposes of subsection (1)(b) above, breach by the transferor of any term (express or implied)—

(a) as to the quality of the goods or their fitness for a purpose;
(b) if the goods are, or are to be, transferred by description, that the goods will correspond with the description;
(c) if the goods are, or are to be, transferred by reference to a sample, that the bulk will correspond with the sample in quality,

shall be deemed to be a material breach.

(3) In subsection (2) above, "consumer contract" has the same meaning as in section 25(1) of the 1977 Act; and for the purposes of that subsection the onus of proving that a contract is not to be regarded as a consumer contract shall lie on the transferor.]

NOTES

This Part (ss 11A–11L) was inserted by the Sale and Supply of Goods Act 1994, s 6, Sch 1, para 1.

[Contracts for the hire of goods]

[11G The contracts concerned]

[(1) In this Act in its application to Scotland a "contract for the hire of goods" means a contract under which one person ("the supplier") hires or agrees to hire goods to another, other than an excepted contract.

(2) For the purposes of this section, an excepted contract means any of the following—

(a) a hire-purchase agreement;
(b) a contract under which goods are (or are to be) hired in exchange for trading stamps on their redemption.

(3) For the purposes of this Act in its application to Scotland a contract is a contract for the hire of goods whether or not services are also provided or to be provided under the contract, and (subject to subsection (2) above) whatever is the nature of the consideration for the hire or agreement to hire.]

NOTES

This Part (ss 11A–11L) was inserted by the Sale and Supply of Goods Act 1994, s 6, Sch 1, para 1.

[11H Implied terms about right to transfer possession etc]

[(1) In a contract for the hire of goods there is an implied term on the part of the supplier that—

(a) in the case of a hire, he has a right to transfer possession of the goods by way of hire for the period of the hire; and

(b) in the case of an agreement to hire, he will have such a right at the time of commencement of the period of the hire.

(2) In a contract for the hire of goods there is also an implied term that the person to whom the goods are hired will enjoy quiet possession of the goods for the period of the hire except so far as the possession may be disturbed by the owner or other person entitled to the benefit of any charge or encumbrance disclosed or known to the person to whom the goods are hired before the contract is made.

(3) The preceding provisions of this section do not affect the right of the supplier to repossess the goods under an express or implied term of the contract.]

NOTES

This Part (ss 11A–11L) was inserted by the Sale and Supply of Goods Act 1994, s 6, Sch 1, para 1.

[11I Implied terms where hire is by description]

[(1) This section applies where, under a contract for the hire of goods, the supplier hires or agrees to hire the goods by description.

(2) In such a case there is an implied term that the goods will correspond with the description.

(3) If under the contract the supplier hires or agrees to hire the goods by reference to a sample as well as by description it is not sufficient that the bulk of the goods corresponds with the sample if the goods do not also correspond with the description.

(4) A contract is not prevented from falling within subsection (1) above by reason only that, being exposed for supply, the goods are selected by the person to whom the goods are hired.]

NOTES

This Part (ss 11A–11L) was inserted by the Sale and Supply of Goods Act 1994, s 6, Sch 1, para 1.

[11J Implied terms about quality or fitness]

[(1) Except as provided by this section and section 11K below and subject to the provisions of any other enactment, there is no implied term about the quality or fitness for any particular purpose of goods hired under a contract for the hire of goods.

(2) Where, under such a contract, the supplier hires goods in the course of a business, there is an implied term that the goods supplied under the contract are of satisfactory quality.

(3) For the purposes of this section and section 11K below, goods are of satisfactory quality if they meet the standard that a reasonable person would regard as satisfactory, taking account of any description of the goods, the consideration for the hire (if relevant) and all the other relevant circumstances.

(4) The term implied by subsection (2) above does not extend to any matter making the quality of goods unsatisfactory—

(a) which is specifically drawn to the attention of the person to whom the goods are hired before the contract is made, or

(b) where that person examines the goods before the contract is made, which that examination ought to reveal; or

(c) where the goods are hired by reference to a sample, which would have been apparent on reasonable examination of the sample.

(5) Subsection (6) below applies where, under a contract for the hire of goods, the supplier hires goods in the course of a business and the person to whom the goods are hired, expressly or by implication, makes known—

(a) to the supplier in the course of negotiations conducted by him in relation to the making of the contract; or

(b) to a credit-broker in the course of negotiations conducted by that broker in relation to goods sold by him to the supplier before forming the subject matter of the contract,

any particular purpose for which the goods are being hired.

(6) In that case there is (subject to subsection (7) below) an implied term that the goods supplied under the contract are reasonably fit for that purpose, whether or not that is a purpose for which such goods are commonly supplied.

(7) Subsection (6) above does not apply where the circumstances show that the person to whom the goods are hired does not rely, or that it is unreasonable for him to rely, on the skill or judgment of the hirer or credit-broker.

(8) An implied term about quality or fitness for a particular purpose may be annexed by usage to a contract for the hire of goods.

(9) The preceding provisions of this section apply to a hire by a person who in the course of a business is acting as agent for another as they apply to a hire by a principal in the course of a business, except where that other is not hiring in the course of a business and either the person to whom the goods are hired knows that fact or reasonable steps are taken to bring it to that person's notice before the contract concerned is made.]

NOTES

This Part (ss 11A–11L) was inserted by the Sale and Supply of Goods Act 1994, s 6, Sch 1, para 1.

[11K Implied terms where hire is by sample]

[(1) This section applies where, under a contract for the hire of goods, the supplier hires or agrees to hire the goods by reference to a sample.

(2) In such a case there is an implied term—

(a) that the bulk will correspond with the sample in quality; and
(b) that the person to whom the goods are hired will have a reasonable opportunity of comparing the bulk with the sample; and
(c) that the goods will be free from any defect, making their quality unsatisfactory, which would not be apparent on reasonable examination of the sample.

(3) For the purposes of this section a supplier hires or agrees to hire goods by reference to a sample where there is an express or implied term to that effect in the contract concerned.]

NOTES

This Part (ss 11A–11L) was inserted by the Sale and Supply of Goods Act 1994, s 6, Sch 1, para 1.

[Exclusion of implied terms, etc]

[11L Exclusion of implied terms etc]

[(1) Where a right, duty or liability would arise under a contract for the transfer of goods or a contract for the hire of goods by implication of law, it may (subject to subsection (2) below and the 1977 Act) be negatived or varied by express agreement, or by the course of dealing between the parties, or by such usage as binds both parties to the contract.

(2) An express term does not negative a term implied by the preceding provisions of this Part of this Act unless inconsistent with it.

(3) Nothing in the preceding provisions of this Part of this Act prejudices the operation of any other enactment or any rule of law whereby any term (other than one relating to quality or fitness) is to be implied in a contract for the transfer of goods or a contract for the hire of goods.]

NOTES

This Part (ss 11A–11L) was inserted by the Sale and Supply of Goods Act 1994, s 6, Sch 1, para 1.

PART II
SUPPLY OF SERVICES

12 The contracts concerned

(1) In this Act a "contract for the supply of a service" means, subject to subsection (2) below, a contract under which a person ("the supplier") agrees to carry out a service.

(2) For the purposes of this Act, a contract of service or apprenticeship is not a contract for the supply of a service.

(3) Subject to subsection (2) above, a contract is a contract for the supply of a service for the purposes of this Act whether or not goods are also—
(a) transferred or to be transferred, or

(b) bailed or to be bailed by way of hire,

under the contract, and whatever is the nature of the consideration for which the service is to be carried out.

(4) The Secretary of State may by order provide that one or more of sections 13 to 15 below shall not apply to services of a description specified in the order, and such an order may make different provision for different circumstances.

(5) The power to make an order under subsection (4) above shall be exercisable by statutory instrument subject to annulment in pursuance of a resolution of either House of Parliament.

13 Implied term about care and skill

In a contract for the supply of a service where the supplier is acting in the course of a business, there is an implied term that the supplier will carry out the service with reasonable care and skill.

14 Implied term about time for performance

(1) Where, under a contract for the supply of a service by a supplier acting in the course of a business, the time for the service to be carried out is not fixed by the contract, left to be fixed in a manner agreed by the contract or determined by the course of dealing between the parties, there is an implied term that the supplier will carry out the service within a reasonable time.

(2) What is a reasonable time is a question of fact.

15 Implied term about consideration

(1) Where, under a contract for the supply of a service, the consideration for the service is not determined by the contract, left to be determined in a manner agreed by the contract or determined by the course of dealing between the parties, there is an implied term that the party contracting with the supplier will pay a reasonable charge.

(2) What is a reasonable charge is a question of fact.

16 Exclusion of implied terms, etc

(1) Where a right, duty or liability would arise under a contract for the supply of a service by virtue of this Part of this Act, it may (subject to subsection (2) below and the 1977 Act) be negatived or varied by express agreement, or by the course of dealing between the parties, or by such usage as binds both parties to the contract.

(2) An express term does not negative a term implied by this Part of this Act unless inconsistent with it.

(3) Nothing in this Part of this Act prejudices—

(a) any rule of law which imposes on the supplier a duty stricter than that imposed by section 13 or 14 above; or

(b) subject to paragraph (*a*) above, any rule of law whereby any term not inconsistent with this Part of this Act is to be implied in a contract for the supply of a service.

(4) This Part of this Act has effect subject to any other enactment which defines or restricts the rights, duties or liabilities arising in connection with a service of any description.

PART III
SUPPLEMENTARY

18 Interpretation: general

(1) In the preceding provisions of this Act and this section—

"bailee", in relation to a contract for the hire of goods means (depending on the context) a person to whom the goods are bailed under the contract, or a person to whom they are to be so bailed, or a person to whom the rights under the contract of either of those persons have passed;

"bailor", in relation to a contract for the hire of goods, means (depending on the context) a person who bails the goods under the contract, or a person who agrees to do so, or a person to whom the duties under the contract of either of those persons have passed;

"business" includes a profession and the activities of any government department or local or public authority;

"credit-broker" means a person acting in the course of a business of credit brokerage carried on by him;

"credit brokerage" means the effecting of introductions—

(a) of individuals desiring to obtain credit to persons carrying on any business so far as it relates to the provision of credit; or
(b) of individuals desiring to obtain goods on hire to persons carrying on a business which comprises or relates to the bailment [or as regards Scotland the hire] of goods under a contract for the hire of goods; or
(c) of individuals desiring to obtain credit, or to obtain goods on hire, to other credit-brokers;

"enactment" means any legislation (including subordinate legislation) of the United Kingdom or Northern Ireland;

"goods" [includes all personal chattels, other than things in action and money, and as regards Scotland all corporeal moveables; and in particular "goods" includes] emblements, industrial growing crops, and things attached to or forming part of the land which are agreed to be severed before the transfer [bailment or hire] concerned or under the contract concerned . . . ;

"hire-purchase agreement" has the same meaning as in the 1974 Act;

"property", in relation to goods, means the general property in them and not merely a special property;

. . .

"redemption", in relation to trading stamps, has the same meaning as in the Trading Stamps Act 1964 or, as respects Northern Ireland, the Trading Stamps Act (Northern Ireland) 1965;

"trading stamps" has the same meaning as in the said Act of 1964 or, as respects

Northern Ireland, the said Act of 1965;

"transferee", in relation to a contract for the transfer of goods, means (depending on the context) a person to whom the property in the goods is transferred under the contract, or a person to whom the property is to be so transferred, or a person to whom the rights under the contract of either of those persons have passed;

"transferor", in relation to a contract for the transfer of goods, means (depending on the context) a person who transfers the property in the goods under the contract, or a person who agrees to do so, or a person to whom the duties under the contract of either of those persons have passed.

(2) In subsection (1) above, in the definitions of bailee, bailor, transferee and transferor, a reference to rights or duties passing is to their passing by assignment [assignation], operation of law or otherwise.

[(3) For the purposes of this Act, the quality of goods includes their state and condition and the following (among others) are in appropriate cases aspects of the quality of goods—

- (a) fitness for all the purposes for which goods of the kind in question are commonly supplied,
- (b) appearance and finish,
- (c) freedom from minor defects,
- (d) safety, and
- (e) durability.

(4) References in this Act to dealing as consumer are to be construed in accordance with Part I of the Unfair Contract Terms Act 1977; and, for the purposes of this Act, it is for the transferor or bailor claiming that the transferee or bailee does not deal as consumer to show that he does not.]

NOTES

Sub-s (1): in definition "credit brokerage" words in square brackets in para (b) inserted, in definition "goods" words in square brackets substituted and words omitted repealed, and definition omitted repealed, by the Sale and Supply of Goods Act 1994, ss 6, 7, Sch 1, para 2, Sch 2, para 6(10), Sch 3.

Sub-s (2): word in square brackets inserted by the Sale and Supply of Goods Act 1994, s 6, Sch 1, para 3.

Sub-ss (3), (4): inserted by the Sale and Supply of Goods Act 1994, s 7, Sch 2, para 6(10).

19 Interpretation: references to Acts

In this Act—

"the 1973 Act" means the Supply of Goods (Implied Terms) Act 1973;
"the 1974 Act" means the Consumer Credit Act 1974;
"the 1977 Act" means the Unfair Contract Terms Act 1977; and
"the 1979 Act" means the Sale of Goods Act 1979.

20 Citation, transitional provisions, commencement and extent

(1) This Act may be cited as the Supply of Goods and Services Act 1982.

(2) The transitional provisions in the Schedule to this Act shall have effect.

(3) Part I of this Act together with section 17 and so much of sections 18 and 19 above as relates to that Part shall not come into operation until 4th January 1983; and Part II of this Act together with so much of sections 18 and 19 above as relates to that Part shall not come into operation until such day as may be appointed by an order made by the Secretary of State.

(4) The power to make an order under subsection (3) above shall be exercisable by statutory instrument.

(5) No provision of this Act applies to a contract made before the provision comes into operation.

(6) This Act [except Part IA, which extends only to Scotland] extends to Northern Ireland [and Parts I and II do not extend] to Scotland.

NOTES

Sub-s (6): first words in square brackets inserted, and final words in square brackets substituted, by the Sale and Supply of Goods Act 1994, s 6, Sch 1, para 4.

Forfeiture Act 1982

1982 CHAPTER 34

An Act to provide for relief for persons guilty of unlawful killing from forfeiture of inheritance and other rights; to enable such persons to apply for financial provision out of the deceased's estate; to provide for the question whether pension and social security benefits have been forfeited to be determined by the Social Security commissioners; and for connected purposes

[13th July 1982]

1 The "forfeiture rule"

(1) In this Act, the "forfeiture rule" means the rule of public policy which in certain circumstances precludes a person who has unlawfully killed another from acquiring a benefit in consequence of the killing.

(2) References in this Act to a person who has unlawfully killed another include a reference to a person who has unlawfully aided, abetted, counselled or procured the death of that other and references in this Act to unlawful killing shall be interpreted accordingly.

2 Power to modify the rule

(1) Where a court determines that the forfeiture rule has precluded a person (in this section referred to as "the offender") who has unlawfully killed another from acquiring any interest in property mentioned in subsection (4) below, the court may make an order under this section modifying the effect of that rule.

(2) The court shall not make an order under this section modifying the effect of the forfeiture rule in any case unless it is satisfied that, having regard to the conduct of the offender and of the deceased and to such other circumstances as appear to the court to be material, the justice of the case requires the effect of the rule to be so modified in that case.

(3) In any case where a person stands convicted of an offence of which unlawful killing is an element, the court shall not make an order under this section modifying the effect of the forfeiture rule in that case unless proceedings for the purpose are brought before the expiry of the period of three months beginning with his conviction.

(4) The interests in property referred to in subsection (1) above are—

- (a) any beneficial interest in property which (apart from the forfeiture rule) the offender would have acquired—
  - (i) under the deceased's will (including, as respects Scotland, any writing having testamentary effect) or the law relating to intestacy or by way of ius relicti, ius relictae or legitim;
  - (ii) on the nomination of the deceased in accordance with the provisions of any enactment;
  - (iii) as a donatio mortis causa made by the deceased; or
  - (iv) under a special destination (whether relating to heritable or moveable property); or
- (b) any beneficial interest in property which (apart from the forfeiture rule) the offender would have acquired in consequence of the death of the deceased, being property which, before the death, was held on trust for any person.

(5) An order under this section may modify the effect of the forfeiture rule in respect of any interest in property to which the determination referred to in subsection (1) above relates and may do so in either or both of the following ways, that is—

- (a) where there is more than one such interest, by excluding the application of the rule in respect of any (but not all) of those interests; and
- (b) in the case of any such interest in property, by excluding the application of the rule in respect of part of the property.

(6) On the making of an order under this section, the forfeiture rule shall have effect for all purposes (including purposes relating to anything done before the order is made) subject to the modifications made by the order.

(7) The court shall not make an order under this section modifying the effect of the forfeiture rule in respect of any interest in property which, in consequence of the rule, has been acquired before the coming into force of this section by a person other than the offender or a person claiming through him.

(8) In this section—

"property" includes any chose in action or incorporeal moveable property; and
"will" includes codicil.

5 Exclusion of murderers

Nothing in this Act or in any order made under section 2 or referred to in section 3(1) of this Act [or in any decision made under section 4(1A) of this Act] shall affect the application of the forfeiture rule in the case of a person who stands convicted of murder.

NOTES

Words in square brackets inserted by the Social Security Act 1986, s 76(4).

7 Short title, etc

(1) This Act may be cited as the Forfeiture Act 1982.

(2) Section 4 of this Act shall come into force on such day as the Secretary of State may appoint by order made by statutory instrument; and sections 1 to 3 and 5 of this Act shall come into force on the expiry of the period of three months beginning with the day on which it is passed.

(3) This Act, except section 6, does not extend to Northern Ireland.

(4) Subject to section 2(7) of this Act, an order under section 2 of this Act or an order referred to in section 3(1) of this Act and made in respect of a person who has unlawfully killed another may be made whether the unlawful killing occurred before or after the coming into force of those sections.

Administration of Justice Act 1982

1982 CHAPTER 53

An Act to make further provision with respect to the administration of justice and matters connected therewith; to amend the law relating to actions for damages for personal injuries, including injuries resulting in death, and to abolish certain actions for loss of services; to amend the law relating to wills; to make further provision with respect to funds in court, statutory deposits and schemes for the common investment of such funds and deposits and certain other funds; to amend the law relating to deductions by employers under attachment of earnings orders; to make further provision with regard to penalties that may be awarded by the Solicitors' Disciplinary Tribunal under section 47 of the Solicitors Act 1974; to make further provision for the appointment of justices of the peace in England and Wales and in relation to temporary vacancies in the membership of the Law Commission; to enable the title register kept by the Chief Land Registrar to be kept otherwise than in documentary form; and to authorise the payment of travelling, subsistence and financial loss allowances for justices of the peace in Northern Ireland

[28th October 1982]

PART I
DAMAGES FOR PERSONAL INJURIES ETC

Abolition of certain claims for damages etc

1 Abolition of right to damages for loss of expectation of life

(1) In an action under the law of England and Wales or the law of Northern Ireland for damages for personal injuries—

- (a) no damages shall be recoverable in respect of any loss of expectation of life caused to the injured person by the injuries; but
- (b) if the injured person's expectation of life has been reduced by the injuries, the court, in assessing damages in respect of pain and suffering caused by the injuries, shall take account of any suffering caused or likely to be caused to him by awareness that his expectation of life has been so reduced.

(2) The reference in subsection (1)(a) above to damages in respect of loss of expectation of life does not include damages in respect of loss of income.

2 Abolition of actions for loss of services etc

No person shall be liable in tort under the law of England and Wales or the law of Northern Ireland—

- (a) to a husband on the ground only of his having deprived him of the services or society of his wife;

(b) to a parent (or person standing in the place of a parent) on the ground only of his having deprived him of the services of a child; or
(c) on the ground only—
(i) of having deprived another of the services of his menial servant;
(ii) of having deprived another of the services of his female servant by raping or seducing her; or
(iii) of enticement of a servant or harbouring a servant.

Maintenance at public expense

5 Maintenance at public expense to be taken into account in assessment of damages

In an action under the law of England and Wales or the law of Northern Ireland for damages for personal injuries (including any such action arising out of a contract) any saving to the injured person which is attributable to his maintenance wholly or partly at public expense in a hospital, nursing home or other institution shall be set off against any income lost by him as a result of his injuries.

PART IX
GENERAL AND SUPPLEMENTARY

77 Extent

(1) Subject to subsection (6) below, the following provisions of this Act—
(a) sections 3, 4 and 6;
(b) Part III;
(c) sections 17 to 22;
(d) Part V;
(e) sections 49 to 57;
(f) sections 65 to 67,

extend to England and Wales only.

(2) Sections 1, 2, 5, 39, 42 to 47, 64 and 74 above extend to England and Wales and Northern Ireland.

(3) Part II of this Act and section 26 above extend to Scotland only and Part VI of this Act applies to Scotland only to the extent specified in section 48 above.

(4) Part VIII of this Act extends to Northern Ireland only.

(5) The repeal of the Wills Act Amendment Act 1852 by section 75 above does not extend to Northern Ireland.

(6) Subject to subsection (5) above, where any enactment repealed or amended or instrument revoked by this Act extends to any part of the United Kingdom, the repeal, amendment or revocation extends to that part.

78 Citation

This Act may be cited as the Administration of Justice Act 1982.

Occupiers' Liability Act 1984

1984 CHAPTER 3

An Act to amend the law of England and Wales as to the liability of persons as occupiers of premises for injury suffered by persons other than their visitors; and to amend the Unfair Contract Terms Act 1977, as it applies to England and Wales, in relation to persons obtaining access to premises for recreational or educational purposes

[13th March 1984]

1 Duty of occupier to persons other than his visitors

(1) The rules enacted by this section shall have effect, in place of the rules of the common law, to determine—

(a) whether any duty is owed by a person as occupier of premises to persons other than his visitors in respect of any risk of their suffering injury on the premises by reason of any danger due to the state of the premises or to things done or omitted to be done on them; and

(b) if so, what that duty is.

(2) For the purposes of this section, the persons who are to be treated respectively as an occupier of any premises (which, for those purposes, include any fixed or movable structure) and as his visitors are—

(a) any person who owes in relation to the premises the duty referred to in section 2 of the Occupiers' Liability Act 1957 (the common duty of care), and

(b) those who are his visitors for the purposes of that duty.

(3) An occupier of premises owes a duty to another (not being his visitor) in respect of any such risk as is referred to in subsection (1) above if—

(a) he is aware of the danger or has reasonable grounds to believe that it exists;

(b) he knows or has reasonable grounds to believe that the other is in the vicinity of the danger concerned or that he may come into the vicinity of the danger (in either case, whether the other has lawful authority for being in that vicinity or not); and

(c) the risk is one against which, in all the circumstances of the case, he may reasonably be expected to offer the other some protection.

(4) Where, by virtue of this section, an occupier of premises owes a duty to another in respect of such a risk, the duty is to take such care as is reasonable in all the circumstances of the case to see that he does not suffer injury on the premises by reason of the danger concerned.

(5) Any duty owed by virtue of this section in respect of a risk may, in an appropriate case, be discharged by taking such steps as are reasonable in all the circumstances of the case to give warning of the danger concerned or to discourage persons from incurring the risk.

(6) No duty is owed by virtue of this section to any person in respect of risks willingly accepted as his by that person (the question whether a risk was so accepted to be decided on the same principles as in other cases in which one person owes a duty of care to another).

[(6A) At any time when the right conferred by section 2(1) of the Countryside and Rights of Way Act 2000 is exercisable in relation to land which is access land for the purposes of Part I of that Act, an occupier of the land owes (subject to subsection (6C) below) no duty by virtue of this section to any person in respect of—

(a) a risk resulting from the existence of any natural feature of the landscape, or any river, stream, ditch or pond whether or not a natural feature, or
(b) a risk of that person suffering injury when passing over, under or through any wall, fence or gate, except by proper use of the gate or of a stile.

(6B) For the purposes of subsection (6A) above, any plant, shrub or tree, of whatever origin, is to be regarded as a natural feature of the landscape.

(6C) Subsection (6A) does not prevent an occupier from owing a duty by virtue of this section in respect of any risk where the danger concerned is due to anything done by the occupier—

(a) with the intention of creating that risk, or
(b) being reckless as to whether that risk is created.]

(7) No duty is owed by virtue of this section to persons using the highway, and this section does not affect any duty owed to such persons.

(8) Where a person owes a duty by virtue of this section, he does not, by reason of any breach of the duty, incur any liability in respect of any loss of or damage to property.

(9) In this section—

"highway" means any part of a highway other than a ferry or waterway;

"injury" means anything resulting in death or personal injury, including any disease and any impairment of physical or mental condition; and

"movable structure" includes any vessel, vehicle or aircraft.

NOTES

Sub-ss (6A)–(6C): inserted by the Countryside and Rights of Way Act 2000, s 13(2).
Date in force: to be appointed: see the Countryside and Rights of Way Act 2000, s 103(3).

3 Application to Crown

Section 1 of this Act shall bind the Crown, but as regards the Crown's liability in tort shall not bind the Crown further than the Crown is made liable in tort by the Crown Proceedings Act 1947.

4 Short title, commencement and extent

(1) This Act may be cited as the Occupiers' Liability Act 1984.

(2) This Act shall come into force at the end of the period of two months beginning with the day on which it is passed.

(3) This Act extends to England and Wales only.

Data Protection Act 1984

1984 CHAPTER 35

An Act to regulate the use of automatically processed information relating to individuals and the provision of services in respect of such information

[12 July 1984]

PART III
RIGHTS OF DATA SUBJECTS

22 Compensation for inaccuracy

(1) An individual who is the subject of personal data held by a data user and who suffers damage by reason of the inaccuracy of the data shall be entitled to compensation from the data user for that damage and for any distress which the individual has suffered by reason of the inaccuracy.

(2) In the case of data which accurately record information received or obtained by the data user from the data subject or a third party, subsection (1) above does not apply if the following requirements have been complied with—

(a) the data indicate that the information was received or obtained as aforesaid or the information has not been extracted from the data except in a form which includes an indication to that effect; and

(b) if the data subject has notified the data user that he regards the information as incorrect or misleading, an indication to that effect has been included in the data or the information has not been extracted from the data except in a form which includes an indication to that effect.

(3) In proceedings brought against any person by virtue of this section it shall be a defence to prove that he had taken such care as in all the circumstances was reasonably required to ensure the accuracy of the data at the material time.

(4) Data are inaccurate for the purposes of this section if incorrect or misleading as to any matter of fact.

NOTES

Whole Act repealed with savings by the Data Protection Act 1998, s 74(2), Sch 16, Pt I, as from a day to be appointed; for savings and transitional provisions see Sch 14, paras 2, 4 thereto.

23 Compensation for loss or unauthorised disclosure

(1) An individual who is the subject of personal data held by a data user or in respect of which services are provided by a person carrying on a computer bureau and who suffers damage by reason of—

(a) *the loss of the data;*
(b) *the destruction of the data without the authority of the data user or, as the case may be, of the person carrying on the bureau; or*
(c) *subject to subsection (2) below, the disclosure of the data, or access having been obtained to the data, without such authority as aforesaid,*

shall be entitled to compensation from the data user or, as the case may be, the person carrying on the bureau for that damage and for any distress which the individual has suffered by reason of the loss, destruction, disclosure or access.

(2) In the case of a registered data user, subsection (1)(c) above does not apply to disclosure to, or access by, any person falling within a description specified pursuant to section 4(3)(d) above in an entry in the register relating to that data user.

(3) In proceedings brought against any person by virtue of this section it shall be a defence to prove that he had taken such care as in all the circumstances was reasonably required to prevent the loss, destruction, disclosure or access in question.

NOTES

Repealed as noted to s 22.

PART V
GENERAL

43 Short title and extent

(1) This Act may be cited as the Data Protection Act 1984.

(2) This Act extends to Northern Ireland.

(3) Her Majesty may by Order in Council direct that this Act shall extend to any of the Channel Islands with such exceptions and modifications as may be specified in the Order.

NOTES

Repealed as noted to s 22.

Building Act 1984

1984 CHAPTER 55

An Act to consolidate certain enactments concerning building and buildings and related matters

[31st October 1984]

PART I
BUILDING REGULATIONS

Power to make building regulations

1 Power to make building regulations

(1) The Secretary of State may, for any of the purposes of—

- (a) securing the health, safety, welfare and convenience of persons in or about buildings and of others who may be affected by buildings or matters connected with buildings,
- (b) furthering the conservation of fuel and power, and
- (c) preventing waste, undue consumption, misuse or contamination of water,

make regulations with respect to the design and construction of buildings and the provision of services, fittings and equipment in or in connection with buildings.

(2) Regulations made under subsection (1) above are known as building regulations.

(3) Schedule 1 to this Act has effect with respect to the matters as to which building regulations may provide.

(4) The power to make building regulations is exercisable by statutory instrument, which is subject to annulment in pursuance of a resolution of either House of Parliament.

Breach of building regulations

38 Civil liability

(1) Subject to this section—

- (a) breach of a duty imposed by building regulations, so far as it causes damage, is actionable, except in so far as the regulations provide otherwise, and
- (b) as regards such a duty, building regulations may provide for a prescribed defence to be available in an action for breach of that duty brought by virtue of this subsection.

(2) Subsection (1) above, and any defence provided for in regulations made by virtue of it, do not apply in the case of a breach of such a duty in connection with a building erected before the date on which that subsection comes into force unless

the regulations imposing the duty apply to or in connection with the building by virtue of section 2(2) above or paragraph 8 of Schedule 1 to this Act.

(3) This section does not affect the extent (if any) to which breach of—

(a) a duty imposed by or arising in connection with this Part of this Act or any other enactment relating to building regulations, or

(b) a duty imposed by building regulations in a case to which subsection (1) above does not apply,

is actionable, or prejudice a right of action that exists apart from the enactments relating to building regulations.

(4) In this section, "damage" includes the death of, or injury to, any person (including any disease and any impairment of a person's physical or mental condition).

PART V
SUPPLEMENTARY

135 Short title and extent

(1) This Act may be cited as the Building Act 1984.

(2) This Act does not extend to Scotland or to Northern Ireland.

Police and Criminal Evidence Act 1984

1984 CHAPTER 60

An Act to make further provision in relation to the powers and duties of the police, persons in police detention, criminal evidence, police discipline and complaints against the police; to provide for arrangements for obtaining the views of the community on policing and for a rank of deputy chief constable; to amend the law relating to the Police Federations and Police Forces and Police Cadets in Scotland; and for connected purposes

[31st October 1984]

PART II
POWERS OF ENTRY, SEARCH AND SEIZURE

Entry and search without search warrant

17 Entry for purpose of arrest etc

(1) Subject to the following provisions of this section, and without prejudice to any other enactment, a constable may enter and search any premises for the purpose—

(a) of executing—

(i) a warrant of arrest issued in connection with or arising out of criminal proceedings; or
(ii) a warrant of commitment issued under section 76 of the Magistrates' Courts Act 1980;

(b) of arresting a person for an arrestable offence;

(c) of arresting a person for an offence under—
(i) section 1 (prohibition of uniforms in connection with political objects) . . . of the Public Order Act 1936;
(ii) any enactment contained in sections 6 to 8 or 10 of the Criminal Law Act 1977 (offences relating to entering and remaining on property);
[(iii) section 4 of the Public Order Act 1986 (fear or provocation of violence);]
[(iv) section 76 of the Criminal Justice and Public Order Act 1994 (failure to comply with interim possession order);]

[(ca) of arresting, in pursuance of section 32(1A) of the Children and Young Persons Act 1969, any child or young person who has been remanded or committed to local authority accommodation under section 23(1) of that Act;

(cb) of recapturing any person who is, or is deemed for any purpose to be, unlawfully at large while liable to be detained—
(i) in a prison, remand centre, young offender institution or secure training centre, or
(ii) in pursuance of [section 92 of the Powers of Criminal Courts (Sentencing) Act 2000] (dealing with children and young persons guilty of grave crimes), in any other place;]

(d) of recapturing [any person whatever] who is unlawfully at large and whom he is pursuing; or

(e) of saving life or limb or preventing serious damage to property.

(2) Except for the purpose specified in paragraph (e) of subsection (1) above, the powers of entry and search conferred by this section—

(a) are only exercisable if the constable has reasonable grounds for believing that the person whom he is seeking is on the premises; and

(b) are limited, in relation to premises consisting of two or more separate dwellings, to powers to enter and search—
(i) any parts of the premises which the occupiers of any dwelling comprised in the premises use in common with the occupiers of any other such dwelling; and
(ii) any such dwelling in which the constable has reasonable grounds for believing that the person whom he is seeking may be.

(3) The powers of entry and search conferred by this section are only exercisable for the purposes specified in subsection (1)(c)(ii) [or (iv)] above by a constable in uniform.

(4) The power of search conferred by this section is only a power to search to the extent that is reasonably required for the purpose for which the power of entry is exercised.

(5) Subject to subsection (6) below, all the rules of common law under which a constable has power to enter premises without a warrant are hereby abolished.

(6) Nothing in subsection (5) above affects any power of entry to deal with or prevent a breach of the peace.

NOTES

Sub-s (1): in para (c)(i) words omitted repealed by the Public Order Act 1986, s 40(3), Sch 3.

Sub-s (1): para (c)(iii) inserted by the Public Order Act 1986, s 40(2), Sch 2, para 7.

Sub-s (1): para (c)(iv) inserted by the Criminal Justice and Public Order Act 1994, s 168(2), Sch 10, para 53(a).

Sub-s (1): paras (ca), (cb) inserted by the Prisoners (Return to Custody) Act 1995, s 2(1).

Sub-s (1): in para (cb)(ii) words "section 92 of the Powers of Criminal Courts (Sentencing) Act 2000" in square brackets substituted by the Powers of Criminal Courts (Sentencing) Act 2000, s 165(1), Sch 9, para 95.

Date in force: 25 August 2000: see the Powers of Criminal Courts (Sentencing) Act 2000, s 168(1).

Sub-s (1): in para (d) words "any person whatever" in square brackets substituted by the Prisoners (Return to Custody) Act 1995, s 2(1).

Sub-s (3): words in square brackets inserted by the Criminal Justice and Public Order Act 1994, s 168(2), Sch 10, para 53(b).

Seizure etc

19 General power of seizure etc

(1) The powers conferred by subsections (2), (3) and (4) below are exercisable by a constable who is lawfully on any premises.

(2) The constable may seize anything which is on the premises if he has reasonable grounds for believing—

(a) that it has been obtained in consequence of the commission of an offence; and

(b) that it is necessary to seize it in order to prevent it being concealed, lost, damaged, altered or destroyed.

(3) The constable may seize anything which is on the premises if he has reasonable grounds for believing—

(a) that it is evidence in relation to an offence which he is investigating or any other offence; and

(b) that it is necessary to seize it in order to prevent the evidence being concealed, lost, altered or destroyed.

(4) The constable may require any information which is *contained in a computer* [stored in any electronic form] and is accessible from the premises to be produced in a form in which it can be taken away and in which it is visible and legible [or from which it can readily be produced in a visible and legible form] if he has reasonable grounds for believing—

(a) that—

(i) it is evidence in relation to an offence which he is investigating or any other offence; or

(ii) it has been obtained in consequence of the commission of an offence; and

(b) that it is necessary to do so in order to prevent it being concealed, lost, tampered with or destroyed.

(5) The powers conferred by this section are in addition to any power otherwise conferred.

(6) No power of seizure conferred on a constable under any enactment (including an enactment contained in an Act passed after this Act) is to be taken to authorise the seizure of an item which the constable exercising the power has reasonable grounds for believing to be subject to legal privilege.

NOTES

Sub-s (4): words "contained in a computer" in italics repealed and subsequent words in square brackets substituted by the Criminal Justice and Police Act 2001, s 70, Sch 2, Pt 2, para 13(1)(a), (2)(a).

Date in force: to be appointed: see the Criminal Justice and Police Act 2001, s 138(2).

Sub-s (4): words from "or from which" to "and legible form" in square brackets inserted by the Criminal Justice and Police Act 2001, s 70, Sch 2, Pt 2, para 13(1)(b), (2)(a).

Date in force: to be appointed: see the Criminal Justice and Police Act 2001, s 138(2).

22 Retention

(1) Subject to subsection (4) below, anything which has been seized by a constable or taken away by a constable following a requirement made by virtue of section 19 or 20 above may be retained so long as is necessary in all the circumstances.

(2) Without prejudice to the generality of subsection (1) above—

(a) anything seized for the purposes of a criminal investigation may be retained, except as provided by subsection (4) below,—

(i) for use as evidence at a trial for an offence; or

(ii) for forensic examination or for investigation in connection with an offence; and

(b) anything may be retained in order to establish its lawful owner, where there are reasonable grounds for believing that it has been obtained in consequence of the commission of an offence.

(3) Nothing seized on the ground that it may be used—

(a) to cause physical injury to any person;

(b) to damage property;

(c) to interfere with evidence; or

(d) to assist in escape from police detention or lawful custody,

may be retained when the person from whom it was seized is no longer in police detention or the custody of a court or is in the custody of a court but has been released on bail.

(4) Nothing may be retained for either of the purposes mentioned in subsection (2)(*a*) above if a photograph or copy would be sufficient for that purpose.

(5) Nothing in this section affects any power of a court to make an order under section 1 of the Police (Property) Act 1897.

[(6) This section also applies to anything retained by the police under section 28H(5) of the Immigration Act 1971.]

NOTES

Sub-s (6): inserted by the Immigration and Asylum Act 1999, s 169(1), Sch 14, para 80(1), (3).

Date in force: 14 February 2000: see SI 2000/168, art 2, Schedule.

PART III
ARREST

24 Arrest without warrant for arrestable offences

(1) The powers of summary arrest conferred by the following subsections shall apply—

- (a) to offences for which the sentence is fixed by law;
- (b) to offences for which a person of *21* [18] years of age or over (not previously convicted) may be sentenced to imprisonment for a term of five years (or might be so sentenced but for the restrictions imposed by section 33 of the Magistrates' Courts Act 1980); and
- (c) to the offences to which subsection (2) below applies,

and in this Act "arrestable offence" means any such offence.

(2) The offences to which this subsection applies are—

- (a) offences for which a person may be arrested under the customs and excise Acts, as defined in section 1(1) of the Customs and Excise Management Act 1979;
- (b) offences under [the Official Secrets Act 1920] that are not arrestable offences by virtue of the term of imprisonment for which a person may be sentenced in respect of them;
- [(bb) offences under any provision of the Official Secrets Act 1989 except section 8(1), (4) or (5);]
- (c) offences under section . . . 22 (causing prostitution of women) or 23 (procuration of girl under 21) of the Sexual Offences Act 1956;
- [(ca) an offence under section 46 of the Criminal Justice and Police Act 2001;]
- (d) offences under section 12(1) (taking motor vehicle or other conveyance without authority etc.) or 25(1) (going equipped for stealing, etc.) of the Theft Act 1968; and
- [(e) any offence under the Football (Offences) Act 1991.]
- [(f) an offence under section 2 of the Obscene Publications Act 1959 (publication of obscene matter);
- (g) an offence under section 1 of the Protection of Children Act 1978 (indecent photographs and pseudo-photographs of children);]
- [(ga) an offence under section 1 of the Sexual Offences Act 1985 (c 44) (kerb-crawling);

(gb) an offence under subsection (4) of section 170 of the Road Traffic Act 1988 (c 52) (failure to stop and report an accident) in respect of an accident to which that section applies by virtue of subsection (1)(a) of that section (accidents causing personal injury);]

[(h) an offence under section 166 of the Criminal Justice and Public Order Act 1994 (sale of tickets by unauthorised persons);]

[(i) an offence under section 19 of the Public Order Act 1986 (publishing, etc material intended or likely to stir up racial hatred);]

[(j) an offence under section 167 of the Criminal Justice and Public Order Act 1994 (touting for hire car services);]

[(k) an offence under section 1(1) of the Prevention of Crime Act 1953 (prohibition of the carrying of offensive weapons without lawful authority or reasonable excuse);

(l) an offence under section 139(1) of the Criminal Justice Act 1988 (offence of having article with blade or point in public place);

(m) an offence under section 139A(1) or (2) of the Criminal Justice Act 1988 (offence of having article with blade or point (or offensive weapon) on school premises)];

[(n) an offence under section 2 of the Protection from Harassment Act 1997 (harassment).]

[(o) an offence under [section 60AA(7)] of the Criminal Justice and Public Order Act 1994 (failing to comply with requirement to remove mask etc);]

[(p) an offence falling within section 32(1)(a) of the Crime and Disorder Act 1998 ([racially or religiously aggravated] harassment);]

[(q) an offence under section 14J or 21C of the Football Spectators Act 1989 (failure to comply with requirements imposed by or under a banning order or a notice under section 21B);]

[(qa) an offence under section 12(4) of the Criminal Justice and Police Act 2001;]

[(r) . . .]

[(s) an offence under section 1(1) or (2) or 6 of the Wildlife and Countryside Act 1981 (taking, possessing, selling etc of wild birds) in respect of a bird included in Schedule 1 to that Act or any part of, or anything derived from, such a bird;

(t) an offence under any of the following provisions of the Wildlife and Countryside Act 1981—

  (i) section 1(5) (disturbance of wild birds),

  (ii) section 9 or 13(1)(a) or (2) (taking, possessing, selling etc of wild animals or plants),

  (iii) section 14 (introduction of new species etc)];

[(u) an offence under section 21C(1) or 21D(1) of the Aviation Security Act 1982 (c 36) (unauthorised presence in restricted zone or on aircraft);

(v) an offence under section 39(1) of the Civil Aviation Act 1982 (c 16) (trespass on aerodrome)].

(3) Without prejudice to section 2 of the Criminal Attempts Act 1981, the powers of summary arrest conferred by the following subsections shall also apply to the offences of—

(a) conspiring to commit any of the offences mentioned in subsection (2) above;

(b) attempting to commit any such offence [other than an offence under section 12(1) of the Theft Act 1968];
(c) inciting, aiding, abetting, counselling or procuring the commission of any such offence;

and such offences are also arrestable offences for the purposes of this Act.

(4) Any person may arrest without a warrant—
(a) anyone who is in the act of committing an arrestable offence;
(b) anyone whom he has reasonable grounds for suspecting to be committing such an offence.

(5) Where an arrestable offence has been committed, any person may arrest without a warrant—
(a) anyone who is guilty of the offence;
(b) anyone whom he has reasonable grounds for suspecting to be guilty of it.

(6) Where a constable has reasonable grounds for suspecting that an arrestable offence has been committed, he may arrest without a warrant anyone whom he has reasonable grounds for suspecting to be guilty of the offence.

(7) A constable may arrest without a warrant—
(a) anyone who is about to commit an arrestable offence;
(b) anyone whom he has reasonable grounds for suspecting to be about to commit an arrestable offence.

NOTES

Sub-s (1): in para (b) number "21" in italics repealed and subsequent number in square brackets substituted by the Criminal Justice and Court Services Act 2000, s 74, Sch 7, Pt II, paras 76, 77.

Date in force: to be appointed: see the Criminal Justice and Court Services Act 2000, s 80(1).

Sub-s (2): in para (b) words "the Official Secrets Act 1920" in square brackets substituted by the Official Secrets Act 1989, s 11(1).

Sub-s (2): para (bb) inserted by the Official Secrets Act 1989, s 11(1).

Sub-s (2): in para (c) words omitted repealed by the Sexual Offences Act 1985, s 5(3), Schedule.

Sub-s (2): para (ca) inserted by the Criminal Justice and Police Act 2001, s 46(6).

Date in force: 1 September 2001: see SI 2001/2223, art 4(c).

Sub-s (2): para (e) as originally enacted repealed by the Criminal Justice Act 1988, s 170(2), Sch 16, new para (e) inserted by the Football Offences Act 1991, s 5(1).

Sub-s (2): paras (f), (g) inserted by the Criminal Justice and Public Order Act 1994, s 85(2).

Sub-s (2): paras (ga), (gb) inserted by the Criminal Justice and Police Act 2001, s 71.

Date in force: 1 October 2001: see SI 2001/3150, art 2(a).

Sub-s (2): para (h) inserted by the Criminal Justice and Public Order Act 1994, s 166(4).

Sub-s (2): para (i) inserted by the Criminal Justice and Public Order Act 1994, s 155.

Sub-s (2): para (j) inserted by the Criminal Justice and Public Order Act 1994, s 167(7).

Sub-s (2): paras (k)–(m) inserted by the Offensive Weapons Act 1996, s 1(1).

Sub-s (2): para (n) inserted by the Protection from Harassment Act 1997, s 2(3).

Sub-s (2): para (o) inserted by the Crime and Disorder Act 1998, s 27(1).

Date in force: 1 March 1999: see SI 1998/3263, art 4.

Sub-s (2): in para (o) words "section 60AA(7)" in square brackets substituted by the Anti-terrorism, Crime and Security Act 2001, s 94(3).

Date in force: 14 December 2001: see the Anti-terrorism, Crime and Security Act 2001, s 127(2)(d).

Sub-s (2): para (p) inserted by the Crime and Disorder Act 1998, s 32(2).

Date in force: 30 September 1998: see SI 1998/2327, art 2(1)(g).

Sub-s (2): in para (p) words "racially or religiously aggravated" in square brackets substituted by the Anti-terrorism, Crime and Security Act 2001, s 39(8).

Date in force: 14 December 2001 (except in relation to anything done before that date): see the Anti-terrorism, Crime and Security Act 2001, ss 42, 127(2)(a).

Sub-s (2): para (q) (as originally inserted by the Crime and Disorder Act 1998, s 84(2)) substituted by the Football (Disorder) Act 2000, s 1, Sch 2, para 2.

Date in force: 28 August 2000: see the Football (Disorder) Act 2000, s 5(1), and SI 2000/2125, art 2.

Sub-s (2): para (qa) inserted by the Criminal Justice and Police Act 2001, s 12(6).

Date in force: 1 September 2001: see SI 2001/2223, art 4(a).

Sub-s (2): para (r) inserted by the Football (Offences and Disorder) Act 1999, s 8(3).

Date in force: 27 September 1999, except in relation to offences committed, or orders made before that date: see the Football (Offences and Disorder) Act 1999, s 12(2), (3).

Sub-s (2): para (r) repealed by the Football (Disorder) Act 2000, s 1, Sch 2, para 2, Sch 3.

Date in force: 28 August 2000: see the Football (Disorder) Act 2000, s 5(1), and SI 2000/2125, art 2.

Sub-s (2): paras (s), (t) inserted by the Countryside and Rights of Way Act 2000, s 81(1), Sch 12, para 13.

Date in force: 30 January 2001: see the Countryside and Rights of Way Act 2000, s 103(2).

Sub-s (2): paras (u), (v) inserted by the Anti-terrorism, Crime and Security Act 2001, s 82(1).

Date in force: 14 February 2002 (in relation to an offence committed or alleged to have been committed after that date): see the Anti-terrorism, Crime and Security Act 2001, ss 82(4), 127(2)(c).

Sub-s (3): in para (b) words in square brackets inserted by the Criminal Justice Act 1988, s 170(1), Sch 15, paras 97, 98.

25 General arrest conditions

(1) Where a constable has reasonable grounds for suspecting that any offence which is not an arrestable offence has been committed or attempted, or is being committed or attempted, he may arrest the relevant person if it appears to him that service of a summons is impracticable or inappropriate because any of the general arrest conditions is satisfied.

(2) In this section "the relevant person" means any person whom the constable has reasonable grounds to suspect of having committed or having attempted to commit the offence or of being in the course of committing or attempting to commit it.

(3) The general arrest conditions are—

- (a) that the name of the relevant person is unknown to, and cannot be readily ascertained by, the constable;
- (b) that the constable has reasonable grounds for doubting whether a name furnished by the relevant person as his name is his real name;
- (c) that—

(i) the relevant person has failed to furnish a satisfactory address for service; or
(ii) the constable has reasonable grounds for doubting whether an address furnished by the relevant person is a satisfactory address for service;

(d) that the constable has reasonable grounds for believing that arrest is necessary to prevent the relevant person—
(i) causing physical injury to himself or any other person;
(ii) suffering physical injury;
(iii) causing loss of or damage to property;
(iv) committing an offence against public decency; or
(v) causing an unlawful obstruction of the highway;

(e) that the constable has reasonable grounds for believing that arrest is necessary to protect a child or other vulnerable person from the relevant person.

(4) For the purposes of subsection (3) above an address is a satisfactory address for service if it appears to the constable—
(a) that the relevant person will be at it for a sufficiently long period for it to be possible to serve him with a summons; or
(b) that some other person specified by the relevant person will accept service of a summons for the relevant person at it.

(5) Nothing in subsection (3)(d) above authorises the arrest of a person under sub-paragraph (iv) of that paragraph except where members of the public going about their normal business cannot reasonably be expected to avoid the person to be arrested.

(6) This section shall not prejudice any power of arrest conferred apart from this section.

PART XI
MISCELLANEOUS AND SUPPLEMENTARY

120 Extent

(1) Subject to the following provisions of this section, this Act extends to England and Wales only.

(2) The following extend to Scotland only—
section 108(4) and (5);
section 110;
section 111;
section 112(1); and
section 119(2), so far as it relates to the provisions of the Pedlars Act 1871 repealed by Part VI of Schedule 7.

(3) The following extend to Northern Ireland only—
section 6(4), and
section 112(2).

(4) The following extend to England and Wales and Scotland—

section 6(1) and (2);
section 7;
section 83(2), so far as it relates to paragraph 8 of Schedule 4;
section 108(1) and (6);
section 109; and
section 119(2), so far as it relates to section 19 of the Pedlars Act 1871.

(5) The following extend to England and Wales, Scotland and Northern Ireland—
section 6(3);
[section 9(2A);]
section 83(2), so far as it relates to paragraph 7(1) of Schedule 4; and
section 114(1).

(6) So far as they relate to proceedings before courts-martial and Standing Civilian Courts, the relevant provisions extend to any place at which such proceedings may be held.

(7) So far as they relate to proceedings before the Courts-Martial Appeal Court, the relevant provisions extend to any place at which such proceedings may be held.

(8) In this section "the relevant provisions" means—
(a) subsection (11) of section 67 above;
(b) subsection (12) of that section so far as it relates to subsection (11);
(c) Parts VII and VIII of this Act, except paragraph 10 of Schedule 3;
(d) subsections (2) and (8) to (12) of section 113 above; and
(e) subsection (13) of that section, so far as it relates to an order under subsection (12).

(9) Except as provided by the foregoing provisions of this section, section 113 above extends to any place to which the Army Act 1955, the Air Force Act 1955 or the Naval Discipline Act 1957 extends.

[(9A)] Section 119(1), so far as it relates to any provision amended by Part II of Schedule 6, extends to any place to which that provision extends.

(10) Section 119(2), so far as it relates—
(a) to any provision contained in—
the Army Act 1955;
the Air Force Act 1955;
the Armed Forces Act 1981; or
the Value Added Tax Act 1983;
(b) to any provision mentioned in Part VI of Schedule 7, other than section 18 of the Pedlars Act 1871,

extends to any place to which that provision extends.

(11) So far as any of the following—
section 115;
in section 118, the definition of "document";
this section;
section 121; and
section 122,

has effect in relation to any other provision of this Act, it extends to any place to which that provision extends.

NOTES

Sub-s (5): words "section 9(2A);" in square brackets inserted by the Criminal Justice and Police Act 2001, s 86(2).

Date in force: 1 August 2001: see SI 2001/2223, art 3(e).

Sub-s (9A): renumbered as such by the Criminal Justice Act 1988, s 170(1), Sch 15, para 101.

122 Short title

This Act may be cited as the Police and Criminal Evidence Act 1984.

Companies Act 1985

1985 CHAPTER 6

An Act to consolidate the greater part of the Companies Acts

[11th March 1985]

PART I
FORMATION AND REGISTRATION OF COMPANIES; JURIDICAL STATUS AND MEMBERSHIP

Chapter I
Company Formation

Registration and its consequences

14 Effect of memorandum and articles

(1) Subject to the provisions of this Act, the memorandum and articles, when registered, bind the company and its members to the same extent as if they respectively had been signed and sealed by each member, and contained covenants on the part of each member to observe all the provisions of the memorandum and of the articles.

(2) Money payable by a member to the company under the memorandum or articles is a debt due from him to the company, and in England and Wales is of the nature of a specialty debt.

Chapter III
A Company's Capacity; Formalities of Carrying on Business

[35 A company's capacity not limited by its memorandum]

[(1) The validity of an act done by a company shall not be called into question on the ground of lack of capacity by reason of anything in the company's memorandum.

(2) A member of a company may bring proceedings to restrain the doing of an act which but for subsection (1) would be beyond the company's capacity; but no such proceedings shall lie in respect of an act to be done in fulfilment of a legal obligation arising from a previous act of the company.

(3) It remains the duty of the directors to observe any limitations on their powers flowing from the company's memorandum; and action by the directors which but for subsection (1) would be beyond the company's capacity may only be ratified by the company by special resolution.

A resolution ratifying such action shall not affect any liability incurred by the directors or any other person; relief from any such liability must be agreed to separately by special resolution.

(4) The operation of this section is restricted by [section 65(1) of the Charities Act 1993] and section 112(3) of the Companies Act 1989 in relation to companies which are charities; and section 322A below (invalidity of certain transactions to which directors or their associates are parties) has effect notwithstanding this section.]

NOTES

Substituted, together with ss 35A, 35B, for s 35 as originally enacted, by the Companies Act 1989, s 108(1).

Sub-s (4): words in square brackets substituted by the Charities Act 1993, s 98(1), Sch 6, para 20(2).

[35A Power of directors to bind the company]

[(1) In favour of a person dealing with a company in good faith, the power of the board of directors to bind the company, or authorise others to do so, shall be deemed to be free of any limitation under the company's constitution.

(2) For this purpose—
- (a) a person "deals with" a company if he is a party to any transaction or other act to which the company is a party;
- (b) a person shall not be regarded as acting in bad faith by reason only of his knowing that an act is beyond the powers of the directors under the company's constitution; and
- (c) a person shall be presumed to have acted in good faith unless the contrary is proved.

(3) The references above to limitations on the directors' powers under the company's constitution include limitations deriving—

(a) from a resolution of the company in general meeting or a meeting of any class of shareholders, or
(b) from any agreement between the members of the company or of any class of shareholders.

(4) Subsection (1) does not affect any right of a member of the company to bring proceedings to restrain the doing of an act which is beyond the powers of the directors; but no such proceedings shall lie in respect of an act to be done in fulfilment of a legal obligation arising from a previous act of the company.

(5) Nor does that subsection affect any liability incurred by the directors, or any other person, by reason of the directors' exceeding their powers.

(6) The operation of this section is restricted by [section 65(1) of the Charities Act 1993] and section 112(3) of the Companies Act 1989 in relation to companies which are charities; and section 322A below (invalidity of certain transactions to which directors or their associates are parties) has effect notwithstanding this section.]

NOTES

Substituted, together with new ss 35, 35B, for s 35 as originally enacted, by the Companies Act 1989, s 108.

Sub-s (6): words in square brackets substituted by the Charities Act 1993, s 98(1), Sch 6, para 20(2).

[35B No duty to enquire as to capacity of company or authority of directors]

[A party to a transaction with a company is not bound to enquire as to whether it is permitted by the company's memorandum or as to any limitation on the powers of the board of directors to bind the company or authorise others to do so.]

NOTES

Substituted, together with new ss 35, 35A, for s 35 as originally enacted, by the Companies Act 1989, s 108.

[36 Company contracts: England and Wales]

[Under the law of England and Wales a contract may be made—
(a) by a company, by writing under its common seal, or
(b) on behalf of a company, by any person acting under its authority, express or implied;

and any formalities required by law in the case of a contract made by an individual also apply, unless a contrary intention appears, to a contract made by or on behalf of a company.]

NOTES

Substituted by the Companies Act 1989, s 130(1).

[36A Execution of documents: England and Wales]

[(1) Under the law of England and Wales the following provisions have effect with respect to the execution of documents by a company.

(2) A document is executed by a company by the affixing of its common seal.

(3) A company need not have a common seal, however, and the following subsections apply whether it does or not.

(4) A document signed by a director and the secretary of a company, or by two directors of a company, and expressed (in whatever form of words) to be executed by the company has the same effect as if executed under the common seal of the company.

(5) A document executed by a company which makes it clear on its face that it is intended by the person or persons making it to be a deed has effect, upon delivery, as a deed; and it shall be presumed, unless a contrary intention is proved, to be delivered upon its being so executed.

(6) In favour of a purchaser a document shall be deemed to have been duly executed by a company if it purports to be signed by a director and the secretary of the company, or by two directors of the company, and, where it makes it clear on its face that it is intended by the person or persons making it to be a deed, to have been delivered upon its being executed.

A "purchaser" means a purchaser in good faith for valuable consideration and includes a lessee, mortgagee or other person who for valuable consideration acquires an interest in property.]

NOTES

Inserted by the Companies Act 1989, s 130(2).

[36B Execution of documents by companies]

[(1) Notwithstanding the provisions of any enactment, a company need not have a company seal.

(2) For the purposes of any enactment—

(a) providing for a document to be executed by a company by affixing its common seal; or

(b) referring (in whatever terms) to a document so executed,

a document signed or subscribed by or on behalf of the company in accordance with the provisions of the Requirements of Writing (Scotland) Act 1995 shall have effect as if so executed.

(3) In this section "enactment" includes an enactment contained in a statutory instrument.]

NOTES

Inserted by the Companies Act 1989, s 130(3).

Substituted by the Requirements of Writing (Scotland) Act 1995, s 14(1), Sch 4, para 51.

[36C Pre-incorporation contracts, deeds and obligations]

[(1) A contract which purports to be made by or on behalf of a company at a time when the company has not been formed has effect, subject to any agreement to the contrary, as one made with the person purporting to act for the company or as agent for it, and he is personally liable on the contract accordingly.

(2) Subsection (1) applies—

(a) to the making of a deed under the law of England and Wales, and

(b) to the undertaking of an obligation under the law of Scotland,

as it applies to the making of a contract.]

NOTES

Inserted by the Companies Act 1989, s 130(4).

PART XXVII

FINAL PROVISIONS

746 Commencement

. . . this Act comes into force on 1st July 1985.

NOTES

Words omitted repealed by the Companies Act 1989, s 212, Sch 24.

747 Citation

This Act may be cited as the Companies Act 1985.

Landlord and Tenant Act 1985

1985 CHAPTER 70

An Act to consolidate certain provisions of the law of landlord and tenant formerly found in the Housing Acts, together with the Landlord and Tenant Act 1962, with amendments to give effect to recommendations of the Law Commission

[30th October 1985]

Implied terms as to fitness for human habitation

8 Implied terms as to fitness for human habitation

(1) In a contract to which this section applies for the letting of a house for human habitation there is implied, notwithstanding any stipulation to the contrary—

(a) a condition that the house is fit for human habitation at the commencement of the tenancy, and

(b) an undertaking that the house will be kept by the landlord fit for human habitation during the tenancy.

(2) The landlord, or a person authorised by him in writing, may at reasonable times of the day, on giving 24 hours' notice in writing, to the tenant or occupier, enter premises to which this section applies for the purpose of viewing their state and condition.

(3)-(5) . . .

(6) In this section "house" includes—

(a) a part of a house, and

(b) any yard, garden, outhouses and appurtenances belonging to the house or usually enjoyed with it.

NOTES

Sub-ss (3)-(5): outside the scope of this work.

10 Fitness for human habitation

In determining for the purposes of this Act whether a house is unfit for human habitation, regard shall be had to its condition in respect of the following matters—

repair,
stability,
freedom from damp,
internal arrangement,
natural lighting,
ventilation,
water supply,
drainage and sanitary conveniences,
facilities for preparation and cooking of food and for the disposal of waste water;

and the house shall be regarded as unfit for human habitation if, and only if, it is so far defective in one or more of those matters that it is not reasonably suitable for occupation in that condition.

Final Provisions

40 Short title, commencement and extent

(1) This Act may be cited as the Landlord and Tenant Act 1985.

(2) This Act comes into force on 1st April 1986.

(3) This Act extends to England and Wales.

Latent Damage Act 1986

1986 CHAPTER 37

An Act to amend the law about limitation of actions in relation to actions for damages for negligence not involving personal injuries; and to provide for a person taking an interest in property to have, in certain circumstances, a cause of action in respect of negligent damage to the property occurring before he takes that interest

[18th July 1986]

Accrual of cause of action to successive owners in respect of latent damage to property

3 Accrual of cause of action to successive owners in respect of latent damage to property

(1) Subject to the following provisions of this section, where—
- (a) a cause of action ("the original cause of action") has accrued to any person in respect of any negligence to which damage to any property in which he has an interest is attributable (in whole or in part); and
- (b) another person acquires an interest in that property after the date on which the original cause of action accrued but before the material facts about the damage have become known to any person who, at the time when he first has knowledge of those facts, has any interest in the property;

a fresh cause of action in respect of that negligence shall accrue to that other person on the date on which he acquires his interest in the property.

(2) A cause of action accruing to any person by virtue of subsection (1) above—
- (a) shall be treated as if based on breach of a duty of care at common law owed to the person to whom it accrues; and
- (b) shall be treated for the purposes of section 14A of the 1980 Act (special time limit for negligence actions where facts relevant to cause of action are not known at date of accrual) as having accrued on the date on which the original cause of action accrued.

(3) Section 28 of the 1980 Act (extension of limitation period in case of disability) shall not apply in relation to any such cause of action.

(4) Subsection (1) above shall not apply in any case where the person acquiring an interest in the damaged property is either—
- (a) a person in whom the original cause of action vests by operation of law; or
- (b) a person in whom the interest in that property vests by virtue of any order made by a court under section 538 of the Companies Act 1985 (vesting of company property in liquidator).

(5) For the purposes of subsection (1)(*b*) above, the material facts about the damage are such facts about the damage as would lead a reasonable person who has

an interest in the damaged property at the time when those facts become known to him to consider it sufficiently serious to justify his instituting proceedings for damages against a defendant who did not dispute liability and was able to satisfy a judgment.

(6) For the purposes of this section a person's knowledge includes knowledge which he might reasonably have been expected to acquire—

(a) from facts observable or ascertainable by him; or

(b) from facts ascertainable by him with the help of appropriate expert advice which it is reasonable for him to seek;

but a person shall not be taken by virtue of this subsection to have knowledge of a fact ascertainable by him only with the help of expert advice so long as he has taken all reasonable steps to obtain (and, where appropriate, to act on) that advice.

(7) This section shall bind the Crown, but as regards the Crown's liability in tort shall not bind the Crown further than the Crown is made liable in tort by the Crown Proceedings Act 1947.

Supplementary

5 Citation, interpretation, commencement and extent

(1) This Act may be cited as the Latent Damage Act 1986.

(2) In this Act—

"the 1980 Act" has the meaning given by section 1; and

"action" includes any proceeding in a court of law, an arbitration and any new claim within the meaning of section 35 of the 1980 Act (new claims in pending actions).

(3) This Act shall come into force at the end of the period of two months beginning with the date on which it is passed.

(4) This Act extends to England and Wales only.

Minors' Contracts Act 1987

1987 CHAPTER 13

An Act to amend the law relating to minors' contracts

[9th April 1987]

2 Guarantees

Where—

(a) a guarantee is given in respect of an obligation of a party to a contract made after the commencement of this Act, and

(b) the obligation is unenforceable against him (or he repudiates the contract) because he was a minor when the contract was made,

the guarantee shall not for that reason alone be unenforceable against the guarantor.

3 Restitution

(1) Where—

(a) a person ("the plaintiff") has after the commencement of this Act entered into a contract with another ("the defendant"), and

(b) the contract is unenforceable against the defendant (or he repudiates it) because he was a minor when the contract was made,

the court may, if it is just and equitable to do so, require the defendant to transfer to the plaintiff any property acquired by the defendant under the contract, or any property representing it.

(2) Nothing in this section shall be taken to prejudice any other remedy available to the plaintiff.

5 Short title, commencement and extent

(1) This Act may be cited as the Minors' Contracts Act 1987.

(2) This Act shall come into force at the end of the period of two months beginning with the date on which it is passed.

(3) This Act extends to England and Wales only.

Crown Proceedings (Armed Forces) Act 1987

1987 CHAPTER 25

An Act to repeal section 10 of the Crown Proceedings Act 1947 and to provide for the revival of that section in certain circumstances

[15th May 1987]

1 Repeal of s 10 of the Crown Proceedings Act 1947

Subject to section 2 below, section 10 of the Crown Proceedings Act 1947 (exclusions from liability in tort in cases involving the armed forces) shall cease to have effect except in relation to anything suffered by a person in consequence of an act or omission committed before the date on which this Act is passed.

2 Revival of s 10

(1) Subject to the following provisions of this section, the Secretary of State may, at any time after the coming into force of section 1 above, by order—

(a) revive the effect of section 10 of the Crown Proceedings Act 1947 either for all purposes or for such purposes as may be described in the order; or

(b) where that section has effect for the time being in pursuance of an order made by virtue of paragraph (*a*) above, provide for that section to cease to have effect either for all of the purposes for which it so has effect or for such of them as may be so described.

(2) The Secretary of State shall not make an order reviving the effect of the said section 10 for any purposes unless it appears to him necessary or expedient to do so—

(a) by reason of any imminent national danger or of any great emergency that has arisen; or

(b) for the purposes of any warlike operations in any part of the world outside the United Kingdom or of any other operations which are or are to be carried out in connection with the warlike activity of any persons in any such part of the world.

(3) Subject to subsection (4) below, an order under this section describing purposes for which the effect of the said section 10 is to be revived, or for which that section is to cease to have effect, may describe those purposes by reference to any matter whatever and may make different provision for different cases, circumstances or persons.

(4) Nothing in any order under this section shall revive the effect of the said section 10, or provide for that section to cease to have effect, in relation to anything suffered by a person in consequence of an act or omission committed before the date on which the order comes into force.

(5) The power to make an order under this section shall be exercisable by statutory instrument subject to annulment in pursuance of a resolution of either House of Parliament.

5 Short title, interpretation and extent

(1) This Act may be cited as the Crown Proceedings (Armed Forces) Act 1987.

(2) For the purposes of the application of any provision of this Act in relation to subsection (2) of section 10 of the Crown Proceedings Act 1947 references in this Act to anything suffered by any person in consequence of an act or omission committed before a particular date shall include references to anything which—

(a) would not, apart from this subsection, be regarded as suffered in consequence of an act or omission; but

(b) is suffered in consequence of the nature or condition at a time before that date of any land, premises, ship, aircraft, hovercraft, or vehicle or of any equipment or supplies.

(3) This Act shall extend to Northern Ireland.

Consumer Protection Act 1987

1987 CHAPTER 43

An Act to make provision with respect to the liability of persons for damage caused by defective products; to consolidate with amendments the Consumer Safety Act 1978 and the Consumer Safety (Amendment) Act 1986; to make provision with respect to the giving of price indications; to amend Part I of the Health and Safety at Work etc Act 1974 and sections 31 and 80 of the Explosives Act 1875; to repeal the Trade Descriptions Act 1972 and the Fabrics (Misdescription) Act 1913; and for connected purposes

[15th May 1987]

PART I
PRODUCT LIABILITY

1 Purpose and construction of Part I

(1) This Part shall have effect for the purpose of making such provision as is necessary in order to comply with the product liability Directive and shall be construed accordingly.

(2) In this Part, except in so far as the context otherwise requires—

. . .

"dependant" and "relative" have the same meanings as they have in, respectively, the Fatal Accidents Act 1976 and the Damages (Scotland) Act 1976;

"producer", in relation to a product, means—

(a) the person who manufactured it;

(b) in the case of a substance which has not been manufactured but has been won or abstracted, the person who won or abstracted it;

(c) in the case of a product which has not been manufactured, won or abstracted but essential characteristics of which are attributable to an industrial or other process having been carried out (for example, in relation to agricultural produce), the person who carried out that process;

"product" means any goods or electricity and (subject to subsection (3) below) includes a product which is comprised in another product, whether by virtue of being a component part or raw material or otherwise; and

"the product liability Directive" means the Directive of the Council of the European Communities, dated 25th July 1985, (No 85/374/EEC) on the approximation of the laws, regulations and administrative provisions of the member States concerning liability for defective products.

(3) For the purposes of this Part a person who supplies any product in which products are comprised, whether by virtue of being component parts or raw materials or otherwise, shall not be treated by reason only of his supply of that product as supplying any of the products so comprised.

NOTES

Sub-s (2): definition "agricultural produce" (omitted) repealed in relation to England and Wales by SI 2000/2771, art 2(1), (2), and in relation to Scotland by SSI 2001/265, art 2(1), (2).

Date in force (in relation to England and Wales): 4 December 2000: see SI 2000/2771, art 1.

Date in force (in relation to Scotland): 19 July 2001: see SSI 2001/265, art 1(1).

2 Liability for defective products

(1) Subject to the following provisions of this Part, where any damage is caused wholly or partly by a defect in a product, every person to whom subsection (2) below applies shall be liable for the damage.

(2) This subsection applies to—
- (a) the producer of the product;
- (b) any person who, by putting his name on the product or using a trade mark or other distinguishing mark in relation to the product, has held himself out to be the producer of the product;
- (c) any person who has imported the product into a member State from a place outside the member States in order, in the course of any business of his, to supply it to another.

(3) Subject as aforesaid, where any damage is caused wholly or partly by a defect in a product, any person who supplied the product (whether to the person who suffered the damage, to the producer of any product in which the product in question is comprised or to any other person) shall be liable for the damage if—
- (a) the person who suffered the damage requests the supplier to identify one or more of the persons (whether still in existence or not) to whom subsection (2) above applies in relation to the product;
- (b) that request is made within a reasonable period after the damage occurs and at a time when it is not reasonably practicable for the person making the request to identify all those persons; and
- (c) the supplier fails, within a reasonable period after receiving the request, either to comply with the request or to identify the person who supplied the product to him.

(4) . . .

(5) Where two or more persons are liable by virtue of this Part for the same damage, their liability shall be joint and several.

(6) This section shall be without prejudice to any liability arising otherwise than by virtue of this Part.

NOTES

Sub-s (4): repealed in relation to England and Wales by SI 2000/2771, art 2(1), (3), and in relation to Scotland by SSI 2001/265, art 2(1), (3).

Date in force (in relation to England and Wales): 4 December 2000: see SI 2000/2771, art 1.

Date in force (in relation to Scotland): 19 July 2001: see SSI 2001/265, art 1.

3 Meaning of "defect"

(1) Subject to the following provisions of this section, there is a defect in a product for the purposes of this Part if the safety of the product is not such as persons generally are entitled to expect; and for those purposes "safety", in relation to a product, shall include safety with respect to products comprised in that product and safety in the context of risks of damage to property, as well as in the context of risks of death or personal injury.

(2) In determining for the purposes of subsection (1) above what persons generally are entitled to expect in relation to a product all the circumstances shall be taken into account, including—

- (a) the manner in which, and purposes for which, the product has been marketed, its get-up, the use of any mark in relation to the product and any instructions for, or warnings with respect to, doing or refraining from doing anything with or in relation to the product;
- (b) what might reasonably be expected to be done with or in relation to the product; and
- (c) the time when the product was supplied by its producer to another;

and nothing in this section shall require a defect to be inferred from the fact alone that the safety of a product which is supplied after that time is greater than the safety of the product in question.

4 Defences

(1) In any civil proceedings by virtue of this Part against any person ("the person proceeded against") in respect of a defect in a product it shall be a defence for him to show—

- (a) that the defect is attributable to compliance with any requirement imposed by or under any enactment or with any Community obligation; or
- (b) that the person proceeded against did not at any time supply the product to another; or
- (c) that the following conditions are satisfied, that is to say—
  - (i) that the only supply of the product to another by the person proceeded against was otherwise than in the course of a business of that person's; and
  - (ii) that section 2(2) above does not apply to that person or applies to him by virtue only of things done otherwise than with a view to profit; or
- (d) that the defect did not exist in the product at the relevant time; or
- (e) that the state of scientific and technical knowledge at the relevant time was not such that a producer of products of the same description as the product in question might be expected to have discovered the defect if it had existed in his products while they were under his control; or
- (f) that the defect—

(i) constituted a defect in a product ("the subsequent product") in which the product in question had been comprised; and

(ii) was wholly attributable to the design of the subsequent product or to compliance by the producer of the product in question with instructions given by the producer of the subsequent product.

(2) In this section "the relevant time", in relation to electricity, means the time at which it was generated, being a time before it was transmitted or distributed, and in relation to any other product, means—

(a) if the person proceeded against is a person to whom subsection (2) of section 2 above applies in relation to the product, the time when he supplied the product to another;

(b) if that subsection does not apply to that person in relation to the product, the time when the product was last supplied by a person to whom that subsection does apply in relation to the product.

5 Damage giving rise to liability

(1) Subject to the following provisions of this section, in this Part "damage" means death or personal injury or any loss of or damage to any property (including land).

(2) A person shall not be liable under section 2 above in respect of any defect in a product for the loss of or any damage to the product itself or for the loss of or any damage to the whole or any part of any product which has been supplied with the product in question comprised in it.

(3) A person shall not be liable under section 2 above for any loss of or damage to any property which, at the time it is lost or damaged, is not—

(a) of a description of property ordinarily intended for private use, occupation or consumption; and

(b) intended by the person suffering the loss or damage mainly for his own private use, occupation or consumption.

(4) No damages shall be awarded to any person by virtue of this Part in respect of any loss of or damage to any property if the amount which would fall to be so awarded to that person, apart from this subsection and any liability for interest, does not exceed £275.

(5) In determining for the purposes of this Part who has suffered any loss of or damage to property and when any such loss or damage occurred, the loss or damage shall be regarded as having occurred at the earliest time at which a person with an interest in the property had knowledge of the material facts about the loss or damage.

(6) For the purposes of subsection (5) above the material facts about any loss of or damage to any property are such facts about the loss or damage as would lead a reasonable person with an interest in the property to consider the loss or damage sufficiently serious to justify his instituting proceedings for damages against a defendant who did not dispute liability and was able to satisfy a judgment.

(7) For the purposes of subsection (5) above a person's knowledge includes knowledge which he might reasonably have been expected to acquire—

(a) from facts observable or ascertainable by him; or

(b) from facts ascertainable by him with the help of appropriate expert advice which it is reasonable for him to seek;

but a person shall not be taken by virtue of this subsection to have knowledge of a fact ascertainable by him only with the help of expert advice unless he has failed to take all reasonable steps to obtain (and, where appropriate, to act on) that advice.

(8) Subsections (5) to (7) above shall not extend to Scotland.

6 Application of certain enactments

(1) Any damage for which a person is liable under section 2 above shall be deemed to have been caused—

(a) for the purposes of the Fatal Accidents Act 1976, by that person's wrongful act, neglect or default;

(b) for the purposes of section 3 of the Law Reform (Miscellaneous Provisions) (Scotland) Act 1940 (contribution among joint wrongdoers), by that person's wrongful act or negligent act or omission;

(c) for the purposes of section 1 of the Damages (Scotland) Act 1976 (rights of relatives of a deceased), by that person's act or omission; and

(d) for the purposes of Part II of the Administration of Justice Act 1982 (damages for personal injuries, etc Scotland), by an act or omission giving rise to liability in that person to pay damages.

(2) Where—

(a) a person's death is caused wholly or partly by a defect in a product, or a person dies after suffering damage which has been so caused;

(b) a request such as mentioned in paragraph (a) of subsection (3) of section 2 above is made to a supplier of the product by that person's personal representatives or, in the case of a person whose death is caused wholly or partly by the defect, by any dependant or relative of that person; and

(c) the conditions specified in paragraphs (b) and (c) of that subsection are satisfied in relation to that request,

this Part shall have effect for the purposes of the Law Reform (Miscellaneous Provisions) Act 1934, the Fatal Accidents Act 1976 and the Damages (Scotland) Act 1976 as if liability of the supplier to that person under that subsection did not depend on that person having requested the supplier to identify certain persons or on the said conditions having been satisfied in relation to a request made by that person.

(3) Section 1 of the Congenital Disabilities (Civil Liability) Act 1976 shall have effect for the purposes of this Part as if—

(a) a person were answerable to a child in respect of an occurrence caused wholly or partly by a defect in a product if he is or has been liable under section 2 above in respect of any effect of the occurrence on a parent of the child, or would be so liable if the occurrence caused a parent of the child to suffer damage;

(b) the provisions of this Part relating to liability under section 2 above applied in relation to liability by virtue of paragraph (a) above under the said section 1; and

(c) subsection (6) of the said section 1 (exclusion of liability) were omitted.

(4) Where any damage is caused partly by a defect in a product and partly by the fault of the person suffering the damage, the Law Reform (Contributory Negligence) Act 1945 and section 5 of the Fatal Accidents Act 1976 (contributory negligence) shall have effect as if the defect were the fault of every person liable by virtue of this Part for the damage caused by the defect.

(5) In subsection (4) above "fault" has the same meaning as in the said Act of 1945.

(6) Schedule 1 to this Act shall have effect for the purpose of amending the Limitation Act 1980 and the Prescription and Limitation (Scotland) Act 1973 in their application in relation to the bringing of actions by virtue of this Part.

(7) It is hereby declared that liability by virtue of this Part is to be treated as liability in tort for the purposes of any enactment conferring jurisdiction on any court with respect to any matter.

(8) Nothing in this Part shall prejudice the operation of section 12 of the Nuclear Installations Act 1965 (rights to compensation for certain breaches of duties confined to rights under that Act).

7 Prohibition on exclusions from liability

The liability of a person by virtue of this Part to a person who has suffered damage caused wholly or partly by a defect in a product, or to a dependant or relative of such a person, shall not be limited or excluded by any contract term, by any notice or by any other provision.

8 Power to modify Part I

(1) Her Majesty may by Order in Council make such modifications of this Part and of any other enactment (including an enactment contained in the following Parts of this Act, or in an Act passed after this Act) as appear to Her Majesty in Council to be necessary or expedient in consequence of any modification of the product liability Directive which is made at any time after the passing of this Act.

(2) An Order in Council under subsection (1) above shall not be submitted to Her Majesty in Council unless a draft of the Order has been laid before, and approved by a resolution of, each House of Parliament.

9 Application of Part I to Crown

(1) Subject to subsection (2) below, this Part shall bind the Crown.

(2) The Crown shall not, as regards the Crown's liability by virtue of this Part, be bound by this Part further than the Crown is made liable in tort or in reparation under the Crown Proceedings Act 1947, as that Act has effect from time to time.

PART II
CONSUMER SAFETY

10 The general safety requirement

(1) A person shall be guilty of an offence if he—
   (a) supplies any consumer goods which fail to comply with the general safety requirement;
   (b) offers or agrees to supply any such goods; or
   (c) exposes or possesses any such goods for supply.

(2) For the purposes of this section consumer goods fail to comply with the general safety requirement if they are not reasonably safe having regard to all the circumstances, including—
   (a) the manner in which, and purposes for which, the goods are being or would be marketed, the get-up of the goods, the use of any mark in relation to the goods and any instructions or warnings which are given or would be given with respect to the keeping, use or consumption of the goods;
   (b) any standards of safety published by any person either for goods of a description which applies to the goods in question or for matters relating to goods of that description; and
   (c) the existence of any means by which it would have been reasonable (taking into account the cost, likelihood and extent of any improvement) for the goods to have been made safer.

(3) For the purposes of this section consumer goods shall not be regarded as failing to comply with the general safety requirement in respect of—
   (a) anything which is shown to be attributable to compliance with any requirement imposed by or under any enactment or with any Community obligation;
   (b) any failure to do more in relation to any matter than is required by—
      (i) any safety regulations imposing requirements with respect to that matter;
      (ii) . . .
      (iii) any provision of any enactment or subordinate legislation imposing such requirements with respect to that matter as are designated for the purposes of this subsection by any such regulations.

(4) In any proceedings against any person for an offence under this section in respect of any goods it shall be a defence for that person to show—
   (a) that he reasonably believed that the goods would not be used or consumed in the United Kingdom; or
   (b) that the following conditions are satisfied, that is to say—

(i) that he supplied the goods, offered or agreed to supply them or, as the case may be, exposed or possessed them for supply in the course of carrying on a retail business; and

(ii) that, at the time he supplied the goods or offered or agreed to supply them or exposed or possessed them for supply, he neither knew nor had reasonable grounds for believing that the goods failed to comply with the general safety requirement; or

(c) that the terms on which he supplied the goods or agreed or offered to supply them or, in the case of goods which he exposed or possessed for supply, the terms on which he intended to supply them—

(i) indicated that the goods were not supplied or to be supplied as new goods; and

(ii) provided for, or contemplated, the acquisition of an interest in the goods by the persons supplied or to be supplied.

(5) For the purposes of subsection (4)(b) above goods are supplied in the course of carrying on a retail business if—

(a) whether or not they are themselves acquired for a person's private use or consumption, they are supplied in the course of carrying on a business of making a supply of consumer goods available to persons who generally acquire them for private use or consumption; and

(b) the descriptions of goods the supply of which is made available in the course of that business do not, to a significant extent, include manufactured or imported goods which have not previously been supplied in the United Kingdom.

(6) A person guilty of an offence under this section shall be liable on summary conviction to imprisonment for a term not exceeding six months or to a fine not exceeding level 5 on the standard scale or to both.

(7) In this section "consumer goods" means any goods which are ordinarily intended for private use or consumption, not being—

(a) growing crops or things comprised in land by virtue of being attached to it;

(b) water, food, feeding stuff or fertiliser;

(c) gas which is, is to be or has been supplied by a person authorised to supply it by or under [section 7A of the Gas Act 1986 (licensing of gas suppliers and gas shippers) or *paragraph 5 of Schedule 2A to that Act (supply to very large customers an exception to prohibition on unlicensed activities)*] [or under Article 8(1)(c) of the Gas (Northern Ireland) Order 1996];

(d) aircraft (other than hang-gliders) or motor vehicles;

(e) controlled drugs or licensed medicinal products;

(f) tobacco.

NOTES

Sub-s (3): para (b)(ii) repealed by SI 1994/2328, reg 6(1).

Sub-s (7): in para (c) words from "section 7A of" to "on unlicensed activities" in square brackets substituted by the Gas Act 1995, s 16(1), Sch 4, para 15(1).

Sub-s (7): in para (c) words from "paragraph 5 of" to "on unlicensed activities)" in italics repealed by the Utilities Act 2000, s 108, Sch 8.

Date in force: to be appointed: see the Utilities Act 2000, s 110(2).

Sub-s (7): in para (c) words "or under Article 8(1)(c) of the Gas (Northern Ireland) Order 1996" in square brackets inserted by the Gas (Northern Ireland) Order 1996, SI 1996/275, art 71(1), Sch 6.

11 Safety regulations

(1) The Secretary of State may by regulations under this section ("safety regulations") make such provision as he considers appropriate for the purposes of section 10(3) above and for the purpose of securing—

- (a) that goods to which this section applies are safe;
- (b) that goods to which this section applies which are unsafe, or would be unsafe in the hands of persons of a particular description, are not made available to persons generally or, as the case may be, to persons of that description; and
- (c) that appropriate information is, and inappropriate information is not, provided in relation to goods to which this section applies.

(2) Without prejudice to the generality of subsection (1) above, safety regulations may contain provision—

- (a) with respect to the composition or contents, design, construction, finish or packing of goods to which this section applies, with respect to standards for such goods and with respect to other matters relating to such goods;
- (b) with respect to the giving, refusal, alteration or cancellation of approvals of such goods, of descriptions of such goods or of standards for such goods;
- (c) with respect to the conditions that may be attached to any approval given under the regulations;
- (d) for requiring such fees as may be determined by or under the regulations to be paid on the giving or alteration of any approval under the regulations and on the making of an application for such an approval or alteration;
- (e) with respect to appeals against refusals, alterations and cancellations of approvals given under the regulations and against the conditions contained in such approvals;
- (f) for requiring goods to which this section applies to be approved under the regulations or to conform to the requirements of the regulations or to descriptions or standards specified in or approved by or under the regulations;
- (g) with respect to the testing or inspection of goods to which this section applies (including provision for determining the standards to be applied in carrying out any test or inspection);
- (h) with respect to the ways of dealing with goods of which some or all do not satisfy a test required by or under the regulations or a standard connected with a procedure so required;
- (i) for requiring a mark, warning or instruction or any other information relating to goods to be put on or to accompany the goods or to be used or provided in some other manner in relation to the goods, and for securing that inappropriate information is not given in relation to goods either by means of misleading marks or otherwise;

(j) for prohibiting persons from supplying, or from offering to supply, agreeing to supply, exposing for supply or possessing for supply, goods to which this section applies and component parts and raw materials for such goods;

(k) for requiring information to be given to any such person as may be determined by or under the regulations for the purpose of enabling that person to exercise any function conferred on him by the regulations.

(3) Without prejudice as aforesaid, safety regulations may contain provision—

(a) for requiring persons on whom functions are conferred by or under section 27 below to have regard, in exercising their functions so far as relating to any provision of safety regulations, to matters specified in a direction issued by the Secretary of State with respect to that provision;

(b) for securing that a person shall not be guilty of an offence under section 12 below unless it is shown that the goods in question do not conform to a particular standard;

(c) for securing that proceedings for such an offence are not brought in England and Wales except by or with the consent of the Secretary of State or the Director of Public Prosecutions;

(d) for securing that proceedings for such an offence are not brought in Northern Ireland except by or with the consent of the Secretary of State or the Director of Public Prosecutions for Northern Ireland;

(e) for enabling a magistrates' court in England and Wales or Northern Ireland to try an information or, in Northern Ireland, a complaint in respect of such an offence if the information was laid or the complaint made within twelve months from the time when the offence was committed;

(f) for enabling summary proceedings for such an offence to be brought in Scotland at any time within twelve months from the time when the offence was committed; and

(g) for determining the persons by whom, and the manner in which, anything required to be done by or under the regulations is to be done.

(4) Safety regulations shall not provide for any contravention of the regulations to be an offence.

(5) Where the Secretary of State proposes to make safety regulations it shall be his duty before he makes them—

(a) to consult such organisations as appear to him to be representative of interests substantially affected by the proposal;

(b) to consult such other persons as he considers appropriate; and

(c) in the case of proposed regulations relating to goods suitable for use at work, to consult the Health and Safety Commission in relation to the application of the proposed regulations to Great Britain;

but the preceding provisions of this subsection shall not to apply in the case of regulations which provide for the regulations to cease to have effect at the end of a period of not more than twelve months beginning with the day on which they come into force and which contain a statement that it appears to the Secretary of State that the need to protect the public requires that the regulations should be made without delay.

(6) The power to make safety regulations shall be exercisable by statutory instrument subject to annulment in pursuance of a resolution of either House of Parliament and shall include power—

(a) to make different provision for different cases; and

(b) to make such supplemental, consequential and transitional provision as the Secretary of State considers appropriate.

(7) This section applies to any goods other than—

(a) growing crops and things comprised in land by virtue of being attached to it;

(b) water, food, feeding stuff and fertiliser;

(c) gas which is, is to be or has been supplied by a person authorised to supply it by or under [section 7A of the Gas Act 1986 (licensing of gas suppliers and gas shippers) *or paragraph 5 of Schedule 2A to that Act (supply to very large customers an exception to prohibition on unlicensed activities)*] [or under Article 8(1)(c) of the Gas (Northern Ireland) Order 1996];

(d) controlled drugs and licensed medicinal products.

NOTES

Sub-s (7): in para (c) words from "section 7A of" to "on unlicensed activities)" in square brackets substituted by the Gas Act 1995, s 16(1), Sch 4, para 15(2).

Sub-s (7): in para (c) words from "or paragraph 5" to "on unlicenced activities)" in italics repealed by the Utilities Act 2000, s 108, Sch 8.

Date in force: to be appointed: see the Utilities Act 2000, s 110(2).

Sub-s (7): in para (c) words "or under Article 8(1)(c) of the Gas (Northern Ireland) Order 1996" in square brackets inserted by the Gas (Northern Ireland) Order 1996, SI 1996/275, art 71(1), Sch 6.

12 Offences against the safety regulations

(1) Where safety regulations prohibit a person from supplying or offering or agreeing to supply any goods or from exposing or possessing any goods for supply, that person shall be guilty of an offence if he contravenes the prohibition.

(2) Where safety regulations require a person who makes or processes any goods in the course of carrying on a business—

(a) to carry out a particular test or use a particular procedure in connection with the making or processing of the goods with a view to ascertaining whether the goods satisfy any requirements of such regulations; or

(b) to deal or not to deal in a particular way with a quantity of the goods of which the whole or part does not satisfy such a test or does not satisfy standards connected with such a procedure,

that person shall be guilty of an offence if he does not comply with the requirement.

(3) If a person contravenes a provision of safety regulations which prohibits or requires the provision, by means of a mark or otherwise, of information of a particular kind in relation to goods, he shall be guilty of an offence.

(4) Where safety regulations require any person to give information to another for the purpose of enabling that other to exercise any function, that person shall be guilty of an offence if—

(a) he fails without reasonable cause to comply with the requirement; or

(b) in giving the information which is required of him—
   (i) he makes any statement which he knows is false in a material particular; or
   (ii) he recklessly makes any statement which is false in a material particular.

(5) A person guilty of an offence under this section shall be liable on summary conviction to imprisonment for a term not exceeding six months or to a fine not exceeding level 5 on the standard scale or to both.

13 Prohibition notices and notices to warn

(1) The Secretary of State may—

(a) serve on any person a notice ("a prohibition notice") prohibiting that person, except with the consent of the Secretary of State, from supplying, or from offering to supply, agreeing to supply, exposing for supply or possessing for supply, any relevant goods which the Secretary of State considers are unsafe and which are described in the notice;

(b) serve on any person a notice ("a notice to warn") requiring that person at his own expense to publish, in a form and manner and on occasions specified in the notice, a warning about any relevant goods which the Secretary of State considers are unsafe, which that person supplies or has supplied and which are described in the notice.

(2) Schedule 2 to this Act shall have effect with respect to prohibition notices and notices to warn; and the Secretary of State may by regulations make provision specifying the manner in which information is to be given to any person under that Schedule.

(3) A consent given by the Secretary of State for the purposes of a prohibition notice may impose such conditions on the doing of anything for which the consent is required as the Secretary of State considers appropriate.

(4) A person who contravenes a prohibition notice or a notice to warn shall be guilty of an offence and liable on summary conviction to imprisonment for a term not exceeding six months or to a fine not exceeding level 5 on the standard scale or to both.

(5) The power to make regulations under subsection (2) above shall be exercisable by statutory instrument subject to annulment in pursuance of a resolution of either House of Parliament and shall include power—

(a) to make different provision for different cases; and

(b) to make such supplemental, consequential and transitional provision as the Secretary of State considers appropriate.

(6) In this section "relevant goods" means—

(a) in relation to a prohibition notice, any goods to which section 11 above applies; and

(b) in relation to a notice to warn, any goods to which that section applies or any growing crops or things comprised in land by virtue of being attached to it.

14 Suspension notices

(1) Where an enforcement authority has reasonable grounds for suspecting that any safety provision has been contravened in relation to any goods, the authority may serve a notice ("a suspension notice") prohibiting the person on whom it is served, for such period ending not more than six months after the date of the notice as is specified therein, from doing any of the following things without the consent of the authority, that is to say, supplying the goods, offering to supply them, agreeing to supply them or exposing them for supply.

(2) A suspension notice served by an enforcement authority in respect of any goods shall—

(a) describe the goods in a manner sufficient to identify them;
(b) set out the grounds on which the authority suspects that a safety provision has been contravened in relation to the goods; and
(c) state that, and the manner in which, the person on whom the notice is served may appeal against the notice under section 15 below.

(3) A suspension notice served by an enforcement authority for the purpose of prohibiting a person for any period from doing the things mentioned in subsection (1) above in relation to any goods may also require that person to keep the authority informed of the whereabouts throughout that period of any of those goods in which he has an interest.

(4) Where a suspension notice has been served on any person in respect of any goods, no further such notice shall be served on that person in respect of the same goods unless—

(a) proceedings against that person for an offence in respect of a contravention in relation to the goods of a safety provision (not being an offence under this section); or
(b) proceedings for the forfeiture of the goods under section 16 or 17 below,

are pending at the end of the period specified in the first-mentioned notice.

(5) A consent given by an enforcement authority for the purposes of subsection (1) above may impose such conditions on the doing of anything for which the consent is required as the authority considers appropriate.

(6) Any person who contravenes a suspension notice shall be guilty of an offence and liable on summary conviction to imprisonment for a term not exceeding six months or to a fine not exceeding level 5 on the standard scale or to both.

(7) Where an enforcement authority serves a suspension notice in respect of any goods, the authority shall be liable to pay compensation to any person having an interest in the goods in respect of any loss or damage caused by reason of the service of the notice if—

(a) there has been no contravention in relation to the goods of any safety provision; and
(b) the exercise of the power is not attributable to any neglect or default by that person.

(8) Any disputed question as to the right to or the amount of any compensation payable under this section shall be determined by arbitration or, in Scotland, by a single arbiter appointed, failing agreement between the parties, by the sheriff.

15 Appeals against suspension notices

(1) Any person having an interest in any goods in respect of which a suspension notice is for the time being in force may apply for an order setting aside the notice.

(2) An application under this section may be made—
- (a) to any magistrates' court in which proceedings have been brought in England and Wales or Northern Ireland—
  - (i) for an offence in respect of a contravention in relation to the goods of any safety provision; or
  - (ii) for the forfeiture of the goods under section 16 below;
- (b) where no such proceedings have been so brought, by way of complaint to a magistrates' court; or
- (c) in Scotland, by summary application to the sheriff.

(3) On an application under this section to a magistrates' court in England and Wales or Northern Ireland the court shall make an order setting aside the suspension notice only if the court is satisfied that there has been no contravention in relation to the goods of any safety provision.

(4) On an application under this section to the sheriff he shall make an order setting aside the suspension notice only if he is satisfied that at the date of making the order—
- (a) proceedings for an offence in respect of a contravention in relation to the goods of any safety provision; or
- (b) proceedings for the forfeiture of the goods under section 17 below,

have not been brought or, having been brought, have been concluded.

(5) Any person aggrieved by an order made under this section by a magistrates' court in England and Wales or Northern Ireland, or by a decision of such a court not to make such an order, may appeal against that order or decision—
- (a) in England and Wales, to the Crown Court;
- (b) in Northern Ireland, to the county court;

and an order so made may contain such provision as appears to the court to be appropriate for delaying the coming into force of the order pending the making and determination of any appeal (including any application under section 111 of the Magistrates' Courts Act 1980 or Article 146 of the Magistrates' Courts (Northern Ireland) Order 1981 (statement of case)).

16 Forfeiture: England and Wales and Northern Ireland

(1) An enforcement authority in England and Wales or Northern Ireland may apply under this section for an order for the forfeiture of any goods on the grounds that there has been a contravention in relation to the goods of a safety provision.

(2) An application under this section may be made—

(a) where proceedings have been brought in a magistrates' court for an offence in respect of a contravention in relation to some or all of the goods of any safety provision, to that court;
(b) where an application with respect to some or all of the goods has been made to a magistrates' court under section 15 above or section 33 below, to that court; and
(c) where no application for the forfeiture of the goods has been made under paragraph (a) or (b) above, by way of complaint to a magistrates' court.

(3) On an application under this section the court shall make an order for the forfeiture of any goods only if it is satisfied that there has been a contravention in relation to the goods of a safety provision.

(4) For the avoidance of doubt it is declared that a court may infer for the purposes of this section that there has been a contravention in relation to any goods of a safety provision if it is satisfied that any such provision has been contravened in relation to goods which are representative of those goods (whether by reason of being of the same design or part of the same consignment or batch or otherwise).

(5) Any person aggrieved by an order made under this section by a magistrates' court, or by a decision of such a court not to make such an order, may appeal against that order or decision—
(a) in England and Wales, to the Crown Court;
(b) in Northern Ireland, to the county court;

and an order so made may contain such provision as appears to the court to be appropriate for delaying the coming into force of the order pending the making and determination of any appeal (including any application under section 111 of the Magistrates' Courts Act 1980 or Article 146 of the Magistrates' Courts (Northern Ireland) Order 1981 (statement of case)).

(6) Subject to subsection (7) below, where any goods are forfeited under this section they shall be destroyed in accordance with such directions as the court may give.

(7) On making an order under this section a magistrates' court may, if it considers it appropriate to do so, direct that the goods to which the order relates shall (instead of being destroyed) be released, to such person as the court may specify, on condition that that person—
(a) does not supply those goods to any person otherwise than as mentioned in section 46(7)(a) or (b) below; and
(b) complies with any order to pay costs or expenses (including any order under section 35 below) which has been made against that person in the proceedings for the order for forfeiture.

18 Power to obtain information

(1) If the Secretary of State considers that, for the purpose of deciding whether—
(a) to make, vary or revoke any safety regulations; or
(b) to serve, vary or revoke a prohibition notice; or
(c) to serve or revoke a notice to warn,

he requires information which another person is likely to be able to furnish, the Secretary of State may serve on the other person a notice under this section.

(2) A notice served on any person under this section may require that person—
- (a) to furnish to the Secretary of State, within a period specified in the notice, such information as is so specified;
- (b) to produce such records as are specified in the notice at a time and place so specified and to permit a person appointed by the Secretary of State for the purpose to take copies of the records at that time and place.

(3) A person shall be guilty of an offence if he—
- (a) fails, without reasonable cause, to comply with a notice served on him under this section; or
- (b) in purporting to comply with a requirement which by virtue of paragraph (a) of subsection (2) above is contained in such a notice—
  - (i) furnishes information which he knows is false in a material particular; or
  - (ii) recklessly furnishes information which is false in a material particular.

(4) A person guilty of an offence under subsection (3) above shall—
- (a) in the case of an offence under paragraph (a) of that subsection, be liable on summary conviction to a fine not exceeding level 5 on the standard scale; and
- (b) in the case of an offence under paragraph (b) of that subsection be liable—
  - (i) on conviction on indictment, to a fine;
  - (ii) on summary conviction, to a fine not exceeding the statutory maximum.

19 Interpretation of Part II

(1) In this Part—

"controlled drug" means a controlled drug within the meaning of the Misuse of Drugs Act 1971;

"feeding stuff" and "fertiliser" have the same meanings as in Part IV of the Agriculture Act 1970;

"food" does not include anything containing tobacco but, subject to that, has the same meaning as in the [Food Safety Act 1990] or, in relation to Northern Ireland, the same meaning as in the [Food Safety (Northern Ireland) Order 1991];

"licensed medicinal product" means—
- (a) any medicinal product within the meaning of the Medicines Act 1968 in respect of which a product licence within the meaning of that Act is for the time being in force; or
- (b) any other article or substance in respect of which any such licence is for the time being in force in pursuance of an order under section 104 or 105 of that Act (application of Act to other articles and substances);

"safe", in relation to any goods, means such that there is no risk, or no risk apart from one reduced to a minimum, that any of the following will (whether immediately or after a definite or indefinite period) cause the death of, or any personal injury to, any person whatsoever, that is to say—

(a) the goods;
(b) the keeping, use or consumption of the goods;
(c) the assembly of any of the goods which are, or are to be, supplied unassembled;
(d) any emission or leakage from the goods or, as a result of the keeping, use or consumption of the goods, from anything else; or
(e) reliance on the accuracy of any measurement, calculation or other reading made by or by means of the goods,

and "safer" and "unsafe" shall be construed accordingly;

"tobacco" includes any tobacco product within the meaning of the Tobacco Products Duty Act 1979 and any article or substance containing tobacco and intended for oral or nasal use.

(2) In the definition of "safe" in subsection (1) above, references to the keeping, use or consumption of any goods are references to—

(a) the keeping, use or consumption of the goods by the persons by whom, and in all or any of the ways or circumstances in which, they might reasonably be expected to be kept, used or consumed; and
(b) the keeping, use or consumption of the goods either alone or in conjunction with other goods in conjunction with which they might reasonably be expected to be kept, used or consumed.

NOTES

Sub-s (1): in definition "food" first words in square brackets substituted by the Food Safety Act 1990, s 59(1), Sch 3, para 37, second words in square brackets substituted by the Food Safety (Northern Ireland) Order 1991, SI 1991/762, art 51(1), Sch 2, para 17.

PART III

MISLEADING PRICE INDICATIONS

20 Offence of giving misleading indication

(1) Subject to the following provisions of this Part, a person shall be guilty of an offence if, in the course of any business of his, he gives (by any means whatever) to any consumers an indication which is misleading as to the price at which any goods, services, accommodation or facilities are available (whether generally or from particular persons).

(2) Subject as aforesaid, a person shall be guilty of an offence if—

(a) in the course of any business of his, he has given an indication to any consumer which, after it was given, has become misleading as mentioned in subsection (1) above; and
(b) some or all of those consumers might reasonably be expected to rely on the indication at a time after it has become misleading; and
(c) he fails to take all such steps as are reasonable to prevent those consumers from relying on the indication.

(3) For the purposes of this section it shall be immaterial—

(a) whether the person who gives or gave the indication is or was acting on his own behalf or on behalf of another;

(b) whether or not that person is the person, or included among the persons, from whom the goods, services, accommodation or facilities are available; and

(c) whether the indication is or has become misleading in relation to all the consumers to whom it is or was given or only in relation to some of them.

(4) A person guilty of an offence under subsection (1) or (2) above shall be liable—

(a) on conviction on indictment, to a fine;

(b) on summary conviction, to a fine not exceeding the statutory maximum.

(5) No prosecution for an offence under subsection (1) or (2) above shall be brought after whichever is the earlier of the following, that is to say—

(a) the end of the period of three years beginning with the day on which the offence was committed; and

(b) the end of the period of one year beginning with the day on which the person bringing the prosecution discovered that the offence had been committed.

[(5A) A person is not guilty of an offence under subsection (1) or (2) above if, in giving the misleading indication which would otherwise constitute an offence under either of those subsections, he is guilty of an offence under section 397 of the Financial Services and Markets Act 2000 (misleading statements and practices).]

(6) In this Part—

"consumer"—

(a) in relation to any goods, means any person who might wish to be supplied with the goods for his own private use or consumption;

(b) in relation to any services or facilities, means any person who might wish to be provided with the services or facilities otherwise than for the purposes of any business of his; and

(c) in relation to any accommodation, means any person who might wish to occupy the accommodation otherwise than for the purposes of any business of his;

"price", in relation to any goods, services, accommodation or facilities, means—

(a) the aggregate of the sums required to be paid by a consumer for or otherwise in respect of the supply of the goods or the provision of the services, accommodation or facilities; or

(b) except in section 21 below, any method which will be or has been applied for the purpose of determining that aggregate.

NOTES

Sub-s (5A): inserted by SI 2001/3649, art 309.

Date in force: 1 December 2001: see SI 2001/3649, art 1.

21 Meaning of "misleading"

(1) For the purposes of section 20 above an indication given to any consumers is misleading as to a price if what is conveyed by the indication, or what those consumers might reasonably be expected to infer from the indication or any omission from it, includes any of the following, that is to say—

(a) that the price is less than in fact it is;
(b) that the applicability of the price does not depend on facts or circumstances on which its applicability does in fact depend;
(c) that the price covers matters in respect of which an additional charge is in fact made;
(d) that a person who in fact has no such expectation—
  (i) expects the price to be increased or reduced (whether or not at a particular time or by a particular amount); or
  (ii) expects the price, or the price as increased or reduced, to be maintained (whether or not for a particular period); or
(e) that the facts or circumstances by reference to which the consumers might reasonably be expected to judge the validity of any relevant comparison made or implied by the indication are not what in fact they are.

(2) For the purposes of section 20 above, an indication given to any consumers is misleading as to a method of determining a price if what is conveyed by the indication, or what those consumers might reasonably be expected to infer from the indication or any omission from it, includes any of the following, that is to say—
(a) that the method is not what in fact it is;
(b) that the applicability of the method does not depend on facts or circumstances on which its applicability does in fact depend;
(c) that the method takes into account matters in respect of which an additional charge will in fact be made;
(d) that a person who in fact has no such expectation—
  (i) expects the method to be altered (whether or not at a particular time or in a particular respect); or
  (ii) expects the method, or that method as altered, to remain unaltered (whether or not for a particular period); or
(e) that the facts or circumstances by reference to which the consumers might reasonably be expected to judge the validity of any relevant comparison made or implied by the indication are not what in fact they are.

(3) For the purposes of subsections (1)(e) and (2)(e) above a comparison is a relevant comparison in relation to a price or method of determining a price if it is made between that price or that method, or any price which has been or may be determined by that method, and—
(a) any price or value which is stated or implied to be, to have been or to be likely to be attributed or attributable to the goods, services, accommodation or facilities in question or to any other goods, services, accommodation or facilities; or
(b) any method, or other method, which is stated or implied to be, to have been or to be likely to be applied or applicable for the determination of the price or value of the goods, services, accommodation or facilities in question or of the price or value of any other goods, services, accommodation or facilities.

22 Application to provision of services and facilities

(1) Subject to the following provisions of this section, references in this Part to services or facilities are references to any services or facilities whatever including, in particular—

(a) the provision of credit or of banking or insurance services and the provision of facilities incidental to the provision of such services;
(b) the purchase or sale of foreign currency;
(c) the supply of electricity;
(d) the provision of a place, other than on a highway, for the parking of a motor vehicle;
(e) the making of arrangements for a person to put or keep a caravan on any land other than arrangements by virtue of which that person may occupy the caravan as his only or main residence.

(2) References in this Part to services shall not include references to services provided to an employer under a contract of employment.

(3) . . .

(4) In relation to a service consisting in the purchase or sale of foreign currency, references in this Part to the method by which the price of the service is determined shall include references to the rate of exchange.

(5) In this section—

. . .

"caravan" has the same meaning as in the Caravan Sites and Control of Development Act 1960;

"contract of employment" and "employer" have the same meanings as in [the Employment Rights Act 1996];

"credit" has the same meaning as in the Consumer Credit Act 1974.

NOTES

Sub-s (3): repealed by SI 2001/3649, art 310(1), (2).

Date in force: 1 December 2001: see SI 2001/3649, art 1.

Sub-s (5): definition ""appointed representative", "authorised person" and "investment business"" (omitted) repealed by SI 2001/3649, art 310(1), (3).

Date in force: 1 December 2001: see SI 2001/3649, art 1.

Sub-s (5): in definition ""contract of employment" and "employer"" words "the Employment Rights Act 1996" in square brackets substituted by the Employment Rights Act 1996, s 240, Sch 1, para 34.

23 Application to provision of accommodation etc

(1) Subject to subsection (2) below, references in this Part to accommodation or facilities being available shall not include references to accommodation or facilities being available to be provided by means of the creation or disposal of an interest in land except where—

(a) the person who is to create or dispose of the interest will do so in the course of any business of his; and
(b) the interest to be created or disposed of is a relevant interest in a new dwelling and is to be created or disposed of for the purpose of enabling that

dwelling to be occupied as a residence, or one of the residences, of the person acquiring the interest.

(2) Subsection (1) above shall not prevent the application of any provision of this Part in relation to—

- (a) the supply of any goods as part of the same transaction as any creation or disposal of an interest in land; or
- (b) the provision of any services or facilities for the purposes of, or in connection with, any transaction for the creation or disposal of such an interest.

(3) In this section—

"new dwelling" means any building or part of a building in Great Britain which—

- (a) has been constructed or adapted to be occupied as a residence; and
- (b) has not previously been so occupied or has been so occupied only with other premises or as more than one residence,

and includes any yard, garden, out-houses or appurtenances which belong to that building or part or are to be enjoyed with it;

"relevant interest"—

- (a) in relation to a new dwelling in England and Wales, means the freehold estate in the dwelling or a leasehold interest in the dwelling for a term of years absolute of more than twenty-one years, not being a term of which twenty-one years or less remains unexpired;
- (b) in relation to a new dwelling in Scotland, means the *dominium utile* [ownership] of the land comprising the dwelling, or a leasehold interest in the dwelling where twenty-one years or more remains unexpired.

NOTES

Sub-s (3): in para (b) of definition "relevant interest" words "dominium utile" repealed and subsequent word in square brackets substituted by the Abolition of Feudal Tenure etc (Scotland) Act 2000, s 76(1), Sch 12, para 49.

Date in force: to be appointed: see the Abolition of Feudal Tenure etc (Scotland) Act 2000, ss 71, 77(2).

24 Defences

(1) In any proceedings against a person for an offence under subsection (1) or (2) of section 20 above in respect of any indication it shall be a defence for that person to show that his acts or omissions were authorised for the purposes of this subsection by regulations made under section 26 below.

(2) In proceedings against a person for an offence under subsection (1) or (2) of section 20 above in respect of an indication published in a book, newspaper, magazine [or film or in a programme included in a programme service (within the meaning of the Broadcasting Act 1990),] it shall be a defence for that person to show that the indication was not contained in an advertisement.

(3) In proceedings against a person for an offence under subsection (1) or (2) of section 20 above in respect of an indication published in an advertisement it shall be a defence for that person to show that—

(a) he is a person who carries on a business of publishing or arranging for the publication of advertisements;
(b) he received the advertisement for publication in the ordinary course of that business; and
(c) at the time of publication he did not know and had no grounds for suspecting that the publication would involve the commission of the offence.

(4) In any proceedings against a person for an offence under subsection (1) of section 20 above in respect of any indication, it shall be a defence for that person to show that—
(a) the indication did not relate to the availability from him of any goods, services, accommodation or facilities;
(b) a price had been recommended to every person from whom the goods, services, accommodation or facilities were indicated as being available;
(c) the indication related to that price and was misleading as to that price only by reason of a failure by any person to follow the recommendation; and
(d) it was reasonable for the person who gave the indication to assume that the recommendation was for the most part being followed.

(5) The provisions of this section are without prejudice to the provisions of section 39 below.

(6) In this section—
"advertisement" includes a catalogue, a circular and a price list;
. . .

NOTES

Sub-s (2): words in square brackets substituted by the Broadcasting Act 1990, s 203(1), Sch 20, para 48.

Sub-s (6): definition omitted repealed by the Broadcasting Act 1990, s 203(1), (3), Sch 20, para 48, Sch 21.

25 Code of practice

(1) The Secretary of State may, after consulting the Director General of Fair Trading and such other persons as the Secretary of State considers it appropriate to consult, by order approve any code of practice issued (whether by the Secretary of State or another person) for the purpose of—
(a) giving practical guidance with respect to any of the requirements of section 20 above; and
(b) promoting what appear to the Secretary of State to be desirable practices as to the circumstances and manner in which any person gives an indication as to the price at which any goods, services, accommodation or facilities are available or indicates any other matter in respect of which any such indication may be misleading.

(2) A contravention of a code of practice approved under this section shall not of itself give rise to any criminal or civil liability, but in any proceedings against any person for an offence under section 20(1) or (2) above—

(a) any contravention by that person of such a code may be relied on in relation to any matter for the purpose of establishing that that person committed the offence or of negativing any defence; and
(b) compliance by that person with such a code may be relied on in relation to any matter for the purpose of showing that the commission of the offence by that person has not been established or that that person has a defence.

(3) Where the Secretary of State approves a code of practice under this section he may, after such consultation as is mentioned in subsection (1) above, at any time by order—
(a) approve any modification of the code; or
(b) withdraw his approval;

and references in subsection (2) above to a code of practice approved under this section shall be construed accordingly.

(4) The power to make an order under this section shall be exercisable by statutory instrument subject to annulment in pursuance of a resolution of either House of Parliament.

26 Power to make regulations

(1) The Secretary of State may, after consulting the Director General of Fair Trading and such other persons as the Secretary of State considers it appropriate to consult, by regulations make provision—
(a) for the purpose of regulating the circumstances and manner in which any person—
  (i) gives any indication as to the price at which any goods, services, accommodation or facilities will be or are available or have been supplied or provided; or
  (ii) indicates any other matter in respect of which any such indication may be misleading;
(b) for the purpose of facilitating the enforcement of the provisions of section 20 above or of any regulations made under this section.

(2) The Secretary of State shall not make regulations by virtue of subsection (1)(a) above except in relation to—
(a) indications given by persons in the course of business; and
(b) such indications given otherwise than in the course of business as—
  (i) are given by or on behalf of persons by whom accommodation is provided to others by means of leases or licences; and
  (ii) relate to goods, services or facilities supplied or provided to those others in connection with the provision of the accommodation.

(3) Without prejudice to the generality of subsection (1) above, regulations under this section may—
(a) prohibit an indication as to a price from referring to such matters as may be prescribed by the regulations;
(b) require an indication as to a price or other matter to be accompanied or supplemented by such explanation or such additional information as may be prescribed by the regulations;

(c) require information or explanations with respect to a price or other matter to be given to an officer of an enforcement authority and to authorise such an officer to require such information or explanations to be given;
(d) require any information or explanation provided for the purposes of any regulations made by virtue of paragraph (b) or (c) above to be accurate;
(e) prohibit the inclusion in indications as to a price or other matter of statements that the indications are not to be relied upon;
(f) provide that expressions used in any indication as to a price or other matter shall be construed in a particular way for the purposes of this Part;
(g) provide that a contravention of any provision of the regulations shall constitute a criminal offence punishable—
 (i) on conviction on indictment, by a fine;
 (ii) on summary conviction, by a fine not exceeding the statutory maximum;
(h) apply any provision of this Act which relates to a criminal offence to an offence created by virtue of paragraph (g) above.

(4) The power to make regulations under this section shall be exercisable by statutory instrument subject to annulment in pursuance of a resolution of either House of Parliament and shall include power—
(a) to make different provision for different cases; and
(b) to make such supplemental, consequential and transitional provision as the Secretary of State considers appropriate.

(5) In this section "lease" includes a sub-lease and an agreement for a lease and a statutory tenancy (within the meaning of the Landlord and Tenant Act 1985 or the Rent (Scotland) Act 1984).

PART IV
ENFORCEMENT OF PARTS II AND III

27 Enforcement

(1) Subject to the following provisions of this section—
(a) it shall be the duty of every weights and measures authority in Great Britain to enforce within their area the safety provisions and the provisions made by or under Part III of this Act; and
(b) it shall be the duty of every district council in Northern Ireland to enforce within their area the safety provisions.

(2) The Secretary of State may by regulations—
(a) wholly or partly transfer any duty imposed by subsection (1) above on a weights and measures authority or a district council in Northern Ireland to such other person who has agreed to the transfer as is specified in the regulations;
(b) relieve such an authority or council of any such duty so far as it is exercisable in relation to such goods as may be described in the regulations.

(3) The power to make regulations under subsection (2) above shall be exercisable by statutory instrument subject to annulment in pursuance of a resolution of either House of Parliament and shall include power—

(a) to make different provision for different cases; and
(b) to make such supplemental, consequential and transitional provision as the Secretary of State considers appropriate.

(4) Nothing in this section shall authorise any weights and measures authority, or any person on whom functions are conferred by regulations under subsection (2) above, to bring proceedings in Scotland for an offence.

28 Test purchases

(1) An enforcement authority shall have power, for the purpose of ascertaining whether any safety provision or any provision made by or under Part III of this Act has been contravened in relation to any goods, services, accommodation or facilities—
(a) to make, or to authorise an officer of the authority to make, any purchase of any goods; or
(b) to secure, or to authorise an officer of the authority to secure, the provision of any services, accommodation or facilities.

(2) Where—
(a) any goods purchased under this section by or on behalf of an enforcement authority are submitted to a test; and
(b) the test leads to—
(i) the bringing of proceedings for an offence in respect of a contravention in relation to the goods of any safety provision or of any provision made by or under Part III of this Act or for the forfeiture of the goods under section 16 or 17 above; or
(ii) the serving of a suspension notice in respect of any goods; and
(c) the authority is requested to do so and it is practicable for the authority to comply with the request,

the authority shall allow the person from whom the goods were purchased or any person who is a party to the proceedings or has an interest in any goods to which the notice relates to have the goods tested.

(3) The Secretary of State may by regulations provide that any test of goods purchased under this section by or on behalf of an enforcement authority shall—
(a) be carried out at the expense of the authority in a manner and by a person prescribed by or determined under the regulations; or
(b) be carried out either as mentioned in paragraph (a) above or by the authority in a manner prescribed by the regulations.

(4) The power to make regulations under subsection (3) above shall be exercisable by statutory instrument subject to annulment in pursuance of a resolution of either House of Parliament and shall include power—
(a) to make different provision for different cases; and
(b) to make such supplemental, consequential and transitional provision as the Secretary of State considers appropriate.

(5) Nothing in this section shall authorise the acquisition by or on behalf of an enforcement authority of any interest in land.

29 Powers of search etc

(1) Subject to the following provisions of this Part, a duly authorised officer of an enforcement authority may at any reasonable hour and on production, if required, of his credentials exercise any of the powers conferred by the following provisions of this section.

(2) The officer may, for the purposes of ascertaining whether there has been any contravention of any safety provision or of any provision made by or under Part III of this Act, inspect any goods and enter any premises other than premises occupied only as a person's residence.

(3) The officer may, for the purpose of ascertaining whether there has been any contravention of any safety provision, examine any procedure (including any arrangements for carrying out a test) connected with the production of any goods.

(4) If the officer has reasonable grounds for suspecting that any goods are manufactured or imported goods which have not been supplied in the United Kingdom since they were manufactured or imported he may—

- (a) for the purpose of ascertaining whether there has been any contravention of any safety provision in relation to the goods, require any person carrying on a business, or employed in connection with a business, to produce any records relating to the business;
- (b) for the purpose of ascertaining (by testing or otherwise) whether there has been any such contravention, seize and detain the goods;
- (c) take copies of, or of any entry in, any records produced by virtue of paragraph (a) above.

(5) If the officer has reasonable grounds for suspecting that there has been a contravention in relation to any goods of any safety provision or of any provision made by or under Part III of this Act, he may—

- (a) for the purpose of ascertaining whether there has been any such contravention, require any person carrying on a business, or employed in connection with a business, to produce any records relating to the business;
- (b) for the purpose of ascertaining (by testing or otherwise) whether there has been any such contravention, seize and detain the goods;
- (c) take copies of, or of any entry in, any records produced by virtue of paragraph (a) above.

(6) The officer may seize and detain—

- (a) any goods or records which he has reasonable grounds for believing may be required as evidence in proceedings for an offence in respect of a contravention of any safety provision or of any provision made by or under Part III of this Act;
- (b) any goods which he has reasonable grounds for suspecting may be liable to be forfeited under section 16 or 17 above.

(7) If and to the extent that it is reasonably necessary to do so to prevent a contravention of any safety provision or of any provision made by or under Part III of this Act, the officer may, for the purpose of exercising his power under subsection (4), (5) or (6) above to seize any goods or records—

(a) require any person having authority to do so to open any container or to open any vending machine; and
(b) himself open or break open any such container or machine where a requirement made under paragraph (a) above in relation to the container or machine has not been complied with.

30 Provisions supplemental to s 29

(1) An officer seizing any goods or records under section 29 above shall inform the following persons that the goods or records have been so seized, that is to say—
(a) the person from whom they are seized; and
(b) in the case of imported goods seized on any premises under the control of the Commissioners of Customs and Excise, the importer of those goods (within the meaning of the Customs and Excise Management Act 1979).

(2) If a justice of the peace—
(a) is satisfied by any written information on oath that there are reasonable grounds for believing either—
(i) that any goods or records which any officer has power to inspect under section 29 above are on any premises and that their inspection is likely to disclose evidence that there has been a contravention of any safety provision or of any provision made by or under Part III of this Act; or
(ii) that such a contravention has taken place, is taking place or is about to take place on any premises; and
(b) is also satisfied by any such information either—
(i) that admission to the premises has been or is likely to be refused and that notice of intention to apply for a warrant under this subsection has been given to the occupier; or
(ii) that an application for admission, or the giving of such a notice, would defeat the object of the entry or that the premises are unoccupied or that the occupier is temporarily absent and it might defeat the object of the entry to await his return,

the justice may by warrant under his hand, which shall continue in force for a period of one month, authorise any officer of an enforcement authority to enter the premises, if need be by force.

(3) An officer entering any premises by virtue of section 29 above or a warrant under subsection (2) above may take with him such other persons and such equipment as may appear to him necessary.

(4) On leaving any premises which a person is authorised to enter by a warrant under subsection (2) above, that person shall, if the premises are unoccupied or the occupier is temporarily absent, leave the premises as effectively secured against trespassers as he found them.

(5) If any person who is not an officer of an enforcement authority purports to act as such under section 29 above or this section he shall be guilty of an offence and liable on summary conviction to a fine not exceeding level 5 on the standard scale.

(6) Where any goods seized by an officer under section 29 above are submitted to a test, the officer shall inform the persons mentioned in subsection (1) above of the result of the test and, if—

(a) proceedings are brought for an offence in respect of a contravention in relation to the goods of any safety provision or of any provision made by or under Part III of this Act or for the forfeiture of the goods under section 16 or 17 above, or a suspension notice is served in respect of any goods; and

(b) the officer is requested to do so and it is practicable to comply with the request,

the officer shall allow any person who is a party to the proceedings or, as the case may be, has an interest in the goods to which the notice relates to have the goods tested.

(7) The Secretary of State may by regulations provide that any test of goods seized under section 29 above by an officer of an enforcement authority shall—

(a) be carried out at the expense of the authority in a manner and by a person prescribed by or determined under the regulations; or

(b) be carried out either as mentioned in paragraph (a) above or by the authority in a manner prescribed by the regulations.

(8) The power to make regulations under subsection (7) above shall be exercisable by statutory instrument subject to annulment in pursuance of a resolution of either House of Parliament and shall include power—

(a) to make different provision for different cases; and

(b) to make such supplemental, consequential and transitional provision as the Secretary of State considers appropriate.

(9) In the application of this section to Scotland, the reference in subsection (2) above to a justice of the peace shall include a reference to a sheriff and the references to written information on oath shall be construed as references to evidence on oath.

(10) In the application of this section to Northern Ireland, the references in subsection (2) above to any information on oath shall be construed as references to any complaint on oath.

31 Power of customs officer to detain goods

(1) A customs officer may, for the purpose of facilitating the exercise by an enforcement authority or officer of such an authority of any functions conferred on the authority or officer by or under Part II of this Act, or by or under this Part in its application for the purposes of the safety provisions, seize any imported goods and detain them for not more than two working days.

(2) Anything seized and detained under this section shall be dealt with during the period of its detention in such manner as the Commissioners of Customs and Excise may direct.

(3) In subsection (1) above the reference to two working days is a reference to a period of forty-eight hours calculated from the time when the goods in question are seized but disregarding so much of any period as falls on a Saturday or Sunday or

on Christmas Day, Good Friday or a day which is a bank holiday under the Banking and Financial Dealings Act 1971 in the part of the United Kingdom where the goods are seized.

(4) In this section and section 32 below "customs officer" means any officer within the meaning of the Customs and Excise Management Act 1979.

32 Obstruction of authorised officer

(1) Any person who—
- (a) intentionally obstructs any officer of an enforcement authority who is acting in pursuance of any provision of this Part or any customs officer who is so acting; or
- (b) intentionally fails to comply with any requirement made of him by any officer of an enforcement authority under any provision of this Part; or
- (c) without reasonable cause fails to give any officer of an enforcement authority who is so acting any other assistance or information which the officer may reasonably require of him for the purposes of the exercise of the officer's functions under any provision of this Part,

shall be guilty of an offence and liable on summary conviction to a fine not exceeding level 5 on the standard scale.

(2) A person shall be guilty of an offence if, in giving any information which is required of him by virtue of subsection (1)(c) above—
- (a) he makes any statement which he knows is false in a material particular; or
- (b) he recklessly makes a statement which is false in a material particular.

(3) A person guilty of an offence under subsection (2) above shall be liable—
- (a) on conviction on indictment, to a fine;
- (b) on summary conviction, to a fine not exceeding the statutory maximum.

33 Appeals against detention of goods

(1) Any person having an interest in any goods which are for the time being detained under any provision of this Part by an enforcement authority or by an officer of such an authority may apply for an order requiring the goods to be released to him or to another person.

(2) An application under this section may be made—
- (a) to any magistrates' court in which proceedings have been brought in England and Wales or Northern Ireland—
  - (i) for an offence in respect of a contravention in relation to the goods of any safety provision or of any provision made by or under Part III of this Act; or
  - (ii) for the forfeiture of the goods under section 16 above;
- (b) where no such proceedings have been so brought, by way of complaint to a magistrates' court; or
- (c) in Scotland, by summary application to the sheriff.

(3) On an application under this section to a magistrates' court or to the sheriff, an order requiring goods to be released shall be made only if the court or sheriff is satisfied—

(a) that proceedings—

(i) for an offence in respect of a contravention in relation to the goods of any safety provision or of any provision made by or under Part III of this Act; or

(ii) for the forfeiture of the goods under section 16 or 17 above,

have not been brought or, having been brought, have been concluded without the goods being forfeited; and

(b) where no such proceedings have been brought, that more than six months have elapsed since the goods were seized.

(4) Any person aggrieved by an order made under this section by a magistrates' court in England and Wales or Northern Ireland, or by a decision of such a court not to make such an order, may appeal against that order or decision—

(a) in England and Wales, to the Crown Court;

(b) in Northern Ireland, to the county court;

and an order so made may contain such provision as appears to the court to be appropriate for delaying the coming into force of the order pending the making and determination of any appeal (including any application under section 111 of the Magistrates' Courts Act 1980 or Article 146 of the Magistrates' Courts (Northern Ireland) Order 1981 (statement of case)).

34 Compensation for seizure and detention

(1) Where an officer of an enforcement authority exercises any power under section 29 above to seize and detain goods, the enforcement authority shall be liable to pay compensation to any person having an interest in the goods in respect of any loss or damage caused by reason of the exercise of the power if—

(a) there has been no contravention in relation to the goods of any safety provision or of any provision made by or under Part III of this Act; and

(b) the exercise of the power is not attributable to any neglect or default by that person.

(2) Any disputed question as to the right to or the amount of any compensation payable under this section shall be determined by arbitration or, in Scotland, by a single arbiter appointed, failing agreement between the parties, by the sheriff.

35 Recovery of expenses of enforcement

(1) This section shall apply where a court—

(a) convicts a person of an offence in respect of a contravention in relation to any goods of any safety provision or of any provision made by or under Part III of this Act; or

(b) makes an order under section 16 or 17 above for the forfeiture of any goods.

(2) The court may (in addition to any other order it may make as to costs or expenses) order the person convicted or, as the case may be, any person having an

interest in the goods to reimburse an enforcement authority for any expenditure which has been or may be incurred by that authority—

(a) in connection with any seizure or detention of the goods by or on behalf of the authority; or
(b) in connection with any compliance by the authority with directions given by the court for the purposes of any order for the forfeiture of the goods.

PART V
MISCELLANEOUS AND SUPPLEMENTAL

36 Amendments of Part I of the Health and Safety at Work etc Act 1974

Part I of the Health and Safety at Work etc Act 1974 (which includes provision with respect to the safety of certain articles and substances) shall have effect with the amendments specified in Schedule 3 to this Act; and, accordingly, the general purposes of that Part of that Act shall include the purpose of protecting persons from the risks protection from which would not be afforded by virtue of that Part but for those amendments.

37 Power of Commissioners of Customs and Excise to disclose information

(1) If they think it appropriate to do so for the purpose of facilitating the exercise by any person to whom subsection (2) below applies of any functions conferred on that person by or under Part II of this Act, or by or under Part IV of this Act in its application for the purposes of the safety provisions, the Commissioners of Customs and Excise may authorise the disclosure to that person of any information obtained for the purposes of the exercise by the Commissioners of their functions in relation to imported goods.

(2) This subsection applies to an enforcement authority and to any officer of an enforcement authority.

(3) A disclosure of information made to any person under subsection (1) above shall be made in such manner as may be directed by the Commissioners of Customs and Excise and may be made through such persons acting on behalf of that person as may be so directed.

(4) Information may be disclosed to a person under subsection (1) above whether or not the disclosure of the information has been requested by or on behalf of that person.

38 Restrictions on disclosure of information

(1) Subject to the following provisions of this section, a person shall be guilty of an offence if he discloses any information—

(a) which was obtained by him in consequence of its being given to any person in compliance with any requirement imposed by safety regulations or regulations under section 26 above;

(b) which consists in a secret manufacturing process or a trade secret and was obtained by him in consequence of the inclusion of the information—
   (i) in written or oral representations made for the purposes of Part I or II of Schedule 2 to this Act; or
   (ii) in a statement of a witness in connection with any such oral representations;

(c) which was obtained by him in consequence of the exercise by the Secretary of State of the power conferred by section 18 above;

(d) which was obtained by him in consequence of the exercise by any person of any power conferred by Part IV of this Act; or

(e) which was disclosed to or through him under section 37 above.

(2) Subsection (1) above shall not apply to a disclosure of information if the information is publicised information or the disclosure is made—

(a) for the purpose of facilitating the exercise of a relevant person's functions under this Act or any enactment or subordinate legislation mentioned in subsection (3) below;

(b) for the purposes of compliance with a Community obligation; or

(c) in connection with the investigation of any criminal offence or for the purposes of any civil or criminal proceedings.

(3) The enactments and subordinate legislation referred to in subsection (2)(a) above are—

(a) the Trade Descriptions Act 1968;

(b) Parts II and III and section 125 of the Fair Trading Act 1973;

(c) the relevant statutory provisions within the meaning of Part I of the Health and Safety at Work etc Act 1974 or within the meaning of the Health and Safety at Work (Northern Ireland) Order 1978;

(d) the Consumer Credit Act 1974;

(e) . . .

(f) . . .

(g) the Estate Agents Act 1979;

(h) the Competition Act 1980;

(i) the Telecommunications Act 1984;

(j) the Airports Act 1986;

(k) the Gas Act 1986;

(l) any subordinate legislation made (whether before or after the passing of this Act) for the purpose of securing compliance with the Directive of the Council of the European Communities, dated 10th September 1984 (No 84/450/EEC) on the approximation of the laws, regulations and administrative provisions of the member States concerning misleading advertising;

[(m) the Electricity Act 1989;]

[(mm) Part IV of the Airports (Northern Ireland) Order 1994;]

[(n) the Electricity (Northern Ireland) Order 1992;]

[(nn) the Gas (Northern Ireland) Order 1996;]

[(o) the Railways Act 1993]

[(p) the Competition Act 1998]

[(q) Part I of the Transport Act 2000].

(4) In subsection (2)(a) above the reference to a person's functions shall include a reference to any function of making, amending or revoking any regulations or order.

(5) A person guilty of an offence under this section shall be liable—
  (a) on summary conviction, to a fine not exceeding the statutory maximum;
  (b) on conviction on indictment, to imprisonment for a term not exceeding two years or to a fine or to both.

(6) In this section—

"publicised information" means any information which has been disclosed in any civil or criminal proceedings or is or has been required to be contained in a warning published in pursuance of a notice to warn; and

"relevant person" means any of the following, that is to say—
  (a) a Minister of the Crown, Government department or Northern Ireland department;
  (b) the [Competition Commission], the Director General of Fair Trading, the Director General of Telecommunications or [the Gas and Electricity Markets Authority] [or the Director General of Electricity Supply for Northern Ireland] [or the Director General of Gas for Northern Ireland] [or the Rail Regulator];
  (c) the Civil Aviation Authority;
  (d) any weights and measures authority, any district council in Northern Ireland or any person on whom functions are conferred by regulations under section 27(2) above;
  (e) any person who is an enforcing authority for the purposes of Part I of the Health and Safety at Work etc Act 1974 or for the purposes of Part II of the Health and Safety at Work (Northern Ireland) Order 1978.

NOTES

Sub-s (3): paras (e), (f) repealed by the Competition Act 1998, s 74(1), (3), Sch 12, para 10(a), Sch 14, Pt I.

Date in force: 1 March 2000: see SI 2000/344, art 2, Schedule.

Sub-s (3): para (m) inserted by the Electricity Act 1989, s 112(1), Sch 16, para 36.

Sub-s (3): para (mm) inserted by the Airports (Northern Ireland) Order 1994, SI 1994/426, art 71(2), Sch 9, para 11.

Sub-s (3): para (n) inserted by the Electricity (Northern Ireland) Order 1992, SI 1992/231, art 95(1), Sch 12, para 31(a).

Sub-s (3): para (nn) inserted by the Gas (Northern Ireland) Order 1996, SI 1996/275, art 71(1), Sch 6.

Sub-s (3): para (o) inserted by the Railways Act 1993, s 152, Sch 12, para 26(2).

Sub-s (3): para (p) inserted by the Competition Act 1998, s 74(1), Sch 12, para 10(b).

Date in force: 11 January 1999: see SI 1998/3166, art 2, Schedule.

Sub-s (3): para (q) inserted by SI 2001/4050, art 2, Schedule, Pt IV, para 19.

Date in force: 21 December 2001: see SI 2001/4050, art 1.

Sub-s (6): in definition "relevant person" in para (b) words "Competition Commission" in square brackets substituted by SI 1999/506, art 22.

Date in force: 1 April 1999: see SI 1999/506, art 1.

Sub-s (6): in definition "relevant person" in para (b) words "the Gas and Electricity Markets Authority" in square brackets substituted (for words as originally inserted in part by the Electricity Act 1989, s 112(1), Sch 16, para 36) by virtue of the Utilities Act 2000, s 3(2).

Date in force: 20 December 2000: see SI 2000/3343, art 2, Schedule.

Sub-s (6): in definition "relevant person" in para (b) words "or the Director General of Electricity Supply for Northern Ireland" in square brackets inserted by SI 1992/231, art 95(1), Sch 12, para 31(b).

Sub-s (6): in definition "relevant person" in para (b) words "or the Director General of Gas for Northern Ireland" in square brackets inserted by the Gas (Northern Ireland) Order 1996, SI 1996/275, art 71(1), Sch 6.

Sub-s (6): in definition "relevant person" in para (b) words "or the Rail Regulator" in square brackets inserted by the Railways Act 1993, s 152, Sch 12, para 26(3).

39 Defence of due diligence

(1) Subject to the following provisions of this section, in proceedings against any person for an offence to which this section applies it shall be a defence for that person to show that he took all reasonable steps and exercised all due diligence to avoid committing the offence.

(2) Where in any proceedings against any person for such an offence the defence provided by subsection (1) above involves an allegation that the commission of the offence was due—

(a) to the act or default of another; or

(b) to reliance on information given by another,

that person shall not, without the leave of the court, be entitled to rely on the defence unless, not less than seven clear days before the hearing of the proceedings, he has served a notice under subsection (3) below on the person bringing the proceedings.

(3) A notice under this subsection shall give such information identifying or assisting in the identification of the person who committed the act or default or gave the information as is in the possession of the person serving the notice at the time he serves it.

(4) It is hereby declared that a person shall not be entitled to rely on the defence provided by subsection (1) above by reason of his reliance on information supplied by another, unless he shows that it was reasonable in all the circumstances for him to have relied on the information, having regard in particular—

(a) to the steps which he took, and those which might reasonably have been taken, for the purpose of verifying the information; and

(b) to whether he had any reason to disbelieve the information.

(5) This section shall apply to an offence under section 10, 12(1), (2) or (3), 13(4), 14(6) or 20(1) above.

40 Liability of persons other than principal offender

(1) Where the commission by any person of an offence to which section 39 above applies is due to an act or default committed by some other person in the course of any business of his, the other person shall be guilty of the offence and may be proceeded against and punished by virtue of this subsection whether or not proceedings are taken against the first-mentioned person.

(2) Where a body corporate is guilty of an offence under this Act (including where it is so guilty by virtue of subsection (1) above) in respect of any act or default

which is shown to have been committed with the consent or connivance of, or to be attributable to any neglect on the part of, any director, manager, secretary or other similar officer of the body corporate or any person who was purporting to act in any such capacity he, as well as the body corporate, shall be guilty of that offence and shall be liable to be proceeded against and punished accordingly.

(3) Where the affairs of a body corporate are managed by its members, subsection (2) above shall apply in relation to the acts and defaults of a member in connection with his functions of management as if he were a director of the body corporate.

41 Civil proceedings

(1) An obligation imposed by safety regulations shall be a duty owed to any person who may be affected by a contravention of the obligation and, subject to any provision to the contrary in the regulations and to the defences and other incidents applying to actions for breach of statutory duty, a contravention of any such obligation shall be actionable accordingly.

(2) This Act shall not be construed as conferring any other right of action in civil proceedings, apart from the right conferred by virtue of Part I of this Act, in respect of any loss or damage suffered in consequence of a contravention of a safety provision or of a provision made by or under Part III of this Act.

(3) Subject to any provision to the contrary in the agreement itself, an agreement shall not be void or unenforceable by reason only of a contravention of a safety provision or of a provision made by or under Part III of this Act.

(4) Liability by virtue of subsection (1) above shall not be limited or excluded by any contract term, by any notice or (subject to the power contained in subsection (1) above to limit or exclude it in safety regulations) by any other provision.

(5) Nothing in subsection (1) above shall prejudice the operation of section 12 of the Nuclear Installations Act 1965 (rights to compensation for certain breaches of duties confined to rights under that Act).

(6) In this section "damage" includes personal injury and death.

42 Reports etc

(1) It shall be the duty of the Secretary of State at least once in every five years to lay before each House of Parliament a report on the exercise during the period to which the report relates of the functions which under Part II of this Act, or under Part IV of this Act in its application for the purposes of the safety provisions, are exercisable by the Secretary of State, weights and measures authorities, district councils in Northern Ireland and persons on whom functions are conferred by regulations made under section 27(2) above.

(2) The Secretary of State may from time to time prepare and lay before each House of Parliament such other reports on the exercise of those functions as he considers appropriate.

(3) Every weights and measures authority, every district council in Northern Ireland and every person on whom functions are conferred by regulations under

subsection (2) of section 27 above shall, whenever the Secretary of State so directs, make a report to the Secretary of State on the exercise of the functions exercisable by that authority or council under that section or by that person by virtue of any such regulations.

(4) A report under subsection (3) above shall be in such form and shall contain such particulars as are specified in the direction of the Secretary of State.

(5) The first report under subsection (1) above shall be laid before each House of Parliament not more than five years after the laying of the last report under section 8(2) of the Consumer Safety Act 1978.

43 Financial provisions

(1) There shall be paid out of money provided by Parliament—

- (a) any expenses incurred or compensation payable by a Minister of the Crown or Government department in consequence of any provision of this Act; and
- (b) any increase attributable to this Act in the sums payable out of money so provided under any other Act.

(2) Any sums received by a Minister of the Crown or Government department by virtue of this Act shall be paid into the Consolidated Fund.

44 Service of documents etc

(1) Any document required or authorised by virtue of this Act to be served on a person may be so served—

- (a) by delivering it to him or by leaving it at his proper address or by sending it by post to him at that address; or
- (b) if the person is a body corporate, by serving it in accordance with paragraph (a) above on the secretary or clerk of that body; or
- (c) if the person is a partnership, by serving it in accordance with that paragraph on a partner or on a person having control or management of the partnership business.

(2) For the purposes of subsection (1) above, and for the purposes of section 7 of the Interpretation Act 1978 (which relates to the service of documents by post) in its application to that subsection, the proper address of any person on whom a document is to be served by virtue of this Act shall be his last known address except that—

- (a) in the case of service on a body corporate or its secretary or clerk, it shall be the address of the registered or principal office of the body corporate;
- (b) in the case of service on a partnership or a partner or a person having the control or management of a partnership business, it shall be the principal office of the partnership;

and for the purposes of this subsection the principal office of a company registered outside the United Kingdom or of a partnership carrying on business outside the United Kingdom is its principal office within the United Kingdom.

(3) The Secretary of State may by regulations make provision for the manner in which any information is to be given to any person under any provision of Part IV of this Act.

(4) Without prejudice to the generality of subsection (3) above regulations made by the Secretary of State may prescribe the person, or manner of determining the person, who is to be treated for the purposes of section 28(2) or 30 above as the person from whom any goods were purchased or seized where the goods were purchased or seized from a vending machine.

(5) The power to make regulations under subsection (3) or (4) above shall be exercisable by statutory instrument subject to annulment in pursuance of a resolution of either House of Parliament and shall include power—

- (a) to make different provision for different cases; and
- (b) to make such supplemental, consequential and transitional provision as the Secretary of State considers appropriate.

45 Interpretation

(1) In this Act, except in so far as the context otherwise requires—

"aircraft" includes gliders, balloons and hovercraft;

"business" includes a trade or profession and the activities of a professional or trade association or of a local authority or other public authority;

"conditional sale agreement", "credit-sale agreement" and "hire-purchase agreement" have the same meanings as in the Consumer Credit Act 1974 but as if in the definitions in that Act "goods" had the same meaning as in this Act;

"contravention" includes a failure to comply and cognate expressions shall be construed accordingly;

"enforcement authority" means the Secretary of State, any other Minister of the Crown in charge of a Government department, any such department and any authority, council or other person on whom functions under this Act are conferred by or under section 27 above;

"gas" has the same meaning as in Part I of the Gas Act 1986;

"goods" includes substances, growing crops and things comprised in land by virtue of being attached to it and any ship, aircraft or vehicle;

"information" includes accounts, estimates and returns;

"magistrates' court", in relation to Northern Ireland, means a court of summary jurisdiction;

. . .

"modifications" includes additions, alterations and omissions, and cognate expressions shall be construed accordingly;

"motor vehicle" has the same meaning as in [the Road Traffic Act 1988];

"notice" means a notice in writing;

"notice to warn" means a notice under section 13(1)(b) above;

"officer", in relation to an enforcement authority, means a person authorised in writing to assist the authority in carrying out its functions under or for the purposes of the enforcement of any of the safety provisions or of any of the provisions made by or under Part III of this Act;

"personal injury" includes any disease and any other impairment of a person's physical or mental condition;

"premises" includes any place and any ship, aircraft or vehicle;

"prohibition notice" means a notice under section 13(1)(a) above;

"records" includes any books or documents and any records in non-documentary form;

"safety provision" means the general safety requirement in section 10 above or any provision of safety regulations, a prohibition notice or a suspension notice;

"safety regulations" means regulations under section 11 above;

"ship" includes any boat and any other description of vessel used in navigation;

"subordinate legislation" has the same meaning as in the Interpretation Act 1978;

"substance" means any natural or artificial substance, whether in solid, liquid or gaseous form or in the form of a vapour, and includes substances that are comprised in or mixed with other goods;

"supply" and cognate expressions shall be construed in accordance with section 46 below;

"suspension notice" means a notice under section 14 above.

(2) Except in so far as the context otherwise requires, references in this Act to a contravention of a safety provision shall, in relation to any goods, include references to anything which would constitute such a contravention if the goods were supplied to any person.

(3) References in this Act to any goods in relation to which any safety provision has been or may have been contravened shall include references to any goods which it is not reasonably practicable to separate from any such goods.

(4) . . .

(5) In Scotland, any reference in this Act to things comprised in land by virtue of being attached to it is a reference to moveables which have become heritable by accession to heritable property.

NOTES

Sub-s (1): in definition "motor vehicle" words in square brackets substituted by the Road Traffic (Consequential Provisions) Act 1988, s 4, Sch 3, para 35; definitions omitted repealed by the Trade Marks Act 1994, s 106(2), Sch 5.

Sub-s (4): repealed by the Trade Marks Act 1994, s 106(2), Sch 5.

46 Meaning of "supply"

(1) Subject to the following provisions of this section, references in this Act to supplying goods shall be construed as references to doing any of the following, whether as principal or agent, that is to say—

(a) selling, hiring out or lending the goods;
(b) entering into a hire-purchase agreement to furnish the goods;
(c) the performance of any contract for work and materials to furnish the goods;
(d) providing the goods in exchange for any consideration (including trading stamps) other than money;
(e) providing the goods in or in connection with the performance of any statutory function; or
(f) giving the goods as a prize or otherwise making a gift of the goods;

and, in relation to gas or water, those references shall be construed as including references to providing the service by which the gas or water is made available for use.

(2) For the purposes of any reference in this Act to supplying goods, where a person ("the ostensible supplier") supplies goods to another person ("the customer") under a hire-purchase agreement, conditional sale agreement or credit-sale agreement or under an agreement for the hiring of goods (other than a hire-purchase agreement) and the ostensible supplier—

- (a) carries on the business of financing the provision of goods for others by means of such agreements; and
- (b) in the course of that business acquired his interest in the goods supplied to the customer as a means of financing the provision of them for the customer by a further person ("the effective supplier"),

the effective supplier and not the ostensible supplier shall be treated as supplying the goods to the customer.

(3) Subject to subsection (4) below, the performance of any contract by the erection of any building or structure on any land or by the carrying out of any other building works shall be treated for the purposes of this Act as a supply of goods in so far as, but only in so far as, it involves the provision of any goods to any person by means of their incorporation into the building, structure or works.

(4) Except for the purposes of, and in relation to, notices to warn or any provision made by or under Part III of this Act, references in this Act to supplying goods shall not include references to supplying goods comprised in land where the supply is effected by the creation or disposal of an interest in the land.

(5) Except in Part I of this Act references in this Act to a person's supplying goods shall be confined to references to that person's supplying goods in the course of a business of his, but for the purposes of this subsection it shall be immaterial whether the business is a business of dealing in the goods.

(6) For the purposes of subsection (5) above goods shall not be treated as supplied in the course of a business if they are supplied, in pursuance of an obligation arising under or in connection with the insurance of the goods, to the person with whom they were insured.

(7) Except for the purposes of, and in relation to, prohibition notices or suspension notices, references in Parts II to IV of this Act to supplying goods shall not include—

- (a) references to supplying goods where the person supplied carries on a business of buying goods of the same description as those goods and repairing or reconditioning them;
- (b) references to supplying goods by a sale of articles as scrap (that is to say, for the value of materials included in the articles rather than for the value of the articles themselves).

(8) Where any goods have at any time been supplied by being hired out or lent to any person, neither a continuation or renewal of the hire or loan (whether on the same or different terms) nor any transaction for the transfer after that time of any

interest in the goods to the person to whom they were hired or lent shall be treated for the purposes of this Act as a further supply of the goods to that person.

(9) A ship, aircraft or motor vehicle shall not be treated for the purposes of this Act as supplied to any person by reason only that services consisting in the carriage of goods or passengers in that ship, aircraft or vehicle, or in its use for any other purpose, are provided to that person in pursuance of an agreement relating to the use of the ship, aircraft or vehicle for a particular period or for particular voyages, flights or journeys.

50 Short title, commencement and transitional provision

(1) This Act may be cited as the Consumer Protection Act 1987.

(2) This Act shall come into force on such day as the Secretary of State may by order made by statutory instrument appoint, and different days may be so appointed for different provisions or for different purposes.

(3) The Secretary of State shall not make an order under subsection (2) above bringing into force the repeal of the Trade Descriptions Act 1972, a repeal of any provision of that Act or a repeal of that Act or of any provision of it for any purposes, unless a draft of the order has been laid before, and approved by a resolution of, each House of Parliament.

(4) An order under subsection (2) above bringing a provision into force may contain such transitional provision in connection with the coming into force of that provision as the Secretary of State considers appropriate.

(5) Without prejudice to the generality of the power conferred by subsection (4) above, the Secretary of State may by order provide for any regulations made under the Consumer Protection Act 1961 or the Consumer Protection Act (Northern Ireland) 1965 to have effect as if made under section 11 above and for any such regulations to have effect with such modifications as he considers appropriate for that purpose.

(6) The power of the Secretary of State by order to make such provision as is mentioned in subsection (5) above, shall, in so far as it is not exercised by an order under subsection (2) above, be exercisable by statutory instrument subject to annulment in pursuance of a resolution of either House of Parliament.

(7) Nothing in this Act or in any order under subsection (2) above shall make any person liable by virtue of Part I of this Act for any damage caused wholly or partly by a defect in a product which was supplied to any person by its producer before the coming into force of Part I of this Act.

(8) Expressions used in subsection (7) above and in Part I of this Act have the same meanings in that subsection as in that Part.

SCHEDULE 2
PROHIBITION NOTICES AND NOTICES TO WARN

Section 13

PART I
PROHIBITION NOTICES

1 A prohibition notice in respect of any goods shall—
- (a) state that the Secretary of State considers that the goods are unsafe;
- (b) set out the reasons why the Secretary of State considers that the goods are unsafe;
- (c) specify the day on which the notice is to come into force; and
- (d) state that the trader may at any time make representations in writing to the Secretary of State for the purpose of establishing that the goods are safe.

2 (1) If representations in writing about a prohibition notice are made by the trader to the Secretary of State, it shall be the duty of the Secretary of State to consider whether to revoke the notice and—
- (a) if he decides to revoke it, to do so;
- (b) in any other case, to appoint a person to consider those representations, any further representations made (whether in writing or orally) by the trader about the notice and the statements of any witnesses examined under this Part of this Schedule.

(2) Where the Secretary of State has appointed a person to consider representations about a prohibition notice, he shall serve a notification on the trader which—
- (a) states that the trader may make oral representations to the appointed person for the purpose of establishing that the goods to which the notice relates are safe; and
- (b) specifies the place and time at which the oral representations may be made.

(3) The time specified in a notification served under sub-paragraph (2) above shall not be before the end of the period of twenty-one days beginning with the day on which the notification is served, unless the trader otherwise agrees.

(4) A person on whom a notification has been served under sub-paragraph (2) above or his representative may, at the place and time specified in the notification—
- (a) make oral representations to the appointed person for the purpose of establishing that the goods in question are safe; and
- (b) call and examine witnesses in connection with the representations.

3 (1) Where representations in writing about a prohibition notice are made by the trader to the Secretary of State at any time after a person has been appointed to consider representations about that notice, then, whether or not the appointed person has made a report to the Secretary of State, the following provisions of this paragraph shall apply instead of paragraph 2 above.

(2) The Secretary of State shall, before the end of the period of one month beginning with the day on which he receives the representations, serve a notification on the trader which states—
- (a) that the Secretary of State has decided to revoke the notice, has decided to vary it or, as the case may be, has decided neither to revoke nor to vary it; or
- (b) that, a person having been appointed to consider representations about the notice, the trader may, at a place and time specified in the notification, make oral representations to the appointed person for the purpose of establishing that the goods to which the notice relates are safe.

(3) The time specified in a notification served for the purposes of sub-paragraph (2)(b) above shall not be before the end of the period of twenty-one days beginning with the day on

which the notification is served, unless the trader otherwise agrees or the time is the time already specified for the purposes of paragraph 2(2)(b) above.

(4) A person on whom a notification has been served for the purposes of sub-paragraph (2)(b) above or his representative may, at the place and time specified in the notification—

(a) make oral representations to the appointed person for the purpose of establishing that the goods in question are safe; and

(b) call and examine witnesses in connection with the representations.

4 (1) Where a person is appointed to consider representations about a prohibition notice, it shall be his duty to consider—

(a) any written representations made by the trader about the notice, other than those in respect of which a notification is served under paragraph 3(2)(a) above;

(b) any oral representations made under paragraph 2(4) or 3(4) above; and

(c) any statements made by witnesses in connection with the oral representations,

and, after considering any matters under this paragraph, to make a report (including recommendations) to the Secretary of State about the matters considered by him and the notice.

(2) It shall be the duty of the Secretary of State to consider any report made to him under sub-paragraph (1) above and, after considering the report, to inform the trader of his decision with respect to the prohibition notice to which the report relates.

5 (1) The Secretary of State may revoke or vary a prohibition notice by serving on the trader a notification stating that the notice is revoked or, as the case may be, is varied as specified in the notification.

(2) The Secretary of State shall not vary a prohibition notice so as to make the effect of the notice more restrictive for the trader.

(3) Without prejudice to the power conferred by section 13(2) of this Act, the service of a notification under sub-paragraph (1) above shall be sufficient to satisfy the requirement of paragraph 4(2) above that the trader shall be informed of the Secretary of State's decision.

PART II
NOTICES TO WARN

6 (1) If the Secretary of State proposes to serve a notice to warn on any person in respect of any goods, the Secretary of State, before he serves the notice, shall serve on that person a notification which—

(a) contains a draft of the proposed notice;

(b) states that the Secretary of State proposes to serve a notice in the form of the draft on that person;

(c) states that the Secretary of State considers that the goods described in the draft are unsafe;

(d) sets out the reasons why the Secretary of State considers that those goods are unsafe; and

(e) states that that person may make representations to the Secretary of State for the purpose of establishing that the goods are safe if, before the end of the period of fourteen days beginning with the day on which the notification is served, he informs the Secretary of State—

(i) of his intention to make representations; and
(ii) whether the representations will be made only in writing or both in writing and orally.

(2) Where the Secretary of State has served a notification containing a draft of a proposed notice to warn on any person, he shall not serve a notice to warn on that person in respect of the goods to which the proposed notice relates unless—
(a) the period of fourteen days beginning with the day on which the notification was served expires without the Secretary of State being informed as mentioned in sub-paragraph (1)(e) above;
(b) the period of twenty-eight days beginning with that day expires without any written representations being made by that person to the Secretary of State about the proposed notice; or
(c) the Secretary of State has considered a report about the proposed notice by a person appointed under paragraph 7(1) below.

7 (1) Where a person on whom a notification containing a draft of a proposed notice to warn has been served—
(a) informs the Secretary of State as mentioned in paragraph 6(1)(e) above before the end of the period of fourteen days beginning with the day on which the notification was served; and
(b) makes written representations to the Secretary of State about the proposed notice before the end of the period of twenty-eight days beginning with that day,

the Secretary of State shall appoint a person to consider those representations, any further representations made by that person about the draft notice and the statements of any witnesses examined under this Part of this Schedule.

(2) Where—
(a) the Secretary of State has appointed a person to consider representations about a proposed notice to warn; and
(b) the person whose representations are to be considered has informed the Secretary of State for the purposes of paragraph 6(1)(e) above that the representations he intends to make will include oral representations,

the Secretary of State shall inform the person intending to make the representations of the place and time at which oral representations may be made to the appointed person.

(3) Where a person on whom a notification containing a draft of a proposed notice to warn has been served is informed of a time for the purposes of sub-paragraph (2) above, that time shall not be—
(a) before the end of the period of twenty-eight days beginning with the day on which the notification was served; or
(b) before the end of the period of seven days beginning with the day on which that person is informed of the time.

(4) A person who has been informed of a place and time for the purposes of sub-paragraph (2) above or his representative may, at that place and time—
(a) make oral representations to the appointed person for the purpose of establishing that the goods to which the proposed notice relates are safe; and
(b) call and examine witnesses in connection with the representations.

8 (1) Where a person is appointed to consider representations about a proposed notice to warn, it shall be his duty to consider—
(a) any written representations made by the person on whom it is proposed to serve the notice; and

(b) in a case where a place and time has been appointed under paragraph 7(2) above for oral representations to be made by that person or his representative, any representations so made and any statements made by witnesses in connection with those representations,

and, after considering those matters, to make a report (including recommendations) to the Secretary of State about the matters considered by him and the proposal to serve the notice.

(2) It shall be the duty of the Secretary of State to consider any report made to him under sub-paragraph (1) above and, after considering the report, to inform the person on whom it was proposed that a notice to warn should be served of his decision with respect to the proposal.

(3) If at any time after serving a notification on a person under paragraph 6 above the Secretary of State decides not to serve on that person either the proposed notice to warn or that notice with modifications, the Secretary of State shall inform that person of the decision; and nothing done for the purposes of any of the preceding provisions of this Part of this Schedule before that person was so informed shall—

(a) entitle the Secretary of State subsequently to serve the proposed notice or that notice with modifications; or
(b) require the Secretary of State, or any person appointed to consider representations about the proposed notice, subsequently to do anything in respect of, or in consequence of, any such representations.

(4) Where a notification containing a draft of a proposed notice to warn is served on a person in respect of any goods, a notice to warn served on him in consequence of a decision made under sub-paragraph (2) above shall either be in the form of the draft or shall be less onerous than the draft.

9 The Secretary of State may revoke a notice to warn by serving on the person on whom the notice was served a notification stating that the notice is revoked.

PART III
GENERAL

10 (1) Where in a notification served on any person under this Schedule the Secretary of State has appointed a time for the making of oral representations or the examination of witnesses, he may, by giving that person such notification as the Secretary of State considers appropriate, change that time to a later time or appoint further times at which further representations may be made or the examination of witnesses may be continued; and paragraphs 2(4), 3(4) and 7(4) above shall have effect accordingly.

(2) For the purposes of this Schedule the Secretary of State may appoint a person (instead of the appointed person) to consider any representations or statements, if the person originally appointed, or last appointed under this sub-paragraph, to consider those representations or statements has died or appears to the Secretary of State to be otherwise unable to act.

11 In this Schedule—

"the appointed person" in relation to a prohibition notice or a proposal to serve a notice to warn, means the person for the time being appointed under this Schedule to consider representations about the notice or, as the case may be, about the proposed notice;

"notification" means a notification in writing;

"trader", in relation to a prohibition notice, means the person on whom the notice is or was served.

Road Traffic Act 1988

1988 CHAPTER 52

An Act to consolidate certain enactments relating to road traffic with amendments to give effect to recommendations of the Law Commission and the Scottish Law Commission

[15th November 1988]

PART I
PRINCIPAL ROAD SAFETY PROVISIONS

Promotion of road safety

38 The Highway Code

(1) The Highway Code shall continue to have effect, subject however to revision in accordance with the following provisions of this section.

(2) Subject to the following provisions of this section, the Secretary of State may from time to time revise the Highway Code by revoking, varying, amending or adding to the provisions of the Code in such manner as he thinks fit.

(3) Where the Secretary of State proposes to revise the Highway Code by making any alterations in the provisions of the Code (other than alterations merely consequential on the passing, amendment or repeal of any statutory provision) he must lay the proposed alterations before both Houses of Parliament and must not make the proposed revision until after the end of a period of forty days beginning with the day on which the alterations were so laid.

(4) If within the period mentioned in subsection (3) above either House resolves that the proposed alterations be not made, the Secretary of State must not make the proposed revision (but without prejudice to the laying before Parliament of further proposals for alteration in accordance with that subsection).

(5) Before revising the Highway Code by making any alterations in its provisions which are required by subsection (3) above to be laid before Parliament, the Secretary of State must consult with such representative organisations as he thinks fit.

(6) The Secretary of State must cause the Highway Code to be printed and may cause copies of it to be sold to the public at such price as he may determine.

(7) A failure on the part of a person to observe a provision of the Highway Code shall not of itself render that person liable to criminal proceedings of any kind but any such failure may in any proceedings (whether civil or criminal, and including proceedings for an offence under the Traffic Acts, the Public Passenger Vehicles Act 1981 or sections 18 to 23 of the Transport Act 1985) be relied upon by any party to the proceedings as tending to establish or negative any liability which is in question in those proceedings.

(8) In this section "the Highway Code" means the code comprising directions for the guidance of persons using roads issued under section 45 of the Road Traffic Act 1930, as from time to time revised under this section or under any previous enactment.

(9) For the purposes of subsection (3) above—

(a) "statutory provision" means a provision contained in an Act or in subordinate legislation within the meaning of the Interpretation Act 1978 (and the reference to the passing or repeal of any such provision accordingly includes the making or revocation of any such provision),

(b) where the proposed alterations are laid before each House of Parliament on different days, the later day shall be taken to be the day on which they were laid before both Houses, and

(c) in reckoning any period of forty days, no account shall be taken of any time during which Parliament is dissolved or prorogued or during which both Houses are adjourned for more than four days.

NOTES

Traffic Acts: Road Traffic Regulation Act 1984, Road Traffic Offenders Act 1988, Road Traffic (Consequential Provisions) Act 1988 (so far as it reproduces the effect of provisions repealed by the Act), Road Traffic Act 1988.

PART VI
THIRD-PARTY LIABILITIES

Compulsory insurance or security against third-party risks

143 Users of motor vehicles to be insured or secured against third-party risks

(1) Subject to the provisions of this Part of this Act—

(a) a person must not use a motor vehicle on a road [or other public place] unless there is in force in relation to the use of the vehicle by that person such a policy of insurance or such a security in respect of third party risks as complies with the requirements of this Part of this Act, and

(b) a person must not cause or permit any other person to use a motor vehicle on a road [or other public place] unless there is in force in relation to the use of the vehicle by that other person such a policy of insurance or such a security in respect of third party risks as complies with the requirements of this Part of this Act.

(2) If a person acts in contravention of subsection (1) above he is guilty of an offence.

(3) A person charged with using a motor vehicle in contravention of this section shall not be convicted if he proves—

(a) that the vehicle did not belong to him and was not in his possession under a contract of hiring or of loan,

(b) that he was using the vehicle in the course of his employment, and

(c) that he neither knew nor had reason to believe that there was not in force in relation to the vehicle such a policy of insurance or security as is mentioned in subsection (1) above.

(4) This Part of this Act does not apply to invalid carriages.

NOTES

Sub-s (1): in para (a) words "or other public place" in square brackets inserted by SI 2000/726, reg 2(1), (2)(a).

Date in force: 3 April 2000: see SI 2000/726, reg 1.

Sub-s (1): in para (b) words "or other public place" in square brackets inserted by SI 2000/726, reg 2(1), (2)(b).

Date in force: 3 April 2000: see SI 2000/726, reg 1.

144 Exceptions from requirement of third-party insurance or security

(1) Section 143 of this Act does not apply to a vehicle owned by a person who has deposited and keeps deposited with the Accountant General of the Supreme Court the sum of [£500,000], at a time when the vehicle is being driven under the owner's control.

[(1A) The Secretary of State may by order made by statutory instrument substitute a greater sum for the sum for the time being specified in subsection (1) above.

(1B) No order shall be made under subsection (1A) above unless a draft of it has been laid before and approved by resolution of each House of Parliament.]

(2) Section 143 does not apply—

(a) to a vehicle owned—

(i) by the council of a county or county district in England and Wales, [the Broads Authority] the Common Council of the City of London, the council of a London borough [a National Park authority], the Inner London Education Authority, [the London Fire and Emergency Planning Authority,] or a joint authority (other than a police authority) established by Part IV of the Local Government Act 1985,

(ii) by a [council constituted under section 2 of the Local Government etc (Scotland) Act 1994] in Scotland, or

(iii) by a joint board or committee in England or Wales, or joint committee in Scotland, which is so constituted as to include among its members representatives of any such council,

at a time when the vehicle is being driven under the owner's control,

(b) to a vehicle owned by a police authority . . ., at a time when it is being driven under the owner's control, or to a vehicle at a time when it is being driven for police purposes by or under the direction of a constable, or by a person employed by a police authority, . . ., or

[(ba) to a vehicle owned by the Service Authority for the National Criminal Intelligence Service or the Service Authority for the National Crime Squad, at a time when it is being driven under the owner's control, or to a vehicle at a time when it is being driven for the purposes of the body maintained by such an Authority by or under the direction of a constable, or by a person employed by such an Authority;]

(c) to a vehicle at a time when it is being driven on a journey to or from any place undertaken for salvage purposes pursuant to Part IX of the [Merchant Shipping Act 1995],

(d) to the use of a vehicle for the purpose of its being provided in pursuance of a direction under section 166(2)(b) of the Army Act 1955 or under the corresponding provision of the Air Force Act 1955,

[(da) to a vehicle owned by a health service body, as defined in section 60(7) of the National Health Service and Community Care Act 1990 [by a Primary Care Trust established under section 16A of the National Health Service Act 1977] [or by the Commission for Health Improvement], at a time when the vehicle is being driven under the owner's control,

(db) to an ambulance owned by a National Health Service trust established under Part I of the National Health Service and Community Care Act 1990 or the National Health Service (Scotland) Act 1978, at a time when a vehicle is being driven under the owner's control,]

(e) to a vehicle which is made available by the Secretary of State to any person, body or local authority in pursuance of section 23 or 26 of the National Health Service Act 1977 at a time when it is being used in accordance with the terms on which it is so made available,

(f) to a vehicle which is made available by the Secretary of State to any local authority, education authority or voluntary organisation in Scotland in pursuance of section 15 or 16 of the National Health Service (Scotland) Act 1978 at a time when it is being used in accordance with the terms on which it is so made available.

NOTES

Sub-s (1): sum in square brackets substituted by the Road Traffic Act 1991, s 20(2).

Sub-ss (1A), (1B): inserted by the Road Traffic Act 1991, s 20(3).

Sub-s (2): in para (a)(i) words "the Broads Authority" in square brackets inserted by the Norfolk and Suffolk Broads Act 1988, s 21, Sch 6, para 9.

Sub-s (2): in para (a)(i) words "a National Park authority" in square brackets inserted by the Environment Act 1995, s 78, Sch 10, para 29.

Sub-s (2): in para (a)(i) words "the London Fire and Emergency Planning Authority," in square brackets inserted by the Greater London Authority Act 1999, s 328, Sch 29, Pt I, para 54.

Date in force: 3 July 2000: see SI 2000/1094, art 4(h).

Sub-s (2): in para (a)(ii) words from "council constituted" to "Act 1994" in square brackets substituted by the Local Government etc (Scotland) Act 1994, s 180(1), Sch 13, para 159(8).

Sub-s (2): in para (b) words omitted repealed by the Greater London Authority Act 1999, ss 325, 423, Sch 27, para 61, Sch 34, Pt VII.

Date in force: 3 July 2000: see SI 2000/1648, art 2, Schedule.

Sub-s (2): para (ba) inserted by the Police Act 1997, s 134(1), Sch 9, para 59.

Date in force: 1 April 1998: see SI 1998/354, art 2(2)(bb).

Sub-s (2): in para (c) words "Merchant Shipping Act 1995" in square brackets substituted by the Merchant Shipping Act 1995, s 314(2), Sch 13, para 85.

Sub-s (2): paras (da), (db) inserted by the National Health Service and Community Care Act 1990, s 60, Sch 8, Pt I, para 4.

Sub-s (2): in para (da) words "by a Primary Care Trust established under section 16A of the National Health Service Act 1977" in square brackets inserted by SI 2000/90, art 3(1), Sch 1, para 23.

Date in force: 8 February 2000: see SI 2000/90, art 1.

Sub-s (2): in para (da) words "or by the Commission for Health Improvement" in square brackets inserted by SI 1999/2795, art 4.

Date in force: 1 November 1999: see SI 1999/2795, art 1(1); for further provision as to the effect of this amendment see art 1(2).

145 Requirements in respect of policies of insurance

(1) In order to comply with the requirements of this Part of this Act, a policy of insurance must satisfy the following conditions.

(2) The policy must be issued by an authorised insurer.

(3) Subject to subsection (4) below, the policy—

(a) must insure such person, persons or classes of persons as may be specified in the policy in respect of any liability which may be incurred by him or them in respect of the death of or bodily injury to any person or damage to property caused by, or arising out of, the use of the vehicle on a road [or other public place] in Great Britain, and

[(aa) must, in the case of a vehicle normally based in the territory of another member State, insure him or them in respect of any civil liability which may be incurred by him or them as a result of an event related to the use of the vehicle in Great Britain if,—

(i) according to the law of that territory, he or they would be required to be insured in respect of a civil liability which would arise under that law as a result of that event if the place where the vehicle was used when the event occurred were in that territory, and

(ii) the cover required by that law would be higher than that required by paragraph (a) above, and]

(b) must[, in the case of a vehicle normally based in Great Britain,] insure him or them in respect of any liability which may be incurred by him or them in respect of the use of the vehicle and of any trailer, whether or not coupled, in the territory other than Great Britain and Gibraltar of each of the member States of the Communities according to

[(i) the law on compulsory insurance against civil liability in respect of the use of vehicles of the State in whose territory the event giving rise to the liability occurred; or

(ii) if it would give higher cover, the law which would be applicable under this Part of this Act if the place where the vehicle was used when that event occurred were in Great Britain; and]

(c) must also insure him or them in respect of any liability which may be incurred by him or them under the provisions of this Part of this Act relating to payment for emergency treatment.

(4) The policy shall not, by virtue of subsection (3)(a) above, be required—

(a) to cover liability in respect of the death, arising out of and in the course of his employment, of a person in the employment of a person insured by the policy or of bodily injury sustained by such a person arising out of and in the course of his employment, or

(b) to provide insurance of more than £250,000 in respect of all such liabilities as may be insured in respect of damage to property caused by, or arising out of, any one accident involving the vehicle, or

(c) to cover liability in respect of damage to the vehicle, or

(d) to cover liability in respect of damage to goods carried for hire or reward in or on the vehicle or in or on any trailer (whether or not coupled) drawn by the vehicle, or

(e) to cover any liability of a person in respect of damage to property in his custody or under his control, or

(f) to cover any contractual liability.

[(4A) In the case of a person—

(a) carried in or upon a vehicle, or

(b) entering or getting on to, or alighting from, a vehicle,

the provisions of paragraph (a) of subsection (4) above do not apply unless cover in respect of the liability referred to in that paragraph is in fact provided pursuant to a requirement of the Employers' Liability (Compulsory Insurance) Act 1969.]

[(5) "Authorised insurer" has the same meaning as in section 95.]

(6) If any person or body of persons ceases to be a member of the Motor Insurers' Bureau, that person or body shall not by virtue of that cease to be treated as an authorised insurer for the purposes of this Part of this Act [or the Road Traffic (NHS Charges) Act 1999]—

(a) in relation to any policy issued by the insurer before ceasing to be such a member, or

(b) in relation to any obligation (whether arising before or after the insurer ceased to be such a member) which the insurer may be called upon to meet under or in consequence of any such policy or under section 157 of this Act [or section 1 of the Act of 1999] by virtue of making a payment in pursuance of such an obligation.

NOTES

Sub-s (3): in para (a) words "or other public place" in square brackets inserted by SI 2000/726, reg 2(1), (3).

Date in force: 3 April 2000: see SI 2000/726, reg 1.

Sub-s (3): para (aa) inserted, in para (b) first words in square brackets inserted and second words in square brackets substituted, by SI 1992/3036, reg 2(1), (2).

Sub-s (4A): inserted by SI 1992/3036, reg 2(3).

Sub-s (5): substituted by SI 2001/3649, art 313.

Date in force: 1 December 2001: see SI 2001/3649, art 1.

Sub-s (6): words "or the Road Traffic (NHS Charges) Act 1999" in square brackets inserted by the Road Traffic (NHS Charges) Act 1999, s 18(1)(a).

Date in force: 5 April 1999: see SI 1999/1075, art 2.

Sub-s (6): in para (b) words "or section 1 of the Act of 1999" in square brackets inserted by the Road Traffic (NHS Charges) Act 1999, s 18(1)(b).

Date in force: 5 April 1999: see SI 1999/1075, art 2.

146 Requirements in respect of securities

(1) In order to comply with the requirements of this Part of this Act, a security must satisfy the following conditions.

(2) The security must be given either by an authorised insurer or by some body of persons which carries on in the United Kingdom the business of giving securities of a like kind and has deposited and keeps deposited with the Accountant General of the Supreme Court the sum of £15,000 in respect of that business.

(3) Subject to subsection (4) below, the security must consist of an undertaking by the giver of the security to make good, subject to any conditions specified in it, any failure by the owner of the vehicle or such other persons or classes of persons as may be specified in the security duly to discharge any liability which may be incurred by him or them, being a liability required under section 145 of this Act to be covered by a policy of insurance.

(4) In the case of liabilities arising out of the use of a motor vehicle on a road [or other public place] in Great Britain the amount secured need not exceed—

- (a) in the case of an undertaking relating to the use of public service vehicles (within the meaning of the Public Passenger Vehicles Act 1981), £25,000,
- (b) in any other case, £5,000.

NOTES

Sub-s (4): words "or other public place" in square brackets inserted by SI 2000/726, reg 2(1), (4).

Date in force: 3 April 2000: see SI 2000/726, reg 1.

147 Issue and surrender of certificates of insurance and of security

(1) A policy of insurance shall be of no effect for the purposes of this Part of this Act unless and until there is delivered by the insurer to the person by whom the policy is effected a certificate (in this Part of this Act referred to as a "certificate of insurance") in the prescribed form and containing such particulars of any conditions subject to which the policy is issued and of any other matters as may be prescribed.

(2) A security shall be of no effect for the purposes of this Part of this Act unless and until there is delivered by the person giving the security to the person to whom it is given a certificate (in this Part of this Act referred to as a "certificate of security") in the prescribed form and containing such particulars of any conditions subject to which the security is issued and of any other matters as may be prescribed.

(3) Different forms and different particulars may be prescribed for the purposes of subsection (1) or (2) above in relation to different cases or circumstances.

(4) Where a certificate has been delivered under this section and the policy or security to which it relates is cancelled by mutual consent or by virtue of any provision in the policy or security, the person to whom the certificate was delivered must, within seven days from the taking effect of the cancellation—

- (a) surrender the certificate to the person by whom the policy was issued or the security was given, or

(b) if the certificate has been lost or destroyed, make a statutory declaration to that effect.

(5) A person who fails to comply with subsection (4) above is guilty of an offence.

148 Avoidance of certain exceptions to policies or securities

(1) Where a certificate of insurance or certificate of security has been delivered under section 147 of this Act to the person by whom a policy has been effected or to whom a security has been given, so much of the policy or security as purports to restrict—

(a) the insurance of the persons insured by the policy, or
(b) the operation of the security,

(as the case may be) by reference to any of the matters mentioned in subsection (2) below shall, as respects such liabilities as are required to be covered by a policy under section 145 of this Act, be of no effect.

(2) Those matters are—

(a) the age or physical or mental condition of persons driving the vehicle,
(b) the condition of the vehicle,
(c) the number of persons that the vehicle carries,
(d) the weight or physical characteristics of the goods that the vehicle carries,
(e) the time at which or the areas within which the vehicle is used,
(f) the horsepower or cylinder capacity or value of the vehicle,
(g) the carrying on the vehicle of any particular apparatus, or
(h) the carrying on the vehicle of any particular means of identification other than any means of identification required to be carried by or under [the Vehicle Excise and Registration Act 1994].

(3) Nothing in subsection (1) above requires an insurer or the giver of a security to pay any sum in respect of the liability of any person otherwise than in or towards the discharge of that liability.

(4) Any sum paid by an insurer or the giver of a security in or towards the discharge of any liability of any person which is covered by the policy or security by virtue only of subsection (1) above is recoverable by the insurer or giver of the security from that person.

(5) A condition in a policy or security issued or given for the purposes of this Part of this Act providing—

(a) that no liability shall arise under the policy or security, or
(b) that any liability so arising shall cease,

in the event of some specified thing being done or omitted to be done after the happening of the event giving rise to a claim under the policy or security, shall be of no effect in connection with such liabilities as are required to be covered by a policy under section 145 of this Act.

(6) Nothing in subsection (5) above shall be taken to render void any provision in a policy or security requiring the person insured or secured to pay to the insurer or the giver of the security any sums which the latter may have become liable to pay

under the policy or security and which have been applied to the satisfaction of the claims of third parties.

(7) Notwithstanding anything in any enactment, a person issuing a policy of insurance under section 145 of this Act shall be liable to indemnify the persons or classes of persons specified in the policy in respect of any liability which the policy purports to cover in the case of those persons or classes of persons.

NOTES

Sub-s (2): words in square brackets substituted by the Vehicle Excise and Registration Act 1994, s 63, Sch 3, para 24(1).

149 Avoidance of certain agreements as to liability towards passengers

(1) This section applies where a person uses a motor vehicle in circumstances such that under section 143 of this Act there is required to be in force in relation to his use of it such a policy of insurance or such a security in respect of third-party risks as complies with the requirements of this Part of this Act.

(2) If any other person is carried in or upon the vehicle while the user is so using it, any antecedent agreement or understanding between them (whether intended to be legally binding or not) shall be of no effect so far as it purports or might be held—

- (a) to negative or restrict any such liability of the user in respect of persons carried in or upon the vehicle as is required by section 145 of this Act to be covered by a policy of insurance, or
- (b) to impose any conditions with respect to the enforcement of any such liability of the user.

(3) The fact that a person so carried has willingly accepted as his the risk of negligence on the part of the user shall not be treated as negativing any such liability of the user.

(4) For the purposes of this section—

- (a) references to a person being carried in or upon a vehicle include references to a person entering or getting on to, or alighting from, the vehicle, and
- (b) the reference to an antecedent agreement is to one made at any time before the liability arose.

150 Insurance or security in respect of private use of vehicle to cover use under car-sharing arrangements

(1) To the extent that a policy or security issued or given for the purposes of this Part of this Act—

- (a) restricts the insurance of the persons insured by the policy or the operation of the security (as the case may be) to use of the vehicle for specified purposes (for example, social, domestic and pleasure purposes) of a non-commercial character, or
- (b) excludes from that insurance or the operation of the security (as the case may be)—

(i) use of the vehicle for hire or reward, or
(ii) business or commercial use of the vehicle, or
(iii) use of the vehicle for specified purposes of a business or commercial character,

then, for the purposes of that policy or security so far as it relates to such liabilities as are required to be covered by a policy under section 145 of this Act, the use of a vehicle on a journey in the course of which one or more passengers are carried at separate fares shall, if the conditions specified in subsection (2) below are satisfied, be treated as falling within that restriction or as not falling within that exclusion (as the case may be).

(2) The conditions referred to in subsection (1) above are—

(a) the vehicle is not adapted to carry more than eight passengers and is not a motor cycle,
(b) the fare or aggregate of the fares paid in respect of the journey does not exceed the amount of the running costs of the vehicle for the journey (which for the purposes of this paragraph shall be taken to include an appropriate amount in respect of depreciation and general wear), and
(c) the arrangements for the payment of fares by the passenger or passengers carried at separate fares were made before the journey began.

(3) Subsections (1) and (2) above apply however the restrictions or exclusions described in subsection (1) are framed or worded.

(4) In subsections (1) and (2) above "fare" and "separate fares" have the same meaning as in section 1(4) of the Public Passenger Vehicles Act 1981.

151 Duty of insurers or persons giving security to satisfy judgment against persons insured or secured against third-party risks

(1) This section applies where, after a certificate of insurance or certificate of security has been delivered under section 147 of this Act to the person by whom a policy has been effected or to whom a security has been given, a judgment to which this subsection applies is obtained.

(2) Subsection (1) above applies to judgments relating to a liability with respect to any matter where liability with respect to that matter is required to be covered by a policy of insurance under section 145 of this Act and either—

(a) it is a liability covered by the terms of the policy or security to which the certificate relates, and the judgment is obtained against any person who is insured by the policy or whose liability is covered by the security, as the case may be, or
(b) it is a liability, other than an excluded liability, which would be so covered if the policy insured all persons or, as the case may be, the security covered the liability of all persons, and the judgment is obtained against any person other than one who is insured by the policy or, as the case may be, whose liability is covered by the security.

(3) In deciding for the purposes of subsection (2) above whether a liability is or would be covered by the terms of a policy or security, so much of the policy or

security as purports to restrict, as the case may be, the insurance of the persons insured by the policy or the operation of the security by reference to the holding by the driver of the vehicle of a licence authorising him to drive it shall be treated as of no effect.

(4) In subsection (2)(b) above "excluded liability" means a liability in respect of the death of, or bodily injury to, or damage to the property of any person who, at the time of the use which gave rise to the liability, was allowing himself to be carried in or upon the vehicle and knew or had reason to believe that the vehicle had been stolen or unlawfully taken, not being a person who—

(a) did not know and had no reason to believe that the vehicle had been stolen or unlawfully taken until after the commencement of his journey, and
(b) could not reasonably have been expected to have alighted from the vehicle.

In this subsection the reference to a person being carried in or upon a vehicle includes a reference to a person entering or getting on to, or alighting from, the vehicle.

(5) Notwithstanding that the insurer may be entitled to avoid or cancel, or may have avoided or cancelled, the policy or security, he must, subject to the provisions of this section, pay to the persons entitled to the benefit of the judgment—

(a) as regards liability in respect of death or bodily injury, any sum payable under the judgment in respect of the liability, together with any sum which, by virtue of any enactment relating to interest on judgments, is payable in respect of interest on that sum,
(b) as regards liability in respect of damage to property, any sum required to be paid under subsection (6) below, and
(c) any amount payable in respect of costs.

(6) This subsection requires—

(a) where the total of any amount paid, payable or likely to be payable under the policy or security in respect of damage to property caused by, or arising out of, the accident in question does not exceed £250,000, the payment of any sum payable under the judgment in respect of the liability, together with any sum which, by virtue of any enactment relating to interest on judgments, is payable in respect of interest on that sum,
(b) where that total exceeds £250,000, the payment of either—
    (i) such proportion of any sum payable under the judgment in respect of the liability as £250,000 bears to that total, together with the same proportion of any sum which, by virtue of any enactment relating to interest on judgments, is payable in respect of interest on that sum, or
    (ii) the difference between the total of any amounts already paid under the policy or security in respect of such damage and £250,000, together with such proportion of any sum which, by virtue of any enactment relating to interest on judgments, is payable in respect of interest on any sum payable under the judgment in respect of the liability as the difference bears to that sum,

whichever is the less, unless not less than £250,000 has already been paid under the policy or security in respect of such damage (in which case nothing is payable).

(7) Where an insurer becomes liable under this section to pay an amount in respect of a liability of a person who is insured by a policy or whose liability is covered by a security, he is entitled to recover from that person—

(a) that amount, in a case where he became liable to pay it by virtue only of subsection (3) above, or

(b) in a case where that amount exceeds the amount for which he would, apart from the provisions of this section, be liable under the policy or security in respect of that liability, the excess.

(8) Where an insurer becomes liable under this section to pay an amount in respect of a liability of a person who is not insured by a policy or whose liability is not covered by a security, he is entitled to recover the amount from that person or from any person who—

(a) is insured by the policy, or whose liability is covered by the security, by the terms of which the liability would be covered if the policy insured all persons or, as the case may be, the security covered the liability of all persons, and

(b) caused or permitted the use of the vehicle which gave rise to the liability.

(9) In this section—

(a) "insurer" includes a person giving a security,

(b) . . .

(c) "liability covered by the terms of the policy or security" means a liability which is covered by the policy or security or which would be so covered but for the fact that the insurer is entitled to avoid or cancel, or has avoided or cancelled, the policy or security.

(10) In the application of this section to Scotland, the words "by virtue of any enactment relating to interest on judgments" in subsections (5) and (6) (in each place where they appear) shall be omitted.

NOTES

Sub-s (9): para (b) repealed by the Road Traffic Act 1991, s 83, Sch 8.

152 Exceptions to section 151

(1) No sum is payable by an insurer under section 151 of this Act—

(a) in respect of any judgment unless, before or within seven days after the commencement of the proceedings in which the judgment was given, the insurer had notice of the bringing of the proceedings, or

(b) in respect of any judgment so long as execution on the judgment is stayed pending an appeal, or

(c) in connection with any liability if, before the happening of the event which was the cause of the death or bodily injury or damage to property giving rise to the liability, the policy or security was cancelled by mutual consent or by virtue of any provision contained in it, and also—

(i) before the happening of that event the certificate was surrendered to the insurer, or the person to whom the certificate was delivered made a statutory declaration stating that the certificate had been lost or destroyed, or

(ii) after the happening of that event, but before the expiration of a period of fourteen days from the taking effect of the cancellation of the policy or security, the certificate was surrendered to the insurer, or the person to whom it was delivered made a statutory declaration stating that the certificate had been lost or destroyed, or

(iii) either before or after the happening of that event, but within that period of fourteen days, the insurer has commenced proceedings under this Act in respect of the failure to surrender the certificate.

(2) Subject to subsection (3) below, no sum is payable by an insurer under section 151 of this Act if, in an action commenced before, or within three months after, the commencement of the proceedings in which the judgment was given, he has obtained a declaration—

(a) that, apart from any provision contained in the policy or security, he is entitled to avoid it on the ground that it was obtained—

(i) by the non-disclosure of a material fact, or

(ii) by a representation of fact which was false in some material particular, or

(b) if he has avoided the policy or security on that ground, that he was entitled so to do apart from any provision contained in it

[and, for the purposes of this section, "material" means of such a nature as to influence the judgment of a prudent insurer in determining whether he will take the risk and, if so, at what premium and on what conditions.]

(3) An insurer who has obtained such a declaration as is mentioned in subsection (2) above in an action does not by reason of that become entitled to the benefit of that subsection as respects any judgment obtained in proceedings commenced before the commencement of that action unless before, or within seven days after, the commencement of that action he has given notice of it to the person who is the plaintiff (or in Scotland pursuer) in those proceedings specifying the non-disclosure or false representation on which he proposes to rely.

(4) A person to whom notice of such an action is so given is entitled, if he thinks fit, to be made a party to it.

NOTES

Sub-s (2): words in square brackets inserted by the Road Traffic Act 1991, s 48, Sch 4, para 66.

153 Bankruptcy, etc, of insured or secured persons not to affect claims by third parties

(1) Where, after a certificate of insurance or certificate of security has been delivered under section 147 of this Act to the person by whom a policy has been effected or to whom a security has been given, any of the events mentioned in subsection (2) below happens, the happening of that event shall, notwithstanding

anything in the Third Parties (Rights Against Insurers) Act 1930, not affect any such liability of that person as is required to be covered by a policy of insurance under section 145 of this Act.

(2) In the case of the person by whom the policy was effected or to whom the security was given, the events referred to in subsection (1) above are—

(a) that he becomes bankrupt or makes a composition or arrangement with his creditors or that his estate is sequestrated or he grants a trust deed for his creditors,

(b) that he dies and—

(i) his estate falls to be administered in accordance with an order under section 421 of the Insolvency Act 1986,

(ii) an award of sequestration of his estate is made, or

(iii) a judicial factor is appointed to administer his estate under section 11A of the Judicial Factors (Scotland) Act 1889,

(c) that if that person is a company—

(i) a winding-up order or an administration order is made with respect to the company,

(ii) a resolution for a voluntary winding-up is passed with respect to the company,

(iii) a receiver or manager of the company's business or undertaking is duly appointed, or

(iv) possession is taken, by or on behalf of the holders of any debentures secured by a floating charge, of any property comprised in or subject to the charge.

(3) Nothing in subsection (1) above affects any rights conferred by the Third Parties (Rights Against Insurers) Act 1930 on the person to whom the liability was incurred, being rights so conferred against the person by whom the policy was issued or the security was given.

PART VII
MISCELLANEOUS AND GENERAL

Supplementary

197 Short title, commencement and extent

(1) This Act may be cited as the Road Traffic Act 1988.

(2) This Act shall come into force, subject to the transitory provisions in Schedule 5 to the Road Traffic (Consequential Provisions) Act 1988, at the end of the period of six months beginning with the day on which it is passed.

(3) This Act, except section 80 and except as provided by section 184, does not extend to Northern Ireland.

Human Organ Transplants Act 1989

1989 CHAPTER 31

An Act to prohibit commercial dealings in human organs intended for transplanting; to restrict the transplanting of such organs between persons who are not genetically related; and for supplementary purposes connected with those matters
[27th July 1989]

1 Prohibition of commercial dealings in human organs

(1) A person is guilty of an offence if in Great Britain he—
- (a) makes or receives any payment for the supply of, or for an offer to supply, an organ which has been or is to be removed from a dead or living person and is intended to be transplanted into another person whether in Great Britain or elsewhere;
- (b) seeks to find a person willing to supply for payment such an organ as is mentioned in paragraph (a) above or offers to supply such an organ for payment;
- (c) initiates or negotiates any arrangement involving the making of any payment for the supply of, or for an offer to supply, such an organ; or
- (d) takes part in the management or control of a body of persons corporate or unincorporate whose activities consist of or include the initiation or negotiation of such arrangements.

(2) Without prejudice to paragraph (b) of subsection (1) above, a person is guilty of an offence if he causes to be published or distributed, or knowingly publishes or distributes, in Great Britain an advertisement—
- (a) inviting persons to supply for payment any such organs as are mentioned in paragraph (*a*) of that subsection or offering to supply any such organs for payment; or
- (b) indicating that the advertiser is willing to initiate or negotiate any such arrangement as is mentioned in paragraph (c) of that subsection.

(3) In this section "payment" means payment in money or money's worth but does not include any payment for defraying or reimbursing—
- (a) the cost of removing, transporting or preserving the organ to be supplied; or
- (b) any expenses or loss of earnings incurred by a person so far as reasonably and directly attributable to his supplying an organ from his body.

(4) In this section ''advertisement" includes any form of advertising whether to the public generally, to any section of the public or individually to selected persons.

(5) A person guilty of an offence under subsection (1) above is liable on summary conviction to imprisonment for a term not exceeding three months or a fine not exceeding level 5 on the standard scale or both; and a person guilty of an offence under subsection (2) above is liable on summary conviction to a fine not exceeding level 5 on that scale.

7 Short title, interpretation, commencement and extent

(1) This Act may be cited as the Human Organ Transplants Act 1989.

(2) In this Act "organ" means any part of a human body consisting of a structured arrangement of tissues which, if wholly removed, cannot be replicated by the body.

(3) Section 1 above shall not come into force until the day after that on which this Act is passed and section 2(1) above shall not come into force until such day as the Secretary of State may appoint by an order made by statutory instrument.

(4) Except for section 6 this Act does not extend to Northern Ireland.

Law of Property (Miscellaneous Provisions) Act 1989

1989 CHAPTER 34

An Act to make new provision with respect to deeds and their execution and contracts for the sale or other disposition of interests in land; and to abolish the rule of law known as the rule in Bain v. Fothergill

[27th July 1989]

2 Contracts for sale etc of land to be made by signed writing

(1) A contract for the sale or other disposition of an interest in land can only be made in writing and only by incorporating all the terms which the parties have expressly agreed in one document or, where contracts are exchanged, in each.

(2) The terms may be incorporated in a document either by being set out in it or by reference to some other document.

(3) The document incorporating the terms or, where contracts are exchanged, one of the documents incorporating them (but not necessarily the same one) must be signed by or on behalf of each party to the contract.

(4) Where a contract for the sale or other disposition of an interest in land satisfies the conditions of this section by reason only of the rectification of one or more documents in pursuance of an order of a court, the contract shall come into being, or be deemed to have come into being, at such time as may be specified in the order.

(5) This section does not apply in relation to—

(a) a contract to grant such a lease as is mentioned in section 54(2) of the Law Property Act 1925 (short leases);

(b) a contract made in the course of a public auction; or

[(c) a contract regulated under the Financial Services and Markets Act 2000, other than a regulated mortgage contract;]

and nothing in this section affects the creation or operation of resulting, implied or constructive trusts.

(6) In this section—

"disposition" has the same meaning as in the Law of Property Act 1925;

"interest in land" means any estate, interest or charge in or over land . . .

["regulated mortgage contract" must be read with—

(a) section 22 of the Financial Services and Markets Act 2000,

(b) any relevant order under that section, and

(c) Schedule 22 to that Act].

(7) Nothing in this section shall apply in relation to contracts made before this section comes into force.

(8) . . .

NOTES

Sub-s (5): para (c) substituted by SI 2001/3649, art 317(1), (2).

Date in force: 1 December 2001: see SI 2001/3649, art 1.

Sub-s (6): in definition "interest in land" words omitted repealed by the Trusts of Land and Appointment of Trustees Act 1996, s 25(2), Sch 4; for savings in relation to entailed interests created before the commencement of that Act, and savings consequential upon the abolition of the doctrine of conversion, see s 25(4), (5) thereof.

Sub-s (6): definition "regulated mortgage contract" inserted by SI 2001/3649, art 317(1), (3).

Date in force: 1 December 2001: see SI 2001/3649, art 1.

Sub-s (8): repeals the Law of Property Act 1925, s 40.

5 Commencement

(1) The provisions of this Act to which this subsection applies shall come into force on such day as the Lord Chancellor may by order made by statutory instrument appoint.

(2) The provisions to which subsection (1) above applies are—

(a) section 1 above; and

(b) section 4 above, except so far as it relates to section 40 of the Law of Property Act 1925.

(3) The provisions of this Act to which this subsection applies shall come into force at the end of the period of two months beginning with the day on which this Act is passed.

(4) The provisions of this Act to which subsection (3) above applies are—

(a) sections 2 and 3 above; and

(b) section 4 above, so far as it relates to section 40 of the Law of Property Act 1925.

6 Citation

(1) This Act may be cited as the Law of Property (Miscellaneous Provisions) Act 1989.

(2) This Act extends to England and Wales only.

Broadcasting Act 1990

1990 CHAPTER 42

An Act to make new provision with respect to the provision and regulation of independent television and sound programme services and of other services provided on television or radio frequencies; to make provision with respect to the provision and regulation of local delivery services; to amend in other respects the law relating to broadcasting and the provision of television and sound programme services and to make provision with respect to the supply and use of information about programmes; to make provision with respect to the transfer of the property, rights and liabilities of the Independent Broadcasting Authority and the Cable Authority and the dissolution of those bodies; to make new provision relating to the Broadcasting Complaints Commission; to provide for the establishment and functions of a Broadcasting Standards Council; to amend the Wireless Telegraphy Acts 1949 to 1967 and the Marine, &c, Broadcasting (Offences) Act 1967; to revoke a class licence granted under the Telecommunications Act 1984 to run broadcast relay systems; and for connected purposes

[1st November 1990]

PART VII
PROHIBITION ON INCLUSION OF OBSCENE AND OTHER MATERIAL IN PROGRAMME SERVICES

Defamation

166 Defamatory material

(1) For the purposes of the law of libel and slander (including the law of criminal libel so far as it relates to the publication of defamatory matter) the publication of words in the course of any programme included in a programme service shall be treated as publication in permanent form.

(2) Subsection (1) above shall apply for the purposes of section 3 of each of the Defamation Acts (slander of title etc) as it applies for the purposes of the law of libel and slander.

(3) . . .

(4) In this section "the Defamation Acts" means the Defamation Act 1952 and the Defamation Act (Northern Ireland) 1955.

(5) Subsections (1) and (2) above do not extend to Scotland.

NOTES

Sub-s (3): repealed by the Defamation Act 1996, s 16, Sch 2.
Date in force: 1 April 1999: see SI 1999/817, art 2(b).

PART X
MISCELLANEOUS AND GENERAL

General

204 Short title, commencement and extent

(1) This Act may be cited as the Broadcasting Act 1990.

(2) This Act shall come into force on such day as the Secretary of State may by order appoint; and different days may be so appointed for different provisions or for different purposes.

(3) Subject to subsections (4) and (5), this Act extends to the whole of the United Kingdom.

(4) In Part VII—
- (a) section 162 and Schedule 15 extend to England and Wales only;
- (b) section 163 extends to Scotland only;
- (c) section 164 extends to England and Wales and Scotland; and
- (d) section 165 extends to Northern Ireland only.

(5) The amendments and repeals in Schedules 20 and 21 have the same extent as the enactments to which they refer.

(6) Her Majesty may by Order in Council direct that any of the provisions of this Act shall extend to the Isle of Man or any of the Channel Islands with such modifications, if any, as appear to Her Majesty to be appropriate.

Environmental Protection Act 1990

1990 CHAPTER 43

An Act to make provision for the improved control of pollution arising from certain industrial and other processes; to re-enact the provisions of the Control of Pollution Act 1974 relating to waste on land with modifications as respects the functions of the regulatory and other authorities concerned in the collection and disposal of waste and to make further provision in relation to such waste; to restate the law defining statutory nuisances and improve the summary procedures for dealing with them, to provide for the termination of the existing controls over offensive trades or businesses and to provide for the extension of the Clean Air Acts to prescribed gases; to amend the law relating to litter and make further provision imposing or conferring powers to impose duties to keep public places clear of litter and clean; to make provision conferring powers in relation to trolleys abandoned on land in the open air; to amend the Radioactive Substances Act 1960; to make provision for the control of genetically modified organisms; to make provision for the abolition of the Nature Conservancy Council and for the creation of councils to replace it and discharge the functions of that Council and, as respects Wales, of the Countryside Commission; to make further provision for the control of the importation, exportation, use, supply or storage of prescribed substances and articles and the importation or exportation of prescribed descriptions of waste; to confer powers to obtain information about potentially hazardous substances; to amend the law relating to the control of hazardous substances on, over or under land; to amend section 107(6) of the Water Act 1989 and sections 31(7)(a), 31A(c)(i) and 32(7)(a) of the Control of Pollution Act 1974; to amend the provisions of the Food and Environment Protection Act 1985 as regards the dumping of waste at sea; to make further provision as respects the prevention of oil pollution from ships; to make provision for and in connection with the identification and control of dogs; to confer powers to control the burning of crop residues; to make provision in relation to financial or other assistance for purposes connected with the environment; to make provision as respects superannuation of employees of the Groundwork Foundation and for remunerating the chairman of the Inland Waterways Amenity Advisory Council; and for purposes connected with those purposes

[1st November 1990]

PART II
WASTE ON LAND

Duty of care etc as respects waste

34 Duty of care etc as respects waste

(1) Subject to subsection (2) below, it shall be the duty of any person who imports, produces, carries, keeps, treats or disposes of controlled waste or, as a broker, has

control of such waste, to take all such measures applicable to him in that capacity as are reasonable in the circumstances—

(a) to prevent any contravention by any other person of section 33 above;

[(aa) to prevent any contravention by any other person of regulation 9 of the Pollution Prevention and Control (England and Wales) Regulations 2000 or of a condition of a permit granted under regulation 10 of those Regulations;]

(b) to prevent the escape of the waste from his control or that of any other person; and

(c) on the transfer of the waste, to secure—

(i) that the transfer is only to an authorised person or to a person for authorised transport purposes; and

(ii) that there is transferred such a written description of the waste as will enable other persons to avoid a contravention of that section [or any condition of a permit granted under regulation 10 of those Regulations] and to comply with the duty under this subsection as respects the escape of waste.

(2) The duty imposed by subsection (1) above does not apply to an occupier of domestic property as respects the household waste produced on the property.

(3) The following are authorised persons for the purpose of subsection (1)(c) above—

(a) any authority which is a waste collection authority for the purposes of this Part;

(b) any person who is the holder of a waste management licence under section 35 below *or of a disposal licence under section 5 of the Control of Pollution Act 1974*;

(c) any person to whom section 33(1) above does not apply by virtue of regulations under subsection (3) of that section;

(d) any person registered as a carrier of controlled waste under section 2 of the Control of Pollution (Amendment) Act 1989;

(e) any person who is not required to be so registered by virtue of regulations under section 1(3) of that Act; and

(f) a waste disposal authority in Scotland.

[(3A) The Secretary of State may by regulations amend subsection (3) above so as to add, whether generally or in such circumstances as may be prescribed in the regulations, any person specified in the regulations, or any description of person so specified, to the persons who are authorised persons for the purposes of subsection (1)(c) above.]

(4) The following are authorised transport purposes for the purposes of subsection (1)(c) above—

(a) the transport of controlled waste within the same premises between different places in those premises;

(b) the transport to a place in Great Britain of controlled waste which has been brought from a country or territory outside Great Britain not having been landed in Great Britain until it arrives at that place; and

(c) the transport by air or sea of controlled waste from a place in Great Britain to a place outside Great Britain;

and "transport" has the same meaning in this subsection as in the Control of Pollution (Amendment) Act 1989.

[(4A) For the purposes of subsection (1)(c)(ii) above—
 (a) a transfer of waste in stages shall be treated as taking place when the first stage of the transfer takes place, and
 (b) a series of transfers between the same parties of waste of the same description shall be treated as a single transfer taking place when the first of the transfers in the series takes place.]

(5) The Secretary of State may, by regulations, make provision imposing requirements on any person who is subject to the duty imposed by subsection (1) above as respects the making and retention of documents and the furnishing of documents or copies of documents.

(6) Any person who fails to comply with the duty imposed by subsection (1) above or with any requirement imposed under subsection (5) above shall be liable—
 (a) on summary conviction, to a fine not exceeding the statutory maximum; and
 (b) on conviction on indictment, to a fine.

(7) The Secretary of State shall, after consultation with such persons or bodies as appear to him representative of the interests concerned, prepare and issue a code of practice for the purpose of providing to persons practical guidance on how to discharge the duty imposed on them by subsection (1) above.

(8) The Secretary of State may from time to time revise a code of practice issued under subsection (7) above by revoking, amending or adding to the provisions of the code.

(9) [A] code of practice prepared in pursuance of subsection (7) above shall be laid
 [(a)] before both Houses of Parliament[; or
 (b) if it relates only to Scotland before the Scottish Parliament].

(10) A code of practice issued under subsection (7) above shall be admissible in evidence and if any provision of such a code appears to the court to be relevant to any question arising in the proceedings it shall be taken into account in determining that question.

(11) Different codes of practice may be prepared and issued under subsection (7) above for different areas.

NOTES

Sub-s (1): para (aa) inserted in relation to England and Wales by SI 2000/1973, Sch 10, Pt 1, paras 2, 4(a); a corresponding amendment has been made in relation to Scotland by SSI 2000/323, reg 3(1), (3)(a).

Date in force (in relation to England and Wales): 1 August 2000: see SI 2000/1973, reg 1(1).

Date in force (in relation to Scotland): 28 September 2000: see SSI 2000/323, reg 1(1).

Sub-s (1): in para (c)(ii) words "or any condition of a permit granted under regulation 10 of those Regulations" in square brackets inserted by SI 2000/1973, reg 39, Sch 10, Pt 1, paras 2, 4(b); a corresponding amendment has been made in relation to Scotland by SSI 2000/323, reg 36, Sch 10, Pt 1, para 3(1), (3)(b).

Date in force (in relation to England and Wales): 1 August 2000: see SI 2000/1973, reg 1(1).

Date in force (in relation to Scotland): 28 September 2000: see SSI 2000/323, reg 1(1).

Sub-s (3): in para (b) words in italics prospectively repealed by s 162 of, and Sch 16, Part II to, this Act, as from a day to be appointed.

Sub-s (3A): inserted by the Environment Act 1995, s 120, Sch 22, para 65.

Sub-s (4A): inserted with retrospective effect, except in relation to any proceedings for failure to comply with the duty imposed by sub-s (1) above which were commenced before 3 November 1994, by the Deregulation and Contracting Out Act 1994, s 33.

Sub-s (9): word "A" in square brackets substituted by SI 1999/1820, art 4, Sch 2, Pt I, para 102(1), (2)(a).

Date in force: 1 July 1999: see SI 1999/1820, art 1(2).

Sub-s (9): reference to "(a)" in square brackets inserted by SI 1999/1820, art 4, Sch 2, Pt I, para 102(1), (2)(b).

Date in force: 1 July 1999: see SI 1999/1820, art 1(2).

Sub-s (9): para (b) and preceding word "; or" in square brackets inserted by SI 1999/1820, art 4, Sch 2, Pt I, para 102(1), (2)(c).

Date in force: 1 July 1999: see SI 1999/1820, art 1(2).

Supplemental

73 Appeals and other provisions relating to legal proceedings and civil liability

(1) An appeal against any decision of a magistrates' court under this Part (other than a decision made in criminal proceedings) shall lie to the Crown Court at the instance of any party to the proceedings in which the decision was given if such an appeal does not lie to the Crown Court by virtue of any other enactment.

(2) In Scotland an appeal against any decision of the sheriff under this Part (other than a decision made in criminal proceedings) shall lie to the Court of Session at the instance of any party to the proceedings in which the decision was given if such an appeal does not lie to the Court of Session by virtue of any other enactment.

(3) Where a person appeals to the Crown Court or the Court of Session against a decision of a magistrates' court or the sheriff dismissing an appeal against any requirement imposed under this Part which was suspended pending determination of that appeal, the requirement shall again be suspended pending the determination of the appeal to the Crown Court or Court of Session.

(4) Where an appeal against a decision of any authority lies to a magistrates' court or to the sheriff by virtue of any provision of this Part, it shall be the duty of the authority to include in any document by which it notifies the decision to the person concerned a statement indicating that such an appeal lies and specifying the time within which it must be brought.

(5) Where on an appeal to any court against or arising out of a decision of any authority under this Part the court varies or reverses the decision it shall be the duty of the authority to act in accordance with the court's decision.

(6) Where any damage is caused by waste which has been deposited in or on land, any person who deposited it, or knowingly caused or knowingly permitted it to be

deposited, in either case so as to commit an offence under section 33(1) or 63(2) above, is liable for the damage except where the damage—

(a) was due wholly to the fault of the person who suffered it; or
(b) was suffered by a person who voluntarily accepted the risk of the damage being caused;

but without prejudice to any liability arising otherwise than under this subsection.

(7) The matters which may be proved by way of defence under section 33(7) above may be proved also by way of defence to an action brought under subsection (6) above.

(8) In subsection (6) above—

"damage" includes the death of, or injury to, any person (including any disease and any impairment of physical or mental condition); and

"fault" has the same meaning as in the Law Reform (Contributory Negligence) Act 1945.

(9) For the purposes of the following enactments—

(a) the Fatal Accidents Act 1976;
(b) the Law Reform (Contributory Negligence) Act 1945; and
(c) the Limitation Act 1980;

and for the purposes of any action of damages in Scotland arising out of the death of, or personal injury to, any person, any damage for which a person is liable under subsection (6) above shall be treated as due to his fault.

[PART IIA
CONTAMINATED LAND]

[78A Preliminary]

[(1) The following provisions have effect for the interpretation of this Part.

(2) "Contaminated land" is any land which appears to the local authority in whose area it is situated to be in such a condition, by reason of substances in, on or under the land, that–

(a) significant harm is being caused or there is a significant possibility of such harm being caused; or
(b) pollution of controlled waters is being, or is likely to be, caused;

and, in determining whether any land appears to be such land, a local authority shall, subject to subsection (5) below, act in accordance with guidance issued by the Secretary of State in accordance with section 78YA below with respect to the manner in which that determination is to be made.

(3) A "special site" is any contaminated land–

(a) which has been designated as such a site by virtue of section 78C(7) or 78D(6) below; and
(b) whose designation as such has not been terminated by the appropriate Agency under section 78Q(4) below.

(4) "Harm" means harm to the health of living organisms or other interference with the ecological systems of which they form part and, in the case of man, includes harm to his property.

(5) The questions–
- (a) what harm is to be regarded as "significant",
- (b) whether the possibility of significant harm being caused is "significant",
- (c) whether pollution of controlled waters is being, or is likely to be caused,

shall be determined in accordance with guidance issued for the purpose by the Secretary of State in accordance with section 78YA below.

(6) Without prejudice to the guidance that may be issued under subsection (5) above, guidance under paragraph (a) of that subsection may make provision for different degrees of importance to be assigned to, or for the disregard of,–
- (a) different descriptions of living organisms or ecological systems;
- (b) different descriptions of places; or
- (c) different descriptions of harm to health or property, or other interference;

and guidance under paragraph (b) of that subsection may make provision for different degrees of possibility to be regarded as "significant" (or as not being "significant") in relation to different descriptions of significant harm.

(7) "Remediation" means–
- (a) the doing of anything for the purpose of assessing the condition of–
  - (i) the contaminated land in question;
  - (ii) any controlled waters affected by that land; or
  - (iii) any land adjoining or adjacent to that land;
- (b) the doing of any works, the carrying out of any operations or the taking of any steps in relation to any such land or waters for the purpose–
  - (i) of preventing or minimising, or remedying or mitigating the effects of, any significant harm, or any pollution of controlled waters, by reason of which the contaminated land is such land; or
  - (ii) of restoring the land or waters to their former state; or
- (c) the making of subsequent inspections from time to time for the purpose of keeping under review the condition of the land or waters;

and cognate expressions shall be construed accordingly.

(8) Controlled waters are "affected by" contaminated land if (and only if) it appears to the enforcing authority that the contaminated land in question is, for the purposes of subsection (2) above, in such a condition, by reason of substances in, on or under the land, that pollution of those waters is being, or is likely to be caused.

(9) The following expressions have the meaning respectively assigned to them–

"the appropriate Agency" means–
- (a) in relation to England and Wales, the Environment Agency;
- (b) in relation to Scotland, the Scottish Environment Protection Agency;

"appropriate person" means any person who is an appropriate person, determined in accordance with section 78F below, to bear responsibility for any thing which is to be done by way of remediation in any particular case;

"charging notice" has the meaning given by section 78P(3)(b) below;

"controlled waters"–

(a) in relation to England and Wales, has the same meaning as in Part III of the Water Resources Act 1991; and

(b) in relation to Scotland, has the same meaning as in section 30A of the Control of Pollution Act 1974;

"creditor" has the same meaning as in the Conveyancing and Feudal Reform (Scotland) Act 1970;

"enforcing authority" means–

(a) in relation to a special site, the appropriate Agency;

(b) in relation to contaminated land other than a special site, the local authority in whose area the land is situated;

"heritable security" has the same meaning as in the Conveyancing and Feudal Reform (Scotland) Act 1970;

"local authority" in relation to England and Wales means–

(a) any unitary authority;

(b) any district council, so far as it is not a unitary authority;

(c) the Common Council of the City of London and, as respects the Temples, the Sub-Treasurer of the Inner Temple and the Under-Treasurer of the Middle Temple respectively;

and in relation to Scotland means a council for an area constituted under section 2 of the Local Government etc (Scotland) Act 1994;

"notice" means notice in writing;

"notification" means notification in writing;

"owner", in relation to any land in England and Wales, means a person (other than a mortgagee not in possession) who, whether in his own right or as trustee for any other person, is entitled to receive the rack rent of the land, or, where the land is not let at a rack rent, would be so entitled if it were so let;

"owner", in relation to any land in Scotland, means a person (other than a creditor in a heritable security not in possession of the security subjects) for the time being entitled to receive or who would, if the land were let, be entitled to receive, the rents of the land in connection with which the word is used and includes a trustee, factor, guardian or curator and in the case of public or municipal land includes the persons to whom the management of the land is entrusted;

"pollution of controlled waters" means the entry into controlled waters of any poisonous, noxious or polluting matter or any solid waste matter;

"prescribed" means prescribed by regulations;

"regulations" means regulations made by the Secretary of State;

"remediation declaration" has the meaning given by section 78H(6) below;

"remediation notice" has the meaning given by section 78E(1) below;

"remediation statement" has the meaning given by section 78H(7) below;

"required to be designated as a special site" shall be construed in accordance with section 78C(8) below;

"substance" means any natural or artificial substance, whether in solid or liquid form or in the form of a gas or vapour;

"unitary authority" means–

(a) the council of a county, so far as it is the council of an area for which there are no district councils;
(b) the council of any district comprised in an area for which there is no county council;
(c) the council of a London borough;
(d) the council of a county borough in Wales.]

NOTES

Inserted by the Environment Act 1995, s 57.

Date in force (for certain purposes): 21 September 1995: see SI 1995/1983, art 3.

Date in force (in relation to England, for remaining purposes): 1 April 2000: see SI 2000/340, art 2(a).

Date in force (in relation to Scotland, for remaining purposes): 14 July 2000: see SSI 2000/180, art 2(1)(a).

Date in force (in relation to Wales, for remaining purposes): 15 September 2001: see SI 2001/3211, art 2(a).

[78B Identification of contaminated land]

[(1) Every local authority shall cause its area to be inspected from time to time for the purpose–
(a) of identifying contaminated land; and
(b) of enabling the authority to decide whether any such land is land which is required to be designated as a special site.

(2) In performing its functions under subsection (1) above a local authority shall act in accordance with any guidance issued for the purpose by the Secretary of State in accordance with section 78YA below.

(3) If a local authority identifies any contaminated land in its area, it shall give notice of that fact to–
(a) the appropriate Agency;
(b) the owner of the land;
(c) any person who appears to the authority to be in occupation of the whole or any part of the land; and
(d) each person who appears to the authority to be an appropriate person;

and any notice given under this subsection shall state by virtue of which of paragraphs (a) to (d) above it is given.

(4) If, at any time after a local authority has given any person a notice pursuant to subsection (3)(d) above in respect of any land, it appears to the enforcing authority that another person is an appropriate person, the enforcing authority shall give notice to that other person–
(a) of the fact that the local authority has identified the land in question as contaminated land; and
(b) that he appears to the enforcing authority to be an appropriate person.]

NOTES

Inserted by the Environment Act 1995, s 57.

Date in force (for certain purposes): 21 September 1995: see SI 1995/1983, art 3.

Date in force (in relation to England, for remaining purposes): 1 April 2000: see SI 2000/340, art 2(a).

Date in force (in relation to Scotland, for remaining purposes): 14 July 2000: see SSI 2000/180, art 2(1)(a).

Date in force (in relation to Wales, for remaining purposes): 15 September 2001: see SI 2001/3211, art 2(a).

[78C Identification and designation of special sites]

[(1) If at any time it appears to a local authority that any contaminated land in its area might be land which is required to be designated as a special site, the authority–

(a) shall decide whether or not the land is land which is required to be so designated; and

(b) if the authority decides that the land is land which is required to be so designated, shall give notice of that decision to the relevant persons.

(2) For the purposes of this section, "the relevant persons" at any time in the case of any land are the persons who at that time fall within paragraphs (a) to (d) below, that is to say–

(a) the appropriate Agency;

(b) the owner of the land;

(c) any person who appears to the local authority concerned to be in occupation of the whole or any part of the land; and

(d) each person who appears to that authority to be an appropriate person.

(3) Before making a decision under paragraph (a) of subsection (1) above in any particular case, a local authority shall request the advice of the appropriate Agency, and in making its decision shall have regard to any advice given by that Agency in response to the request.

(4) If at any time the appropriate Agency considers that any contaminated land is land which is required to be designated as a special site, that Agency may give notice of that fact to the local authority in whose area the land is situated.

(5) Where notice under subsection (4) above is given to a local authority, the authority shall decide whether the land in question–

(a) is land which is required to be designated as a special site, or

(b) is not land which is required to be so designated,

and shall give notice of that decision to the relevant persons.

(6) Where a local authority makes a decision falling within subsection (1)(b) or (5)(a) above, the decision shall, subject to section 78D below, take effect on the day after whichever of the following events first occurs, that is to say–

(a) the expiration of the period of twenty-one days beginning with the day on which the notice required by virtue of subsection (1)(b) or, as the case may be, (5)(a) above is given to the appropriate Agency; or

(b) if the appropriate Agency gives notification to the local authority in question that it agrees with the decision, the giving of that notification;

and where a decision takes effect by virtue of this subsection, the local authority shall give notice of that fact to the relevant persons.

(7) Where a decision that any land is land which is required to be designated as a special site takes effect in accordance with subsection (6) above, the notice given under subsection (1)(b) or, as the case may be, (5)(a) above shall have effect, as from the time when the decision takes effect, as the designation of that land as such a site.

(8) For the purposes of this Part, land is required to be designated as a special site if, and only if, it is land of a description prescribed for the purposes of this subsection.

(9) Regulations under subsection (8) above may make different provision for different cases or circumstances or different areas or localities and may, in particular, describe land by reference to the area or locality in which it is situated.

(10) Without prejudice to the generality of his power to prescribe any description of land for the purposes of subsection (8) above, the Secretary of State, in deciding whether to prescribe a particular description of contaminated land for those purposes, may, in particular, have regard to–

- (a) whether land of the description in question appears to him to be land which is likely to be in such a condition, by reason of substances in, on or under the land that–
  - (i) serious harm would or might be caused, or
  - (ii) serious pollution of controlled waters would be, or would be likely to be, caused; or
- (b) whether the appropriate Agency is likely to have expertise in dealing with the kind of significant harm, or pollution of controlled waters, by reason of which land of the description in question is contaminated land.]

NOTES

Inserted by the Environment Act 1995, s 57.

Date in force (for certain purposes): 21 September 1995: see SI 1995/1983, art 3.

Date in force (in relation to England, for remaining purposes): 1 April 2000: see SI 2000/340, art 2(a).

Date in force (in relation to Scotland, for remaining purposes): 14 July 2000: see SSI 2000/180, art 2(1)(a).

Date in force (in relation to Wales, for remaining purposes): 15 September 2001: see SI 2001/3211, art 2(a).

[78D Referral of special site decisions to the Secretary of State]

[(1) In any case where–

- (a) a local authority gives notice of a decision to the appropriate Agency pursuant to subsection (1)(b) or (5)(b) of section 78C above, but
- (b) before the expiration of the period of twenty-one days beginning with the day on which that notice is so given, that Agency gives the local authority notice that it disagrees with the decision, together with a statement of its reasons for disagreeing,

the authority shall refer the decision to the Secretary of State and shall send to him a statement of its reasons for reaching the decision.

(2) Where the appropriate Agency gives notice to a local authority under paragraph (b) of subsection (1) above, it shall also send to the Secretary of State a copy of the notice and of the statement given under that paragraph.

(3) Where a local authority refers a decision to the Secretary of State under subsection (1) above, it shall give notice of that fact to the relevant persons.

(4) Where a decision of a local authority is referred to the Secretary of State under subsection (1) above, he–

(a) may confirm or reverse the decision with respect to the whole or any part of the land to which it relates; and

(b) shall give notice of his decision on the referral–

(i) to the relevant persons; and

(ii) to the local authority.

(5) Where a decision of a local authority is referred to the Secretary of State under subsection (1) above, the decision shall not take effect until the day after that on which the Secretary of State gives the notice required by subsection (4) above to the persons there mentioned and shall then take effect as confirmed or reversed by him.

(6) Where a decision which takes effect in accordance with subsection (5) above is to the effect that at least some land is land which is required to be designated as a special site, the notice given under subsection (4)(b) above shall have effect, as from the time when the decision takes effect, as the designation of that land as such a site.

(7) In this section "the relevant persons" has the same meaning as in section 78C above.]

NOTES

Inserted by the Environment Act 1995, s 57.

Date in force (for certain purposes): 21 September 1995: see SI 1995/1983, art 3.

Date in force (in relation to England, for remaining purposes): 1 April 2000: see SI 2000/340, art 2(a).

Date in force (in relation to Scotland, for remaining purposes): 14 July 2000: see SSI 2000/180, art 2(1)(a).

Date in force (in relation to Wales, for remaining purposes): 15 September 2001: see SI 2001/3211, art 2(a).

[78E Duty of enforcing authority to require remediation of contaminated land etc]

[(1) In any case where–

(a) any land has been designated as a special site by virtue of section 78C(7) or 78D(6) above, or

(b) a local authority has identified any contaminated land (other than a special site) in its area,

the enforcing authority shall, in accordance with such procedure as may be prescribed and subject to the following provisions of this Part, serve on each person who is an appropriate person a notice (in this Part referred to as a "remediation notice") specifying what that person is to do by way of remediation and the periods within which he is required to do each of the things so specified.

(2) Different remediation notices requiring the doing of different things by way of remediation may be served on different persons in consequence of the presence of different substances in, on or under any land or waters.

(3) Where two or more persons are appropriate persons in relation to any particular thing which is to be done by way of remediation, the remediation notice served on each of them shall state the proportion, determined under section 78F(7) below, of the cost of doing that thing which each of them respectively is liable to bear.

(4) The only things by way of remediation which the enforcing authority may do, or require to be done, under or by virtue of this Part are things which it considers reasonable, having regard to–

(a) the cost which is likely to be involved; and
(b) the seriousness of the harm, or pollution of controlled waters, in question.

(5) In determining for any purpose of this Part–

(a) what is to be done (whether by an appropriate person, the enforcing authority or any other person) by way of remediation in any particular case,
(b) the standard to which any land is, or waters are, to be remediated pursuant to the notice, or
(c) what is, or is not, to be regarded as reasonable for the purposes of subsection (4) above,

the enforcing authority shall have regard to any guidance issued for the purpose by the Secretary of State.

(6) Regulations may make provision for or in connection with–

(a) the form or content of remediation notices; or
(b) any steps of a procedural nature which are to be taken in connection with, or in consequence of, the service of a remediation notice.]

NOTES

Inserted by the Environment Act 1995, s 57.

Date in force (for certain purposes): 21 September 1995: see SI 1995/1983, art 3.

Date in force (in relation to England, for remaining purposes): 1 April 2000: see SI 2000/340, art 2(a).

Date in force (in relation to Scotland, for remaining purposes): 14 July 2000: see SSI 2000/180, art 2(1)(a).

Date in force (in relation to Wales, for remaining purposes): 15 September 2001: see SI 2001/3211, art 2(a).

[78F Determination of the appropriate person to bear responsibility for remediation]

[(1) This section has effect for the purpose of determining who is the appropriate person to bear responsibility for any particular thing which the enforcing authority determines is to be done by way of remediation in any particular case.

(2) Subject to the following provisions of this section, any person, or any of the persons, who caused or knowingly permitted the substances, or any of the substances, by reason of which the contaminated land in question is such land to be in, on or under that land is an appropriate person.

(3) A person shall only be an appropriate person by virtue of subsection (2) above in relation to things which are to be done by way of remediation which are to any extent referable to substances which he caused or knowingly permitted to be present in, on or under the contaminated land in question.

(4) If no person has, after reasonable inquiry, been found who is by virtue of subsection (2) above an appropriate person to bear responsibility for the things which are to be done by way of remediation, the owner or occupier for the time being of the contaminated land in question is an appropriate person.

(5) If, in consequence of subsection (3) above, there are things which are to be done by way of remediation in relation to which no person has, after reasonable inquiry, been found who is an appropriate person by virtue of subsection (2) above, the owner or occupier for the time being of the contaminated land in question is an appropriate person in relation to those things.

(6) Where two or more persons would, apart from this subsection, be appropriate persons in relation to any particular thing which is to be done by way of remediation, the enforcing authority shall determine in accordance with guidance issued for the purpose by the Secretary of State whether any, and if so which, of them is to be treated as not being an appropriate person in relation to that thing.

(7) Where two or more persons are appropriate persons in relation to any particular thing which is to be done by way of remediation, they shall be liable to bear the cost of doing that thing in proportions determined by the enforcing authority in accordance with guidance issued for the purpose by the Secretary of State.

(8) Any guidance issued for the purposes of subsection (6) or (7) above shall be issued in accordance with section 78YA below.

(9) A person who has caused or knowingly permitted any substance ("substance A") to be in, on or under any land shall also be taken for the purposes of this section to have caused or knowingly permitted there to be in, on or under that land any substance which is there as a result of a chemical reaction or biological process affecting substance A.

(10) A thing which is to be done by way of remediation may be regarded for the purposes of this Part as referable to the presence of any substance notwithstanding that the thing in question would not have to be done–

(a) in consequence only of the presence of that substance in any quantity; or

(b) in consequence only of the quantity of that substance which any particular person caused or knowingly permitted to be present.]

NOTES

Inserted by the Environment Act 1995, s 57.

Date in force (for certain purposes): 21 September 1995: see SI 1995/1983, art 3.

Date in force (in relation to England, for remaining purposes): 1 April 2000: see SI 2000/340, art 2(a).

Date in force (in relation to Scotland, for remaining purposes): 14 July 2000: see SSI 2000/180, art 2(1)(a).

Date in force (in relation to Wales, for remaining purposes): 15 September 2001: see SI 2001/3211, art 2(a).

[78G Grant of, and compensation for, rights of entry etc]

[(1) A remediation notice may require an appropriate person to do things by way of remediation, notwithstanding that he is not entitled to do those things.

(2) Any person whose consent is required before any thing required by a remediation notice may be done shall grant, or join in granting, such rights in relation to any of the relevant land or waters as will enable the appropriate person to comply with any requirements imposed by the remediation notice.

(3) Before serving a remediation notice, the enforcing authority shall reasonably endeavour to consult every person who appears to the authority–

(a) to be the owner or occupier of any of the relevant land or waters, and
(b) to be a person who might be required by subsection (2) above to grant, or join in granting, any rights,

concerning the rights which that person may be so required to grant.

(4) Subsection (3) above shall not preclude the service of a remediation notice in any case where it appears to the enforcing authority that the contaminated land in question is in such a condition, by reason of substances in, on or under the land, that there is imminent danger of serious harm, or serious pollution of controlled waters, being caused.

(5) A person who grants, or joins in granting, any rights pursuant to subsection (2) above shall be entitled, on making an application within such period as may be prescribed and in such manner as may be prescribed to such person as may be prescribed, to be paid by the appropriate person compensation of such amount as may be determined in such manner as may be prescribed.

(6) Without prejudice to the generality of the regulations that may be made by virtue of subsection (5) above, regulations by virtue of that subsection may make such provision in relation to compensation under this section as may be made by regulations by virtue of subsection (4) of section 35A above in relation to compensation under that section.

(7) In this section, "relevant land or waters" means–

(a) the contaminated land in question;
(b) any controlled waters affected by that land; or
(c) any land adjoining or adjacent to that land or those waters.]

NOTES

Inserted by the Environment Act 1995, s 57.

Date in force (for certain purposes): 21 September 1995: see SI 1995/1983, art 3.

Date in force (in relation to England, for remaining purposes): 1 April 2000: see SI 2000/340, art 2(a).

Date in force (in relation to Scotland, for remaining purposes): 14 July 2000: see SSI 2000/180, art 2(1)(a).

Date in force (in relation to Wales, for remaining purposes): 15 September 2001: see SI 2001/3211, art 2(a).

[78H Restrictions and prohibitions on serving remediation notices]

[(1) Before serving a remediation notice, the enforcing authority shall reasonably endeavour to consult–

(a) the person on whom the notice is to be served,

(b) the owner of any land to which the notice relates,

(c) any person who appears to that authority to be in occupation of the whole or any part of the land, and

(d) any person of such other description as may be prescribed,

concerning what is to be done by way of remediation.

(2) Regulations may make provision for, or in connection with, steps to be taken for the purposes of subsection (1) above.

(3) No remediation notice shall be served on any person by reference to any contaminated land during any of the following periods, that is to say–

(a) the period–

(i) beginning with the identification of the contaminated land in question pursuant to section 78B(1) above, and

(ii) ending with the expiration of the period of three months beginning with the day on which the notice required by subsection (3)(d) or, as the case may be, (4) of section 78B above is given to that person in respect of that land;

(b) if a decision falling within paragraph (b) of section 78C(1) above is made in relation to the contaminated land in question, the period beginning with the making of the decision and ending with the expiration of the period of three months beginning with–

(i) in a case where the decision is not referred to the Secretary of State under section 78D above, the day on which the notice required by section 78C(6) above is given, or

(ii) in a case where the decision is referred to the Secretary of State under section 78D above, the day on which he gives the notice required by subsection (4)(b) of that section;

(c) if the appropriate Agency gives a notice under subsection (4) of section 78C above to a local authority in relation to the contaminated land in question, the period beginning with the day on which that notice is given and ending with the expiration of the period of three months beginning with–

(i) in a case where notice is given under subsection (6) of that section, the day on which that notice is given;
(ii) in a case where the authority makes a decision falling within subsection (5)(b) of that section and the appropriate Agency fails to give notice under paragraph (b) of section 78D(1) above, the day following the expiration of the period of twenty-one days mentioned in that paragraph; or
(iii) in a case where the authority makes a decision falling within section 78C(5)(b) above which is referred to the Secretary of State under section 78D above, the day on which the Secretary of State gives the notice required by subsection (4)(b) of that section.

(4) Neither subsection (1) nor subsection (3) above shall preclude the service of a remediation notice in any case where it appears to the enforcing authority that the land in question is in such a condition, by reason of substances in, on or under the land, that there is imminent danger of serious harm, or serious pollution of controlled waters, being caused.

(5) The enforcing authority shall not serve a remediation notice on a person if and so long as any one or more of the following conditions is for the time being satisfied in the particular case, that is to say–

(a) the authority is satisfied, in consequence of section 78E(4) and (5) above, that there is nothing by way of remediation which could be specified in a remediation notice served on that person;
(b) the authority is satisfied that appropriate things are being, or will be, done by way of remediation without the service of a remediation notice on that person;
(c) it appears to the authority that the person on whom the notice would be served is the authority itself; or
(d) the authority is satisfied that the powers conferred on it by section 78N below to do what is appropriate by way of remediation are exercisable.

(6) Where the enforcing authority is precluded by virtue of section 78E(4) or (5) above from specifying in a remediation notice any particular thing by way of remediation which it would otherwise have specified in such a notice, the authority shall prepare and publish a document (in this Part referred to as a "remediation declaration") which shall record–

(a) the reasons why the authority would have specified that thing; and
(b) the grounds on which the authority is satisfied that it is precluded from specifying that thing in such a notice.

(7) In any case where the enforcing authority is precluded, by virtue of paragraph (b), (c) or (d) of subsection (5) above, from serving a remediation notice, the responsible person shall prepare and publish a document (in this Part referred to as a "remediation statement") which shall record–

(a) the things which are being, have been, or are expected to be, done by way of remediation in the particular case;
(b) the name and address of the person who is doing, has done, or is expected to do, each of those things; and

(c) the periods within which each of those things is being, or is expected to be, done.

(8) For the purposes of subsection (7) above, the "responsible person" is–

(a) in a case where the condition in paragraph (b) of subsection (5) above is satisfied, the person who is doing or has done, or who the enforcing authority is satisfied will do, the things there mentioned; or

(b) in a case where the condition in paragraph (c) or (d) of that subsection is satisfied, the enforcing authority.

(9) If a person who is required by virtue of subsection (8)(a) above to prepare and publish a remediation statement fails to do so within a reasonable time after the date on which a remediation notice specifying the things there mentioned could, apart from subsection (5) above, have been served, the enforcing authority may itself prepare and publish the statement and may recover its reasonable costs of doing so from that person.

(10) Where the enforcing authority has been precluded by virtue only of subsection (5) above from serving a remediation notice on an appropriate person but–

(a) none of the conditions in that subsection is for the time being satisfied in the particular case, and

(b) the authority is not precluded by any other provision of this Part from serving a remediation notice on that appropriate person,

the authority shall serve a remediation notice on that person; and any such notice may be so served without any further endeavours by the authority to consult persons pursuant to subsection (1) above, if and to the extent that that person has bean consulted pursuant to that subsection concerning the things which will be specified in the notice.]

NOTES

Inserted by the Environment Act 1995, s 57.

Date in force (for certain purposes): 21 September 1995: see SI 1995/1983, art 3.

Date in force (in relation to England, for remaining purposes): 1 April 2000: see SI 2000/340, art 2(a).

Date in force (in relation to Scotland, for remaining purposes): 14 July 2000: see SSI 2000/180, art 2(1)(a).

Date in force (in relation to Wales, for remaining purposes): 15 September 2001: see SI 2001/3211, art 2(a).

[78J Restrictions on liability relating to the pollution of controlled waters]

[(1) This section applies where any land is contaminated land by virtue of paragraph (b) of subsection (2) of section 78A above (whether or not the land is also contaminated land by virtue of paragraph (a) of that subsection).

(2) Where this section applies, no remediation notice given in consequence of the land in question being contaminated land shall require a person who is an appropriate person by virtue of section 78F(4) or (5) above to do anything by way of remediation to that or any other land, or any waters, which he could not have

been required to do by such a notice had paragraph (b) of section 78A(2) above (and all other references to pollution of controlled waters) been omitted from this Part.

(3) If, in a case where this section applies, a person permits, has permitted, or might permit, water from an abandoned mine or part of a mine–

(a) to enter any controlled waters, or

(b) to reach a place from which it is or, as the case may be, was likely, in the opinion of the enforcing authority, to enter such waters,

no remediation notice shall require him in consequence to do anything by way of remediation (whether to the contaminated land in question or to any other land or waters) which he could not have been required to do by such a notice had paragraph (b) of section 78A(2) above (and all other references to pollution of controlled waters) been omitted from this Part.

(4) Subsection (3) above shall not apply to the owner or former operator of any mine or part of a mine if the mine or part in question became abandoned after 31st December 1999.

(5) In determining for the purposes of subsection (4) above whether a mine or part of a mine became abandoned before, on or after 31st December 1999 in a case where the mine or part has become abandoned on two or more occasions, of which–

(a) at least one falls on or before that date, and

(b) at least one falls after that date,

the mine or part shall be regarded as becoming abandoned after that date (but without prejudice to the operation of subsection (3) above in relation to that mine or part at, or in relation to, any time before the first of those occasions which falls after that date).

(6) Where, immediately before a part of a mine becomes abandoned, that part is the only part of the mine not falling to be regarded as abandoned for the time being, the abandonment of that part shall not be regarded for the purposes of subsection (4) or (5) above as constituting the abandonment of the mine, but only of that part of it.

(7) Nothing in subsection (2) or (3) above prevents the enforcing authority from doing anything by way of remediation under section 78N below which it could have done apart from that subsection, but the authority shall not be entitled under section 78P below to recover from any person any part of the cost incurred by the authority in doing by way of remediation anything which it is precluded by subsection (2) or (3) above from requiring that person to do.

(8) In this section "mine" has the same meaning as in the Mines and Quarries Act 1954.]

NOTES

Inserted by the Environment Act 1995, s 57.

Date in force (for certain purposes): 21 September 1995: see SI 1995/1983, art 3.

Date in force (in relation to England, for remaining purposes): 1 April 2000: see SI 2000/340, art 2(a).

Date in force (in relation to Scotland, for remaining purposes): 14 July 2000: see SSI 2000/180, art 2(1)(a).

Date in force (in relation to Wales, for remaining purposes): 15 September 2001: see SI 2001/3211, art 2(a).

[78K Liability in respect of contaminating substances which escape to other land]

[(1) A person who has caused or knowingly permitted any substances to be in, on or under any land shall also be taken for the purposes of this Part to have caused or, as the case may be, knowingly permitted those substances to be in, on or under any other land to which they appear to have escaped.

(2) Subsections (3) and (4) below apply in any case where it appears that any substances are or have been in, on or under any land (in this section referred to as "land A") as a result of their escape, whether directly or indirectly, from other land in, on or under which a person caused or knowingly permitted them to be.

(3) Where this subsection applies, no remediation notice shall require a person–

- (a) who is the owner or occupier of land A, and
- (b) who has not caused or knowingly permitted the substances in question to be in, on or under that land,

to do anything by way of remediation to any land or waters (other than land or waters of which he is the owner or occupier) in consequence of land A appearing to be in such a condition, by reason of the presence of those substances in, on or under it, that significant harm is being caused, or there is a significant possibility of such harm being caused, or that pollution of controlled waters is being, or is likely to be caused.

(4) Where this subsection applies, no remediation notice shall require a person–

- (a) who is the owner or occupier of land A, and
- (b) who has not caused or knowingly permitted the substances in question to be in, on or under that land,

to do anything by way of remediation in consequence of any further land in, on or under which those substances or any of them appear to be or to have been present as a result of their escape from land A ("land B") appearing to be in such a condition; by reason of the presence of those substances in, on or under it, that significant harm is being caused, or there is a significant possibility of such harm being caused, or that pollution of controlled waters is being, or is likely to be caused, unless he is also the owner or occupier of land B.

(5) In any case where–

- (a) a person ("person A") has caused or knowingly permitted any substances to be in, on, or under any land,
- (b) another person ("person B") who has not caused or knowingly permitted those substances to be in, on or under that land becomes the owner or occupier of that land, and
- (c) the substances, or any of the substances, mentioned in paragraph (a) above appear to have escaped to other land,

no remediation notice shall require person B to do anything by way of remediation to that other land in consequence of the apparent acts or omissions of person A, except to the extent that person B caused or knowingly permitted the escape.

(6) Nothing in subsection (3), (4) or (5) above prevents the enforcing authority from doing anything by way of remediation under section 78N below which it could have done apart from that subsection, but the authority shall not be entitled under section 78P below to recover from any person any part of the cost incurred by the authority in doing by way of remediation anything which it is precluded by subsection (3), (4) or (5) above from requiring that person to do.

(7) In this section, "appear" means appear to the enforcing authority, and cognate expressions shall be construed accordingly.]

NOTES

Inserted by the Environment Act 1995, s 57.

Date in force (for certain purposes): 21 September 1995: see SI 1995/1983, art 3.

Date in force (in relation to England, for remaining purposes): 1 April 2000: see SI 2000/340, art 2(a).

Date in force (in relation to Scotland, for remaining purposes): 14 July 2000: see SSI 2000/180, art 2(1)(a).

Date in force (in relation to Wales, for remaining purposes): 15 September 2001: see SI 2001/3211, art 2(a).

[78L Appeals against remediation notices]

[(1) A person on whom a remediation notice is served may, within the period of twenty-one days beginning with the day on which the notice is served, appeal against the notice–

(a) if it was served by a local authority, to a magistrates' court or, in Scotland, to the sheriff by way of summary application; or

(b) if it was served by the appropriate Agency, to the Secretary of State;

and in the following provisions of this section "the appellate authority" means the magistrates' court, the sheriff or the Secretary of State, as the case may be.

(2) On any appeal under subsection (1) above the appellate authority–

(a) shall quash the notice, if it is satisfied that there is a material defect in the notice; but

(b) subject to that, may confirm the remediation notice, with or without modification, or quash it.

(3) Where an appellate authority confirms a remediation notice, with or without modification, it may extend the period specified in the notice for doing what the notice requires to be done.

(4) Regulations may make provision with respect to–

(a) the grounds on which appeals under subsection (1) above may be made;

(b) the cases in which, grounds on which, court or tribunal to which, or person at whose instance, an appeal against a decision of a magistrates' court or sheriff court in pursuance of an appeal under subsection (1) above shall lie; or

(c) the procedure on an appeal under subsection (1) above or on an appeal by virtue of paragraph (b) above.

(5) Regulations under subsection (4) above may (among other things)–

(a) include provisions comparable to those in section 290 of the Public Health Act 1936 (appeals against notices requiring the execution of works);

(b) prescribe the cases in which a remediation notice is, or is not, to be suspended until the appeal is decided, or until some other stage in the proceedings;

(c) prescribe the cases in which the decision on an appeal may in some respects be less favourable to the appellant than the remediation notice against which he is appealing;

(d) prescribe the cases in which the appellant may claim that a remediation notice should have been served on some other person and prescribe the procedure to be followed in those cases;

(e) make provision as respects–

(i) the particulars to be included in the notice of appeal;

(ii) the persons on whom notice of appeal is to be served and the particulars, if any, which are to accompany the notice; and

(iii) the abandonment of an appeal;

(f) make different provision for different cases or classes of case.

(6) This section, so far as relating to appeals to the Secretary of State, is subject to section 114 of the Environment Act 1995 (delegation or reference of appeals etc).]

NOTES

Inserted by the Environment Act 1995, s 57.

Date in force (for certain purposes): 21 September 1995: see SI 1995/1983, art 3.

Date in force (in relation to England, for remaining purposes): 1 April 2000: see SI 2000/340, art 2(a).

Date in force (in relation to Scotland, for remaining purposes): 14 July 2000: see SSI 2000/180, art 2(1)(a).

Date in force (in relation to Wales, for remaining purposes): 15 September 2001: see SI 2001/3211, art 2(a).

[78M Offences of not complying with a remediation notice]

[(1) If a person on whom an enforcing authority serves a remediation notice fails, without reasonable excuse, to comply with any of the requirements of the notice, he shall be guilty of an offence.

(2) Where the remediation notice in question is one which was required by section 78E(3) above to state, in relation to the requirement which has not been complied with, the proportion of the cost involved which the person charged with the offence is liable to bear, it shall be a defence for that person to prove that the only reason why he has not complied with the requirement is that one or more of the other persons who are liable to bear a proportion of that cost refused, or was not able, to comply with the requirement.

(3) Except in a case falling within subsection (4) below, a person who commits an offence under subsection (1) above shall be liable, on summary conviction, to a fine

not exceeding level 5 on the standard scale and to a further fine of an amount equal to one-tenth of level 5 on the standard scale for each day on which the failure continues after conviction of the offence and before the enforcing authority has begun to exercise its powers by virtue of section 78N(3)(c) below.

(4) A person who commits an offence under subsection (1) above in a case where the contaminated land to which the remediation notice relates is industrial, trade or business premises shall be liable on summary conviction to a fine not exceeding £20,000 or such greater sum as the Secretary of State may from time to time by order substitute and to a further fine of an amount equal to one-tenth of that sum for each day on which the failure continues after conviction of the offence and before the enforcing authority has begun to exercise its powers by virtue of section 78N(3)(c) below.

(5) If the enforcing authority is of the opinion that proceedings for an offence under this section would afford an ineffectual remedy against a person who has failed to comply with any of the requirements of a remediation notice which that authority has served on him, that authority may take proceedings in the High Court or, in Scotland, in any court of competent jurisdiction, for the purpose of securing compliance with the remediation notice.

(6) In this section, "industrial, trade or business premises" means premises used for any industrial, trade or business purposes or premises not so used on which matter is burnt in connection with any industrial, trade or business process, and premises are used for industrial purposes where they are used for the purposes of any treatment or process as well as where they are used for the purpose of manufacturing.

(7) No order shall be made under subsection (4) above unless a draft of the order has been laid before, and approved by a resolution of, each House of Parliament.]

NOTES

Inserted by the Environment Act 1995, s 57.

Date in force (for certain purposes): 21 September 1995: see SI 1995/1983, art 3.

Date in force (in relation to England, for remaining purposes): 1 April 2000: see SI 2000/340, art 2(a).

Date in force (in relation to Scotland, for remaining purposes): 14 July 2000: see SSI 2000/180, art 2(1)(a).

Date in force (in relation to Wales, for remaining purposes): 15 September 2001: see SI 2001/3211, art 2(a).

[78N Powers of the enforcing authority to carry out remediation]

[(1) Where this section applies, the enforcing authority shall itself have power, in a case falling within paragraph (a) or (b) of section 78E(1) above, to do what is appropriate by way of remediation to the relevant land or waters.

(2) Subsection (1) above shall not confer power on the enforcing authority to do anything by way of remediation if the authority would, in the particular case, be precluded by section 78YB below from serving a remediation notice requiring that thing to be done.

(3) This section applies in each of the following cases, that is to say–

(a) where the enforcing authority considers it necessary to do anything itself by way of remediation for the purpose of preventing the occurrence of any serious harm, or serious pollution of controlled waters, of which there is imminent danger;

(b) where an appropriate person has entered into a written agreement with the enforcing authority for that authority to do, at the cost of that person, that which he would otherwise be required to do under this Part by way of remediation;

(c) where a person on whom the enforcing authority serves a remediation notice fails to comply with any of the requirements of the notice;

(d) where the enforcing authority is precluded by section 78J or 78K above from including something by way of remediation in a remediation notice;

(e) where the enforcing authority considers that, were it to do some particular thing by way of remediation, it would decide, by virtue of subsection (2) of section 78P below or any guidance issued under that subsection,–

(i) not to seek to recover under subsection (1) of that section any of the reasonable cost incurred by it in doing that thing; or

(ii) to seek so to recover only a portion of that cost;

(f) where no person has, after reasonable inquiry, been found who is an appropriate person in relation to any particular thing.

(4) Subject to section 78E(4) and (5) above, for the purposes of this section, the things which it is appropriate for the enforcing authority to do by way of remediation are–

(a) in a case falling within paragraph (a) of subsection (3) above, anything by way of remediation which the enforcing authority considers necessary for the purpose mentioned in that paragraph;

(b) in a case falling within paragraph (b) of that subsection, anything specified in, or determined under, the agreement mentioned in that paragraph;

(c) in a case falling within paragraph (c) of that subsection, anything which the person mentioned in that paragraph was required to do by virtue of the remediation notice;

(d) in a case falling within paragraph (d) of that subsection, anything by way of remediation which the enforcing authority is precluded by section 78J or 78K above from including in a remediation notice;

(e) in a case falling within paragraph (e) or (f) of that subsection, the particular thing mentioned in the paragraph in question.

(5) In this section "the relevant land or waters" means–

(a) the contaminated land in question;

(b) any controlled waters affected by that land; or

(c) any land adjoining or adjacent to that land or those waters.]

NOTES

Inserted by the Environment Act 1995, s 57.

Date in force (for certain purposes): 21 September 1995: see SI 1995/1983, art 3.

Date in force (in relation to England, for remaining purposes): 1 April 2000: see SI 2000/340, art 2(a).

Date in force (in relation to Scotland, for remaining purposes): 14 July 2000: see SSI 2000/180, art 2(1)(a).

Date in force (in relation to Wales, for remaining purposes): 15 September 2001: see SI 2001/3211, art 2(a).

[78P Recovery of, and security for, the cost of remediation by the enforcing authority]

[(1) Where, by virtue of section 78N(3)(a), (c), (e) or (f) above, the enforcing authority does any particular thing by way of remediation, it shall be entitled, subject to sections 78J(7) and 78K(6) above, to recover the reasonable cost incurred in doing it from the appropriate person or, if there are two or more appropriate persons in relation to the thing in question, from those persons in proportions determined pursuant to section 78F(7) above.

(2) In deciding whether to recover the cost, and, if so, how much of the cost, which it is entitled to recover under subsection (1) above, the enforcing authority shall have regard–

- (a) to any hardship which the recovery may cause to the person from whom the cost is recoverable; and
- (b) to any guidance issued by the Secretary of State for the purposes of this subsection.

(3) Subsection (4) below shall apply in any case where–

- (a) any cost is recoverable under subsection (1) above from a person–
  - (i) who is the owner of any premises which consist of or include the contaminated land in question; and
  - (ii) who caused or knowingly permitted the substances, or any of the substances, by reason of which the land is contaminated land to be in, on or under the land; and
- (b) the enforcing authority serves a notice under this subsection (in this Part referred to as a "charging notice") on that person.

(4) Where this subsection applies–

- (a) the cost shall carry interest, at such reasonable rate as the enforcing authority may determine, from the date of service of the notice until the whole amount is paid; and
- (b) subject to the following provisions of this section, the cost and accrued interest shall be a charge on the premises mentioned in subsection (3)(a)(i) above.

(5) A charging notice shall–

- (a) specify the amount of the cost which the enforcing authority claims is recoverable;
- (b) state the effect of subsection (4) above and the rate of interest determined by the authority under that subsection; and
- (c) state the effect of subsections (7) and (8) below.

(6) On the date on which an enforcing authority serves a charging notice on a person, the authority shall also serve a copy of the notice on every other person

who, to the knowledge of the authority, has an interest in the premises capable of being affected by the charge.

(7) Subject to any order under subsection (9)(b) or (c) below, the amount of any cost specified in a charging notice and the accrued interest shall be a charge on the premises–

(a) as from the end of the period of twenty-one days beginning with the service of the charging notice, or

(b) where an appeal is brought under subsection (8) below, as from the final determination or (as the case may be) the withdrawal, of the appeal,

until the cost and interest are recovered.

(8) A person served with a charging notice or a copy of a charging notice may appeal against the notice to a county court within the period of twenty-one days beginning with the date of service.

(9) On an appeal under subsection (8) above, the court may–

(a) confirm the notice without modification;

(b) order that the notice is to have effect with the substitution of a different amount for the amount originally specified in it; or

(c) order that the notice is to be of no effect.

(10) Regulations may make provision with respect to–

(a) the grounds on which appeals under this section may be made; or

(b) the procedure on any such appeal.

(11) An enforcing authority shall, for the purpose of enforcing a charge under this section, have all the same powers and remedies under the Law of Property Act 1925, and otherwise, as if it were a mortgagee by deed having powers of sale and lease, of accepting surrenders of leases and of appointing a receiver.

(12) Where any cost is a charge on premises under this section, the enforcing authority may by order declare the cost to be payable with interest by instalments within the specified period until the whole amount is paid.

(13) In subsection (12) above–

"interest" means interest at the rate determined by the enforcing authority under subsection (4) above; and

"the specified period" means such period of thirty years or less from the date of service of the charging notice as is specified in the order.

(14) Subsections (3) to (13) above do not extend to Scotland.]

NOTES

Inserted by the Environment Act 1995, s 57.

Date in force (for certain purposes): 21 September 1995: see SI 1995/1983, art 3.

Date in force (in relation to England, for remaining purposes): 1 April 2000: see SI 2000/340, art 2(a).

Date in force (in relation to Scotland, for remaining purposes): 14 July 2000: see SSI 2000/180, art 2(1)(a).

Date in force (in relation to Wales, for remaining purposes): 15 September 2001: see SI 2001/3211, art 2(a).

[78Q Special sites]

[(1) If, in a case where a local authority has served a remediation notice, the contaminated land in question becomes a special site, the appropriate Agency may adopt the remediation notice and, if it does so,–

(a) it shall give notice of its decision to adopt the remediation notice to the appropriate person and to the local authority;

(b) the remediation notice shall have effect, as from the time at which the appropriate Agency decides to adopt it, as a remediation notice given by that Agency; and

(c) the validity of the remediation notice shall not be affected by–

(i) the contaminated land having become a special site;

(ii) the adoption of the remediation notice by the appropriate Agency; or

(iii) anything in paragraph (b) above.

(2) Where a local authority has, by virtue of section 78N above, begun to do any thing, or any series of things, by way of remediation–

(a) the authority may continue doing that thing, or that series of things, by virtue of that section, notwithstanding that the contaminated land in question becomes a special site; and

(b) section 78P above shall apply in relation to the reasonable cost incurred by the authority in doing that thing or those things as if that authority were the enforcing authority.

(3) If and so long as any land is a special site, the appropriate Agency may from time to time inspect that land for the purpose of keeping its condition under review.

(4) If it appears to the appropriate Agency that a special site is no longer land which is required to be designated as such a site, the appropriate Agency may give notice–

(a) to the Secretary of State, and

(b) to the local authority in whose area the site is situated,

terminating the designation of the land in question as a special site as from such date as may be specified in the notice.

(5) A notice under subsection (4) above shall not prevent the land, or any of the land, to which the notice relates being designated as a special site on a subsequent occasion.

(6) In exercising its functions under subsection (3) or (4) above, the appropriate Agency shall act in accordance with any guidance given for the purpose by the Secretary of State.]

NOTES

Inserted by the Environment Act 1995, s 57.

Date in force (for certain purposes): 21 September 1995: see SI 1995/1983, art 3.

Date in force (in relation to England, for remaining purposes): 1 April 2000: see SI 2000/340, art 2(a).

Date in force (in relation to Scotland, for remaining purposes): 14 July 2000: see SSI 2000/180, art 2(1)(a).

Date in force (in relation to Wales, for remaining purposes): 15 September 2001: see SI 2001/3211, art 2(a).

[78R Registers]

[(1) Every enforcing authority shall maintain a register containing prescribed particulars of or relating to–

(a) remediation notices served by that authority;
(b) appeals against any such remediation notices;
(c) remediation statements or remediation declarations prepared and published under section 78H above;
(d) in relation to an enforcing authority in England and Wales, appeals against charging notices served by that authority;
(e) notices under subsection (1)(b) or (5)(a) of section 78C above which have effect by virtue of subsection (7) of that section as the designation of any land as a special site;
(f) notices under subsection (4)(b) of section 78D above which have effect by virtue of subsection (6) of that section as the designation of any land as a special site;
(g) notices given by or to the enforcing authority under section 78Q(4) above terminating the designation of any land as a special site;
(h) notifications given to that authority by persons–
  (i) on whom a remediation notice has been served, or
  (ii) who are or were required by virtue of section 78H(8)(a) above to prepare and publish a remediation statement,

  of what they claim has been done by them by way of remediation;
(j) notifications given to that authority by owners or occupiers of land–
  (i) in respect of which a remediation notice has been served, or
  (ii) in respect of which a remediation statement has been prepared and published,

  of what they claim has been done on the land in question by way of remediation;
(k) convictions for such offences under section 78M above as may be prescribed;
(l) such other matters relating to contaminated land as may be prescribed;

but that duty is subject to sections 78S and 78T below.

(2) The form of, and the descriptions of information to be contained in, notifications for the purposes of subsection (1)(h) or (j) above may be prescribed by the Secretary of State.

(3) No entry made in a register by virtue of subsection (1)(h) or (j) above constitutes a representation by the body maintaining the register or, in a case where the entry is made by virtue of subsection (6) below, the authority which sent the copy of the particulars in question pursuant to subsection (4) or (5) below–

(a) that what is stated in the entry to have been done has in fact been done; or
(b) as to the manner in which it has been done.

(4) Where any particulars are entered on a register maintained under this section by the appropriate Agency, the appropriate Agency shall send a copy of those

particulars to the local authority in whose area is situated the land to which the particulars relate.

(5) In any case where–
- (a) any land is treated by virtue of section 78X(2) below as situated in the area of a local authority other than the local authority in whose area it is in fact situated, and
- (b) any particulars relating to that land are entered on the register maintained under this section by the local authority in whose area the land is so treated as situated,

that authority shall send a copy of those particulars to the local authority in whose area the land is in fact situated.

(6) Where a local authority receives a copy of any particulars sent to it pursuant to subsection (4) or (5) above, it shall enter those particulars on the register maintained by it under this section.

(7) Where information of any description is excluded by virtue of section 78T below from any register maintained under this section, a statement shall be entered in the register indicating the existence of information of that description.

(8) It shall be the duty of each enforcing authority–
- (a) to secure that the registers maintained by it under this section are available, at all reasonable times, for inspection by the public free of charge; and
- (b) to afford to members of the public facilities for obtaining copies of entries, on payment of reasonable charges;

and, for the purposes of this subsection, places may be prescribed by the Secretary of State at which any such registers or facilities as are mentioned in paragraph (a) or (b) above are to be available or afforded to the public in pursuance of the paragraph in question.

(9) Registers under this section may be kept in any form.]

NOTES

Inserted by the Environment Act 1995, s 57.

Date in force (for certain purposes): 21 September 1995: see SI 1995/1983, art 3.

Date in force (in relation to England, for remaining purposes): 1 April 2000: see SI 2000/340, art 2(a).

Date in force (in relation to Scotland, for remaining purposes): 14 July 2000: see SSI 2000/180, art 2(1)(a).

Date in force (in relation to Wales, for remaining purposes): 15 September 2001: see SI 2001/3211, art 2(a).

[78S Exclusion from registers of information affecting national security]

[(1) No information shall be included in a register maintained under section 78R above if and so long as, in the opinion of the Secretary of State, the inclusion in the register of that information, or information of that description, would be contrary to the interests of national security.

(2) The Secretary of State may, for the purpose of securing the exclusion from registers of information to which subsection (1) above applies, give to enforcing authorities directions–

(a) specifying information, or descriptions of information, to be excluded from their registers; or

(b) specifying descriptions of information to be referred to the Secretary of State for his determination;

and no information referred to the Secretary of State in pursuance of paragraph (b) above shall be included in any such register until the Secretary of State determines that it should be so included.

(3) The enforcing authority shall notify the Secretary of State of any information which it excludes from the register in pursuance of directions under subsection (2) above.

(4) A person may, as respects any information which appears to him to be information to which subsection (1) above may apply, give a notice to the Secretary of State specifying the information and indicating its apparent nature; and, if he does so–

(a) he shall notify the enforcing authority that he has done so; and

(b) no information so notified to the Secretary of State shall be included in any such register until the Secretary of State has determined that it should be so included.]

NOTES

Inserted by the Environment Act 1995, s 57.

Date in force (for certain purposes): 21 September 1995: see SI 1995/1983, art 3.

Date in force (in relation to England, for remaining purposes): 1 April 2000: see SI 2000/340, art 2(a).

Date in force (in relation to Scotland, for remaining purposes): 14 July 2000: see SI 2000/1986, art 2.

Date in force (in relation to Wales, for remaining purposes): 15 September 2001: see SI 2001/3211, art 2(a).

[78T Exclusion from registers of certain confidential information]

[(1) No information relating to the affairs of any individual or business shall be included in a register maintained under section 78R above, without the consent of that individual or the person for the time being carrying on that business, if and so long as the information–

(a) is, in relation to him, commercially confidential; and

(b) is not required to be included in the register in pursuance of directions under subsection (7) below;

but information is not commercially confidential for the purposes of this section unless it is determined under this section to be so by the enforcing authority or, on appeal, by the Secretary of State.

(2) Where it appears to an enforcing authority that any information which has been obtained by the authority under or by virtue of any provision of this Part might be commercially confidential, the authority shall–

(a) give to the person to whom or whose business it relates notice that that information is required to be included in the register unless excluded under this section; and
(b) give him a reasonable opportunity–
  (i) of objecting to the inclusion of the information on the ground that it is commercially confidential; and
  (ii) of making representations to the authority for the purpose of justifying any such objection;

and, if any representations are made, the enforcing authority shall, having taken the representations into account, determine whether the information is or is not commercially confidential.

(3) Where, under subsection (2) above, an authority determines that information is not commercially confidential–
(a) the information shall not be entered in the register until the end of the period of twenty-one days beginning with the date on which the determination is notified to the person concerned;
(b) that person may appeal to the Secretary of State against the decision;

and, where an appeal is brought in respect of any information, the information shall not be entered in the register until the end of the period of seven days following the day on which the appeal is finally determined or withdrawn.

(4) An appeal under subsection (3) above shall, if either party to the appeal so requests or the Secretary of State so decides, take or continue in the form of a hearing (which must be held in private).

(5) Subsection (10) of section 15 above shall apply in relation to an appeal under subsection (3) above as it applies in relation to an appeal under that section.

(6) Subsection (3) above is subject to section 114 of the Environment Act 1995 (delegation or reference of appeals etc).

(7) The Secretary of State may give to the enforcing authorities directions as to specified information, or descriptions of information, which the public interest requires to be included in registers maintained under section 78R above notwithstanding that the information may be commercially confidential.

(8) Information excluded from a register shall be treated as ceasing to be commercially confidential for the purposes of this section at the expiry of the period of four years beginning with the date of the determination by virtue of which it was excluded; but the person who furnished it may apply to the authority for the information to remain excluded from the register on the ground that it is still commercially confidential and the authority shall determine whether or not that is the case.

(9) Subsections (3) to (6) above shall apply in relation to a determination under subsection (8) above as they apply in relation to a determination under subsection (2) above.

(10) Information is, for the purposes of any determination under this section, commercially confidential, in relation to any individual or person, if its being

contained in the register would prejudice to an unreasonable degree the commercial interests of that individual or person.

(11) For the purposes of subsection (10) above, there shall be disregarded any prejudice to the commercial interests of any individual or person so far as relating only to the value of the contaminated land in question or otherwise to the ownership or occupation of that land.]

NOTES

Inserted by the Environment Act 1995, s 57.

Date in force (for certain purposes): 21 September 1995: see SI 1995/1983, art 3.

Date in force (in relation to England, for remaining purposes): 1 April 2000: see SI 2000/340, art 2(a).

Date in force (in relation to Scotland, for remaining purposes): 14 July 2000: see SSI 2000/180, art 2(1)(a).

Date in force (in relation to Wales, for remaining purposes): 15 September 2001: see SI 2001/3211, art 2(a).

PART IX
GENERAL

164 Short title, commencement and extent

(1) This Act may be cited as the Environmental Protection Act 1990.

(2) The following provisions of the Act shall come into force at the end of the period of two months beginning with the day on which it is passed, namely—

sections 79 to 85;
section 97;
section 99;
section 105 in so far as it relates to paragraphs 7, 13, 14 and 15 of Schedule 5;
section 140;
section 141;
section 142;
section 145;
section 146;
section 148;
section 153;
section 154;
section 155;
section 157;
section 160;
section 161;
section 162(1) in so far as it relates to paragraphs 4, 5, 7, 8, 9, 18, 22, 24 and 31(4)(b) of Schedule 15; but, in the case of paragraph 22, in so far only as that paragraph inserts a paragraph (m) into section 7(4) of the Act of 1984;
section 162(2) in so far as it relates to Part III of Schedule 16 and, in Part IX of that Schedule, the repeal of section 100 of the Control of Pollution Act 1974;
section 162(5);
section 163.

(3) The remainder of this Act (except this section) shall come into force on such day as the Secretary of State may by order appoint and different days may be appointed for different provisions or different purposes.

(4) Only the following provisions of this Act (together with this section) extend to Northern Ireland, namely—

section 3(5) to (8);

section 62(2)(e) in so far as it relates to importation;

Part V;

Part VI in so far as it relates to importation and, without that restriction, section 127(2) in so far as it relates to the continental shelf;

section 140 in so far as it relates to importation;

section 141;

section 142 in so far as it relates to importation;

section 146;

section 147;

section 148;

section 153 except subsection (1)(k) and (m);

section 156 in so far as it relates to Part VI and sections 140, 141 and 142 in so far as they extend to Northern Ireland and in so far as it relates to the Radioactive Substances Act 1960;

section 158 in so far as it relates to Part VI and sections 140, 141 and 142 in so far as they extend to Northern Ireland.

(5) Where any enactment amended or repealed by this Act extends to any part of the United Kingdom, the amendment or repeal extends to that part, subject, however, to any express provision in Schedule 15 or 16.

Access to Neighbouring Land Act 1992

1992 CHAPTER 23

An Act to enable persons who desire to carry out works to any land which are reasonably necessary for the preservation of that land to obtain access to neighbouring land in order to do so; and for purposes connected therewith

[16th March 1992]

1 Access orders

(1) A person—

(a) who, for the purpose of carrying out works to any land (the "dominant land"), desires to enter upon any adjoining or adjacent land (the "servient land"), and

(b) who needs, but does not have, the consent of some other person to that entry,

may make an application to the court for an order under this section ("an access order") against that other person.

(2) On an application under this section, the court shall make an access order if, and only if, it is satisfied—

(a) that the works are reasonably necessary for the preservation of the whole or any part of the dominant land; and

(b) that they cannot be carried out, or would be substantially more difficult to carry out, without entry upon the servient land;

but this subsection is subject to subsection (3) below.

(3) The court shall not make an access order in any case where it is satisfied that, were it to make such an order—

(a) the respondent or any other person would suffer interference with, or disturbance of, his use or enjoyment of the servient land, or

(b) the respondent, or any other person (whether of full age or capacity or not) in occupation of the whole or any part of the servient land, would suffer hardship,

to such a degree by reason of the entry (notwithstanding any requirement of this Act or any term or condition that may be imposed under it) that it would be unreasonable to make the order.

(4) Where the court is satisfied on an application under this section that it is reasonably necessary to carry out any basic preservation works to the dominant land, those works shall be taken for the purposes of this Act to be reasonably necessary for the preservation of the land; and in this subsection "basic preservation works" means any of the following, that is to say—

(a) the maintenance, repair or renewal of any part of a building or other structure comprised in, or situate on, the dominant land;

(b) the clearance, repair or renewal of any drain, sewer, pipe or cable so comprised or situate;

(c) the treatment, cutting back, felling, removal or replacement of any hedge, tree, shrub or other growing thing which is so comprised and which is, or is in danger of becoming, damaged, diseased, dangerous, insecurely rooted or dead;

(d) the filling in, or clearance, of any ditch so comprised;

but this subsection is without prejudice to the generality of the works which may, apart from it, be regarded by the court as reasonably necessary for the preservation of any land.

(5) If the court considers it fair and reasonable in all the circumstances of the case, works may be regarded for the purposes of this Act as being reasonably necessary for the preservation of any land (or, for the purposes of subsection (4) above, as being basic preservation works which it is reasonably necessary to carry out to any land) notwithstanding that the works incidentally involve—

(a) the making of some alteration, adjustment or improvement to the land, or

(b) the demolition of the whole or any part of a building or structure comprised in or situate upon the land.

(6) Where any works are reasonably necessary for the preservation of the whole or any part of the dominant land, the doing to the dominant land of anything which is requisite for, incidental to, or consequential on, the carrying out of those works shall

be treated for the purposes of this Act as the carrying out of works which are reasonably necessary for the preservation of that land; and references in this Act to works, or to the carrying out of works, shall be construed accordingly.

(7) Without prejudice to the generality of subsection (6) above, if it is reasonably necessary for a person to inspect the dominant land—

- (a) for the purpose of ascertaining whether any works may be reasonably necessary for the preservation of the whole or any part of that land,
- (b) for the purpose of making any map or plan, or ascertaining the course of any drain, sewer, pipe or cable, in preparation for, or otherwise in connection with, the carrying out of works which are so reasonably necessary, or
- (c) otherwise in connection with the carrying out of any such works,

the making of such an inspection shall be taken for the purposes of this Act to be the carrying out to the dominant land of works which are reasonably necessary for the preservation of that land; and references in this Act to works, or to the carrying out of works, shall be construed accordingly.

3 Effect of access order

(1) An access order requires the respondent, so far as he has power to do so, to permit the applicant or any of his associates to do anything which the applicant or associate is authorised or required to do under or by virtue of the order or this section.

(2) Except as otherwise provided by or under this Act, an access order authorises the applicant or any of his associates, without the consent of the respondent,—

- (a) to enter upon the servient land for the purpose of carrying out the specified works;
- (b) to bring on to that land, leave there during the period permitted by the order and, before the end of that period, remove, such materials, plant and equipment as are reasonably necessary for the carrying out of those works; and
- (c) to bring on to that land any waste arising from the carrying out of those works, if it is reasonably necessary to do so in the course of removing it from the dominant land;

but nothing in this Act or in any access order shall authorise the applicant or any of his associates to leave anything in, on or over the servient land (otherwise than in discharge of their duty to make good that land) after their entry for the purpose of carrying out works to the dominant land ceases to be authorised under or by virtue of the order.

(3) An access order requires the applicant—

- (a) to secure that any waste arising from the carrying out of the specified works is removed from the servient land forthwith;
- (b) to secure that, before the entry ceases to be authorised under or by virtue of the order, the servient land is, so far as reasonably practicable, made good; and

(c) to indemnify the respondent against any damage which may be caused to the servient land or any goods by the applicant or any of his associates which would not have been so caused had the order not been made;

but this subsection is subject to subsections (4) and (5) below.

(4) In making an access order, the court may vary or exclude, in whole or in part,—

(a) any authorisation that would otherwise be conferred by subsection (2)(b) or (c) above; or

(b) any requirement that would otherwise be imposed by subsection (3) above.

(5) Without prejudice to the generality of subsection (4) above, if the court is satisfied that it is reasonably necessary for any such waste as may arise from the carrying out of the specified works to be left on the servient land for some period before removal, the access order may, in place of subsection (3)(a) above, include provision—

(a) authorising the waste to be left on that land for such period as may be permitted by the order; and

(b) requiring the applicant to secure that the waste is removed before the end of that period.

(6) Where the applicant or any of his associates is authorised or required under or by virtue of an access order or this section to enter, or do any other thing, upon the servient land, he shall not (as respects that access order) be taken to be a trespasser from the beginning on account of his, or any other person's, subsequent conduct.

(7) For the purposes of this section, the applicant's "associates" are such number of persons (whether or not servants or agents of his) whom he may reasonably authorise under this subsection to exercise the power of entry conferred by the access order as may be reasonably necessary for carrying out the specified works.

9 Short title, commencement and extent

(1) This Act may be cited as the Access to Neighbouring Land Act 1992.

(2) This Act shall come into force on such day as the Lord Chancellor may by order made by statutory instrument appoint.

(3) This Act extends to England and Wales only.

Carriage of Goods by Sea Act 1992

1992 CHAPTER 50

An Act to replace the Bills of Lading Act 1855 with new provision with respect to bills of lading and certain other shipping documents

[16th July 1992]

1 Shipping documents etc to which Act applies

(1) This Act applies to the following documents, that is to say—
- (a) any bill of lading;
- (b) any sea waybill; and
- (c) any ship's delivery order.

(2) References in this Act to a bill of lading—
- (a) do not include references to a document which is incapable of transfer either by indorsement or, as a bearer bill, by delivery without indorsement; but
- (b) subject to that, do include references to a received for shipment bill of lading.

(3) References in this Act to a sea waybill are references to any document which is not a bill of lading but—
- (a) is such a receipt for goods as contains or evidences a contract for the carriage of goods by sea; and
- (b) identifies the person to whom delivery of the goods is to be made by the carrier in accordance with that contract.

(4) References in this Act to a ship's delivery order are references to any document which is neither a bill of lading nor a sea waybill but contains an undertaking which—
- (a) is given under or for the purposes of a contract for the carriage by sea of the goods to which the document relates, or of goods which include those goods; and
- (b) is an undertaking by the carrier to a person identified in the document to deliver the goods to which the document relates to that person.

(5) The Secretary of State may by regulations make provision for the application of this Act to cases where a telecommunication system or any other information technology is used for effecting transactions corresponding to—
- (a) the issue of a document to which this Act applies;
- (b) the indorsement, delivery or other transfer of such a document; or
- (c) the doing of anything else in relation to such a document.

(6) Regulations under subsection (5) above may—
- (a) make such modifications of the following provisions of this Act as the Secretary of State considers appropriate in connection with the application of this Act to any case mentioned in that subsection; and
- (b) contain supplemental, incidental, consequential and transitional provision;

and the power to make regulations under that subsection shall be exercisable by statutory instrument subject to annulment in pursuance of a resolution of either House of Parliament.

2 Rights under shipping documents

(1) Subject to the following provisions of this section, a person who becomes—

(a) the lawful holder of a bill of lading;

(b) the person who (without being an original party to the contract of carriage) is the person to whom delivery of the goods to which a sea waybill relates is to be made by the carrier in accordance with that contract; or

(c) the person to whom delivery of the goods to which a ship's delivery order relates is to be made in accordance with the undertaking contained in the order,

shall (by virtue of becoming the holder of the bill or, as the case may be, the person to whom delivery is to be made) have transferred to and vested in him all rights of suit under the contract of carriage as if he had been a party to that contract.

(2) Where, when a person becomes the lawful holder of a bill of lading, possession of the bill no longer gives a right (as against the carrier) to possession of the goods to which the bill relates, that person shall not have any rights transferred to him by virtue of subsection (1) above unless he becomes the holder of the bill—

(a) by virtue of a transaction effected in pursuance of any contractual or other arrangements made before the time when such a right to possession ceased to attach to possession of the bill; or

(b) as a result of the rejection to that person by another person of goods or documents delivered to the other person in pursuance of any such arrangements.

(3) The rights vested in any person by virtue of the operation of subsection (1) above in relation to a ship's delivery order—

(a) shall be so vested subject to the terms of the order; and

(b) where the goods to which the order relates form a part only of the goods to which the contract of carriage relates, shall be confined to rights in respect of the goods to which the order relates.

(4) Where, in the case of any document to which this Act applies—

(a) a person with any interest or right in or in relation to goods to which the document relates sustains loss or damage in consequence of a breach of the contract of carriage; but

(b) subsection (1) above operates in relation to that document so that rights of suit in respect of that breach are vested in another person,

the other person shall be entitled to exercise those rights for the benefit of the person who sustained the loss or damage to the same extent as they could have been exercised if they had been vested in the person for whose benefit they are exercised.

(5) Where rights are transferred by virtue of the operation of subsection (1) above in relation to any document, the transfer for which that subsection provides shall extinguish any entitlement to those rights which derives—

(a) where that document is a bill of lading, from a person's having been an original party to the contract of carriage; or
(b) in the case of any document to which this Act applies, from the previous operation of that subsection in relation to that document;

but the operation of that subsection shall be without prejudice to any rights which derive from a person's having been an original party to the contract contained in, or evidenced by, a sea waybill and, in relation to a ship's delivery order, shall be without prejudice to any rights deriving otherwise than from the previous operation of that subsection in relation to that order.

3 Liabilities under shipping documents

(1) Where subsection (1) of section 2 of this Act operates in relation to any document to which this Act applies and the person in whom rights are vested by virtue of that subsection—
(a) takes or demands delivery from the carrier of any of the goods to which the document relates;
(b) makes a claim under the contract of carriage against the carrier in respect of any of those goods; or
(c) is a person who, at a time before those rights were vested in him, took or demanded delivery from the carrier of any of those goods,

that person shall (by virtue of taking or demanding delivery or making the claim or, in a case falling within paragraph (c) above, of having the rights vested in him) become subject to the same liabilities under that contract as if he had been a party to that contract.

(2) Where the goods to which a ship's delivery order relates form a part only of the goods to which the contract of carriage relates, the liabilities to which any person is subject by virtue of the operation of this section in relation to that order shall exclude liabilities in respect of any goods to which the order does not relate.

(3) This section, so far as it imposes liabilities under any contract on any person, shall be without prejudice to the liabilities under the contract of any person as an original party to the contract.

4 Representations in bills of lading

A bill of lading which—
(a) represents goods to have been shipped on board a vessel or to have been received for shipment on board a vessel; and
(b) has been signed by the master of the vessel or by a person who was not the master but had the express, implied or apparent authority of the carrier to sign bills of lading,

shall, in favour of a person who has become the lawful holder of the bill, be conclusive evidence against the carrier of the shipment of the goods or, as the case may be, of their receipt for shipment.

5 Interpretation etc

(1) In this Act—

"bill of lading", "sea waybill" and "ship's delivery order" shall be construed in accordance with section 1 above;

"the contract of carriage"—

(a) in relation to a bill of lading or sea waybill, means the contract contained in or evidenced by that bill or waybill; and

(b) in relation to a ship's delivery order, means the contract under or for the purposes of which the undertaking contained in the order is given;

"holder", in relation to a bill of lading, shall be construed in accordance with subsection (2) below;

"information technology" includes any computer or other technology by means of which information or other matter may be recorded or communicated without being reduced to documentary form; and

"telecommunication system" has the same meaning as in the Telecommunications Act 1984.

(2) References in this Act to the holder of a bill of lading are references to any of the following persons, that is to say—

(a) a person with possession of the bill who, by virtue of being the person identified in the bill, is the consignee of the goods to which the bill relates;

(b) a person with possession of the bill as a result of the completion, by delivery of the bill, of any indorsement of the bill or , in the case of a bearer bill, of any other transfer of the bill;

(c) a person with possession of the bill as a result of any transaction by virtue of which he would have become a holder falling within paragraph (a) or (b) above had not the transaction been effected at a time when possession of the bill no longer gave a right (as against the carrier) to possession of the goods to which the bill relates;

and a person shall be regarded for the purposes of this Act as having become the lawful holder of a bill of lading wherever he has become the holder of the bill in good faith.

(3) References in this Act to a person's being identified in a document include references to his being identified by a description which allows for the identity of the person in question to be varied, in accordance with the terms of the document, after its issue; and the reference in section 1(3)(b) of this Act to a document's identifying a person shall be construed accordingly.

(4) Without prejudice to sections 2(2) and 4 above, nothing in this Act shall preclude its operation in relation to a case where the goods to which a document relates—

(a) cease to exist after the issue of the document; or

(b) cannot be identified (whether because they are mixed with other goods or for any other reason);

and references in this Act to the goods to which a document relates shall be construed accordingly.

(5) The preceding provisions of this Act shall have effect without prejudice to the application, in relation to any case, of the rules (the Hague-Visby Rules) which for the time being have the force of law by virtue of section 1 of the Carriage of Goods by Sea Act 1971.

6 Short title, repeal, commencement and extent

(1) This Act may be cited as the Carriage of Goods by Sea Act 1992.

(2) . . .

(3) This Act shall come into force at the end of the period of two months beginning with the day on which it is passed; but nothing in this Act shall have effect in relation to any document issued before the coming into force of this Act.

(4) This Act extends to Northern Ireland.

NOTES

Sub-s (2): repeals the Bills of Lading Act 1855.

Trade Union and Labour Relations (Consolidation) Act 1992

1992 CHAPTER 52

An Act to consolidate the enactments relating to collective labour relations, that is to say, to trade unions, employers' associations, industrial relations and industrial action

[16th July 1992]

PART I
TRADE UNIONS

Chapter I
Introductory

Meaning of "trade union"

1 Meaning of "trade union"

In this Act a "trade union" means an organisation (whether temporary or permanent)—

(a) which consists wholly or mainly of workers of one or more descriptions and whose principal purposes include the regulation of relations between workers of that description or those descriptions and employers or employers' associations; or

(b) which consists wholly or mainly of—

(i) constituent or affiliated organisations which fulfil the conditions in paragraph (a) (or themselves consist wholly or mainly of constituent or affiliated organisations which fulfil those conditions), or
(ii) representatives of such constituent or affiliated organisations,

and whose principal purposes include the regulation of relations between workers and employers or between workers and employers' associations, or the regulation of relations between its constituent or affiliated organisations.

Certification as independent trade union

5 Meaning of "independent trade union"

In this Act an "independent trade union" means a trade union which—
(a) is not under the domination or control of an employer or group of employers or of one or more employers' associations, and
(b) is not liable to interference by an employer or any such group or association (arising out of the provision of financial or material support or by any other means whatsoever) tending towards such control;

and references to "independence", in relation to a trade union, shall be construed accordingly.

Chapter II
Status and Property of Trade Unions

General

10 Quasi-corporate status of trade unions

(1) A trade union is not a body corporate but—
(a) it is capable of making contracts;
(b) it is capable of suing and being sued in its own name, whether in proceedings relating to property or founded on contract or tort or any other cause of action; and
(c) proceedings for an offence alleged to have been committed by it or on its behalf may be brought against it in its own name.

(2) A trade union shall not be treated as if it were a body corporate except to the extent authorised by the provisions of this Part.

(3) A trade union shall not be registered—
(a) as a company under the Companies Act 1985, or
(b) under the Friendly Societies Act 1974 or the Industrial and Provident Societies Act 1965;

and any such registration of a trade union (whenever effected) is void.

11 Exclusion of common law rules as to restraint of trade

(1) The purposes of a trade union are not, by reason only that they are in restraint of trade, unlawful so as—

(a) to make any member of the trade union liable to criminal proceedings for conspiracy or otherwise, or
(b) to make any agreement or trust void or voidable.

(2) No rule of a trade union is unlawful or unenforceable by reason only that it is in restraint of trade.

Property of trade union

15 Prohibition on use of funds to indemnify unlawful conduct

(1) It is unlawful for property of a trade union to be applied in or towards—
(a) the payment for an individual of a penalty which has been or may be imposed on him for an offence or for contempt of court,
(b) the securing of any such payment, or
(c) the provision of anything for indemnifying an individual in respect of such a penalty.

(2) Where any property of a trade union is so applied for the benefit of an individual on whom a penalty has been or may be imposed, then—
(a) in the case of a payment, an amount equal to the payment is recoverable by the union from him, and
(b) in any other case, he is liable to account to the union for the value of the property applied.

(3) If a trade union fails to bring or continue proceedings which it is entitled to bring by virtue of subsection (2), a member of the union who claims that the failure is unreasonable may apply to the court on that ground for an order authorising him to bring or continue the proceedings on the union's behalf and at the union's expense.

(4) In this section "penalty", in relation to an offence, includes an order to pay compensation and an order for the forfeiture of any property; and references to the imposition of a penalty for an offence shall be construed accordingly.

(5) The Secretary of State may by order designate offences in relation to which the provisions of this section do not apply.

Any such order shall be made by statutory instrument which shall be subject to annulment in pursuance of a resolution of either House of Parliament.

(6) This section does not affect—
(a) any other enactment, any rule of law or any provision of the rules of a trade union which makes it unlawful for the property of a trade union to be applied in a particular way; or
(b) any other remedy available to a trade union, the trustees of its property or any of its members in respect of an unlawful application of the union's property.

(7) In this section "member", in relation to a trade union consisting wholly or partly of, or of representatives of, constituent or affiliated organisations, includes a member of any of the constituent or affiliated organisations.

16 Remedy against trustees for unlawful use of union property

(1) A member of a trade union who claims that the trustees of the union's property—

- (a) have so carried out their functions, or are proposing so to carry out their functions, as to cause or permit an unlawful application of the union's property, or
- (b) have complied, or are proposing to comply, with an unlawful direction which has been or may be given, or purportedly given, to them under the rules of the union,

may apply to the court for an order under this section.

(2) In a case relating to property which has already been unlawfully applied, or to an unlawful direction that has already been complied with, an application under this section may be made only by a person who was a member of the union at the time when the property was applied or, as the case may be, the direction complied with.

(3) Where the court is satisfied that the claim is well-founded, it shall make such order as it considers appropriate.

The court may in particular—

- (a) require the trustees (if necessary, on behalf of the union) to take all such steps as may be specified in the order for protecting or recovering the property of the union;
- (b) appoint a receiver of, or in Scotland a judicial factor on, the property of the union;
- (c) remove one or more of the trustees.

(4) Where the court makes an order under this section in a case in which—

- (a) property of the union has been applied in contravention of an order of any court, or in compliance with a direction given in contravention of such an order, or
- (b) the trustees were proposing to apply property in contravention of such an order or to comply with any such direction,

the court shall by its order remove all the trustees except any trustee who satisfies the court that there is a good reason for allowing him to remain a trustee.

(5) Without prejudice to any other power of the court, the court may on an application for an order under this section grant such interlocutory relief (in Scotland, such interim order) as it considers appropriate.

(6) This section does not affect any other remedy available in respect of a breach of trust by the trustees of a trade union's property.

(7) In this section "member", in relation to a trade union consisting wholly or partly of, or of representatives of, constituent or affiliated organisations, includes a member of any of the constituent or affiliated organisations.

Liability of trade unions in proceedings in tort

20 Liability of trade union in certain proceedings in tort

(1) Where proceedings in tort are brought against a trade union—

(a) on the ground that an act—

(i) induces another person to break a contract or interferes or induces another person to interfere with its performance, or

(ii) consists in threatening that a contract (whether one to which the union is a party or not) will be broken or its performance interfered with, or that the union will induce another person to break a contract or interfere with its performance, or

(b) in respect of an agreement or combination by two or more persons to do or to procure the doing of an act which, if it were done without any such agreement or combination, would be actionable in tort on such a ground,

then, for the purpose of determining in those proceedings whether the union is liable in respect of the act in question, that act shall be taken to have been done by the union if, but only if, it is to be taken to have been authorised or endorsed by the trade union in accordance with the following provisions.

(2) An act shall be taken to have been authorised or endorsed by a trade union if it was done, or was authorised or endorsed—

(a) by any person empowered by the rules to do, authorise or endorse acts of the kind in question, or

(b) by the principal executive committee or the president or general secretary, or

(c) by any other committee of the union or any other official of the union (whether employed by it or not).

(3) For the purposes of paragraph (c) of subsection (2)—

(a) any group of persons constituted in accordance with the rules of the union is a committee of the union; and

(b) an act shall be taken to have been done, authorised or endorsed by an official if it was done, authorised or endorsed by, or by any member of, any group of persons of which he was at the material time a member, the purposes of which included organising or co-ordinating industrial action.

(4) The provisions of paragraphs (b) and (c) of subsection (2) apply notwithstanding anything in the rules of the union, or in any contract or rule of law, but subject to the provisions of section 21 (repudiation by union of certain acts).

(5) Where for the purposes of any proceedings an act is by virtue of this section taken to have been done by a trade union, nothing in this section shall affect the liability of any other person, in those or any other proceedings, in respect of that act.

(6) In proceedings arising out of an act which is by virtue of this section taken to have been done by a trade union, the power of the court to grant an injunction or interdict includes power to require the union to take such steps as the court considers appropriate for ensuring—

(a) that there is no, or no further, inducement of persons to take part or to continue to take part in industrial action, and

(b) that no person engages in any conduct after the granting of the injunction or interdict by virtue of having been induced before it was granted to take part or to continue to take part in industrial action.

The provisions of subsections (2) to (4) above apply in relation to proceedings for failure to comply with any such injunction or interdict as they apply in relation to the original proceedings.

(7) In this section "rules", in relation to a trade union, means the written rules of the union and any other written provision forming part of the contract between a member and the other members.

21 Repudiation by union of certain acts

(1) An act shall not be taken to have been authorised or endorsed by a trade union by virtue only of paragraph (c) of section 20(2) if it was repudiated by the executive, president or general secretary as soon as reasonably practicable after coming to the knowledge of any of them.

(2) Where an act is repudiated—
 (a) written notice of the repudiation must be given to the committee or official in question, without delay, and
 (b) the union must do its best to give individual written notice of the fact and date of repudiation, without delay—
  (i) to every member of the union who the union has reason to believe is taking part, or might otherwise take part, in industrial action as a result of the act, and
  (ii) to the employer of every such member.

(3) The notice given to members in accordance with paragraph (b)(i) of subsection (2) must contain the following statement—

'Your union has repudiated the call (or calls) for industrial action to which this notice relates and will give no support to unofficial industrial action taken in response to it (or them). If you are dismissed while taking unofficial industrial action, you will have no right to complain of unfair dismissal.'

(4) If subsection (2) or (3) is not complied with, the repudiation shall be treated as ineffective.

(5) An act shall not be treated as repudiated if at any time after the union concerned purported to repudiate it the executive, president or general secretary has behaved in a manner which is inconsistent with the purported repudiation.

(6) The executive, president or general secretary shall be treated as so behaving if, on a request made to any of them within [three months] of the purported repudiation by a person who—
 (a) is a party to a commercial contract whose performance has been or may be interfered with as a result of the act in question, and
 (b) has not been given written notice by the union of the repudiation,

it is not forthwith confirmed in writing that the act has been repudiated.

(7) In this section "commercial contract" means any contract other than—

(a) a contract of employment, or
(b) any other contract under which a person agrees personally to do work or perform services for another.

NOTES

Sub-s (6): words in square brackets substituted by the Trade Union Reform and Employment Rights Act 1993, s 49(1), Sch 7, para 17.

22 Limit on damages awarded against trade unions in actions in tort

(1) This section applies to any proceedings in tort brought against a trade union, except—
(a) proceedings for personal injury as a result of negligence, nuisance or breach of duty;
(b) proceedings for breach of duty in connection with the ownership, occupation, possession, control or use of property;
(c) proceedings brought by virtue of Part I of the Consumer Protection Act 1987 (product liability).

(2) In any proceedings in tort to which this section applies the amount which may be awarded against the union by way of damages shall not exceed the following limit—

Number of members of union	*Maximum award of damages*
Less than 5,000	£10,000
5,000 or more but less than 25,000	£50,000
25,000 or more but less than 100,000	£125,000
100,000 or more	£250,000

(3) The Secretary of State may by order amend subsection (2) so as to vary any of the sums specified; and the order may make such transitional provision as the Secretary of State considers appropriate.

(4) Any such order shall be made by statutory instrument which shall be subject to annulment in pursuance of a resolution of either House of Parliament.

(5) In this section—

"breach of duty" means breach of a duty imposed by any rule of law or by or under any enactment;

"personal injury" includes any disease and any impairment of a person's physical or mental condition; and

"property" means any property, whether real or personal (or in Scotland, heritable or moveable).

PART VII
MISCELLANEOUS AND GENERAL

Final provisions

302 Commencement

This Act comes into force at the end of the period of three months beginning with the day on which it is passed.

303 Short title

This Act may be cited as the Trade Union and Labour Relations (Consolidation) Act 1992.

Railways Act 1993

1993 CHAPTER 43

An Act to provide for the appointment and functions of a Rail Regulator and a Director of Passenger Rail Franchising and of users' consultative committees for the railway industry and for certain ferry services; to make new provision with respect to the provision of railway services and the persons by whom they are to be provided or who are to secure their provision; to make provision for and in connection with the grant and acquisition of rights over, and the disposal or other transfer and vesting of, any property, rights or liabilities by means of which railway services are, or are to be, provided; to amend the functions of the British Railways Board; to make provision with respect to the safety of railways and the protection of railway employees and members of the public from personal injury and other risks arising from the construction or operation of railways; to make further provision with respect to transport police; to make provision with respect to certain railway pension schemes; to make provision for and in connection with the payment of grants and subsidies in connection with railways and in connection with the provision of facilities for freight haulage by inland waterway; to make provision in relation to tramways and other guided transport systems; and for connected purposes

[5th November 1993]

PART I
THE PROVISION OF RAILWAY SERVICES

Closures

50 Exclusion of liability for breach of statutory duty

(1) The obligations of the [Authority], imposed by or under any provision of this Part—

- (a) to comply with any closure conditions,
- (b) . . .
- (c) to secure the provision of any services, or
- (d) to secure the operation of any additional railway asset,

shall not give rise to any form of duty or liability enforceable by civil proceedings for breach of statutory duty.

(2) Subject to section 57 below, the obligations of—

- (a) any service operator (within the meaning of section 37 above), imposed by or under section 37(1) above, not to discontinue any railway passenger services,
- (b) any operator (within the meaning of section 48 above), imposed by or under section 48(3) above, not to discontinue any experimental passenger services, or

(c) any operator of an additional railway asset, imposed by or under section 39(1) or 41(1) above, not to discontinue the operation of any additional railway asset,

shall not give rise to any form of duty or liability enforceable by civil proceedings for breach of statutory duty.

NOTES

Sub-s (1): word "Authority" in square brackets substituted by the Transport Act 2000, s 215, Sch 16, paras 8, 33.

Date in force: 1 February 2001: see SI 2001/57, art 3(1), Sch 2, Pt I (as amended by SI 2001/115, art 2(1), (2)).

Sub-s (1): para (b) repealed by the Transport Act 2000, s 274, Sch 31, Pt IV.

Date in force: 1 February 2001: see SI 2001/57, art 3(1), Sch 2, Pt I.

PART II
RE-ORGANISATION OF THE RAILWAYS

Transfer schemes: supplemental provision

93 Assignment of employees to particular parts of undertakings

(1) Schemes may be made—

(a) assigning such qualifying employees, or qualifying employees of such a class or description, as may be specified in the scheme to such part of their employer's undertaking as may be so specified;

(b) modifying the terms and conditions of employment of those employees; and

(c) providing for the payment of compensation to any of those employees by his employer in respect of any overall detriment incurred by the employee in consequence of any modifications made by the scheme to his terms and conditions of employment.

(2) A scheme shall be made only for the purpose of facilitating, or otherwise in contemplation of, or in connection with,—

(a) the disposal of the undertaking, or part of the undertaking, of the Board or of a wholly owned subsidiary of the Board;

(b) the transfer, by virtue of a transfer scheme, of any property, rights or liabilities—

(i) from the Board or a wholly owned subsidiary of the Board to any such subsidiary or to a publicly owned railway company or a company wholly owned by the Franchising Director; or

(ii) from a company wholly owned by the Franchising Director to another such company;

(c) the provision of railway passenger services, or the operation of additional railway assets, under a franchise agreement, in circumstances where a previous franchise agreement relating to the provision of those services or the operation of those assets comes, or has come, to an end;

(d) the performance of any duty imposed on the Franchising Director by any provision of Part I above to secure—

(i) the provision of any railway passenger services;
(ii) the operation of any network or part of a network;
(iii) the operation of any station or light maintenance depot, or any part of a station or light maintenance depot; or

(e) the exercise of the power conferred on the Franchising Director by section 30 above to secure the operation of any additional railway assets.

(3) The power to make a scheme shall be exercisable—

(a) by the Board, in respect of employees of the Board or of any wholly owned subsidiary of the Board; or

(b) by the Franchising Director, in respect of employees of any company which is wholly owned by the Franchising Director.

(4) Where a scheme modifies the terms and conditions of employment of any person, the person's terms and conditions of employment after the modification takes effect must overall, and taking account of the amount or value of any compensation payable to him by virtue of subsection (1)(c) above in respect of any such detriment as is there mentioned, be no less favourable to him than his terms and conditions of employment before the modification takes effect.

(5) The duty imposed on an employer by section 4 of [the Employment Rights Act 1996] (requirement for written statement in respect of certain changes relating to an employee's employment) shall extend to all of the modifications made by a scheme to a qualifying employee's terms and conditions of employment, as if those modifications were changes required to be dealt with in a written statement under that section.

(6) If any qualifying employee whose terms and conditions of employment are modified by a scheme is aggrieved—

(a) at the provisions made by the scheme with respect to the payment of compensation, so far as applicable in his case, or

(b) at the fact that the scheme does not make any such provision,

he may make a written complaint to the maker of the scheme not later than twelve weeks after the date of issue of the written statement required by section 4 of [the Employment Rights Act 1996] in consequence of the modifications made by the scheme in the qualifying employee's terms and conditions of employment.

(7) Any complaint under subsection (6) above shall be referred to, and determined by, such arbitrator as may be agreed by the qualifying employee and the person to whom the complaint was made or, at the request of either of them, by a panel of three arbitrators appointed by the Secretary of State and consisting of—

(a) a person who appears to the Secretary of State to be representative of employers in the railway industry;

(b) a person who appears to the Secretary of State to be representative of employees in the railway industry; and

(c) an independent chairman.

(8) A scheme may make such incidental, consequential, supplemental or transitional provision as appears necessary or expedient to the person making the scheme.

(9) A scheme may make different provision for different qualifying employees or for qualifying employees of different classes or descriptions.

(10) A scheme shall not come into force unless it has been approved by the Secretary of State or until such date as the Secretary of State may, after consultation with the maker of the scheme, specify for the purpose in giving his approval.

(11) In the application of this section in relation to Scotland, any reference to an arbitrator shall be taken as a reference to an arbiter.

(12) In the application of this section to Northern Ireland, for any reference to section 4 of [the Employment Rights Act 1996] there shall be substituted a reference to section 4(4) to (6B) of the Contracts of Employment and Redundancy Payments Act (Northern Ireland) 1965.

(13) In this section—

"qualifying employee", in the case of any scheme, means a person who, immediately before the coming into force of that scheme—

(a) is an employee of—

(i) the Board;

(ii) a wholly owned subsidiary of the Board; or

(iii) a company which is wholly owned by the Franchising Director; and

(b) is not assigned solely to duties in that part of his employer's undertaking to which he is, or is to be, assigned by that scheme;

"scheme" means a scheme under this section;

and expressions used in this section and in Part I above have the same meaning in this section as they have in that Part.

NOTES

Repealed by the Transport Act 2000, s 274, Sch 31, Pt IV.

Date in force: to be appointed: see the Transport Act 2000, s 275(1).

Sub-ss (5), (6), (12): words in square brackets substituted by the Employment Rights Act 1996, s 240, Sch 1, para 60(1), (2).

PART III
MISCELLANEOUS, GENERAL AND SUPPLEMENTAL PROVISIONS

Statutory authority

122 Statutory authority as a defence to actions in nuisance etc

(1) Subject to the following provisions of this section—

(a) any person shall have authority—

(i) to use, or to cause or permit any agent or independent contractor of his to use, rolling stock on any track, or

(ii) to use, or to cause or permit any agent or independent contractor of his to use, any land comprised in a network, station or light maintenance depot for or in connection with the provision of network services, station services or light maintenance services, and

(b) any person who is the owner or occupier of any land shall have authority to authorise, consent to or acquiesce in—

(i) the use by another of rolling stock on any track comprised in that land, or

(ii) the use by another of that land for or in connection with the provision of network services, station services or light maintenance services,

if and so long as the qualifying conditions are satisfied in the particular case.

(2) For the purposes of this section, the "qualifying conditions" are—

(a) in relation to any use of rolling stock on track—

(i) that the track is comprised in a network, station or light maintenance depot, and

(ii) that the operator of that network, station or light maintenance depot is the holder of an appropriate licence or has the benefit of an appropriate licence exemption; and

(b) in relation to any use of land for or in connection with the provision of network services, station services or light maintenance services, that the operator of the network, station or light maintenance depot in question is the holder of an appropriate licence or has the benefit of an appropriate licence exemption.

(3) The authority conferred by this section is conferred only for the purpose of providing a defence of statutory authority—

(a) in England and Wales—

(i) in any proceedings, whether civil or criminal, in nuisance; or

(ii) in any civil proceedings, other than proceedings for breach of statutory duty, in respect of the escape of things from land;

(b) in Scotland, in any civil proceedings on the ground of nuisance where the rule of strict liability applies, other than proceedings for breach of statutory duty.

(4) Nothing in this section shall be construed as excluding a defence of statutory authority otherwise available under or by virtue of any enactment.

(5) The owner or occupier of any land shall be regarded for the purposes of this section as "acquiescing" in—

(a) any use by another of rolling stock on track comprised in that land, or

(b) any use of that land by another for or in connection with the provision of network services, station services or light maintenance services,

notwithstanding that it is not within his power to put an end to that use by that other.

(6) For the purposes of this section—

(a) any reference to the use of rolling stock on track includes a reference to the carriage of any passengers or other persons, or any goods, of any class or description for any purpose on or by means of that rolling stock on that track; and

(b) rolling stock shall be regarded as "used" on any track at any time when it is present on that track, irrespective of whether the rolling stock is comprised in a train or not, whether the rolling stock is moving or stationary and, if moving, irrespective of the means by which the motion is caused.

(7) In this section—

"appropriate licence", in relation to the operator of a network, station or light maintenance depot, means a licence which authorises him to be the operator of that network, station or light maintenance depot;

"appropriate licence exemption", in relation to the operator of a network, station or light maintenance depot, means any such licence exemption as exempts him from the requirement to hold the licence that would otherwise be the appropriate licence in his case;

and expressions used in this section and in Part I above have the same meaning in this section as they have in that Part.

Supplemental

154 Short title, commencement and extent

(1) This Act may be cited as the Railways Act 1993.

(2) Except for section 1 and Schedule 1 (which come into force on the passing of this Act), this Act shall come into force on such day as may be specified in an order made by the Secretary of State; and different days may be so specified—

(a) for different provisions;
(b) for different purposes of the same provision; and
(c) for different areas within the United Kingdom.

(3) The following provisions of this Act extend to Northern Ireland—

[(a) section 36(1), (4) and (5);]
(b) subsections (1), (2), (4) and (5) of section 66;
[(c) sections 124 and 129(3);]
(d) section 131;
(e) section 134;
(f) sections 143, 144, 146, 147(1) and (2) and 149 to 152, so far as relating to provisions of this Act which so extend;
(g) section 153;
(h) this section;
(j) paragraphs 6, 7 and 8 of Schedule 1, paragraph 10 of Schedule 2 and paragraph 9 of Schedule 3;
(k) Schedules 8 and 9;
(l) Schedule 11;
(m) the amendments and repeals made by Schedules 12 and 14, other than those relating to—

(i) section 6 of the Regulation of Railways Act 1889,
(ii) the Railway Fires Act 1905, and
(iii) the Railway Fires Act (1905) Amendment Act 1923,
to the extent that the enactments to which they relate so extend.

(4) Except as provided in subsection (3) above, this Act does not extend to Northern Ireland.

NOTES

Sub-s (3): para (a) substituted by the Transport Act 2000, s 252, Sch 27, paras 17, 44(1), (2).

Date in force: 1 February 2001: see SI 2001/57, art 3(1), Sch 2, Pt I.

Sub-s (3): para (c) substituted by the Transport Act 2000, s 252, Sch 27, paras 17, 44(1), (3).

Date in force: 1 February 2001: see SI 2001/57, art 3(1), Sch 2, Pt I.

Criminal Justice and Public Order Act 1994

1994 CHAPTER 33

An Act to make further provision in relation to criminal justice (including employment in the prison service); to amend or extend the criminal law and powers for preventing crime and enforcing that law; to amend the Video Recordings Act 1984; and for purposes connected with those purposes

[3rd November 1994]

PART IV
POLICE POWERS

Powers of police to stop and search

60 Powers to stop and search in anticipation of violence

[(1) If a police officer of or above the rank of inspector reasonably believes—

(a) that incidents involving serious violence may take place in any locality in his police area, and that it is expedient to give an authorisation under this section to prevent their occurrence, or

(b) that persons are carrying dangerous instruments or offensive weapons in any locality in his police area without good reason,

he may give an authorisation that the powers conferred by this section are to be exercisable at any place within that locality for a specified period not exceeding 24 hours.]

(2) . . .

(3) If it appears to [an officer of or above the rank of] superintendent that it is expedient to do so, having regard to offences which have, or are reasonably suspected to have, been committed in connection with any [activity] falling within the authorisation, he may direct that the authorisation shall continue in being for a further [24] hours.

[(3A) If an inspector gives an authorisation under subsection (1) he must, as soon as it is practicable to do so, cause an officer of or above the rank of superintendent to be informed.]

(4) This section confers on any constable in uniform power—

(a) to stop any pedestrian and search him or anything carried by him for offensive weapons or dangerous instruments;

(b) to stop any vehicle and search the vehicle, its driver and any passenger for offensive weapons or dangerous instruments.

[(4A) *This section also confers on any constable in uniform power—*

(a) to require any person to remove any item which the constable reasonably believes that person is wearing wholly or mainly for the purpose of concealing his identity;

(b) to seize any item which the constable reasonably believes any person intends to wear wholly or mainly for that purpose.]

(5) A constable may, in the exercise of [the powers conferred by subsection (4) above], stop any person or vehicle and make any search he thinks fit whether or not he has any grounds for suspecting that the person or vehicle is carrying weapons or articles of that kind.

(6) If in the course of a search under this section a constable discovers a dangerous instrument or an article which he has reasonable grounds for suspecting to be an offensive weapon, he may seize it.

(7) This section applies (with the necessary modifications) to ships, aircraft and hovercraft as it applies to vehicles.

(8) A person who fails

[(a) to stop, or to stop a vehicle; *or*

(b) *to remove an item worn by him,*]

when required to do so by a constable in the exercise of his powers under this section shall be liable on summary conviction to imprisonment for a term not exceeding one month or to a fine not exceeding level 3 on the standard scale or both.

(9) Any authorisation under this section shall be in writing signed by the officer giving it and shall specify [the grounds on which it is given and] the locality in which and the period during which the powers conferred by this section are exercisable and a direction under subsection (3) above shall also be given in writing or, where that is not practicable, recorded in writing as soon as it is practicable to do so.

[(9A) The preceding provisions of this section, so far as they relate to an authorisation by a member of the British Transport Police Force (including one who for the time being has the same powers and privileges as a member of a police force for a police area), shall have effect as if the references to a locality in his police area were references to any locality in or in the vicinity of any policed premises, or to the whole or any part of any such premises.]

(10) Where a vehicle is stopped by a constable under this section, the driver shall be entitled to obtain a written statement that the vehicle was stopped under the powers conferred by this section if he applies for such a statement not later than the end of the period of twelve months from the day on which the vehicle was stopped . . .

[(10A) A person who is searched by a constable under this section shall be entitled to obtain a written statement that he was searched under the powers conferred by this section if he applies for such a statement not later than the end of the period of twelve months from the day on which he was searched.]

(11) In this section—

["British Transport Police Force" means the constables appointed under section 53 of the British Transport Commission Act 1949;]

"dangerous instruments" means instruments which have a blade or are sharply pointed;

"offensive weapon" has the meaning given by section 1(9) of the Police and Criminal Evidence Act 1984 [or, in relation to Scotland, section 47(4) of the Criminal Law (Consolidation) (Scotland) Act 1995] ;

["policed premises", in relation to England and Wales, has the meaning given by section 53(3) of the British Transport Commission Act 1949 and, in relation to Scotland, means those places where members of the British Transport Police Force have the powers, protection and privileges of a constable under section 53(4)(a) of that Act (as it relates to Scotland);] and

"vehicle" includes a caravan as defined in section 29(1) of the Caravan Sites and Control of Development Act 1960.

[(11A) For the purposes of this section, a person carries a dangerous instrument or an offensive weapon if he has it in his possession.]

(12) The powers conferred by this section are in addition to and not in derogation of, any power otherwise conferred.

NOTES

Sub-s (1): substituted by the Knives Act 1997, s 8(1), (2).

Date in force: 1 March 1999: see SI 1999/5, art 2.

Sub-s (2): repealed by the Knives Act 1997, s 8(1), (3).

Date in force: 1 March 1999: see SI 1999/5, art 2.

Sub-s (3): words "an officer of or above the rank of" in square brackets substituted by the Knives Act 1997, s 8(1), (4)(a).

Date in force: 1 March 1999: see SI 1999/5, art 2.

Sub-s (3): word "activity" in square brackets substituted by the Knives Act 1997, s 8(1), (4)(b).

Date in force: 1 March 1999: see SI 1999/5, art 2.

Sub-s (3): number "24" in square brackets substituted by the Knives Act 1997, s 8(1), (4)(c).

Date in force: 1 March 1999: see SI 1999/5, art 2.

Sub-s (3A): inserted by the Knives Act 1997, s 8(1), (5).
Date in force: 1 March 1999: see SI 1999/5, art 2.
Sub-s (4A): inserted by the Crime and Disorder Act 1998, s 25(1).
Date in force: 1 March 1999: see SI 1998/3263, art 4.
Sub-s (4A): repealed, except in relation to Scotland, by the Anti-terrorism, Crime and Security Act 2001, s 125, Sch 8, Pt 6.
Date in force: 14 December 2001: see the Anti-terrorism, Crime and Security Act 2001, s 127(2)(i).
Sub-s (5): words "the powers conferred by subsection (4) above" in square brackets substituted by the Crime and Disorder Act 1998, s 25(2).
Date in force: 1 March 1999: see SI 1998/3263, art 4.
Sub-s (8): paras (a), (b) substituted by the Crime and Disorder Act 1998, s 25(3).
Date in force: 1 March 1999: see SI 1998/3263, art 4.
Sub-s (8): para (b) and word "or" in italics immediately preceding it repealed, except in relation to Scotland, by the Anti-terrorism, Crime and Security Act 2001, s 125, Sch 8, Pt 6.
Date in force: 14 December 2001: see the Anti-terrorism, Crime and Security Act 2001, s 127(2)(i).
Sub-s (9): words "the grounds on which it is given and" in square brackets inserted by the Knives Act 1997, s 8(1), (6).
Date in force: 1 March 1999: see SI 1999/5, art 2.
Sub-s (9A): inserted by the Anti-terrorism, Crime and Security Act 2001, s 101, Sch 7, paras 15, 16(1), (2).
Date in force: 14 December 2001: see the Anti-terrorism, Crime and Security Act 2001, s 127(2)(f).
Sub-s (10): words omitted repealed by the Knives Act 1997, s 8(1), (7).
Date in force: 1 March 1999: see SI 1999/5, art 2.
Sub-s (10A): inserted by the Knives Act 1997, s 8(1), (8).
Date in force: 1 March 1999: see SI 1999/5, art 2.
Sub-s (11): definition "British Transport Police Force" inserted by the Anti-terrorism, Crime and Security Act 2001, s 101, Sch 7, paras 15, 16(1), (3)(a).
Date in force: 14 December 2001: see the Anti-terrorism, Crime and Security Act 2001, s 127(2)(f).
Sub-s (11): in definition "offensive weapon" words from "or, in relation" to "Act 1995" in square brackets inserted by the Knives Act 1997, s 8(1), (9).
Date in force: 1 March 1999: see SI 1999/5, art 2.
Sub-s (11): definition "policed premises" inserted by the Anti-terrorism, Crime and Security Act 2001, s 101, Sch 7, paras 15, 16(1), (3)(b).
Date in force: 14 December 2001: see the Anti-terrorism, Crime and Security Act 2001, s 127(2)(f).
Sub-s (11A): inserted by the Knives Act 1997, s 8(1), (10).
Date in force: 1 March 1999: see SI 1999/5, art 2.

[60AA Powers to require removal of disguises]

[(1) Where—

(a) an authorisation under section 60 is for the time being in force in relation to any locality for any period, or

(b) an authorisation under subsection (3) that the powers conferred by subsection (2) shall be exercisable at any place in a locality is in force for any period,

those powers shall be exercisable at any place in that locality at any time in that period.

(2) This subsection confers power on any constable in uniform—

(a) to require any person to remove any item which the constable reasonably believes that person is wearing wholly or mainly for the purpose of concealing his identity;

(b) to seize any item which the constable reasonably believes any person intends to wear wholly or mainly for that purpose.

(3) If a police officer of or above the rank of inspector reasonably believes—

(a) that activities may take place in any locality in his police area that are likely (if they take place) to involve the commission of offences, and

(b) that it is expedient, in order to prevent or control the activities, to give an authorisation under this subsection,

he may give an authorisation that the powers conferred by this section shall be exercisable at any place within that locality for a specified period not exceeding twenty-four hours.

(4) If it appears to an officer of or above the rank of superintendent that it is expedient to do so, having regard to offences which—

(a) have been committed in connection with the activities in respect of which the authorisation was given, or

(b) are reasonably suspected to have been so committed,

he may direct that the authorisation shall continue in force for a further twenty-four hours.

(5) If an inspector gives an authorisation under subsection , he must, as soon as it is practicable to do so, cause an officer of or above the rank of superintendent to be informed.

(6) Any authorisation under this section—

(a) shall be in writing and signed by the officer giving it; and

(b) shall specify—

(i) the grounds on which it is given;

(ii) the locality in which the powers conferred by this section are exercisable;

(iii) the period during which those powers are exercisable;

and a direction under subsection (4) shall also be given in writing or, where that is not practicable, recorded in writing as soon as it is practicable to do so.

(7) A person who fails to remove an item worn by him when required to do so by a constable in the exercise of his power under this section shall be liable, on summary conviction, to imprisonment for a term not exceeding one month or to a fine not exceeding level 3 on the standard scale or both.

(8) The preceding provisions of this section, so far as they relate to an authorisation by a member of the British Transport Police Force (including one who for the time being has the same powers and privileges as a member of a police force for a police area), shall have effect as if references to a locality or to a locality in his police area were references to any locality in or in the vicinity of any policed premises, or to the whole or any part of any such premises.

(9) In this section "British Transport Police Force" and "policed premises" each has the same meaning as in section 60.

(10) The powers conferred by this section are in addition to, and not in derogation of, any power otherwise conferred.

(11) This section does not extend to Scotland.]

NOTES

Inserted by the Anti-terrorism, Crime and Security Act 2001, s 94(1).

Date in force: 14 December 2001: see the Anti-terrorism, Crime and Security Act 2001, s 127(2)(d).

[60A Retention and disposal of things seized under section 60]

[(1) Any things seized by a constable under section 60 [or 60AA] may be retained in accordance with regulations made by the Secretary of State under this section.

(2) The Secretary of State may make regulations regulating the retention and safe keeping, and the disposal and destruction in prescribed circumstances, of such things.

(3) Regulations under this section may make different provisions for different classes of things or for different circumstances.

(4) The power to make regulations under this section shall be exercisable by statutory instrument which shall be subject to annulment in pursuance of a resolution of either House of Parliament.]

NOTES

Inserted by the Crime and Disorder Act 1998, s 26.

Date in force (for certain purposes): 1 December 1998: see SI 1998/2327, art 4(1A).

Date in force (for remaining purposes): 1 March 1999: see SI 1998/3263, art 4.

Sub-s (1): words "or 60AA" in square brackets inserted by the Anti-terrorism, Crime and Security Act 2001, s 94(2).

Date in force: 14 December 2001: see the Anti-terrorism, Crime and Security Act 2001, s 127(2)(d).

[60B Arrest without warrant for offences under section 60: Scotland]

[In Scotland, where a constable reasonably believes that a person has committed or is committing an offence under section 60(8) he may arrest that person without warrant.]

NOTES

Inserted by the Crime and Disorder Act 1998, s 27(2).

Date in force: 1 March 1999: see SI 1998/3263, art 4.

PART V
PUBLIC ORDER: COLLECTIVE TRESPASS OR NUISANCE ON LAND

Powers to remove trespassers on land

61 Power to remove trespassers on land

(1) If the senior police officer present at the scene reasonably believes that two or more persons are trespassing on land and are present there with the common purpose of residing there for any period, that reasonable steps have been taken by or on behalf of the occupier to ask them to leave and—

(a) that any of those persons has caused damage to the land or to property on the land or used threatening, abusive or insulting words or behaviour towards the occupier, a member of his family or an employee or agent of his, or
(b) that those persons have between them six or more vehicles on the land,

he may direct those persons, or any of them, to leave the land and to remove any vehicles or other property they have with them on the land.

(2) Where the persons in question are reasonably believed by the senior police officer to be persons who were not originally trespassers but have become trespassers on the land, the officer must reasonably believe that the other conditions specified in subsection (1) are satisfied after those persons became trespassers before he can exercise the power conferred by that subsection.

(3) A direction under subsection (1) above, if not communicated to the persons referred to in subsection (1) by the police officer giving the direction, may be communicated to them by any constable at the scene.

(4) If a person knowing that a direction under subsection (1) above has been given which applies to him—

(a) fails to leave the land as soon as reasonably practicable, or
(b) having left again enters the land as a trespasser within the period of three months beginning with the day on which the direction was given,

he commits an offence and is liable on summary conviction to imprisonment for a term not exceeding three months or a fine not exceeding level 4 on the standard scale, or both.

(5) A constable in uniform who reasonably suspects that a person is committing an offence under this section may arrest him without a warrant.

(6) In proceedings for an offence under this section it is a defence for the accused to show—

(a) that he was not trespassing on the land, or
(b) that he had a reasonable excuse for failing to leave the land as soon as reasonably practicable or, as the case may be, for again entering the land as a trespasser.

(7) In its application in England and Wales to common land this section has effect as if in the preceding subsections of it—

(a) references to trespassing or trespassers were references to acts and persons doing acts which constitute either a trespass as against the occupier or an infringement of the commoners' rights; and
(b) references to "the occupier" included the commoners or any of them or, in the case of common land to which the public has access, the local authority as well as any commoner.

(8) Subsection (7) above does not—
(a) require action by more than one occupier; or
(b) constitute persons trespassers as against any commoner or the local authority if they are permitted to be there by the other occupier.

(9) In this section—
"common land" means common land as defined in section 22 of the Commons Registration Act 1965;
"commoner" means a person with rights of common as defined in section 22 of the Commons Registration Act 1965;
"land" does not include—
(a) buildings other than—
(i) agricultural buildings within the meaning of, in England and Wales, paragraphs 3 to 8 of Schedule 5 to the Local Government Finance Act 1988 or, in Scotland, section 7(2) of the Valuation and Rating (Scotland) Act 1956, or
(ii) scheduled monuments within the meaning of the Ancient Monuments and Archaeological Areas Act 1979;
(b) land forming part of—
(i) a highway unless *it falls within the classifications in section 54 of the Wildlife and Countryside Act 1981 (footpath, bridleway or byway open to all traffic or road used as a public path)* [it is a footpath, bridleway or byway open to all traffic within the meaning of Part III of the Wildlife and Countryside Act 1981, is a restricted byway within the meaning of Part II of the Countryside and Rights of Way Act 2000] or is a cycle track under the Highways Act 1980 or the Cycle Tracks Act 1984; or
(ii) a road within the meaning of the Roads (Scotland) Act 1984 unless it falls within the definitions in section 151(2)(a)(ii) or (b) (footpaths and cycle tracks) of that Act or is a bridleway within the meaning of section 47 of the Countryside (Scotland) Act 1967;
"the local authority", in relation to common land, means any local authority which has powers in relation to the land under section 9 of the Commons Registration Act 1965;
"occupier" (and in subsection (8) "the other occupier") means—

(a) in England and Wales, the person entitled to possession of the land by virtue of an estate or interest held by him; and
(b) in Scotland, the person lawfully entitled to natural possession of the land;

"property", in relation to damage to property on land, means—
(a) in England and Wales, property within the meaning of section 10(1) of the Criminal Damage Act 1971; and
(b) in Scotland, either—
(i) heritable property other than land; or
(ii) corporeal moveable property,

and "damage" includes the deposit of any substance capable of polluting the land;

"trespass" means, in the application of this section—
(a) in England and Wales, subject to the extensions effected by subsection (7) above, trespass as against the occupier of the land;
(b) in Scotland, entering, or as the case may be remaining on, land without lawful authority and without the occupier's consent; and

"trespassing" and "trespasser" shall be construed accordingly;

"vehicle" includes—
(a) any vehicle, whether or not it is in a fit state for use on roads, and includes any chassis or body, with or without wheels, appearing to have formed part of such a vehicle, and any load carried by, and anything attached to, such a vehicle; and
(b) a caravan as defined in section 29(1) of the Caravan Sites and Control of Development Act 1960;

and a person may be regarded for the purposes of this section as having a purpose of residing in a place notwithstanding that he has a home elsewhere.

NOTES

Sub-s (9): in definition "land" in para (b)(i) words from "it falls within" to "a public path)" in italics repealed and subsequent words in square brackets substituted by the Countryside and Rights of Way Act 2000, s 51, Sch 5, Pt II, para 17.

Date in force: to be appointed: see the Countryside and Rights of Way Act 2000, s 103(3).

62 Supplementary powers of seizure

(1) If a direction has been given under section 61 and a constable reasonably suspects that any person to whom the direction applies has, without reasonable excuse—
(a) failed to remove any vehicle on the land which appears to the constable to belong to him or to be in his possession or under his control; or
(b) entered the land as a trespasser with a vehicle within the period of three months beginning with the day on which the direction was given,

the constable may seize and remove that vehicle.

(2) In this section, "trespasser" and "vehicle" have the same meaning as in section 61.

Powers in relation to raves

63 Powers to remove persons attending or preparing for a rave

(1) This section applies to a gathering on land in the open air of 100 or more persons (whether or not trespassers) at which amplified music is played during the night (with or without intermissions) and is such as, by reason of its loudness and duration and the time at which it is played, is likely to cause serious distress to the inhabitants of the locality; and for this purpose

(a) such a gathering continues during intermissions in the music and, where the gathering extends over several days, throughout the period during which amplified music is played at night (with or without intermissions); and

(b) "music" includes sounds wholly or predominantly characterised by the emission of a succession of repetitive beats.

(2) If, as respects any land in the open air, a police officer of at least the rank of superintendent reasonably believes that—

(a) two or more persons are making preparations for the holding there of a gathering to which this section applies,

(b) ten or more persons are waiting for such a gathering to begin there, or

(c) ten or more persons are attending such a gathering which is in progress,

he may give a direction that those persons and any other persons who come to prepare or wait for or to attend the gathering are to leave the land and remove any vehicles or other property which they have with them on the land.

(3) A direction under subsection (2) above, if not communicated to the persons referred to in subsection (2) by the police officer giving the direction, may be communicated to them by any constable at the scene.

(4) Persons shall be treated as having had a direction under subsection (2) above communicated to them if reasonable steps have been taken to bring it to their attention.

(5) A direction under subsection (2) above does not apply to an exempt person.

(6) If a person knowing that a direction has been given which applies to him—

(a) fails to leave the land as soon as reasonably practicable, or

(b) having left again enters the land within the period of 7 days beginning with the day on which the direction was given,

he commits an offence and is liable on summary conviction to imprisonment for a term not exceeding three months or a fine not exceeding level 4 on the standard scale, or both.

(7) In proceedings for an offence under this section it is a defence for the accused to show that he had a reasonable excuse for failing to leave the land as soon as reasonably practicable or, as the case may be, for again entering the land.

(8) A constable in uniform who reasonably suspects that a person is committing an offence under this section may arrest him without a warrant.

(9) This section does not apply—

(a) in England and Wales, to a gathering licensed by an entertainment licence; or

(b) in Scotland, to a gathering in premises which, by virtue of section 41 of the Civic Government (Scotland) Act 1982, are licensed to be used as a place of public entertainment.

(10) In this section—

"entertainment licence" means a licence granted by a local authority under—

(a) Schedule 12 to the London Government Act 1963;

(b) section 3 of the Private Places of Entertainment (Licensing) Act 1967; or

(c) Schedule 1 to the Local Government (Miscellaneous Provisions) Act 1982;

"exempt person", in relation to land (or any gathering on land), means the occupier, any member of his family and any employee or agent of his and any person whose home is situated on the land;

"land in the open air" includes a place partly open to the air;

"local authority" means—

(a) in Greater London, a London borough council or the Common Council of the City of London;

(b) in England outside Greater London, a district council or the council of the Isles of Scilly;

(c) in Wales, a county council or county borough council; and

"occupier", "trespasser" and "vehicle" have the same meaning as in section 61.

(11) Until 1st April 1996, in this section "local authority" means, in Wales, a district council.

64 Supplementary powers of entry and seizure

(1) If a police officer of at least the rank of superintendent reasonably believes that circumstances exist in relation to any land which would justify the giving of a direction under section 63 in relation to a gathering to which that section applies he may authorise any constable to enter the land for any of the purposes specified in subsection (2) below.

(2) Those purposes are—

(a) to ascertain whether such circumstances exist; and

(b) to exercise any power conferred on a constable by section 63 or subsection (4) below.

(3) A constable who is so authorised to enter land for any purpose may enter the land without a warrant.

(4) If a direction has been given under section 63 and a constable reasonably suspects that any person to whom the direction applies has, without reasonable excuse—

(a) failed to remove any vehicle or sound equipment on the land which appears to the constable to belong to him or to be in his possession or under his control; or

(b) entered the land as a trespasser with a vehicle or sound equipment within the period of 7 days beginning with the day on which the direction was given,

the constable may seize and remove that vehicle or sound equipment.

(5) Subsection (4) above does not authorise the seizure of any vehicle or sound equipment of an exempt person.

(6) In this section—

"exempt person" has the same meaning as in section 63;

"sound equipment" means equipment designed or adapted for amplifying music and any equipment suitable for use in connection with such equipment, and "music" has the same meaning as in section 63; and

"vehicle" has the same meaning as in section 61.

65 Raves: power to stop persons from proceeding

(1) If a constable in uniform reasonably believes that a person is on his way to a gathering to which section 63 applies in relation to which a direction under section 63(2) is in force, he may, subject to subsections (2) and (3) below—

(a) stop that person, and

(b) direct him not to proceed in the direction of the gathering.

(2) The power conferred by subsection (1) above may only be exercised at a place within 5 miles of the boundary of the site of the gathering.

(3) No direction may be given under subsection (1) above to an exempt person.

(4) If a person knowing that a direction under subsection (1) above has been given to him fails to comply with that direction, he commits an offence and is liable on summary conviction to a fine not exceeding level 3 on the standard scale.

(5) A constable in uniform who reasonably suspects that a person is committing an offence under this section may arrest him without a warrant.

(6) In this section, "exempt person" has the same meaning as in section 63.

66 Power of court to forfeit sound equipment

(1) Where a person is convicted of an offence under section 63 in relation to a gathering to which that section applies and the court is satisfied that any sound equipment which has been seized from him under section 64(4), or which was in his possession or under his control at the relevant time, has been used at the gathering the court may make an order for forfeiture under this subsection in respect of that property.

(2) The court may make an order under subsection (1) above whether or not it also deals with the offender in respect of the offence in any other way and without regard to any restrictions on forfeiture in any enactment.

(3) In considering whether to make an order under subsection (1) above in respect of any property a court shall have regard—

(a) to the value of the property; and

(b) to the likely financial and other effects on the offender of the making of the order (taken together with any other order that the court contemplates making).

(4) An order under subsection (1) above shall operate to deprive the offender of his rights, if any, in the property to which it relates, and the property shall (if not already in their possession) be taken into the possession of the police.

(5) Except in a case to which subsection (6) below applies, where any property has been forfeited under subsection (1) above, a magistrates' court may, on application by a claimant of the property, other than the offender from whom it was forfeited under subsection (1) above, make an order for delivery of the property to the applicant if it appears to the court that he is the owner of the property.

(6) In a case where forfeiture under subsection (1) above has been by order of a Scottish court, a claimant such as is mentioned in subsection (5) above may, in such manner as may be prescribed by act of adjournal, apply to that court for an order for the return of the property in question.

(7) No application shall be made under subsection (5), or by virtue of subsection (6), above by any claimant of the property after the expiration of 6 months from the date on which an order under subsection (1) above was made in respect of the property.

(8) No such application shall succeed unless the claimant satisfies the court either that he had not consented to the offender having possession of the property or that he did not know, and had no reason to suspect, that the property was likely to be used at a gathering to which section 63 applies.

(9) An order under subsection (5), or by virtue of subsection (6), above shall not affect the right of any person to take, within the period of 6 months from the date of an order under subsection (5), or as the case may be by virtue of subsection (6), above, proceedings for the recovery of the property from the person in possession of it in pursuance of the order, but on the expiration of that period the right shall cease.

(10) The Secretary of State may make regulations for the disposal of property, and for the application of the proceeds of sale of property, forfeited under subsection (1) above where no application by a claimant of the property under subsection (5), or by virtue of subsection (6), above has been made within the period specified in subsection (7) above or no such application has succeeded.

(11) The regulations may also provide for the investment of money and for the audit of accounts.

(12) The power to make regulations under subsection (10) above shall be exercisable by statutory instrument which shall be subject to annulment in pursuance of a resolution of either House of Parliament.

(13) In this section—

"relevant time", in relation to a person—

- (a) convicted in England and Wales of an offence under section 63, means the time of his arrest for the offence or of the issue of a summons in respect of it;
- (b) so convicted in Scotland, means the time of his arrest for, or of his being cited as an accused in respect of, the offence;

"sound equipment" has the same meaning as in section 64.

Retention and charges for seized property

67 Retention and charges for seized property

(1) Any vehicles which have been seized and removed by a constable under section 62(1) or 64(4) may be retained in accordance with regulations made by the Secretary of State under subsection (3) below.

(2) Any sound equipment which has been seized and removed by a constable under section 64(4) may be retained until the conclusion of proceedings against the person from whom it was seized for an offence under section 63.

(3) The Secretary of State may make regulations—
- (a) regulating the retention and safe keeping and the disposal and the destruction in prescribed circumstances of vehicles; and
- (b) prescribing charges in respect of the removal, retention, disposal and destruction of vehicles.

(4) Any authority shall be entitled to recover from a person from whom a vehicle has been seized such charges as may be prescribed in respect of the removal, retention, disposal and destruction of the vehicle by the authority.

(5) Regulations under subsection (3) above may make different provisions for different classes of vehicles or for different circumstances.

(6) Any charges under subsection (4) above shall be recoverable as a simple contract debt.

(7) Any authority having custody of vehicles under regulations under subsection (3) above shall be entitled to retain custody until any charges under subsection (4) are paid.

(8) The power to make regulations under subsection (3) above shall be exercisable by statutory instrument which shall be subject to annulment in pursuance of a resolution of either House of Parliament.

(9) In this section—

"conclusion of proceedings" against a person means—
- (a) his being sentenced or otherwise dealt with for the offence or his acquittal;
- (b) the discontinuance of the proceedings; or
- (c) the decision not to prosecute him,

whichever is the earlier;

"sound equipment" has the same meaning as in section 64; and

"vehicle" has the same meaning as in section 61.

Disruptive trespassers

68 Offence of aggravated trespass

(1) A person commits the offence of aggravated trespass if he trespasses on land in the open air and, in relation to any lawful activity which persons are engaging in or

are about to engage in on that or adjoining land in the open air, does there anything which is intended by him to have the effect—

- (a) of intimidating those persons or any of them so as to deter them or any of them from engaging in that activity,
- (b) of obstructing that activity, or
- (c) of disrupting that activity.

(2) Activity on any occasion on the part of a person or persons on land is "lawful" for the purposes of this section if he or they may engage in the activity on the land on that occasion without committing an offence or trespassing on the land.

(3) A person guilty of an offence under this section is liable on summary conviction to imprisonment for a term not exceeding three months or a fine not exceeding level 4 on the standard scale, or both.

(4) A constable in uniform who reasonably suspects that a person is committing an offence under this section may arrest him without a warrant.

(5) In this section "land" does not include—

- (a) the highways and roads excluded from the application of section 61 by paragraph (b) of the definition of "land" in subsection (9) of that section; or
- (b) a road within the meaning of the Roads (Northern Ireland) Order 1993.

69 Powers to remove persons committing or participating in aggravated trespass

(1) If the senior police officer present at the scene reasonably believes—

- (a) that a person is committing, has committed or intends to commit the offence of aggravated trespass on land in the open air; or
- (b) that two or more persons are trespassing on land in the open air and are present there with the common purpose of intimidating persons so as to deter them from engaging in a lawful activity or of obstructing or disrupting a lawful activity,

he may direct that person or (as the case may be) those persons (or any of them) to leave the land.

(2) A direction under subsection (1) above, if not communicated to the persons referred to in subsection (1) by the police officer giving the direction, may be communicated to them by any constable at the scene.

(3) If a person knowing that a direction under subsection (1) above has been given which applies to him—

- (a) fails to leave the land as soon as practicable, or
- (b) having left again enters the land as a trespasser within the period of three months beginning with the day on which the direction was given,

he commits an offence and is liable on summary conviction to imprisonment for a term not exceeding three months or a fine not exceeding level 4 on the standard scale, or both.

(4) In proceedings for an offence under subsection (3) it is a defence for the accused to show—

(a) that he was not trespassing on the land, or

(b) that he had a reasonable excuse for failing to leave the land as soon as practicable or, as the case may be, for again entering the land as a trespasser.

(5) A constable in uniform who reasonably suspects that a person is committing an offence under this section may arrest him without a warrant.

(6) In this section "lawful activity" and "land" have the same meaning as in section 68.

PART XII
MISCELLANEOUS AND GENERAL

General

172 Short title, commencement and extent

(1) This Act may be cited as the Criminal Justice and Public Order Act 1994.

(2) With the exception of section 82 and subject to subsection (4) below, this Act shall come into force on such day as the Secretary of State or, in the case of sections 52 and 53, the Lord Chancellor may appoint by order made by statutory instrument, and different days may be appointed for different provisions or different purposes.

(3) Any order under subsection (2) above may make such transitional provisions and savings as appear to the authority making the order necessary or expedient in connection with any provision brought into force by the order.

(4) The following provisions and their related amendments, repeals and revocations shall come into force on the passing of this Act, namely sections 5 to 15 (and Schedules 1 and 2), 61, 63, 65, 68 to 71, 77 to 80, 81, 83, 90, Chapters I and IV of Part VIII, sections 142 to 148, 150, 158(1), (3) and (4), 166, 167, 171, paragraph 46 of Schedule 9 and this section.

(5) No order shall be made under subsection (6) of section 166 above unless a draft of the order has been laid before, and approved by a resolution of, each House of Parliament.

(6) For the purposes of subsection (4) above—

(a) the following are the amendments related to the provisions specified in that subsection, namely, in Schedule 10, paragraphs 26, 35, 36, 59, 60 and 63(1), (3), (4) and (5);

(b) the repeals and revocations related to the provisions specified in that subsection are those specified in the Note at the end of Schedule 11.

(7) Except as regards any provisions applied under section 39 and subject to the following provisions, this Act extends to England and Wales only.

(8) Sections 47(3), 49, [60 to 67], 70, 71, 81, 82, 146(4), 157(1), 163, 169 and 170 also extend to Scotland.

(9) Section 83(1) extends to England and Wales and Northern Ireland.

(10) This section, sections 68, 69, 83(3) to (5), 88 to 92, 136 to 141, 156, 157(2), (3), (4), (5) and (9), 158, 159, 161, 162, 164, 165, 168, 171 and Chapter IV of Part VIII extend to the United Kingdom and sections 158 and 159 also extend to the Channel Islands and the Isle of Man.

(11) Sections 93, 95 and 101(8), so far as relating to the delivery of prisoners to or from premises situated in a part of the British Islands outside England and Wales, extend to that part of those Islands.

(12) Sections 102(1) to (3), 104, 105 and 117, so far as relating to the transfer of prisoners to or from premises situated in a part of the British Islands outside Scotland, extend to that part of those Islands, but otherwise Chapter II of Part VIII extends to Scotland only.

(13) Sections 47(4), 83(2), 84(5) to (7), 87, Part IX, sections 145(2), 146(2), 148, 151(2), 152(2), 153, 157(7) and 160(2) extend to Scotland only.

(14) Sections 118, 120, 121 and 125, so far as relating to the delivery of prisoners to or from premises situated in a part of the British Islands outside Northern Ireland, extend to that part of those islands, but otherwise Chapter III of Part VIII extends to Northern Ireland only.

(15) Sections 53, 84(8) to (11), 85(4) to (6), 86(2), 145(3), 147 and 157(8) extend to Northern Ireland only.

(16) Where any enactment is amended, repealed or revoked by Schedule 9, 10 or 11 to this Act the amendment, repeal or revocation has the same extent as that enactment; except that Schedules 9 and 11 do not extend to Scotland in so far as they relate to section 17(1) of the Video Recordings Act 1984.

NOTES

Sub-s (8): words "60 to 67" in square brackets substituted by the Knives Act 1997, s 8(1), (11).

Date in force: 1 March 1999: see SI 1999/5, art 2.

Criminal Injuries Compensation Act 1995

1995 CHAPTER 53

An Act to provide for the establishment of a scheme for compensation for criminal injuries

[8th November 1995]

1 The Criminal Injuries Compensation Scheme

(1) The Secretary of State shall make arrangements for the payment of compensation to, or in respect of, persons who have sustained one or more criminal injuries.

(2) Any such arrangements shall include the making of a scheme providing, in particular, for—
(a) the circumstances in which awards may be made; and
(b) the categories of person to whom awards may be made.

(3) The scheme shall be known as the Criminal Injuries Compensation Scheme.

(4) In this Act—

"adjudicator" means a person appointed by the Secretary of State [or the Scottish Ministers] under section 5(1)(b);

"award" means an award of compensation made in accordance with the provisions of the Scheme;

"claims officer" means a person appointed by the Secretary of State under section 3(4)(b);

"compensation" means compensation payable under an award;

"criminal injury", "loss of earnings" and "special expenses" have such meaning as may be specified;

"the Scheme" means the Criminal Injuries Compensation Scheme;

"Scheme manager" means a person appointed by the Secretary of State to have overall responsibility for managing the provisions of the Scheme (other than those to which section 5(2) applies); and

"specified" means specified by the Scheme.

NOTES

Sub-s (4): in definition "adjudicator" words "or the Scottish Ministers" in square brackets inserted by SI 1999/1747, art 3, Sch 10, Pt II, para 2(1), (2).

Date in force: 1 July 1999: see SI 1999/1747, art 1, and SI 1998/3178, art 3.

2 Basis on which compensation is to be calculated

(1) The amount of compensation payable under an award shall be determined in accordance with the provisions of the Scheme.

(2) Provision shall be made for—
(a) a standard amount of compensation, determined by reference to the nature of the injury;
(b) in such cases as may be specified, an additional amount of compensation calculated with respect to loss of earnings;
(c) in such cases as may be specified, an additional amount of compensation calculated with respect to special expenses; and
(d) in cases of fatal injury, such additional amounts as may be specified or otherwise determined in accordance with the Scheme.

(3) Provision shall be made for the standard amount to be determined—
(a) in accordance with a table ("the Tariff") prepared by the Secretary of State as part of the Scheme and such other provisions of the Scheme as may be relevant; or
(b) where no provision is made in the Tariff with respect to the injury in question, in accordance with such provisions of the Scheme as may be relevant.

(4) The Tariff shall show, in respect of each description of injury mentioned in the Tariff, the standard amount of compensation payable in respect of that description of injury.

(5) An injury may be described in the Tariff in such a way, including by reference to the nature of the injury, its severity or the circumstances in which it was sustained, as the Secretary of State considers appropriate.

(6) The Secretary of State may at any time alter the Tariff—
- (a) by adding to the descriptions of injury mentioned there;
- (b) by removing a description of injury;
- (c) by increasing or reducing the amount shown as the standard amount of compensation payable in respect of a particular description of injury; or
- (d) in such other way as he considers appropriate.

(7) The Scheme may—
- (a) provide for amounts of compensation not to exceed such maximum amounts as may be specified;
- (b) include such transitional provision with respect to any alteration of its provisions relating to compensation as the Secretary of State considers appropriate.

3 Claims and awards

(1) The Scheme may, in particular, include provision—
- (a) as to the circumstances in which an award may be withheld or the amount of compensation reduced;
- (b) for an award to be made subject to conditions;
- (c) for the whole or any part of any compensation to be repayable in specified circumstances;
- (d) for compensation to be held subject to trusts, in such cases as may be determined in accordance with the Scheme;
- (e) requiring claims under the Scheme to be made within such periods as may be specified by the Scheme; and
- (f) imposing other time limits.

(2) Where, in accordance with any provision of the Scheme, it falls to one person to satisfy another as to any matter, the standard of proof required shall be that applicable in civil proceedings.

(3) Where, in accordance with any provision of the Scheme made by virtue of subsection (1)(c), any amount falls to be repaid it shall be recoverable as a debt due to the Crown.

(4) The Scheme shall include provision for claims for compensation to be determined and awards and payments of compensation to be made—
- (a) if a Scheme manager has been appointed, by persons appointed for the purpose by the Scheme manager; but
- (b) otherwise by persons ("claims officers") appointed for the purpose by the Secretary of State.

(5) A claims officer—

(a) shall be appointed on such terms and conditions as the Secretary of State considers appropriate; but

(b) shall not be regarded as having been appointed to exercise functions of the Secretary of State or to act on his behalf.

(6) No decision taken by a claims officer shall be regarded as having been taken by, or on behalf of, the Secretary of State.

(7) If a Scheme manager has been appointed—

(a) he shall not be regarded as exercising functions of the Secretary of State or as acting on his behalf; and

(b) no decision taken by him or by any person appointed by him shall be regarded as having been taken by, or on behalf of, the Secretary of State.

7 Inalienability of awards

(1) Every assignment (or, in Scotland, assignation) of, or charge on, an award and every agreement to assign or charge an award shall be void.

(2) On the bankruptcy of a person in whose favour an award is made (or, in Scotland, on the sequestration of such a person's estate), the award shall not pass to any trustee or other person acting on behalf of his creditors.

9 Financial provisions

(1) The Secretary of State may pay such remuneration, allowances or gratuities to or in respect of claims officers and other persons appointed by him under this Act (other than adjudicators) as he considers appropriate.

(2) The Secretary of State may pay, or make such payments towards the provision of, such remuneration, pensions, allowances or gratuities to or in respect of adjudicators, as he considers appropriate.

(3) The Secretary of State may make such payments by way of compensation for loss of office to any adjudicator who is removed from office under section 5(7), as he considers appropriate.

(4) Sums required for the payment of compensation in accordance with the Scheme shall be provided by the Secretary of State out of money provided by Parliament.

(5) Where a Scheme manager has been appointed, the Secretary of State may make such payments to him, in respect of the discharge of his functions in relation to the Scheme, as the Secretary of State considers appropriate.

(6) Any expenses incurred by the Secretary of State under this Act shall be paid out of money provided by Parliament.

[(6A) Any expenses incurred by the Secretary of State under subsection (6) above as regards Scotland shall be reimbursed to the Secretary of State by the Scottish Ministers.]

(7) Any sums received by the Secretary of State under any provision of the Scheme made by virtue of section 3(1)(c) shall be paid by him into the Consolidated Fund.

NOTES

Sub-s (6A): inserted by SI 1999/1820, art 4, Sch 2, Pt I, para 123(1), (6).
Date in force: 1 July 1999: see SI 1999/1820, art 1(2).

13 Short title and extent

(1) This Act may be cited as the Criminal Injuries Compensation Act 1995.

(2) This Act does not extend to Northern Ireland.

Police Act 1996

1996 CHAPTER 16

An Act to consolidate the Police Act 1964, Part IX of the Police and Criminal Evidence Act 1984, Chapter I of Part I of the Police and Magistrates' Courts Act 1994 and certain other enactments relating to the police

[22nd May 1996]

Chapter II
Disciplinary and Other Proceedings

88 Liability for wrongful acts of constables

(1) The chief officer of police for a police area shall be liable in respect of torts committed by constables under his direction and control in the performance or purported performance of their functions in like manner as a master is liable in respect of torts committed by his servants in the course of their employment, and accordingly shall in respect of any such tort be treated for all purposes as a joint tortfeasor.

(2) There shall be paid out of the police fund—
- (a) any damages or costs awarded against the chief officer of police in any proceedings brought against him by virtue of this section and any costs incurred by him in any such proceedings so far as not recovered by him in the proceedings; and
- (b) any sum required in connection with the settlement of any claim made against the chief officer of police by virtue of this section, if the settlement is approved by the police authority.

(3) Any proceedings in respect of a claim made by virtue of this section shall be brought against the chief officer of police for the time being or, in the case of a vacancy in that office, against the person for the time being performing the functions

of the chief officer of police; and references in subsections (1) and (2) to the chief officer of police shall be construed accordingly.

(4) A police authority may, in such cases and to such extent as appear to it to be appropriate, pay out of the police fund—

(a) any damages or costs awarded against a person to whom this subsection applies in proceedings for a tort committed by that person,

(b) any costs incurred and not recovered by such a person in such proceedings, and

(c) any sum required in connection with the settlement of a claim that has or might have given rise to such proceedings.

(5) Subsection (4) applies to a person who is—

(a) a member of the police force maintained by the police authority,

(b) a constable for the time being required to serve with that force by virtue of section 24 or 98 [of this Act or section 23 of the Police Act 1997], or

(c) a special constable appointed for the authority's police area.

NOTES

-s (5): in para (b) words "of this Act or section 23 of the Police Act 1997" in square brackets inserted by the Police Act 1997, s 134(1), Sch 9, para 85.

Date in force: 1 April 1998: see SI 1998/354, art 2(2)(bb).

PART V
MISCELLANEOUS AND GENERAL

Supplemental

106 Short title

This Act may be cited as the Police Act 1996.

Defamation Act 1996

1996 CHAPTER 31

An Act to amend the law of defamation and to amend the law of limitation with respect to actions for defamation or malicious falsehood

[4th July 1996]

Responsibility for publication

1 Responsibility for publication

(1) In defamation proceedings a person has a defence if he shows that—

(a) he was not the author, editor or publisher of the statement complained of,

(b) he took reasonable care in relation to its publication, and

(c) he did not know, and had no reason to believe, that what he did caused or contributed to the publication of a defamatory statement.

(2) For this purpose "author", "editor" and "publisher" have the following meanings, which are further explained in subsection (3)—

"author" means the originator of the statement, but does not include a person who did not intend that his statement be published at all;

"editor" means a person having editorial or equivalent responsibility for the content of the statement or the decision to publish it; and

"publisher" means a commercial publisher, that is, a person whose business is issuing material to the public, or a section of the public, who issues material containing the statement in the course of that business.

(3) A person shall not be considered the author, editor or publisher of a statement if he is only involved—

(a) in printing, producing, distributing or selling printed material containing the statement;
(b) in processing, making copies of, distributing, exhibiting or selling a film or sound recording (as defined in Part I of the Copyright, Designs and Patents Act 1988) containing the statement;
(c) in processing, making copies of, distributing or selling any electronic medium in or on which the statement is recorded, or in operating or providing any equipment, system or service by means of which the statement is retrieved, copied, distributed or made available in electronic form;
(d) as the broadcaster of a live programme containing the statement in circumstances in which he has no effective control over the maker of the statement;
(e) as the operator of or provider of access to a communications system by means of which the statement is transmitted, or made available, by a person over whom he has no effective control.

In a case not within paragraphs (a) to (e) the court may have regard to those provisions by way of analogy in deciding whether a person is to be considered the author, editor or publisher of a statement.

(4) Employees or agents of an author, editor or publisher are in the same position as their employer or principal to the extent that they are responsible for the content of the statement or the decision to publish it.

(5) In determining for the purposes of this section whether a person took reasonable care, or had reason to believe that what he did caused or contributed to the publication of a defamatory statement, regard shall be had to—

(a) the extent of his responsibility for the content of the statement or the decision to publish it,
(b) the nature or circumstances of the publication, and
(c) the previous conduct or character of the author, editor or publisher.

(6) This section does not apply to any cause of action which arose before the section came into force.

Offer to make amends

2 Offer to make amends

(1) A person who has published a statement alleged to be defamatory of another may offer to make amends under this section.

(2) The offer may be in relation to the statement generally or in relation to a specific defamatory meaning which the person making the offer accepts that the statement conveys ("a qualified offer").

(3) An offer to make amends—
(a) must be in writing,
(b) must be expressed to be an offer to make amends under section 2 of the Defamation Act 1996, and
(c) must state whether it is a qualified offer and, if so, set out the defamatory meaning in relation to which it is made.

(4) An offer to make amends under this section is an offer—
(a) to make a suitable correction of the statement complained of and a sufficient apology to the aggrieved party,
(b) to publish the correction and apology in a manner that is reasonable and practicable in the circumstances, and
(c) to pay to the aggrieved party such compensation (if any), and such costs, as may be agreed or determined to be payable.

The fact that the offer is accompanied by an offer to take specific steps does not affect the fact that an offer to make amends under this section is an offer to do all the things mentioned in paragraphs (a) to (c).

(5) An offer to make amends under this section may not be made by a person after serving a defence in defamation proceedings brought against him by the aggrieved party in respect of the publication in question.

(6) An offer to make amends under this section may be withdrawn before it is accepted; and a renewal of an offer which has been withdrawn shall be treated as a new offer.

3 Accepting an offer to make amends

(1) If an offer to make amends under section 2 is accepted by the aggrieved party, the following provisions apply.

(2) The party accepting the offer may not bring or continue defamation proceedings in respect of the publication concerned against the person making the offer, but he is entitled to enforce the offer to make amends, as follows.

(3) If the parties agree on the steps to be taken in fulfilment of the offer, the aggrieved party may apply to the court for an order that the other party fulfil his offer by taking the steps agreed.

(4) If the parties do not agree on the steps to be taken by way of correction, apology and publication, the party who made the offer may take such steps as he thinks appropriate, and may in particular—

(a) make the correction and apology by a statement in open court in terms approved by the court, and
(b) give an undertaking to the court as to the manner of their publication.

(5) If the parties do not agree on the amount to be paid by way of compensation, it shall be determined by the court on the same principles as damages in defamation proceedings.

The court shall take account of any steps taken in fulfilment of the offer and (so far as not agreed between the parties) of the suitability of the correction, the sufficiency of the apology and whether the manner of their publication was reasonable in the circumstances, and may reduce or increase the amount of compensation accordingly.

(6) If the parties do not agree on the amount to be paid by way of costs, it shall be determined by the court on the same principles as costs awarded in court proceedings.

(7) The acceptance of an offer by one person to make amends does not affect any cause of action against another person in respect of the same publication, subject as follows.

(8) In England and Wales or Northern Ireland, for the purposes of the Civil Liability (Contribution) Act 1978—
(a) the amount of compensation paid under the offer shall be treated as paid in bona fide settlement or compromise of the claim; and
(b) where another person is liable in respect of the same damage (whether jointly or otherwise), the person whose offer to make amends was accepted is not required to pay by virtue of any contribution under section 1 of that Act a greater amount than the amount of the compensation payable in pursuance of the offer.

(9) In Scotland—
(a) subsection (2) of section 3 of the Law Reform (Miscellaneous Provisions) (Scotland) Act 1940 (right of one joint wrongdoer as respects another to recover contribution towards damages) applies in relation to compensation paid under an offer to make amends as it applies in relation to damages in an action to which that section applies; and
(b) where another person is liable in respect of the same damage (whether jointly or otherwise), the person whose offer to make amends was accepted is not required to pay by virtue of any contribution under section 3(2) of that Act a greater amount than the amount of compensation payable in pursuance of the offer.

(10) Proceedings under this section shall be heard and determined without a jury.

4 Failure to accept offer to make amends

(1) If an offer to make amends under section 2, duly made and not withdrawn, is not accepted by the aggrieved party, the following provisions apply.

(2) The fact that the offer was made is a defence (subject to subsection (3)) to defamation proceedings in respect of the publication in question by that party against the person making the offer.

A qualified offer is only a defence in respect of the meaning to which the offer related.

(3) There is no such defence if the person by whom the offer was made knew or had reason to believe that the statement complained of—

(a) referred to the aggrieved party or was likely to be understood as referring to him, and

(b) was both false and defamatory of that party;

but it shall be presumed until the contrary is shown that he did not know and had no reason to believe that was the case.

(4) The person who made the offer need not rely on it by way of defence, but if he does he may not rely on any other defence.

If the offer was a qualified offer, this applies only in respect of the meaning to which the offer related.

(5) The offer may be relied on in mitigation of damages whether or not it was relied on as a defence.

Limitation

5 Limitation of actions: England and Wales

(1)–(5) . . .

(6) The amendments made by this section apply only to causes of action arising after the section comes into force.

NOTES

Sub-ss (1)–(5): substitute the Limitation Act 1980, ss 4A, 32A and amend ss 28, 36.

6 Limitation of actions: Northern Ireland

(1)–(4) . . .

(5) The amendments made by this section apply only to causes of action arising after the section comes into force.

NOTES

Sub-ss (1)–(4): amend the Limitation (Northern Ireland) Order 1989, SI 1989/1339, arts 6, 48, 51

The meaning of a statement

7 Ruling on the meaning of a statement

In defamation proceedings the court shall not be asked to rule whether a statement is arguably capable, as opposed to capable, of bearing a particular meaning or meanings attributed to it.

8 Summary disposal of claim

(1) In defamation proceedings the court may dispose summarily of the plaintiff's claim in accordance with the following provisions.

(2) The court may dismiss the plaintiff's claim if it appears to the court that it has no realistic prospect of success and there is no reason why it should be tried.

(3) The court may give judgment for the plaintiff and grant him summary relief (see section 9) if it appears to the court that there is no defence to the claim which has a realistic prospect of success, and that there is no other reason why the claim should be tried.

Unless the plaintiff asks for summary relief, the court shall not act under this subsection unless it is satisfied that summary relief will adequately compensate him for the wrong he has suffered.

(4) In considering whether a claim should be tried the court shall have regard to—

- (a) whether all the persons who are or might be defendants in respect of the publication complained of are before the court;
- (b) whether summary disposal of the claim against another defendant would be inappropriate;
- (c) the extent to which there is a conflict of evidence;
- (d) the seriousness of the alleged wrong (as regards the content of the statement and the extent of publication); and
- (e) whether it is justifiable in the circumstances to proceed to a full trial.

(5) Proceedings under this section shall be heard and determined without a jury.

9 Meaning of summary relief

(1) For the purposes of section 8 (summary disposal of claim) "summary relief" means such of the following as may be appropriate—

- (a) a declaration that the statement was false and defamatory of the plaintiff;
- (b) an order that the defendant publish or cause to be published a suitable correction and apology;
- (c) damages not exceeding £10,000 or such other amount as may be prescribed by order of the Lord Chancellor;
- (d) an order restraining the defendant from publishing or further publishing the matter complained of.

(2) The content of any correction and apology, and the time, manner, form and place of publication, shall be for the parties to agree.

If they cannot agree on the content, the court may direct the defendant to publish or cause to be published a summary of the court's judgment agreed by the parties or settled by the court in accordance with rules of court.

If they cannot agree on the time, manner, form or place of publication, the court may direct the defendant to take such reasonable and practicable steps as the court considers appropriate.

(3) Any order under subsection (1)(c) shall be made by statutory instrument which shall be subject to annulment in pursuance of a resolution of either House of Parliament.

10 Summary disposal: rules of court

(1) Provision may be made by rules of court as to the summary disposal of the plaintiff's claim in defamation proceedings.

(2) Without prejudice to the generality of that power, provision may be made—
- (a) authorising a party to apply for summary disposal at any stage of the proceedings;
- (b) authorising the court at any stage of the proceedings—
  - (i) to treat any application, pleading or other step in the proceedings as an application for summary disposal, or
  - (ii) to make an order for summary disposal without any such application;
- (c) as to the time for serving pleadings or taking any other step in the proceedings in a case where there are proceedings for summary disposal;
- (d) requiring the parties to identify any question of law or construction which the court is to be asked to determine in the proceedings;
- (e) as to the nature of any hearing on the question of summary disposal, and in particular—
  - (i) authorising the court to order affidavits or witness statements to be prepared for use as evidence at the hearing, and
  - (ii) requiring the leave of the court for the calling of oral evidence, or the introduction of new evidence, at the hearing;
- (f) authorising the court to require a defendant to elect, at or before the hearing, whether or not to make an offer to make amends under section 2.

11 Summary disposal: application to Northern Ireland

In their application to Northern Ireland the provisions of sections 8 to 10 (summary disposal of claim) apply only to proceedings in the High Court.

Evidence of convictions

12 Evidence of convictions

(1) . . .

The amendments made by this subsection apply only where the trial of the action begins after this section comes into force.

(2) . . .

The amendments made by this subsection apply only for the purposes of an action begun after this section comes into force, whenever the cause of action arose.

(3) . . .

The amendments made by this subsection apply only where the trial of the action begins after this section comes into force.

NOTES

Sub-s (1): words omitted amend the Civil Evidence Act 1968, s 13.

Sub-s (2): words omitted amend the Law Reform (Miscellaneous Provisions) (Scotland) Act 1968, s 12.

Sub-s (3): words omitted amend the Civil Evidence Act (Northern Ireland) 1971, s 9.

Evidence concerning proceedings in Parliament

13 Evidence concerning proceedings in Parliament

(1) Where the conduct of a person in or in relation to proceedings in Parliament is in issue in defamation proceedings, he may waive for the purposes of those proceedings, so far as concerns him, the protection of any enactment or rule of law which prevents proceedings in Parliament being impeached or questioned in any court or place out of Parliament.

(2) Where a person waives that protection—
- (a) any such enactment or rule of law shall not apply to prevent evidence being given, questions being asked or statements, submissions, comments or findings being made about his conduct, and
- (b) none of those things shall be regarded as infringing the privilege of either House of Parliament.

(3) The waiver by one person of that protection does not affect its operation in relation to another person who has not waived it.

(4) Nothing in this section affects any enactment or rule of law so far as it protects a person (including a person who has waived the protection referred to above) from legal liability for words spoken or things done in the course of, or for the purposes of or incidental to, any proceedings in Parliament.

(5) Without prejudice to the generality of subsection (4), that subsection applies to—
- (a) the giving of evidence before either House or a committee;
- (b) the presentation or submission of a document to either House or a committee;
- (c) the preparation of a document for the purposes of or incidental to the transacting of any such business;
- (d) the formulation, making or publication of a document, including a report, by or pursuant to an order of either House or a committee; and
- (e) any communication with the Parliamentary Commissioner for Standards or any person having functions in connection with the registration of members' interests.

In this subsection "a committee" means a committee of either House or a joint committee of both Houses of Parliament.

Statutory privilege

14 Reports of court proceedings absolutely privileged

(1) A fair and accurate report of proceedings in public before a court to which this section applies, if published contemporaneously with proceedings, is absolutely privileged.

(2) A report of proceedings which by an order of the court, or as a consequence of any statutory provision, is required to be postponed shall be treated as published contemporaneously if it is published as soon as practicable after publication is permitted.

(3) This section applies to—
- (a) any court in the United Kingdom,
- (b) the European Court of Justice or any court attached to that court,
- (c) the European Court of Human Rights, and
- (d) any international criminal tribunal established by the Security Council of the United Nations or by an international agreement to which the United Kingdom is a party.

In paragraph (a) "court" includes any tribunal or body exercising the judicial power of the State.

(4) . . .

NOTES

Sub-s (4): amends the Rehabilitation of Offenders Act 1974, s 8(6) and the Rehabilitation of Offenders (Northern Ireland) Order 1978, SI 1978/1908, art 9(6).

15 Reports, &c protected by qualified privilege

(1) The publication of any report or other statement mentioned in Schedule 1 to this Act is privileged unless the publication is shown to be made with malice, subject as follows.

(2) In defamation proceedings in respect of the publication of a report or other statement mentioned in Part II of that Schedule, there is no defence under this section if the plaintiff shows that the defendant—
- (a) was requested by him to publish in a suitable manner a reasonable letter or statement by way of explanation or contradiction, and
- (b) refused or neglected to do so.

For this purpose "in a suitable manner" means in the same manner as the publication complained of or in a manner that is adequate and reasonable in the circumstances.

(3) This section does not apply to the publication to the public, or a section of the public, of matter which is not of public concern and the publication of which is not for the public benefit.

(4) Nothing in this section shall be construed—
  (a) as protecting the publication of matter the publication of which is prohibited by law, or
  (b) as limiting or abridging any privilege subsisting apart from this section.

Supplementary provisions

17 Interpretation

(1) In this Act—

"publication" and "publish", in relation to a statement, have the meaning they have for the purposes of the law of defamation generally, but "publisher" is specially defined for the purposes of section 1;

"statement" means words, pictures, visual images, gestures or any other method of signifying meaning; and

"statutory provision" means—
  (a) a provision contained in an Act or in subordinate legislation within the meaning of the Interpretation Act 1978,
  [(aa)a provision contained in an Act of the Scottish Parliament or in an instrument made under such an Act,] or
  (b) a statutory provision within the meaning given by section 1(f) of the Interpretation Act (Northern Ireland) 1954.

(2) In this Act as it applies to proceedings in Scotland—

"costs" means expenses; and

"plaintiff" and "defendant" mean pursuer and defender.

NOTES

Sub-s (1): in definition "statutory provision" para (aa) inserted by the Scotland Act 1998, s 125, Sch 8, para 33(2).

Date in force: 6 May 1999: see SI 1998/3178, art 2(2), Sch 3.

General provisions

18 Extent

(1) The following provisions of this Act extend to England and Wales—

section 1 (responsibility for publication),

sections 2 to 4 (offer to make amends), except section 3(9),

section 5 (time limit for actions for defamation or malicious falsehood),

section 7 (ruling on the meaning of a statement),

sections 8 to 10 (summary disposal of claim),

section 12(1) (evidence of convictions),

section 13 (evidence concerning proceedings in Parliament),

sections 14 and 15 and Schedule 1 (statutory privilege),

section 16 and Schedule 2 (repeals) so far as relating to enactments extending to England and Wales,

section 17 (interpretation),

this subsection,

section 19 (commencement) so far as relating to provisions which extend to England and Wales, and

section 20 (short title and saving).

(2) The following provisions of this Act extend to Scotland—

section 1 (responsibility for publication),

sections 2 to 4 (offer to make amends), except section 3(8),

section 12(2) (evidence of convictions),

section 13 (evidence concerning proceedings in Parliament),

sections 14 and 15 and Schedule 1 (statutory privilege),

section 16 and Schedule 2 (repeals) so far as relating to enactments extending to Scotland,

section 17 (interpretation),

this subsection,

section 19 (commencement) so far as relating to provisions which extend to Scotland, and

section 20 (short title and saving).

(3) The following provisions of this Act extend to Northern Ireland—

section 1 (responsibility for publication),

sections 2 to 4 (offer to make amends), except section 3(9),

section 6 (time limit for actions for defamation or malicious falsehood),

section 7 (ruling on the meaning of a statement),

sections 8 to 11 (summary disposal of claim),

section 12(3) (evidence of convictions),

section 13 (evidence concerning proceedings in Parliament),

sections 14 and 15 and Schedule 1 (statutory privilege),

section 16 and Schedule 2 (repeals) so far as relating to enactments extending to Northern Ireland,

section 17(1) (interpretation),

this subsection,

section 19 (commencement) so far as relating to provisions which extend to Northern Ireland, and

section 20 (short title and saving).

19 Commencement

(1) Sections 18 to 20 (extent, commencement and other general provisions) come into force on Royal Assent.

(2) The following provisions of this Act come into force at the end of the period of two months beginning with the day on which this Act is passed—

section 1 (responsibility for publication),

sections 5 and 6 (time limit for actions for defamation or malicious falsehood),

section 12 (evidence of convictions),

section 13 (evidence concerning proceedings in Parliament),

section 16 and the repeals in Schedule 2, so far as consequential on the above provisions, and

section 17 (interpretation), so far as relating to the above provisions.

(3) The provisions of this Act otherwise come into force on such day as may be appointed—

(a) for England and Wales or Northern Ireland, by order of the Lord Chancellor, or

(b) for Scotland, by order of the Secretary of State,

and different days may be appointed for different purposes.

(4) Any such order shall be made by statutory instrument and may contain such transitional provisions as appear to the Lord Chancellor or Secretary of State to be appropriate.

20 Short title and saving

(1) This Act may be cited as the Defamation Act 1996.

(2) Nothing in this Act affects the law relating to criminal libel.

SCHEDULE 1
QUALIFIED PRIVILEGE

Section 15

PART I
STATEMENTS HAVING QUALIFIED PRIVILEGE WITHOUT EXPLANATION OR CONTRADICTION

1 A fair and accurate report of proceedings in public of a legislature anywhere in the world.

2 A fair and accurate report of proceedings in public before a court anywhere in the world.

3 A fair and accurate report of proceedings in public of a person appointed to hold a public inquiry by a government or legislature anywhere in the world.

4 A fair and accurate report of proceedings in public anywhere in the world of an international organisation or an international conference.

5 A fair and accurate copy of or extract from any register or other document required by law to be open to public inspection.

6 A notice or advertisement published by or on the authority of a court, or of a judge or officer of a court, anywhere in the world.

7 A fair and accurate copy of or extract from matter published by or on the authority of a government or legislature anywhere in the world.

8 A fair and accurate copy of or extract from matter published anywhere in the world by an international organisation or an international conference.

PART II
STATEMENTS PRIVILEGED SUBJECT TO EXPLANATION OR CONTRADICTION

9 (1) A fair and accurate copy of or extract from a notice or other matter issued for the information of the public by or on behalf of—

(a) a legislature in any member State or the European Parliament;

(b) the government of any member State, or any authority performing governmental functions in any member State or part of a member State, or the European Commission;

(c) an international organisation or international conference.

(2) In this paragraph "governmental functions" includes police functions.

10 A fair and accurate copy of or extract from a document made available by a court in any member State or the European Court of Justice (or any court attached to that court), or by a judge or officer of any such court.

11 (1) A fair and accurate report of proceedings at any public meeting or sitting in the United Kingdom of—

(a) a local authority or local authority committee;

[(aa) in the case of a local authority which are operating executive arrangements, the executive of that authority or a committee of that executive;]

(b) a justice or justices of the peace acting otherwise than as a court exercising judicial authority;

(c) a commission, tribunal, committee or person appointed for the purposes of any inquiry by any statutory provision, by Her Majesty or by a Minister of the Crown [a member of the Scottish Executive] or a Northern Ireland Department;

(d) a person appointed by a local authority to hold a local inquiry in pursuance of any statutory provision;

(e) any other tribunal, board, committee or body constituted by or under, and exercising functions under, any statutory provision.

[(1A) In the case of a local authority which are operating executive arrangements, a fair and accurate record of any decision made by any member of the executive where that record is required to be made and available for public inspection by virtue of section 22 of the Local Government Act 2000 or of any provision in regulations made under that section.]

(2) *In sub-paragraph (1)(a)*— [In sub-paragraphs (1)(a)[, (1)(aa)] and (1A)— . . .]

"local authority" means—

(a) in relation to England and Wales, a principal council within the meaning of the Local Government Act 1972, any body falling within any paragraph of section 100J(1) of that Act or an authority or body to which the Public Bodies (Admission to Meetings) Act 1960 applies,

(b) in relation to Scotland, a council constituted under section 2 of the Local Government etc (Scotland) Act 1994 or an authority or body to which the Public Bodies (Admission to Meetings) Act 1960 applies,

(c) in relation to Northern Ireland, any authority or body to which sections 23 to 27 of the Local Government Act (Northern Ireland) 1972 apply; and

"local authority committee" means any committee of a local authority or of local authorities, and includes—

(a) any committee or sub-committee in relation to which sections 100A to 100D of the Local Government Act 1972 apply by virtue of section 100E of that Act (whether or not also by virtue of section 100J of that Act), and

(b) any committee or sub-committee in relation to which sections 50A to 50D of the Local Government (Scotland) Act 1973 apply by virtue of section 50E of that Act.

[(2A) In sub-paragraphs (1) and (1A)—

"executive" and "executive arrangements" have the same meaning as in Part II of the Local Government Act 2000.]

(3) A fair and accurate report of any corresponding proceedings in any of the Channel Islands or the Isle of Man or in another member State.

12 (1) A fair and accurate report of proceedings at any public meeting held in a member State.

(2) In this paragraph a "public meeting" means a meeting bona fide and lawfully held for a lawful purpose and for the furtherance or discussion of a matter of public concern, whether admission to the meeting is general or restricted.

13 (1) A fair and accurate report of proceedings at a general meeting of a UK public company.

(2) A fair and accurate copy of or extract from any document circulated to members of a UK public company—

(a) by or with the authority of the board of directors of the company,
(b) by the auditors of the company, or
(c) by any member of the company in pursuance of a right conferred by any statutory provision.

(3) A fair and accurate copy of or extract from any document circulated to members of a UK public company which relates to the appointment, resignation, retirement or dismissal of directors of the company.

(4) In this paragraph "UK public company" means—

(a) a public company within the meaning of section 1(3) of the Companies Act 1985 or Article 12(3) of the Companies (Northern Ireland) Order 1986, or
(b) a body corporate incorporated by or registered under any other statutory provision, or by Royal Charter, or formed in pursuance of letters patent.

(5) A fair and accurate report of proceedings at any corresponding meeting of, or copy of or extract from any corresponding document circulated to members of, a public company formed under the law of any of the Channel Islands or the Isle of Man or of another member State.

14 A fair and accurate report of any finding or decision of any of the following descriptions of association, formed in the United Kingdom or another member State, or of any committee or governing body of such an association—

(a) an association formed for the purpose of promoting or encouraging the exercise of or interest in any art, science, religion or learning, and empowered by its constitution to exercise control over or adjudicate on matters of interest or concern to the association, or the actions or conduct of any person subject to such control or adjudication;
(b) an association formed for the purpose of promoting or safeguarding the interests of any trade, business, industry or profession, or of the persons carrying on or engaged in any trade, business, industry or profession, and empowered by its constitution to exercise control over or adjudicate upon matters connected with that trade, business, industry or profession, or the actions or conduct of those persons;
(c) an association formed for the purpose of promoting or safeguarding the interests of a game, sport or pastime to the playing or exercise of which members of the public are invited or admitted, and empowered by its constitution to exercise control over or adjudicate upon persons connected with or taking part in the game, sport or pastime;
(d) an association formed for the purpose of promoting charitable objects or other objects beneficial to the community and empowered by its constitution to exercise control over or to adjudicate on matters of interest or concern to the association, or the actions or conduct of any person subject to such control or adjudication.

15 (1) A fair and accurate report of, or copy of or extract from, any adjudication, report, statement or notice issued by a body, officer or other person designated for the purposes of this paragraph—

(a) for England and Wales or Northern Ireland, by order of the Lord Chancellor, and

(b) for Scotland, by order of the Secretary of State.

(2) An order under this paragraph shall be made by statutory instrument which shall be subject to annulment in pursuance of a resolution of either House of Parliament.

NOTES

Para 11: sub-para (1)(aa) inserted in relation to England by SI 2002/1057, arts 2(h), 12(b); a corresponding amendment has been made in relation to Wales by SI 2002/808, arts 2(p), 30(a), (see Miscellaneous note below).

Date in force (in relation to England): 6 May 2002: see SI 2002/1057, art 1(1).

Para 11: in sub-para (1)(c) words "a member of the Scottish Executive" in square brackets inserted by the Scotland Act 1998, s 125, Sch 8, para 33(3).

Date in force: 6 May 1999: see SI 1998/3178, art 2(2), Sch 3.

Para 11: sub-para (1A) inserted in relation to England by SI 2001/2237, arts 1(2), 2(q), 31(b), and in relation to Wales by SI 2002/808, arts 2(p), 30(b).

Date in force (in relation to England): 11 July 2001: see SI 2001/2237, art 1(1).

Date in force (in relation to Wales): 1 April 2002: see SI 2002/808, art 1(1).

Para 11: in sub-para (2) words "In sub-paragraph (1)(a)—" in italics repealed and subsequent words in square brackets substituted in relation to England by SI 2001/2237, arts 1(2), 2(q), 31(c), and in relation to Wales by SI 2002/808, arts 2(p), 30(c).

Date in force (in relation to England): 11 July 2001: see SI 2001/2237, art 1(1).

Date in force (in relation to Wales): 1 April 2002: see SI 2002/808, art 1(1).

Para 11: in sub-para (2) reference to ", (1)(aa)" in square brackets inserted, in relation to England, by SI 2002/1057, arts 2(h), 12(c)(i).

Date in force: 6 May 2002: see SI 2002/1057, art 1(1).

Para 11: in sub-para (2) definition "executive" and "executive arrangements" (omitted) repealed, in relation to England, by SI 2002/1057, arts 2(h), 12(c)(ii).

Date in force: 6 May 2002: see SI 2002/1057, art 1(1).

Para 11: sub-para (2A) inserted, in relation to England, by SI 2002/1057, arts 2(h), 12(d).

Date in force: 6 May 2002: see SI 2002/1057, art 1(1).

PART III
SUPPLEMENTARY PROVISIONS

16 (1) In this Schedule—

"court" includes any tribunal or body exercising the judicial power of the State;

"international conference" means a conference attended by representatives of two or more governments;

"international organisation" means an organisation of which two or more governments are members, and includes any committee or other subordinate body of such an organisation; and

"legislature" includes a local legislature.

(2) References in this Schedule to a member State include any European dependent territory of a member State.

(3) In paragraphs 2 and 6 "court" includes—

(a) the European Court of Justice (or any court attached to that court) and the Court of Auditors of the European Communities,

(b) the European Court of Human Rights,

(c) any international criminal tribunal established by the Security Council of the United Nations or by an international agreement to which the United Kingdom is a party, and

(d) the International Court of Justice and any other judicial or arbitral tribunal deciding matters in dispute between States.

(4) In paragraphs 1, 3 and 7 "legislature" includes the European Parliament.

17 (1) Provision may be made by order identifying—
- (a) for the purposes of paragraph 11, the corresponding proceedings referred to in sub-paragraph (3);
- (b) for the purposes of paragraph 13, the corresponding meetings and documents referred to in sub-paragraph (5).

(2) An order under this paragraph may be made—
- (a) for England and Wales or Northern Ireland, by the Lord Chancellor, and
- (b) for Scotland, by the Secretary of State.

(3) An order under this paragraph shall be made by statutory instrument which shall be subject to annulment in pursuance of a resolution of either House of Parliament.

Damages Act 1996

1996 CHAPTER 48

An Act to make new provision in relation to damages for personal injury, including injury resulting in death

[24th July 1996]

1 Assumed rate of return on investment of damages

(1) In determining the return to be expected from the investment of a sum awarded as damages for future pecuniary loss in an action for personal injury the court shall, subject to and in accordance with rules of court made for the purposes of this section, take into account such rate of return (if any) as may from time to time be prescribed by an order made by the Lord Chancellor.

(2) Subsection (1) above shall not however prevent the court taking a different rate of return into account if any party to the proceedings shows that it is more appropriate in the case in question.

(3) An order under subsection (1) above may prescribe different rates of return for different classes of case.

(4) Before making an order under subsection (1) above the Lord Chancellor shall consult the Government Actuary and the Treasury; and any order under that subsection shall be made by statutory instrument subject to annulment in pursuance of a resolution of either House of Parliament.

[(5) In the application of this section to Scotland—
- (a) for the reference to the Lord Chancellor in subsections (1) and (4) there is substituted a reference to the Scottish Ministers; and
- (b) in subsection (4)—

(i) "and the Treasury" is omitted; and
(ii) for "either House of Parliament" there is substituted "the Scottish Parliament".]

NOTES

Sub-s (5): substituted by SI 1999/1820, art 4, Sch 2, Pt I, para 126(1), (2).
Date in force: 1 July 1999: see SI 1999/1820, art 1(2).

2 Consent orders for periodical payments

(1) A court awarding damages in an action for personal injury may, with the consent of the parties, make an order under which the damages are wholly or partly to take the form of periodical payments.

(2) In this section "damages" includes an interim payment which the court, by virtue of rules of court in that behalf, orders the defendant to make to the plaintiff (or, in the application of this section to Scotland, the defender to make to the pursuer).

(3) This section is without prejudice to any powers exercisable apart from this section.

3 Provisional damages and fatal accident claims

(1) This section applies where a person—
(a) is awarded provisional damages; and
(b) subsequently dies as a result of the act or omission which gave rise to the cause of action for which the damages were awarded.

(2) The award of the provisional damages shall not operate as a bar to an action in respect of that person's death under the Fatal Accidents Act 1976.

(3) Such part (if any) of—
(a) the provisional damages; and
(b) any further damages awarded to the person in question before his death,

as was intended to compensate him for pecuniary loss in a period which in the event falls after his death shall be taken into account in assessing the amount of any loss of support suffered by the person or persons for whose benefit the action under the Fatal Accidents Act 1976 is brought.

(4) No award of further damages made in respect of that person after his death shall include any amount for loss of income in respect of any period after his death.

(5) In this section "provisional damages" means damages awarded by virtue of subsection (2)(a) of section 32A of the Supreme Court Act 1981 or section 51 of the County Courts Act 1984 and "further damages" means damages awarded by virtue of subsection (2)(b) of either of those sections.

(6) Subsection (2) above applies whether the award of provisional damages was before or after the coming into force of that subsection; and subsections (3) and (4) apply to any award of damages under the 1976 Act or, as the case may be, further damages after the coming into force of those subsections.

(7) In the application of this section to Northern Ireland—
  (a) for references to the Fatal Accidents Act 1976 there shall be substituted references to the Fatal Accidents (Northern Ireland) Order 1977;
  (b) for the reference to subsection (2)(a) and (b) of section 32A of the Supreme Court Act 1981 and section 51 of the County Courts Act 1984 there shall be substituted a reference to paragraph 10(2)(a) and (b) of Schedule 6 to the Administration of Justice Act 1982.

4 Enhanced protection for structured settlement annuitants

(1) In relation to an annuity purchased for a person pursuant to a structured settlement from an authorised insurance company within the meaning of the Policyholders Protection Act 1975 (and in respect of which that person as annuitant is accordingly the policyholder for the purposes of that Act) sections 10 and 11 of that Act (protection in the event of liquidation of the insurer) [as applied by any transitional provisions made by order under section 426 of the 2000 Act] shall have effect as if any reference to ninety per cent of the amount of the liability, of any future benefit or of the value attributed to the policy were a reference to the full amount of the liability, benefit or value.

(2) Those sections [as applied by any transitional provisions made by order under section 426 of the 2000 Act] shall also have effect as mentioned in subsection (1) above in relation to an annuity purchased from an authorised insurance company within the meaning of the 1975 Act pursuant to any order incorporating terms corresponding to those of a structured settlement which a court makes when awarding damages for personal injury.

(3) Those sections [as applied by any transitional provisions made by order under section 426 of the 2000 Act] shall also have effect as mentioned in subsection (1) above in relation to an annuity purchased from or otherwise provided by an authorised insurance company within the meaning of the 1975 Act pursuant to terms corresponding to those of a structured settlement contained in an agreement made by—
  (a) the Motor Insurers' Bureau; or
  (b) a Domestic Regulations Insurer,

in respect of damages for personal injury which the Bureau or Insurer undertakes to pay in satisfaction of a claim or action against an uninsured driver.

[(3A) In relation to an annuity—
  (a) purchased for a person pursuant to a structured settlement from an authorised insurer;
  (b) purchased from such an insurer pursuant to any order of the kind referred to in subsection (2); or
  (c) purchased from or otherwise provided by such an insurer pursuant to terms corresponding to those of a structured settlement contained in an agreement of the kind referred to in subsection (3)

any long term insurance provision in the Financial Services Compensation Scheme has effect in accordance with subsection (3B).

(3B) To the extent that any long term insurance provision limits the obligation of the scheme manager to make payments or secure continuity of insurance by reference to any amount less than the full amount of any liability, benefit or value due under a contract of long term insurance, the provision has effect as if the reference to that amount were a reference to the full amount of the liability, benefit or value.

(3C) In this section—

"the 2000 Act" means the Financial Services and Markets Act 2000;

"authorised insurer" means an authorised person within the meaning of the 2000 Act with permission under that Act to effect or carry out contracts of insurance as principal;

"Financial Services Compensation Scheme" means the Financial Services Compensation Scheme referred to in section 213(2) of the Financial Services and Markets Act 2000;

"long term insurance provision" means any provision in the Financial Services Compensation Scheme requiring the scheme manager to—

- (a) pay compensation in respect of a liability of an authorised insurer in liquidation under a contract of long term insurance;
- (b) secure continuity of insurance for parties to contracts of long term insurance in the event that an authorised insurer goes into liquidation; or
- (c) secure that payments are made in respect of benefits falling due under contracts of long term insurance during any period while the scheme manager is seeking to make arrangements to secure continuity of insurance as mentioned in (b) above;

"scheme manager" means a body corporate established in accordance with section 212(1) of the 2000 Act.

(3D) In subsections (3B) and (3C) above—

- (a) a reference to a contract of long term insurance must be read with—
  - (i) section 22 of the 2000 Act;
  - (ii) any relevant order under that section; and
  - (iii) Schedule 2 to that Act;
- (b) an authorised insurer is in liquidation when—
  - (i) a resolution has been passed in accordance with the provisions of the Insolvency Act 1986 or (as the case may be) of the Insolvency (Northern Ireland) Order 1989 for the voluntary winding up of the insurer, otherwise than merely for the purpose of reconstruction of the insurer or of amalgamation with another insurer; or
  - (ii) without any such resolution having been passed beforehand, an order has been made for the winding up of the insurer by the court under that Act or that Order.]

(4) In subsection (3) above "the Motor Insurers' Bureau" means the company of that name incorporated on 14th June 1946 under the Companies Act 1929 and "a Domestic Regulations Insurer" has the meaning given in the Bureau's Domestic Regulations.

(5) [Subsections (1) to (3) of this section apply] if the liquidation of the authorised insurance company begins (within the meaning of the 1975 Act) after the coming into force of this section irrespective of when the annuity was purchased or provided.

[(6) Subsections (3A) to (3D) of this section apply if the liquidation of the authorised insurer begins (within the meaning of subsection (3D)) after the coming into force of section 19 of the 2000 Act, irrespective of when the annuity was purchased or provided.]

NOTES

Sub-ss (1)–(3): words "as applied by any transitional provisions made by order under section 426 of the 2000 Act" in square brackets inserted by SI 2001/3649, art 350(a).

Date in force: 1 December 2001: see SI 2001/3649, art 1.

Sub-ss (3A)–(3D): inserted by SI 2001/3649, art 350(b).

Date in force: 1 December 2001: see SI 2001/3649, art 1.

Sub-s (5): words "Subsections (1) to (3) of this section apply" in square brackets substituted by SI 2001/3649, art 350(c).

Date in force: 1 December 2001: see SI 2001/3649, art 1.

Sub-s (6): inserted by SI 2001/3649, art 350(d).

Date in force: 1 December 2001: see SI 2001/3649, art 1.

5 Meaning of structured settlement

(1) In section 4 above a "structured settlement" means an agreement settling a claim or action for damages for personal injury on terms whereby—

- (a) the damages are to consist wholly or partly of periodical payments; and
- (b) the person to whom the payments are to be made is to receive them as the annuitant under one or more annuities purchased for him by the person against whom the claim or action is brought or, if he is insured against the claim, by his insurer.

(2) The periodical payments may be for the life of the claimant, for a specified period or of a specified number or minimum number or include payments of more than one of those descriptions.

(3) The amounts of the periodical payments (which need not be at a uniform rate or payable at uniform intervals) may be—

- (a) specified in the agreement, with or without provision for increases of specified amounts or percentages; or
- (b) subject to adjustment in a specified manner so as to preserve their real value; or
- (c) partly specified as mentioned in paragraph (a) above and partly subject to adjustment as mentioned in paragraph (b) above.

(4) The annuity or annuities must be such as to provide the annuitant with sums which as to amount and time of payment correspond to the periodical payments described in the agreement.

(5) Payments in respect of the annuity or annuities may be received on behalf of the annuitant by another person or received and held on trust for his benefit under a trust of which he is, during his lifetime, the sole beneficiary.

(6) The Lord Chancellor may by an order made by statutory instrument provide that there shall for the purposes of this section be treated as an insurer any body specified in the order, being a body which, though not an insurer, appears to him to fulfil corresponding functions in relation to damages for personal injury claimed or awarded against persons of any class or description, and the reference in subsection (1)(b) above to a person being insured against the claim and his insurer shall be construed accordingly.

(7) In the application of subsection (6) above to Scotland for the reference to the Lord Chancellor there shall be substituted a reference to the Secretary of State.

(8) Where—

(a) an agreement is made settling a claim or action for damages for personal injury on terms whereby the damages are to consist wholly or partly of periodical payments;

(b) the person against whom the claim or action is brought (or, if he is insured against the claim, his insurer) purchases one or more annuities; and

(c) a subsequent agreement is made under which the annuity is, or the annuities are, assigned in favour of the person entitled to the payments (so as to secure that from a future date he receives the payments as the annuitant under the annuity or annuities),

then, for the purposes of section 4 above, the agreement settling the claim or action shall be treated as a structured settlement and any such annuity assigned in favour of that person shall be treated as an annuity purchased for him pursuant to the settlement.

(9) Subsections (2) to (7) above shall apply to an agreement to which subsection (8) above applies as they apply to a structured settlement as defined in subsection (1) above (the reference in subsection (6) to subsection (1)(b) being read as a reference to subsection (8)(b)).

6 Guarantees for public sector settlements

(1) This section applies where—

(a) a claim or action for damages for personal injury is settled on terms corresponding to those of a structured settlement as defined in section 5 above except that the person to whom the payments are to be made is not to receive them as mentioned in subsection (1)(b) of that section; or

(b) a court awarding damages for personal injury makes an order incorporating such terms.

(2) If it appears to a Minister of the Crown that the payments are to be made by a body in relation to which he has, by virtue of this section, power to do so, he may guarantee the payments to be made under the agreement or order.

(3) The bodies in relation to which a Minister may give such a guarantee shall, subject to subsection (4) below, be such bodies as are designated in relation to the relevant government department by guidelines agreed upon between that department and the Treasury.

(4) A guarantee purporting to be given by a Minister under this section shall not be invalidated by any failure on his part to act in accordance with such guidelines as are mentioned in subsection (3) above.

(5) A guarantee under this section shall be given on such terms as the Minister concerned may determine but those terms shall in every case require the body in question to reimburse the Minister, with interest, for any sums paid by him in fulfilment of the guarantee.

(6) Any sums required by a Minister for fulfilling a guarantee under this section shall be defrayed out of money provided by Parliament and any sums received by him by way of reimbursement or interest shall be paid into the Consolidated Fund.

(7) A Minister who has given one or more guarantees under this section shall, as soon as possible after the end of each financial year, lay before each House of Parliament a statement showing what liabilities are outstanding in respect of the guarantees in that year, what sums have been paid in that year in fulfilment of the guarantees and what sums (including interest) have been recovered in that year in respect of the guarantees or are still owing.

(8) In this section "government department" means any department of Her Majesty's government in the United Kingdom and for the purposes of this section a government department is a relevant department in relation to a Minister if he has responsibilities in respect of that department.

[(8A) In the application of subsection (3) above to Scotland, for the words from "guidelines" to the end there shall be substituted "the Minister".]

[(8B) In the application of this section to Scotland, "relevant government department" shall be read as if it was a reference to any part of the Scottish Administration and subsection (8) shall cease to have effect.]

(9) The Schedule to this Act has effect for conferring corresponding powers on Northern Ireland departments.

NOTES

Sub-s (8A): inserted by the Scotland Act 1998, s 125, Sch 8, para 34.
Date in force: 1 July 1999: see SI 1998/3178, art 2(1).
Sub-s (8B): inserted by SI 1999/1820, art 4, Sch 2, Pt I, para 126(1), (3).
Date in force: 1 July 1999: see SI 1999/1820, art 1(2).

7 Interpretation

(1) Subject to subsection (2) below, in this Act "personal injury" includes any disease and any impairment of a person's physical or mental condition and references to a claim or action for personal injury include references to such a claim or action brought by virtue of the Law Reform (Miscellaneous Provisions) Act 1934 and to a claim or action brought by virtue of the Fatal Accidents Act 1976.

(2) In the application of this Act to Scotland "personal injury" has the meaning given by section 10(1) of the Damages (Scotland) Act 1976.

(3) In the application of subsection (1) above to Northern Ireland for the references to the Law Reform (Miscellaneous Provisions) Act 1934 and to the Fatal Accidents

Act 1976 there shall be substituted respectively references to the Law Reform (Miscellaneous Provisions) Act (Northern Ireland) 1937 and the Fatal Accidents (Northern Ireland) Order 1977.

8 Short title, extent and commencement

(1) This Act may be cited as the Damages Act 1996.

(2) Section 3 does not extend to Scotland but, subject to that, this Act extends to the whole of the United Kingdom.

(3) This Act comes into force at the end of the period of two months beginning with the day on which it is passed.

SCHEDULE

GUARANTEES BY NORTHERN IRELAND DEPARTMENTS FOR PUBLIC SECTOR SETTLEMENTS

Section 6(9)

1 This Schedule applies where—

(a) a claim or action for damages for personal injury is settled on terms corresponding to those of a structured settlement as defined in section 5 of this Act except that the person to whom the payments are to be made is not to receive them as mentioned in subsection (1)(b) of that section; or

(b) a court awarding damages for personal injury makes an order incorporating such terms.

2 If it appears to a Northern Ireland department that the payments are to be made by a body in relation to which that department has, by virtue of this Schedule, power to do so, that department may guarantee the payments to be made under the agreement or order.

3 The bodies in relation to which a Northern Ireland department may give such a guarantee shall, subject to paragraph 4 below, be such bodies as are designated in relation to that department by guidelines agreed upon between that department and the Department of Finance and Personnel in Northern Ireland.

4 A guarantee purporting to be given by a Northern Ireland department under this Schedule shall not be invalidated by any failure on the part of that department to act in accordance with such guidelines as are mentioned in paragraph 3 above.

5 A guarantee under this Schedule shall be given on such terms as the Northern Ireland department concerned may determine but those terms shall in every case require the body in question to reimburse that department, with interest, for any sums paid by that department in fulfilment of the guarantee.

6 A Northern Ireland department which has given one or more guarantees under this Schedule shall, as soon as possible after the end of each financial year, lay before the Northern Ireland Assembly a statement showing what liabilities are outstanding in respect of the guarantees in that year, what sums have been paid in that year in fulfilment of the guarantees and what sums (including interest) have been recovered in that year in respect of the guarantees or are still owing.

Broadcasting Act 1996

1996 CHAPTER 55

An Act to make new provision about the broadcasting in digital form of television and sound programme services and the broadcasting in that form on television or radio frequencies of other services; to amend the Broadcasting Act 1990; to make provision about rights to televise sporting or other events of national interest; to amend in other respects the law relating to the provision of television and sound programme services; to provide for the establishment and functions of a Broadcasting Standards Commission and for the dissolution of the Broadcasting Complaints Commission and the Broadcasting Standards Council; to make provision for the transfer to other persons of property, rights and liabilities of the British Broadcasting Corporation relating to their transmission network; and for connected purposes

[24th July 1996]

PART V
THE BROADCASTING STANDARDS COMMISSION

Complaints

121 Certain statements etc protected by qualified privilege for purposes of defamation

(1) For the purposes of the law relating to defamation—

(a) publication of any statement in the course of the consideration by the BSC of, and their adjudication on, a fairness complaint,

(b) publication by the BSC of directions under section 119(1) relating to a fairness complaint, or

(c) publication of a report of the BSC, so far as the report relates to fairness complaints,

is privileged unless the publication is shown to be made with malice.

(2) Nothing in subsection (1) shall be construed as limiting any privilege subsisting apart from that subsection.

PART VIII
MISCELLANEOUS AND GENERAL

General

150 Short title and extent

(1) This Act may be cited as the Broadcasting Act 1996.

(2) This Act, except paragraph 27 of Schedule 10, extends to Northern Ireland.

(3) Section 204(6) of the 1990 Act (power to extend to Isle of Man and Channel Islands) applies to the provisions of this Act amending that Act.

(4) Her Majesty may by Order in Council direct that any of the other provisions of this Act shall extend to the Isle of Man or any of the Channel Islands with such modifications, if any, as appear to Her Majesty to be appropriate.

Justices of the Peace Act 1997

1997 CHAPTER 25

An Act to consolidate the Justices of the Peace Act 1979 and provisions of Part IV of the Police and Magistrates' Courts Act 1994.

[19th March 1997]

PART V
PROTECTION AND INDEMNIFICATION OF JUSTICES AND JUSTICES' CLERKS

51 Immunity for acts within jurisdiction

[(1)] No action shall lie against any justice of the peace or justices' clerk in respect of any act or omission of his—

(a) in the execution of his duty—

(i) as such a justice; or

(ii) as such a clerk exercising, by virtue of any statutory provision, any of the functions of a single justice; and

(b) with respect to any matter within his jurisdiction.

[(2) In this section references to a justices' clerk include any person appointed by a magistrates' courts committee to assist a justices' clerk.]

NOTES

Sub-s (1): numbered as such by the Access to Justice Act 1999, s 100.
Date in force: 1 April 2001: see SI 2001/916, art 2(b)(i).
Sub-s (2): inserted by the Access to Justice Act 1999, s 100.
Date in force: 1 April 2001: see SI 2001/916, art 2(b)(i).

52 Immunity for certain acts beyond jurisdiction

[(1)] An action shall lie against any justice of the peace or justices' clerk in respect of any act or omission of his—

(a) in the purported execution of his duty—

(i) as such a justice; or

(ii) as such a clerk exercising, by virtue of any statutory provision, any of the functions of a single justice; but

(b) with respect to a matter which is not within his jurisdiction,

if, but only if, it is proved that he acted in bad faith.

[(2) In this section references to a justices' clerk include any person appointed by a magistrates' courts committee to assist a justices' clerk.]

NOTES

Sub-s (1): numbered as such by the Access to Justice Act 1999, s 100.
Date in force: 1 April 2001: see SI 2001/916, art 2(b)(i).
Sub-s (2): inserted by the Access to Justice Act 1999, s 100.
Date in force: 1 April 2001: see SI 2001/916, art 2(b)(i).

PART VIII
MISCELLANEOUS AND SUPPLEMENTARY PROVISIONS

74 Commencement

(1) Subject to—
- (a) subsection (2) below; and
- (b) paragraphs 7(2)(1) and 8 of Schedule 4 to this Act,

this Act shall come into force at the end of the period of three months beginning with the day on which it is passed (and any reference in this Act to the commencement of this Act is a reference to its coming into force at the end of that period).

(2) If section 82 of and Schedule 7 to the Police and Magistrates' Courts Act 1994 have not come into force before the commencement of this Act, then section 50 of and Schedule 3 to this Act shall come into force on the relevant commencement date.

(3) In subsection (2) above "relevant commencement date" means—
- (a) if before the commencement of this Act a date on or after the date of that commencement has been appointed by an order under section 94 of the Police and Magistrates' Courts Act 1994 (commencement and transitional provisions) as the date on which section 82 of and Schedule 7 to that Act are to come into force, the date so appointed; and
- (b) otherwise, such date as the Lord Chancellor may by order appoint.

(4) Subsections (4), (5), (7) and (8) of section 94 of the Police and Magistrates' Courts Act 1994 shall apply to an order under subsection (3)(b) above as they would apply to an order under subsection (2) of that section.

75 Short title and extent

(1) This Act may be cited as the Justices of the Peace Act 1997.

(2) Subject to subsections (3) and (4) below, any amendment, repeal or revocation contained in Schedule 5 or 6 to this Act has the same extent as the provision it amends, repeals or revokes.

(3) In Schedule 5 to this Act—
- (a) paragraphs 2 and 5 extend to England and Wales only; and
- (b) paragraph 9 extends to the United Kingdom.

(4) In Schedule 6 to this Act, the repeal of section 70 of the Criminal Procedure and Investigations Act 1996 extends to England and Wales only.

(5) Subject to subsections (2) to (4) above, this Act extends to England and Wales only.

Social Security (Recovery of Benefits) Act 1997

1997 CHAPTER 27

An Act to re-state, with amendments, Part IV of the Social Security Administration Act 1992

[19th March 1997]

Introductory

1 Cases in which this Act applies

(1) This Act applies in cases where—
- (a) a person makes a payment (whether on his own behalf or not) to or in respect of any other person in consequence of any accident, injury or disease suffered by the other, and
- (b) any listed benefits have been, or are likely to be, paid to or for the other during the relevant period in respect of the accident, injury or disease.

(2) The reference above to a payment in consequence of any accident, injury or disease is to a payment made—
- (a) by or on behalf of a person who is, or is alleged to be, liable to any extent in respect of the accident, injury or disease, or
- (b) in pursuance of a compensation scheme for motor accidents;

but does not include a payment mentioned in Part I of Schedule 1.

(3) Subsection (1)(a) applies to a payment made—
- (a) voluntarily, or in pursuance of a court order or an agreement, or otherwise, and
- (b) in the United Kingdom or elsewhere.

(4) In a case where this Act applies—
- (a) the "injured person" is the person who suffered the accident, injury or disease,
- (b) the "compensation payment" is the payment within subsection (1)(a), and
- (c) "recoverable benefit" is any listed benefit which has been or is likely to be paid as mentioned in subsection (1)(b).

2 Compensation payments to which this Act applies

This Act applies in relation to compensation payments made on or after the day on which this section comes into force, unless they are made in pursuance of a court order or agreement made before that day.

3 The relevant period

(1) In relation to a person ("the claimant") who has suffered any accident, injury or disease, "the relevant period" has the meaning given by the following subsections.

(2) Subject to subsection (4), if it is a case of accident or injury, the relevant period is the period of five years immediately following the day on which the accident or injury in question occurred.

(3) Subject to subsection (4), if it is a case of disease, the relevant period is the period of five years beginning with the date on which the claimant first claims a listed benefit in consequence of the disease.

(4) If at any time before the end of the period referred to in subsection (2) or (3)—
- (a) a person makes a compensation payment in final discharge of any claim made by or in respect of the claimant and arising out of the accident, injury or disease, or
- (b) an agreement is made under which an earlier compensation payment is treated as having been made in final discharge of any such claim,

the relevant period ends at that time.

Certificates of recoverable benefits

4 Applications for certificates of recoverable benefits

(1) Before a person ("the compensator") makes a compensation payment he must apply to the Secretary of State for a certificate of recoverable benefits.

(2) Where the compensator applies for a certificate of recoverable benefits, the Secretary of State must—
- (a) send to him a written acknowledgement of receipt of his application, and
- (b) subject to subsection (7), issue the certificate before the end of the following period.

(3) The period is—
- (a) the prescribed period, or
- (b) if there is no prescribed period, the period of four weeks,

which begins with the day following the day on which the application is received.

(4) The certificate is to remain in force until the date specified in it for that purpose.

(5) The compensator may apply for fresh certificates from time to time.

(6) Where a certificate of recoverable benefits ceases to be in force, the Secretary of State may issue a fresh certificate without an application for one being made.

(7) Where the compensator applies for a fresh certificate while a certificate ("the existing certificate") remains in force, the Secretary of State must issue the fresh certificate before the end of the following period.

(8) The period is—

(a) the prescribed period, or
(b) if there is no prescribed period, the period of four weeks,

which begins with the day following the day on which the existing certificate ceases to be in force.

(9) For the purposes of this Act, regulations may provide for the day on which an application for a certificate of recoverable benefits is to be treated as received.

5 Information contained in certificates

(1) A certificate of recoverable benefits must specify, for each recoverable benefit—

(a) the amount which has been or is likely to have been paid on or before a specified date, and
(b) if the benefit is paid or likely to be paid after the specified date, the rate and period for which, and the intervals at which, it is or is likely to be so paid.

(2) In a case where the relevant period has ended before the day on which the Secretary of State receives the application for the certificate, the date specified in the certificate for the purposes of subsection (1) must be the day on which the relevant period ended.

(3) In any other case, the date specified for those purposes must not be earlier than the day on which the Secretary of State received the application.

(4) The Secretary of State may estimate, in such manner as he thinks fit, any of the amounts, rates or periods specified in the certificate.

(5) Where the Secretary of State issues a certificate of recoverable benefits, he must provide the information contained in the certificate to—

(a) the person who appears to him to be the injured person, or
(b) any person who he thinks will receive a compensation payment in respect of the injured person.

(6) A person to whom a certificate of recoverable benefits is issued or who is provided with information under subsection (5) is entitled to particulars of the manner in which any amount, rate or period specified in the certificate has been determined, if he applies to the Secretary of State for those particulars.

Liability of person paying compensation

6 Liability to pay Secretary of State amount of benefits

(1) A person who makes a compensation payment in any case is liable to pay to the Secretary of State an amount equal to the total amount of the recoverable benefits.

(2) The liability referred to in subsection (1) arises immediately before the compensation payment or, if there is more than one, the first of them is made.

(3) No amount becomes payable under this section before the end of the period of 14 days following the day on which the liability arises.

(4) Subject to subsection (3), an amount becomes payable under this section at the end of the period of 14 days beginning with the day on which a certificate of recoverable benefits is first issued showing that the amount of recoverable benefit to which it relates has been or is likely to have been paid before a specified date.

7 Recovery of payments due under section 6

(1) This section applies where a person has made a compensation payment but—
- (a) has not applied for a certificate of recoverable benefits, or
- (b) has not made a payment to the Secretary of State under section 6 before the end of the period allowed under that section.

(2) The Secretary of State may—
- (a) issue the person who made the compensation payment with a certificate of recoverable benefits, if none has been issued, or
- (b) issue him with a copy of the certificate of recoverable benefits or (if more than one has been issued) the most recent one,

and (in either case) issue him with a demand that payment of any amount due under section 6 be made immediately.

(3) The Secretary of State may, in accordance with subsections (4) and (5), recover the amount for which a demand for payment is made under subsection (2) from the person who made the compensation payment.

(4) If the person who made the compensation payment resides or carries on business in England and Wales and a county court so orders, any amount recoverable under subsection (3) is recoverable by execution issued from the county court or otherwise as if it were payable under an order of that court.

(5) If the person who made the payment resides or carries on business in Scotland, any amount recoverable under subsection (3) may be enforced in like manner as an extract registered decree arbitral bearing a warrant for execution issued by the sheriff court of any sheriffdom in Scotland.

(6) A document bearing a certificate which—
- (a) is signed by a person authorised to do so by the Secretary of State, and

(b) states that the document, apart from the certificate, is a record of the amount recoverable under subsection (3),

is conclusive evidence that that amount is so recoverable.

(7) A certificate under subsection (6) purporting to be signed by a person authorised to do so by the Secretary of State is to be treated as so signed unless the contrary is proved.

Reduction of compensation payment

8 Reduction of compensation payment

(1) This section applies in a case where, in relation to any head of compensation listed in column 1 of Schedule 2—

(a) any of the compensation payment is attributable to that head, and

(b) any recoverable benefit is shown against that head in column 2 of the Schedule.

(2) In such a case, any claim of a person to receive the compensation payment is to be treated for all purposes as discharged if—

(a) he is paid the amount (if any) of the compensation payment calculated in accordance with this section, and

(b) if the amount of the compensation payment so calculated is nil, he is given a statement saying so by the person who (apart from this section) would have paid the gross amount of the compensation payment.

(3) For each head of compensation listed in column 1 of the Schedule for which paragraphs (a) and (b) of subsection (1) are met, so much of the gross amount of the compensation payment as is attributable to that head is to be reduced (to nil, if necessary) by deducting the amount of the recoverable benefit or, as the case may be, the aggregate amount of the recoverable benefits shown against it.

(4) Subsection (3) is to have effect as if a requirement to reduce a payment by deducting an amount which exceeds that payment were a requirement to reduce that payment to nil.

(5) The amount of the compensation payment calculated in accordance with this section is—

(a) the gross amount of the compensation payment,

less

(b) the sum of the reductions made under subsection (3),

(and, accordingly, the amount may be nil).

9 Section 8: supplementary

(1) A person who makes a compensation payment calculated in accordance with section 8 must inform the person to whom the payment is made—

(a) that the payment has been so calculated, and

(b) of the date for payment by reference to which the calculation has been made.

(2) If the amount of a compensation payment calculated in accordance with section 8 is nil, a person giving a statement saying so is to be treated for the purposes of this Act as making a payment within section 1(1)(a) on the day on which he gives the statement.

(3) Where a person—
 (a) makes a compensation payment calculated in accordance with section 8, and
 (b) if the amount of the compensation payment so calculated is nil, gives a statement saying so,

he is to be treated, for the purpose of determining any rights and liabilities in respect of contribution or indemnity, as having paid the gross amount of the compensation payment.

(4) For the purposes of this Act—
 (a) the gross amount of the compensation payment is the amount of the compensation payment apart from section 8, and
 (b) the amount of any recoverable benefit is the amount determined in accordance with the certificate of recoverable benefits.

Reviews and appeals

10 Review of certificates of recoverable benefits

(1) The Secretary of State may review any certificate of recoverable benefits if he is satisfied—
 (a) that it was issued in ignorance of, or was based on a mistake as to, a material fact, or
 (b) that a mistake (whether in computation or otherwise) has occurred in its preparation.

[(1) Any certificate of recoverable benefits may be reviewed by the Secretary of State—
 (a) either within the prescribed period or in prescribed cases or circumstances; and
 (b) either on an application made for the purpose or on his own initiative.]

(2) On a review under this section the Secretary of State may either—
 (a) confirm the certificate, or
 (b) (subject to subsection (3)) issue a fresh certificate containing such variations as he considers appropriate [or
 (c) revoke the certificate].

(3) The Secretary of State may not vary the certificate so as to increase the total amount of the recoverable benefits unless it appears to him that the variation is required as a result of the person who applied for the certificate supplying him with incorrect or insufficient information.

NOTES

Sub-s (1): substituted by the Social Security Act 1998, s 86(1), Sch 7, para 149(1).

Date in force (to the extent the making of regulations is authorised): 4 March 1999: see SI 1999/528, art 2(a), Schedule.

Date in force (for remaining purposes, except in relation to housing benefit, council tax benefit or decisions to which the Social Security Contributions (Transfer of Functions, etc) Act 1999 (Commencement No 1 and Transitional Provisions) Order 1999, SI 1999/527, art 4(6) applies): 29 November 1999: see SI 1999/3178, art 2(1), Sch 1.

Date in force (for remaining purposes): to be appointed: see the Social Security Act 1998, s 87(2).

Sub-s (2): para (c) and the word "or" immediately preceding it inserted by the Social Security Act 1998, s 86(1), Sch 7, para 149(2).

Date in force (except in relation to housing benefit, council tax benefit or decisions to which the Social Security Contributions (Transfer of Functions, etc) Act 1999 (Commencement No 1 and Transitional Provisions) Order 1999, SI 1999/527, art 4(6) applies): 29 November 1999: see SI 1999/3178, art 2(1), Sch 1.

Date in force (for remaining purposes): to be appointed: see the Social Security Act 1998, s 87(2).

11 Appeals against certificates of recoverable benefits

(1) An appeal against a certificate of recoverable benefits may be made on the ground—

(a) that any amount, rate or period specified in the certificate is incorrect, or
(b) that listed benefits which have been, or are likely to be, paid otherwise than in respect of the accident, injury or disease in question have been brought into account [or
(c) that listed benefits which have not been, and are not likely to be, paid to the injured person during the relevant period have been brought into account, or
(d) that the payment on the basis of which the certificate was issued is not a payment within section 1(1)(a)].

(2) An appeal under this section may be made by—

(a) the person who applied for the certificate of recoverable benefits, or
[(aa) (in a case where that certificate was issued under section 7(2)(a)) the person to whom it was so issued, or]
(b) (in a case where the amount of the compensation payment has been calculated under section 8) the injured person or other person to whom the payment is made.

(3) No appeal may be made under this section until—

(a) the claim giving rise to the compensation payment has been finally disposed of, and
(b) the liability under section 6 has been discharged.

(4) For the purposes of subsection (3)(a), if an award of damages in respect of a claim has been made under or by virtue of—

(a) section 32A(2)(a) of the Supreme Court Act 1981,
(b) section 12(2)(a) of the Administration of Justice Act 1982, or
(c) section 51(2)(a) of the County Courts Act 1984,

(orders for provisional damages in personal injury cases), the claim is to be treated as having been finally disposed of.

(5) Regulations may make provision—

(a) as to the manner in which, and the time within which, appeals under this section may be made,
(b) as to the procedure to be followed where such an appeal is made, and
(c) for the purpose of enabling any such appeal to be treated as an application for review under section 10.

(6) *Regulations under subsection (5)(c) may (among other things) provide that the circumstances in which a review may be carried out are not to be restricted to those specified in section 10(1).*

NOTES

Sub-s (1): paras (c), (d) and the word "or" immediately preceding it inserted by the Social Security Act 1998, s 86(1), Sch 7, para 150(1).

Date in force (except in relation to housing benefit, council tax benefit or decisions to which the Social Security Contributions (Transfer of Functions, etc) Act 1999 (Commencement No 1 and Transitional Provisions) Order 1999, SI 1999/527, art 4(6) applies): 29 November 1999: see SI 1999/3178, art 2(1), Sch 1.

Date in force (for remaining purposes): to be appointed: see the Social Security Act 1998, s 87(2).

Sub-s (2): para (aa) inserted by the Social Security Act 1998, s 86(1), Sch 7, para 150(2).

Date in force (except in relation to housing benefit, council tax benefit or decisions to which the Social Security Contributions (Transfer of Functions, etc) Act 1999 (Commencement No 1 and Transitional Provisions) Order 1999, SI 1999/527, art 4(6) applies): 29 November 1999: see SI 1999/3178, art 2(1), Sch 1.

Date in force (for remaining purposes): to be appointed: see the Social Security Act 1998, s 87(2).

Sub-s (6): repealed by the Social Security Act 1998, s 86(1), (2), Sch 7, para 150(3), Sch 8.

Date in force (except in relation to housing benefit, council tax benefit or decisions to which the Social Security Contributions (Transfer of Functions, etc) Act 1999 (Commencement No 1 and Transitional Provisions) Order 1999, SI 1999/527, art 4(6) applies): 29 November 1999: see SI 1999/3178, art 2(1), Sch 1.

Date in force (for remaining purposes): to be appointed: see the Social Security Act 1998, s 87(2).

12 Reference of questions to medical appeal tribunal

(1) The Secretary of State must refer to a medical appeal tribunal any question mentioned in subsection (2) arising for determination on an appeal under section 11.

(2) The questions are any concerning—

(a) any amount, rate or period specified in the certificate of recoverable benefits, or
(b) whether listed benefits which have been, or are likely to be, paid otherwise than in respect of the accident, injury or disease in question have been brought into account.

[(1) The Secretary of State must refer an appeal under section 11 to an appeal tribunal.]

(3) In determining *any question referred to it under subsection (1)* [any appeal under section 11], the tribunal must take into account any decision of a court relating to the same, or any similar, issue arising in connection with the accident, injury or disease in question.

(4) On *a reference under subsection (1) a medical appeal tribunal* [an appeal under section 11 an appeal tribunal] may either—

(a) confirm the amounts, rates and periods specified in the certificate of recoverable benefits, or

(b) specify any variations which are to be made on the issue of a fresh certificate under subsection (5) [or

(c) declare that the certificate of recoverable benefits is to be revoked].

(5) When the Secretary of State has received *the decisions of the tribunal on the questions referred to it under subsection (1), he must in accordance with those decisions* [the decision of the tribunal on the appeal under section 11, he must in accordance with that decision] either—

(a) confirm the certificate against which the appeal was brought, or

(b) issue a fresh certificate [or

(c) revoke the certificate].

(6) *Regulations may make provision—*

(a) as to the manner in which, and the time within which, a reference under subsection (1) is to be made, and

(b) as to the procedure to be followed where such a reference is made.

(7) Regulations *under subsection (6)(b)* may (among other things) provide for the non-disclosure of medical advice or medical evidence given or submitted following a reference under subsection (1).

(8) *In this section "medical appeal tribunal" means a medical appeal tribunal constituted under section 50 of the Social Security Administration Act 1992.*

NOTES

Sub-ss (1), (2): substituted, by subsequent sub-s (1) in square brackets, by the Social Security Act 1998, s 86(1), Sch 7, para 151(1).

Date in force (except in relation to decisions to which the Social Security Contributions (Transfer of Functions, etc) Act 1999 (Commencement No 1 and Transitional Provisions) Order 1999, SI 1999/527, art 4(6) applies): 29 November 1999: see SI 1999/3178, art 2(1), Sch 1.

Date in force (for remaining purposes): to be appointed: see the Social Security Act 1998, s 87(2).

Sub-s (3): words "any question referred to it under subsection (1)" in italics repealed and subsequent words in square brackets substituted by the Social Security Act 1998, s 86(1), Sch 7, para 151(2).

Date in force (except in relation to decisions to which the Social Security Contributions (Transfer of Functions, etc) Act 1999 (Commencement No 1 and Transitional Provisions) Order 1999, SI 1999/527, art 4(6) applies): 29 November 1999: see SI 1999/3178, art 2(1), Sch 1.

Date in force (for remaining purposes): to be appointed: see the Social Security Act 1998, s 87(2).

Sub-s (4): words "a reference under subsection (1) a medical appeal tribunal" in italics repealed and subsequent words in square brackets substituted by the Social Security Act 1998, s 86(1), Sch 7, para 151(3)(a).

Date in force (except in relation to decisions to which the Social Security Contributions (Transfer of Functions, etc) Act 1999 (Commencement No 1 and Transitional Provisions) Order 1999, SI 1999/527, art 4(6) applies): 29 November 1999: see SI 1999/3178, art 2(1), Sch 1.

Date in force (for remaining purposes): to be appointed: see the Social Security Act 1998, s 87(2).

Sub-s (4): para (c) and the word "or" immediately preceding it inserted by the Social Security Act 1998, s 86(1), Sch 7, para 151(3)(b).

Date in force (except in relation to decisions to which the Social Security Contributions (Transfer of Functions, etc) Act 1999 (Commencement No 1 and Transitional Provisions) Order 1999, SI 1999/527, art 4(6) applies): 29 November 1999: see SI 1999/3178, art 2(1), Sch 1.

Date in force (for remaining purposes): to be appointed: see the Social Security Act 1998, s 87(2).

Sub-s (5): words from "the decisions of the tribunal" to "those decisions" in italics repealed and subsequent words in square brackets substituted by the Social Security Act 1998, s 86(1), Sch 7, para 151(4)(a).

Date in force (except in relation to decisions to which the Social Security Contributions (Transfer of Functions, etc) Act 1999 (Commencement No 1 and Transitional Provisions) Order 1999, SI 1999/527, art 4(6) applies): 29 November 1999: see SI 1999/3178, art 2(1), Sch 1.

Date in force (for remaining purposes): to be appointed: see the Social Security Act 1998, s 87(2).

Sub-s (5): para (c) and the word "or" immediately preceding it inserted by the Social Security Act 1998, s 86(1), Sch 7, para 151(4)(b).

Date in force (except in relation to decisions to which the Social Security Contributions (Transfer of Functions, etc) Act 1999 (Commencement No 1 and Transitional Provisions) Order 1999, SI 1999/527, art 4(6) applies): 29 November 1999: see SI 1999/3178, art 2(1), Sch 1.

Date in force (for remaining purposes): to be appointed: see the Social Security Act 1998, s 87(2).

Sub-s (6): repealed by the Social Security Act 1998, s 86(1), (2), Sch 7, para 151(5)(a), Sch 8.

Date in force (except in relation to decisions to which the Social Security Contributions (Transfer of Functions, etc) Act 1999 (Commencement No 1 and Transitional Provisions) Order 1999, SI 1999/527, art 4(6) applies): 29 November 1999: see SI 1999/3178, art 2(1), Sch 1.

Date in force (for remaining purposes): to be appointed: see the Social Security Act 1998, s 87(2).

Sub-s (7): words "under subsection (6)(b)" in italics repealed by the Social Security Act 1998, s 86(1), (2), Sch 7, para 151(5)(b), Sch 8.

Date in force (except in relation to decisions to which the Social Security Contributions (Transfer of Functions, etc) Act 1999 (Commencement No 1 and Transitional Provisions) Order 1999, SI 1999/527, art 4(6) applies): 29 November 1999: see SI 1999/3178, art 2(1), Sch 1.

Date in force (for remaining purposes): to be appointed: see the Social Security Act 1998, s 87(2).

Sub-s (8): repealed by the Social Security Act 1998, s 86(1), (2), Sch 7, para 151(5)(c), Sch 8.

Date in force (except in relation to decisions to which the Social Security Contributions (Transfer of Functions, etc) Act 1999 (Commencement No 1 and Transitional Provisions) Order 1999, SI 1999/527, art 4(6) applies): 29 November 1999: see SI 1999/3178, art 2(1), Sch 1.

Date in force (for remaining purposes): to be appointed: see the Social Security Act 1998, s 87(2).

13 Appeal to Social Security Commissioner

(1) An appeal may be made to a Commissioner against any decision of *a medical appeal tribunal* [an appeal tribunal] under section 12 on the ground that the decision was erroneous in point of law.

(2) An appeal under this section may be made by—

(a) the Secretary of State,

(b) the person who applied for the certificate of recoverable benefits, *or*

[(bb) (in a case where that certificate was issued under section 7(2)(a)) the person to whom it was so issued, or]

(c) (in a case where the amount of the compensation payment has been calculated in accordance with section 8) the injured person or other person to whom the payment is made.

(3) *Subsections (7) to (10) of section 23 of the Social Security Administration Act 1992* [Subsections (7) to (12) of section 14 of the Social Security Act 1998] apply to appeals under this section as they apply to appeals under that section.

(4) *In this section "Commissioner" has the same meaning as in the Social Security Administration Act 1992 (see section 191).*

NOTES

Sub-s (1): words "a medical appeal tribunal" in italics repealed and subsequent words in square brackets substituted by the Social Security Act 1998, s 86(1), Sch 7, para 152(1).

Date in force (except in relation to decisions to which the Social Security Contributions (Transfer of Functions, etc) Act 1999 (Commencement No 1 and Transitional Provisions) Order 1999, SI 1999/527, art 4(6) applies): 29 November 1999: see SI 1999/3178, art 2(1), Sch 1.

Date in force (for remaining purposes): to be appointed: see the Social Security Act 1998, s 87(2).

Sub-s (2): word "or" in italics at the end of para (b) repealed by the Social Security Act 1998, s 86(1), (2), Sch 7, para 152(2)(a), Sch 8.

Date in force (except in relation to housing benefit, council tax benefit or decisions to which the Social Security Contributions (Transfer of Functions, etc) Act 1999 (Commencement No 1 and Transitional Provisions) Order 1999, SI 1999/527, art 4(6) applies): 29 November 1999: see SI 1999/3178, art 2(1), Sch 1.

Date in force (for remaining purposes): to be appointed: see the Social Security Act 1998, s 87(2).

Sub-s (2): para (bb) inserted by the Social Security Act 1998, s 86(1), Sch 7, para 152(2)(b).

Date in force (except in relation to housing benefit, council tax benefit or decisions to which the Social Security Contributions (Transfer of Functions, etc) Act 1999 (Commencement No 1 and Transitional Provisions) Order 1999, SI 1999/527, art 4(6) applies): 29 November 1999: see SI 1999/3178, art 2(1), Sch 1.

Date in force (for remaining purposes): to be appointed: see the Social Security Act 1998, s 87(2).

Sub-s (3): words from "Subsections (7) to (10)" to "Act 1992" in italics repealed and subsequent words in square brackets substituted by the Social Security Act 1998, s 86(1), Sch 7, para 152(3).

Date in force (except in relation to housing benefit, council tax benefit or decisions to which the Social Security Contributions (Transfer of Functions, etc) Act 1999 (Commencement No 1 and Transitional Provisions) Order 1999, SI 1999/527, art 4(6) applies): 29 November 1999: see SI 1999/3178, art 2(1), Sch 1.

Date in force (for remaining purposes): to be appointed: see the Social Security Act 1998, s 87(2).

Sub-s (4): repealed by the Social Security Act 1998, s 86(1), (2), Sch 7, para 152(4), Sch 8.

Date in force (except in relation to housing benefit, council tax benefit or decisions to which the Social Security Contributions (Transfer of Functions, etc) Act 1999 (Commencement No 1 and Transitional Provisions) Order 1999, SI 1999/527, art 4(6) applies): 29 November 1999: see SI 1999/3178, art 2(1), Sch 1.

Date in force (for remaining purposes): to be appointed: see the Social Security Act 1998, s 87(2).

14 Reviews and appeals: supplementary

(1) This section applies in cases where a fresh certificate of recoverable benefits is issued as a result of a review under section 10 or an appeal under section 11.

(2) If—

- (a) a person has made one or more payments to the Secretary of State under section 6, and
- (b) in consequence of the review or appeal, it appears that the total amount paid is more than the amount that ought to have been paid,

regulations may provide for the Secretary of State to pay the difference to that person, or to the person to whom the compensation payment is made, or partly to one and partly to the other.

(3) If—

- (a) a person has made one or more payments to the Secretary of State under section 6, and
- (b) in consequence of the review or appeal, it appears that the total amount paid is less than the amount that ought to have been paid,

regulations may provide for that person to pay the difference to the Secretary of State.

(4) Regulations under this section may provide—

- (a) for the re-calculation in accordance with section 8 of the amount of any compensation payment,
- (b) for giving credit for amounts already paid, and
- (c) for the payment by any person of any balance or the recovery from any person of any excess,

and may provide for any matter by modifying this Act.

Courts

15 Court orders

(1) This section applies where a court makes an order for a compensation payment to be made in any case, unless the order is made with the consent of the injured person and the person by whom the payment is to be made.

(2) The court must, in the case of each head of compensation listed in column 1 of Schedule 2 to which any of the compensation payment is attributable, specify in the order the amount of the compensation payment which is attributable to that head.

16 Payments into court

(1) Regulations may make provision (including provision modifying this Act) for any case in which a payment into court is made.

(2) The regulations may (among other things) provide—
- (a) for the making of a payment into court to be treated in prescribed circumstances as the making of a compensation payment,
- (b) for application for, and issue of, certificates of recoverable benefits, and
- (c) for the relevant period to be treated as ending on a date determined in accordance with the regulations.

(3) Rules of court may make provision governing practice and procedure in such cases.

(4) This section does not extend to Scotland.

17 Benefits irrelevant to assessment of damages

In assessing damages in respect of any accident, injury or disease, the amount of any listed benefits paid or likely to be paid is to be disregarded.

Reduction of compensation: complex cases

18 Lump sum and periodical payments

(1) Regulations may make provision (including provision modifying this Act) for any case in which two or more compensation payments in the form of lump sums are made by the same person to or in respect of the injured person in consequence of the same accident, injury or disease.

(2) The regulations may (among other things) provide—
- (a) for the re-calculation in accordance with section 8 of the amount of any compensation payment,
- (b) for giving credit for amounts already paid, and
- (c) for the payment by any person of any balance or the recovery from any person of any excess.

(3) For the purposes of subsection (2), the regulations may provide for the gross amounts of the compensation payments to be aggregated and for—

(a) the aggregate amount to be taken to be the gross amount of the compensation payment for the purposes of section 8,
(b) so much of the aggregate amount as is attributable to a head of compensation listed in column 1 of Schedule 2 to be taken to be the part of the gross amount which is attributable to that head;

and for the amount of any recoverable benefit shown against any head in column 2 of that Schedule to be taken to be the amount determined in accordance with the most recent certificate of recoverable benefits.

(4) Regulations may make provision (including provision modifying this Act) for any case in which, in final settlement of the injured person's claim, an agreement is entered into for the making of—
(a) periodical compensation payments (whether of an income or capital nature), or
(b) periodical compensation payments and lump sum compensation payments.

(5) Regulations made by virtue of subsection (4) may (among other things) provide—
(a) for the relevant period to be treated as ending at a prescribed time,
(b) for the person who is to make the payments under the agreement to be treated for the purposes of this Act as if he had made a single compensation payment on a prescribed date.

(6) A periodical payment may be a compensation payment for the purposes of this section even though it is a small payment (as defined in Part II of Schedule 1).

19 Payments by more than one person

(1) Regulations may make provision (including provision modifying this Act) for any case in which two or more persons ("the compensators") make compensation payments to or in respect of the same injured person in consequence of the same accident, injury or disease.

(2) In such a case, the sum of the liabilities of the compensators under section 6 is not to exceed the total amount of the recoverable benefits, and the regulations may provide for determining the respective liabilities under that section of each of the compensators.

(3) The regulations may (among other things) provide in the case of each compensator—
(a) for determining or re-determining the part of the recoverable benefits which may be taken into account in his case,
(b) for calculating or re-calculating in accordance with section 8 the amount of any compensation payment,
(c) for giving credit for amounts already paid, and
(d) for the payment by any person of any balance or the recovery from any person of any excess.

Miscellaneous

20 Amounts overpaid under section 6

(1) Regulations may make provision (including provision modifying this Act) for cases where a person has paid to the Secretary of State under section 6 any amount ("the amount of the overpayment") which he was not liable to pay.

(2) The regulations may provide—
- (a) for the Secretary of State to pay the amount of the overpayment to that person, or to the person to whom the compensation payment is made, or partly to one and partly to the other, or
- (b) for the receipt by the Secretary of State of the amount of the overpayment to be treated as the recovery of that amount.

(3) Regulations made by virtue of subsection (2)(b) are to have effect in spite of anything in section 71 of the Social Security Administration Act 1992 (overpayments—general).

(4) The regulations may also (among other things) provide—
- (a) for the re-calculation in accordance with section 8 of the amount of any compensation payment,
- (b) for giving credit for amounts already paid, and
- (c) for the payment by any person of any balance or the recovery from any person of any excess.

(5) This section does not apply in a case where section 14 applies.

21 Compensation payments to be disregarded

(1) If, when a compensation payment is made, the first and second conditions are met, the payment is to be disregarded for the purposes of sections 6 and 8.

(2) The first condition is that the person making the payment—
- (a) has made an application for a certificate of recoverable benefits which complies with subsection (3), and
- (b) has in his possession a written acknowledgment of the receipt of his application.

(3) An application complies with this subsection if it—
- (a) accurately states the prescribed particulars relating to the injured person and the accident, injury or disease in question, and
- (b) specifies the name and address of the person to whom the certificate is to be sent.

(4) The second condition is that the Secretary of State has not sent the certificate to the person, at the address, specified in the application, before the end of the period allowed under section 4.

(5) In any case where—
- (a) by virtue of subsection (1), a compensation payment is disregarded for the purposes of sections 6 and 8, but

(b) the person who made the compensation payment nevertheless makes a payment to the Secretary of State for which (but for subsection (1)) he would be liable under section 6,

subsection (1) is to cease to apply in relation to the compensation payment.

(6) If, in the opinion of the Secretary of State, circumstances have arisen which adversely affect normal methods of communication—

(a) he may by order provide that subsection (1) is not to apply during a specified period not exceeding three months, and

(b) he may continue any such order in force for further periods not exceeding three months at a time.

22 Liability of insurers

(1) If a compensation payment is made in a case where—

(a) a person is liable to any extent in respect of the accident, injury or disease, and

(b) the liability is covered to any extent by a policy of insurance,

the policy is also to be treated as covering any liability of that person under section 6.

(2) Liability imposed on the insurer by subsection (1) cannot be excluded or restricted.

(3) For that purpose excluding or restricting liability includes—

(a) making the liability or its enforcement subject to restrictive or onerous conditions,

(b) excluding or restricting any right or remedy in respect of the liability, or subjecting a person to any prejudice in consequence of his pursuing any such right or remedy, or

(c) excluding or restricting rules of evidence or procedure.

(4) Regulations may in prescribed cases limit the amount of the liability imposed on the insurer by subsection (1).

(5) This section applies to policies of insurance issued before (as well as those issued after) its coming into force.

(6) References in this section to policies of insurance and their issue include references to contracts of insurance and their making.

23 Provision of information

(1) Where compensation is sought in respect of any accident, injury or disease suffered by any person ("the injured person"), the following persons must give the Secretary of State the prescribed information about the injured person—

(a) anyone who is, or is alleged to be, liable in respect of the accident, injury or disease, and

(b) anyone acting on behalf of such a person.

(2) A person who receives or claims a listed benefit which is or is likely to be paid in respect of an accident, injury or disease suffered by him, must give the Secretary of State the prescribed information about the accident, injury or disease.

(3) Where a person who has received a listed benefit dies, the duty in subsection (2) is imposed on his personal representative.

(4) Any person who makes a payment (whether on his own behalf or not)—
(a) in consequence of, or
(b) which is referable to any costs (in Scotland, expenses) incurred by reason of,

any accident, injury or disease, or any damage to property, must, if the Secretary of State requests him in writing to do so, give the Secretary of State such particulars relating to the size and composition of the payment as are specified in the request.

(5) The employer of a person who suffers or has suffered an accident, injury or disease, and anyone who has been the employer of such a person at any time during the relevant period, must give the Secretary of State the prescribed information about the payment of statutory sick pay in respect of that person.

(6) In subsection (5) "employer" has the same meaning as it has in Part XI of the Social Security Contributions and Benefits Act 1992.

(7) A person who is required to give information under this section must do so in the prescribed manner, at the prescribed place and within the prescribed time.

(8) Section 1 does not apply in relation to this section.

24 Power to amend Schedule 2

(1) The Secretary of State may by regulations amend Schedule 2.

(2) A statutory instrument which contains such regulations shall not be made unless a draft of the instrument has been laid before and approved by resolution of each House of Parliament.

Provisions relating to Northern Ireland

25 Corresponding provision for Northern Ireland

An Order in Council made under paragraph 1(1)(b) of Schedule 1 to the Northern Ireland Act 1974 which contains a statement that it is made only for purposes corresponding to those of the provisions of this Act—
(a) shall not be subject to sub-paragraphs (4) and (5) of paragraph 1 of that Schedule (affirmative resolution of both Houses of Parliament), but
(b) shall be subject to annulment in pursuance of a resolution of either House of Parliament.

26 Residence of the injured person

(1) In a case where this Act applies, if the injured person's address is in Northern Ireland—

(a) the person making the compensation payment must apply for a certificate under the Northern Ireland provisions, and may not make any separate application for a certificate of recoverable benefits,

(b) any certificate issued as a result under the Northern Ireland provisions—

(i) is to be treated as including a certificate of recoverable benefits,

(ii) must state that it is to be so treated, and

(iii) must state that any payment required to be made to the Secretary of State under this Act is to be made to the Northern Ireland Department as his agent, and

(c) any payment made pursuant to a certificate so issued is to be applied—

(i) first towards discharging the liability of the person making the compensation payment under the Northern Ireland provisions, and

(ii) then, as respects any remaining balance, towards discharging his liability under section 6.

(2) In a case where the Northern Ireland provisions apply, if the injured person's address is in any part of Great Britain—

(a) the person making the compensation payment must apply for a certificate of recoverable benefits, and may not make any separate application for a certificate under the Northern Ireland provisions,

(b) any certificate of recoverable benefits issued as a result—

(i) is to be treated as including a certificate under the Northern Ireland provisions,

(ii) must state that it is to be so treated, and

(iii) must state that any payment required to be made to the Northern Ireland Department under the Northern Ireland provisions is to be made to the Secretary of State as its agent, and

(c) any payment made pursuant to a certificate of recoverable benefits so issued is to be applied—

(i) first towards discharging the liability of the person making the compensation payment under section 6, and

(ii) then, as respects any remaining balance, towards discharging his liability under the Northern Ireland provisions.

(3) In this section—

(a) "the injured person's address" is the address first notified in writing to the person making the payment by or on behalf of the injured person as his residence (or, if he has died, by or on behalf of the person entitled to receive the compensation payment as the injured person's last residence),

(b) "Northern Ireland Department" means the Department of Health and Social Services for Northern Ireland,

(c) "the Northern Ireland provisions" means—

(i) any legislation corresponding to this Act (other than this section and section 27) and having effect in Northern Ireland, and

(ii) this section and section 27,

and

(d) any reference in relation to the Northern Ireland provisions to—

(i) the injured person, means the injured person within the meaning of those provisions,
(ii) a certificate, means a certificate under those provisions corresponding to the certificate of recoverable benefits, and
(iii) a compensation payment, means a compensation payment within the meaning of those provisions.

27 Jurisdiction of courts

(1) In a case where this Act applies, if immediately before making a compensation payment a person—
(a) is not resident and does not have a place of business in Great Britain, but
(b) is resident or has a place of business in Northern Ireland,

subsections (4) and (5) of section 7 apply in relation to him as if at that time he were resident or had a place of business in the relevant part of Great Britain.

(2) In a case where the Northern Ireland provisions apply, if immediately before making a compensation payment a person—
(a) is not resident and does not have a place of business in Northern Ireland, but
(b) is resident or has a place of business in any part of Great Britain,

any provision of the Northern Ireland provisions corresponding to subsection (4) or (5) of section 7 applies in relation to him as if at that time he were resident or had a place of business in Northern Ireland.

(3) In this section—
(a) "the relevant part of Great Britain" means—
(i) the part of Great Britain in which the injured person is or was most recently resident (as determined by any written statement given to the person making the payment by or on behalf of the injured person or, if he has died, by or on behalf of the person entitled to receive the compensation payment), or
(ii) if no such statement has been given, such part of Great Britain as may be prescribed, and
(b) "the Northern Ireland provisions" and references to compensation payments in relation to such provisions have the same meaning as in section 26.

General

28 The Crown

This Act applies to the Crown.

29 General interpretation

In this Act—

["appeal tribunal" means an appeal tribunal constituted under Chapter I of Part I of the Social Security Act 1998;]

"benefit" means any benefit under the Social Security Contributions and Benefits Act 1992, a jobseeker's allowance or mobility allowance,

["Commissioner" has the same meaning as in Chapter II of Part I of the Social Security Act 1998 (see section 39);]

"compensation scheme for motor accidents" means any scheme or arrangement under which funds are available for the payment of compensation in respect of motor accidents caused, or alleged to have been caused, by uninsured or unidentified persons,

"listed benefit" means a benefit listed in column 2 of Schedule 2,

"payment" means payment in money or money's worth, and related expressions are to be interpreted accordingly,

"prescribed" means prescribed by regulations, and

"regulations" means regulations made by the Secretary of State.

NOTES

Definition "appeal tribunal" inserted by the Social Security Act 1998, s 86(1), Sch 7, para 153(a).

Date in force (except in relation to housing benefit, council tax benefit or decisions to which the Social Security Contributions (Transfer of Functions, etc) Act 1999 (Commencement No 1 and Transitional Provisions) Order 1999, SI 1999/527, art 4(6) applies): 29 November 1999: see SI 1999/3178, art 2(1), Sch 1.

Date in force (for remaining purposes): to be appointed: see the Social Security Act 1998, s 87(2).

Definition "Commissioner" inserted by the Social Security Act 1998, s 86(1), Sch 7, para 153(b).

Date in force (except in relation to housing benefit, council tax benefit or decisions to which the Social Security Contributions (Transfer of Functions, etc) Act 1999 (Commencement No 1 and Transitional Provisions) Order 1999, SI 1999/527, art 4(6) applies): 29 November 1999: see SI 1999/3178, art 2(1), Sch 1.

Date in force (for remaining purposes): to be appointed: see the Social Security Act 1998, s 87(2).

30 Regulations and orders

(1) Any power under this Act to make regulations or an order is exercisable by statutory instrument.

(2) A statutory instrument containing regulations or an order under this Act (other than regulations under section 24 or an order under section 34) shall be subject to annulment in pursuance of a resolution of either House of Parliament.

(3) Regulations under section 20, under section 24 amending the list of benefits in column 2 of Schedule 2 or under paragraph 9 of Schedule 1 may not be made without the consent of the Treasury.

(4) Subsections (4), (5), (6) and (9) of section 189 of the Social Security Administration Act 1992 (regulations and orders—general) apply for the purposes of this Act as they apply for the purposes of that.

31 Financial arrangements

(1) There are to be paid out of the National Insurance Fund any expenses of the Secretary of State in making payments under section 14 or 20 to the extent that he estimates that those payments relate to sums paid out of that Fund.

(2) There are to be paid out of money provided by Parliament—

(a) any expenses of the Secretary of State in making payments under section 14 or 20 to the extent that he estimates that those payments relate to sums paid out of the Consolidated Fund, and

(b) (subject to subsection (1)) any other expenses of the Secretary of State incurred in consequence of this Act.

(3) Any sums paid to the Secretary of State under section 6 or 14 are to be paid—

(a) into the Consolidated Fund, to the extent that the Secretary of State estimates that the sums relate to payments out of money provided by Parliament, and

(b) into the National Insurance Fund, to the extent that he estimates that they relate to payments out of that Fund.

32 Power to make transitional, consequential etc provisions

(1) Regulations may make such transitional and consequential provisions, and such savings, as the Secretary of State considers necessary or expedient in preparation for, in connection with, or in consequence of—

(a) the coming into force of any provision of this Act, or

(b) the operation of any enactment repealed or amended by a provision of this Act during any period when the repeal or amendment is not wholly in force.

(2) Regulations under this section may (among other things) provide—

(a) for compensation payments in relation to which, by virtue of section 2, this Act does not apply to be treated as payments in relation to which this Act applies,

(b) for compensation payments in relation to which, by virtue of section 2, this Act applies to be treated as payments in relation to which this Act does not apply, and

(c) for the modification of any enactment contained in this Act or referred to in subsection (1)(b) in its application to any compensation payment.

33 Consequential amendments and repeals

(1) Schedule 3 (which makes consequential amendments) is to have effect.

(2) The enactments shown in Schedule 4 are repealed to the extent specified in the third column.

34 Short title, commencement and extent

(1) This Act may be cited as the Social Security (Recovery of Benefits) Act 1997.

(2) Sections 1 to 24, 26 to 28 and 33 are to come into force on such day as the Secretary of State may by order appoint, and different days may be appointed for different purposes.

(3) Apart from sections 25 to 27, section 33 so far as it relates to any enactment which extends to Northern Ireland, and this section this Act does not extend to Northern Ireland.

SCHEDULE 1
COMPENSATION PAYMENTS

Section 1

PART I
EXEMPTED PAYMENTS

1 Any small payment (defined in Part II of this Schedule).

2 Any payment made to or for the injured person under [section 130 of the Powers of Criminal Courts (Sentencing) Act 2000] or section 249 of the Criminal Procedure (Scotland) Act 1995 (compensation orders against convicted persons).

3 Any payment made in the exercise of a discretion out of property held subject to a trust in a case where no more than 50 per cent by value of the capital contributed to the trust was directly or indirectly provided by persons who are, or are alleged to be, liable in respect of—

(a) the accident, injury or disease suffered by the injured person, or
(b) the same or any connected accident, injury or disease suffered by another.

4 Any payment made out of property held for the purposes of any prescribed trust (whether the payment also falls within paragraph 3 or not).

5 [(1)] Any payment made to the injured person by an [insurer] under the terms of any contract of insurance entered into between the injured person and [the insurer] before—

(a) the date on which the injured person first claims a listed benefit in consequence of the disease in question, or
(b) the occurrence of the accident or injury in question.

[(2) "Insurer" means—

(a) a person who has permission under Part 4 of the Financial Services and Markets Act 2000 to effect or carry out contracts of insurance; or
(b) an EEA firm of the kind mentioned in paragraph 5(d) of Schedule 3 to that Act which has permission under paragraph 15 of that Schedule (as a result of qualifying for authorisation under paragraph 12 of that Schedule) to effect or carry out contracts of insurance.

(3) Sub-paragraph (2) must be read with—

(a) section 22 of the Financial Services and Markets Act 2000;
(b) any relevant order under that section; and
(c) Schedule 2 to that Act.]

6 Any redundancy payment falling to be taken into account in the assessment of damages in respect of an accident, injury or disease.

7 So much of any payment as is referable to costs.

8 Any prescribed payment.

NOTES

Para 2: words "section 130 of the Powers of Criminal Courts (Sentencing) Act 2000" in square brackets substituted by the Powers of Criminal Courts (Sentencing) Act 2000, s 165(1), Sch 9, para 181.

Date in force: 25 August 2000: see the Powers of Criminal Courts (Sentencing) Act 2000, s 168(1).

Para 5: sub-para (1) numbered as such by SI 2001/3649, art 358(1), (2).

Date in force: 1 December 2001: see SI 2001/3649, art 1.

Para 5: in sub-para (1) words "insurer" and "the insurer" in square brackets substituted by SI 2001/3649, art 358(1), (3)(a).

Date in force: 1 December 2001: see SI 2001/3649, art 1.

Para 5: sub-paras (2), (3) inserted by SI 2001/3649, art 358(1), (4).

Date in force: 1 December 2001: see SI 2001/3649, art 1.

PART II
POWER TO DISREGARD SMALL PAYMENTS

9 (1) Regulations may make provision for compensation payments to be disregarded for the purposes of sections 6 and 8 in prescribed cases where the amount of the compensation payment, or the aggregate amount of two or more connected compensation payments, does not exceed the prescribed sum.

(2) A compensation payment disregarded by virtue of this paragraph is referred to in paragraph 1 as a "small payment".

(3) For the purposes of this paragraph—

(a) two or more compensation payments are "connected" if each is made to or in respect of the same injured person and in respect of the same accident, injury or disease, and

(b) any reference to a compensation payment is a reference to a payment which would be such a payment apart from paragraph 1.

SCHEDULE 2
CALCULATION OF COMPENSATION PAYMENT

Section 8

(1) *Head of compensation*	(2) *Benefit*
1 Compensation for earnings lost during the relevant period	. . . Disablement pension payable under section 103 of the 1992 Act Incapacity benefit Income support Invalidity pension and allowance Jobseeker's allowance Reduced earnings allowance Severe disablement allowance Sickness benefit Statutory sick pay Unemployability supplement Unemployment benefit
2 Compensation for cost of care incurred during the relevant period	Attendance allowance Care component of disability living allowance Disablement pension increase payable under section 104 or 105 of the 1992 Act

3 Compensation for loss of mobility during the relevant period	Mobility allowance Mobility component of disability living allowance

NOTES

1 (1) References to incapacity benefit, invalidity pension and allowance, severe disablement allowance, sickness benefit and unemployment benefit also include any income support paid with each of those benefits on the same instrument of payment or paid concurrently with each of those benefits by means of an instrument for benefit payment.

(2) For the purpose of this Note, income support includes personal expenses addition, special transitional additions and transitional addition as defined in the Income Support (Transitional) Regulations 1987.

2 Any reference to statutory sick pay—
- (a) includes only 80 per cent of payments made between 6th April 1991 and 5th April 1994, and
- (b) does not include payments made on or after 6th April 1994.

3 In this Schedule "the 1992 Act" means the Social Security Contributions and Benefits Act 1992.

NOTES

Para 1: in column (2), words omitted repealed by the Tax Credits Act 1999, ss 2(3), 19(4), Sch 2, para 18(1)(a), Sch 6.

Date in force: 5 October 1999, except in relation to cases where the payments or likely payments referred to in s 1(1)(b) hereof are for a payment period beginning before that date: see the Tax Credits Act 1999, s 20(2), Sch 2, para 18(2).

Protection from Harassment Act 1997

1997 CHAPTER 40

An Act to make provision for protecting persons from harassment and similar conduct

[21st March 1997]

England and Wales

1 Prohibition of harassment

(1) A person must not pursue a course of conduct—
- (a) which amounts to harassment of another, and
- (b) which he knows or ought to know amounts to harassment of the other.

(2) For the purposes of this section, the person whose course of conduct is in question ought to know that it amounts to harassment of another if a reasonable

person in possession of the same information would think the course of conduct amounted to harassment of the other.

(3) Subsection (1) does not apply to a course of conduct if the person who pursued it shows—

(a) that it was pursued for the purpose of preventing or detecting crime,
(b) that it was pursued under any enactment or rule of law or to comply with any condition or requirement imposed by any person under any enactment, or
(c) that in the particular circumstances the pursuit of the course of conduct was reasonable.

2 Offence of harassment

(1) A person who pursues a course of conduct in breach of section 1 is guilty of an offence.

(2) A person guilty of an offence under this section is liable on summary conviction to imprisonment for a term not exceeding six months, or a fine not exceeding level 5 on the standard scale, or both.

(3) In section 24(2) of the Police and Criminal Evidence Act 1984 (arrestable offences), after paragraph (m) there is inserted—

"(n) an offence under section 2 of the Protection from Harassment Act 1997 (harassment).".

3 Civil remedy

(1) An actual or apprehended breach of section 1 may be the subject of a claim in civil proceedings by the person who is or may be the victim of the course of conduct in question.

(2) On such a claim, damages may be awarded for (among other things) any anxiety caused by the harassment and any financial loss resulting from the harassment.

(3) Where—

(a) in such proceedings the High Court or a county court grants an injunction for the purpose of restraining the defendant from pursuing any conduct which amounts to harassment, and
(b) the plaintiff considers that the defendant has done anything which he is prohibited from doing by the injunction,

the plaintiff may apply for the issue of a warrant for the arrest of the defendant.

(4) An application under subsection (3) may be made—

(a) where the injunction was granted by the High Court, to a judge of that court, and
(b) where the injunction was granted by a county court, to a judge or district judge of that or any other county court.

(5) The judge or district judge to whom an application under subsection (3) is made may only issue a warrant if—

(a) the application is substantiated on oath, and
(b) the judge or district judge has reasonable grounds for believing that the defendant has done anything which he is prohibited from doing by the injunction.

(6) Where—
(a) the High Court or a county court grants an injunction for the purpose mentioned in subsection (3)(a), and
(b) without reasonable excuse the defendant does anything which he is prohibited from doing by the injunction,

he is guilty of an offence.

(7) Where a person is convicted of an offence under subsection (6) in respect of any conduct, that conduct is not punishable as a contempt of court.

(8) A person cannot be convicted of an offence under subsection (6) in respect of any conduct which has been punished as a contempt of court.

(9) A person guilty of an offence under subsection (6) is liable—
(a) on conviction on indictment, to imprisonment for a term not exceeding five years, or a fine, or both, or
(b) on summary conviction, to imprisonment for a term not exceeding six months, or a fine not exceeding the statutory maximum, or both.

4 Putting people in fear of violence

(1) A person whose course of conduct causes another to fear, on at least two occasions, that violence will be used against him is guilty of an offence if he knows or ought to know that his course of conduct will cause the other so to fear on each of those occasions.

(2) For the purposes of this section, the person whose course of conduct is in question ought to know that it will cause another to fear that violence will be used against him on any occasion if a reasonable person in possession of the same information would think the course of conduct would cause the other so to fear on that occasion.

(3) It is a defence for a person charged with an offence under this section to show that—
(a) his course of conduct was pursued for the purpose of preventing or detecting crime,
(b) his course of conduct was pursued under any enactment or rule of law or to comply with any condition or requirement imposed by any person under any enactment, or
(c) the pursuit of his course of conduct was reasonable for the protection of himself or another or for the protection of his or another's property.

(4) A person guilty of an offence under this section is liable—
(a) on conviction on indictment, to imprisonment for a term not exceeding five years, or a fine, or both, or
(b) on summary conviction, to imprisonment for a term not exceeding six months, or a fine not exceeding the statutory maximum, or both.

(5) If on the trial on indictment of a person charged with an offence under this section the jury find him not guilty of the offence charged, they may find him guilty of an offence under section 2.

(6) The Crown Court has the same powers and duties in relation to a person who is by virtue of subsection (5) convicted before it of an offence under section 2 as a magistrates' court would have on convicting him of the offence.

5 Restraining orders

(1) A court sentencing or otherwise dealing with a person ("the defendant") convicted of an offence under section 2 or 4 may (as well as sentencing him or dealing with him in any other way) make an order under this section.

(2) The order may, for the purpose of protecting the victim of the offence, or any other person mentioned in the order, from further conduct which—

- (a) amounts to harassment, or
- (b) will cause a fear of violence,

prohibit the defendant from doing anything described in the order.

(3) The order may have effect for a specified period or until further order.

(4) The prosecutor, the defendant or any other person mentioned in the order may apply to the court which made the order for it to be varied or discharged by a further order.

(5) If without reasonable excuse the defendant does anything which he is prohibited from doing by an order under this section, he is guilty of an offence.

(6) A person guilty of an offence under this section is liable—

- (a) on conviction on indictment, to imprisonment for a term not exceeding five years, or a fine, or both, or
- (b) on summary conviction, to imprisonment for a term not exceeding six months, or a fine not exceeding the statutory maximum, or both.

7 Interpretation of this group of sections

(1) This section applies for the interpretation of sections 1 to 5.

(2) References to harassing a person include alarming the person or causing the person distress.

(3) A "course of conduct" must involve conduct on at least two occasions.

[(3A) A person's conduct on any occasion shall be taken, if aided, abetted, counselled or procured by another—

- (a) to be conduct on that occasion of the other (as well as conduct of the person whose conduct it is); and
- (b) to be conduct in relation to which the other's knowledge and purpose, and what he ought to have known, are the same as they were in relation to what was contemplated or reasonably foreseeable at the time of the aiding, abetting, counselling or procuring.]

(4) "Conduct" includes speech.

NOTES

Sub-s (3A): inserted by the Criminal Justice and Police Act 2001, s 44(1).

Date in force: 1 August 2001 (in relation to any aiding, abetting, counselling or procuring that takes place after that date): see the Criminal Justice and Police Act 2001, ss 44(2), 138(2) and SI 2001/2223, art 3(b).

General

12 National security, etc

(1) If the Secretary of State certifies that in his opinion anything done by a specified person on a specified occasion related to—

(a) national security,
(b) the economic well-being of the United Kingdom, or
(c) the prevention or detection of serious crime,

and was done on behalf of the Crown, the certificate is conclusive evidence that this Act does not apply to any conduct of that person on that occasion.

(2) In subsection (1), "specified" means specified in the certificate in question.

(3) A document purporting to be a certificate under subsection (1) is to be received in evidence and, unless the contrary is proved, be treated as being such a certificate.

16 Short title

This Act may be cited as the Protection from Harassment Act 1997.

Police Act 1997

1997 CHAPTER 50

An Act to make provision for the National Criminal Intelligence Service and the National Crime Squad; to make provision about entry on and interference with property and with wireless telegraphy in the course of the prevention or detection of serious crime; to make provision for the Police Information Technology Organisation; to provide for the issue of certificates about criminal records; to make provision about the administration and organisation of the police; to repeal certain enactments about rehabilitation of offenders; and for connected purposes.

[21st March 1997]

PART II
THE NATIONAL CRIME SQUAD

Miscellaneous

86 Liability for wrongful acts of constables etc

(1) The Director General of the National Crime Squad shall be liable in respect of torts committed by constables under his direction and control in the performance or purported performance of their functions in like manner as a master is liable in respect of torts committed by his servants in the course of their employment, and accordingly shall in respect of any such tort be treated for all purposes as a joint tortfeasor.

(2) There shall be paid out of the NCS service fund—

- (a) any damages or costs awarded against the Director General in any proceedings brought against him by virtue of this section and any costs incurred by him in any such proceedings so far as not recovered by him in the proceedings, and
- (b) any sum required in connection with the settlement of any claim made against the Director General by virtue of this section, if the settlement is approved by the NCS Service Authority.

(3) Any proceedings in respect of a claim made by virtue of this section shall be brought against the Director General of the National Crime Squad for the time being or, in the case of a vacancy in that office, against the person for the time being performing the functions of the Director General; and references in subsections (1) and (2) to the Director General shall be construed accordingly.

(4) The NCS Service Authority may, in such cases and to such extent as appear to it to be appropriate, pay out of the NCS service fund—

- (a) any damages or costs awarded against a person to whom this subsection applies in proceedings for a tort committed by that person,
- (b) any costs incurred and not recovered by such a person in such proceedings, and

(c) any sum required in connection with the settlement of a claim that has or might have given rise to such proceedings.

(5) Subsection (4) applies to a person who is—

(a) a member of the National Crime Squad, or

(b) a constable for the time being required to serve with the National Crime Squad by virtue of section 23 above or section 24 or 98 of the Police Act 1996.

PART VII
GENERAL

138 Short title

This Act may be cited as the Police Act 1997.

Local Government (Contracts) Act 1997

1997 CHAPTER 65

An Act to make provision about the powers of local authorities (including probation committees and the Receiver for the Metropolitan Police District) to enter into contracts; to enable expenditure of local authorities making administrative arrangements for magistrates' courts to be treated for some purposes as not being capital expenditure; and for connected purposes.

[27th November 1997]

Contracts for provision of assets or services

1 Functions to include power to enter into contracts

(1) Every statutory provision conferring or imposing a function on a local authority confers power on the local authority to enter into a contract with another person for the provision or making available of assets or services, or both, (whether or not together with goods) for the purposes of, or in connection with, the discharge of the function by the local authority.

(2) Where—

(a) a local authority enters into a contract such as is mentioned in subsection (1) ("the provision contract") under any statutory provision, and

(b) in connection with the provision contract, a person ("the financier") makes a loan to, or provides any other form of finance for, a party to the provision contract other than the local authority, the statutory provision also confers power on the local authority to enter into a contract with the financier, or any insurer of or trustee for the financier, in connection with the provision contract.

(3) The following are local authorities for the purposes of this Act—

(a) any authority with respect to the finances of which Part IV of the Local Government and Housing Act 1989 has effect at the time in question,

(b) any probation committee, [and]

(c) *the Receiver for the Metropolitan Police District, and*

(d) any local authority or joint board as defined in section 235(1) of the Local Government (Scotland) Act 1973.

(4) In this Act "assets" means assets of any description (whether tangible or intangible), including (in particular) land, buildings, roads, works, plant, machinery, vehicles, vessels, apparatus, equipment and computer software.

(5) Regulations may be made amending subsection (4).

NOTES

Sub-s (3): in para (b) word "and" in square brackets inserted by the Greater London Authority Act 1999, s 325, Sch 27, para 116.

Date in force: to be appointed: see the Greater London Authority Act 1999, s 425(2).

Sub-s (3): para (c) repealed by the Greater London Authority Act 1999, ss 325, 423, Sch 27, para 116, Sch 34, Pt VII.

Date in force: to be appointed: see the Greater London Authority Act 1999, s 425(2).

Certified contracts

2 Certified contracts to be intra vires

(1) Where a local authority has entered into a contract, the contract shall, if it is a certified contract, have effect (and be deemed always to have had effect) as if the local authority had had power to enter into it (and had exercised that power properly in entering into it).

(2) For the purposes of this Act a contract entered into by a local authority is a certified contract if (and, subject to subsections (3) and (4), only if) the certification requirements have been satisfied by the local authority with respect to the contract and they were so satisfied before the end of the certification period.

(3) A contract entered into by a local authority shall be treated as a certified contract during the certification period if the contract provides that the certification requirements are intended to be satisfied by the local authority with respect to the contract before the end of that period.

(4) Where a local authority has entered into a contract which is a certified contract ("the existing contract") and the existing contract is replaced by a contract entered into by it with a person or persons not identical with the person or persons with whom it entered into the existing contract, the replacement contract is also a certified contract if—

(a) the period for which it operates or is intended to operate ends at the same time as the period for which the existing contract was to operate, and

(b) apart from that, its provisions are the same as those of the existing contract.

(5) In this Act "the certification period", in relation to a contract entered into by a local authority, means the period of six weeks beginning with the day on which the local authority entered into the contract.

(6) Subsection (1) is subject to section 5 (special provisions about judicial reviews and audit reviews).

(7) The application of subsection (1) in relation to a contract entered into by a local authority does not affect any claim for damages made by a person who is not (and has never been) a party to the contract in respect of a breach by the local authority of any duty to do, or not to do, something before entering into the contract (including, in particular, any such duty imposed by a statutory provision for giving effect to any Community obligation relating to public procurement or by section 17(1) of the Local Government Act 1988).

3 The certification requirements

(1) In this Act "the certification requirements", in relation to a contract entered into by a local authority, means the requirements specified in subsections (2) to (4).

(2) The requirement specified in this subsection is that the local authority must have issued a certificate (whether before or after the contract is entered into)—

(a) including details of the period for which the contract operates or is to operate,

(b) describing the purpose of the contract,

(c) containing a statement that the contract is or is to be a contract falling within section 4(3) or (4),

(d) stating that the local authority had or has power to enter into the contract and specifying the statutory provision, or each of the statutory provisions, conferring the power,

(e) stating that a copy of the certificate has been or is to be given to each person to whom a copy is required to be given by regulations,

(f) dealing in a manner prescribed by regulations with any matters required by regulations to be dealt with in certificates under this section, and

(g) confirming that the local authority has complied with or is to comply with any requirement imposed by regulations with respect to the issue of certificates under this section.

(3) The requirement specified in this subsection is that the local authority must have secured that the certificate is signed by any person who is required by regulations to sign it.

(4) The requirement specified in this subsection is that the local authority must have obtained consent to the issue of a certificate under this section from each of the persons with whom the local authority has entered, or is to enter, into the contract.

4 Certified contracts: supplementary

(1) Where the certification requirements have been satisfied in relation to a contract by a local authority, the certificate which has been issued shall have effect

(and be deemed always to have had effect) as if the local authority had had power to issue it (and had exercised that power properly in issuing it); and a certificate which has been so issued is not invalidated by reason that anything in the certificate is inaccurate or untrue.

(2) Where the certification requirements have been satisfied in relation to a contract by a local authority within section 1(3)(a) or (d), the local authority shall secure that throughout the period for which the contract operates—

(a) a copy of the certificate which has been issued is open to inspection by members of the public at all reasonable times without payment, and

(b) members of the public are afforded facilities for obtaining copies of that certificate on payment of a reasonable fee.

(3) A contract entered into by a local authority falls within this subsection if—

(a) it is entered into with another person for the provision or making available of services (whether or not together with assets or goods) for the purposes of or in connection with, the discharge by the local authority of any of its functions, and

(b) it operates, or is intended to operate, for a period of at least five years.

(4) A contract entered into by a local authority falls within this subsection if it is entered into, in connection with a contract falling within subsection (3), with—

(a) a person who, in connection with that contract, makes a loan to, or provides any other form of finance for, a party to that contract other than the local authority, or

(b) any insurer of or trustee for such a person.

(5) Regulations may be made amending subsection (3) or (4).

5 Special provision for judicial reviews and audit reviews

(1) Section 2(1) does not apply for the purposes of determining any question arising on—

(a) an application for judicial review, or

(b) an audit review,

as to whether a local authority had power to enter into a contract (or exercised any power properly in entering into a contract).

(2) Section 2(1) has effect subject to any determination or order made in relation to a certified contract on—

(a) an application for judicial review, or

(b) an audit review.

(3) Where, on an application for judicial review or an audit review relating to a certified contract entered into by a local authority, a court—

(a) is of the opinion that the local authority did not have power to enter into the contract (or exercised any power improperly in entering into it), but

(b) (having regard in particular to the likely consequences for the financial position of the local authority, and for the provision of services to the public, of a decision that the contract should not have effect) considers that the contract should have effect, the court may determine that the contract has (and always has had) effect as if the local authority had had power to enter into it (and had exercised that power properly in entering into it).

(4) In this section and sections 6 and 7 references to an application for judicial review include any appeal (or further appeal) against a determination or order made on such an application.

6 Relevant discharge terms

(1) No determination or order made in relation to a certified contract on—
- (a) an application for judicial review, or
- (b) an audit review,

shall affect the enforceability of any relevant discharge terms relating to the contract.

(2) In this section and section 7 "relevant discharge terms", in relation to a contract entered into by a local authority, means terms—
- (a) which have been agreed by the local authority and any person with whom the local authority entered into the contract,
- (b) which either form part of the contract or constitute or form part of another agreement entered into by them not later than the day on which the contract was entered into, and
- (c) which provide for a consequence mentioned in subsection (3) to ensue in the event of the making of a determination or order in relation to the contract on an application for judicial review or an audit review.

(3) Those consequences are—
- (a) the payment of compensatory damages (measured by reference to loss incurred or loss of profits or to any other circumstances) by one of the parties to the other,
- (b) the adjustment between the parties of rights and liabilities relating to any assets or goods provided or made available under the contract, or
- (c) both of those things.

(4) Where a local authority has agreed relevant discharge terms with any person with whom it has entered into a contract and the contract is a certified contract, the relevant discharge terms shall have effect (and be deemed always to have had effect) as if the local authority had had power to agree them (and had exercised that power properly in agreeing them).

7 Absence of relevant discharge terms

(1) Subsection (2) applies where—
- (a) the result of a determination or order made by a court on an application for judicial review or an audit review is that a certified contract does not have effect, and
- (b) there are no relevant discharge terms having effect between the local authority and a person who is a party to the contract.

(2) That person shall be entitled to be paid by the local authority such sums (if any) as he would have been entitled to be paid by the local authority if the contract—

(a) had had effect until the time when the determination or order was made, but
(b) had been terminated at that time by acceptance by him of a repudiatory breach by the local authority.

(3) For the purposes of this section the circumstances in which there are no relevant discharge terms having effect between the local authority and a person who is a party to the contract include (as well as circumstances in which no such terms have been agreed) circumstances in which the result of a determination or order of a court, made (despite section 6(4)) on an application for judicial review or an audit review, is that such terms do not have effect.

Supplementary

12 Short title, commencement and extent

(1) This Act may be cited as the Local Government (Contracts) Act 1997.

(2) Sections 2 to 9 shall not come into force until a day appointed by the Secretary of State by order made by statutory instrument; and different days may be appointed for different provisions or purposes.

(3) Sections 1 to 9 apply to any contract which a local authority enters into after 12th June 1997; but in relation to a contract entered into before the day on which section 2 comes into force "the certification period" means the period of six weeks beginning with that day.

(4) Section 10 does not extend to Scotland.

(5) This Act does not extend to Northern Ireland.

Late Payment of Commercial Debts (Interest) Act 1998

1998 CHAPTER 20

An Act to make provision with respect to interest on the late payment of certain debts arising under commercial contracts for the supply of goods or services; and for connected purposes.

[11th June 1998]

PART I
STATUTORY INTEREST ON QUALIFYING DEBTS

1 Statutory interest

(1) It is an implied term in a contract to which this Act applies that any qualifying debt created by the contract carries simple interest subject to and in accordance with this Part.

(2) Interest carried under that implied term (in this Act referred to as "statutory interest") shall be treated, for the purposes of any rule of law or enactment (other than this Act) relating to interest on debts, in the same way as interest carried under an express contract term.

(3) This Part has effect subject to Part II (which in certain circumstances permits contract terms to oust or vary the right to statutory interest that would otherwise be conferred by virtue of the term implied by subsection (1)).

2 Contracts to which Act applies

(1) This Act applies to a contract for the supply of goods or services where the purchaser and the supplier are each acting in the course of a business, other than an excepted contract.

(2) In this Act "contract for the supply of goods or services" means—
- (a) a contract of sale of goods; or
- (b) a contract (other than a contract of sale of goods) by which a person does any, or any combination, of the things mentioned in subsection (3) for a consideration that is (or includes) a money consideration.

(3) Those things are—
- (a) transferring or agreeing to transfer to another the property in goods;
- (b) bailing or agreeing to bail goods to another by way of hire or, in Scotland, hiring or agreeing to hire goods to another; and
- (c) agreeing to carry out a service.

(4) For the avoidance of doubt a contract of service or apprenticeship is not a contract for the supply of goods or services.

(5) The following are excepted contracts—
(a) a consumer credit agreement;
(b) a contract intended to operate by way of mortgage, pledge, charge or other security; and
(c) *a contract of a description specified in an order made by the Secretary of State.*

(6) *An order under subsection (5)(c) may specify a description of contract by reference to any feature of the contract (including the parties).*

(7) In this section—

"business" includes a profession and the activities of any government department or local or public authority;

"consumer credit agreement" has the same meaning as in the Consumer Credit Act 1974;

"contract of sale of goods" and "goods" have the same meaning as in the Sale of Goods Act 1979;

["government department" includes any part of the Scottish Administration;]

"property in goods" means the general property in them and not merely a special property.

NOTES

Sub-s (5): para (c) repealed, in relation to Scotland, by SSI 2002/335, reg 2(1), (2).

Date in force: 7 August 2002 (except in relation to contracts made before that date): see SSI 2002/335, regs 1(1), 4.

Sub-s (6): repealed, in relation to Scotland, by SSI 2002/335, reg 2(1), (2).

Date in force: 7 August 2002 (except in relation to contracts made before that date): see SSI 2002/335, regs 1(1), 4.

Sub-s (7): definition "government department" inserted by SI 1999/1820, art 4, Sch 2, Pt I, para 132.

Date in force: 1 July 1999: see SI 1999/1820, art 1(2).

[2A Application of the Act to Advocates]

[The provisions of this Act apply to a transaction in respect of which fees are paid for professional services to a member of the Faculty of Advocates as they apply to a contract for the supply of services for the purpose of this Act.]

NOTES

Inserted, in relation to Scotland, by SSI 2002/335, reg 2(1), (3).

Date in force: 7 August 2002 (except in relation to contracts made before that date): see SSI 2002/335, regs 1(1), 4.

3 Qualifying debts

(1) A debt created by virtue of an obligation under a contract to which this Act applies to pay the whole or any part of the contract price is a "qualifying debt" for the purposes of this Act, unless (when created) the whole of the debt is prevented from carrying statutory interest by this section.

(2) A debt does not carry statutory interest if or to the extent that it consists of a sum to which a right to interest or to charge interest applies by virtue of any enactment (other than section 1 of this Act).

This subsection does not prevent a sum from carrying statutory interest by reason of the fact that a court, arbitrator or arbiter would, apart from this Act, have power to award interest on it.

(3) A debt does not carry (and shall be treated as never having carried) statutory interest if or to the extent that a right to demand interest on it, which exists by virtue of any rule of law, is exercised.

(4) *A debt does not carry statutory interest if or to the extent that it is of a description specified in an order made by the Secretary of State.*

(5) *Such an order may specify a description of debt by reference to any feature of the debt (including the parties or any other feature of the contract by which it is created).*

NOTES

Sub-ss (4), (5): repealed, in relation to Scotland, by SSI 2002/335, reg 2(1), (4).

Date in force: 7 August 2002 (except in relation to contracts made before that date): see SSI 2002/335, regs 1(1), 4.

4 Period for which statutory interest runs

(1) Statutory interest runs in relation to a qualifying debt in accordance with this section (unless section 5 applies).

(2) Statutory interest starts to run on the day after the relevant day for the debt, at the rate prevailing under section 6 at the end of the relevant day.

(3) Where the supplier and the purchaser agree a date for payment of the debt (that is, the day on which the debt is to be created by the contract), that is the relevant day unless the debt relates to an obligation to make an advance payment.

A date so agreed may be a fixed one or may depend on the happening of an event or the failure of an event to happen.

(4) Where the debt relates to an obligation to make an advance payment, the relevant day is the day on which the debt is treated by section 11 as having been created.

(5) In any other case, the relevant day is the last day of the period of 30 days beginning with—

- (a) the day on which the obligation of the supplier to which the debt relates is performed; or
- (b) the day on which the purchaser has notice of the amount of the debt or (where that amount is unascertained) the sum which the supplier claims is the amount of the debt,

whichever is the later.

(6) Where the debt is created by virtue of an obligation to pay a sum due in respect of a period of hire of goods, subsection (5)(a) has effect as if it referred to the last day of that period.

(7) Statutory interest ceases to run when the interest would cease to run if it were carried under an express contract term.

(8) In this section "advance payment" has the same meaning as in section 11.

5 Remission of statutory interest

(1) This section applies where, by reason of any conduct of the supplier, the interests of justice require that statutory interest should be remitted in whole or part in respect of a period for which it would otherwise run in relation to a qualifying debt.

(2) If the interests of justice require that the supplier should receive no statutory interest for a period, statutory interest shall not run for that period.

(3) If the interests of justice require that the supplier should receive statutory interest at a reduced rate for a period, statutory interest shall run at such rate as meets the justice of the case for that period.

(4) Remission of statutory interest under this section may be required—

(a) by reason of conduct at any time (whether before or after the time at which the debt is created); and

(b) for the whole period for which statutory interest would otherwise run or for one or more parts of that period.

(5) In this section "conduct" includes any act or omission.

[5A Compensation arising out of late payment]

[(1) Once statutory interest begins to run in relation to a qualifying debt, the supplier shall be entitled to a fixed sum (in addition to the statutory interest on the debt).

(2) That sum shall be—

(a) for a debt less than £1000, the sum of £40;

(b) for a debt of £1000 or more, but less than £10,000, the sum of £70;

(c) for a debt of £10,000 or more, the sum of £100.

(3) The obligation to pay an additional fixed sum under this section in respect of a qualifying debt shall be treated as part of the term implied by section 1(1) in the contract creating the debt.]

NOTES

Inserted, in relation to Scotland, by SSI 2002/335, reg 2(1), (5).

Date in force: 7 August 2002 (except in relation to contracts made before that date): see SSI 2002/335, regs 1(1), 4.

6 Rate of statutory interest

(1) The Secretary of State shall by order made with the consent of the Treasury set the rate of statutory interest by prescribing—
- (a) a formula for calculating the rate of statutory interest; or
- (b) the rate of statutory interest.

(2) Before making such an order the Secretary of State shall, among other things, consider the extent to which it may be desirable to set the rate so as to—
- (a) protect suppliers whose financial position makes them particularly vulnerable if their qualifying debts are paid late; and
- (b) deter generally the late payment of qualifying debts.

PART II

CONTRACT TERMS RELATING TO LATE PAYMENT OF QUALIFYING DEBTS

7 Purpose of Part II

(1) This Part deals with the extent to which the parties to a contract to which this Act applies may by reference to contract terms oust or vary the right to statutory interest that would otherwise apply when a qualifying debt created by the contract (in this Part referred to as "the debt") is not paid.

(2) This Part applies to contract terms agreed before the debt is created; after that time the parties are free to agree terms dealing with the debt.

(3) This Part has effect without prejudice to any other ground which may affect the validity of a contract term.

8 Circumstances where statutory interest may be ousted or varied

(1) Any contract terms are void to the extent that they purport to exclude the right to statutory interest in relation to the debt, unless there is a substantial contractual remedy for late payment of the debt.

(2) Where the parties agree a contractual remedy for late payment of the debt that is a substantial remedy, statutory interest is not carried by the debt (unless they agree otherwise).

(3) The parties may not agree to vary the right to statutory interest in relation to the debt unless either the right to statutory interest as varied or the overall remedy for late payment of the debt is a substantial remedy.

(4) Any contract terms are void to the extent that they purport to—
- (a) confer a contractual right to interest that is not a substantial remedy for late payment of the debt, or
- (b) vary the right to statutory interest so as to provide for a right to statutory interest that is not a substantial remedy for late payment of the debt,

unless the overall remedy for late payment of the debt is a substantial remedy.

(5) Subject to this section, the parties are free to agree contract terms which deal with the consequences of late payment of the debt.

9 Meaning of "substantial remedy"

(1) A remedy for the late payment of the debt shall be regarded as a substantial remedy unless—

(a) the remedy is insufficient either for the purpose of compensating the supplier for late payment or for deterring late payment; and

(b) it would not be fair or reasonable to allow the remedy to be relied on to oust or (as the case may be) to vary the right to statutory interest that would otherwise apply in relation to the debt.

(2) In determining whether a remedy is not a substantial remedy, regard shall be had to all the relevant circumstances at the time the terms in question are agreed.

(3) In determining whether subsection (1)(b) applies, regard shall be had (without prejudice to the generality of subsection (2)) to the following matters—

(a) the benefits of commercial certainty;

(b) the strength of the bargaining positions of the parties relative to each other;

(c) whether the term was imposed by one party to the detriment of the other (whether by the use of standard terms or otherwise); and

(d) whether the supplier received an inducement to agree to the term.

10 Interpretation of Part II

(1) In this Part—

"contract term" means a term of the contract creating the debt or any other contract term binding the parties (or either of them);

"contractual remedy" means a contractual right to interest or any contractual remedy other than interest;

"contractual right to interest" includes a reference to a contractual right to charge interest;

"overall remedy", in relation to the late payment of the debt, means any combination of a contractual right to interest, a varied right to statutory interest or a contractual remedy other than interest;

"substantial remedy" shall be construed in accordance with section 9.

(2) In this Part a reference (however worded) to contract terms which vary the right to statutory interest is a reference to terms altering in any way the effect of Part I in relation to the debt (for example by postponing the time at which interest starts to run or by imposing conditions on the right to interest).

(3) In this Part a reference to late payment of the debt is a reference to late payment of the sum due when the debt is created (excluding any part of that sum which is prevented from carrying statutory interest by section 3).

PART III
GENERAL AND SUPPLEMENTARY

11 Treatment of advance payments of the contract price

(1) A qualifying debt created by virtue of an obligation to make an advance payment shall be treated for the purposes of this Act as if it was created on the day mentioned in subsection (3), (4) or (5) (as the case may be).

(2) In this section "advance payment" means a payment falling due before the obligation of the supplier to which the whole contract price relates ("the supplier's obligation") is performed, other than a payment of a part of the contract price that is due in respect of any part performance of that obligation and payable on or after the day on which that part performance is completed.

(3) Where the advance payment is the whole contract price, the debt shall be treated as created on the day on which the supplier's obligation is performed.

(4) Where the advance payment is a part of the contract price, but the sum is not due in respect of any part performance of the supplier's obligation, the debt shall be treated as created on the day on which the supplier's obligation is performed.

(5) Where the advance payment is a part of the contract price due in respect of any part performance of the supplier's obligation, but is payable before that part performance is completed, the debt shall be treated as created on the day on which the relevant part performance is completed.

(6) Where the debt is created by virtue of an obligation to pay a sum due in respect of a period of hire of goods, this section has effect as if—
- (a) references to the day on which the supplier's obligation is performed were references to the last day of that period; and
- (b) references to part performance of that obligation were references to part of that period.

(7) For the purposes of this section an obligation to pay the whole outstanding balance of the contract price shall be regarded as an obligation to pay the whole contract price and not as an obligation to pay a part of the contract price.

12 Conflict of laws

(1) This Act does not have effect in relation to a contract governed by the law of a part of the United Kingdom by choice of the parties if—
- (a) there is no significant connection between the contract and that part of the United Kingdom; and
- (b) but for that choice, the applicable law would be a foreign law.

(2) This Act has effect in relation to a contract governed by a foreign law by choice of the parties if—
- (a) but for that choice, the applicable law would be the law of a part of the United Kingdom; and
- (b) there is no significant connection between the contract and any country other than that part of the United Kingdom.

(3) In this section—
"contract" means a contract falling within section 2(1); and
"foreign law" means the law of a country outside the United Kingdom.

13 Assignments, etc

(1) The operation of this Act in relation to a qualifying debt is not affected by—
(a) any change in the identity of the parties to the contract creating the debt; or
(b) the passing of the right to be paid the debt, or the duty to pay it (in whole or in part) to a person other than the person who is the original creditor or the original debtor when the debt is created.

(2) Any reference in this Act to the supplier or the purchaser is a reference to the person who is for the time being the supplier or the purchaser or, in relation to a time after the debt in question has been created, the person who is for the time being the creditor or the debtor, as the case may be.

(3) Where the right to be paid part of a debt passes to a person other than the person who is the original creditor when the debt is created, any reference in this Act to a debt shall be construed as (or, if the context so requires, as including) a reference to part of a debt.

(4) A reference in this section to the identity of the parties to a contract changing, or to a right or duty passing, is a reference to it changing or passing by assignment or assignation, by operation of law or otherwise.

14 Contract terms relating to the date for payment of the contract price

(1) This section applies to any contract term which purports to have the effect of postponing the time at which a qualifying debt would otherwise be created by a contract to which this Act applies.

(2) Sections 3(2)(b) and 17(1)(b) of the Unfair Contract Terms Act 1977 (no reliance to be placed on certain contract terms) shall apply in cases where such a contract term is not contained in written standard terms of the purchaser as well as in cases where the term is contained in such standard terms.

(3) In this section "contract term" has the same meaning as in section 10(1).

15 Orders and regulations

(1) Any power to make an order or regulations under this Act is exercisable by statutory instrument.

(2) Any statutory instrument containing an order or regulations under this Act, other than an order under section 17(2), shall be subject to annulment in pursuance of a resolution of either House of Parliament.

16 Interpretation

(1) In this Act—

"contract for the supply of goods or services" has the meaning given in section 2(2);

"contract price" means the price in a contract of sale of goods or the money consideration referred to in section 2(2)(b) in any other contract for the supply of goods or services;

"purchaser" means (subject to section 13(2)) the buyer in a contract of sale or the person who contracts with the supplier in any other contract for the supply of goods or services;

"qualifying debt" means a debt falling within section 3(1);

"statutory interest" means interest carried by virtue of the term implied by section 1(1); and

"supplier" means (subject to section 13(2)) the seller in a contract of sale of goods or the person who does one or more of the things mentioned in section 2(3) in any other contract for the supply of goods or services.

(2) In this Act any reference (however worded) to an agreement or to contract terms includes a reference to both express and implied terms (including terms established by a course of dealing or by such usage as binds the parties).

17 Short title, commencement and extent

(1) This Act may be cited as the Late Payment of Commercial Debts (Interest) Act 1998.

(2) This Act (apart from this section) shall come into force on such day as the Secretary of State may by order appoint; and different days may be appointed for different descriptions of contract or for other different purposes.

An order under this subsection may specify a description of contract by reference to any feature of the contract (including the parties).

(3) The Secretary of State may by regulations make such transitional, supplemental or incidental provision (including provision modifying any provision of this Act) as the Secretary of State may consider necessary or expedient in connection with the operation of this Act while it is not fully in force.

(4) This Act does not affect contracts of any description made before this Act comes into force for contracts of that description.

(5) This Act extends to Northern Ireland.

Data Protection Act 1998

1998 CHAPTER 29

An Act to make new provision for the regulation of the processing of information relating to individuals, including the obtaining, holding, use or disclosure of such information.

[16th July 1998]

PART I
PRELIMINARY

1 Basic interpretative provisions

(1) In this Act, unless the context otherwise requires—

"data" means information which—

(a) is being processed by means of equipment operating automatically in response to instructions given for that purpose,

(b) is recorded with the intention that it should be processed by means of such equipment,

(c) is recorded as part of a relevant filing system or with the intention that it should form part of a relevant filing system, *or*

(d) does not fall within paragraph (a), (b) or (c) but forms part of an accessible record as defined by section 68; [or

(e) is recorded information held by a public authority and does not fall within any of paragraphs (a) to (d);]

"data controller" means, subject to subsection (4), a person who (either alone or jointly or in common with other persons) determines the purposes for which and the manner in which any personal data are, or are to be, processed;

"data processor", in relation to personal data, means any person (other than an employee of the data controller) who processes the data on behalf of the data controller;

"data subject" means an individual who is the subject of personal data;

"personal data" means data which relate to a living individual who can be identified—

(a) from those data, or

(b) from those data and other information which is in the possession of, or is likely to come into the possession of, the data controller,

and includes any expression of opinion about the individual and any indication of the intentions of the data controller or any other person in respect of the individual;

"processing", in relation to information or data, means obtaining, recording or holding the information or data or carrying out any operation or set of operations on the information or data, including—

(a) organisation, adaptation or alteration of the information or data,
(b) retrieval, consultation or use of the information or data,
(c) disclosure of the information or data by transmission, dissemination or otherwise making available, or
(d) alignment, combination, blocking, erasure or destruction of the information or data;

["public authority" has the same meaning as in the Freedom of Information Act 2000;]

"relevant filing system" means any set of information relating to individuals to the extent that, although the information is not processed by means of equipment operating automatically in response to instructions given for that purpose, the set is structured, either by reference to individuals or by reference to criteria relating to individuals, in such a way that specific information relating to a particular individual is readily accessible.

(2) In this Act, unless the context otherwise requires—
(a) "obtaining" or "recording", in relation to personal data, includes obtaining or recording the information to be contained in the data, and
(b) "using" or "disclosing", in relation to personal data, includes using or disclosing the information contained in the data.

(3) In determining for the purposes of this Act whether any information is recorded with the intention—
(a) that it should be processed by means of equipment operating automatically in response to instructions given for that purpose, or
(b) that it should form part of a relevant filing system,

it is immaterial that it is intended to be so processed or to form part of such a system only after being transferred to a country or territory outside the European Economic Area.

(4) Where personal data are processed only for purposes for which they are required by or under any enactment to be processed, the person on whom the obligation to process the data is imposed by or under that enactment is for the purposes of this Act the data controller.

[(5) In paragraph (e) of the definition of "data" in subsection (1), the reference to information "held" by a public authority shall be construed in accordance with section 3(2) of the Freedom of Information Act 2000.

(6) Where section 7 of the Freedom of Information Act 2000 prevents Parts I to V of that Act from applying to certain information held by a public authority, that information is not to be treated for the purposes of paragraph (e) of the definition of "data" in subsection (1) as held by a public authority.]

NOTES

Sub-s (1): in definition "data" word "or" at the end of para (c) repealed by the Freedom of Information Act 2000, ss 68(1), (2), 86, Sch 8, Pt III.

Date in force: 30 November 2005 (unless the Secretary of State by order appoints an earlier date): see the Freedom of Information Act 2000, s 87(3).

Sub-s (1): in definition "data" para (e) and the word "or" immediately preceding it inserted by the Freedom of Information Act 2000, s 68(1), (2)(a).

Date in force: 30 November 2005 (unless the Secretary of State by order appoints an earlier date): see the Freedom of Information Act 2000, s 87(3).

Sub-s (1): definition "public authority" inserted by the Freedom of Information Act 2000, s 68(1), (2)(b).

Date in force: 30 November 2005 (unless the Secretary of State by order appoints an earlier date): see the Freedom of Information Act 2000, s 87(3).

Sub-ss (5), (6): inserted by the Freedom of Information Act 2000, s 68(1), (3).

Date in force: 30 November 2005 (unless the Secretary of State by order appoints an earlier date): see the Freedom of Information Act 2000, s 87(3).

2 Sensitive personal data

In this Act "sensitive personal data" means personal data consisting of information as to—

(a) the racial or ethnic origin of the data subject,
(b) his political opinions,
(c) his religious beliefs or other beliefs of a similar nature,
(d) whether he is a member of a trade union (within the meaning of the Trade Union and Labour Relations (Consolidation) Act 1992,
(e) his physical or mental health or condition,
(f) his sexual life,
(g) the commission or alleged commission by him of any offence, or
(h) any proceedings for any offence committed or alleged to have been committed by him, the disposal of such proceedings or the sentence of any court in such proceedings.

3 The special purposes

In this Act "the special purposes" means any one or more of the following—

(a) the purposes of journalism,
(b) artistic purposes, and
(c) literary purposes.

4 The data protection principles

(1) References in this Act to the data protection principles are to the principles set out in Part I of Schedule 1.

(2) Those principles are to be interpreted in accordance with Part II of Schedule 1.

(3) Schedule 2 (which applies to all personal data) and Schedule 3 (which applies only to sensitive personal data) set out conditions applying for the purposes of the first principle; and Schedule 4 sets out cases in which the eighth principle does not apply.

(4) Subject to section 27(1), it shall be the duty of a data controller to comply with the data protection principles in relation to all personal data with respect to which he is the data controller.

5 Application of Act

(1) Except as otherwise provided by or under section 54, this Act applies to a data controller in respect of any data only if—

(a) the data controller is established in the United Kingdom and the data are processed in the context of that establishment, or

(b) the data controller is established neither in the United Kingdom nor in any other EEA State but uses equipment in the United Kingdom for processing the data otherwise than for the purposes of transit through the United Kingdom.

(2) A data controller falling within subsection (1)(b) must nominate for the purposes of this Act a representative established in the United Kingdom.

(3) For the purposes of subsections (1) and (2), each of the following is to be treated as established in the United Kingdom—

(a) an individual who is ordinarily resident in the United Kingdom,

(b) a body incorporated under the law of, or of any part of, the United Kingdom,

(c) a partnership or other unincorporated association formed under the law of any part of the United Kingdom, and

(d) any person who does not fall within paragraph (a), (b) or (c) but maintains in the United Kingdom—

(i) an office, branch or agency through which he carries on any activity, or

(ii) a regular practice;

and the reference to establishment in any other EEA State has a corresponding meaning.

6 The Commissioner and the Tribunal

[(1) For the purposes of this Act and of the Freedom of Information Act 2000 there shall be an officer known as the Information Commissioner (in this Act referred to as "the Commissioner").]

(2) The Commissioner shall be appointed by Her Majesty by Letters Patent.

[(3) For the purposes of this Act and of the Freedom of Information Act 2000 there shall be a tribunal known as the Information Tribunal (in this Act referred to as "the Tribunal").]

(4) The Tribunal shall consist of—

(a) a chairman appointed by the Lord Chancellor after consultation with the [Secretary of State],

(b) such number of deputy chairmen so appointed as the Lord Chancellor may determine, and

(c) such number of other members appointed by the [Lord Chancellor] as he may determine.

(5) The members of the Tribunal appointed under subsection (4)(a) and (b) shall be—

(a) persons who have a 7 year general qualification, within the meaning of section 71 of the Courts and Legal Services Act 1990,

(b) advocates or solicitors in Scotland of at least 7 years' standing, or

(c) members of the bar of Northern Ireland or solicitors of the Supreme Court of Northern Ireland of at least 7 years' standing.

(6) The members of the Tribunal appointed under subsection (4)(c) shall be—

(a) persons to represent the interests of data subjects,

[(aa) persons to represent the interests of those who make requests for information under the Freedom of Information Act 2000,]

(b) persons to represent the interests of data controllers [and

(bb) persons to represent the interests of public authorities].

(7) Schedule 5 has effect in relation to the Commissioner and the Tribunal.

NOTES

Sub-s (1): substituted by the Freedom of Information Act 2000, s 18(4), Sch 2, Pt I, para 13(1), (2).

Date in force: 30 January 2001: see the Freedom of Information Act 2000, s 87(2)(c).

Sub-s (3): substituted by the Freedom of Information Act 2000, s 18(4), Sch 2, Pt I, para 13(1), (3).

Date in force: 14 May 2001: see SI 2001/1637, art 2(b).

Sub-s (4): in para (a) words "Secretary of State" in square brackets substituted by virtue of SI 1999/678, art 2(1), Schedule.

Date in force: 19 May 1999: see SI 1999/678, art 1.

Sub-s (4): in para (c) words "Lord Chancellor" in square brackets substituted by SI 2001/3500, art 8, Sch 2, Pt I, para 6(1)(a).

Date in force: 26 November 2001: see SI 2001/3500, art 1(2).

Sub-s (6): para (aa) substituted, for original word "and" at the end of para (a), by the Freedom of Information Act 2000, s 18(4), Sch 2, Pt II, para 16(a).

Date in force: 14 May 2001: see SI 2001/1637, art 2(b).

Sub-s (6): para (bb) and the word "and" immediately preceding it inserted by the Freedom of Information Act 2000, s 18(4), Sch 2, Pt II, para 16(b).

Date in force: 14 May 2001: see SI 2001/1637, art 2(b).

PART II
RIGHTS OF DATA SUBJECTS AND OTHERS

7 Right of access to personal data

(1) Subject to the following provisions of this section and to *sections 8 and 9* [sections 8, 9 and 9A], an individual is entitled—

(a) to be informed by any data controller whether personal data of which that individual is the data subject are being processed by or on behalf of that data controller,

(b) if that is the case, to be given by the data controller a description of—

(i) the personal data of which that individual is the data subject,

(ii) the purposes for which they are being or are to be processed, and

(iii) the recipients or classes of recipients to whom they are or may be disclosed,

(c) to have communicated to him in an intelligible form—

(i) the information constituting any personal data of which that individual is the data subject, and
(ii) any information available to the data controller as to the source of those data, and

(d) where the processing by automatic means of personal data of which that individual is the data subject for the purpose of evaluating matters relating to him such as, for example, his performance at work, his creditworthiness, his reliability or his conduct, has constituted or is likely to constitute the sole basis for any decision significantly affecting him, to be informed by the data controller of the logic involved in that decision-taking.

(2) A data controller is not obliged to supply any information under subsection (1) unless he has received—
(a) a request in writing, and
(b) except in prescribed cases, such fee (not exceeding the prescribed maximum) as he may require.

[(3) Where a data controller—
(a) reasonably requires further information in order to satisfy himself as to the identity of the person making a request under this section and to locate the information which that person seeks, and
(b) has informed him of that requirement,

the data controller is not obliged to comply with the request unless he is supplied with that further information.]

(4) Where a data controller cannot comply with the request without disclosing information relating to another individual who can be identified from that information, he is not obliged to comply with the request unless—
(a) the other individual has consented to the disclosure of the information to the person making the request, or
(b) it is reasonable in all the circumstances to comply with the request without the consent of the other individual.

(5) In subsection (4) the reference to information relating to another individual includes a reference to information identifying that individual as the source of the information sought by the request; and that subsection is not to be construed as excusing a data controller from communicating so much of the information sought by the request as can be communicated without disclosing the identity of the other individual concerned, whether by the omission of names or other identifying particulars or otherwise.

(6) In determining for the purposes of subsection (4)(b) whether it is reasonable in all the circumstances to comply with the request without the consent of the other individual concerned, regard shall be had, in particular, to—
(a) any duty of confidentiality owed to the other individual,
(b) any steps taken by the data controller with a view to seeking the consent of the other individual,
(c) whether the other individual is capable of giving consent, and
(d) any express refusal of consent by the other individual.

(7) An individual making a request under this section may, in such cases as may be prescribed, specify that his request is limited to personal data of any prescribed description.

(8) Subject to subsection (4), a data controller shall comply with a request under this section promptly and in any event before the end of the prescribed period beginning with the relevant day.

(9) If a court is satisfied on the application of any person who has made a request under the foregoing provisions of this section that the data controller in question has failed to comply with the request in contravention of those provisions, the court may order him to comply with the request.

(10) In this section—

"prescribed" means prescribed by the [Lord Chancellor] by regulations;

"the prescribed maximum" means such amount as may be prescribed;

"the prescribed period" means forty days or such other period as may be prescribed;

"the relevant day", in relation to a request under this section, means the day on which the data controller receives the request or, if later, the first day on which the data controller has both the required fee and the information referred to in subsection (3).

(11) Different amounts or periods may be prescribed under this section in relation to different cases.

NOTES

Sub-s (1): words "sections 8 and 9" in italics repealed and subsequent words in square brackets substituted by the Freedom of Information Act 2000, s 69(1).

Date in force: 30 November 2005 (unless the Secretary of State by order appoints an earlier date): see the Freedom of Information Act 2000, s 87(3).

Sub-s (3): substituted by the Freedom of Information Act 2000, s 73, Sch 6, para 1.

Date in force: 14 May 2001: see SI 2001/1637, art 2(d).

Sub-s (10): in definition "prescribed" words "Lord Chancellor" in square brackets substituted by SI 2001/3500, art 8, Sch 2, Pt I, para 6(1)(b).

Date in force: 26 November 2001: see SI 2001/3500, art 1(2).

8 Provisions supplementary to section 7

(1) The [Lord Chancellor] may by regulations provide that, in such cases as may be prescribed, a request for information under any provision of subsection (1) of section 7 is to be treated as extending also to information under other provisions of that subsection.

(2) The obligation imposed by section 7(1)(c)(i) must be complied with by supplying the data subject with a copy of the information in permanent form unless—

(a) the supply of such a copy is not possible or would involve disproportionate effort, or

(b) the data subject agrees otherwise;

and where any of the information referred to in section 7(1)(c)(i) is expressed in terms which are not intelligible without explanation the copy must be accompanied by an explanation of those terms.

(3) Where a data controller has previously complied with a request made under section 7 by an individual, the data controller is not obliged to comply with a subsequent identical or similar request under that section by that individual unless a reasonable interval has elapsed between compliance with the previous request and the making of the current request.

(4) In determining for the purposes of subsection (3) whether requests under section 7 are made at reasonable intervals, regard shall be had to the nature of the data, the purpose for which the data are processed and the frequency with which the data are altered.

(5) Section 7(1)(d) is not to be regarded as requiring the provision of information as to the logic involved in any decision-taking if, and to the extent that, the information constitutes a trade secret.

(6) The information to be supplied pursuant to a request under section 7 must be supplied by reference to the data in question at the time when the request is received, except that it may take account of any amendment or deletion made between that time and the time when the information is supplied, being an amendment or deletion that would have been made regardless of the receipt of the request.

(7) For the purposes of section 7(4) and (5) another individual can be identified from the information being disclosed if he can be identified from that information, or from that and any other information which, in the reasonable belief of the data controller, is likely to be in, or to come into, the possession of the data subject making the request.

NOTES

Sub-s (1): words "Lord Chancellor" in square brackets substituted by SI 2001/3500, art 8, Sch 2, Pt I, para 6(1)(c).

Date in force: 26 November 2001: see SI 2001/3500, art 1(2).

9 Application of section 7 where data controller is credit reference agency

(1) Where the data controller is a credit reference agency, section 7 has effect subject to the provisions of this section.

(2) An individual making a request under section 7 may limit his request to personal data relevant to his financial standing, and shall be taken to have so limited his request unless the request shows a contrary intention.

(3) Where the data controller receives a request under section 7 in a case where personal data of which the individual making the request is the data subject are being processed by or on behalf of the data controller, the obligation to supply information under that section includes an obligation to give the individual making

the request a statement, in such form as may be prescribed by the [Lord Chancellor] by regulations, of the individual's rights—

(a) under section 159 of the Consumer Credit Act 1974 , and

(b) to the extent required by the prescribed form, under this Act.

NOTES

Sub-s (3): words "Lord Chancellor" in square brackets substituted by SI 2001/3500, art 8, Sch 2, Pt I, para 6(1)(d).

Date in force: 26 November 2001: see SI 2001/3500, art 1(2).

[9A Unstructured personal data held by public authorities]

[(1) In this section "unstructured personal data" means any personal data falling within paragraph (e) of the definition of "data" in section 1(1), other than information which is recorded as part of, or with the intention that it should form part of, any set of information relating to individuals to the extent that the set is structured by reference to individuals or by reference to criteria relating to individuals.

(2) A public authority is not obliged to comply with subsection (1) of section 7 in relation to any unstructured personal data unless the request under that section contains a description of the data.

(3) Even if the data are described by the data subject in his request, a public authority is not obliged to comply with subsection (1) of section 7 in relation to unstructured personal data if the authority estimates that the cost of complying with the request so far as relating to those data would exceed the appropriate limit.

(4) Subsection (3) does not exempt the public authority from its obligation to comply with paragraph (a) of section 7(1) in relation to the unstructured personal data unless the estimated cost of complying with that paragraph alone in relation to those data would exceed the appropriate limit.

(5) In subsections (3) and (4) "the appropriate limit" means such amount as may be prescribed by the [Lord Chancellor] by regulations, and different amounts may be prescribed in relation to different cases.

(6) Any estimate for the purposes of this section must be made in accordance with regulations under section 12(5) of the Freedom of Information Act 2000.]

NOTES

Inserted by the Freedom of Information Act 2000, s 69(2).

Date in force (in so far as this section confers powers to make regulations): 30 November 2000: see the Freedom of Information Act 2000, s 87(1)(m).

Date in force (for remaining purposes): 30 November 2005 (unless the Secretary of State by order appoints an earlier date): see the Freedom of Information Act 2000, s 87(3).

Sub-s (5): words "Lord Chancellor" in square brackets substituted by SI 2001/3500, art 8, Sch 2, Pt I, para 6(1)(e).

Date in force: 26 November 2001: see SI 2001/3500, art 1(2).

10 Right to prevent processing likely to cause damage or distress

(1) Subject to subsection (2), an individual is entitled at any time by notice in writing to a data controller to require the data controller at the end of such period as is reasonable in the circumstances to cease, or not to begin, processing, or processing for a specified purpose or in a specified manner, any personal data in respect of which he is the data subject, on the ground that, for specified reasons—

(a) the processing of those data or their processing for that purpose or in that manner is causing or is likely to cause substantial damage or substantial distress to him or to another, and

(b) that damage or distress is or would be unwarranted.

(2) Subsection (1) does not apply—

(a) in a case where any of the conditions in paragraphs 1 to 4 of Schedule 2 is met, or

(b) in such other cases as may be prescribed by the [Lord Chancellor] by order.

(3) The data controller must within twenty-one days of receiving a notice under subsection (1) ("the data subject notice") give the individual who gave it a written notice—

(a) stating that he has complied or intends to comply with the data subject notice, or

(b) stating his reasons for regarding the data subject notice as to any extent unjustified and the extent (if any) to which he has complied or intends to comply with it.

(4) If a court is satisfied, on the application of any person who has given a notice under subsection (1) which appears to the court to be justified (or to be justified to any extent), that the data controller in question has failed to comply with the notice, the court may order him to take such steps for complying with the notice (or for complying with it to that extent) as the court thinks fit.

(5) The failure by a data subject to exercise the right conferred by subsection (1) or section 11(1) does not affect any other right conferred on him by this Part.

NOTES

Sub-s (2): in para (b) words "Lord Chancellor" in square brackets substituted by SI 2001/3500, art 8, Sch 2, Pt I, para 6(1)(f).

Date in force: 26 November 2001: see SI 2001/3500, art 1(2).

11 Right to prevent processing for purposes of direct marketing

(1) An individual is entitled at any time by notice in writing to a data controller to require the data controller at the end of such period as is reasonable in the circumstances to cease, or not to begin, processing for the purposes of direct marketing personal data in respect of which he is the data subject.

(2) If the court is satisfied, on the application of any person who has given a notice under subsection (1), that the data controller has failed to comply with the notice, the court may order him to take such steps for complying with the notice as the court thinks fit.

[(2A) This section shall not apply in relation to the processing of such data as are mentioned in paragraph (1) of regulation 8 of the Telecommunications (Data Protection and Privacy) Regulations 1999 (processing of telecommunications billing data for certain marketing purposes) for the purposes mentioned in paragraph (2) of that regulation.]

(3) In this section "direct marketing" means the communication (by whatever means) of any advertising or marketing material which is directed to particular individuals.

NOTES

Sub-s (2A): inserted by SI 1999/2093, reg 3(3), Sch 1, Pt II, para 3.
Date in force: 1 March 2000: see SI 1999/2093, reg 1(2)(b).

13 Compensation for failure to comply with certain requirements

(1) An individual who suffers damage by reason of any contravention by a data controller of any of the requirements of this Act is entitled to compensation from the data controller for that damage.

(2) An individual who suffers distress by reason of any contravention by a data controller of any of the requirements of this Act is entitled to compensation from the data controller for that distress if—

- (a) the individual also suffers damage by reason of the contravention, or
- (b) the contravention relates to the processing of personal data for the special purposes.

(3) In proceedings brought against a person by virtue of this section it is a defence to prove that he had taken such care as in all the circumstances was reasonably required to comply with the requirement concerned.

PART VI
MISCELLANEOUS AND GENERAL

General

75 Short title, commencement and extent

(1) This Act may be cited as the Data Protection Act 1998.

(2) The following provisions of this Act—

- (a) sections 1 to 3,
- (b) section 25(1) and (4),
- (c) section 26,
- (d) sections 67 to 71,
- (e) this section,
- (f) paragraph 17 of Schedule 5,
- (g) Schedule 11,
- (h) Schedule 12, and
- (i) so much of any other provision of this Act as confers any power to make subordinate legislation,

shall come into force on the day on which this Act is passed.

(3) The remaining provisions of this Act shall come into force on such day as the [Lord Chancellor] may by order appoint; and different days may be appointed for different purposes.

(4) The day appointed under subsection (3) for the coming into force of section 56 must not be earlier than the first day on which sections 112, 113 and 115 of the Police Act 1997 (which provide for the issue by the Secretary of State of criminal conviction certificates, criminal record certificates and enhanced criminal record certificates) are all in force.

(5) Subject to subsection (6), this Act extends to Northern Ireland.

(6) Any amendment, repeal or revocation made by Schedule 15 or 16 has the same extent as that of the enactment or instrument to which it relates.

NOTES

Sub-s (3): words "Lord Chancellor" in square brackets substituted by SI 2001/3500, art 8, Sch 2, Pt I, para 6(1)(w).

Date in force: 26 November 2001: see SI 2001/3500, art 1(2).

Contracts (Rights of Third Parties) Act 1999

1999 CHAPTER 31

An Act to make provision for the enforcement of contractual terms by third parties.
[11th November 1999]

1 Right of third party to enforce contractual term

(1) Subject to the provisions of this Act, a person who is not a party to a contract (a "third party") may in his own right enforce a term of the contract if—
- (a) the contract expressly provides that he may, or
- (b) subject to subsection (2), the term purports to confer a benefit on him.

(2) Subsection (1)(b) does not apply if on a proper construction of the contract it appears that the parties did not intend the term to be enforceable by the third party.

(3) The third party must be expressly identified in the contract by name, as a member of a class or as answering a particular description but need not be in existence when the contract is entered into.

(4) This section does not confer a right on a third party to enforce a term of a contract otherwise than subject to and in accordance with any other relevant terms of the contract.

(5) For the purpose of exercising his right to enforce a term of the contract, there shall be available to the third party any remedy that would have been available to

him in an action for breach of contract if he had been a party to the contract (and the rules relating to damages, injunctions, specific performance and other relief shall apply accordingly).

(6) Where a term of a contract excludes or limits liability in relation to any matter references in this Act to the third party enforcing the term shall be construed as references to his availing himself of the exclusion or limitation.

(7) In this Act, in relation to a term of a contract which is enforceable by a third party—

"the promisor" means the party to the contract against whom the term is enforceable by the third party, and

"the promisee" means the party to the contract by whom the term is enforceable against the promisor.

2 Variation and rescission of contract

(1) Subject to the provisions of this section, where a third party has a right under section 1 to enforce a term of the contract, the parties to the contract may not, by agreement, rescind the contract, or vary it in such a way as to extinguish or alter his entitlement under that right, without his consent if—

(a) the third party has communicated his assent to the term to the promisor,
(b) the promisor is aware that the third party has relied on the term, or
(c) the promisor can reasonably be expected to have foreseen that the third party would rely on the term and the third party has in fact relied on it.

(2) The assent referred to in subsection (1)(a)—

(a) may be by words or conduct, and
(b) if sent to the promisor by post or other means, shall not be regarded as communicated to the promisor until received by him.

(3) Subsection (1) is subject to any express term of the contract under which—

(a) the parties to the contract may by agreement rescind or vary the contract without the consent of the third party, or
(b) the consent of the third party is required in circumstances specified in the contract instead of those set out in subsection (1)(a) to (c).

(4) Where the consent of a third party is required under subsection (1) or (3), the court or arbitral tribunal may, on the application of the parties to the contract, dispense with his consent if satisfied—

(a) that his consent cannot be obtained because his whereabouts cannot reasonably be ascertained, or
(b) that he is mentally incapable of giving his consent.

(5) The court or arbitral tribunal may, on the application of the parties to a contract, dispense with any consent that may be required under subsection (1)(c) if satisfied that it cannot reasonably be ascertained whether or not the third party has in fact relied on the term.

(6) If the court or arbitral tribunal dispenses with a third party's consent, it may impose such conditions as it thinks fit, including a condition requiring the payment of compensation to the third party.

(7) The jurisdiction conferred on the court by subsections (4) to (6) is exercisable by both the High Court and a county court.

3 Defences etc available to promisor

(1) Subsections (2) to (5) apply where, in reliance on section 1, proceedings for the enforcement of a term of a contract are brought by a third party.

(2) The promisor shall have available to him by way of defence or set-off any matter that—

(a) arises from or in connection with the contract and is relevant to the term, and

(b) would have been available to him by way of defence or set-off if the proceedings had been brought by the promisee.

(3) The promisor shall also have available to him by way of defence or set-off any matter if—

(a) an express term of the contract provides for it to be available to him in proceedings brought by the third party, and

(b) it would have been available to him by way of defence or set-off if the proceedings had been brought by the promisee.

(4) The promisor shall also have available to him—

(a) by way of defence or set-off any matter, and

(b) by way of counterclaim any matter not arising from the contract,

that would have been available to him by way of defence or set-off or, as the case may be, by way of counterclaim against the third party if the third party had been a party to the contract.

(5) Subsections (2) and (4) are subject to any express term of the contract as to the matters that are not to be available to the promisor by way of defence, set-off or counterclaim.

(6) Where in any proceedings brought against him a third party seeks in reliance on section 1 to enforce a term of a contract (including, in particular, a term purporting to exclude or limit liability), he may not do so if he could not have done so (whether by reason of any particular circumstances relating to him or otherwise) had he been a party to the contract.

4 Enforcement of contract by promisee

Section 1 does not affect any right of the promisee to enforce any term of the contract.

5 Protection of party promisor from double liability

Where under section 1 a term of a contract is enforceable by a third party, and the promisee has recovered from the promisor a sum in respect of—

(a) the third party's loss in respect of the term, or

(b) the expense to the promisee of making good to the third party the default of the promisor, then, in any proceedings brought in reliance on that section by the third party, the court or arbitral tribunal shall reduce any award to the third party to such extent as it thinks appropriate to take account of the sum recovered by the promisee.

6 Exceptions

(1) Section 1 confers no rights on a third party in the case of a contract on a bill of exchange, promissory note or other negotiable instrument.

(2) Section 1 confers no rights on a third party in the case of any contract binding on a company and its members under section 14 of the Companies Act 1985.

[(2A) Section 1 confers no rights on a third party in the case of any incorporation document of a limited liability partnership or any limited liability partnership agreement as defined in the Limited Liability Partnerships Regulations 2001 (SI No 2001/1090).]

(3) Section 1 confers no right on a third party to enforce—
- (a) any term of a contract of employment against an employee,
- (b) any term of a worker's contract against a worker (including a home worker), or
- (c) any term of a relevant contract against an agency worker.

(4) In subsection (3)—
- (a) "contract of employment", "employee", "worker's contract", and "worker" have the meaning given by section 54 of the National Minimum Wage Act 1998,
- (b) "home worker" has the meaning given by section 35(2) of that Act,
- (c) "agency worker" has the same meaning as in section 34(1) of that Act, and
- (d) "relevant contract" means a contract entered into, in a case where section 34 of that Act applies, by the agency worker as respects work falling within subsection (1)(a) of that section.

(5) Section 1 confers no rights on a third party in the case of—
- (a) a contract for the carriage of goods by sea, or
- (b) a contract for the carriage of goods by rail or road, or for the carriage of cargo by air, which is subject to the rules of the appropriate international transport convention,

except that a third party may in reliance on that section avail himself of an exclusion or limitation of liability in such a contract.

(6) In subsection (5) "contract for the carriage of goods by sea" means a contract of carriage—
- (a) contained in or evidenced by a bill of lading, sea waybill or a corresponding electronic transaction, or
- (b) under or for the purposes of which there is given an undertaking which is contained in a ship's delivery order or a corresponding electronic transaction.

(7) For the purposes of subsection (6)—
- (a) "bill of lading", "sea waybill" and "ship's delivery order" have the same meaning as in the Carriage of Goods by Sea Act 1992, and

(b) a corresponding electronic transaction is a transaction within section 1(5) of that Act which corresponds to the issue, indorsement, delivery or transfer of a bill of lading, sea waybill or ship's delivery order.

(8) In subsection (5) "the appropriate international transport convention" means—

(a) in relation to a contract for the carriage of goods by rail, the Convention which has the force of law in the United Kingdom under section 1 of the International Transport Conventions Act 1983,

(b) in relation to a contract for the carriage of goods by road, the Convention which has the force of law in the United Kingdom under section 1 of the Carriage of Goods by Road Act 1965, and

(c) in relation to a contract for the carriage of cargo by air—

(i) the Convention which has the force of law in the United Kingdom under section 1 of the Carriage by Air Act 1961, or

(ii) the Convention which has the force of law under section 1 of the Carriage by Air (Supplementary Provisions) Act 1962, or

(iii) either of the amended Conventions set out in Part B of Schedule 2 or 3 to the Carriage by Air Acts (Application of Provisions) Order 1967.

NOTES

Sub-s (2A): inserted by SI 2001/1090, reg 9(1), Sch 5, para 20.
Date in force: 6 April 2001: see SI 2001/1090, reg 1.

7 Supplementary provisions relating to third party

(1) Section 1 does not affect any right or remedy of a third party that exists or is available apart from this Act.

(2) Section 2(2) of the Unfair Contract Terms Act 1977 (restriction on exclusion etc of liability for negligence) shall not apply where the negligence consists of the breach of an obligation arising from a term of a contract and the person seeking to enforce it is a third party acting in reliance on section 1.

(3) In sections 5 and 8 of the Limitation Act 1980 the references to an action founded on a simple contract and an action upon a specialty shall respectively include references to an action brought in reliance on section 1 relating to a simple contract and an action brought in reliance on that section relating to a specialty.

(4) A third party shall not, by virtue of section 1(5) or 3(4) or (6), be treated as a party to the contract for the purposes of any other Act (or any instrument made under any other Act).

8 Arbitration provisions

(1) Where—

(a) a right under section 1 to enforce a term ("the substantive term") is subject to a term providing for the submission of disputes to arbitration ("the arbitration agreement"), and

(b) the arbitration agreement is an agreement in writing for the purposes of Part I of the Arbitration Act 1996, the third party shall be treated for the purposes of that Act as a party to the arbitration agreement as regards disputes between himself and the promisor relating to the enforcement of the substantive term by the third party.

(2) Where—

(a) a third party has a right under section 1 to enforce a term providing for one or more descriptions of dispute between the third party and the promisor to be submitted to arbitration ("the arbitration agreement"),

(b) the arbitration agreement is an agreement in writing for the purposes of Part I of the Arbitration Act 1996, and

(c) the third party does not fall to be treated under subsection (1) as a party to the arbitration agreement,

the third party shall, if he exercises the right, be treated for the purposes of that Act as a party to the arbitration agreement in relation to the matter with respect to which the right is exercised, and be treated as having been so immediately before the exercise of the right.

9 Northern Ireland

(1) In its application to Northern Ireland, this Act has effect with the modifications specified in subsections (2) and (3).

(2) In section 6(2), for "section 14 of the Companies Act 1985" there is substituted "Article 25 of the Companies (Northern Ireland) Order 1986".

(3) In section 7, for subsection (3) there is substituted—

> "(3) In Articles 4(a) and 15 of the Limitation (Northern Ireland) Order 1989, the references to an action founded on a simple contract and an action upon an instrument under seal shall respectively include references to an action brought in reliance on section 1 relating to a simple contract and an action brought in reliance on that section relating to a contract under seal.".

(4) In the Law Reform (Husband and Wife) (Northern Ireland) Act 1964, the following provisions are hereby repealed—

(a) section 5, and

(b) in section 6, in subsection (1)(a), the words "in the case of section 4" and "and in the case of section 5 the contracting party" and, in subsection (3), the words "or section 5".

10 Short title, commencement and extent

(1) This Act may be cited as the Contracts (Rights of Third Parties) Act 1999.

(2) This Act comes into force on the day on which it is passed but, subject to subsection (3), does not apply in relation to a contract entered into before the end of the period of six months beginning with that day.

(3) The restriction in subsection (2) does not apply in relation to a contract which—

(a) is entered into on or after the day on which this Act is passed, and

(b) expressly provides for the application of this Act.

(4) This Act extends as follows—
  (a) section 9 extends to Northern Ireland only;
  (b) the remaining provisions extend to England and Wales and Northern Ireland only.

Electronic Communications Act 2000

2000 CHAPTER 7

An Act to make provision to facilitate the use of electronic communications and electronic data storage; to make provision about the modification of licences granted under section 7 of the Telecommunications Act 1984; and for connected purposes.

[25th May 2000]

PART II
FACILITATION OF ELECTRONIC COMMERCE, DATA STORAGE, ETC

7 Electronic signatures and related certificates

(1) In any legal proceedings—
  (a) an electronic signature incorporated into or logically associated with a particular electronic communication or particular electronic data, and
  (b) the certification by any person of such a signature,

shall each be admissible in evidence in relation to any question as to the authenticity of the communication or data or as to the integrity of the communication or data.

(2) For the purposes of this section an electronic signature is so much of anything in electronic form as—
  (a) is incorporated into or otherwise logically associated with any electronic communication or electronic data; and
  (b) purports to be so incorporated or associated for the purpose of being used in establishing the authenticity of the communication or data, the integrity of the communication or data, or both.

(3) For the purposes of this section an electronic signature incorporated into or associated with a particular electronic communication or particular electronic data is certified by any person if that person (whether before or after the making of the communication) has made a statement confirming that—
  (a) the signature,
  (b) a means of producing, communicating or verifying the signature, or
  (c) a procedure applied to the signature,

is (either alone or in combination with other factors) a valid means of establishing the authenticity of the communication or data, the integrity of the communication or data, or both.

8 Power to modify legislation

(1) Subject to subsection (3), the appropriate Minister may by order made by statutory instrument modify the provisions of—

(a) any enactment or subordinate legislation, or

(b) any scheme, licence, authorisation or approval issued, granted or given by or under any enactment or subordinate legislation,

in such manner as he may think fit for the purpose of authorising or facilitating the use of electronic communications or electronic storage (instead of other forms of communication or storage) for any purpose mentioned in subsection (2).

(2) Those purposes are—

(a) the doing of anything which under any such provisions is required to be or may be done or evidenced in writing or otherwise using a document, notice or instrument;

(b) the doing of anything which under any such provisions is required to be or may be done by post or other specified means of delivery;

(c) the doing of anything which under any such provisions is required to be or may be authorised by a person's signature or seal, or is required to be delivered as a deed or witnessed;

(d) the making of any statement or declaration which under any such provisions is required to be made under oath or to be contained in a statutory declaration;

(e) the keeping, maintenance or preservation, for the purposes or in pursuance of any such provisions, of any account, record, notice, instrument or other document;

(f) the provision, production or publication under any such provisions of any information or other matter;

(g) the making of any payment that is required to be or may be made under any such provisions.

(3) The appropriate Minister shall not make an order under this section authorising the use of electronic communications or electronic storage for any purpose, unless he considers that the authorisation is such that the extent (if any) to which records of things done for that purpose will be available will be no less satisfactory in cases where use is made of electronic communications or electronic storage than in other cases.

(4) Without prejudice to the generality of subsection (1), the power to make an order under this section shall include power to make an order containing any of the following provisions—

(a) provision as to the electronic form to be taken by any electronic communications or electronic storage the use of which is authorised by an order under this section;

(b) provision imposing conditions subject to which the use of electronic communications or electronic storage is so authorised;

(c) provision, in relation to cases in which any such conditions are not satisfied, for treating anything for the purposes of which the use of such communications or storage is so authorised as not having been done;

(d) provision, in connection with anything so authorised, for a person to be able to refuse to accept receipt of something in electronic form except in such circumstances as may be specified in or determined under the order;
(e) provision, in connection with any use of electronic communications so authorised, for intermediaries to be used, or to be capable of being used, for the transmission of any data or for establishing the authenticity or integrity of any data;
(f) provision, in connection with any use of electronic storage so authorised, for persons satisfying such conditions as may be specified in or determined under the regulations to carry out functions in relation to the storage;
(g) provision, in relation to cases in which the use of electronic communications or electronic storage is so authorised, for the determination of any of the matters mentioned in subsection (5), or as to the manner in which they may be proved in legal proceedings;
(h) provision, in relation to cases in which fees or charges are or may be imposed in connection with anything for the purposes of which the use of electronic communications or electronic storage is so authorised, for different fees or charges to apply where use is made of such communications or storage;
(i) provision, in relation to any criminal or other liabilities that may arise (in respect of the making of false or misleading statements or otherwise) in connection with anything for the purposes of which the use of electronic communications or electronic storage is so authorised, for corresponding liabilities to arise in corresponding circumstances where use is made of such communications or storage;
(j) provision requiring persons to prepare and keep records in connection with any use of electronic communications or electronic storage which is so authorised;
(k) provision requiring the production of the contents of any records kept in accordance with an order under this section;
(l) provision for a requirement imposed by virtue of paragraph (j) or (k) to be enforceable at the suit or instance of such person as may be specified in or determined in accordance with the order;
(m) any such provision, in relation to electronic communications or electronic storage the use of which is authorised otherwise than by an order under this section, as corresponds to any provision falling within any of the preceding paragraphs that may be made where it is such an order that authorises the use of the communications or storage.

(5) The matters referred to in subsection (4)(g) are—
(a) whether a thing has been done using an electronic communication or electronic storage;
(b) the time at which, or date on which, a thing done using any such communication or storage was done;
(c) the place where a thing done using such communication or storage was done;
(d) the person by whom such a thing was done; and
(e) the contents, authenticity or integrity of any electronic data.

(6) An order under this section—

(a) shall not (subject to paragraph (b)) require the use of electronic communications or electronic storage for any purpose; but

(b) may make provision that a period of notice specified in the order must expire before effect is given to a variation or withdrawal of an election or other decision which—

(i) has been made for the purposes of such an order; and

(ii) is an election or decision to make use of electronic communications or electronic storage.

(7) The matters in relation to which provision may be made by an order under this section do not include any matter under the care and management of the Commissioners of Inland Revenue or any matter under the care and management of the Commissioners of Customs and Excise.

(8) In this section references to doing anything under the provisions of any enactment include references to doing it under the provisions of any subordinate legislation the power to make which is conferred by that enactment.

9 Section 8 orders

(1) In this Part "the appropriate Minister" means (subject to subsections (2) and (7) and section 10(1))—

(a) in relation to any matter with which a department of the Secretary of State is concerned, the Secretary of State;

(b) in relation to any matter with which the Treasury is concerned, the Treasury; and

(c) in relation to any matter with which any Government department other than a department of the Secretary of State or the Treasury is concerned, the Minister in charge of the other department.

(2) Where in the case of any matter—

(a) that matter falls within more than one paragraph of subsection (1),

(b) there is more than one such department as is mentioned in paragraph (c) of that subsection that is concerned with that matter, or

(c) both paragraphs (a) and (b) of this subsection apply,

references, in relation to that matter, to the appropriate Minister are references to any one or more of the appropriate Ministers acting (in the case of more than one) jointly.

(3) Subject to subsection (4) and section 10(6), a statutory instrument containing an order under section 8 shall be subject to annulment in pursuance of a resolution of either House of Parliament.

(4) Subsection (3) does not apply in the case of an order a draft of which has been laid before Parliament and approved by a resolution of each House.

(5) An order under section 8 may—

(a) provide for any conditions or requirements imposed by such an order to be framed by reference to the directions of such persons as may be specified in or determined in accordance with the order;

(b) provide that any such condition or requirement is to be satisfied only where a person so specified or determined is satisfied as to specified matters.

(6) The provision made by such an order may include—
(a) different provision for different cases;
(b) such exceptions and exclusions as the person making the order may think fit; and
(c) any such incidental, supplemental, consequential and transitional provision as he may think fit;

and the provision that may be made by virtue of paragraph (c) includes provision modifying any enactment or subordinate legislation or any scheme, licence, authorisation or approval issued, granted or given by or under any enactment or subordinate legislation.

(7) In the case of any matter which is not one of the reserved matters within the meaning of the Scotland Act 1998 or in respect of which functions are, by virtue of section 63 of that Act, exercisable by the Scottish Ministers instead of by or concurrently with a Minister of the Crown, this section and section 8 shall apply to Scotland subject to the following modifications—
(a) subsections (1) and (2) of this section are omitted;
(b) any reference to the appropriate Minister is to be read as a reference to the Secretary of State;
(c) any power of the Secretary of State, by virtue of paragraph (b), to make an order under section 8 may also be exercised by the Scottish Ministers with the consent of the Secretary of State; and
(d) where the Scottish Ministers make an order under section 8—
(i) any reference to the Secretary of State (other than a reference in this subsection) shall be construed as a reference to the Scottish Ministers; and
(ii) any reference to Parliament or to a House of Parliament shall be construed as a reference to the Scottish Parliament.

10 Modifications in relation to Welsh matters

(1) For the purposes of the exercise of the powers conferred by section 8 in relation to any matter the functions in respect of which are exercisable by the National Assembly for Wales, the appropriate Minister is the Secretary of State.

(2) Subject to the following provisions of this section, the powers conferred by section 8, so far as they fall within subsection (3), shall be exercisable by the National Assembly for Wales, as well as by the appropriate Minister.

(3) The powers conferred by section 8 fall within this subsection to the extent that they are exercisable in relation to—
(a) the provisions of any subordinate legislation made by the National Assembly for Wales;
(b) so much of any other subordinate legislation as makes provision the power to make which is exercisable by that Assembly;
(c) any power under any enactment to make provision the power to make which is so exercisable;

(d) the giving, sending or production of any notice, account, record or other document or of any information to or by a body mentioned in subsection (4); or

(e) the publication of anything by a body mentioned in subsection (4).

(4) Those bodies are—

(a) the National Assembly for Wales;

(b) any body specified in Schedule 4 to the Government of Wales Act 1998 (Welsh public bodies subject to reform by that Assembly);

(c) any other such body as may be specified for the purposes of this section by an order made by the Secretary of State with the consent of that Assembly.

(5) The National Assembly for Wales shall not make an order under section 8 except with the consent of the Secretary of State.

(6) Section 9(3) shall not apply to any order made under section 8 by the National Assembly for Wales.

(7) Nothing in this section shall confer any power on the National Assembly for Wales to modify any provision of the Government of Wales Act 1998.

(8) The power of the Secretary of State to make an order under subsection (4)(c)—

(a) shall include power to make any such incidental, supplemental, consequential and transitional provision as he may think fit; and

(b) shall be exercisable by statutory instrument subject to annulment in pursuance of a resolution of either House of Parliament.

Supplemental

15 General interpretation

(1) In this Act, except in so far as the context otherwise requires—

"document" includes a map, plan, design, drawing, picture or other image;

"communication" includes a communication comprising sounds or images or both and a communication effecting a payment;

"electronic communication" means a communication transmitted (whether from one person to another, from one device to another or from a person to a device or vice versa)—

(a) by means of a telecommunication system (within the meaning of the Telecommunications Act 1984); or

(b) by other means but while in an electronic form;

"enactment" includes—

(a) an enactment passed after the passing of this Act,

(b) an enactment comprised in an Act of the Scottish Parliament, and

(c) an enactment contained in Northern Ireland legislation,

but does not include an enactment contained in Part I or II of this Act;

"modification" includes any alteration, addition or omission, and cognate expressions shall be construed accordingly;

"record" includes an electronic record; and

"subordinate legislation" means—

(a) any subordinate legislation (within the meaning of the Interpretation Act 1978);
(b) any instrument made under an Act of the Scottish Parliament; or
(c) any statutory rules (within the meaning of the Statutory Rules (Northern Ireland) Order 1979).

(2) In this Act—
(a) references to the authenticity of any communication or data are references to any one or more of the following—
(i) whether the communication or data comes from a particular person or other source;
(ii) whether it is accurately timed and dated;
(iii) whether it is intended to have legal effect;
and
(b) references to the integrity of any communication or data are references to whether there has been any tampering with or other modification of the communication or data.

(3) References in this Act to something's being put into an intelligible form include references to its being restored to the condition in which it was before any encryption or similar process was applied to it.

16 Short title, commencement, extent

(1) This Act may be cited as the Electronic Communications Act 2000.

(2) Part I of this Act and sections 7, 11 and 12 shall come into force on such day as the Secretary of State may by order made by statutory instrument appoint; and different days may be appointed under this subsection for different purposes.

(3) An order shall not be made for bringing any of Part I of this Act into force for any purpose unless a draft of the order has been laid before Parliament and approved by a resolution of each House.

(4) If no order for bringing Part I of this Act into force has been made under subsection (2) by the end of the period of five years beginning with the day on which this Act is passed, that Part shall, by virtue of this subsection, be repealed at the end of that period.

(5) This Act extends to Northern Ireland.

PART II

STATUTORY INSTRUMENTS

General Product Safety Regulations 1994

1994 No 2328

NOTES

Made - - - 5th September 1994

1 Citation and commencement

[(1)] These Regulations may be cited as the General Product Safety Regulations 1994 and shall come into force on 3rd October 1994.

[(2) Nothing in these Regulations applies to a medicinal product for human use to which the Medicines for Human Use (Marketing Authorizations Etc) Regulations 1994 apply.]

NOTES

Para (1): numbered as such by SI 1994/3144, reg 11, Sch 7, para 21(b).
Para (2): inserted by SI 1994/3144, reg 11, Sch 7, para 21(c).

2 Interpretation

(1) In these Regulations—

"the 1968 Act" means the Medicines Act 1968;

"the 1987 Act" means the Consumer Protection Act 1987;

"the 1990 Act" means the Food Safety Act 1990;

"commercial activity" includes a business and a trade;

"consumer" means a consumer acting otherwise than in the course of a commercial activity;

"dangerous product" means any product other than a safe product;

"distributor" means any professional in the supply chain whose activity does not affect the safety properties of a product;

"enforcement authority" means the Secretary of State, any other Minister of the Crown in charge of a Government Department, any such department and any authority, council and other person on whom functions under these Regulations are imposed by or under regulation 11;

"general safety requirement" means the requirement in regulation 7;

"the GPS Directive" means Council Directive 92/59/EEC on general product safety;

"the 1991 Order" means the Food Safety (Northern Ireland) Order 1991;

"producer" means

(a) the manufacturer of the product, when he is established in the Community, and includes any person presenting himself as the manufacturer by affixing to the product his name, trade mark or other distinctive mark, or the person who reconditions the product;

(b) when the manufacturer is not established in the Community—

(i) if the manufacturer does not have a representative established in the Community, the importer of the product;

(ii) in all other cases, the manufacturer's representative; and

(c) other professionals in the supply chain, insofar as their activities may affect the safety properties of a product placed on the market;

"product" means any product intended for consumers or likely to be used by consumers, supplied whether for consideration or not in the course of a commercial activity and whether new, used or reconditioned; provided, however, a product which is used exclusively in the context of a commercial activity even if it is used for or by a consumer shall not be regarded as a product for the purposes of these Regulations provided always and for the avoidance of doubt this exception shall not extend to the supply of such a product to a consumer;

"safe product" means any product which, under normal or reasonably foreseeable conditions of use, including duration, does not present any risk or only the minimum risks compatible with the product's use, considered as acceptable and consistent with a high level of protection for the safety and health of persons, taking into account in particular—

(a) the characteristics of the product, including its composition, packaging, instructions for assembly and maintenance;

(b) the effect on other products, where it is reasonably foreseeable that it will be used with other products;

(c) the presentation of the product, the labelling, any instructions for its use and disposal and any other indication or information provided by the producer; and

(d) the categories of consumers at serious risk when using the product, in particular children,

and the fact that higher levels of safety may be obtained or other products presenting a lesser degree of risk may be available shall not of itself cause the product to be considered other than a safe product.

(2) References in these Regulations to the "Community" are references to the European Economic Area established under the Agreement signed at Oporto on 2nd May 1992 as adjusted by the Protocol signed at Brussels on 17th March 1993.

3 Application and revocation

These Regulations do not apply to—

(a) second-hand products which are antiques;

(b) products supplied for repair or reconditioning before use, provided the supplier clearly informs the person to whom he supplies the product to that effect; or

(c) any product where there are specific provisions in rules of Community law governing all aspects of the safety of the product.

4

The requirements of these Regulations apply to a product where the product is the subject of provisions of Community law other than the GPS Directive insofar as those provisions do not make specific provision governing an aspect of the safety of the product.

5

For the purposes of these Regulations the provisions of section 10 of the 1987 Act to the extent that they impose general safety requirements which must be complied with if products are to be—

(i) placed on the market, offered or agreed to be placed on the market or exposed or possessed to be placed on the market by producers; or

(ii) supplied, offered or agreed to be supplied or exposed or possessed to be supplied by distributors,

are hereby disapplied.

7

No producer shall place a product on the market unless the product is a safe product.

8 Requirement as to information

(1) Within the limits of his activity, a producer shall—

(a) provide consumers with the relevant information to enable them to assess the risks inherent in a product throughout the normal or reasonably foreseeable period of its use, where such risks are not immediately obvious without adequate warnings, and to take precautions against those risks; and

(b) adopt measures commensurate with the characteristics of the products which he supplies, to enable him to be informed of the risks which these products might present and to take appropriate action, including, if necessary, withdrawing the product in question from the market to avoid those risks.

(2) The measures referred to in sub-paragraph (b) of paragraph (1) above may include, whenever appropriate—

(i) marking of the products or product batches in such a way that they can be identified;

(ii) sample testing of marketed products;

(iii) investigating complaints; and

(iv) keeping distributors informed of such monitoring.

9 Requirements of distributors

A distributor shall act with due care in order to help ensure compliance with the requirements of regulation 7 above and, in particular, without limiting the generality of the foregoing—

(a) a distributor shall not supply products to any person which he knows, or should have presumed, on the basis of the information in his possession and as a professional, are dangerous products; and

(b) within the limits of his activities, a distributor shall participate in monitoring the safety of products placed on the market, in particular by passing on information on the product risks and cooperating in the action taken to avoid those risks.

10 Presumption of conformity and product assessment

(1) Where in relation to any product such product conforms to the specific rules of the law of the United Kingdom laying down the health and safety requirements which the product must satisfy in order to be marketed there shall be a presumption that, until the contrary is proved, the product is a safe product.

(2) Where no specific rules as are mentioned or referred to in paragraph (1) exist, the conformity of a product to the general safety requirement shall be assessed taking into account—

- (i) voluntary national standards of the United Kingdom giving effect to a European standard; or
- (ii) Community technical specifications; or
- (iii) if there are no such voluntary national standards of the United Kingdom or Community technical specifications—
  - (aa) standards drawn up in the United Kingdom; or
  - (bb) the codes of good practice in respect of health and safety in the product sector concerned; or
  - (cc) the state of the art and technology

and the safety which consumers may reasonably expect.

11 Enforcement

For the purposes of providing for the enforcement of these Regulations—

- (a) section 13 of the 1987 Act (prohibition notices and notices to warn) shall (to the extent that it does not already do so) apply to products as it applies to relevant goods under that section;
- (b) the requirements of these Regulations shall constitute safety provisions for the purposes of sections 14 (suspension notices), 15 (appeals against suspension notices), 16 (forfeiture: England, Wales and Northern Ireland), 17 (forfeiture: Scotland) and 18 (power to obtain information) of the 1987 Act;
- (c)
  - (i) subject to paragraph (ii) below a weights and measures authority in Great Britain and a district council in Northern Ireland shall have the same duty to enforce these Regulations as they have in relation to Part II of the 1987 Act, and Part IV, sections 37 and 38 and subsections (3) and (4) of section 42 of that Act shall apply accordingly;
  - (ii) without prejudice to the provisions of paragraphs (a) and (b) above and sub-paragraph (i) above, insofar as these Regulations apply:—

(aa) to products licensed in accordance with the provisions of the 1968 Act [or authorised in accordance with the provisions of the Marketing Authorisations for Veterinary Medicinal Products Regulations 1994] [or which are the subject of a marketing authorization within the meaning of the Medicines for Human Use (Marketing Authorizations Etc) Regulations 1994], it shall be the duty of the enforcement authority as defined in section 132(1) of the 1968 Act to enforce or to secure the enforcement of these Regulations and sections 108 to 115 and section 119 of and Schedule 3 to that Act shall apply accordingly as if these Regulations were regulations made under the said Act;

(bb) in relation to food within the meaning of section 1 of the 1990 Act, it shall be the duty of each food authority as defined in section 5 of the 1990 Act to enforce or to secure the enforcement of these Regulations, within its area, in Great Britain and sections 9, 29, 30 and 32 of that Act shall apply accordingly as if these Regulations were food safety requirements made under the said Act and section 10 of that Act shall apply as if these Regulations were regulations made under Part II of that Act; and

(cc) in relation to food within the meaning of article 2 of the 1991 Order, it shall be the duty of the relevant enforcement authority as provided for in article 26 of that Order to enforce or to secure enforcement of these Regulations in Northern Ireland and articles 8, 29, 30, 31 and 33 of that Order shall apply accordingly as if these Regulations were food safety requirements made under that Order and article 9 of that Order shall apply as if these Regulations were regulations made under Part II of that Order;

(d) in sections 13(4) and 14(6) of the 1987 Act for the words "six months" there shall be substituted "three months"; and

(e) nothing in this regulation shall authorise any enforcement authority to bring proceedings in Scotland for an offence.

NOTES

First words in square brackets inserted by SI 1994/3142, reg 21, Sch 5, para 29; final words in square brackets inserted by SI 1994/3144, reg 11, Sch 7, para 21.

12 Offences and preparatory acts

Any person who contravenes regulation 7 or 9(a) shall be guilty of an offence.

13

No producer or distributor shall—

(a) offer or agree to place on the market any dangerous product or expose or possess any such product for placing on the market; or

(b) offer or agree to supply any dangerous product or expose or possess any such product for supply, and any person who contravenes the requirements of this regulation shall be guilty of an offence.

14 Defence of due diligence

(1) Subject to the following paragraphs of this regulation, in proceedings against any person for an offence under these Regulations it shall be a defence for that person to show that he took all reasonable steps and exercised all due diligence to avoid committing the offence.

(2) Where in any proceedings against any person for such an offence the defence provided by paragraph (1) above involves an allegation that the commission of the offence was due—

(a) to the act or default of another, or
(b) to reliance on information given by another,

that person shall not, without leave of the court, be entitled to rely on the defence unless, not less than seven days before, in England, Wales and Northern Ireland, the hearing of the proceedings or, in Scotland, the trial diet, he has served a notice under paragraph (3) below on the person bringing the proceedings.

(3) A notice under this paragraph shall give such information identifying or assisting in the identification of the person who committed the act or default or gave the information as is in the possession of the person serving the notice at the time he serves it.

(4) It is hereby declared that a person shall not be entitled to rely on the defence provided in paragraph (1) above by reason of his reliance on information supplied by another, unless he shows that it was reasonable in all the circumstances for him to have relied on the information, having regard in particular—

(a) to the steps which he took, and those which might reasonably have been taken, for the purpose of verifying the information; and
(b) to whether he had any reason to disbelieve the information.

(5) It is hereby declared that a person shall not be entitled to rely on the defence provided by paragraph (1) above or by section 39(1) of the 1987 Act (defence of due diligence) if he has contravened regulation 9(b).

15 Liability of persons other than principal offender

(1) Where the commission by any person of an offence to which regulation 14 above applies is due to the act or default committed by some other person in the course of a commercial activity of his, the other person shall be guilty of an offence and may be proceeded against and punished by virtue of this paragraph whether or not proceedings are taken against the first-mentioned person.

(2) Where a body corporate is guilty of an offence under these Regulations (including where it is so guilty by virtue of paragraph (1) above) in respect of any act or default which is shown to have been committed with the consent or connivance of, or to be attributable to any neglect on the part of any director, manager, secretary or other similar officer of the body corporate or any person who

was purporting to act in any such capacity he, as well as the body corporate, shall be guilty of that offence and shall be liable to be proceeded against and punished accordingly.

(3) Where the affairs of a body corporate are managed by its members, paragraph (2) above shall apply in relation to the acts and defaults of a member in connection with his functions of management as if he were a director of the body corporate.

(4) Where a Scottish partnership is guilty of an offence under regulation 14 above (including where it is so guilty by virtue of paragraph (1) above) in respect of any act or default which is shown to have been committed with the consent or connivance of, or to be attributable to any neglect on the part of, a partner in the partnership, he, as well as the partnership, shall be guilty of that offence and shall be liable to be proceeded against and punished accordingly.

16 Extension of the time for bringing summary proceedings

(1) Notwithstanding section 127 of the Magistrates' Courts Act 1980 and article 19 of the Magistrates' Courts (Northern Ireland) Order 1981, in England, Wales and Northern Ireland a magistrates' court may try an information (in the case of England and Wales) or a complaint (in the case of Northern Ireland) in respect of proceedings for an offence under regulation 12 or 13 above if (in the case of England and Wales) the information is laid or (in the case of Northern Ireland) the complaint is made within twelve months from the date of the offence.

(2) Notwithstanding section 331 of the Criminal Procedure (Scotland) Act 1975, in Scotland summary proceedings for an offence under regulation 12 or 13 above may be commenced at any time within twelve months from the date of the offence.

(3) For the purposes of paragraph (2) above, section 331(3) of the Criminal Procedure (Scotland) Act 1975 shall apply as it applies for the purposes of that section.

17 Penalties

A person guilty of an offence under regulation 12 or 13 above shall be liable on summary conviction to—

(a) imprisonment for a term not exceeding three months; or
(b) a fine not exceeding level 5 on the standard scale;

or to both.

18 Duties of enforcement authorities

(1) Every enforcement authority shall give immediate notice to the Secretary of State of any action taken by it to prohibit or restrict the supply of any product or forfeit or do any other thing in respect of any product for the purposes of these Regulations.

(2) The requirements of paragraph (1) above shall not apply in the case of any action taken in respect of any second-hand product.

Provision and Use of Work Equipment Regulations 1998

1998 No 2306

NOTES

Made ....15th September 1998
Laid before Parliament...25th September 1998
Coming into force ....5th December 1998

PART I
INTRODUCTION

1 Citation and commencement

These Regulations may be cited as the Provision and Use of Work Equipment Regulations 1998 and shall come into force on 5th December 1998.

2 Interpretation

(1) In these Regulations, unless the context otherwise requires—

"the 1974 Act" means the Health and Safety at Work etc Act 1974;

"employer" except in regulation 3(2) and (3) includes a person to whom the requirements imposed by these Regulations apply by virtue of regulation 3(3)(a) and (b);

"essential requirements" means requirements described in regulation 10(1);

"the Executive" means the Health and Safety Executive;

"inspection" in relation to an inspection under paragraph (1) or (2) of regulation 6—

- (a) means such visual or more rigorous inspection by a competent person as is appropriate for the purpose described in the paragraph;
- (b) where it is appropriate to carry out testing for the purpose, includes testing the nature and extent of which are appropriate for the purpose;

"power press" means a press or press brake for the working of metal by means of tools, or for die proving, which is power driven and which embodies a flywheel and clutch;

"thorough examination" in relation to a thorough examination under paragraph (1), (2), (3) or (4) of regulation 32—

- (a) means a thorough examination by a competent person;
- (b) includes testing the nature and extent of which are appropriate for the purpose described in the paragraph;

"use" in relation to work equipment means any activity involving work equipment and includes starting, stopping, programming, setting, transporting, repairing, modifying, maintaining, servicing and cleaning;

"work equipment" means any machinery, appliance, apparatus, tool or installation for use at work (whether exclusively or not);

and related expressions shall be construed accordingly.

(2) Any reference in regulations 32 to 34 or Schedule 3 to a guard or protection device is a reference to a guard or protection device provided for the tools of a power press.

(3) Any reference in regulation 32 or 33 to a guard or protection device being on a power press shall, in the case of a guard or protection device designed to operate while adjacent to a power press, be construed as a reference to its being adjacent to it.

(4) Any reference in these Regulations to—
- (a) a numbered regulation or Schedule is a reference to the regulation or Schedule in these Regulations so numbered; and
- (b) a numbered paragraph is a reference to the paragraph so numbered in the regulation in which the reference appears.

3 Application

(1) These Regulations shall apply—
- (a) in Great Britain; and
- (b) outside Great Britain as sections 1 to 59 and 80 to 82 of the 1974 Act apply by virtue of the Health and Safety at Work etc Act 1974 (Application outside Great Britain) Order 1995 ("the 1995 Order").

(2) The requirements imposed by these Regulations on an employer in respect of work equipment shall apply to such equipment provided for use or used by an employee of his at work.

(3) The requirements imposed by these Regulations on an employer shall also apply—
- (a) to a self-employed person, in respect of work equipment he uses at work;
- (b) subject to paragraph (5), to a person who has control to any extent of—
  - (i) work equipment;
  - (ii) a person at work who uses or supervises or manages the use of work equipment; or
  - (iii) the way in which work equipment is used at work,

  and to the extent of his control.

(4) Any reference in paragraph (3)(b) to a person having control is a reference to a person having control in connection with the carrying on by him of a trade, business or other undertaking (whether for profit or not).

(5) The requirements imposed by these Regulations shall not apply to a person in respect of work equipment supplied by him by way of sale, agreement for sale or hire-purchase agreement.

(6) Subject to paragraphs (7) to (10), these Regulations shall not impose any obligation in relation to a ship's work equipment (whether that equipment is used on or off the ship).

(7) Where merchant shipping requirements are applicable to a ship's work equipment, paragraph (6) shall relieve the shore employer of his obligations under these Regulations in respect of that equipment only where he has taken all reasonable steps to satisfy himself that the merchant shipping requirements are being complied with in respect of that equipment.

(8) In a case where the merchant shipping requirements are not applicable to the ship's work equipment by reason only that for the time being there is no master, crew or watchman on the ship, those requirements shall nevertheless be treated for the purpose of paragraph (7) as if they were applicable.

(9) Where the ship's work equipment is used in a specified operation paragraph (6) shall not apply to regulations 7 to 9, 11 to 13, 20 to 22 and 30 (each as applied by regulation 3).

(10) Paragraph (6) does not apply to a ship's work equipment provided for use or used in an activity (whether carried on in or outside Great Britain) specified in the 1995 Order save that it does apply to—

(a) the loading, unloading, fuelling or provisioning of the ship; or
(b) the construction, reconstruction, finishing, refitting, repair, maintenance, cleaning or breaking up of the ship.

(11) In this regulation—

"master" has the meaning assigned to it by section 313(1) of the Merchant Shipping Act 1995;

"merchant shipping requirements" means the requirements of regulations 3 and 4 of the Merchant Shipping (Guarding of Machinery and Safety of Electrical Equipment) Regulations 1988 and regulations 5 to 10 of the Merchant Shipping (Hatches and Lifting Plant) Regulations 1988;

"ship" has the meaning assigned to it by section 313(1) of the Merchant Shipping Act 1995 save that it does not include an offshore installation;

"shore employer" means an employer of persons (other than the master and crew of any ship) who are engaged in a specified operation;

"specified operation" means an operation in which the ship's work equipment is used—

(a) by persons other than the master and crew; or
(b) where persons other than the master and crew are liable to be exposed to a risk to their health or safety from its use.

PART II
GENERAL

4 Suitability of work equipment

(1) Every employer shall ensure that work equipment is so constructed or adapted as to be suitable for the purpose for which it is used or provided.

(2) In selecting work equipment, every employer shall have regard to the working conditions and to the risks to the health and safety of persons which exist in the premises or undertaking in which that work equipment is to be used and any additional risk posed by the use of that work equipment.

(3) Every employer shall ensure that work equipment is used only for operations for which, and under conditions for which, it is suitable.

[(4) In this regulation "suitable"—

(a) subject to sub-paragraph (b), means suitable in any respect which it is reasonably foreseeable will affect the health or safety of any person;

(b) in relation to—

(i) an offensive weapon within the meaning of section 1(4) of the Prevention of Crime Act 1953 provided for use as self-defence or as deterrent equipment; and

(ii) work equipment provided for use for arrest or restraint,

by a person who holds the office of constable or an appointment as police cadet, means suitable in any respect which it is reasonably foreseeable will affect the health or safety of such person.]

NOTES

Para (4): substituted by SI 1999/860, reg 5(1).
Date in force: 14 April 1999: see SI 1999/860, reg 1.

5 Maintenance

(1) Every employer shall ensure that work equipment is maintained in an efficient state, in efficient working order and in good repair.

(2) Every employer shall ensure that where any machinery has a maintenance log, the log is kept up to date.

6 Inspection

(1) Every employer shall ensure that, where the safety of work equipment depends on the installation conditions, it is inspected—

(a) after installation and before being put into service for the first time; or

(b) after assembly at a new site or in a new location,

to ensure that it has been installed correctly and is safe to operate.

(2) Every employer shall ensure that work equipment exposed to conditions causing deterioration which is liable to result in dangerous situations is inspected—

(a) at suitable intervals; and

(b) each time that exceptional circumstances which are liable to jeopardise the safety of the work equipment have occurred,

to ensure that health and safety conditions are maintained and that any deterioration can be detected and remedied in good time.

(3) Every employer shall ensure that the result of an inspection made under this regulation is recorded and kept until the next inspection under this regulation is recorded.

(4) Every employer shall ensure that no work equipment—

(a) leaves his undertaking; or

(b) if obtained from the undertaking of another person, is used in his undertaking, unless it is accompanied by physical evidence that the last inspection required to be carried out under this regulation has been carried out.

(5) This regulation does not apply to—
(a) a power press to which regulations 32 to 35 apply;
(b) a guard or protection device for the tools of such power press;
(c) work equipment for lifting loads including persons;
(d) winding apparatus to which the Mines (Shafts and Winding) Regulations 1993 apply;
(e) work equipment required to be inspected by regulation 29 of the Construction (Health, Safety and Welfare) Regulations 1996.

7 Specific risks

(1) Where the use of work equipment is likely to involve a specific risk to health or safety, every employer shall ensure that—
(a) the use of that work equipment is restricted to those persons given the task of using it; and
(b) repairs, modifications, maintenance or servicing of that work equipment is restricted to those persons who have been specifically designated to perform operations of that description (whether or not also authorised to perform other operations).

(2) The employer shall ensure that the persons designated for the purposes of sub-paragraph (b) of paragraph (1) have received adequate training related to any operations in respect of which they have been so designated.

8 Information and instructions

(1) Every employer shall ensure that all persons who use work equipment have available to them adequate health and safety information and, where appropriate, written instructions pertaining to the use of the work equipment.

(2) Every employer shall ensure that any of his employees who supervises or manages the use of work equipment has available to him adequate health and safety information and, where appropriate, written instructions pertaining to the use of the work equipment.

(3) Without prejudice to the generality of paragraphs (1) or (2), the information and instructions required by either of those paragraphs shall include information and, where appropriate, written instructions on—
(a) the conditions in which and the methods by which the work equipment may be used;
(b) foreseeable abnormal situations and the action to be taken if such a situation were to occur; and
(c) any conclusions to be drawn from experience in using the work equipment.

(4) Information and instructions required by this regulation shall be readily comprehensible to those concerned.

9 Training

(1) Every employer shall ensure that all persons who use work equipment have received adequate training for purposes of health and safety, including training in the methods which may be adopted when using the work equipment, any risks which such use may entail and precautions to be taken.

(2) Every employer shall ensure that any of his employees who supervises or manages the use of work equipment has received adequate training for purposes of health and safety, including training in the methods which may be adopted when using the work equipment, any risks which such use may entail and precautions to be taken.

10 Conformity with Community requirements

(1) Every employer shall ensure that an item of work equipment has been designed and constructed in compliance with any essential requirements, that is to say requirements relating to its design or construction in any of the instruments listed in Schedule 1 (being instruments which give effect to Community directives concerning the safety of products).

(2) Where an essential requirement applied to the design or construction of an item of work equipment, the requirements of regulations 11 to 19 and 22 to 29 shall apply in respect of that item only to the extent that the essential requirement did not apply to it.

(3) This regulation applies to items of work equipment provided for use in the premises or undertaking of the employer for the first time after 31st December 1992.

11 Dangerous parts of machinery

(1) Every employer shall ensure that measures are taken in accordance with paragraph (2) which are effective—

- (a) to prevent access to any dangerous part of machinery or to any rotating stock-bar; or
- (b) to stop the movement of any dangerous part of machinery or rotating stock-bar before any part of a person enters a danger zone.

(2) The measures required by paragraph (1) shall consist of—

- (a) the provision of fixed guards enclosing every dangerous part or rotating stock-bar where and to the extent that it is practicable to do so, but where or to the extent that it is not, then
- (b) the provision of other guards or protection devices where and to the extent that it is practicable to do so, but where or to the extent that it is not, then
- (c) the provision of jigs, holders, push-sticks or similar protection appliances used in conjunction with the machinery where and to the extent that it is practicable to do so, but where or to the extent that it is not, then
- (d) the provision of information, instruction, training and supervision.

(3) All guards and protection devices provided under sub-paragraphs (a) or (b) of paragraph (2) shall—

- (a) be suitable for the purpose for which they are provided;

(b) be of good construction, sound material and adequate strength;
(c) be maintained in an efficient state, in efficient working order and in good repair;
(d) not give rise to any increased risk to health or safety;
(e) not be easily bypassed or disabled;
(f) be situated at sufficient distance from the danger zone;
(g) not unduly restrict the view of the operating cycle of the machinery, where such a view is necessary;
(h) be so constructed or adapted that they allow operations necessary to fit or replace parts and for maintenance work, restricting access so that it is allowed only to the area where the work is to be carried out and, if possible, without having to dismantle the guard or protection device.

(4) All protection appliances provided under sub-paragraph (c) of paragraph (2) shall comply with sub-paragraphs (a) to (d) and (g) of paragraph (3).

(5) In this regulation—

"danger zone" means any zone in or around machinery in which a person is exposed to a risk to health or safety from contact with a dangerous part of machinery or a rotating stock-bar;

"stock-bar" means any part of a stock-bar which projects beyond the head-stock of a lathe.

12 Protection against specified hazards

(1) Every employer shall take measures to ensure that the exposure of a person using work equipment to any risk to his health or safety from any hazard specified in paragraph (3) is either prevented, or, where that is not reasonably practicable, adequately controlled.

(2) The measures required by paragraph (1) shall—
(a) be measures other than the provision of personal protective equipment or of information, instruction, training and supervision, so far as is reasonably practicable; and
(b) include, where appropriate, measures to minimise the effects of the hazard as well as to reduce the likelihood of the hazard occurring.

(3) The hazards referred to in paragraph (1) are—
(a) any article or substance falling or being ejected from work equipment;
(b) rupture or disintegration of parts of work equipment;
(c) work equipment catching fire or overheating;
(d) the unintended or premature discharge of any article or of any gas, dust, liquid, vapour or other substance which, in each case, is produced, used or stored in the work equipment;
(e) the unintended or premature explosion of the work equipment or any article or substance produced, used or stored in it.

(4) For the purposes of this regulation "adequately" means adequately having regard only to the nature of the hazard and the nature and degree of exposure to the risk.

(5) This regulation shall not apply where any of the following Regulations apply in respect of any risk to a person's health or safety for which such Regulations require measures to be taken to prevent or control such risk, namely—

(a) the Ionising Radiations Regulations 1985;
(b) the Control of Asbestos at Work Regulations 1987;
(c) the Control of Substances Hazardous to Health Regulations 1994;
(d) the Noise at Work Regulations 1989;
(e) the Construction (Head Protection) Regulations 1989;
(f) the Control of Lead at Work Regulations 1998.

13 High or very low temperature

Every employer shall ensure that work equipment, parts of work equipment and any article or substance produced, used or stored in work equipment which, in each case, is at a high or very low temperature shall have protection where appropriate so as to prevent injury to any person by burn, scald or sear.

14 Controls for starting or making a significant change in operating conditions

(1) Every employer shall ensure that, where appropriate, work equipment is provided with one or more controls for the purposes of—

(a) starting the work equipment (including re-starting after a stoppage for any reason); or
(b) controlling any change in the speed, pressure or other operating conditions of the work equipment where such conditions after the change result in risk to health and safety which is greater than or of a different nature from such risks before the change.

(2) Subject to paragraph (3), every employer shall ensure that, where a control is required by paragraph (1), it shall not be possible to perform any operation mentioned in sub-paragraph (a) or (b) of that paragraph except by a deliberate action on such control.

(3) Paragraph (1) shall not apply to re-starting or changing operating conditions as a result of the normal operating cycle of an automatic device.

15 Stop controls

(1) Every employer shall ensure that, where appropriate, work equipment is provided with one or more readily accessible controls the operation of which will bring the work equipment to a safe condition in a safe manner.

(2) Any control required by paragraph (1) shall bring the work equipment to a complete stop where necessary for reasons of health and safety.

(3) Any control required by paragraph (1) shall, if necessary for reasons of health and safety, switch off all sources of energy after stopping the functioning of the work equipment.

(4) Any control required by paragraph (1) shall operate in priority to any control which starts or changes the operating conditions of the work equipment.

16 Emergency stop controls

(1) Every employer shall ensure that, where appropriate, work equipment is provided with one or more readily accessible emergency stop controls unless it is not necessary by reason of the nature of the hazards and the time taken for the work equipment to come to a complete stop as a result of the action of any control provided by virtue of regulation 15(1).

(2) Any control required by paragraph (1) shall operate in priority to any control required by regulation 15(1).

17 Controls

(1) Every employer shall ensure that all controls for work equipment are clearly visible and identifiable, including by appropriate marking where necessary.

(2) Except where necessary, the employer shall ensure that no control for work equipment is in a position where any person operating the control is exposed to a risk to his health or safety.

(3) Every employer shall ensure where appropriate—

(a) that, so far as is reasonably practicable, the operator of any control is able to ensure from the position of that control that no person is in a place where he would be exposed to any risk to his health or safety as a result of the operation of that control, but where or to the extent that it is not reasonably practicable;

(b) that, so far as is reasonably practicable, systems of work are effective to ensure that, when work equipment is about to start, no person is in a place where he would be exposed to a risk to his health or safety as a result of the work equipment starting, but where neither of these is reasonably practicable;

(c) that an audible, visible or other suitable warning is given by virtue of regulation 24 whenever work equipment is about to start.

(4) Every employer shall take appropriate measures to ensure that any person who is in a place where he would be exposed to a risk to his health or safety as a result of the starting or stopping of work equipment has sufficient time and suitable means to avoid that risk.

18 Control systems

(1) Every employer shall—

(a) ensure, so far as is reasonably practicable, that all control systems of work equipment are safe; and

(b) are chosen making due allowance for the failures, faults and constraints to be expected in the planned circumstances of use.

(2) Without prejudice to the generality of paragraph (1), a control system shall not be safe unless—

(a) its operation does not create any increased risk to health or safety;

(b) it ensures, so far as is reasonably practicable, that any fault in or damage to any part of the control system or the loss of supply of any source of energy used by the work equipment cannot result in additional or increased risk to health or safety;

(c) it does not impede the operation of any control required by regulation 15 or 16.

19 Isolation from sources of energy

(1) Every employer shall ensure that where appropriate work equipment is provided with suitable means to isolate it from all its sources of energy.

(2) Without prejudice to the generality of paragraph (1), the means mentioned in that paragraph shall not be suitable unless they are clearly identifiable and readily accessible.

(3) Every employer shall take appropriate measures to ensure that re-connection of any energy source to work equipment does not expose any person using the work equipment to any risk to his health or safety.

20 Stability

Every employer shall ensure that work equipment or any part of work equipment is stabilised by clamping or otherwise where necessary for purposes of health or safety.

21 Lighting

Every employer shall ensure that suitable and sufficient lighting, which takes account of the operations to be carried out, is provided at any place where a person uses work equipment.

22 Maintenance operations

Every employer shall take appropriate measures to ensure that work equipment is so constructed or adapted that, so far as is reasonably practicable, maintenance operations which involve a risk to health or safety can be carried out while the work equipment is shut down, or in other cases—

(a) maintenance operations can be carried out without exposing the person carrying them out to a risk to his health or safety; or

(b) appropriate measures can be taken for the protection of any person carrying out maintenance operations which involve a risk to his health or safety.

23 Markings

Every employer shall ensure that work equipment is marked in a clearly visible manner with any marking appropriate for reasons of health and safety.

24 Warnings

(1) Every employer shall ensure that work equipment incorporates any warnings or warning devices which are appropriate for reasons of health and safety.

(2) Without prejudice to the generality of paragraph (1), warnings given by warning devices on work equipment shall not be appropriate unless they are unambiguous, easily perceived and easily understood.

PART III
MOBILE WORK EQUIPMENT

25 Employees carried on mobile work equipment

Every employer shall ensure that no employee is carried by mobile work equipment unless—

(a) it is suitable for carrying persons; and
(b) it incorporates features for reducing to as low as is reasonably practicable risks to their safety, including risks from wheels or tracks.

26 Rolling over of mobile work equipment

(1) Every employer shall ensure that where there is a risk to an employee riding on mobile work equipment from its rolling over, it is minimised by—

(a) stabilising the work equipment;
(b) a structure which ensures that the work equipment does no more than fall on its side;
(c) a structure giving sufficient clearance to anyone being carried if it overturns further than that; or
(d) a device giving comparable protection.

(2) Where there is a risk of anyone being carried by mobile work equipment being crushed by its rolling over, the employer shall ensure that it has a suitable restraining system for him.

(3) This regulation shall not apply to a fork-lift truck having a structure described in sub-paragraph (b) or (c) of paragraph (1).

(4) Compliance with this regulation is not required where—

(a) it would increase the overall risk to safety;
(b) it would not be reasonably practicable to operate the mobile work equipment in consequence; or
(c) in relation to an item of work equipment provided for use in the undertaking or establishment before 5th December 1998 it would not be reasonably practicable.

27 Overturning of fork-lift trucks

Every employer shall ensure that a fork-lift truck to which regulation 26(3) refers and which carries an employee is adapted or equipped to reduce to as low as is reasonably practicable the risk to safety from its overturning.

28 Self-propelled work equipment

Every employer shall ensure that, where self-propelled work equipment may, while in motion, involve risk to the safety of persons—

(a) it has facilities for preventing its being started by an unauthorised person;
(b) it has appropriate facilities for minimising the consequences of a collision where there is more than one item of rail-mounted work equipment in motion at the same time;
(c) it has a device for braking and stopping;
(d) where safety constraints so require, emergency facilities operated by readily accessible controls or automatic systems are available for braking and stopping the work equipment in the event of failure of the main facility;
(e) where the driver's direct field of vision is inadequate to ensure safety, there are adequate devices for improving his vision so far as is reasonably practicable;
(f) if provided for use at night or in dark places—
 (i) it is equipped with lighting appropriate to the work to be carried out; and
 (ii) is otherwise sufficiently safe for such use;
(g) if it, or anything carried or towed by it, constitutes a fire hazard and is liable to endanger employees, it carries appropriate fire-fighting equipment, unless such equipment is kept sufficiently close to it.

29 Remote-controlled self-propelled work equipment

Every employer shall ensure that where remote-controlled self-propelled work equipment involves a risk to safety while in motion—
(a) it stops automatically once it leaves its control range; and
(b) where the risk is of crushing or impact it incorporates features to guard against such risk unless other appropriate devices are able to do so.

30 Drive shafts

(1) Where the seizure of the drive shaft between mobile work equipment and its accessories or anything towed is likely to involve a risk to safety every employer shall—
(a) ensure that the work equipment has a means of preventing such seizure; or
(b) where such seizure cannot be avoided, take every possible measure to avoid an adverse effect on the safety of an employee.

(2) Every employer shall ensure that—
(a) where mobile work equipment has a shaft for the transmission of energy between it and other mobile work equipment; and
(b) the shaft could become soiled or damaged by contact with the ground while uncoupled,

the work equipment has a system for safeguarding the shaft.

PART IV
POWER PRESSES

31 Power presses to which Part IV does not apply

Regulations 32 to 35 shall not apply to a power press of a kind which is described in Schedule 2.

32 Thorough examination of power presses, guards and protection devices

(1) Every employer shall ensure that a power press is not put into service for the first time after installation, or after assembly at a new site or in a new location unless—

(a) it has been thoroughly examined to ensure that it—
  (i) has been installed correctly; and
  (ii) would be safe to operate; and
(b) any defect has been remedied.

(2) Every employer shall ensure that a guard, other than one to which paragraph (3) relates, or protection device is not put into service for the first time on a power press unless—

(a) it has been thoroughly examined when in position on that power press to ensure that it is effective for its purpose; and
(b) any defect has been remedied.

(3) Every employer shall ensure that that part of a closed tool which acts as a fixed guard is not used on a power press unless—

(a) it has been thoroughly examined when in position on any power press in the premises to ensure that it is effective for its purpose; and
(b) any defect has been remedied.

(4) For the purpose of ensuring that health and safety conditions are maintained, and that any deterioration can be detected and remedied in good time, every employer shall ensure that—

(a) every power press is thoroughly examined, and its guards and protection devices are thoroughly examined when in position on that power press—
  (i) at least every 12 months, where it has fixed guards only; or
  (ii) at least every 6 months, in other cases; and
  (iii) each time that exceptional circumstances have occurred which are liable to jeopardise the safety of the power press or its guards or protection devices; and
(b) any defect is remedied before the power press is used again.

(5) Where a power press, guard or protection device was before the coming into force of these Regulations required to be thoroughly examined by regulation 5(2) of the Power Presses Regulations 1965 the first thorough examination under paragraph (4) shall be made before the date by which a thorough examination would have been required by regulation 5(2) had it remained in force.

(6) Paragraph (4) shall not apply to that part of a closed tool which acts as a fixed guard.

(7) In this regulation "defect" means a defect notified under regulation 34 other than a defect which has not yet become a danger to persons.

33 Inspection of guards and protection devices

(1) Every employer shall ensure that a power press is not used after the setting, re-setting or adjustment of its tools, save in trying out its tools or save in die proving, unless—

- (a) its every guard and protection device has been inspected and tested while in position on the power press by a person appointed in writing by the employer who is—
  - (i) competent; or
  - (ii) undergoing training for that purpose and acting under the immediate supervision of a competent person,

  and who has signed a certificate which complies with paragraph (3); or
- (b) the guards and protection devices have not been altered or disturbed in the course of the adjustment of its tools.

(2) Every employer shall ensure that a power press is not used after the expiration of the fourth hour of a working period unless its every guard and protection device has been inspected and tested while in position on the power press by a person appointed in writing by the employer who is—

- (a) competent; or
- (b) undergoing training for that purpose and acting under the immediate supervision of a competent person,

and who has signed a certificate which complies with paragraph (3).

(3) A certificate referred to in this regulation shall—

- (a) contain sufficient particulars to identify every guard and protection device inspected and tested and the power press on which it was positioned at the time of the inspection and test;
- (b) state the date and time of the inspection and test; and
- (c) state that every guard and protection device on the power press is in position and effective for its purpose.

(4) In this regulation "working period", in relation to a power press, means—

- (a) the period in which the day's or night's work is done; or
- (b) in premises where a shift system is in operation, a shift.

34 Reports

(1) A person making a thorough examination for an employer under regulation 32 shall—

- (a) notify the employer forthwith of any defect in a power press or its guard or protection device which in his opinion is or could become a danger to persons;

(b) as soon as is practicable make a report of the thorough examination to the employer in writing authenticated by him or on his behalf by signature or equally secure means and containing the information specified in Schedule 3; and

(c) where there is in his opinion a defect in a power press or its guard or protection device which is or could become a danger to persons, send a copy of the report as soon as is practicable to the enforcing authority for the premises in which the power press is situated.

(2) A person making an inspection and test for an employer under regulation 33 shall forthwith notify the employer of any defect in a guard or protection device which in his opinion is or could become a danger to persons and the reason for his opinion.

35 Keeping of information

(1) Every employer shall ensure that the information in every report made pursuant to regulation 34(1) is kept available for inspection for 2 years after it is made.

(2) Every employer shall ensure that a certificate under regulation 33(1)(a)(ii) or (2)(b) is kept available for inspection—

(a) at or near the power press to which it relates until superseded by a later certificate; and

(b) after that, until 6 months have passed since it was signed.

PART V
MISCELLANEOUS

36 Exemption for the armed forces

(1) The Secretary of State for Defence may, in the interests of national security, by a certificate in writing exempt any of the home forces, any visiting force or any headquarters from any requirement or prohibition imposed by these Regulations and any such exemption may be granted subject to conditions and to a limit of time and may be revoked by the said Secretary of State by a certificate in writing at any time.

(2) In this regulation—

(a) "the home forces" has the same meaning as in section 12(1) of the Visiting Forces Act 1952;

(b) "headquarters" has the same meaning as in article 3(2) of the Visiting Forces and International Headquarters (Application of Law) Order 1965;

(c) "visiting force" has the same meaning as it does for the purposes of any provision of Part I of the Visiting Forces Act 1952.

37 Transitional provision

The requirements in regulations 25 to 30 shall not apply to work equipment provided for use in the undertaking or establishment before 5th December 1998 until 5th December 2002.

SCHEDULE 1
INSTRUMENTS WHICH GIVE EFFECT TO COMMUNITY DIRECTIVES CONCERNING THE SAFETY OF PRODUCTS

Regulation 10

(1) Title	(2) Reference
The Construction Plant and Equipment (Harmonisation of Noise Emission Standards) Regulations 1985	SI 1985/1968, amended by SI 1989/1127
The Construction Plant and Equipment (Harmonisation of Noise Emission Standards) Regulations 1988	SI 1988/361, amended by SI 1992/488, 1995/2357
The Electro-medical Equipment (EEC Requirements) Regulations 1988	SI 1988/1586, amended by SI 1994/3017
The Low Voltage Electrical Equipment (Safety) Regulations 1989	SI 1989/728, amended by SI 1994/3260
The Construction Products Regulations 1991	SI 1991/1620, amended by SI 1994/3051
The Simple Pressure Vessels (Safety) Regulations 1991	SI 1991/2749, amended by SI 1994/3098
The Lawnmowers (Harmonisation of Noise Emission Standards) Regulations 1992	SI 1992/168
The Gas Appliances (Safety) Regulations 1992	SI 1992/711
The Electromagnetic Compatibility Regulations 1992	SI 1992/2372, amended by SI 1994/3080
The Supply of Machinery (Safety) Regulations 1992	SI 1992/3073, amended by SI 1994/2063
The Personal Protective Equipment (EC Directive) Regulations 1992	SI 1992/3139, amended by SI 1993/3074, 1994/2326, 1996/3039
The Active Implantable Medical Devices Regulations 1992	SI 1992/3146, amended by SI 1995/1671
The Medical Devices Regulations 1994	SI 1994/3017
The Electrical Equipment (Safety) Regulations 1994	SI 1994/3260
The Gas Appliances (Safety) Regulations 1995	SI 1995/1629
The Equipment and Protective Systems Intended for Use in Potentially Explosive Atmospheres Regulations 1996	SI 1996/192
The Lifts Regulations 1997	SI 1997/831
[The Pressure Equipment Regulations 1999	SI 1999/2001]
[The Noise Emission in the Environment by Equipment for use Outdoors Regulations 2001	SI 2001/1701]

NOTES

Entry relating to "The Pressure Equipment Regulations 1999" inserted by SI 1999/2001, reg 29(1).

Date in force: 29 November 1999: see SI 1999/2001, reg 1(3).

Entry relating to "The Noise Emission in the Environment by Equipment for use Outdoors Regulations 2001" inserted by SI 2001/1701, reg 22(1).
Date in force: 3 July 2001: see SI 2001/1701, reg 1(3).

SCHEDULE 2
POWER PRESSES TO WHICH REGULATIONS 32 TO 35 DO NOT APPLY

Regulation 31

1 A power press for the working of hot metal.

2 A power press not capable of a stroke greater than 6 millimetres.

3 A guillotine.

4 A combination punching and shearing machine, turret punch press or similar machine for punching, shearing or cropping.

5 A machine, other than a press brake, for bending steel sections.

6 A straightening machine.

7 An upsetting machine.

8 A heading machine.

9 A riveting machine.

10 An eyeletting machine.

11 A press-stud attaching machine.

12 A zip fastener bottom stop attaching machine.

13 A stapling machine.

14 A wire stitching machine.

15 A power press for the compacting of metal powders.

SCHEDULE 3
INFORMATION TO BE CONTAINED IN A REPORT OF A THOROUGH EXAMINATION OF A POWER PRESS, GUARD OR PROTECTION DEVICE

Regulation 34(1)(b)

1 The name of the employer for whom the thorough examination was made.

2 The address of the premises at which the thorough examination was made.

3 In relation to each item examined—
- (a) that it is a power press, interlocking guard, fixed guard or other type of guard or protection device;
- (b) where known its make, type and year of manufacture;
- (c) the identifying mark of—
  - (i) the manufacture,
  - (ii) the employer.

4 In relation to the first thorough examination of a power press after installation or after assembly at a new site or in a new location—
- (a) that it is such thorough examination;
- (b) either that it has been installed correctly and would be safe to operate or the respects in which it has not been installed correctly or would not be safe to operate;

(c) identification of any part found to have a defect, and a description of the defect.

5 In relation to a thorough examination of a power press other than one to which paragraph 4 relates—

(a) that it is such other thorough examination;

(b) either that the power press would be safe to operate or the respects in which it would not be safe to operate;

(c) identification of any part found to have a defect which is or could become a danger to persons, and a description of the defect.

6 In relation to a thorough examination of a guard or protection device—

(a) either that it is effective for its purpose or the respects in which it is not effective for its purpose;

(b) identification of any part found to have a defect which is or could become a danger to persons, and a description of the defect.

7 Any repair, renewal or alteration required to remedy a defect found to be a danger to persons.

8 In the case of a defect which is not yet but could become a danger to persons—

(a) the time by which it could become such danger;

(b) any repair, renewal or alteration required to remedy it.

9 Any other defect which requires remedy.

10 Any repair, renewal or alteration referred to in paragraph 7 which has already been effected.

11 The date on which any defect referred to in paragraph 8 was notified to the employer under regulation 34(1)(a).

12 The qualification and address of the person making the report; that he is self-employed or if employed, the name and address of his employer.

13 The date of the thorough examination.

14 The date of the report.

15 The name of the person making the report and where different the name of the person signing or otherwise authenticating it.

Employers' Liability (Compulsory Insurance) Regulations 1998

1998 No 2573

NOTES

Made....13th October 1998
Laid before Parliament....27th October 1998
Coming into force....1st January 1999

1 Citation, commencement and interpretation

(1) These Regulations may be cited as the Employers' Liability (Compulsory Insurance) Regulations 1998 and shall come into force on 1st January 1999.

(2) In these Regulations—

"the 1969 Act" means the Employers' Liability (Compulsory Insurance) Act 1969;

"associated structure" means, in relation to an offshore installation, a vessel, aircraft or hovercraft attendant on the installation or any floating structure used in connection with the installation;

"company" has the same meaning as in section 735 of the Companies Act 1985;

"inspector" means an inspector duly authorised by the Secretary of State under section 4(2)(b) of the 1969 Act;

"offshore installation" has the same meaning as in the Offshore Installations and Pipeline Works (Management and Administration) Regulations 1995;

"relevant employee" means an employee—

(a) who is ordinarily resident in the United Kingdom; or
(b) who, though not ordinarily resident in the United Kingdom, has been employed on or from an offshore installation or associated structure for a continuous period of not less than 7 days; or
(c) who, though not ordinarily resident in Great Britain, is present in Great Britain in the course of employment for a continuous period of not less than 14 days; and

"subsidiary" has the same meaning as in section 736 of the Companies Act 1985.

2 Prohibition of certain conditions in policies of insurance

(1) For the purposes of the 1969 Act, there is prohibited in any contract of insurance any condition which provides (in whatever terms) that no liability (either generally or in respect of a particular claim) shall arise under the policy, or that any such liability so arising shall cease, if—

(a) some specified thing is done or omitted to be done after the happening of the event giving rise to a claim under the policy;
(b) the policy holder does not take reasonable care to protect his employees against the risk of bodily injury or disease in the course of their employment;
(c) the policy holder fails to comply with the requirements of any enactment for the protection of employees against the risk of bodily injury or disease in the course of their employment; or
(d) the policy holder does not keep specified records or fails to provide the insurer with or make available to him information from such records.

(2) For the purposes of the 1969 Act there is also prohibited in a policy of insurance any condition which requires—

(a) a relevant employee to pay; or
(b) an insured employer to pay the relevant employee,

the first amount of any claim or any aggregation of claims.

(3) Paragraphs (1) and (2) above do not prohibit for the purposes of the 1969 Act a condition in a policy of insurance which requires the employer to pay or contribute

any sum to the insurer in respect of the satisfaction of any claim made under the contract of insurance by a relevant employee or any costs and expenses incurred in relation to any such claim.

3 Limit of amount of compulsory insurance

(1) Subject to paragraph (2) below, the amount for which an employer is required by the 1969 Act to insure and maintain insurance in respect of relevant employees under one or more policies of insurance shall be, or shall in aggregate be not less than £5 million in respect of—

(a) a claim relating to any one or more of those employees arising out of any one occurrence; and

(b) any costs and expenses incurred in relation to any such claim.

(2) Where an employer is a company with one or more subsidiaries, the requirements of paragraph (1) above shall be taken to apply to that company with any subsidiaries together, as if they were a single employer.

4 Issue of certificates of insurance

(1) Every authorised insurer who enters into a contract of insurance with an employer in accordance with the 1969 Act shall issue the employer with a certificate of insurance in the form, and containing the particulars, set out in Schedule 1 to these Regulations.

(2) The certificate shall be issued by the insurer not later than thirty days after the date on which the insurance commences or is renewed.

(3) Where a contract of insurance for the purposes of the 1969 Act is entered into together with one or more other contracts of insurance which jointly provide insurance cover of no less than £5 million, the certificate shall specify both—

(a) the amount in excess of which insurance cover is provided by the policy; and

(b) the maximum amount of that cover.

(4) An employer shall retain each certificate issued to him under this regulation, or a copy of each such certificate, for a period of 40 years beginning on the date on which the insurance to which it relates commences or is renewed.

(5) Where the employer is a company, retaining in any eye readable form a copy of a certificate in any one of the ways authorised by sections 722 and 723 of the Companies Act 1985 shall count as keeping a copy of it for the purposes of paragraph (4) above.

(6) In any case where it is intended that a contract of insurance for the purposes of the 1969 Act is to be effective, not only in Great Britain, but also—

(a) in Northern Ireland, the Isle of Man, the Island of Guernsey, the Island of Jersey or the Island of Alderney;

(b) in any waters outside the United Kingdom to which the 1969 Act may have been applied by any enactment, the form set out in Schedule 1 to these Regulations may be modified by a reference to the relevant law which is applicable and a statement that the policy to which it relates satisfies the requirements of that law.

5 Display and production of copies of certificates of insurance

(1) Subject to paragraph (4) below, an employer who has been issued with a certificate in accordance with regulation 4 above shall display one or more copies of it, in accordance with paragraphs (2) and (3) below, at each place of business at which he employs any relevant employee of the class or description to which such certificate relates.

(2) Any relevant certificate which is required to be displayed in accordance with paragraph (1) above, shall be displayed in such number and in such positions and be of such size and legibility that they may be easily seen and read by any relevant employees, and shall be reasonably protected from being defaced or damaged.

(3) Copies of a certificate which are required to be displayed in accordance with paragraph (1) above shall be kept on display until the date of expiry or earlier termination of the approved policy mentioned in the certificate.

(4) The requirements of paragraphs (1), (2) and (3) above do not apply where an employer employs a relevant employee on or from an offshore installation or associated structure, but in such a case the employer shall produce, at the request of that employee and within the period of ten days from such request, a copy of the certificate which relates to that employee.

6 Production of certificates of insurance to an Inspector

An employer who is required by a written notice issued by an inspector to do so shall produce or send to any person specified in the notice, at the address and within the time specified in the notice—

- (a) either the original or a copy of every certificate issued to him under regulation 4 above which relates to a period of insurance current at the date of issue of the notice;
- (b) either the original or a copy of every certificate issued to him under regulation 4 above and retained by him in accordance with regulation 4(4) above.

7 Inspection of policies of insurance

Where a certificate is required to be issued to an employer in accordance with regulation 4 above, the employer shall during the currency of the insurance permit the policy of insurance or a copy of it to be inspected by an inspector—

- (a) at such reasonable time as the inspector may require;
- (b) at such place of business of the employer (which, in the case of an employer who is a company, may include its registered office) as the inspector may require.

8 Production by inspectors of evidence of authority

Any inspector shall, if so required when visiting any premises for the purposes of the 1969 Act, produce to an employer or his agent some duly authenticated document showing that he is authorised by the Secretary of State under section 4(2)(b) of the 1969 Act.

9 Employers exempted from insurance

(1) The employers specified in Schedule 2 to these Regulations are exempted from the requirement of the 1969 Act to insure and maintain insurance.

(2) The exemption applies to all cases to which that requirement would otherwise apply, except that for the employers specified in paragraphs 1, 12, 13 and 14 it applies only so far as is mentioned in those paragraphs.

10 Revocations and transitional

(1) Subject to paragraphs (2) and (3) below, the instruments specified in column 1 of Schedule 3 to these Regulations are hereby revoked to the extent specified in column 3 of that Schedule.

(2) Subject to paragraphs (4) and (5) below, in the case of an insurance policy commenced before, and current at, 1st January 1999, regulations 2 to 6 of, and the Schedule to, the 1971 Regulations shall continue to apply, instead of regulations 2 to 6 of, and Schedule 1 to, these Regulations, until the expiry or renewal of the policy or until 1st January 2000, whichever is the earlier.

(3) The certificate required to be issued by regulation 4(1) of these Regulations in respect of insurance commenced or renewed on or after 1st January 1999 but before 1st April 1999 may, instead of being in the prescribed form, be in the form and contain the particulars specified in the Schedule to the 1971 Regulations.

(4) Every authorised insurer who has issued a certificate in the form, and containing the particulars, specified in the Schedule to the 1971 Regulations in respect of insurance current at 1st April 2000 shall replace it by that date with a certificate in the prescribed form and the replacement shall then be the relevant certificate for the purposes of regulation 5 of these Regulations.

(5) The certificates to which regulation 4(4) of these Regulations applies include any certificate of which a copy is required to be displayed or maintained by regulation 6(1) of the 1971 Regulations immediately before 1st January 1999, and any such certificate shall be treated for the purposes of regulation 6 of these Regulations as having been issued under regulation 4 of these Regulations.

(6) Regulation 7 of these Regulations applies where a certificate is required, in accordance with paragraph (2) above, to be issued in accordance with the 1971 Regulations as it applies where a certificate is required to be issued in accordance with regulation 4 of these Regulations.

(7) In this regulation—

"in the prescribed form" means in the form, and containing the particulars, required by regulation 4(1) and (3) of, and Schedule 1 to, these Regulations;

"the 1971 Regulations" means the Employers' Liability (Compulsory Insurance) General Regulations 1971 as in force on 31st December 1998, including those Regulations as applied by the Employers' Liability (Compulsory Insurance) (Offshore Installations) Regulations 1975.

SCHEDULE 1

Regulation 4

"CERTIFICATE OF EMPLOYERS' LIABILITY INSURANCE

(Where required by regulation 5 of the Employers' Liability (Compulsory Insurance) Regulations 1998 (the Regulations), one or more copies of this certificate must be displayed at each place of business at which the policy holder employs persons covered by the policy)

Policy No.. .. ..

1 Name of policy holder.

2 Date of commencement of insurance policy.

3 Date of expiry of insurance policy.

We hereby certify that subject to paragraph 2:—

1 the policy to which this certificate relates satisfies the requirements of the relevant law applicable in [Great Britain]; and

2

(a) the minimum amount of cover provided by this policy is no less than £5 million; or

(b) the cover provided under this policy relates to claims in excess of [£] but not exceeding [£].

Signed on behalf of .. .. (Authorised Insurer)

.. .. Signature

Notes

(a) *Where the employer is a company to which regulation 3(2) of the Regulations applies, the certificate shall state in a prominent place, either that the policy covers the holding company and all its subsidiaries, or that the policy covers the holding company and all its subsidiaries except any specifically excluded by name, or that the policy covers the holding company and only the named subsidiaries.*

(b) *Specify applicable law as provided for in regulation 4(6) of the Regulations.*

(c) *See regulation 3(1) of the Regulations and delete whichever of paragraphs 2(a) or 2(b) does not apply. Where 2(b) is applicable, specify the amount of cover provided by the relevant policy."*

SCHEDULE 2
EMPLOYERS EXEMPTED FROM INSURANCE

Regulation 9

1 A person who for the time being holds a current certificate issued by a government department [or the Scottish Ministers] [or the National Assembly for Wales] stating that claims established against that person in respect of any liability to such employees of the kind mentioned in section 1(1) of the 1969 Act as are mentioned in the certificate will, to any extent to which they are incapable of being satisfied by that person, be satisfied out of money provided by Parliament [or, in the case of a certificate issued by the Scottish Ministers, out of the Scottish Consolidated Fund] [or, in the case of a certificate issued by the National Assembly for Wales, out of monies provided by that Assembly]; but only in respect of employees covered by the certificate.

2 The Government of any foreign state or Commonwealth country.

3 Any inter-governmental organisation which by virtue of any enactment is to be treated as a body corporate.

4 Any subsidiary of any such body as is mentioned in section 3(1)(b) of the 1969 Act (which exempts any body corporate established by or under any enactment for the carrying on of any industry or part of an industry, or of any undertaking, under national ownership or control) and any company of which two or more such bodies are members and which would, if those bodies were a single corporate body, be a subsidiary of that body corporate.

5 Any Passenger Transport Executive and any subsidiary thereof.

6 London Regional Transport, and any of its subsidiaries or joint subsidiaries within the meaning of section 51(5) of the Transport Act 1968.

7 The Commission for the New Towns.

8 The Qualifications and Curriculum Authority.

9 Any voluntary management committee of an approved bail or approved probation hostel within the meaning of the Probation Service Act 1993.

10 Any magistrates' courts committee established under the Justices of the Peace Act 1997.

11 Any probation committee established under the Probation Service Act 1993.

12 Any employer who is a member of a mutual insurance association of shipowners or of shipowners and others, in respect of any liability to an employee of the kind mentioned in section 1(1) of the 1969 Act against which the employer is insured for the time being with that association for an amount not less than that required by the 1969 Act and regulations under it, being an employer who holds a certificate issued by that association to the effect that he is so insured in relation to that employee.

13 Any licensee within the meaning of the Nuclear Installations Act 1965, in respect of any liability to pay compensation under that Act to any of his employees in respect of a breach of duty imposed on him by virtue of section 7 of that Act.

14 Any employer to the extent he is required to insure and maintain insurance by subsection (1) of section 1 of the 1969 Act against liability for bodily injury sustained by his employee when the employee is—

(i) carried in or upon a vehicle; or
(ii) entering or getting on to, or alighting from, a vehicle,

in the circumstances specified in that subsection and where that bodily injury is caused by or, arises out of, the use by the employer of a vehicle on a road; and the expression "road", "use" and "vehicle" have the same meanings as in Part VI of the Road Traffic Act 1988.

NOTES

Para 1: words "or the Scottish Ministers" in square brackets inserted by SI 1999/1820, art 4, Sch 2, Pt II, para 165(1), (2).

Date in force: 1 July 1999: see SI 1999/1820, art 1(2).

Para 1: words "or the National Assembly for Wales" in square brackets inserted by SI 2000/253, art 7, Sch 5, para 8(1), (2).

Date in force: 16 February 2000: see SI 2000/253, art 1(2).

Para 1: words from "or, in the case" to "Scottish Consolidated Fund" in square brackets inserted by SI 1999/1820, art 4, Sch 2, Pt II, para 165(1), (3).

Date in force: 1 July 1999: see SI 1999/1820, art 1(2).

Para 1: words from "or, in the case of" to "provided by that Assembly" in square brackets inserted by SI 2000/253, art 7, Sch 5, para 8(1), (3).

Date in force: 16 February 2000: see SI 2000/253, art 1(2).

Unfair Terms in Consumer Contracts Regulations 1999

1999 No 2083

NOTES

Made ...... 22nd July 1999
Laid before Parliament ...... 22nd July 1999
Coming into force ...... 1st October 1999

1 Citation and commencement

These Regulations may be cited as the Unfair Terms in Consumer Contracts Regulations 1999 and shall come into force on 1st October 1999.

3 Interpretation

(1) In these Regulations—

"the Community" means the European Community;

"consumer" means any natural person who, in contracts covered by these Regulations, is acting for purposes which are outside his trade, business or profession;

"court" in relation to England and Wales and Northern Ireland means a county court or the High Court, and in relation to Scotland, the Sheriff or the Court of Session;

"Director" means the Director General of Fair Trading;

"EEA Agreement" means the Agreement on the European Economic Area signed at Oporto on 2nd May 1992 as adjusted by the protocol signed at Brussels on 17th March 1993;

"Member State" means a State which is a contracting party to the EEA Agreement;

"notified" means notified in writing;

"qualifying body" means a person specified in Schedule 1;

"seller or supplier" means any natural or legal person who, in contracts covered by these Regulations, is acting for purposes relating to his trade, business or profession, whether publicly owned or privately owned;

"unfair terms" means the contractual terms referred to in regulation 5.

(2) In the application of these Regulations to Scotland for references to an "injunction" or an "interim injunction" there shall be substituted references to an "interdict" or "interim interdict" respectively.

4 Terms to which these Regulations apply

(1) These Regulations apply in relation to unfair terms in contracts concluded between a seller or a supplier and a consumer.

(2) These Regulations do not apply to contractual terms which reflect—
- (a) mandatory statutory or regulatory provisions (including such provisions under the law of any Member State or in Community legislation having effect in the United Kingdom without further enactment);
- (b) the provisions or principles of international conventions to which the Member States or the Community are party.

5 Unfair Terms

(1) A contractual term which has not been individually negotiated shall be regarded as unfair if, contrary to the requirement of good faith, it causes a significant imbalance in the parties' rights and obligations arising under the contract, to the detriment of the consumer.

(2) A term shall always be regarded as not having been individually negotiated where it has been drafted in advance and the consumer has therefore not been able to influence the substance of the term.

(3) Notwithstanding that a specific term or certain aspects of it in a contract has been individually negotiated, these Regulations shall apply to the rest of a contract if an overall assessment of it indicates that it is a pre-formulated standard contract.

(4) It shall be for any seller or supplier who claims that a term was individually negotiated to show that it was.

(5) Schedule 2 to these Regulations contains an indicative and non-exhaustive list of the terms which may be regarded as unfair.

6 Assessment of unfair terms

(1) Without prejudice to regulation 12, the unfairness of a contractual term shall be assessed, taking into account the nature of the goods or services for which the contract was concluded and by referring, at the time of conclusion of the contract, to all the circumstances attending the conclusion of the contract and to all the other terms of the contract or of another contract on which it is dependent.

(2) In so far as it is in plain intelligible language, the assessment of fairness of a term shall not relate—
- (a) to the definition of the main subject matter of the contract, or
- (b) to the adequacy of the price or remuneration, as against the goods or services supplied in exchange.

7 Written contracts

(1) A seller or supplier shall ensure that any written term of a contract is expressed in plain, intelligible language.

(2) If there is doubt about the meaning of a written term, the interpretation which is most favourable to the consumer shall prevail but this rule shall not apply in proceedings brought under regulation 12.

8 Effect of unfair term

(1) An unfair term in a contract concluded with a consumer by a seller or supplier shall not be binding on the consumer.

(2) The contract shall continue to bind the parties if it is capable of continuing in existence without the unfair term.

9 Choice of law clauses

These Regulations shall apply notwithstanding any contract term which applies or purports to apply the law of a non-Member State, if the contract has a close connection with the territory of the Member States.

10 Complaints—consideration by Director

(1) It shall be the duty of the Director to consider any complaint made to him that any contract term drawn up for general use is unfair, unless—

(a) the complaint appears to the Director to be frivolous or vexatious; or
(b) a qualifying body has notified the Director that it agrees to consider the complaint.

(2) The Director shall give reasons for his decision to apply or not to apply, as the case may be, for an injunction under regulation 12 in relation to any complaint which these Regulations require him to consider.

(3) In deciding whether or not to apply for an injunction in respect of a term which the Director considers to be unfair, he may, if he considers it appropriate to do so, have regard to any undertakings given to him by or on behalf of any person as to the continued use of such a term in contracts concluded with consumers.

11 Complaints—consideration by qualifying bodies

(1) If a qualifying body specified in Part One of Schedule 1 notifies the Director that it agrees to consider a complaint that any contract term drawn up for general use is unfair, it shall be under a duty to consider that complaint.

(2) Regulation 10(2) and (3) shall apply to a qualifying body which is under a duty to consider a complaint as they apply to the Director.

12 Injunctions to prevent continued use of unfair terms

(1) The Director or, subject to paragraph (2), any qualifying body may apply for an injunction (including an interim injunction) against any person appearing to the

Director or that body to be using, or recommending use of, an unfair term drawn up for general use in contracts concluded with consumers.

(2) A qualifying body may apply for an injunction only where—
  (a) it has notified the Director of its intention to apply at least fourteen days before the date on which the application is made, beginning with the date on which the notification was given; or
  (b) the Director consents to the application being made within a shorter period.

(3) The court on an application under this regulation may grant an injunction on such terms as it thinks fit.

(4) An injunction may relate not only to use of a particular contract term drawn up for general use but to any similar term, or a term having like effect, used or recommended for use by any person.

13 Powers of the Director and qualifying bodies to obtain documents and information

(1) The Director may exercise the power conferred by this regulation for the purpose of—
  (a) facilitating his consideration of a complaint that a contract term drawn up for general use is unfair; or
  (b) ascertaining whether a person has complied with an undertaking or court order as to the continued use, or recommendation for use, of a term in contracts concluded with consumers.

(2) A qualifying body specified in Part One of Schedule 1 may exercise the power conferred by this regulation for the purpose of—
  (a) facilitating its consideration of a complaint that a contract term drawn up for general use is unfair; or
  (b) ascertaining whether a person has complied with—
    (i) an undertaking given to it or to the court following an application by that body, or
    (ii) a court order made on an application by that body,

  as to the continued use, or recommendation for use, of a term in contracts concluded with consumers.

(3) The Director may require any person to supply to him, and a qualifying body specified in Part One of Schedule 1 may require any person to supply to it—
  (a) a copy of any document which that person has used or recommended for use, at the time the notice referred to in paragraph (4) below is given, as a pre-formulated standard contract in dealings with consumers;
  (b) information about the use, or recommendation for use, by that person of that document or any other such document in dealings with consumers.

(4) The power conferred by this regulation is to be exercised by a notice in writing which may—
  (a) specify the way in which and the time within which it is to be complied with; and
  (b) be varied or revoked by a subsequent notice.

(5) Nothing in this regulation compels a person to supply any document or information which he would be entitled to refuse to produce or give in civil proceedings before the court.

(6) If a person makes default in complying with a notice under this regulation, the court may, on the application of the Director or of the qualifying body, make such order as the court thinks fit for requiring the default to be made good, and any such order may provide that all the costs or expenses of and incidental to the application shall be borne by the person in default or by any officers of a company or other association who are responsible for its default.

14 Notification of undertakings and orders to Director

A qualifying body shall notify the Director—

(a) of any undertaking given to it by or on behalf of any person as to the continued use of a term which that body considers to be unfair in contracts concluded with consumers;

(b) of the outcome of any application made by it under regulation 12, and of the terms of any undertaking given to, or order made by, the court;

(c) of the outcome of any application made by it to enforce a previous order of the court.

15 Publication, information and advice

(1) The Director shall arrange for the publication in such form and manner as he considers appropriate, of—

(a) details of any undertaking or order notified to him under regulation 14;

(b) details of any undertaking given to him by or on behalf of any person as to the continued use of a term which the Director considers to be unfair in contracts concluded with consumers;

(c) details of any application made by him under regulation 12, and of the terms of any undertaking given to, or order made by, the court;

(d) details of any application made by the Director to enforce a previous order of the court.

(2) The Director shall inform any person on request whether a particular term to which these Regulations apply has been—

(a) the subject of an undertaking given to the Director or notified to him by a qualifying body; or

(b) the subject of an order of the court made upon application by him or notified to him by a qualifying body;

and shall give that person details of the undertaking or a copy of the order, as the case may be, together with a copy of any amendments which the person giving the undertaking has agreed to make to the term in question.

(3) The Director may arrange for the dissemination in such form and manner as he considers appropriate of such information and advice concerning the operation of these Regulations as may appear to him to be expedient to give to the public and to all persons likely to be affected by these Regulations.

SCHEDULE 1
Qualifying Bodies

Regulation 3

PART ONE

[1 The Information Commissioner.

2 The Gas and Electricity Markets Authority.

3 The Director General of Electricity Supply for Northern Ireland.

4 The Director General of Gas for Northern Ireland.

5 The Director General of Telecommunications.

6 The Director General of Water Services.

7 The Rail Regulator.

8 Every weights and measures authority in Great Britain.

9 The Department of Enterprise, Trade and Investment in Northern Ireland.

10 The Financial Services Authority.]

NOTES

Substituted by SI 2001/1186, reg 2(b).
Date in force: 1 May 2001: see SI 2001/1186, reg 1.

PART TWO

11 Consumers' Association

SCHEDULE 2
Indicative and Non-Exhaustive List of Terms which may be Regarded as Unfair

Regulation 5(5)

1 Terms which have the object or effect of—

(a) excluding or limiting the legal liability of a seller or supplier in the event of the death of a consumer or personal injury to the latter resulting from an act or omission of that seller or supplier;

(b) inappropriately excluding or limiting the legal rights of the consumer vis-à-vis the seller or supplier or another party in the event of total or partial non-performance or inadequate performance by the seller or supplier of any of the contractual obligations, including the option of offsetting a debt owed to the seller or supplier against any claim which the consumer may have against him;

(c) making an agreement binding on the consumer whereas provision of services by the seller or supplier is subject to a condition whose realisation depends on his own will alone;

(d) permitting the seller or supplier to retain sums paid by the consumer where the latter decides not to conclude or perform the contract, without providing for the consumer to receive compensation of an equivalent amount from the seller or supplier where the latter is the party cancelling the contract;

(e) requiring any consumer who fails to fulfil his obligation to pay a disproportionately high sum in compensation;

(f) authorising the seller or supplier to dissolve the contract on a discretionary basis where the same facility is not granted to the consumer, or permitting the seller or supplier to retain the sums paid for services not yet supplied by him where it is the seller or supplier himself who dissolves the contract;

(g) enabling the seller or supplier to terminate a contract of indeterminate duration without reasonable notice except where there are serious grounds for doing so;

(h) automatically extending a contract of fixed duration where the consumer does not indicate otherwise, when the deadline fixed for the consumer to express his desire not to extend the contract is unreasonably early;

(i) irrevocably binding the consumer to terms with which he had no real opportunity of becoming acquainted before the conclusion of the contract;

(j) enabling the seller or supplier to alter the terms of the contract unilaterally without a valid reason which is specified in the contract;

(k) enabling the seller or supplier to alter unilaterally without a valid reason any characteristics of the product or service to be provided;

(l) providing for the price of goods to be determined at the time of delivery or allowing a seller of goods or supplier of services to increase their price without in both cases giving the consumer the corresponding right to cancel the contract if the final price is too high in relation to the price agreed when the contract was concluded;

(m) giving the seller or supplier the right to determine whether the goods or services supplied are in conformity with the contract, or giving him the exclusive right to interpret any term of the contract;

(n) limiting the seller's or supplier's obligation to respect commitments undertaken by his agents or making his commitments subject to compliance with a particular formality;

(o) obliging the consumer to fulfil all his obligations where the seller or supplier does not perform his;

(p) giving the seller or supplier the possibility of transferring his rights and obligations under the contract, where this may serve to reduce the guarantees for the consumer, without the latter's agreement;

(q) excluding or hindering the consumer's right to take legal action or exercise any other legal remedy, particularly by requiring the consumer to take disputes exclusively to arbitration not covered by legal provisions, unduly restricting the evidence available to him or imposing on him a burden of proof which, according to the applicable law, should lie with another party to the contract.

2 Scope of paragraphs 1(g), (j) and (l)

(a) Paragraph 1(g) is without hindrance to terms by which a supplier of financial services reserves the right to terminate unilaterally a contract of indeterminate duration without notice where there is a valid reason, provided that the supplier is required to inform the other contracting party or parties thereof immediately.

(b) Paragraph 1(j) is without hindrance to terms under which a supplier of financial services reserves the right to alter the rate of interest payable by the consumer or due to the latter, or the amount of other charges for financial services without notice where there is a valid reason, provided that the supplier is required to inform the other contracting party or parties thereof at the earliest opportunity and that the latter are free to dissolve the contract immediately.

Paragraph 1(j) is also without hindrance to terms under which a seller or supplier reserves the right to alter unilaterally the conditions of a contract of indeterminate duration, provided that he is required to inform the consumer with reasonable notice and that the consumer is free to dissolve the contract.

(c) Paragraphs 1(g), (j) and (l) do not apply to:
—transactions in transferable securities, financial instruments and other products or services where the price is linked to fluctuations in a stock exchange quotation or index or a financial market rate that the seller or supplier does not control;
—contracts for the purchase or sale of foreign currency, traveller's cheques or international money orders denominated in foreign currency.

(d) Paragraph 1(1) is without hindrance to price indexation clauses, where lawful, provided that the method by which prices vary is explicitly described.

PART III

LAW COMMISSION PROPOSED BILLS

(Draft) Contributory Negligence Bill

(Law Com No 219)

A Bill to provide for reducing the damages recoverable for breach of a contractual duty to take reasonable care or exercise reasonable skill in cases where the claimant's failure to take reasonable care has contributed to the damage suffered by him

[1993]

1 Contributory negligence in claims for breach of contract

(1) Where by virtue of an express or implied term of a contract a party is under a duty to take reasonable care or exercise reasonable skill or both in the performance of the contract and the party to whom that duty is owed suffers damage as the result—

(a) partly of a breach of that duty; and
(b) partly of his own failure to take reasonable care for the protection of himself or his interests,

the damages recoverable by that party on a claim in respect of the damage shall be reduced to such extent as the court thinks just and equitable having regard to the claimant's share in the responsibility for the damage.

(2) Subsection (1) above does not apply if the parties have agreed (in whatever terms and whether expressly or by implication) that the damages for breach of the contract are not to be reduced as there mentioned, for example by specifying a sum payable in the event of breach and constituting liquidated damages.

(3) Where subsection (1) above applies the court, in deciding whether and, if so, to what extent the damages recoverable by the claimant are to be reduced—

(a) shall disregard anything done or omitted by him before the contract was entered into; but
(b) shall have regard to the nature of the contract and the mutual obligations of the parties,

and in other respects shall apply the like principles as those applicable under section 1(1) of the Law Reform (Contributory Negligence) Act 1945.

(4) Where the damages recoverable by any person are reduced by virtue of subsection (1) above the court shall find and record what the damages would have been without the reduction.

(5) In subsection (1) above references to the party by or to whom the duty under the contract is owed include references to any person subject to, or entitled to the performance of, that duty by virtue of assignment or otherwise.

(6) In this section "the court" means, in relation to any claim, the court or arbitrator by whom the claim falls to be determined and "damage" includes loss of life and personal injury.

2 Consequential amendments

(1) In section 4(3) of the Crown Proceedings Act 1947 (Crown bound by Law Reform (Contributory Negligence) Act 1945) after "1945" there shall be inserted "and the Contributory Negligence Act 1993".

(2) In section 5 of the Fatal Accidents Act 1976 (reduction of damages under that Act if Law Reform (Contributory Negligence) Act 1945 would have reduced the damages recoverable in an action brought for the benefit of the deceased's estate) there shall be added at the end "and likewise if the damages in an action so brought would be reduced under section 1(1) of the Contributory Negligence Act 1993".

(3) In section 2(3)(b) of the Civil Liability (Contribution) Act 1978 (limit on liability of contributor) after "the Law Reform (Contributory Negligence) Act 1945" there shall be inserted ", the Contributory Negligence Act 1993".

3 Short title, commencement, saving and extent

(1) This Act may be cited as the Contributory Negligence Act 1993.

(2) This Act comes into force at the end of the period of two months beginning with the day on which it is passed.

(3) This Act does not apply to any contract entered into before the coming into force of this Act.

(4) This Act does not extend to Scotland or Northern Ireland.

(Draft) Restitution (Mistakes of Law) Bill

(Law Com No 227)

An Act to make provision in relation to claims made in any proceedings for restitution in respect of acts done under mistake

[1994]

1 Claims to which Act applies

(1) In this Act "mistake claim" means a claim made in any proceedings for restitution of a sum in respect of an act done under mistake.

(2) In this Act "act" includes anything which may found a claim for restitution, that is to say, the making of a payment, the conferring of a non-pecuniary benefit or the doing of work.

2 Abrogation of mistake of law rule

The classification of a mistake as a mistake of law or as a mistake of fact shall not of itself be material to the determination of a mistake claim; and no such claim shall be denied on the ground that the alleged mistake is a mistake of law.

3 Effect on mistake claim of judicial change in the law

(1) An act done in accordance with a settled view of the law shall not be regarded as founding a mistake claim by reason only that a subsequent decision of a court or tribunal departs from that view.

(2) A view of the law may be regarded for the purposes of this section as having been settled at any time notwithstanding that it was not held unanimously or had not been the subject of a decision by a court or tribunal.

4 Savings

(1) This Act does not affect any mistake claim (whenever made) in respect of an act done before the date on which this Act comes into force.

(2) Without prejudice to the generality of subsection (1), nothing in this Act shall be taken to affect any question as to the existence or operation before that date of any rule whereby a mistake claim would be denied by reason of the alleged mistake being a mistake of law.

(3) An enactment which has the effect of excluding or restricting the right to bring a mistake claim in any particular circumstances shall have the same effect on any right to bring a mistake claim in those circumstances that may arise by virtue of section 2.

(4) In subsection (3) "enactment" includes an enactment comprised in subordinate legislation within the meaning of the interpretation Act 1978.

5 Short title, commencement and extent

(1) This Act may be cited as the Restitution (Mistakes of Law) Act 1994.

(2) This Act shall come into force on such day as the Lord Chancellor may appoint by order made by statutory instrument.

(3) This Act extends to England and Wales only.

(Draft) Damages Bill

(Law Com No 247)

An Act to amend certain rules, and to clarify certain rules, of the law of damages [1997]

PART I
PUNITIVE DAMAGES

Introduction

1 Introduction

(1) This Part amends certain rules, and clarifies certain rules, relating to punitive damages.

(2) Punitive damages are damages which were commonly called exemplary before the passing of this Act.

Main provisions

2 The court's functions

If liability in respect of a cause of action is established a decision whether punitive damages should be awarded, or what their amount should be, must not be left to a jury.

3 Availability of punitive damages

(1) Punitive damages may be awarded only if permitted by this section.

(2) Punitive damages may be awarded only if they are claimed.

(3) Punitive damages may be awarded in respect of any tort or any equitable wrong.

(4) Punitive damages may be awarded in respect of any wrong arising under an Act if—

(a) a person may recover compensation or damages in respect of the wrong, and
(b) an award of punitive damages would be consistent with the policy of that Act.

(5) If a tort or an equitable wrong arises under an Act, subsection (4) applies to it and subsection (3) does not.

(6) Punitive damages may be awarded only if the defendant's conduct shows a deliberate and outrageous disregard of the plaintiff's rights.

(7) Punitive damages may be awarded only if the court believes that—

(a) the defendant's conduct is such that the court should punish him for it, and

(b) the other remedies available are inadequate to do that.

(8) Punitive damages may be awarded whether or not another remedy is granted.

(9) The fact that the defendant's conduct falls outside the following categories is not a ground for refusing to award punitive damages—

(a) oppressive, arbitrary or unconstitutional conduct by a servant of the government;

(b) conduct calculated to make a profit which might exceed compensation payable to the plaintiff.

(10) The court may regard deterring the defendant and others from similar conduct as an object of punishment.

4 Other sanctions

(1) In deciding whether to award punitive damages the court must have regard to the principle that they must not usually be awarded if, at any time before the decision falls to be made, the defendant has been convicted of an offence involving the conduct concerned.

(2) In deciding whether to award punitive damages the court must take account of any sanction imposed in respect of the conduct concerned as a result of action (such as an employer's disciplinary proceedings) not involving conviction of an offence.

(3) In applying subsection (1) the court must ignore section 1C of the Powers of Criminal Courts Act 1973 (which provides that a conviction discharging an offender absolutely or conditionally is not deemed a conviction for certain purposes).

5 Amount of punitive damages

(1) In deciding the amount of punitive damages the court must have regard to these principles—

(a) the amount must not exceed the minimum needed to punish the defendant for his conduct;

(b) the amount must be proportionate to the gravity of the defendant's conduct.

(2) In deciding the amount of punitive damages the court must take account of these matters—

(a) the defendant's state of mind;

(b) the nature of the rights infringed by the defendant;

(c) the nature and extent of any loss or harm the defendant caused or intended to cause by his conduct;

(d) the nature and extent of any benefit the defendant derived or intended to derive from his conduct:

(e) any other matter the court considers relevant (except the defendant's means, which are dealt with in section 6).

(3) The court may regard deterring the defendant and others from similar conduct as an object of punishment.

6 The defendant's means

(1) If the court decides to award punitive damages it must indicate the amount it has in mind to award irrespective of the defendant's means.

(2) If the defendant shows that he does not have the means to discharge an award of that amount without undue hardship, the court must take account of his means in deciding the amount of punitive damages to award.

(3) If an amount awarded as punitive damages would have been more but for subsection (2) the court must record what the amount awarded would have been but for that subsection.

(4) The defendant's means include anything falling to be paid under a contract of insurance against the risk of an award of punitive damages.

Multiple parties

7 More than one person wronged

(1) This section applies if conduct constitutes, or is alleged to constitute, torts or other wrongs against two or more persons (the persons wronged).

(2) In deciding whether to award punitive damages or the amount of punitive damages to award (whether to one or more of the persons wronged)—
- (a) the court must take account of any settlement or compromise by any persons of a claim in respect of the conduct, but
- (b) the court may not take account of any such settlement or compromise unless the defendant consents to it doing so.

(3) If the court awards punitive damages to two or more of the persons wronged the aggregate amount awarded must be such that, while it takes account of the fact that more than one party is awarded punitive damages, it does not punish the defendant excessively.

(4) If the court awards punitive damages to one or more of the persons wronged no later claim may be made for punitive damages as regards the conduct.

8 More than one wrongdoer

(1) Any liability of two or more persons in respect of punitive damages is several (and not joint or joint and several).

(2) Subsection (1) has effect subject to the law relating to—
- (a) vicarious liability;
- (b) the liability of a partner for the conduct of another partner.

(3) If the liability of two or more persons in respect of punitive damages is several no contribution in respect of the damages may be recovered by any of them from any other under section 1 of the Civil Liability (Contribution) Act 1978.

Other provisions

9 Insurance against punitive damages

(1) It is not contrary to public policy for the risk of an award of punitive damages to be the subject of a contract of insurance.

(2) No provision of an Act or of subordinate legislation must be taken to require the risk of an award of punitive damages to be the subject of a contract of insurance.

10 Standard of proof

If it is sought to establish a matter relating to the question whether punitive damages should be awarded, or to the question of their amount, the civil (not the criminal) standard of proof must be satisfied.

11 Vicarious liability

(1) A person may be vicariously liable to pay punitive damages in respect of another's conduct.

(2) In a case where, if punitive damages were to be awarded, a person would be vicariously liable to pay them in respect of another's conduct—
- (a) references to the defendant in sections 3 to 5 are to that other;
- (b) section 5(2)(e) applies as if "defendant's means, which are dealt with in section 6" read "means of the person vicariously liable or the person in respect of whose conduct he is vicariously liable".

(3) If the court decides to award punitive damages and a person is vicariously liable to pay them in respect of another's conduct, references to the defendant and his means in section 6 are to the person vicariously liable and his means.

PART II
CERTAIN OTHER DAMAGES

12 Restitutionary damages for outrageous conduct

(1) Restitutionary damages may be awarded if—
- (a) a tort or an equitable wrong is committed, and
- (b) the defendant's conduct shows a deliberate and outrageous disregard of the plaintiff's rights.

(2) Restitutionary damages may be awarded if a wrong arising under an Act is committed and each of these conditions is fulfilled—
- (a) a person may recover compensation or damages in respect of the wrong,
- (b) an award of restitutionary damages would be consistent with the policy of that Act, and
- (c) the defendant's conduct shows a deliberate and outrageous disregard of the plaintiff's rights.

(3) If a tort or an equitable wrong arises under an Act, subsection (2) applies to it and subsection (1) does not.

(4) If—

(a) it falls to be decided whether subsection (1)(b) or (2)(c) is satisfied in relation to a plaintiff, and

(b) punitive damages are claimed in the same proceedings (whether by that plaintiff or not),

the decision whether subsection (1)(b) or (2)(c) is satisfied must not be left to a jury.

(5) Subsections (1) and (2) do not prejudice any power to award restitutionary damages in other cases.

13 Certain damages for mental distress

(1) This section applies to damages which were commonly called aggravated before the passing of this Act and which—

(a) are awarded against a person in respect of his motive or exceptional conduct, but

(b) are not punitive damages or restitutionary damages.

(2) Damages to which this section applies may be awarded only to compensate for mental distress and must not be intended to punish.

PART III

MISCELLANEOUS AND GENERAL

Miscellaneous

14 Amendment of other legislation

(1) Section 1 of the Law Reform (Miscellaneous Provisions) Act 1934 (effect of death on certain causes of action) is amended as mentioned in subsections (2) and (3).

(2) Subsection (2)(a)(i) (damages recoverable for benefit of estate not to include exemplary damages) is repealed.

(3) After subsection (2) insert—

"(2A) Where a cause of action survives against the estate of a deceased person under this section, any damages recoverable against the estate may not include punitive damages.

(2B) Where a cause of action survives for the benefit of the estate of a deceased person under this section, any damages recoverable for the benefit of the estate may include punitive damages.

(2C) References in subsections (2A) and (2B) of this section to punitive damages are to damages to which Part I of the Damages Act 1997 relates."

(4) In section 13(2) of the Reserve and Auxiliary Forces (Protection of Civil Interests) Act 1951 (in certain proceedings the court may take account of the defendant's conduct with a view, if the court thinks fit, to awarding exemplary damages)—

(a) for "exemplary" substitute "punitive";
(b) at the end insert "; and the reference here to punitive damages is to damages to which Part I of the Damages Act 1997 relates".

(5) In the Copyright, Designs and Patents Act 1988, sections 97(2), 191J(2) and 229(3) (power to award additional damages for infringement of copyright, performer's property rights or design right) are repealed in consequence of section 3(4) of this Act.

General

15 Interpretation

(1) For the purposes of this Act this section interprets the following expressions (here listed alphabetically)—
(a) Act;
(b) conduct;
(c) equitable wrong;
(d) punitive damages;
(e) restitutionary damages;
(f) subordinate legislation.

(2) "Act" includes a local and personal or private Act.

(3) A reference to conduct includes a reference to omissions; and a reference to a person's conduct includes a reference to his conduct subsequent to that giving rise to the cause of action concerned.

(4) Each of the following is an equitable wrong—
(a) a breach of fiduciary duty;
(b) breach of confidence;
(c) procuring or assisting a breach of fiduciary duty.

(5) References to punitive damages are to be construed in accordance with section 1(2).

(6) Restitutionary damages are damages designed to remove a benefit derived by a person from his tort or other wrong.

(7) "Subordinate legislation" means Orders in Council, orders, rules, regulations, schemes, warrants, byelaws and other instruments made under any Act.

16 Commencement

(1) Nothing in this Act affects a cause of action accruing before such day as the Lord Chancellor may appoint by order made by statutory instrument.

(2) Different days may be appointed for different provisions or for different purposes.

(3) An order under this section may include such supplementary, incidental, consequential or transitional provisions as appear to the Lord Chancellor to be necessary or expedient.

17 Extent

This Act extends to England and Wales only.

18 Citation

This Act may be cited as the Damages Act 1997.

(Draft) Negligence (Psychiatric Illness) Bill

(Law Com No 249)

An Act to amend and clarify the law relating to liability in negligence for psychiatric illness

[1998]

New duties of care

1 Close tie: duty of care

(1) Subsection (2) imposes a duty of care for the purposes of the tort of negligence, and that subsection has effect subject to (and only to) subsections (3) to (6).

(2) A person (the defendant) owes a duty to take reasonable care to avoid causing another person (the plaintiff) to suffer a recognisable psychiatric illness as a result of the death, injury or imperilment of a third person (the immediate victim) if it is reasonably foreseeable that the defendant's act or omission might cause the plaintiff to suffer such an illness.

(3) The defendant must be taken not to have owed the duty unless—

- (a) his act or omission caused the death, injury or imperilment of the immediate victim, and
- (b) the plaintiff and the immediate victim had a close tie of love and affection immediately before the act or omission occurred or immediately before the onset of the plaintiff's illness (or both).

(4) The duty is not imposed if the court is satisfied that its imposition would not be just and reasonable—

- (a) because of any factor by virtue of which the defendant owed no duty of care to the immediate victim,
- (b) because the immediate victim voluntarily accepted the risk that the defendant's act or omission might cause his death, injury or imperilment, or
- (c) because the plaintiff was involved in conduct which is illegal or contrary to public policy.

(5) The duty is not imposed if the plaintiff—

(a) voluntarily accepted the risk of suffering the illness, or
(b) excluded the duty.

(6) The duty is not imposed if a provision which is contained in or made under another enactment, or which has the force of law by virtue of another enactment, regulates the defendant's duty to the plaintiff as regards the act or omission in place of the common law rules of the tort of negligence.

2 Close tie: duty of care if defendant is victim

(1) Subsection (2) imposes a duty of care for the purposes of the tort of negligence, and that subsection has effect subject to (and only to) subsections (3) to (6).

(2) A person (the defendant) owes a duty to take reasonable care to avoid causing another person (the plaintiff) to suffer a recognisable psychiatric illness as a result of the death, injury or imperilment of the defendant if it is reasonably foreseeable that the defendant's act or omission might cause the plaintiff to suffer such an illness.

(3) The defendant must be taken not to have owed the duty unless—
(a) his act or omission caused his death, injury or imperilment, and
(b) the plaintiff and the defendant had a close tie of love and affection immediately before the act or omission occurred or immediately before the onset of the plaintiff's illness (or both).

(4) The duty is not imposed if the court is satisfied that its imposition would not be just and reasonable—
(a) because the defendant chose to cause his death, injury or imperilment, or
(b) because the plaintiff was involved in conduct which is illegal or contrary to public policy.

(5) The duty is not imposed if the plaintiff—
(a) voluntarily accepted the risk of suffering the illness, or
(b) excluded the duty.

(6) The duty is not imposed if a provision which is contained in or made under another enactment, or which has the force of law by virtue of another enactment, regulates the defendant's duty to the plaintiff as regards the act or omission in place of the common law rules of the tort of negligence.

3 Meaning of close tie

(1) Subsections (2) to (5) have effect to determine whether for the purposes of section 1 the plaintiff and the immediate victim had a close tie of love and affection at a particular time.

(2) If at the time concerned the plaintiff fell within any of the categories listed in subsection (4) he and the immediate victim must be conclusively taken to have had a close tie of love and affection at that time.

(3) Otherwise it is for the plaintiff to show that he and the immediate victim had a close tie of love and affection at the time concerned.

(4) The categories are—

(a) the immediate victim's spouse;
(b) either parent of the immediate victim;
(c) any child of the immediate victim;
(d) any brother or sister of the immediate victim;
(e) the immediate victim's cohabitant.

(5) The plaintiff was the immediate victim's cohabitant at the time concerned if and only if—
(a) though not married to each other, they lived together as man and wife for a period of at least two years immediately before the time concerned, or
(b) though of the same gender, they had a relationship equivalent to that described in paragraph (a) for such a period.

(6) Subsections (2) to (5) also have effect to determine whether for the purposes of section 2 the plaintiff and the defendant had a close tie of love and affection at a particular time, reading references in those subsections to the immediate victim as references to the defendant.

Common law duty of care

4 Close tie: abolition of common law duty

The common law duty of care under the tort of negligence is abolished to the extent that (apart from this section)—
(a) it would arise in respect of a recognisable psychiatric illness suffered by a person (A) as a result of the death, injury or imperilment of another (B),
(b) it would depend on the existence of a close tie of love and affection between A and B, and
(c) it would be imposed on the person (whether B or a third person) causing the death, injury or imperilment.

5 Removal of certain restrictions

(1) This section amends and clarifies the law relating to a claim which—
(a) is founded on the common law duty of care under the tort of negligence, and
(b) is made in respect of a recognisable psychiatric illness.

(2) It is not a condition of the claim's success that the illness was induced by a shock.

(3) The court may allow the claim even if the illness results from the defendant causing his own death, injury or imperilment.

General

6 Commencement

(1) Sections 1 to 4 apply if the act or omission causing the death, injury or imperilment occurs on or after the appointed day.

(2) Section 5 applies if the defendant's act or omission occurs on or after the appointed day.

(3) The appointed day is such day as the Lord Chancellor appoints for the purposes of this Act by order made by statutory instrument.

7 Extent

This Act extends to England and Wales only.

8 Citation

This Act may be cited as the Negligence (Psychiatric Illness) Act 1998.